ALL · IN · ONE

Network+
Certification

EXAM GUIDE

SECOND EDITION

ALL · IN · ONE

Network+
Certification

EXAM GUIDE

SECOND EDITION

Michael Meyers

Osborne / McGraw-Hill
New York • Chicago • San Francisco • Lisbon
London • Madrid • Mexico City • Milan • New Delhi
San Juan • Seoul • Singapore • Sydney • Toronto

Osborne/**McGraw-Hill**
2600 Tenth Street
Berkeley, California 94710
U.S.A.

To arrange bulk purchase discounts for sales promotions, premiums, or fund-raisers, please contact McGraw-Hill/Osborne at the above address. For information on translations or book distributors outside the U.S.A., please see the International Contact Information page immediately following the index of this book.

Network+ Certification All-in-One Exam Guide, Second Edition

7890 DOC DOC 01987654

Book p/n 0-07-213162-4 and CD p/n 0-07-213163-2
parts of
ISBN 0-07-213164-0

Publisher	**Technical Editor**
Brandon A. Nordin	Tom McIntyre
Vice President & Associate Publisher	**Copy Editors**
Scott Rogers	Mike McGee
	Dennis Weaver
Acquisitions Editor	**Compositor**
Michael Sprague	MacAllister Publishing Services, LLC
Project Editor	**Cover Design**
Jody McKenzie	Greg Scott
Acquisitions Coordinator	
Jessica Wilson	

This book was composed with QuarkXpress™.

DEDICATION

I'd like to dedicate this book to everyone I've ever snarked during a game
of Half-Life, rail-gunned in Quake, or mowed down with a
Level Three sentry gun in Team Fortress. Make no mistake,
though—I don't apologize, and I'd do it again in a heartbeat.

ACKNOWLEDGMENTS

I'd like to acknowledge the legions of people who contributed their talents to make this book possible:

To my in-house Editor-in-Chief, Scott Jernigan: I'm really looking forward to meeting you at the water bottle inside the Habitrail. You will be toast.

To Cary Dier, Editor Extraordinaire: I tried to warn you—but you still came to work for me! Hmm, my back hurts. Bring out the Table!

To Brian Schwarz, Libby Ingrassia Schwarz, and Nigel Kendrick: Your voices can be heard echoing, occasionally heckling, and once even yodeling in this book. It wouldn't have been nearly as nice without you!

To Jessica Wilson, Love Goddess . . . err . . . Acquisitions Coordinator over at Osborne/McGraw-Hill: My hat is off to you—handling us Total folks with such aplomb is no small feat!

To Michael Sprague: *Nil illegitimus carborundum.*

To Jody McKenzie, our superb Project Editor on the Left Coast and her wonderful copyeditors, Mike McGee and Dennis Weaver: You did a fabulous job and made what could have been a gruesome process into a fairly pleasurable experience.

To Molly Applegate and the talented folks at MacAllister Publishing in the fine city of Indianapolis: Once again, you have done excellent work!

Special thanks to Tom MacIntyre, the technical editor for the book: Stay warm up there in the Great White North, my friend!

To the rest of the folks at Total's Houston HQ—Cindy, John, John, Roger, Dana, Martin, David, Dudley, Janelle, Amber, Kathy, Mandy, Missy, and of course, Bambi: Thanks for all your hard work putting this book together. You guys are the greatest!

Finally, a special thanks to Alison and Emily: You are always first in my world.

ABOUT THE AUTHOR

Michael Meyers is the industry's leading authority on Network+ Certification. He is the president and founder of Total Seminars, LLC, a major provider of PC and Network repair seminars for thousands of organizations throughout the world and a member of CompTIA.

Mike has written numerous popular certification books, including the best-selling *A+ Certification All-in-One Exam Guide.*

BRIEF CONTENTS

CONTENTS

Introduction

In this chapter, you will

- Understand the importance of Network+ Certification
- Discover the structure and goals of the exam
- Find out the "where, when, and how much" of the exam
- Plan a strategy to pass

Why Network+ anyway? Aren't there enough network certifications as it is? Heck, the entire concept of IT certifications began with the Novell NetWare CNE way back in the mid-1980s. Add the Microsoft MCSE to that mix and you have a slew of network certifications already in existence. So, why add to the pile?

The networking side of our business clearly does not suffer from a lack of vendor-specific tests and certifications, and these certifications provide a great way to get (and keep) a job. The *Microsoft Certified Professional* (MCP), *Microsoft Certified Systems Engineer* (MCSE), and *Certified Novell Engineer* (CNE), as well as a few niche players like the *Cisco Certified Network Associate* (CCNA) and *Cisco Certified Internetwork Expert* (CCIE), have opened doors for many who have decided to pursue those certifications.

The vendor-specific certifications, however, fail to address one very important group of people: those who have basic skills that are not specific to any one hardware type or software package—the people, in other words, who have taken the time to understand conceptually how computers and networks operate. These *general practitioners* form the cornerstone of the IT industry. They set up Windows systems to link into NT or Windows 2000 networks. They know how to set the TCP/IP information to access the Internet. They know a network cable from a telephone cable. The vendor-specific certifications fail to test these more generic skills comprehensively.

Further, attaining a vendor-specific certification can cost you a lot in terms of time and money. For many of these vendor-specific certifications you must take a series of tests to get the full certifications. The tuition for courses or boot camps or even the self-study programs, and the amount of work involved in getting those certifications, can be intimidating. By contrast, with the vendor-neutral Network+ Certification you take only one test and get a lifelong certification that never needs updating.

Most techs get their Network+ Certification after becoming A+ certified. Network+ opens the way to several certification paths for those interested in continuing their certifications. Over the past several years, companies offering vendor-specific certifications have begun to respect the need for a Network+ Certification. In fact, many have adopted the Network+ certifications into their programs. After you become Network+ certified, for example, Novell automatically notifies you that you have received credit for its Network Technologies test. Hence, if you decide to focus on Novell, you will already have one test under your belt! Interested in Lotus Notes? You meet Lotus' networking competency requirement for CLP Domino Messaging Administrator R4 certification when you become Network+ certified.

Welcome to Network+ Certification!

What Is Network+ Certification?

Network+ Certification is an industry-wide, vendor-neutral certification program developed and sponsored by the Computing Technology Industry Association (CompTIA). The Network+ Certification shows that you have a basic competency in the physical support of networking systems and knowledge of the conceptual aspects of networking. The test covers the knowledge that a network technician with at least 18 to 24 months of networking experience should have. CompTIA recommends A+ knowledge or background, but does not require an A+ Certification to take the Network+ exam. You achieve a Network+ Certification by taking one computer-based, 65-question multiple-choice examination. To date, nearly 10,000 technicians have become Network+ certified.

A Network+ certified candidate knows the OSI 7-layer model and understands the significance and protocols of each layer. The successful Network+ candidate can explain the essential roles, tasks, installation, and basic troubleshooting of networking components as well as hardware and networking protocols.

Network+ Certification enjoys wide recognition throughout the IT industry. At first, it rode in on the coattails of the successful A+ Certification program, but it now stands on its own in the networking industry. Having a Network+ Certification notably improves your ability to get and keep a job. It also serves as a stepping stone to more networking certificate programs.

What Is CompTIA?

CompTIA is a nonprofit industry trade association based in Lombard, Illinois. More than 8,000 computer resellers, value-added resellers, distributors, manufacturers, and training companies from all over the world are members of CompTIA.

CompTIA was founded in 1982. The following year, CompTIA began offering the A+ Certification exam. Despite a shaky start, A+ Certification is now widely recognized as a de facto requirement for entrance into the PC industry. Because the A+ exam covers networking only lightly, CompTIA decided to establish a vendor-neutral test covering basic networking skills. So, in April 1999, CompTIA unveiled the Network+ Certification exam.

CompTIA provides certifications for a variety of areas in the computer industry, offers opportunities for its members to interact, and represents its members' interests to government bodies. CompTIA certifications include A+, Network+, I-Net+, and Server+, to name a few. Check out the CompTIA web site at http://www.comptia.org for details on other certifications.

Virtually every company of consequence in the IT industry is a member of CompTIA. Here are a few of the biggies:

3COM	Adobe	AST	Digital
Black Box	Canon	Compaq	Hewlett-Packard
Epson	Fujitsu	Hayes	Lexmark
IBM	Intel	Iomega	Minolta
Lotus	Micro House	Microsoft	Novell
NEC	NETGEAR	Netscape	Peachtree
Old Data	Oracle	Panasonic	Symantec
Rockwell	Sun Microsystems	Sybex	AT&T
Toshiba	Total Seminars, LLC (that's my company)		Plus about 8,000 more!

The New Network+ Certification Exam Release

CompTIA constantly works to provide tests that cover the latest technologies, and as part of that effort, they periodically update their test objectives, domains, and test questions. In January 2002, CompTIA released the newest version of the Network+ exam. This book covers all you need to know to pass the 2002 revision of the Network+ Certification exam.

How Do I Become Network+ Certified?

To become Network+ certified, you simply pass one computer-based, multiple-choice exam. There are no prerequisites for taking the Network+ exam, and no networking experience is needed. There is no required training course, nor any training materials to buy. You do not have to use an authorized training center, but you do have to pay a testing fee and must actually sit for the test. You will immediately know whether you passed or failed. Should you pass, that's all it takes. You are now Network+ certified. There are no annual dues, and no continuing education requirements.

Now for the details:

CompTIA does recommend that you have at least nine months of experience and A+ knowledge, but this is not a requirement. Note the word *recommend*. You may not *need* to have experience or A+ knowledge, but from personal experience, both of these help! In particular, A+ knowledge comes in very handy on I/O address and IRQ questions, as well as on connector questions. As for experience, keep in mind that Network+ is mostly a practical exam. Those who have been out there supporting real networks will find many of the questions reminiscent of the types of problems they have actually seen on Local Area Networks (LANs). The bottom line is that you'll probably have a much easier time on the Network+ exam if you have some A+ experience under your belt.

What Are the Tests Like and How Are They Structured?

The Network+ test contains 72 questions, which you have 90 minutes to complete. To pass, you must score at least 646 on a scale of 100–900.

The table that follows lists the CompTIA Network+ domains and the percentage of the test that each represents.

Network+ Certification Exam Domain Areas	Percent of Examination
1.0 Media and Topologies	20 percent
2.0 Protocols and Standards	25 percent
3.0 Network Implementation	23 percent
4.0 Network Support	32 percent
Total	100 percent

The Network+ exam is extremely practical. Questions often present real-life scenarios and ask you to determine the best solution. Network+ loves troubleshooting. Let me repeat: many of the test objectives deal with direct, real-world troubleshooting. Be prepared to troubleshoot both hardware and software failures, and to answer both the "What do you do next?" and "What is most likely the problem?" types of questions.

A qualified Network+ test candidate can install and configure a PC to connect to a network. This includes installing and testing a network card, configuring drivers, and loading all network software. The exam will test you on the different topologies, standards, and cabling.

Expect conceptual questions about the OSI 7-layer model. While this model rarely comes into play during the daily grind of supporting a network, you need to know the functions and protocols for each layer to pass the Network+ exam. You can also expect questions on most of the protocol suites, with heavy emphasis on the TCP/IP suite.

NOTE: In the past, CompTIA has made changes to the content of the exams as well as the score necessary to pass it! Count on that trend to continue. Do not assume they'll wait for a major revision! Always check the CompTIA web site before scheduling your exam. Be prepared!

How Do I Take the Tests?

Prometric/Thompson (formerly known as Sylvan Prometric) and Virtual University Enterprise (VUE) administer the actual Network+ tests. There are thousands of Prometric and VUE testing centers across the United States and Canada as well as in over 75 other countries around the world. You may take the exam at any testing center. In the United States and Canada, call Prometric at 800-77MICRO or VUE at 877-551-7587 to locate the nearest testing center and schedule the exam. International customers should go to CompTIA's web site at http://www.comptia.org, click Search, and then select Find Test Center Location. This page lists contact phone numbers for both Prometric and VUE by areas of the world.

You must pay for the exam when you call to schedule. Be prepared to hold for a while. Have your Social Security number (or international equivalent) and a credit card ready when you call. Both Prometric and VUE will be glad to invoice you, but you won't be able to take the test until they receive full payment. Both Prometric and VUE offer complete listings of all available testing centers online, although only VUE offers you the ability to select the closest training center and schedule your exams online. To view the lists of testing centers, visit their web sites at http://www.prometric.com and http://www.vue.com. If you require any special accommodations, both Prometric and VUE will be able to assist you, although your selection of testing locations may be a bit more limited.

How Much Does the Test Cost?

The cost of the exam depends on whether you work for a CompTIA member or not. At this writing, the cost for non-CompTIA members was $199.00 (U.S.). International prices vary; see the CompTIA web site for international pricing. Of course, prices are subject to change without notice, so always check the CompTIA web site for current pricing!

Very few people pay full price for the exam. Virtually every organization that provides Network+ training and testing offers discount vouchers. Total Seminars (800-446-6004 or 281-922-4166) is one place to pick up discount vouchers. If you work for a CompTIA member, you can get discount vouchers at significant savings. No one should ever pay full price for the Network+ exam!

How to Pass the Network+ Exam

The single most important thing to remember about the Network+ Certification is that CompTIA designed it to test the knowledge of a technician with as little as nine months of experience—so keep it simple! Think in terms of practical knowledge. Read the book, take the practice tests on the CD in the back of the book, review any topics you missed, and you'll pass with flying colors.

Is it safe to assume that it's probably been a while since you've taken an exam? Consequently, has it been a while since you've had to *study* for an exam? If you're nodding your head yes, you'll probably want to read the next sections. They lay out a proven strategy to help you study for the Network+ exam, and pass it. Try it. It works. The Force is with you, young Skywalker . . .

Obligate Yourself

The very first step you should take is to schedule the exam. Ever heard the old adage that heat and pressure make diamonds? Well, if you don't give yourself a little "heat," you'll end up procrastinating and unnecessarily delay taking the exam. Even worse, you may end up not taking the exam at all. Do yourself a favor. Determine how much time you need to study (see the next section), then call Prometric or VUE and schedule the exam for a time not long from now. Afterward, sit back and let your anxieties wash over you. Suddenly it will become a lot easier to turn off the television and crack open the book! Keep in mind that Prometric and VUE let you schedule an exam only a few *weeks* in advance, at most. If you schedule an exam and can't make it, you must reschedule at least a day in advance or lose your money.

Set Aside the Right Amount of Study Time

After helping thousands of techs get their Network+ Certification, we at Total Seminars have developed a pretty good feel for the amount of study time needed to pass the Network+ exam. Table 1-1 will help you plan how much study time you must devote to the Network+ exam. Keep in mind that these are averages. If you're not a great student or if you're a little on the nervous side, add another 10 percent. Equally, if you're the type who can learn an entire semester of geometry in one night, reduce the numbers by 10 percent. To use this table, just circle the values that are most accurate for you, and add them up to get the number of study hours.

A complete neophyte will need at least 120 hours of study time. An experienced network technician with A+ and MCSE or CNE will only need about 24 hours.

Keep in mind that these are estimates. Study habits also come into play here. A person with solid study habits (you know who you are) can reduce the number by 15 percent. People with poor study habits should increase that number by 20 percent.

The total hours of study you need is _____.

Studying for the Test

Now that you have a feel for how long it's going to take, you need a strategy for studying. The following has proven itself to be an excellent game plan for cramming the knowledge from the study materials into your head. Try it. It works!

This strategy has two alternate paths. The first path is designed for highly experienced technicians who have a strong knowledge of PCs and networking and want to concentrate on *just* what's on the exam. Let's call this group the Fast Track group. The second path, and the one I'd strongly recommend, is geared toward people like me: the ones

Table 1-1 Study Hours Guide

Type of Experience	Amount of Experience			
	None	Once or Twice	Every Now and Then	Quite a Bit
Installing structured network cabling	10	8	6	1
Installing network cards	8	7	2	1
Installing RAID devices	4	2	1	1
Building PCs from scratch	4	4	1	0
Installing NetWare using IP	8	8	6	1
Installing an NT/2000 server using IP	8	8	5	1
Configuring a DHCP server	1	1	0	0
Configuring a WINS server	1	1	0	0
Configuring Internet dial-ups	5	4	2	1
Supporting an NT/2000 n etwork	6	5	3	2
Supporting a NetWare network	6	5	3	1
Supporting a UNIX network	4	4	1	1
Supporting a Windows 9x/ME network	3	3	2	2
Installing/troubleshooting routers	3	3	1	1
Installing/troubleshooting hubs	2	2	1	1
Creating tape backups	1	1	0	0

who want to know *why* things work, who want to wrap their arms completely around a concept, as opposed to regurgitating answers just to pass the Network+ exam. Let's call this group the Brainiacs.

To provide for both types of learners, I have broken down most of the chapters into three parts:

- **Historical/Conceptual**   It's not on the Network+ exam, but it's knowledge that will help you understand more clearly what *is* on the Network+ exam.

- **Test Specific**   Topics that clearly fit under the Network+ Certification domains.

- **Beyond Network+**   More advanced issues that probably will not be on the Network+ exam.

The beginning of each of these areas is clearly marked with a large banner that looks like this:

Historical/Conceptual

If you consider yourself a Fast Tracker, skip everything but the Test Specific section in each chapter. After reading the Test Specific section, jump immediately to the End of Chapter questions, which concentrate on information in the Test Specific section. If you run into problems, review the Historical/Conceptual sections in that chapter. Be aware that you may need to skip back to previous chapters to get the Historical/Conceptual information you need for a later chapter.

 NOTE: Not every chapter will have all three sections!

After going through every chapter as described, do the free practice exams on the CD-ROM that accompanies the book. First, do them in practice mode, then switch to final mode. Once you start hitting in the 800 range, go take the test!

Brainiacs should first read the book—the *whole* book. Read it as though you're reading a novel, starting on page one and going all the way through. Don't skip around on the first read-through, even if you are a highly experienced tech. Because there are terms and concepts that build on each other, skipping around will make you confused, and you'll just end up closing the book and firing up your favorite PC game. Your goal on this first read is to understand *concepts*—to understand the whys, not just the hows. It is very helpful to have a network available while you're doing this.

You will notice a lot of historical information—the Historical/Conceptual sections—which you may be tempted to skip. Don't! Understanding how some of the older stuff worked will help you appreciate the reason behind modern networking features and how they function.

After you have completed the first read-through, cozy up for a second. This time try to knock out one chapter at a sitting. Concentrate on the Test Specific sections. Get a highlighter and mark the phrases and sentences that bring out major points. Take a hard look at the pictures and tables, noting how they illustrate the concepts.

Once you have read and studied the material in the book, check your knowledge with the practice exams included on the CD-ROM at the back of the book. The exams can be taken in practice mode or final mode. In practice mode, you are allowed to check references in the book (if you want) before you answer each question, and each question is graded immediately. In final mode, you must answer all the questions before you are given a test score. In each case, you can review a results summary that tells you which questions you missed, what the right answer is, and where to study further.

NOTE: For those who'd like some questions that are above and beyond the norm, you can purchase a CD-ROM with extra exams from Total Seminars (www.totalsem.com) You don't need them to pass the exam, but if you want some additional practice, they're a great deal!!

Use the results of the exams to see where you need to bone up, then study some more and try them again. Continue retaking the exams and reviewing the topics you missed until you are consistently scoring in the 800 range. When you've reached that point, you are ready to pass the Network+ exam!

If you have any problems or questions, or if you just want to argue about something, feel free to send an e-mail to the author at michaelm@totalsem.com.

For additional information about the Network+ exam, contact CompTIA directly at its web site: http://www.comptia.org.

Good Luck!

Mike Meyers

PART I

Everything You Ever Really Wanted to Know About Networking

Network Fundamentals

In this chapter, you will

- Look at the history of networking
- Understand the goal of networking
- Understand the concept of servers and clients
- Understand the concept of sharing resources

Every once in a while, a completely obsolete technology or way of doing things will resurface years later in a recognizable, but dramatically changed, form to fix a problem in the world of computing. Most techs refer to this phenomenon as "everything old is new again," and it holds up as a truism in the IT industry. From a tech's standpoint, this means that learning how things used to be done can often shed light on or solve problems that come up much later. In short, know your history! Let's start with a look at the evolution of networking.

Historical/Conceptual

At the beginning of real computing back in the late 1960s, the world used large, individual mainframe computers. Though the word *mainframe* in this context may sound impressive, the computers sitting in our offices and homes today have far more computing power than the archaic systems of that era. Nevertheless, those early mainframes were the cutting edge of technology at the time, capable enough even to put men on the moon! This cutting edge cachet, combined with the fact that mainframes always lived behind locked doors in faraway rooms tended by geeky acolytes, gave them an aura of exclusivity and mystery that still exists today.

One aspect of mainframes *did* make them very special: there just weren't that many of them. So, how do you share one of these big whopper systems, ensuring that many people can do their work simultaneously? The earliest answer was very simple: you stood in line. (See Figure 2-1.) Early mainframes didn't have a monitor and keyboard the way PCs do today. (If you're under 35, you probably think I'm making this up, but stay with me.) If a keyboard did exist, it was on a single, large typewriter-like console in the computer room, and the acolytes used it to give the system detailed operating commands, like telling it to look in a specific memory address for a piece of data or program code.

Most systems loaded programs using punch cards or magnetic tape. You, as the powerless user, stood in line with your tape or stack of cards and took a number. You submitted your "job" to a person behind a counter and came back an hour (or a day) later to receive a stack of readout paper along with your cards or tape. If you were lucky, you got a meaningful and relevant result and shouted, "Eureka!" or some other dandy phrase, much to the annoyance of the other programmers. Just as often, however, you got back a pile of gibberish or an error code, at which point you went back to the keypuncher and tried to figure out what you'd done wrong. In short, early mainframe computing wasn't pretty—but it beat the heck out of doing the calculations by hand!

Fairly quickly, mainframes began to use CRT terminals and keyboards. But let's get one thing straight: These were *not* networks in any way! The terminals were simply data

Figure 2-1 Standing in line

entry ports that enabled you to compose your programs. (Forget about ready-to-go applications—if you wanted to run a computer program for some purpose, you usually had to write it first!) The terminals themselves had no CPUs or other computer chips at all. They were strictly I/O devices, like the keyboard and monitor on a modern PC. That's why we use the term *dumb terminal* when referring to these ancient devices. (See Figure 2-2.)

Mainframe computers grew more sophisticated during the late '60s and '70s, incorporating features such as mass storage (hard drives) and more sophisticated operating systems to let multiple mainframe users access common data on that mass storage. Users enjoyed the ability to access common data on one mainframe, but that still wasn't networking because the data was only on one computer. By the late '60s, however, scientists and researchers saw the benefits of enabling users on one mainframe computer to share data with users on other mainframes.

The concept of sharing data between mainframes sounded great, but presented huge challenges. How could they connect mainframes that were often hundreds, if not

Figure 2-2   A typical dumb terminal from the '70s

Figure 2-3 What will it take for us to be able to talk?

thousands, of miles apart? Also, by this time many locations had acquired several mainframes, but often from different manufacturers who used totally different operating systems, data formats, and interfaces. How could they get totally different machines to share data as depicted in Figure 2-3? A lot of smart people were going to have to work hard to come up with a way to hook computers together in this structure we eventually came to call a *network*.

Remote terminals offered an early, but somewhat limited, method for accessing remote computers. A remote terminal used a modem and conventional phone lines to connect to some far-flung system across town or across the world. The downside to remote terminals was that they did not allow *sharing* of information. Using a remote terminal, you could access the remote computer, but *not* your local computer. Using your local terminal, you could not access the remote computer. Sure, it was better than no remote access at all, but this still left something to be desired!

Let's go back to the late 1960s and see what the early creators of networking had to face to answer this big question: How can we enable two separate computer systems to share data?

Before we begin, you should understand that no one group or person invented networking. The beginnings of networking can be traced to a number of now-famous research papers that discussed the myriad issues involved in making a network work. Researchers spent years theorizing about networking, long before any real network ever existed. Most people agree that the first practical network ever created was ARPANET. ARPANET was conceived by an organization called the Advanced Research Projects Agency (ARPA).

ARPA was created in 1958 by President Eisenhower, the same president who created another important network, the Interstate Highway System. ARPA is more commonly referred to as DARPA (Defense Advanced Research Projects Agency), and is still in existence today (www.darpa.mil). Its name was changed from ARPA to DARPA in 1972, back to ARPA in 1993, and back to DARPA again in 1996, so I'll refer to it as DARPA in this book. DARPA is a consortium of federal organizations and researchers who work on a number of highly technical projects for the U.S. government. It was DARPA that first funded a small project to pull together the existing mass of theoretical research and try to create a practical, working network.

Understanding Networking

Folks often make two big mistakes when they initially attempt to understand networking. First, they fail to appreciate the phenomenal *complexity* of even the simplest networks. Second, they fail to understand the *goal* of networking, which is *not* to share data. I'll deal with the complexity issue in a moment. Right now, let's think about the goal of networking. The magic word here is *sharing*.

A single mainframe computer with a zillion terminals can't really share. Granted, all those terminals provide multiple access points to its data, but keep in mind that all the data is on that one system. In order for something to be a network, there must be *more than one* system. This is a critical issue, and one that comes up even in today's post-mainframe world.

 NOTE: A network must consist of more than one separate system.

Test Specific

Let's get back to the concept of sharing. Assuming we have more than one system, what is there on the other system that we want to access? Put another way, what do we want to share?

What to Share

"What do we want to share?" was one of the biggest questions for the folks who first invented networks. To your average, modern office worker, this may seem like a silly question—why, we want to share files and printers, right? Well, the answer didn't seem as obvious back then as it does today. Sure, they wanted to share files, but they were also smart enough to appreciate that they couldn't even *begin* to guess what else they might want to share in the far-off future. Thank goodness! More than anything else, they wanted to create some type of standardized networking structure, hardware, and software that would allow a network to grow and adapt as new uses came to light. Almost no one could have imagined something as amazing as the World Wide Web back in the late '60s—but they still managed to create a networking methodology that enabled existing networks to integrate the technology of the World Wide Web easily when it later came along.

Networks enable computers to share *resources*. A resource is anything that a particular device on a particular network wants to share with other systems. Typical resources include files, folders, and printers. But there are other types of resources, ones that aren't nearly as simple to visualize. For example, e-mail is a resource for transferring messages. Further, networks enable computers to share functions, like program execution, as well as files. To log into a remote computer and run a program on that machine, for example, all you need is a terminal emulation tool like Telnet and a working network connection. Sharing resources, therefore, means much more than simply sharing files! We'll look at all of these resources and more as the book progresses, but for now just accept the concept that virtually anything that one computer can serve up to another computer is a resource.

Servers and Clients

Okay, so a network centers around the concept of shared resources—cool. Now we need to determine who shares, and who simply accesses the shared resource. That's where the terms *server* and *client* come into play. A server is a system on a network that shares resources, while a client is a system that accesses a shared resource.

I can hear you right now: "But Mike, I thought a server was one of those big super PCs that hide in closets!" Well, yes, we do call those servers, but that is a special use of the word. Any system that shares resources on a network will work best if it has extra power to handle all of the incoming requests for its shared resources. In response to this need, the PC industry makes higher-powered systems specifically designed to meet the extra demands of *serving up* resources. And everybody calls them . . . you guessed it: servers!

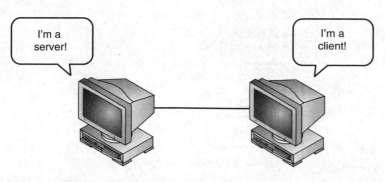

Figure 2-4   I'm a server! I'm a client!

The key addition you must make to create a network server, however, is not special hardware, but rather *software*. Any system that wants to share its resources must run a *serving program*. By the same token, a client system must run a *client program* to access shared resources on a network. (See Figure 2-4.) Thus, even though servers tend to be the musclemen of the PC world, *any* system able to run a serving program can be a server.

If any system running a server program is a server, then can there be more than one server on a network? For that matter, can one system run multiple serving programs? Heck, yes! It's done all the time. In my office, for example, I have one computer that runs at least seven different serving programs, sharing everything from files to e-mail to a web site. Depending on the time of day, my office also contains roughly a dozen different systems that serve up something.

The final thing to appreciate is that a system can be both a server *and* a client at the same time. With the exception of Novell NetWare, every operating system that can do networking (Windows, UNIX/Linux, and Macintosh) enables systems to act both as servers and as clients at the same time. (See Figure 2-5.)

In my office, every PC on the network is both a server and a client. This setup is common in office environments because it facilitates sharing both work files and common peripherals, like printers.

Making Shared Resources Useable

Okay, so servers share resources and clients access those shared resources. The last big conceptual question is: how do we make sure that a client system—and the human using it—can actually use a shared resource? The answer to this one is simple. A shared

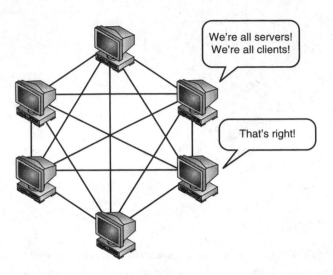

Figure 2-5   We're all servers! We're all clients!

resource must look and act as if it were local to the client system's hard drive. It may be okay and even useful, for example, if the icon of a shared folder looks slightly different on the screen—blue instead of yellow, say, or with an added symbol—but it should be similar enough that you can tell it's a folder. Even more importantly, it should interact with the client system's file manager or word processing software just as if it were local to that system. An example of a typical shared folder in Windows 2000 is shown in the following illustration:

Moe's files

A resource that isn't shared is like a picture of a big fat warm-from-the-oven chocolate chip cookie—you can drool all you want, but it doesn't do you any good because you can't have it!

The Goal of Networking

You are now armed with three critical pieces of information about what a network must do: it must have shared resources, there must always be a client and a server, and shared resources must look or at least act like local resources. By putting these three features together, we can finally define the entire reason to use networks—what I like to call the Big Kahuna of Networking, but which my English teacher would prefer to call the Goal of Networking:

The goal of networking is to enable remote systems (servers) to share their resources with accessing systems (clients) in such a way that the shared resources are comprehensible to the client systems.

That's it. That statement, in a nutshell, defines the entire reason networks exist. Now that you understand *why* computers use networks, you can begin the very interesting process of learning how a network functions.

Chapter Review

Questions

1. Which of the following statements are true of all servers? (Choose two.)
   a. Servers access resources on client computers.
   b. Servers make resources available for client computers to access.
   c. Servers have special server hardware installed.
   d. Servers have special server software installed.

2. Which of the following is *not* a resource that can be shared by a server?
   a. Mouse
   b. Printer
   c. Folder
   d. File

3. Which of the following network operating systems *cannot* act as both a client and a server simultaneously?
   a. Windows 2000
   b. Linux
   c. Macintosh
   d. Novell NetWare

4. Which of the following is necessary to have a network?
   a. An Ethernet connection
   b. At least one server and two clients

    c. More than one system

    d. A remote terminal

5. The goal of networking is
   a. To enable remote systems to connect to each other efficiently and to access each other's files.
   b. To enable remote systems to share resources with accessing systems in such a way that the shared resources are comprehensible to the accessing systems.
   c. To enable servers to access resources on one or more client systems in such a way that the shared resources are comprehensible to the accessing systems.
   d. To enable users on remote terminals to access mainframe systems as if they were directly connected to those systems.

Answers

1. **B, D.** Servers must have server software installed. This software is what enables them to serve up resources to client computers. Hardware upgrades can help a server handle its workload, but are not required.

2. **A.** A mouse is not a resource that would typically be shared on a network.

3. **D.** Novell NetWare cannot act as both a client and a server simultaneously. All of the other operating systems can.

4. **C.** To have a network you must have more than one system. A mainframe connected to dumb terminals, whether remote or local, is still just a single system.

5. **B.** The goal of networking is to enable remote systems to share resources with accessing systems in such a way that the shared resources are comprehensible to the accessing systems.

Building a Network with OSI

In this chapter, you will

- Look at a conceptual overview of network hardware and software functions
- Understand the physical aspect of networking
- Understand the concept of a system sending and receiving data
- Learn the hardware aspect of networking
- Learn the basics of the TCP/IP protocol
- Understand the concept of accessing a system on a network
- Understand the concept and functions of the OSI seven-layer model

Let's look at a typical network situation you might find in many small offices today: a network of PCs all running the Windows 2000 operating system at a company called Wheebo, Inc. The Windows 2000 operating system has complete network functionality built in, making Windows 2000 a network operating system (NOS) as well as a standard operating system. The Wheebo network uses a popular cabling system called unshielded twisted pair. Just keep in mind that other networks may use other types of cabling or even wireless connections. The specific type of NOS and cabling used by the network really don't matter for purposes of this chapter's more conceptual overview, but to avoid getting thousands of e-mails saying "my cabling doesn't look like that!" I will specify that this particular network uses UTP cabling.

Historical/Conceptual

The goal of this chapter is not to give you gritty technical details on how a network functions. This chapter simply provides you with a conceptual overview of the many hardware and software components involved in the process of making a network function. Again, don't be misled by the fact that I'm using Windows 2000 or UTP cabling in my Wheebo examples—every part of this process works almost, if not exactly, the same way in every type of network. So sit back, gather your wits about you, and let's take a look inside the visible network!

NOTE: This section is a conceptual overview of the hardware and software functions of a network. Your network may have different hardware or software, but it will share the same functions!

So, without further ado, let's head over to Wheebo, Inc. and start by taking a look at the overall network. As in most offices, virtually everyone has their own PC for personal use. Figure 3-1 shows two workers, Janelle and Dana. Janelle and Dana handle all of the administrative functions at Wheebo and as a result, often need to exchange data between their two PCs. Janelle just completed a new employee handbook in Microsoft Word and wants Dana to check it for accuracy. Janelle could transfer a copy of the file

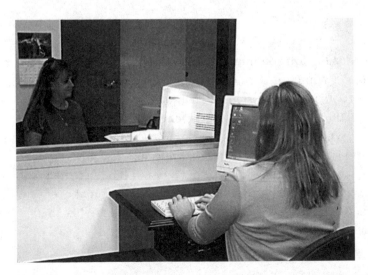

Figure 3-1   Janelle and Dana—happy workers!

to Dana's computer by the tried and true *Sneakernet* method, saving the file on a floppy disk and walking it over to her, but thanks to the wonders of computer networking, she doesn't have to get out of her chair. Let's watch in detail the process by which the network gives Dana direct access to Janelle's computer so she can copy the Word document from Janelle's system to her own.

Long before Janelle ever saved the Word document on her system, when the systems were first installed, someone who knew what they were doing performed a number of setups and configurations to make the systems of Janelle, Dana, and everyone else at Wheebo, Inc. part of a common network. All this setup activity resulted in multiple layers of hardware and software working together behind the scenes to get that Word document from Janelle's system to Dana's. Let's start by examining the different pieces, and then return to the process of Dana grabbing that Word document.

Test Specific

Let's Get Physical

Clearly the network needs a physical channel through which it can move bits of data between systems. Most networks use a cable like the one shown in Figure 3-2. This cable, known in the networking industry as *unshielded twisted pair* (UTP), contains

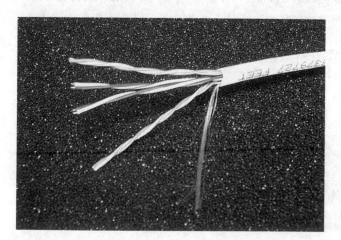

Figure 3-2 UTP network cable showing wires

either four or eight wires that transmit data. The Wheebo network's UTP cable uses only four: two for sending data and two for receiving.

Another key piece of hardware the network uses is a special device called a *hub*, often tucked away in a closet somewhere (Figure 3-3). Each system on the network has its own cable that runs to the hub. Think of the hub as something like one of the old-time telephone switchboards, where operators created connections between persons who called in wanting to reach other telephone users. A hub departs from the switchboard/operator analogy in one way: the hub doesn't connect the "caller" to one specific "callee." Instead, the hub passes along the data received from one system to *all* the other systems, leaving the systems themselves to sort out which of them are actually the intended recipients. Remember this fact, because it becomes a very important concept later.

Okay, back to the hardware, because there's another key piece you will be hearing a lot about: the *network interface card* or NIC (pronounced "nick"). The real magic of a network starts with the NIC, which serves as the interface between the PC and the network. While NICs come in a wide array of shapes and sizes, the ones at Wheebo look like Figure 3-4.

When installed in a PC, the NIC looks like Figure 3-5. Note the cable running from the back of the NIC into the wall—that cable runs all the way back to the hub.

Now that you have a picture of all the pieces, here's a diagram of the network cabling system (Figure 3-6). I'll build on this diagram as I delve deeper into the network process.

The NIC

To understand networks, you must understand what takes place inside a NIC. If you look at the previous diagram, you'll notice that all the networked systems connect to the same hub. The network must provide a mechanism that gives each system a unique identifier, like a telephone number, so that data is delivered to the right system. That's one of the most important jobs of a NIC. Inside every NIC, burned onto some type of

Figure 3-3   Typical hub

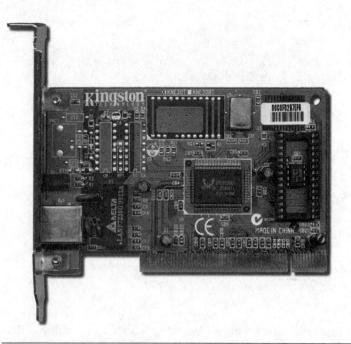

Figure 3-4   Typical NIC

Figure 3-5   NIC in a PC

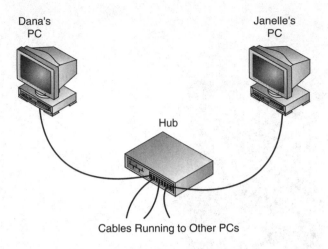

Figure 3-6   The Wheebo network

ROM chip, is special firmware containing a unique identifier with a 48-bit value called the *Media Access Control address* (MAC address). No two NICs ever share the same MAC address—ever. The companies that make NICs must contact the IEEE (Institute of Electrical and Electronics Engineers) and request a block of MAC addresses that they then burn into the ROMs on the NICs. Many NIC makers also print the MAC address on the surface of the NIC, as shown in Figure 3-7. Note that this NIC shows the MAC address in hexadecimal notation. Count the number of hex characters—since each hex character represents four bits, it takes 12 hex characters to represent 48 bits. The MAC address in Figure 3-7 is 004005-5B7151, although in print it appears as 00-40-05-5B-71-51. The first six digits, in this example 00-40-05, represent the number of the manufacturer of the NIC card. The last six digits, in this example 5B-71-51, are the manufacturer's serial number for that NIC card.

All NICs will respond to software requests for their MAC address. Would you like to see the MAC address for your NIC? On Window 9*x* systems, run the WINIPCFG command to see the MAC address (Figure 3-8).

On Windows NT/2000 systems, running IPCONFIG /ALL from a command prompt displays the MAC address (Figure 3-9).

Okay, so every NIC in the world has a unique thingy called a MAC address, but how is it used? Ah, that's where the fun begins! Recall that computer data is binary, which is to say streams of ones and zeros. NICs send and receive this binary data as pulses of

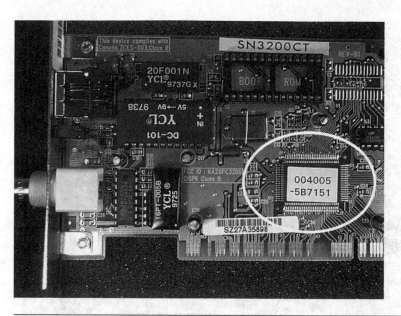

Figure 3-7 NIC with printed MAC address

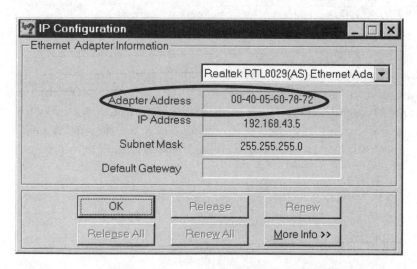

Figure 3-8 WINIPCFG (showing MAC address circled)

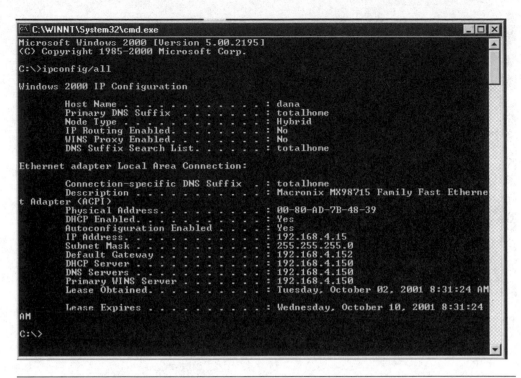

```
C:\WINNT\System32\cmd.exe                                           _ □ ×
Microsoft Windows 2000 [Version 5.00.2195]
(C) Copyright 1985-2000 Microsoft Corp.

C:\>ipconfig/all

Windows 2000 IP Configuration

        Host Name . . . . . . . . . . . . : dana
        Primary DNS Suffix  . . . . . . . : totalhome
        Node Type . . . . . . . . . . . . : Hybrid
        IP Routing Enabled. . . . . . . . : No
        WINS Proxy Enabled. . . . . . . . : No
        DNS Suffix Search List. . . . . . : totalhome

Ethernet adapter Local Area Connection:

        Connection-specific DNS Suffix  . : totalhome
        Description . . . . . . . . . . . : Macronix MX98715 Family Fast Etherne
t Adapter (ACPI)
        Physical Address. . . . . . . . . : 00-80-AD-7B-48-39
        DHCP Enabled. . . . . . . . . . . : Yes
        Autoconfiguration Enabled . . . . : Yes
        IP Address. . . . . . . . . . . . : 192.168.4.15
        Subnet Mask . . . . . . . . . . . : 255.255.255.0
        Default Gateway . . . . . . . . . : 192.168.4.152
        DHCP Server . . . . . . . . . . . : 192.168.4.150
        DNS Servers . . . . . . . . . . . : 192.168.4.150
        Primary WINS Server . . . . . . . : 192.168.4.150
        Lease Obtained. . . . . . . . . . : Tuesday, October 02, 2001 8:31:24 AM

        Lease Expires . . . . . . . . . . : Wednesday, October 10, 2001 8:31:24
AM

C:\>
```

Figure 3-9 IPCONFIG/ALL (MAC address is listed as Physical Address)

electricity, light, or radio waves. The NICs that use electricity to send and receive data are the most common, so let's consider that type of NIC. The exact process by which a NIC uses electricity to send and receive data is exceedingly complicated, but lucky for you, not necessary to understand. Instead, just think of a *charge* on the wire as a *one*, and *no charge* as a *zero*. A chunk of data moving in pulses across a wire might look something like Figure 3-10.

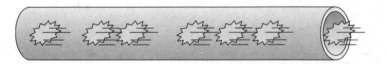

Figure 3-10 Data pulses on a wire

Figure 3-11 Oscilloscope readout of the voltages on the wire

Figure 3-12 Ones and zeros

If you put an oscilloscope on the wire measuring voltage, you'd see something like Figure 3-11.

Now, remembering that the pulses represent binary data, visualize instead a string of ones and zeros moving across the wire (Figure 3-12).

Once you understand how data moves along the wire, the next question becomes: how does the network get the right data to the right system? Data is sent across networks in discrete chunks called *frames*. A frame is basically a container for a chunk of data moving across a network. The NIC creates and sends as well as receives and reads these frames. I like to visualize an imaginary table inside every NIC that acts as a frame creation and reading station. I see frames as those pneumatic canisters you see when you go to a drive-in teller at a bank. A little guy inside the network card—named Nick, naturally!—builds these pneumatic canisters (the frames) on the table and then shoots them out on the wire to the hub (Figure 3-13).

Figure 3-13 A frame-building table inside a NIC

NOTE: There are a number of different frame types used in different networks. All NICs on the same network must use the same frame type or they will not be able to communicate with other NICs. Fortunately, almost all modern NICs can automatically determine the type of frame in use on a particular network and adjust to send and receive that type of frame.

Here's where the MAC address becomes important. Figure 3-14 shows a generic frame. Each rectangle represents a string of ones and zeros—you will see this type of frame representation used quite often, so you should become comfortable with it (even though I still prefer to see frames as pneumatic canisters!). Note that the frame begins with the MAC address of the NIC to which the data is to be sent, followed by the MAC address of the sending NIC. Then comes the data, followed by a special bit of checking information called the Cyclic Redundancy Check (CRC) that the receiving NIC uses to verify the data got to it correctly.

So what does the data look like? Well, we don't know, nor do we care. The data may be a part of a file, a piece of a print job, or part of a web page. NICs don't care about this. The NIC simply takes whatever data is passed to it via its device driver and sends it to the correct system. Special software will take care of *what* data gets sent and what happens to that data when it arrives. This is the beauty of imagining frames as little pneumatic canisters (Figure 3-15). A canister can carry anything from dirt to diamonds —within certain size limitations—which has no bearing on how the canister works, does it?

Recipient's MAC address	Sender's MAC address	Data	CRC

Figure 3-14   Generic frame

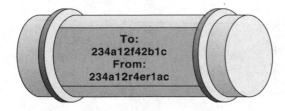

Figure 3-15   Frame as a canister

Like a canister, a frame can only hold a certain amount of data. Different networks use different sizes of frames, but generally a single frame holds about 1500 bytes of data. This raises a new question: what happens when the data to be sent is larger than the frame size? Well, the sending system's software must chop the data up into nice, frame-sized chunks. The receiving system's software must then recombine the data chunks as they come in from the network. But this disassembling and reassembling activity isn't the job of the NIC. The data itself includes special numbering to handle this issue.

When a frame goes out on the network, every system on that network receives the frame. I like to visualize a frame sliding onto the NIC's frame assembly table, where the electronics of the NIC inspect it. However, only the NIC to which the frame is addressed will process it—the other NICs simply erase it when they see that it is not addressed to their MAC address. This is very important to appreciate: *every* frame sent on a network is received by *every* NIC, but only the NIC with the matching MAC address will actually process that particular frame (Figure 3-16).

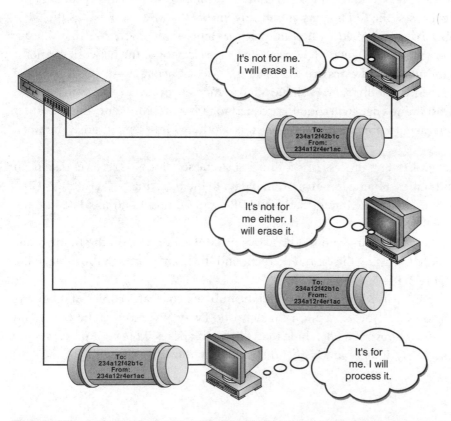

Figure 3-16   All NICs getting a frame but only one actually processing it

Getting the Data on the Line

The process of actually getting data onto the wire and then picking that data off the wire is amazingly complicated. For instance, what happens to keep two NICs from speaking at the same time? Because all of the data sent by one NIC is read by every other NIC on the network, only one system may speak at a time. Networks use frames to restrict the amount of data a NIC can send at one time, giving all NICs a chance to send data over the network in a reasonable span of time. Dealing with this and many other issues requires sophisticated electronics, but lucky for us the NICs handle these issues completely on their own without any help from us. So thankfully, while the folks who design NICs worry about all these details, we don't have to!

Getting to Know You

Now that we have a few basic concepts, let's look at how a network moves a frame from one system to another. Each step in the process raises important questions. First of all, how does a sending NIC know the MAC address of the NIC to which it is sending the data? In most cases, the sending system already knows the MAC address, as the NICs had probably communicated earlier and each system stores that data. If it doesn't already know the MAC address, a NIC may send a *broadcast* onto the network to ask for it. Certain unique IP addresses are assigned as *broadcast addresses*—if a NIC sends a frame to a broadcast address, every single NIC on the network will process that frame. That broadcast frame's data will contain a request for a system's MAC address. The other systems will then respond, although *how* this works varies tremendously between networks.

The basic send/receive process is as follows: First, the sending NIC receives data from the NOS and builds a frame to transport that data to the receiving NIC (Figure 3-17).

After the NIC creates the frame, it adds the CRC and dumps it and the data into the frame (Figure 3-18).

Next, it puts the receiving and sending systems' MAC addresses on the frame, waits until no other NIC is using the cable, and then sends the frame through the cable to the network (Figure 3-19).

The frame propagates down the wire into the hub, which creates copies of the frame and sends it to every other system on the network. Every NIC receives the frame and checks the MAC address. If a NIC finds that a frame is addressed to it, it processes the frame (Figure 3-20); if the frame is not addressed to it, the NIC erases it.

Figure 3-17 Building the frame

Figure 3-18 Adding the data and the CRC to the frame

So, what happens to the data when it gets to the *correct* NIC? Well, first the receiving NIC uses the CRC to verify the data is valid. If it is, the NIC strips off all the framing information and sends the data to the software—the NOS—for processing. The NIC doesn't care what the software does with the data—its job stops the moment it passes

Figure 3-19   Sending the frame

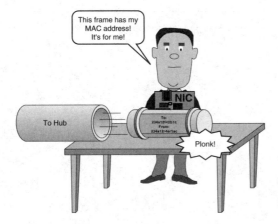

Figure 3-20   Receiving the Frame

on the data to the NOS. We *are* interested, however. You will learn what happens to that data when I talk about the NOS in more depth later in the book.

The Two Aspects of Hardware

There are basically two aspects to networking hardware: cabling and NICs. A network's cabling must provide a way for pieces of data to move from one system to another. It provides a shared method, such as a hub, for multiple systems to access the network. The NIC is, of course, physically connected to the cable, but a NIC does far more than simply connect a PC to a network. The NIC creates and destroys frames. It holds the all-important MAC address, the unique identifier that guides data packets to the correct NIC. Finally, the NIC creates a CRC on the end of each packet so the receiving NIC can verify that the data inside is in good shape.

Beyond the Single Wire

Getting data from one system to another in a simple network takes relatively little effort on the part of the NICs, which all use the same frame type and share the same hub. But what happens when you start to use the network for more complex functions? What if someone wants to use a modem to dial into Janelle's system? Modems connect to a network in a totally different way—they don't use MAC addresses and their frame types are unique. Or what if Wheebo merges with a company that uses Macintosh computers and a different type of cabling? In these situations, you can't put these different systems on the same cable—the different frame types alone make them incompatible! (Figure 3-21.) You need some method besides MAC addresses to provide each system on the network with a unique identifier. You need special software that creates a unique identifier and that works with any type of NIC, any type of frame, and any type of hardware.

This special software—usually called a *network protocol*—exists in almost every network-capable operating system. A network protocol not only has to create unique identifiers for each system, it must also create a set of communication rules for issues like how to handle data chopped up into multiple packets, and how to deal with these really cool network tools called *routers*. I'd love to stop and explain routers right now,

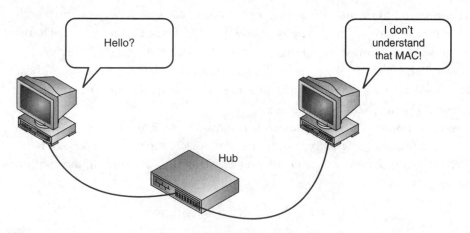

Figure 3-21 We can't speak to each other!

but routers won't make much sense until you understand network protocols. So let's talk about network protocols first, and then we'll look at routers.

You may not realize it, but you've probably heard of network protocols before—the most famous one is called *TCP/IP*, which is part of every system that accesses the Internet. To be accurate, TCP/IP is really two sets of network protocols—that's why there's a slash between TCP and IP. TCP stands for *Transmission Control Protocol*, and IP stands for *Internet Protocol*. IP is the network protocol I need to discuss first; rest assured, however, I'll cover TCP in plenty of detail later!

NOTE: TCP/IP is the most famous network protocol, but there are plenty of others!

The IP protocol is primarily concerned with making sure that packets get where they need to go on the network. It does this by giving each device on the network a unique name. Every network protocol uses some type of naming convention, but no two protocols do it the same way. IP uses a rather unique dotted-octal numbering system based on four 8-bit numbers. Each 8-bit number ranges from 0 to 255, and the four numbers are separated by periods. (If you don't see how 8-bit numbers can range from 0 to 255, don't worry. By the end of this book, you'll understand these in more detail than you ever believed possible!) A typical IP address might look like this:

192.168.4.232

No two devices on the same network share the same IP address; if two machines accidentally receive the same address, a nasty error will occur. These IP addresses don't just magically appear—they must be configured. Some IP networks take advantage of a groovy tool called Dynamic Host Configuration Protocol (DHCP) to configure these values. Here's the network diagram again, this time showing the IP and MAC addresses for each system (Figure 3-22).

Once every computer has an IP address, the network protocol has to be able to do the data transfer, no matter what type of frame or hardware the various computers are running. To do this, a network protocol also uses frames—actually, frames within frames!

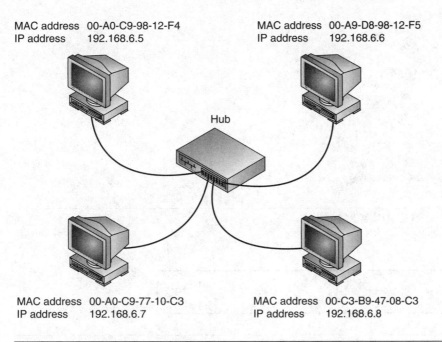

MAC address   00-A0-C9-98-12-F4
IP address   192.168.6.5

MAC address   00-A9-D8-98-12-F5
IP address   192.168.6.6

Hub

MAC address   00-A0-C9-77-10-C3
IP address   192.168.6.7

MAC address   00-C3-B9-47-08-C3
IP address   192.168.6.8

Figure 3-22   IP and MAC address for each system on the network

There's Frames in Them Thar Frames!

Whoa! Frames within frames? What are you talking about, Mike? Never fear, I'll show you. When the network protocol gets hold of data coming from higher layers of software, it places its own packet around it. We call this a *packet* so it won't be confused with the *frame* that the NIC will add later. Figure 3-23 shows a typical IP data packet; notice the similarity to the frames you saw earlier. Warning: this is a highly simplified IP packet—I am not including lots of little parts of the IP packet in this diagram because they are not important to what you need to understand right now—but don't worry, you'll see them later in the book!

Data Type	Packet Count	Recipient's IP address	Sender's IP address	Data

Figure 3-23   IP packet

Figure 3-24   An IP packet in a frame

Frame	Packet	Data	CRC

Figure 3-25   An IP packet with frame added

But IP packets don't leave their PC home naked. Each IP packet is handed to the NIC, which then encloses the IP packet in a regular frame, creating, in essence, *a packet within a frame*. I like to visualize the packet as an envelope, with the envelope in the pneumatic canister frame (Figure 3-24). A more conventional drawing would look like Figure 3-25.

All very nice, you say, but why hassle with this *packet in a frame* business when you could just use MAC addresses? For that matter, why even bother with this IP thing in the first place? Good question, if I do say so myself! Let me explain . . .

Let's say that Janelle wants to access the Internet from her PC. To make this possible, we will connect the Wheebo network to the Internet by adding a *router* (Figure 3-26).

Basically, routers are devices that link networks to other networks. This router has two connections. One is really just a built-in NIC that runs from the router to the hub. The other connection links the router to a telephone line. And therein lies our answer: telephone systems *don't use MAC addresses*. They use their own type of frame that has nothing to do with MAC addresses. If you tried to send a regular network frame on a phone line—well, actually I don't know exactly what would happen, but I assure you it doesn't work! Therefore when a router receives an IP packet inside a frame added by a NIC, it peels off that frame and replaces it with the type of frame the phone system needs (Figure 3-27).

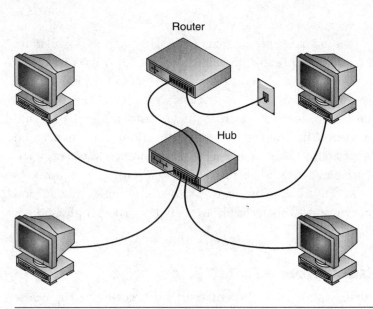

Figure 3-26 Adding a router to the network

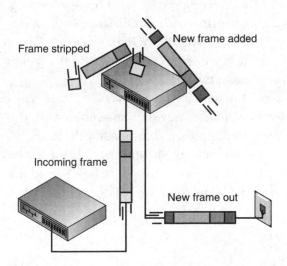

Figure 3-27 Router removing network frame and adding one for telephone line

Once the network frame is gone, so are the MAC addresses! Thus, you need some *other* naming system the router can use to get the data to the right computer—and that's why you use IP addresses on a network! Here's the most frequent come-back I get from students when I teach this: "Well, Mike, if I have a network that does not go out to the Internet, do I still need to do all this IP stuff?" My answer: "No, actually, you don't!" There are other network protocols, some of which are much easier to use than IP and require almost no configuration. The problem is they don't work on the Internet, and most networks *do* require the ability to communicate over the Internet as well as internally. Thus the question becomes, why go to the hassle of installing two protocols when one will do? Sure, you can install many, many protocols on one computer, and sometimes you have to, but most network techs like to keep their lives simple, and I'm one of them!

Assembly and Disassembly—TCP

Most data is much larger than a single frame and as a result must get chopped up before it is sent across a network. When the network protocol receives a file, web page, print job, or anything else from a higher layer, it must be able to receive that data, chop it into packet-sized chunks, organize the packets for the benefit of the receiving system, send them, and verify that all of them made it. The receiving system must be able to recognize a series of incoming packets as one data transmission, and reassemble them correctly. Remember when I broke up TCP/IP into TCP and IP? Well, one of TCP's jobs is to do this assembly/disassembly function. Can you guess how it does it? That's right, it puts *another* packet inside the packet! Let's look at the steps.

The network protocol must break down the data into a sequence of identifiably related packets so that the receiving system will know how to reassemble them. Figure 3-28 shows a sample TCP packet—note the Sequence Number and the Acknowledgement Number. These two fields let the systems exchanging data track the data packets. The receiving system knows, based on the Sequence Numbers, how to organize the packets, and the sending system knows, based on the Acknowledgement Number, whether a packet has been received.

Source Port	Destination Port	Sequence Number	Acknowledgement Number	Data

Figure 3-28 Sample TCP packet

The Visible Network just keeps getting more and more complex, doesn't it? And you still haven't actually seen the Word document get copied, have you? Don't worry, you're almost there—just a few more pieces to go!

Talking on a Network

Now that you understand that the system uses software to assemble and disassemble data packets, what's next? In a network, any one system may be talking to many other systems at any given moment. For example, Janelle's PC has a printer used by all the Wheebo systems, so there's a better than average chance that as Dana tries to access the Word document, another system will be sending a print job to Janelle's PC (Figure 3-29). Her system must be able to direct these incoming files, print jobs, web pages, and so on to the right programs (Figure 3-30). Additionally, the NOS must enable one system to make a connection to another system to verify that the other system can handle whatever operation the initiating system wants to perform. If Bill's system wants to send a print job to Janelle's printer, it first contacts Janelle's system to ensure that it is

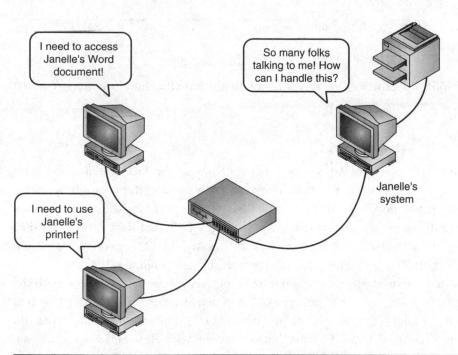

Figure 3-29   So many folks talking to me! How can I handle this?

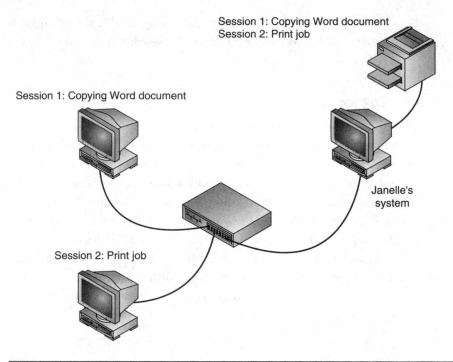

Figure 3-30 Each request becomes a session.

ready to handle the print job. We typically call the software that handles this part of networking the *session software*.

Standardized Formats

One of the most powerful aspects of a network lies in the fact that it works with (almost) any operating system. Today's networks easily connect, for example, a Macintosh system to a Windows 2000 PC, despite the fact that these very different operating systems use different formats for many types of data. Different data formats used to drive us crazy back in the days before word processors (like Microsoft Word) could import or export a thousand other word processor formats (Figure 3-31).

This created the motivation for standardized formats that anyone—at least with the right program—could read from any type of computer. Specialized file formats, such as Adobe's very popular Portable Document Format (PDF) for documents and Postscript for printing, provide standard formats that any system, regardless of the operating system, can read, write, and edit (Figure 3-32).

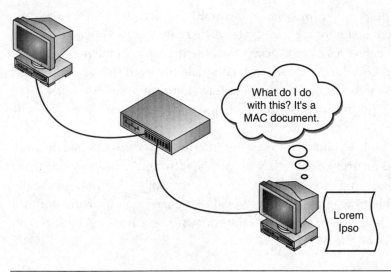

Figure 3-31   What do I do with this?

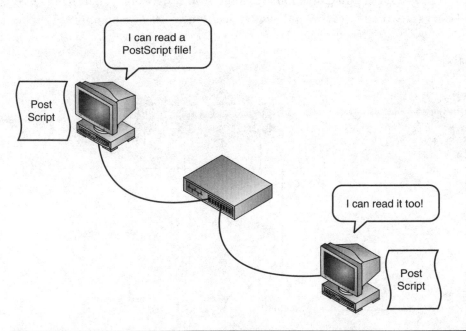

Figure 3-32   MACs and PCs both recognize Adobe Postscript.

Another function that comes into play at this point is encryption. Many networks encrypt data to prevent unauthorized access. One great example is a *Virtual Private Network* (VPN). A VPN enables a system to access a private network via the Internet. Folks who live on the road love VPNs, because they eliminate the need to dial directly into the private network's server via a telephone line. Traveling employees can link securely into their company's private network using whatever Internet access is available to them locally (Figure 3-33).

The big problem with sending data over the Internet is security. Even a low-end hacker knows how to intercept data packets as they float by and can look inside to see what those packets contain. Encryption stops these hackers cold—they may get the file, but they won't be able to read it if it is encrypted. For encryption to work, both the sending and the receiving system must know the encryption method and must be able to encrypt and decrypt on the fly (Figure 3-34).

Network Applications

The last and most visible part of any network is the software applications that use it. If you want to copy a file residing on another system in your network, you need an application like My Network Places in Windows that lets you access files on remote systems.

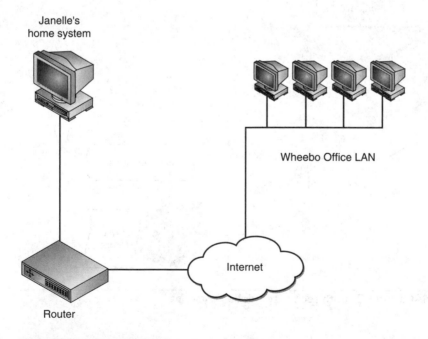

Figure 3-33 VPN diagram

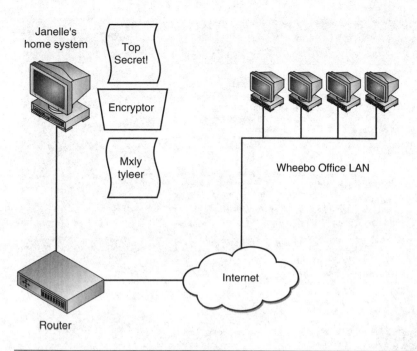

Figure 3-34 Same VPN diagram, showing encryption/decryption

If you want to view web pages, you need a web browser like Internet Explorer or Netscape Navigator. The people who use a network experience it through an application. A user may know nothing about all the other parts of a network, but still know how to open an e-mail application to retrieve mail (Figure 3-35).

Applications may include a number of additional functions, such as encryption, user authentication, and tools to control the look of the data. But these functions are specific to the given applications. In other words, if you want to put a password on your Word document, you must use the password functions of Word to do so.

How Dana Gets Her Document

Okay, you've now seen all the different parts of the network—keep in mind that not all networks contain all of these pieces. Certain functions, such as encryption, may or may not be present depending on the needs of the particular network. With that understanding, let's watch the network function as Dana gets Janelle's Word document.

Dana has two choices for accessing Janelle's Word document. She can access the document by opening Word on her system, selecting File | Open, and taking the file off

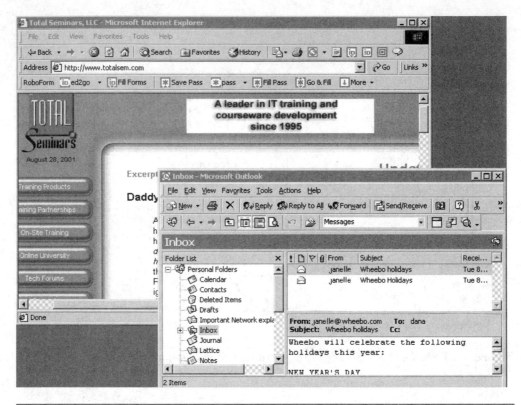

Figure 3-35 Network applications at work

Janelle's Desktop; or she can use My Computer or Windows Explorer to copy the Word file from Janelle's Desktop to her computer, then open her own copy of the file in Word. Dana wants to make changes to the document, so she chooses to copy it over to her system. This will leave an original copy on Janelle's system so Janelle can still use it if she doesn't like Dana's changes.

Dana's goal is simply to copy the file from Janelle's Desktop to her system. Let's watch it happen. The process begins when Dana opens her My Network Places application. The My Network Places application shows her all of the computers on the Wheebo network along with their shared resources (Figure 3-36).

Both systems are PCs running Word, so Dana doesn't need to worry about incompatible data formats. This network does not use any encryption, but it does use authentication. As soon as Dana clicks the icon for Janelle's system in My Network Places, the two systems begin to communicate. Janelle's system checks a database of usernames

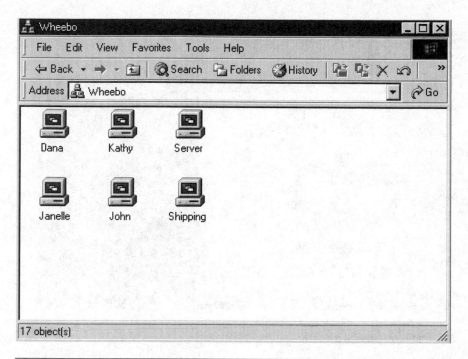

Figure 3-36   My Network Places

and privileges to see what Dana can and cannot do on Janelle's system. This checking process takes place a number of times during the process as Dana accesses various shared folders on Janelle's system. By this time, a session has been established between the two machines. Dana now opens the shared folder and locates the Word Document. To copy the file, she drags and drops the Word document icon from her My Network Places onto her Desktop (Figure 3-37).

This simple act starts a series of actions. First, Janelle's system begins to chop the Word document into packets and assign each a sequence number so that Dana's system will know how to reassemble them when they arrive on her system (Figure 3-38).

After Janelle's system chops the packets, each one gets the address of Dana's system as well as Janelle's address (Figure 3-39).

The packets now get sent to the NIC for transfer. The NIC adds a frame around each packet that contains the MAC addresses for Dana's and Janelle's systems (Figure 3-40).

As the NIC assembles each frame, it checks the network cabling to see if the cable is busy. If not, it sends the frame down the wire. The frame goes through the hub and off

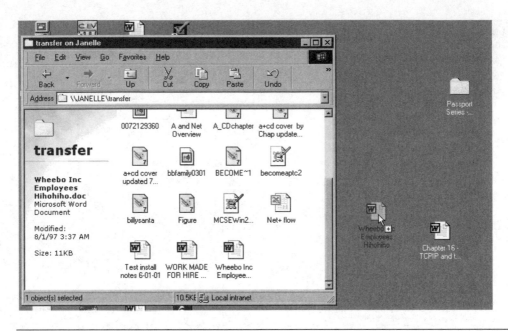

Figure 3-37 Moving the Word document

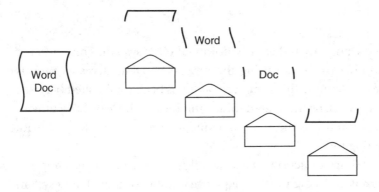

Figure 3-38 Janelle's system chopping packets

to every other NIC in the network. Each NIC looks at the MAC address. All the other systems discard the frame, but Dana's system sees its MAC address and grabs it (Figure 3-41).

As Dana's NIC begins to take in frames, it checks each one using the CRC to insure the validity of the data in the frame. After verifying the data, the NIC strips off both the

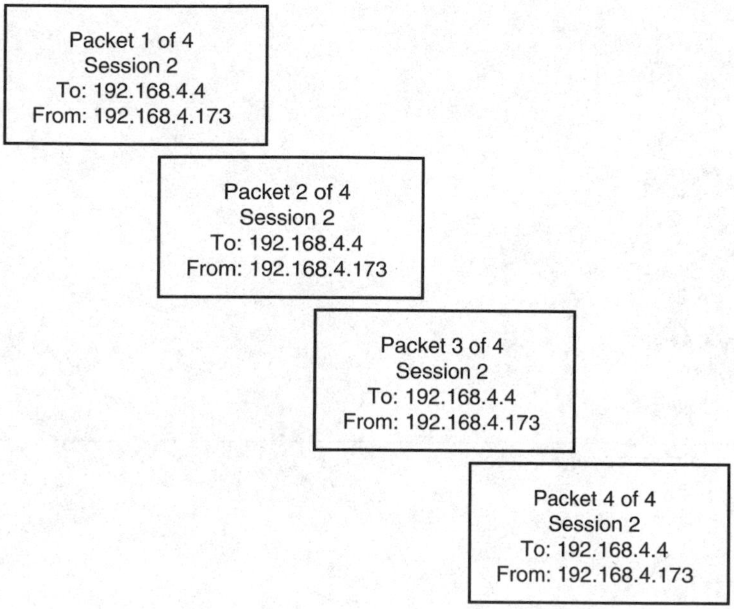

Packet 1 of 4
Session 2
To: 192.168.4.4
From: 192.168.4.173
Packet 2 of 4
Session 2
To: 192.168.4.4
From: 192.168.4.173
Packet 3 of 4
Session 2
To: 192.168.4.4
From: 192.168.4.173
Packet 4 of 4
Session 2
To: 192.168.4.4
From: 192.168.4.173

Figure 3-39 Adding packet headers

Packet 4 of 4
Session 2
Packet 3 of 4
Session 2
Packet 2 of 4
Session 2
To:192.168.4.4
From: 192.168.4.173
NIC
To:
234a12f42b1c
From:
234a12r4er1ac

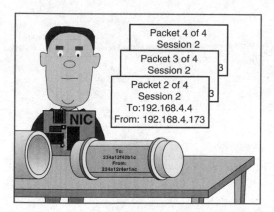

Figure 3-40 Frame being assembled

Figure 3-41 Dana's system grabbing a frame

Figure 3-42 Stripping off the frame and CRC

frame and CRC and passes the packet to the NOS (Figure 3-42). The NOS has the job of inspecting each packet to make sure the data gets to the right place.

Dana's system then begins to reassemble the individual packets back into the complete Word document. If Dana's system fails to receive one of the packets, it simply requests that Janelle's computer resend it (Figure 3-43).

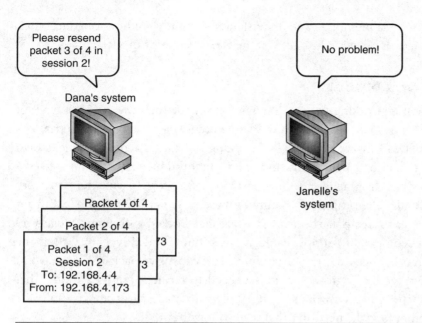

Figure 3-43   Please resend packet 3 of 4.

Once Dana's system reassembles the completed Word document, it sends the document to the proper application, in this case Windows Explorer—better known as the Desktop. Once the system copies the file to the Desktop, the network applications erase the session connection information from each system and prepare for what Dana and Janelle may want to do next.

The most amazing part of this process is that the user sees virtually none of it. Dana simply opened her My Network Places, located Janelle's system, located the shared folder followed by the Word document, and then just dragged and dropped it onto her Desktop—all of the many networking steps executed automatically and transparently to get the job done. This is the beauty and mystery of networks.

The OSI Seven-Layer Model

Well, weren't you impressed with the way I described all of the network functions, breaking them down into perfect little discrete chunks? As much as I'd love to take credit for this, I must admit that I'm simply using a very special concept called the *OSI seven-layer model*. Folks who want to understand networks—and who want to pass the

Network+ exam—must memorize and understand this handy method for conceptualizing computer networks. Let's take a look at the OSI seven-layer model.

Biography of a Model

In the early days of networking, lots of different folks made their own unique types of networks. For the most part they worked well, but because each was created separately, these different networks were incapable of working together. Each one had its own hardware, drivers, naming conventions, and many other unique features that created a lot of headaches and heartaches for anyone who had to try to get them to work together. Additionally, the proprietary nature of these early networks made it difficult for other companies to create hardware or software that worked with them. It was very common for one company to supply cabling, NICs, hubs, and drivers as well as the NOS for their brand of network, in one complete and expensive package! If the world of networking was going to grow, someone needed to create a guide, a model that described the functions of a network so that people who made hardware and software could work together to make networks that worked together well.

The other big problem lay in the use of jargon. The networking industry is rife with terms that can have more than one meaning depending on who's talking and in what context. The deeper you delve into networking, the worse the jargon gets. Terms such as protocol, gateway, and switch, for example, can have vastly different meanings depending on the context of the conversation. To prevent confusion, the International Organization for Standardization, known as the ISO, proposed the Open System Interconnection (OSI) model. The OSI seven-layer model provides a precise terminology for discussing networks. Before reviewing it, let's clarify a few of the most badly mauled terms used in the networking industry.

 NOTE: ISO may look like a misspelled acronym, but it's actually a word, derived from the Greek word isos, which means equal.

Protocols

The word *protocol* serves as a good example of this terminology confusion. In normal English, the term protocol usually refers to a formal procedure for doing something. For example, a specific protocol exists for a meeting between two heads of state. If the President of Mexico comes to the United States to visit the U.S. President, many issues have to be decided in advance. Does the U.S. President meet the Mexican President at the airport or wait for him at the White House? Who walks into a joint press conference first? Who gets to make the announcement about a new agreement? Protocols supply the answers in advance, keeping everyone from using the wrong fork. Networking protocols work the same way, setting the rules for communication.

Even a simple exchange of data between two computers involves many distinct protocols. In computer networking, the term *protocol* describes any predetermined set of rules that defines how two devices or pieces of software should communicate with each other. When Dana uploads a file from her computer to a server on the Internet, she thinks she's doing just one thing, but in reality, lots of things are happening behind the scenes. When Dana transfers a file using a file transfer utility program like WS_FTP32, numerous protocols come into play. The *File Transfer Protocol* (FTP) specifies how two programs running on two different computers can exchange the file. The Transmission Control Protocol (TCP) controls how the two computers break the file up into smaller pieces on the sending machine and reassemble it on the receiving end. The Internet Protocol (IP) determines the proper routing of the data across multiple routers, and the NIC and cabling protocols handle the actual delivery of the frames. The OSI model provides a more precise terminology that clarifies the relationships between the various protocols used.

The Seven Layers

Most network documentation uses the OSI seven-layer model to define more precisely the role played by each protocol. The OSI model also provides a common jargon that network techs can use to describe the function of any network protocol. The model breaks up the task of networking computers into seven distinct layers, each of which addresses an essential networking task. The seven layers are

- **Layer 7** Application
- **Layer 6** Presentation
- **Layer 5** Session
- **Layer 4** Transport
- **Layer 3** Network
- **Layer 2** Data Link
- **Layer 1** Physical

This list may seem upside down, but the OSI model is conceptualized that way, with the Physical layer on the bottom, sending data "up" to the Data Link layer, which in turn sends information up to the Network layer, and so on until it reaches the Application layer, which sends data it generates back "down" through the layers until it reaches the Physical layer and is sent out as ones and zeros.

NOTE: Be sure to memorize both the name and number of each OSI layer. Network techs use terms such as "Layer 4" and "Transport layer" synonymously.

Each layer defines a challenge in computer networking, and the protocols that operate at that layer offer solutions to those challenges. The OSI model encourages modular design in networking, meaning that each protocol is designed to deal with a specific layer and to have as little to do with the operation of other layers as possible. Each protocol needs to understand the protocols handling the layers directly above and below it, but it can and should be oblivious to the protocols handling the other layers.

NOTE: Keep in mind that these layers are not laws of physics—anybody who wants to design a network can do it any way they want. While many protocols fit neatly into one of the seven layers, others do not.

Layer 1: What Do These Electrical Signals Mean? The Physical Layer

Layer 1, the Physical layer, defines the physical form taken by data when it travels across a cable. While other layers deal with ones and zeros, the physical layer defines the rules for turning those ones and zeros into actual electrical signals traveling over a copper cable (or light passing through a fiber optic cable, or radio waves generated by a wireless network, and so on). Figure 3-44 shows a sending NIC turning a string of ones and zeros into an electrical signal, and a receiving NIC turning it back into the same string of ones and zeros. Unless both ends of the transmission agree in advance on the physical layer rules, successful communication is not possible. The Physical layer adds no additional information to the data packet—it is concerned solely with transmitting the data provided by the layers above it.

The Physical layer is one of the few parts of the OSI seven-layer model that you actually see. The cabling and hubs handle these functions.

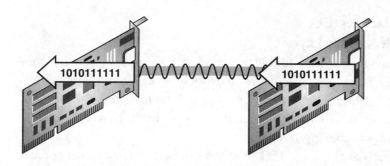

Figure 3-44 The Physical layer turns binary code into a physical signal and back into ones and zeros.

Layer 2: How Do Devices Use the Wire? The Data Link Layer

The Data Link layer defines the rules for accessing and using the Physical layer. The majority of the Data Link functions take place inside the NIC. The Data Link layer specifies the rules for identifying devices on the network, determining which machine should use the network at a given moment, and checking for errors in the data received from the Physical layer. Note that the functions performed at this layer affect only one sender and recipient. Data Link information does not persist beyond that single transaction, but is re-created each time the packet is transmitted to a new host.

The Data Link layer is actually divided into two sublayers: Media Access Control (MAC) and Logical Link Control (LLC). The LLC sublayer is important enough to have its own IEEE standard: 802.2 (IEEE 802.x is an important set of networking standards I'll be talking more about later). The LLC sublayer is conceptually *above* the MAC sublayer, that is, between it and the Network layer (OSI Layer 3). The MAC sublayer controls access to the Physical layer, or shared media. It encapsulates data to be sent from the system, adding source and destination MAC addresses, error-checking information, and a frame, and decapsulates data received by the system. It is also responsible for data collision avoidance and resolution in half-duplex mode. The LLC sublayer provides an interface with the Network layer protocols. It supplies protocol-specific logical links (ports) called *Service Access Points* (SAPs) that ensure the protocols of the source and destination systems match (so TCP/IP talks to TCP/IP, for example). It is responsible for the ordered delivery of frames, including retransmission of missing or corrupt packets, and for flow control (moderating data flow so one system doesn't overwhelm the other).

Layer 3: How Do Packets Get
from A to B? The Network Layer

The Network layer defines the rules for adding information to the data packet that controls how routers move it from its source on one network to its destination on a different network. At this point, the packet contains the data to be transferred, the Network layer information, and the Data Link information. The data itself, however, actually contains information about other layers as well.

The IP protocol operates at this layer. Packets are routed across the Internet (or any TCP/IP network) using the unique IP addresses of the sending and receiving systems.

Layer 4: Breaking Data Up and Putting
It Back Together: The Transport Layer

The Transport layer breaks up data it receives from the upper layers into smaller pieces for *transport* within the data packets created at the lower levels. Most networks have a packet limit of fewer than 1500 bytes, including the information generated by the various layers of the OSI model. As we discussed previously, a chunk of data larger than 1500 bytes must be broken into smaller pieces on the sending node and reassembled at the receiving node. The protocols that typically handle this job include NetBEUI, SPX, and, of course, TCP. These protocols also handle other functions, such as checking for errors.

The Transport layer is the pivotal layer that guarantees smooth communication between the lower layers (1 through 3) and the upper layers (5 through 7). The lower layers concern themselves with moving data from point A to point B on the network, without regard for the actual content of the data. The upper layers deal with specific types of requests involving that data. This separation allows applications using the network to remain blissfully unconcerned about the workings of the underlying hardware.

Layer 5: How Do Machines Keep Track of
Who They Are Talking to? The Session Layer

The Session layer manages the connections between machines on the network. Suppose machine A receives one file from machine B, another from machine C, and sends a third file to machine D. Machine A needs some means to track its connections so that it sends the right response to the right computer. Protocols such as NetBIOS and Sockets give networked systems the means to track and manage connections. A computer managing connections is like a short order cook keeping track of orders. Just as a cook must track which meals go with which ticket, a computer on a network must track which data should be sent out to which machine.

Layer 6: What Language Is This?
The Presentation Layer

The job of the Presentation layer is to present data from the sending system in a form that the applications on the receiving system can understand. This enables different applications—Word and WordPerfect, for example—to communicate with each other despite the fact that they use different methods to represent the same data.

Most computer systems store text. A DOS or Windows 9*x* system usually stores text using a series of 8-bit codes known as ASCII (American Standard Code for Information Interchange), but a Windows NT, 2000, or XP system uses 16-bit Unicode to store text. The Windows 9*x* system would store the letter **A** as 01000001, while the Windows NT system would store the same letter A as 0000000001000001. The end users, of course, do not care about the difference between ASCII and Unicode—they just want to see the letter **A**. The Presentation layer smoothes over these differences.

The OSI model treats the Presentation layer as a distinct layer, but most real-world network operating systems fold its functions into programs that also handle either Application or Session layer functions. In fact, most network operating systems ignore the Presentation layer completely. Why? Because modern versions of Word and Word-Perfect, to use my earlier example, now do this job for themselves!

NOTE: Although not purely network protocols, Adobe Systems' PostScript printer language and Acrobat/PDF file format handle a typical Presentation layer problem: enabling users to view or print the same file even if they use different operating systems or printers. PostScript is a device-independent printer language designed to ensure that any two PostScript-compatible printers will produce exactly the same output regardless of the manufacturer. Adobe's PDF file format takes device-independence a step further, enabling any system running an Acrobat viewer to view and print a PDF file precisely the way the author intended, regardless of what operating system or printer it uses. PostScript and Acrobat are both Presentation layer tools that hide the differences between systems.

Layer 7: How Do Programmers Write Applications
that Use the Network? The Application Layer

The Application layer in the OSI model defines a set of tools that programs can use to access the network. Application layer programs provide services to the programs that the users themselves see. Web browsing is a good example. Bob launches his browser, either Netscape or Internet Explorer, to access a web site. These programs use the Hyper-Text Transfer Protocol (HTTP) to request data (usually HTML documents) from a web server. HTTP is not an executable program. It is a protocol, a set of rules, that enables two other programs—the web browser and the web server—to communicate successfully with each other.

The APIs used by Microsoft networking also operate at the Application layer. An *API* is an Application Program Interface, a special set of commands that allows applications such as Microsoft Word to request services from an operating system. When Microsoft Word displays My Network Places in a **Save As** dialog box, for example, it does not access the network directly. Instead, it uses the networking APIs. By providing a standard set of APIs that operate at the OSI's Application layer, Microsoft makes it easy for programmers writing applications like Microsoft Word or Lotus 1-2-3 to access the network without knowing any of the details of the network.

OSI Is the Key

The networking industry relies heavily on the OSI seven-layer model to describe the many functions that take place in a network. This chapter introduced these layers to you. Throughout the rest of the book, you'll find plenty of references to these layers as you examine every part of the network.

Chapter Review

Questions

1. A hub sends data:
   a. Only to the receiving system.
   b. Only to the sending system.
   c. To all the systems connected to the hub.
   d. Only to the server.

2. The unique identifier on a NIC is known as a(n):
   a. IP address
   b. Media Access Control address
   c. ISO number
   d. Packet ID number

3. What Windows 9x utility do you use to find the MAC address for a system?
   a. WINIPCFG
   b. IPCONFIG
   c. PING
   d. MAC

4. On a Windows NT or 2000 system, what utility do you use to find its MAC address?
   a. WINIPCFG
   b. IPCONFIG
   c. PING
   d. MAC

5. A NIC sends data in discrete chunks called:
   a. Segments
   b. Sections
   c. Frames
   d. Layers

6. A frame begins with the MAC address of the:
   a. Receiving system
   b. Sending system
   c. Network
   d. Router

7. A frame ends with a special bit called the Cyclic Redundancy Check (CRC). The CRC's job is:
   a. To cycle data across the network
   b. To verify that the MAC addresses are correct
   c. To verify that the data arrived correctly
   d. To verify that the IP address is correct

8. Which of the following is an example of a MAC address?
   a. 0 – 255
   b. 00-50-56-A3-04-0C
   c. SBY3M7
   d. 192.168.4.13

9. Which layer of the OSI seven-layer model controls the assembly and disassembly of data?
   a. Application layer
   b. Presentation layer
   c. Session layer
   d. Transport layer

10. Which layer of the OSI seven-layer model keeps track of a system's connections in order to send the right response to the right computer?
    a. Application layer
    b. Presentation layer
    c. Session layer
    d. Transport layer

11. Which of the following OSI layers converts the ones and zeros to electrical signals and places theses signals on the cable?
    a. Physical layer
    b. Transport layer
    c. Network layer
    d. Data Link layer

12. Which layer of the OSI model involves routing?
    a. Physical layer
    b. Transport layer
    c. Network layer
    d. Data Link layer

13. Which layer of the OSI model makes sure the data is in a readable format for the Application layer?
    a. Application layer
    b. Presentation layer
    c. Session layer
    d. Transport layer

14. Which layer of the OSI model includes HTTP?
    a. Application layer
    b. Presentation layer
    c. Session layer
    d. Transport layer

Answers

1. **C.** Data comes into a hub through one wire, and is then sent out through all of the other wires. A hub sends data to all the systems connected to it.

2. **B.** The unique identifier on a network interface card is called the Media Access Control (MAC) address.

3. **A.** All versions of Windows 9x can use the WINIPCFG command to find the MAC address. The last 9x versions (SE and ME) could also use IPCONFIG.

4. **B.** You can determine the MAC address on a Windows 2000 or NT system using the IPCONFIG /ALL command.

5. **C.** Data is sent in discrete chunks called *frames*.

6. **A.** The frame begins with the MAC address of the receiving NIC, followed by the MAC address of the sending NIC, followed in turn by the data.

7. **C.** The data is followed by a special bit of checking information called the Cyclic Redundancy Check that the receiving NIC uses to verify that the data arrived correctly.

8. **B.** A MAC address is a 48-bit value, and no two NICs ever share the same MAC address—ever. 00-50-56-A3-04-0C is a MAC address. Answer D (192.168.4.13) is an IP address.

9. **D.** The Transport layer controls the assembly and disassembly of data.

10. **C.** The Session layer keeps track of a system's connections in order to send the right response to the right computer.

11. **A.** The Physical layer converts ones and zeros to electrical signals and then places these signals on the cable.

12. **C.** Routing takes place at the Network layer.

13. **B.** The Presentation layer translates the data into a readable format for the Application layer.

14. **A.** The Application layer includes the HTTP protocol, which allows the web browser and the web server to communicate with each other.

PART II

The Basic LAN

Hardware Concepts

In this chapter, you will

- Understand hardware concepts
- Learn the different types of network topology
- Learn the different types of cabling
- Understand the concept of IEEE standards
- Learn the IEEE standards

Historical/Conceptual

Every network must provide some method to get data from one system to another. In most cases, this method consists of some type of cabling (usually copper or fiber optic) running between systems, although wireless methods are starting to become more popular. In this chapter, you will learn about the most common types of cabling used in today's networks, as well as the critical, magical concept called topology.

Topology

Topology is a general description of how computers *connect* to each other, without regard to how they actually communicate. The most common network technologies are bus, ring, star, and mesh. Figure 4-1 shows all four types: a *bus topology*, where all computers connect to the network via a central bus cable; a *ring topology*, where all computers on the network attach to a central ring of cable; a *star topology*, where the computers on the

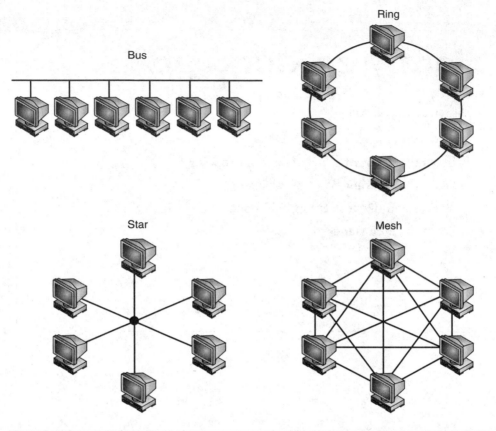

Figure 4-1   Bus, ring, star, and mesh topologies

network connect to a central wiring point (usually called a hub); and a *mesh topology*, where each computer has a dedicated line to every other computer. Mesh topologies rarely appear in the real world because of the excessive number of cables involved. Make sure you know these four topologies!

While a topology describes the method by which systems in a network connect, the topology alone doesn't describe a number of other features necessary to make a cabling system work. The term *bus topology*, for example, describes a network that consists of some number of machines connected to the network via the same piece of cable. Notice that this definition of a bus topology leaves a lot of questions unanswered. What is the cable made of? How long can it be? How do the machines decide which machine should send data at a specific moment? A network based on a bus topology can answer these questions in a number of different ways. Over the years, particular manufacturers and standards bodies created several specific technologies based on different topologies. These technologies use the topologies as a starting point, but they then build on them to create a variety of answers for these questions. These technologies have names like Ethernet, Token Ring, or FDDI. Later chapters will describe all of these network technologies in great detail, but for now, concentrate on learning the different topologies.

NOTE: Make sure you know your topologies!

Test Specific

Hybrid Topologies

Even though the Network+ test wants you to know these four types of topologies, almost none of them actually exist in real networks today. Two of the topologies, star and mesh, are totally obsolete. Networks based on ring topology were once quite common but now are much less so. So, you're probably thinking that only leaves bus topology. True, sort of. Unfortunately, bus topology has faded away, too. So what's the answer? Well, bus topology has evolved into a special type of bus topology called star bus. A *star bus topology* is a hybrid of the star and bus topologies. Star bus networks use a physical star design that provides improved stability and a logical bus that maintains compatibility with existing Ethernet standards. Star bus is overwhelmingly the most common topology used today. Let's take a look at the star and the bus topologies and then see how the star bus topology eliminates a number of problems inherent to both the plain old star and plain old bus topologies.

In a star topology, all nodes connect to a central wiring point, as shown earlier in Figure 4-1. The key advantage of the star topology is that a break in the cable affects only the machine connected to that cable. In Figure 4-2, machine C cannot communicate with any other node, but machines A, B, D, E, and F are unaffected.

So star topology sounds pretty spiffy. Why complicate things by using star bus topology? Why not just use the plain old star topology? The answer lies more in market share and compatibility than in any aspect of star bus that makes it more attractive than plain

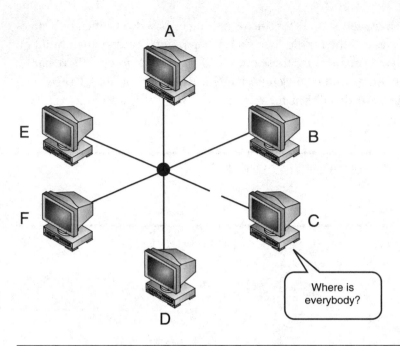

Figure 4-2 In a star topology, a broken cable affects only the machine connected to it.

old star. You see, for many years Ethernet technology used a bus topology. Ethernet networks using this bus topology became the predominant technology. One technology, called ArcNet, used the plain star topology, but enjoyed only a small following. Eventually the Ethernet folks created a new type of Ethernet technology using the star bus topology. Because this new technology was completely compatible with the older Ethernet bus technologies, there was no incentive to switch to ArcNet for the benefits of star topology, and *every* incentive to use the new star bus-based Ethernet. Thus, even though the star topology boasts an equally robust, fault tolerant cabling system, pure star topologies do not exist in modern computer networks.

NOTE: Fault tolerance refers to a system's capability to continue functioning even when some part of the system has failed. When bad things happen, a robust system continues to operate, at least to some degree. Thus, the more robust the system, the more fault tolerant it is.

In a network, physical topology describes the layout of the wires, while logical topology describes the behavior of the electronics. The star bus topology used in Ethernet networks employs a physical star and a logical bus. The nodes physically connect to a hub sitting in a central location (see Figure 4-3), forming a star. The hub contains circuitry that takes incoming frames from one cable and repeats them to every other wire on the network. We use the term *nodes* to describe the other wires. Logically, the nodes behave as though they are attached directly to the bus, as you can see illustrated in Figure 4-4, but have the advantage that in the case where one wire gets cut, only one system goes off the network.

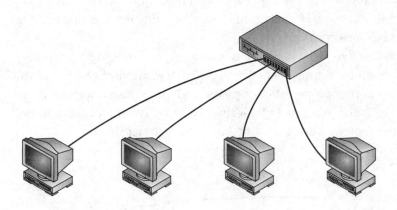

Figure 4-3   A 10BaseT network, with each node connected to the hub

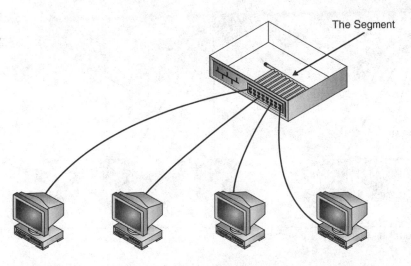

Figure 4-4   A 10BaseT hub contains the electronic equivalent of a properly terminated Ethernet segment.

Star bus is not the only hybrid topology. Many years ago, IBM invented a technology called Token Ring that employs a unique type of hybrid technology called *star ring*. Star ring works basically the same way as star bus; the only difference is that instead of a logical bus, it uses a logical ring. Token Ring once held a large part of the installed base of networks, but this has slipped considerably over the years as many networks have switched to Ethernet. Token Ring still has a fairly large installed base, however, and the Network+ exam expects you to know its topology. Be warned: in many cases the Token Ring topology is simply referred to as a star even though in reality it is star ring (see Figure 4-5)—be prepared to answer either way!

In this section, you saw that every network uses some type of topology. A topology simply describes a method for getting data from one system to another. Make sure you know the four basic types of topology: star, ring, bus, and mesh. Also understand that two hybrid types of topologies, star bus and star ring, exist in networks today. Most networks use the star bus topology, but a substantial minority use star ring.

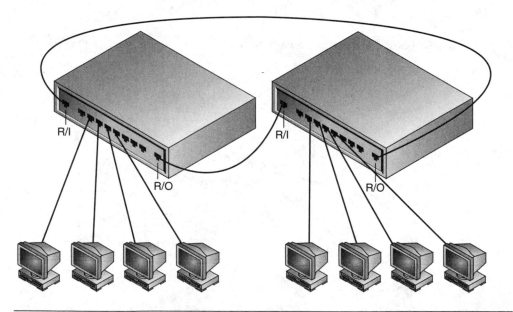

Figure 4-5   Token Ring topology is a star ring.

Cabling

The vast majority of networked systems are linked together using some type of cabling. This section reviews cables from yesterday's, today's, and tomorrow's networks. Keep in mind that folks who network look at cabling differently than people who run cables for a living. In this chapter, we will look just at the cabling types used in today's networks. Don't worry about what type of network uses these cables—that's a completely separate topic covered in the next two chapters.

Some cabling types are used by a variety of networks, while other networks use their own unique cabling. Many of the cables I'll discuss have uses outside the networking industry. You will probably recognize a number of them from their use in cable TV, recording equipment, and telephone systems. Remember, just because it's listed here, don't assume a particular cable type is only used in networks!

All cables used in the networking industry separate into three distinct groups: coaxial (coax), twisted pair, and fiber optic. Let's look at all three.

Coax

Coaxial cable contains a central conductor wire, surrounded by an insulating material, which in turn is surrounded by a braided metal shield (see Figure 4-6). The cable is referred to as coaxial (*coax* for short) because the center wire and the braided metal shield share a common axis or centerline (see Figure 4-7).

Coaxial cable is designed to shield data transmissions from *electro-magnetic interference* (*EMI*). Many devices in the typical office environment generate magnetic fields, including lights, fans, copy machines, and refrigerators. When a metal wire encounters these magnetic fields, electrical current is generated along the wire. This extra current can shut down a network because it is easily misinterpreted as a signal by devices like NICs. To prevent EMI from affecting the network, the outer mesh layer of a coaxial cable shields the center wire (on which the data is actually transmitted) from interference (see Figure 4-8).

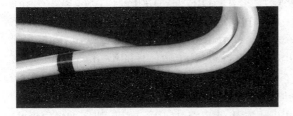

Figure 4-6   Thick coaxial cable (RG-8), with a black band marked every 2.5 meters

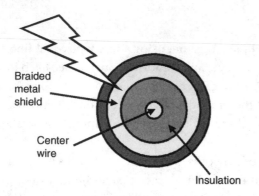

Figure 4-7   Cut-away view of a coaxial cable

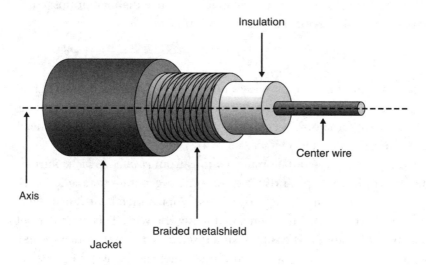

Figure 4-8   The braided metal shield prevents interference from reaching the center wire.

Only three types of coax cable have ever been used in networking: RG-58, RG-6, and the unique Thick Ethernet RG-8. All coax cables have an *RG* rating. RG ratings were developed by the military to provide a quick reference for the different types of coax. The only important measure of coax cabling is its *Ohm rating*, a relative measure of the *resistance* (or to be precise, *characteristic impedance*) on the cable. You may run across coax cables that look similar (on the outside at least) to some of the cables shown here; nevertheless they may not have acceptable Ohm ratings. Fortunately, most coax cable types display their Ohm ratings on the cables themselves (see Figure 4-9).

Figure 4-9   Ohm rating on a coax cable

 NOTE: Know the Ohm ratings for these cable types!

RG-8

RG-8, often referred to as *Thick Ethernet*, is the oldest and least-used cabling type still in use. It gets the name Thick Ethernet from the fact that it is used exclusively in one and only one type of network technology—you guessed it, Thick Ethernet! You'll see more on Thick Ethernet in the next chapter, but for now make sure you can recognize this type of cabling (see Figure 4-10).

RG-8 is rated at 50 Ohms and has a distinct yellow or orange/brown color. The color issue makes Thick Ethernet cabling rather unique, as almost all other types of cabling have no fixed color. Some cable types come in a veritable rainbow of colors!

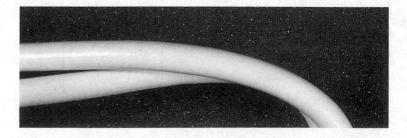

Figure 4-10   RG-8 Thick Ethernet cable

RG-6

RG-6 cable (rated at 75 Ohms) is virtually never installed in networks these days, but you should know about it nonetheless (see Figure 4-11.) If you think RG-6 resembles what your cable TV guy hitched up to your television, you aren't imagining things—cable TV uses RG-6 coax.

RG-58

Today, RG-58 stands alone as the only coax cable type still in widespread use. It works with the still popular *Thin Ethernet* network technology (something you'll learn about in the next chapter). At first glance, RG-58 may look like RG-6, but its 50-Ohm rating makes it very different on the inside (see Figure 4-12)!

Twisted Pair

The most overwhelmingly common type of cabling used in networks consists of twisted pairs of cables. Networks use two types of twisted pair cabling: *shielded twisted pair* (*STP*) and *unshielded twisted pair* (*UTP*). Twisted pair cabling for networks is composed of multiple pairs of wires twisted around each other at specific intervals. The twists serve to reduce interference, called *crosstalk*; the more twists, the less crosstalk.

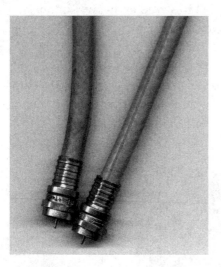

Figure 4-11   RG-6 coax cable

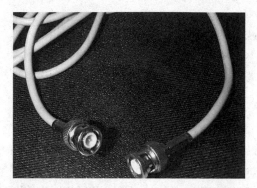

Figure 4-12 RG-58 coax cable

Shielded Twisted Pair

Shielded twisted pair (STP) cabling, as its name implies, consists of twisted pairs of wires surrounded by shielding to protect them from EMI. The Network+ exam barely touches STP cabling, but I'll throw it in for completeness. STP cabling doesn't blend well with telephone cabling, and as a result is pretty much confined to one type of network technology, called Token Ring (see Chapter 6), and a few very high-speed networking technologies. There's nothing wrong with STP; in fact, STP prices have dropped so much they're now fairly close to UTP! But UTP's hegemony is so complete today that STP continues to disappear. Figure 4-13 shows the most common STP type: the venerable IBM type 1 cable used in Token Ring network technology.

Figure 4-13 IBM type 1 Shielded Twisted Pair cable

Installing STP cable makes even the most experienced network tech shudder. STP is usually installed above drop ceilings on racks or hooks. It is less susceptible to electronic interference, so the need to avoid potential EMI sources diminishes. You must ground the STP cable shielding, because if you don't, the shielding will turn into an antenna; needless to say, this usually causes significant problems for the network!

Unshielded Twisted Pair

Unshielded twisted pair (UTP) is by far the most common type of network cabling used today. UTP consists of twisted pairs of wires surrounded by a plastic jacket (see Figure 4-14). This jacket does *not* provide any protection from EMI, so some care must be used when installing UTP cabling.

Although more sensitive to interference than coaxial cable, UTP cabling provides an inexpensive and flexible means to cable networks. Take care when installing UTP—many other applications, especially telephone systems, employ the same cabling and connectors. UTP cabling is subject to strict standards regarding the proper crimping of the connectors. Because it has such a wide array of uses, UTP comes in a variety of grades called category or *CAT* ratings (see Table 4-1).

As most networks are designed to run at speeds of up to 100 MHz, most new cabling installations use Category 5 (CAT 5) cabling, although the improved CAT 5e is quickly gaining ground. CAT 5 cabling costs only a few more pennies per foot than Category 3 cabling, and has the advantage of allowing for future upgrades. Because labor, not

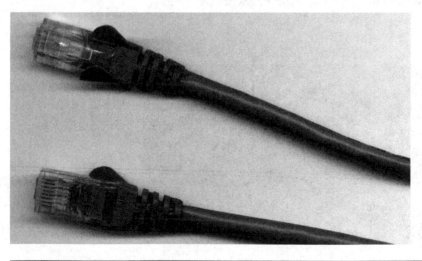

Figure 4-14   UTP cabling

Table 4-1   CAT Ratings for UTP Cables

Category 1	Regular analog phone lines—not used for data communications
Category 2	Supports speeds up to 4 megabits per second
Category 3	Supports speeds up to 16 megabits per second
Category 4	Supports speeds up to 20 megabits per second
Category 5 (5e)	Supports speeds up to 100 megabits per second

materials, constitutes the major expense when cabling a new network, it makes sense to install CAT 5 in your network from the beginning, even if the network will initially use 10BaseT. Why pay a cable installer to wire the network for CAT 3 today, only to pay him again in two years to wire it for CAT 5 when you upgrade to a higher-speed network? Because so few cable installers use Category 3 cabling anymore, the higher-grade CAT 5 cabling can sometimes be cheaper than CAT 3 cabling. The category level of a piece of cable is usually written on the cable itself (see Figure 4-15).

Fiber Optic

Fiber optic cabling transmits *light* rather than electricity, making it very attractive for both high-EMI areas and very long distance transmissions. While most copper cables cannot carry data more than a few hundred meters at best, fiber optic cabling will operate, depending on the implementation, for distances of up to *10 kilometers*. A fiber optic cable has three components: the fiber itself; the *cladding*, which is the part that makes the light reflect down the fiber; and the insulating jacket. Fiber optic cabling is manufactured with many different diameters of fiber and cladding. In a convenient bit of standardization, cable manufacturers use a two-number designator to define fiber optic cables according to their fiber and cladding measurements. The most common fiber

Figure 4-15   Markings on a UTP cable show its category level.

optic cable size is 62.5/125 μm. Almost all network technologies that use fiber optic cable require pairs of fibers. In response to the demand for two-pair cabling, manufacturers often connect two fibers together like a lamp cord to create the popular *duplex* fiber optic cabling (Figure 4-16).

Light can be sent down a fiber optic cable as regular light or as laser light. The two types of light require totally different fiber optic cables. Most network technologies that use fiber optics use LEDs (Light Emitting Diodes) to send light signals. LED fiber uses *multimode* fiber optic cabling. Network technologies that use laser light use *single-mode* fiber optic cabling. Using laser light and single-mode fiber optic cables enables a network to achieve phenomenally high transfer rates over incredibly long distances. Single-mode cable is currently quite rare; if you see fiber optic cabling, you can be relatively sure it's multimode.

Installing fiber optic cabling is basically a love/hate arrangement. On the love side, fiber optics don't use electricity, so you can ignore the electrical interference issue. Also, fiber optic cabling can reach up to 10,000 meters. This depends on the networking technology used, of course, and the most common network technology that uses fiber optic has a much lower limit of *only* 1000 meters! On the hate side of the fiber optic equation, there is the chore of actually getting it into the walls. Fiber optic cabling installations are tedious and difficult, although fiber optic manufacturers continue to make new strides in easing the job. Fiber optic cabling is fragile and will fail if it is bent much. My advice: leave this job to a professional cable installer.

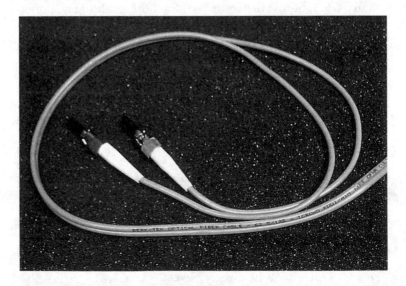

Figure 4-16   Duplex fiber optic cable

Know Thy Cables

Concentrate on UTP—that's where the hardest Network+ questions lie. Don't forget to give STP and fiber a quick pass as well, to understand why you would pick one type of cabling over another. Even though Network+ doesn't test too hard on cabling, this is important information that you will use in the real networking world.

Networking Industry Standards—IEEE

The *Institute of Electrical and Electronics Engineers* (*IEEE*) defines industry-wide standards that promote the use and implementation of technology. In February of 1980, a new committee called the 802 working group took over the job of defining network cabling standards from the private sector. The IEEE 802 committee recognizes that no single cabling solution can work in all situations and provides a variety of cabling standards with cryptic names, including Token Ring, 10BaseT, and Gigabit Ethernet.

IEEE committees define standards for a wide variety of electronics. The names of these committees are often used to refer to the standards they publish. The IEEE 1284 committee, for example, sets standards for parallel communication. Have you ever seen a printer cable marked "IEEE 1284-compliant," as in Figure 4-17? It means the manufacturer followed the rules set by the IEEE 1284 committee. Another committee you may have heard of is the IEEE 1394 committee, which controls the FireWire standard.

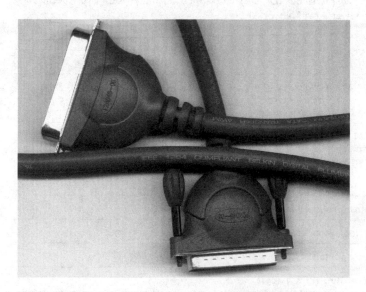

Figure 4-17 An IEEE 1284-compliant printer cable

The IEEE 802 committee sets the standards for networking. Although the original plan was to define a single, universal standard for networking, it quickly became apparent that no single solution would work for all needs. The 802 committee was split up into smaller subcommittees, with names such as IEEE 802.3 and IEEE 802.5. Table 4-2 shows the currently recognized IEEE 802 subcommittees and their areas of jurisdiction.

Table 4-2   IEEE 802 Subcommittees

IEEE 802	LAN/MAN Overview & Architecture
IEEE 802.1	LAN/MAN Bridging and Management (Higher Layer LAN Protocols)
802.1s	Multiple Spanning Tree
802.1w	Rapid Reconfiguration of Spanning Tree
802.1x	Port-based Network Access Control
IEEE 802.2	Logical Link Control (LLC)
IEEE 802.3	CSMA/CD access method (Ethernet)
802.3ae	10 Gigabit Ethernet
IEEE 802.4	Token Passing Bus access method and Physical layer specifications
IEEE 802.5	Token Ring access method and Physical layer specifications
IEEE 802.6	Distributed Queue Dual Bus (DQDB) access method and Physical layer specifications (Metropolitan Area Networks)
IEEE 802.7	Broadband LAN
IEEE 802.8	Fiber Optic
IEEE 802.9	Isochronous LANs (standard withdrawn)
IEEE 802.10	Interoperable LAN/MAN Security
IEEE 802.11	Wireless LAN Medium Access Control (MAC) and Physical layer specifications
IEEE 802.12	Demand-priority access method, Physical Layer, and repeater specifications
IEEE 802.13	Not used
IEEE 802.14	Cable Modems (proposed standard withdrawn)
IEEE 802.15	Wireless Personal Area Network (WPAN)
IEEE 802.16	Wireless Metropolitan Area Network (Wireless MAN)
IEEE 802.17	Resilient Packet Ring (RPR) Access

PART II

 EXAM TIP: Memorize the 802.2, 802.3, 802.5, and 802.11 standards. Ignore the rest.

Some of these committees deal with technologies that didn't quite make it, and the committees associated with those standards—such as IEEE 802.4, Token Bus—have become dormant. When preparing for the Network+ exam, concentrate on the IEEE 802.3, 802.5, and 802.11 standards. The others rarely impact the life of a network tech directly. You'll see each of the three main 802 standards in detail in later chapters.

Chapter Review

Questions

1. Which of the following standards defines Token Ring networks?
    a. IEEE 802.3
    b. IEEE 802.5
    c. EIA/TIA 568A
    d. IEEE 1284

2. Token Ring networks use a _____ physical topology and a _____ logical topology.
    a. mesh, ring
    b. ring, star
    c. star, ring
    d. ring, bus

3. Of the topologies listed, which one is the most fault tolerant and has the most redundancy?
    a. mesh
    b. bus
    c. star
    d. ring

4. What term is used to describe the physical layout of network components?
   a. segmentation
   b. map
   c. topology
   d. protocol

5. Which of the following IEEE standards defines wireless networking?
   a. 802.8
   b. 802.9
   c. 802.10
   d. 802.11

6. Which IEEE standard defines the CSMA/CD access method?
   a. 802.2
   b. 802.3
   c. 802.4
   d. 802.5

7. Which of the following is NOT a coaxial cable?
   a. RJ-45
   b. RG-58
   c. RG-8
   d. RG-6

8. Which network topology connects nodes with a central ring of cable?
   a. star
   b. bus
   c. ring
   d. mesh

9. Which network topology uses a central hub?
   a. star
   b. bus
   c. ring
   d. mesh

10. Which of the following network topologies is the easiest to configure?
    a. star
    b. bus
    c. ring
    d. mesh

Answers

1. **B.** IEEE 802.5 defines Token Ring networks. EIA/TIA 568A is a cabling standard for UTP cabling that is used in both Token Ring and Ethernet networks.

2. **C.** Token Ring networks use a star physical topology and a ring logical topology.

3. **A.** Mesh topology is the most fault tolerant and has the most redundancy because each computer has a dedicated connection to every other computer on the network.

4. **C.** Topology is the term used to describe the layout of a network: how computers connect to each other without regard to how they actually communicate.

5. **D.** The IEEE 802.11 standard defines wireless networking.

6. **B.** The IEEE 802.3 standard defines the CSMA/CD access method, part of the Ethernet standard.

7. **A.** RJ-45 is a type of connector for unshielded twisted-pair cabling. All the others are types of coaxial cable.

8. **C.** The aptly named ring topology connects nodes with a central ring of cable.

9. **A.** A star topology uses a central hub.

10. **A.** A star topology is the easiest to configure.

Ethernet Basics

In this chapter, you will

- Understand the concept of Ethernet
- Learn how Ethernet works
- Learn how Ethernet organizes and transmits data
- Understand Ethernet's CSMA/CD
- Learn the specifics of Ethernet
- Learn the different cabling systems' specifications
- Understand the functions of repeaters and bridges

Historical/Conceptual

In the beginning, there were no networks. Computers were isolated, solitary islands of information in a teeming sea of proto-geeks. If you wanted to move a file from one machine to another—and proto-geeks were as much into that as modern geeks—you had to use *Sneakernet*, which meant you saved the file on a disk, laced up your tennis shoes, and hiked over to the other system. All that walking was no doubt producing lots of health benefits; but proto-geeks were, frankly, not all that into health benefits—they were into speed, power, and technological coolness in general (sound familiar?). Thus, you will not be surprised to hear there was broad agreement on the need to replace Sneakernet with a faster and more efficient method of sharing data.

In 1973, Xerox answered this challenge by developing *Ethernet*, a networking technology based on a bus topology. The Ethernet standard, which predominates in today's networks, defines many issues involved in transferring data between computer systems. The original Ethernet used a single piece of coaxial cable to connect several computers, enabling them to transfer data at a rate of up to 3 Mbps. Although slow by today's standards, this early version of Ethernet was, needless to say, a huge improvement over Sneakernet methods, and served as the foundation for all later versions of Ethernet. It remained a largely in-house technology within Xerox until 1979, when Xerox decided to look for partners to help promote Ethernet as an industry standard. Working with Digital Equipment Corporation (DEC) and Intel, they published what became the Digital-Intel-Xerox (DIX) standard. Running on coaxial cable, the DIX standard enabled multiple computers to communicate with each other at a screaming 10 Mbps. Although 10 Mbps represents the low end of standard network speeds today, at the time it was revolutionary.

Ethernet or IEEE 802.3?

Today the IEEE 802.3 standard has completely supplanted the original Ethernet standard, and the term *Ethernet* refers to any network based on the IEEE 802.3 standard. Occasionally, you will see references that imply that IEEE 802.3 and Ethernet are not the same thing. Technically, that might be true. For many years, Ethernet referred specifically to the original Xerox Ethernet standard, whereas IEEE 802.3 referred to the standard set forth some years later by the IEEE. The IEEE 802.3 standard differs in a few relatively minor details from the original Xerox standard, and early on it was important for the designers of certain pieces of software and hardware to make a distinction as to which standard they were following. If someone corrects you when you use the term Ethernet to refer to the IEEE 802.3 standard, they are technically correct. If they get obnoxious about it, feel free to quote them Grandma Erna's golden rule: *You might be right, but you won't have any friends.* The remainder of this book follows common parlance and uses the terms Ethernet and IEEE 802.3 interchangeably.

Ethernet is not one network technology, but rather a family of network technologies that share the same basic bus topology, frame type, and network access method. So with that, let's see how Ethernet works.

How Ethernet Works

Ethernet's designers faced the same challenges as the designers of any network: how to send data across the wire, how to identify the sending and receiving computers, and how to determine which computer should use the shared cable at what time. The engineers resolved these issues by using data packets that contain MAC addresses to identify computers on the network, and using a process called CSMA/CD to determine which machine should access the wire at any given time. You saw some of this in action in Chapter 3, but now I need to introduce you to a bunch of new terms, so let's look at each of these solutions.

Organizing the Data: Packets

All computer networks break data transmitted between computers into smaller pieces called *packets* or *frames*, as you'll recall from Chapter 3. Using packets addresses two issues for Ethernet networks. First, it prevents any single machine from monopolizing the shared bus cable. Second, packets make the process of retransmitting lost data more efficient.

 EXAM TIP: The terms packet and frame are often used interchangeably.

The process you saw earlier of transferring a large word processing document between two computers illustrates these two issues. First, if the sending computer sends the document as a single piece, it will monopolize the cable and prevent other machines from using it. Using packets allows computers to share the cable, with each computer sending a few pieces of data whenever they have access to the cable. Second, in the real world, bad things can happen to good data. When errors occur during transmission, only the damaged packets need to be retransmitted. If, for example, a large word processing document were transmitted as a single piece, the entire file would need to be retransmitted. Breaking the file up into smaller pieces enables the computer to retransmit only the damaged portions. Because of their benefits—shared access and reduced retransmission—virtually all networking technologies use packets.

An Ethernet packet contains four basic pieces of information: the actual data to be sent, the Media Access Control (MAC) address of the packet's source, the MAC address of the intended recipient, and a Cyclic Redundancy Check (CRC) code. Figure 5-1 shows a simplified data packet.

MAC Addresses

Each computer on an Ethernet, called a *node*, must have a unique identifying address. Ethernet identifies the machines on a network using special 48-bit binary addresses known as *MAC addresses* (see Chapter 3). A 48-bit address provides for 2^{48} possible

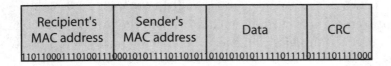

Recipient's MAC address	Sender's MAC address	Data	CRC

Figure 5-1   A simplified Ethernet data packet

MAC addresses. 2^{48} equals 281,474,976,710,656, which means that an Ethernet network can conceivably have more than 281 trillion machines! (Other factors limit Ethernet networks to a much smaller size).

The machine used to write this paragraph has a Linksys PCMCIA Ethernet card whose MAC address is 000000001110000010011000000000010000100100001110. Just try saying that three times fast! To make it easier for network technicians to talk about MAC addresses, they are usually written in hexadecimal notation. Instead of writing 000000001110000010011000000000010000100100001110, a tech would write 00 E0 98 01 09 0E. Even the hexadecimal number isn't exactly simple, but at least it's easier to deal with than the binary version!

NOTE: Every device that has a MAC address is called a node.

Before manufacturing my Ethernet card, Linksys applied to the IEEE for a block of addresses; it was assigned the set of addresses matching the form 00 E0 98 *xx xx xx*. The IEEE assigned Linksys what it calls an *Organizationally Unique Identifier* (OUI), which comprises the first 24 bits (00 E0 98); the second 24 bits are the *Device ID*. It is the responsibility of Linksys to give each NIC it manufactures a unique address, combining its OUI with a never-to-be-reused Device ID to produce a MAC address somewhere in the range between 00 E0 98 *00 00 00* and 00 E0 98 *FF FF FF*. If Linksys ever exhausts this pool of 2^{24} addresses (approximately 16 million), the company can apply to the IEEE for more.

To determine the MAC address of a specific NIC, use the diagnostic utility that comes with the card (see Figure 5-2). Also, as mentioned in Chapter 3, you can run WINIPCFG (Win9*x*) or IPCONFG (WinNT/2000) or just look for a MAC address label on the NIC itself.

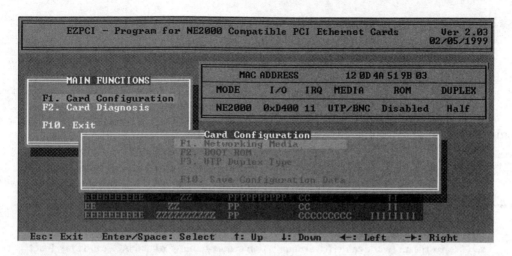

Figure 5-2 Most NIC setup disks include a diagnostic utility that will display the MAC address of the NIC.

Using MAC Addresses

MAC addresses allow each machine on the network to determine which data packets to process. When a computer sends out a data packet, it transmits it across the wire in both directions, as shown Figure 5-3. All of the other computers on the network listen to the wire and examine the packet to see if it contains their MAC address. If not, they ignore the packet. If a machine sees a packet with its MAC address, it opens the packet and begins processing the data.

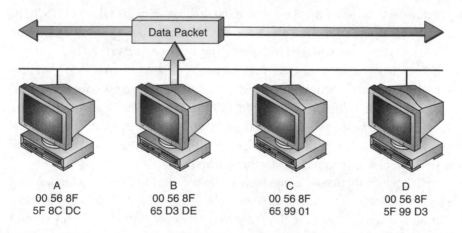

Figure 5-3 A computer on the network sends out a packet.

This system of allowing each machine to decide which packets it will process may be efficient, but because *any* device connected to the network cable can potentially capture *any* data packet transmitted across the wire, plain Ethernet carries a significant security vulnerability. Network diagnostic programs, commonly called *packet sniffers,* can order a NIC to run in *promiscuous mode.* When running in promiscuous mode, the NIC processes *all* the packets it sees on the cable, regardless of their MAC addresses. Packet sniffers are valuable troubleshooting tools in the right hands, but Ethernet provides no protections against their unscrupulous use. If data security is important, consider installing some type of additional encryption software to safeguard the data.

NOTE: MAC stands for Media Access Control, which simply means that the MAC address has something to do with how machines on the network control access to the network cable (the media). Don't worry about what MAC stands for. Just remember that the MAC address is a unique identifier for each machine on the network.

NOTE: Don't confuse MAC addresses with IP addresses. They serve a different purpose.

CRC Error Correction

The Cyclic Redundancy Check (CRC) code in a data packet enables Ethernet nodes to recognize when bad things happen to good data. Machines on a network must be able to detect when data has been damaged in transit. In order to detect errors, the computers on an Ethernet network attach a special code to each packet. When creating an Ethernet packet, the sending machine runs the data through a special mathematical formula and attaches the result, called the *CRC,* to the packet. The receiving machine opens up the packet, performs the same calculation, and compares its answer with the one included with the packet. If the CRC codes do not match, the receiving machine will ask the sending machine to retransmit that packet.

At this point, those crafty network engineers have solved two of the problems facing them by using data packets to organize the data to be sent, and MAC addresses to identify machines on the network. But the challenge of determining which machine should send data at which time required another solution: CSMA/CD.

Test Specific

CSMA/CD, or Who Gets to Send the Next Packet?

Ethernet networks use a system called *Carrier Sense, Multiple Access/Collision Detection* (CSMA/CD) to determine which computer should use a shared cable at a given moment. *Carrier sense* means that each node using the network examines the cable before sending a data packet (see Figure 5-4). If another machine is using the network, the node will detect traffic and wait until the cable is free. If it detects no traffic, the node will send out its data packet.

Multiple Access means that all machines have equal access to the wire. If the line is free, an Ethernet node does not need approval to use the wire—it just uses it. From the point of view of Ethernet, it does not matter what function the node is performing. It could be a desktop system running Windows XP or a high-end file server running Windows 2000 Server or Novell NetWare. As far as Ethernet is concerned, a node is a node is a node, and access to the cable is assigned strictly on a first-come, first-served basis.

Figure 5-4 A node on an Ethernet network listens for traffic before it sends out a data packet.

So what happens if two machines listening to the cable simultaneously decide that it is free and try to send a packet? When two computers try to use the cable simultaneously, a *collision* occurs, and both of the transmissions are lost (see Figure 5-5). A collision resembles the effect of two people talking simultaneously: the listener hears a mixture of two voices, and can't understand either one.

Both machines will detect the fact that a collision has occurred by listening to their own transmissions. People talking on the telephone use a similar technique to know whether or not they are the only ones speaking at a particular moment. By comparing the words they speak with the sounds they hear, they know whether or not other people are talking. If a person hears words he or she didn't say, he or she knows someone else is also talking (see Figure 5-6).

Ethernet nodes do the same thing. They compare their own transmissions with the transmission they are receiving over the cable and can detect if another node has transmitted at the same time (Figure 5-7). If they detect a collision, both nodes immediately stop transmitting. They then each generate a random number and wait for a random period of time. If you imagine that each machine rolls its magic electronic dice and waits for that number of seconds, you wouldn't be too far from the truth, except that the amount of time an Ethernet node waits to retransmit is much shorter than one second (see Figure 5-8). Whichever node generates the lowest random number begins its retransmission first, winning the competition to use the wire. The losing node then sees traffic on the wire, and waits for the wire to be free again before attempting to retransmit its data.

CSMA/CD has the benefit of being very simple to program into Ethernet devices such as NIC cards. The Token Ring method of determining access to a shared cable,

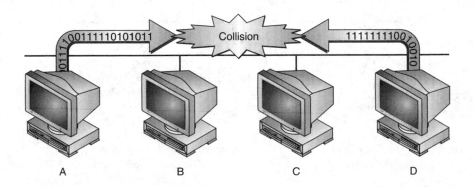

Figure 5-5   When two machines transmit simultaneously, their data packets collide.

Figure 5-6   Two people talking at the same time can tell they are not the only ones talking.

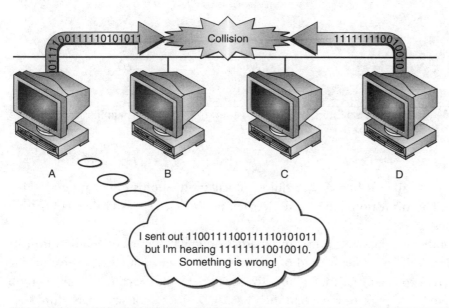

Figure 5-7   An Ethernet node detects a collision.

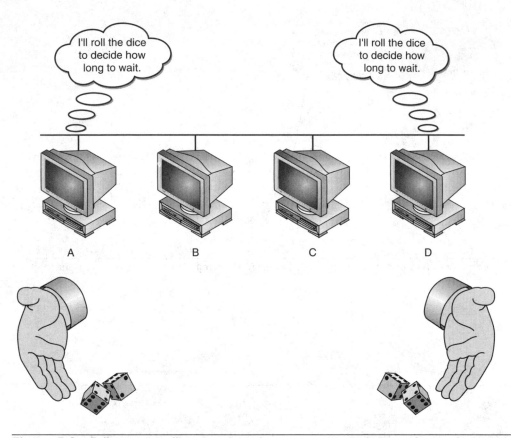

Figure 5-8 Following a collision, each node generates a random number and waits to try again.

discussed in detail in Chapter 7, requires much more sophisticated programming algorithms. For this reason, Ethernet devices tend to be less expensive than competing technologies.

That simplicity comes at a price: an Ethernet node will waste some amount of its time dealing with collisions instead of sending data. To illustrate this waste, and the chaos inherent to CSMA/CD, imagine a five-node network. Machines A and C both have outgoing data packets and begin the CSMA/CD process for sending traffic. They examine the cable and determine that no other node is currently sending out data (Carrier Sense). Because the cable is available, both A and C assume they are free to use it (Multiple Access). When they begin sending their respective data packets, they detect that another station is also sending data (Collision Detection). Nodes A and C both generate a random number and begin counting down. Sticking with the dice analogy, assume node A rolls a 5 and node C rolls a 6. They begin counting down. 1, 2, 3, WAIT! Node E just started sending! Node E had no involvement in the original collision, and has no idea that nodes A and C are contending for the right to use the cable. All E knows is that no device is using the cable at this moment. According to the CSMA/CD rules, E can begin sending. Nodes A and C have both lost out, and now must wait again for the cable to be free.

The chaotic CSMA/CD method of determining access to the cable explains experiences common to users of Ethernet networks. At 9:00 on a Monday morning, 100 users sit down at approximately the same time and type in their names and passwords to log in to their Ethernet network. Virtually every station on the network contends for the use of the cable at the same time, causing massive collisions and attempted retransmissions. Only rarely will the end users receive any kind of error message caused by high levels of traffic. Instead, they will perceive that the network is running slowly. The Ethernet NICs will continue to retry transmission and will eventually send the data packets successfully. Only in the event that the collisions get so severe that a packet cannot be sent after 16 retries will the sending station give up, resulting in an error of some kind being reported to the user.

Every Ethernet network wastes some amount of its available bandwidth dealing with these collisions. The typical Ethernet network is advertised to run at either 10 or 100 Mbps, but that advertised speed assumes that no collisions ever take place! In reality, collisions are a normal part of the operation of an Ethernet network.

Termination

The use of CSMA/CD in the real world has physical consequences for Ethernet networks. Most Ethernet networks use copper cabling to transmit their data packets as electrical signals. When an electrical signal travels down a copper wire, several things happen when the signal reaches the end of the wire. Some of the energy radiates out as radio waves, the cable functioning like the antennae on a radio transmitter. But some of the energy reflects off the end of the wire and travels back up the wire (see Figure 5-9). When the other Ethernet nodes on the network attempt to send, they check the cable and misinterpret that reflection as another node sending out data packets. They wait for the reflection to dissipate before sending. Unfortunately, the reflections quickly build up to a point that the network looks permanently busy to all of the nodes attached to it (see Figure 5-10).

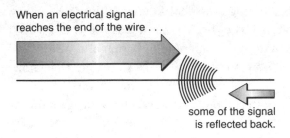

When an electrical signal
reaches the end of the wire . . .

some of the signal
is reflected back.

Figure 5-9 When electricity hits the end of the wire, some of the electricity comes back up the wire as a reflection.

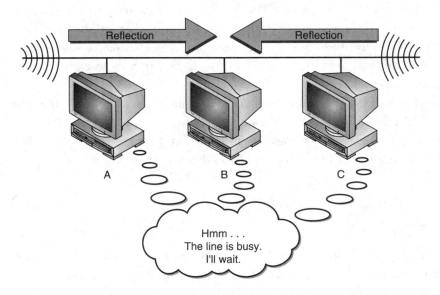

Reflection

Reflection

A   B   C

Hmm . . .
The line is busy.
I'll wait.

Figure 5-10 Reflections look like a busy signal to the computers attached to the network.

In order to prevent these reflections, a *terminating resistor* must be connected at each end of the segment (see Figure 5-11). This resistor absorbs the reflections, thereby enabling the segment to function properly. A CSMA/CD network using copper cabling won't function properly unless both ends of the network bus cable are terminated with terminating resistors.

Figure 5-11   Two 50-Ohm terminating resistors of the type used with 10Base2 cable

Cable Breaks

The use of CSMA/CD in Ethernet networks causes some interesting behavior when the cable breaks. Figure 5-12 shows a five-node network connected to a single segment of cable. If the piece of cable between computer A and computer B breaks, computer A will not be able to communicate with the rest of the machines (see Figure 5-13). But that's not the end of the trouble, because a break anywhere in the bus cable causes a loss of

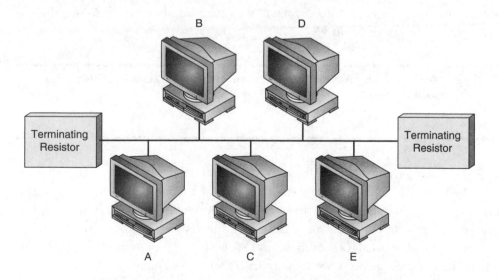

Figure 5-12   An Ethernet network with five computers

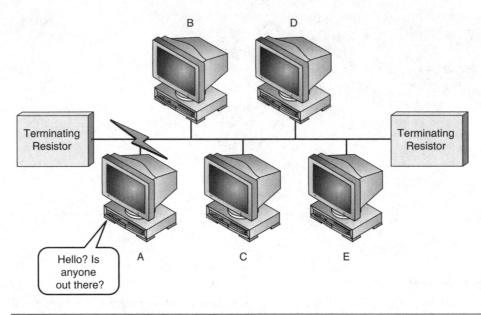

Figure 5-13   A cable break cuts computer A off from the rest of the network.

termination in the cable. This results in reflections in both directions, prompting all the nodes on the network to go into perpetual waiting mode (see Figure 5-14), thereby shutting down the entire network.

> **NOTE:**   **The bus cable that computers on an Ethernet network connect to is called a segment.**

Now we have the answers to many of the questions that faced those early Ethernet designers. MAC addresses identify each machine on the network. CSMA/CD determines which machine should have access to the cable when. But all this remains in the realm of theory—we still need to build the thing! Numerous questions must be answered. What kind of cables should we use? What should they be made of? How long can they be? For these answers, we look to the IEEE 802.3 standard.

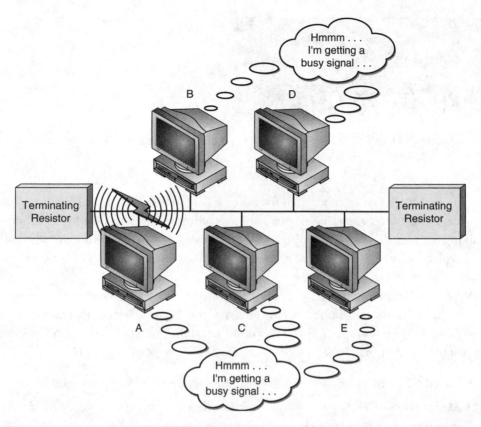

Figure 5-14 Reflections caused by the cable break bring the whole network down.

Ethernet Cabling Systems

The IEEE 802.3 committee recognizes that no single cabling solution can work in all situations, so it provides a variety of cabling standards, featuring cryptic names like 10Base5, 10Base2, 10BaseT, and 100BaseTX. This chapter will concentrate on the Ethernet cabling systems based on coaxial cabling (10Base5 and 10Base2), while the next chapter will discuss Ethernet cabling based on other cable types, such as twisted-pair (10BaseT and 100baseTX) and fiber optic (100BaseFX).

10Base5

In the beginning, the term *Ethernet* referred specifically to a CSMA/CD network running over a thick RG-8 coaxial cable like the one shown in Figure 5-15. Although not required by any standard, the cable was almost always yellow. Network techs refer to

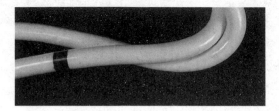

Figure 5-15 Thick Ethernet cable (RG-8) has a black band marking every 2.5 meters.

the original thick yellow cable used for Ethernet as Thick Ethernet, or Thicknet. Thicknet has the heaviest shielding of any cabling commonly used for 10 Mbps Ethernet, making it an excellent choice for high interference environments. Because of its rigidity and typical color, the less formal among us occasionally refer to RG-8 cable as *yellow cable* or *frozen yellow garden hose*.

When the IEEE took charge of the Ethernet standard, it created a more structured way to refer to the various Ethernet cabling systems, and began referring to Thick Ethernet as *10Base5*, a term that specifies the speed of the cabling system, its signaling type, and its distance limitations. 10Base5 breaks down as follows (see Figure 5-16):

- **Speed** The *10* in 10Base5 signifies an Ethernet network that runs at 10 Mbps.
- **Signal type** The *Base* in 10Base5 signifies that 10Base5 uses baseband signaling, meaning there is a single signal on the cable.
- **Distance** The *5* in 10Base5 indicates that 10Base5 cables may not be longer than 500 meters.

Baseband vs. Broadband

Data signals can be sent over a network cable in two ways: broadband and baseband. Cable television is an example of broadband transmission. The single piece of coaxial cable that comes into your home carries multiple signals, and a small box allows you to

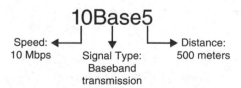

Figure 5-16 The term 10Base5 provides three key pieces of information.

select specific channels. Broadband creates these separate channels through a process called *Frequency Division Multiplexing*. Each channel is actually a different frequency of signal. Your television or cable box filters out all but the frequency you want to see. Baseband is a much simpler process. It simply sends a single signal over the cable (see Figure 5-17). With the exception of the rarely used 10Broad36 standard, Ethernet networks use baseband signaling which employs very simple *transceivers* (the devices that transmit and receive signals on the cable) because they only need to distinguish between three states on the cable: one, zero, and idle. Broadband transceivers must be more complex because they have to be able to distinguish those three states on multiple channels within the same cable. Because of its relative simplicity, most computer networks use baseband signaling.

NOTE: The dominance of baseband signaling may not last forever. Cable modems, which connect computers to the Internet using the same cable used for cable television, use broadband signaling. As cable modems become more popular, the networking industry may reexamine the use of broadband signaling in other types of networks.

500 Meters per 10Base5 Segment

10Base5 segments cannot be longer than 500 meters. A *segment* is the single length of cable, connected on either end to a hub, router, switch or bridge, to which the computers on an Ethernet network connect. The terminating resistors at each end of the segment define the ends of the segment (see Figure 5-18). The 500-meter segment limitation applies to the *entire* segment, not to the length of the cable between any two machines.

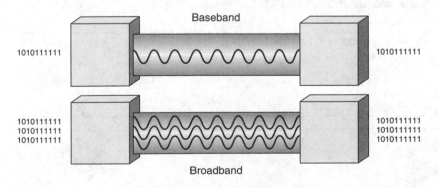

Figure 5-17   Baseband signaling sends a single signal at any given instant, whereas broadband signaling sends multiple signals on separate frequencies.

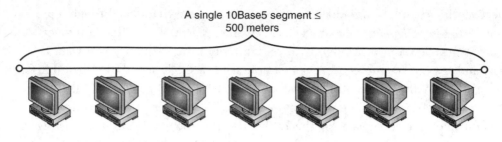

Figure 5-18 A 10Base5 Ethernet segment

The 10Base5 cabling standard strictly defines how nodes connect to the segment. Unlike nodes in many other cabling systems, 10Base5 nodes do not connect directly to the bus cable. Instead, 10Base5 NICs use a 15-pin female DB connector (called an AUI connector) to connect to an external transceiver (see Figure 5-19). This connector is physically identical to the MIDI and joystick connectors found on most soundcards. Confusing your Ethernet connection with these cables not only drops the node off the network, it makes those flight simulator games much more challenging!

The cable between a NIC and a transceiver can be up to 50 meters long, but the external transceivers must be placed exactly at 2.5-meter intervals along the Ethernet cable (see Figure 5-20). Remember that black band on the cable in Figure 5-15? Those black bands, spaced every 2.5 meters, help technicians space the connections properly when

Figure 5-19 An AUI connector on a 10Base5 NIC

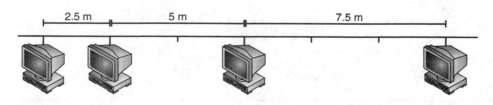

Figure 5-20 10Base5 requires that nodes be spaced at 2.5-meter intervals.

installing the cable. Figure 5-21 shows the connection between a 10Base5 transceiver and a NIC. Because 10Base5 uses an extremely stiff cable, the cables were often run through the ceiling, with *drop cables* used to connect the cable to the individual NICs (see Figure 5-22). A maximum of 100 nodes can be attached to each 10Base5 segment.

Why Not 10Base5?

Although some organizations continue to use 10Base5 cabling, most new 10 Mbps installations use either 10Base2 or 10BaseT. Although all three of these types of cabling run at 10 Mbps, the RG-8 cable used in 10Base5 networks costs more than either

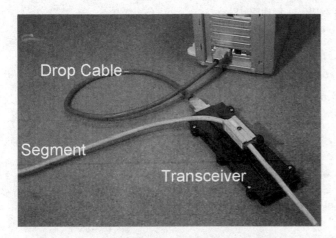

Figure 5-21   A 10Base5 transceiver connected to a NIC drop cable

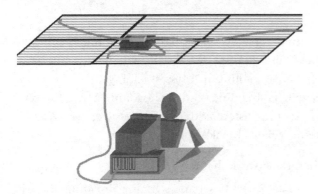

Figure 5-22   10Base5 uses drop cables to connect individual NICs to the segment, typically installed in the ceiling.

10Base2 or 10BaseT, both for material and for installation. Organizations mainly continue to use 10Base5 where it is already installed or in high-interference environments that require RG-8's heavy shielding.

10Base5 Summary

- Speed: 10 Mbps
- Signal type: Baseband
- Distance: 500 meters/segment
- No more than 100 nodes per segment
- Nodes must be spaced at 2.5 meter intervals
- Cables marked with a black band every 2.5 meters to ease installation
- The thick coaxial cable used for 10Base5 is almost always yellow, although nothing in the standard requires that color
- Expensive cost per foot compared to other cabling systems
- Typically uses yellow cables, but not required by the standard
- Known as Thick Ethernet or Thicknet

 NOTE: 10Base5 will become even less common as fiber optic cabling, which is immune to electrical interference and has even more generous distance limitations, becomes less expensive.

10Base2

10Base2 can be used in many of the same instances as 10Base5, but is much easier to install and much less expensive. 10Base2 uses RG-58 coaxial cable with BNC connectors, as shown in Figure 5-23. Although RG-58 cabling has less shielding than the more expensive RG-8 cabling used in 10Base5, its shielding is adequate for most installations.

The IEEE 802.3 committee tried to stay consistent with their *name-signal type-distance* scheme for naming Ethernet. The term *10Base2* breaks down as follows:

- **Speed**   The *10* signifies an Ethernet network that runs at 10 Mbps.
- **Signal type**   *Base* signifies that 10Base2 uses baseband signaling, meaning there is a single signal on the cable.
- **Distance**   The *2* indicates 10Base2 cables may not be longer than 185 meters.

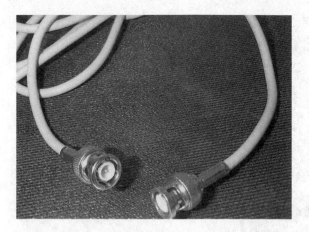

Figure 5-23   A piece of RG-58 coaxial cabling with BNC connectors

How does the 2 in 10Base2 translate into 185 meters? Don't ask—just live with it. Maybe at some point in the process, the distance limitation really was 200 meters and the IEEE later decided it had to be shortened. Maybe they thought 10Base1.85 looked funny and went for the closest round number. Who knows? Your job is to memorize the fact that the distance limitation for 10Base2 is 185 meters.

10Base2 has several advantages that make it the preferred choice for running Ethernet over coaxial cable, even though it allows only 30 computers per segment, far fewer than 10Base5. 10Base2 costs much less to install than 10Base5. RG-58 cabling costs significantly less per foot than 10Base5's RG-8 cabling. 10Base2's spacing requirements are also much less strict: computers must be spaced at least 0.5 meters apart, but do not have to be spaced at a specific interval as required by 10Base5. RG-58's greater flexibility makes modifying and extending 10Base2 segments relatively painless. Except for instances that require the longer distance or greater shielding of 10Base5, network technicians today choose 10Base2 for running Ethernet over coaxial cabling.

Connectors

The connectors used in 10Base2 networks make 10Base2 much easier to install and support than 10Base5. Unlike 10Base5's awkward requirement for external transceivers, 10Base2 NICs have a built-in transceiver and connect to the bus cable using a *BNC* connector (see Figure 5-24). The BNC connector provides an easy way to separate the center wire, which transmits data, from the outer shield, which protects the center wire from interference (see Figure 5-25).

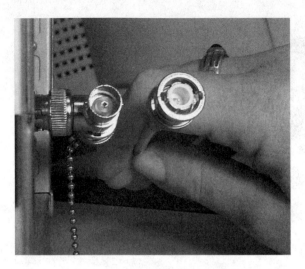

Figure 5-24   Male and female BNC connectors

Figure 5-25   The BNC connector keeps the center wire and the shield from touching.

BNC connectors are crimped onto the wire using a crimping tool like the one shown in Figure 5-26. *Crimping* means to bend the metal of the connector around the cable to secure it to the cable. A properly crimped BNC connector keeps the center wire electrically insulated from the shield. An improperly crimped BNC connector allows the shield and the center wire to make electrical contact, creating a short in the cable (see Figure 5-27). A *short*, or short circuit, allows electricity to pass between the center wire and the shield. Because any current on the shield caused by interference will be conducted to the center strand, machines on the network will assume the network is busy and will not transmit data. The effect of a short circuit is the same as a break in the cable: The entire network goes down.

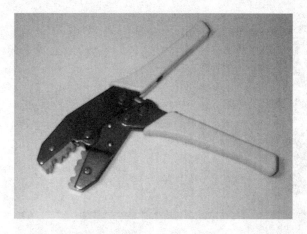

Figure 5-26 A typical crimping tool used for putting BNC connectors on a piece of RG-58 coaxial cable

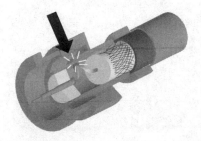

Figure 5-27 A poorly crimped cable allows electricity to pass between the shield and the center wire, creating a short.

> **NOTE:** The origins of the acronym BNC have been lost. Some of the possible things it could stand for include Bayonet Nut Connector, Bayonet Navy Connector, British Naval Connector, Bayonet Neil Cofflin (purported inventor), and according to a long-time manufacturer of the devices, BNC stands for Bayonet Nut Coupling. My advice: If you can recognize a BNC connector, know what it's for, and know how to use one, then you don't need to worry about the acronym!

10Base2 requires the use of a T-connector (see Figure 5-28) when connecting devices to the cable. The stem of the T-connector plugs into the female connector on the Ethernet NIC, and the two pieces of coaxial cable are plugged into either end of the top bar

Figure 5-28   A T-connector

Figure 5-29   A T-connector with an RG-58 cable attached to either side

(see Figure 5-29). In the event the Ethernet node sits at the end of the cable, a terminating resistor takes the place of one of the cables (see Figure 5-30). All BNC connectors, including terminators and T-connectors, should be locked into place; you do this by turning their locking rings (see Figure 5-31). Although BNC connectors are basically easy to use, mistakes can happen. One frequent novice mistake is to connect a BNC connector directly to the female connection on a NIC (see Figure 5-32). While the connector locks in place just fine, the network will not function because there is no place to attach the terminating resistor.

Figure 5-30   A T-connector with a terminating resistor attached

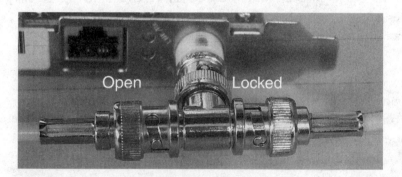

Figure 5-31   The BNC connector on the right is locked into place; the one on the left is not.

Figure 5-32   BNC connectors should never be attached directly to the NIC.

10Base2 Summary

- Speed: 10 Mbps

- Signal type: Baseband

- Distance: 185 meters/segment

- No more than 30 nodes per segment

- Nodes must be spaced at least 0.5 meters apart

- Inexpensive cost per foot compared to 10Base5

- Known as Thin Ethernet, Thinnet, and sometimes Cheapernet

10Base2 offers a cheap and quick way to network a small number of computers using coaxial cable and Ethernet. Larger networks typically use twisted pair wiring for Ethernet, but 10Base2 retains a strong installed base in smaller networks. 10Base2 retains the basic mechanisms of Ethernet: CSMA/CD, MAC addresses, and the Ethernet packet format. Rather than designing a new networking technology from scratch, 10Base2's designers built on proven, existing technology.

Repeaters

Some networks function perfectly well within the limitations of 10Base2 and 10Base5. For some organizations, however, the limitations of these cabling systems are unacceptable. Organizations that need longer distance limits, more computers, more fault tolerance, or the ability to combine different cabling systems can add repeaters to their networks.

NOTE: Repeaters only operate at layer 1 of the OSI model, the Physical layer (you have memorized these, right?).

A *repeater* is a device that takes all data packets it receives from one Ethernet segment and repeats them, that is, retransmits them, on another segment. Figure 5-33 shows a typical Ethernet repeater. An Ethernet repeater does exactly what it advertises: it takes packets from one Ethernet segment and repeats them on another. A repeater takes the incoming electrical signals, translates them into binary code, and then retransmits the electrical signals. A repeater does not function as an amplifier. *Amplifiers* boost signals, flaws and all, like a copy machine duplicating a bad original. A repeater, in contrast,

Figure 5-33   A typical Ethernet repeater

recreates the signals from scratch. Repeaters address the need for more computers, greater distances, improved fault tolerance, and integration of different cabling systems, but cannot do anything to deal with the downside of these larger networks: increased traffic.

Repeater Benefits

Repeaters have four key benefits. First, they extend the distance that a network can cover. Second, they increase the number of machines that can connect to the network. Third, they provide a measure of fault tolerance, limiting the impact of cable breaks to the segment on which the break occurs. Fourth, they can link different types of cabling segments together.

A repeater increases the maximum possible distance between machines by linking together two segments. Each segment retains its own distance limitation. If a repeater connects two 10Base2 segments, for example, the maximum distance that can separate two machines on different segments is 2×185, or 370 meters (see Figure 5-34). Using this equation, two 10Base5 segments connected by a repeater can cover 1,000 meters (2×500 meters).

In addition to increasing the distance covered by a single Ethernet network, repeaters also increase the number of machines that can connect to the network. A network with a repeater connecting two 10Base2 segments can have 2 segments $\times$ 30 nodes per segment, or 60 computers attached to it (see Figure 5-35).

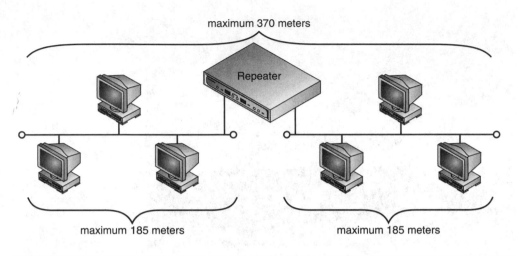

Figure 5-34 Two 10Base2 segments connected by a repeater can cover 370 meters.

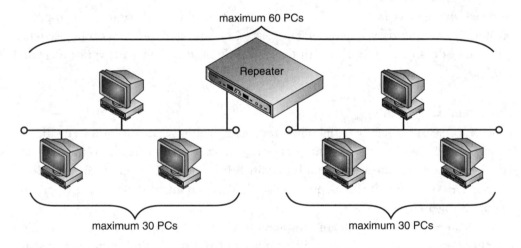

Figure 5-35 Repeaters increase the number of machines that can be connected to the network.

 NOTE: See Chapter 6 for a discussion of the 5-4-3 rule for information about limits to the number of repeaters that can exist on a network.

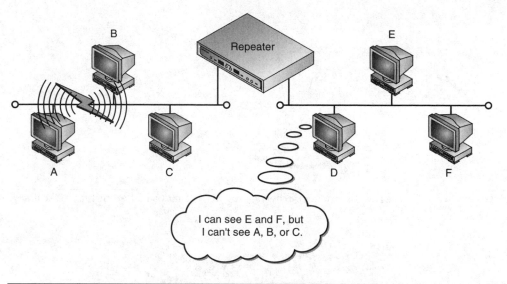

Figure 5-36   Cable breaks affect only the segment on which the break occurs.

Repeaters also add a degree of *fault tolerance* to a network. If one of the segments breaks, only that segment will fail. Computers on the adjacent segment will continue to function, unaffected when communicating within their own segment. The segment with the cable break fails because of reflections, but the segment on the far side of the repeater remains properly terminated and functions normally (see Figure 5-36).

NOTE: Fault tolerance is the capability of a system to continue functioning even after some part of the system has failed.

As an added benefit, repeaters can give network designers the flexibility to combine different cabling types on the same network. Both 10Base5 and 10Base2 use exactly the same packet structure (that is, the actual ones and zeroes used are identical). Thus a repeater can connect a 10Base5 and a 10Base2 segment without difficulty (see Figure 5-37). Many repeaters come with both AUI and BNC connectors for that purpose (see Figure 5-38).

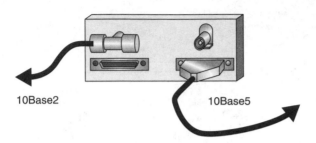

Repeater

10Base2

10Base5

Figure 5-37   A repeater can connect Ethernet segments that use different types of cabling.

Figure 5-38   A typical Ethernet repeater with both AUI connectors for 10Base5 and BNC connectors for 10Base2

Repeaters Repeat Traffic, They Don't Manage It

Repeaters are not smart devices—they repeat every data packet they hear, regardless of its origin. Because the repeater repeats all packets that hit the wire, without regard to the source or destination, the rules of CSMA/CD apply to the entire network as a whole. If two computers on two different segments connected by a repeater both transmit a packet at the same time, a collision will result. Thus using repeaters to build larger networks can lead to traffic jams, meaning more traffic and slower overall performance.

In Figure 5-39, computers A, B, and C connect to segment 1; computers D, E, and F connect to segment 2. Computer A transmits a packet to computer C, which sits on the same side of the repeater. Computers D, E, and F, sitting on the far side of the repeater, do not need to hear the packets sent between computers A and C; however, the repeater sends the packets to their network segment anyway. Machines on segment 1 cannot transmit while machines on segment 2 are using the network and vice versa. Because all of the machines, regardless of the network segment to which they attach, can potentially have collisions with all of the other machines, segments 1 and 2 are both consid-

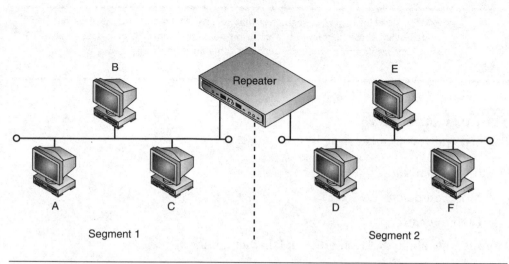

Figure 5-39   Two Ethernet segments connected by a repeater

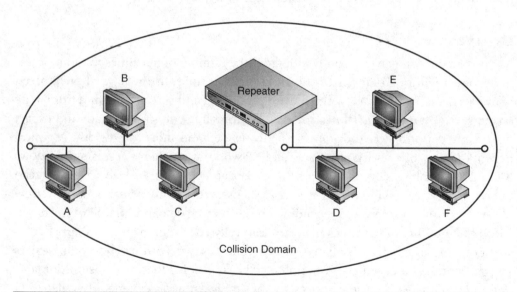

Figure 5-40   A single collision domain

ered part of the same *collision domain* (see Figure 5-40). Even when using repeaters, an Ethernet network functions like a single CB radio channel: Only one user can talk and be understood at any given time.

NOTE: A set of Ethernet segments that receive all traffic generated by any node within those segments is a collision domain. Chapter 6 discusses devices that can break a network into multiple collision domains.

Repeater Summary

Repeaters provide four key benefits:

- Increased distance
- More computers
- Fault tolerance
- Interoperability between different Ethernet cabling systems

Repeaters operate only at the Physical layer of the OSI model.

Repeaters do not help reduce or manage network traffic, but their other attributes make them important tools for network technicians and architects.

Bridges

As the demands on network bandwidth grow, the number of machines that can peacefully coexist within an Ethernet collision domain shrinks. In the days of DOS-based network clients accessing a few small word processing and spreadsheet files from a file server, several hundred machines could sit on the same collision domain and expect reasonable performance. Today, many networks demand more bandwidth. A typical network might consist of Windows 9x and XP workstation clients accessing Windows NT or 2000 database servers, NetWare file servers, and UNIX-based web servers. Instead of occasionally accessing a few files on a server, users constantly demand a wide variety of services from their servers. Depending on the specific demands placed on its bandwidth, the number of machines that can peacefully coexist on a single Ethernet collision domain can vary from as many as 100 to as few as two. Fortunately, certain devices —such as bridges and routers—can link together multiple Ethernet collision domains to form larger networks. These devices do not simply connect networks. They also filter traffic between the networks, preserving precious bandwidth. Let's look at bridges next, but save the more complex router discussion for a later chapter.

Bridges filter and forward traffic between two or more networks based on the MAC addresses contained in the data packets. To *filter* traffic means to stop it from crossing from one network to the next; to *forward* traffic means to pass traffic originating on one

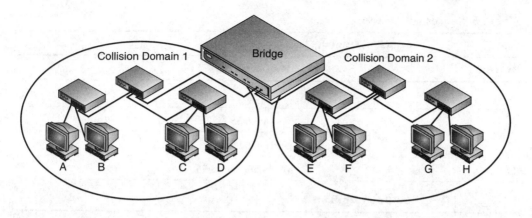

Figure 5-41   Two Ethernet collision domains connected by a bridge

side of the bridge to the other. Figure 5-41 shows two Ethernet collision domains connected by a bridge. The bridge is represented as a simple box because the physical appearance of a bridge can vary a great deal. The bridge can be a stand-alone device that looks similar to an Ethernet repeater or hub, or it might be a PC with two NICs running special bridging software. The bridge might even be built into a multifunction device that provides other functions in addition to acting as a bridge.

How Bridges Function

Ethernet bridges behave just like repeaters when first plugged in. In the network shown in Figure 5-41, machine A sends a data packet to machine D. Because machines A, B, C, and D all lie on the same collision domain, they will all receive that data packet. When the data packet destined for machine D hits the bridge, the bridge does not know the location of machine D, and forwards the packet to collision domain 2. At this point, the bridge begins building a list of machines, and makes a note that it received a data packet from machine A's MAC address from collision domain 1. Now that the bridge knows the location of at least one machine, it can begin filtering. When machine D responds to machine A, the bridge will not forward the packet to collision domain 2 because it knows that the destination of the data packet lies on the same collision domain from which it originated.

Eventually, each machine will have sent out at least one data packet and the bridge will have a full list of each machine's MAC address and location. For the example used here, the table would look something like Table 5-1, but without the letters for each machine. Bridges only care about MAC addresses—they could not care less what designations (like letters or names) we mere mortals assign to our machines.

Table 5-1 Collision Domain

Collision Domain 1	
Machine	**MAC address**
A	00 45 5D 32 5E 72
B	9F 16 C6 55 4D EE
C	9F 16 C6 99 DF F1
D	00 45 5D 75 D3 95
Collision Domain 2	
E	9F 16 C6 85 E5 55
F	9F 16 C6 DD 41 11
G	00 45 5D 00 25 19
H	9F 16 C6 88 58 F5

Once the bridge has a complete table listing, each machine's MAC address and the side of the bridge on which it sits, it can look at every incoming packet and decide whether or not to forward it to the other side. If machine C sends a packet to machine D, machines A and B will receive that packet as well because the hubs between them and machine C lack the ability to decide what to forward. The hubs are repeaters, and they repeat everything. The more sophisticated bridge recognizes that no machine on collision domain 2 needs to see the packet destined for machine D on collision domain 1 and filters the packet accordingly.

 NOTE: Bridges operate at layer 2 of the OSI model, which you should know (again, you have memorized these, right?) is the Data Link layer.

Bridges provide two key benefits: relief from the 5-4-3 rule and the ability to segment traffic. Chapter 6 goes into this in much more detail, but, simply put, the purpose of the 5-4-3 rule is to prevent undetected collisions. With a bridge, machines do not need to be within 5 segments, 4 repeaters, and 3 populated segments of machines on the far side of the bridge—they simply must be within 5-4-3 of the bridge itself. Once a packet reaches the bridge, the bridge takes over the responsibility of sending it to its final destination. If the bridge forwards a packet that collides with another packet, the bridge, not the original source machine, detects the collision and retransmits the packet. Bridges also provide a performance benefit by breaking the network up into independent pieces. In the previous example, machine A can send a packet to machine D at exactly the same instant machine G sends a packet to machine H, without causing a collision. When no traffic crosses the bridge, the bridge effectively doubles the bandwidth of the network as a whole.

Most network traffic is *unicast* traffic, destined for a single machine, and bridges can easily make decisions about whether to filter or forward these packets. A *broadcast* is a packet directed to all machines. Bridges always forward broadcast traffic. Network devices use broadcast addresses to discover information about the network. Human beings like to call machines by names, like *Titan* or *Sales20*. In order for a machine on the network to find out the MAC address of the machine named Titan, it sends out a special broadcast packet that says, "If your name is Titan, please send me a response with your MAC address." Every machine on the network must examine that broadcast and determine whether or not its name is Titan. Most machines think, "Hmm . . . that's not me," and ignore the broadcast. The machine named Titan, however, will respond back with a unicast packet for the machine that sent the broadcast packet, telling it Titan's MAC address. Because the bridge does not know the MAC address of the intended recipient of the broadcast, it plays it safe and forwards all broadcast traffic. This increases traffic on both sides of the bridge, but allows all functions that rely on broadcasts to work correctly.

Machines on either side of the bridge can remain blissfully unaware of the bridge's presence. When bridges retransmit a packet, they copy it precisely, even using the originating machine's MAC address as the source MAC address in the packet. Adding a bridge to a network does not require you to reconfigure any of the other nodes on the network. Simply rewire the cabling and the bridge takes care of the rest. The transparent nature of bridges makes them the easiest way to break an Ethernet network into multiple collision domains.

Because bridges forward data packets without changing the packets themselves, the packet format used on each side of the bridge must be the same. The previous examples discuss bridges that connect two Ethernet networks. Bridges also exist for other technologies, such as Token Ring (see Chapter 7). Bridges cannot, however, connect an Ethernet network to a Token Ring network, because of differences in the way they structure packets.

NOTE: Terminology Alert! To be absolutely precise, the type of bridging described here is transparent bridging. Some documentation, especially documentation that deals with networking theory, will refer to translational bridges, which can translate between different packet formats. Translational bridges rarely, if ever, appear in Ethernet or Token Ring networks. You can assume the term bridge refers to the transparent type unless specifically told otherwise.

Bridges also lack the ability to handle multiple routes between machines. Figure 5-42 shows a network with multiple bridges that create a bridging loop. When machine A transmits a packet, bridges 2 and 3 will both forward the packet to bridge 1, making it appear to bridge 1 that machine A lies on both sides of bridge 1. The bridging loop confuses each of the other bridges in the same way. According to the simplified routing rules discussed previously, the bridges would forward a packet bound for machine A endlessly. To prevent this excess traffic, bridges should not be allowed to form loops. Most bridges use a technique called the *Spanning Tree Algorithm* to detect bridging loops and automatically disable bridges that form loops. Do not use bridges to provide multiple routes between nodes.

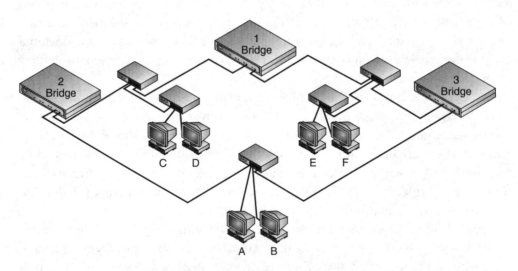

Figure 5-42 Loops can confuse bridges and should be avoided.

EXAM TIP: The Network+ exam does not cover the Spanning Tree Algorithm. The term is mentioned here only for completeness.

Bridge Summary

- Bridges filter or forward traffic based on the MAC addresses contained in each data packet.

- Bridges always forward broadcast packets.

- Bridges operate at the Data Link layer of the OSI model.

- Bridges can only connect two networks using the same type of data packets (for example, Ethernet to Ethernet, or Token Ring to Token Ring).

- Bridges learn the MAC addresses of machines on each network by listening to the cable.

- Bridges cannot be used to provide multiple routes between machines.

Bridges filter some unnecessary traffic, preserving precious network bandwidth. They free Ethernet networks from the limitations imposed by the 5-4-3 rule and increase the available bandwidth on a network by filtering traffic. Bridges do have limitations, however. They cannot connect dissimilar networks and cannot take advantage of multiple routes between nodes. Overcoming these challenges requires another type of device: a router. I'll save the router discussion for later in the book.

Chapter Review

Questions

1. Which Ethernet cabling standard is limited to 10 Megabits per second (Mbps) and can support cable segments up to a maximum distance of 185 meters?
   a. 10Base5
   b. 10Base2
   c. 10BaseT
   d. 10BaseF

2. Which Ethernet cabling standard is limited to 10 Mbps and can support cable segments up to a maximum distance of 500 meters?
   a. 10Base5
   b. 10Base2
   c. 10BaseT
   d. 10BaseF

3. Bridges operate at which layer of the OSI model?
   a. Physical
   b. Data Link
   c. Network
   d. Transport

4. Which of the following requires an external transceiver?
   a. 10Base5
   b. 10Base2
   c. 10BaseT
   d. 10BaseF

5. What kind of topology does 10Base2 use?
   a. Mesh
   b. Bus
   c. Star
   d. Ring

6. What kind of cable does 10Base2 use?
   a. RJ-45
   b. RJ-58
   c. RG-45
   d. RG-58

7. The first 24 bits of a MAC address are called a(n):
   a. Device ID
   b. Data ID
   c. Unique Manufacturing Identifier
   d. Organizationally Unique Identifier

8. The second 24 bits of a MAC address are called a(n):
   a. Device ID
   b. Data ID
   c. Unique Manufacturing Identifier
   d. Organizationally Unique Identifier

9. The type of connector used in 10Base2 is called a(n):
    a. AUI
    b. RJ-45
    c. BNC
    d. RG-8

10. The type of connector used in 10Base5 is called a(n):
    a. AUI
    b. RJ-45
    c. BNC
    d. RG-8

Answers

1. **B.** 10Base2 is the Ethernet cabling standard that is limited to 10 Mbps and can support cable segments up to a maximum distance of 185 meters.

2. **A.** 10Base5 is the Ethernet cabling standard that is limited to 10 Mbps and can support cable segments up to a maximum distance of 500 meters.

3. **B.** Bridges operate at the Data Link layer of the OSI model.

4. **A.** 10Base5 requires an external transceiver. 10Base2 transceivers are built into the NIC.

5. **B.** 10Base2 Ethernet uses a bus topology.

6. **D.** 10Base2 uses RG-58 coaxial cable. RJ-45 is a type of connector used with unshielded twisted-pair wiring. RJ-58 and RG-45 are not common network terms.

7. **D.** The first 24 bits of a MAC address are called the Organizationally Unique Identifier.

8. **A.** The second 24 bits of a MAC address are called the Device ID.

9. **C.** 10Base2 networks use BNC connectors.

10. **A.** 10Base5 networks use AUI connectors.

Modern Ethernet

In this chapter, you will

- Understand the concept of Star bus topology
- Learn the limits and specifications of 10BaseT
- Understand how to connect segments
- Understand the 5-4-3 rule
- Understand the concepts and specifications of high-speed Ethernet, including Fast Ethernet
- Learn the limits and specifications of 100BaseT, 100BaseTX, 1000BaseT, 1000BaseCX, 1000BaseSX, and 1000BaseLX
- Understand the functions of switched Ethernet, Full-duplex Ethernet, and Gigabit Ethernet

Historical/Conceptual

The first generation of Ethernet network technologies enjoyed substantial adoption in the networking world, but their bus topology continued to be their Achilles' heel—any break in the bus would shut down the network completely. Additionally, the relatively high cost of coaxial cable was much more than the UTP cabling used in other types of cabling installations. In 1990, the IEEE unveiled a new Ethernet standard that eliminated both of these issues: the now predominant 10BaseT. Let's take an in-depth look at 10BaseT, from its topology to its technology, and see why 10BaseT and the newer Ethernet technologies based on it now dominate the networking world.

What Is a Star Bus Topology?

10BaseT discards the pure bus topology of 10Base2 and 10Base5, employing instead the star bus topology. A *star bus topology* is a hybrid of the star and bus topologies. Star bus networks use a physical star that provides improved stability and a logical bus that maintains compatibility with existing Ethernet standards. In a star topology, all nodes connect to a central wiring point, as shown in Figure 6-1. The key advantage of the star topology is that a break in the cable affects only the machine connected to that cable. While the star topology boasts a more robust, fault-tolerant cabling system, pure star topologies do not exist in modern computer networks.

The physical topology describes the layout of the wires, while the logical topology depicts the behavior of the electronics. Physically, the nodes connect to a hub sitting in a central location, forming a star (see Figure 6-2). The hub contains circuitry that mimics a terminated Ethernet segment (see Figure 6-3). Logically, the nodes behave as though attached directly to the segment, sharing the segment according to the same CSMA/CD rules used for 10Base2 and 10Base5. Using the star bus topology maintains consistency with previous Ethernet standards such as CSMA/CD, but provides the stability of a star topology: If a cable gets cut, only one node drops off the network.

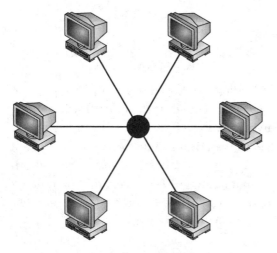

Figure 6-1   A star bus topology

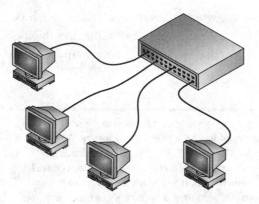

Figure 6-2   A 10BaseT network, with each node connected to the hub

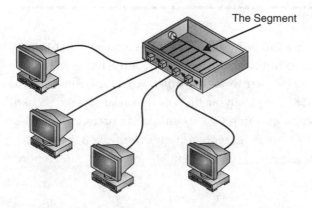

Figure 6-3   A 10BaseT hub contains the electronic equivalent of a properly terminated Ethernet segment.

10BaseT

The term *10BaseT* describes an Ethernet cabling system that uses a star bus topology. Except for the cable used, 10BaseT NICs behave much the same way as 10Base2 or 10Base5 NICs, and use precisely the same packet structure. Machines still identify other machines by their MAC addresses and use CSMA/CD to determine when to use the shared segment. They operate at the same speed, 10 Mbps. The key difference between 10BaseT and its pure bus topology predecessors is the location of the Ethernet segment.

In 10Base2 or 10Base5 installations, the segment winds its way around the network. In 10BaseT, the segment lies protected inside the hub. Although 10BaseT shares the logical bus structure of 10Base2 and 10Base5, it has its own cabling system and unique limitations.

NOTE: Terminology Alert! Depending on who you talk to, you may hear 10BaseT called a star topology, a bus topology, or a star bus topology. Which term a particular tech uses to describe 10BaseT's topology often depends on her job description. For someone whose primary job is installing cable, 10BaseT is a star. A tech crawling through ceiling tiles and punching holes in walls does not care how the electronics that will use the cable actually function. Similarly, a software engineer writing a device driver for an Ethernet NIC could not care less where the cables go; she thinks of 10BaseT as a bus. Engineers need to think about all the rules associated with a bus topology: CSMA/CD, MAC addresses, and so on. Many techs split the difference. Rather than saying that 10BaseT uses a physical star topology and a logical bus topology, they say that 10BaseT uses a star bus topology.

By using this hybrid *star bus topology*, 10BaseT enjoys the key benefit of a star topology: fault tolerance. The hub is really nothing more than a multicasting repeater, in that it repeats the signal coming in from one port to all the other ports. The hub has no interest in MAC addresses and works completely at the OSI Physical layer, just like 10Base2 or 10Base5 repeaters. If a cable running to a specific node breaks, the break affects only that computer because the Ethernet segment itself is unbroken (see Figure 6-4). If the segment itself breaks *inside* the hub, as shown in Figure 6-5, then the entire network goes down.

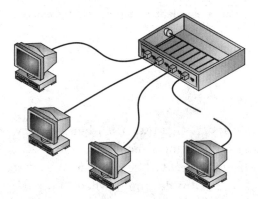

Figure 6-4 Because the Ethernet segment is protected inside the hub and remains unbroken, the break in the cable affects only one machine.

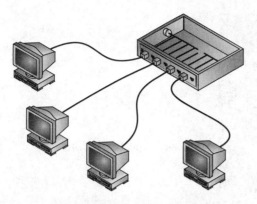

Figure 6-5   If the segment inside the hub breaks, then the entire segment fails.

 NOTE: **Please don't crack open your Ethernet hubs looking for a piece of coaxial cable—it won't be there. The interior of an Ethernet hub contains a circuit board that serves the same function as the coaxial segments used in 10Base5 and 10Base2. When a hub fails, there is no cable inside of it to break. Instead, some part of the circuit board fails. The effect is the same, of course: If the hub fails, the entire segment fails.**

The name *10BaseT* tries to follow the naming convention used for earlier Ethernet cabling systems. The number *10* refers to the speed: 10 Mbps. The word *Base* refers to the signaling type: baseband. The letter *T*, however, does not refer to a distance limitation like the 2 in 10Base2 or the 5 in 10Base5. Instead, it refers to the type of cable used: twisted pair. 10BaseT uses unshielded twisted pair (UTP) cabling.

UTP

Officially, 10BaseT uses a two-pair unshielded twisted pair (UTP), but for years everyone has been using four-pair wiring to connect devices to the hub, as insurance against the possible requirements of newer types of networking (see Figure 6-6). (Thank goodness they did! As you will soon see, newer forms of Ethernet need all four pairs.) Although it is more sensitive to interference than coaxial cable, UTP cabling provides an inexpensive and flexible means to cable physical star networks. Take care when installing UTP—because many other applications employ the same cabling and connectors, UTP cabling has strict standards for the proper crimping of the connectors and comes in a variety of grades, not all of which can support 10BaseT.

Figure 6-6 A typical four-pair unshielded twisted pair cable

Figure 6-7 An RJ-45 connector

UTP cabling uses an RJ-45 connector (Figure 6-7). Each pin on the RJ-45 connects to a single wire inside the cable; this enables devices to put voltage on the individual wires within the cable. The pins on the RJ-45 are numbered from 1 to 8, as shown in Figure 6-8. The 10BaseT standard designates some of these numbered wires for specific purposes. As mentioned earlier, although the cable has four pairs, 10BaseT uses only two of the pairs. Instead of using a single wire both to receive and to transmit data, 10BaseT devices use pins 1 and 2 to send data, and pins 3 and 6 to receive data. Even though one pair of wires sends data and another receives data, a 10BaseT device cannot

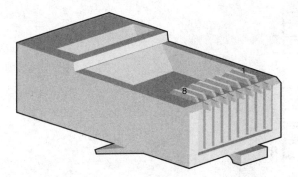

Figure 6-8   The pins on an RJ-45 connector are numbered 1 through 8.

send and receive simultaneously. The rules of CSMA/CD still apply. Only one device can use the segment contained in the hub without causing a collision.

Although 10BaseT Ethernet uses only four wires, cable manufacturers included the remaining four wires for compatibility with other standards. Other technologies, including Token Ring networks and telephone systems, employ the same UTP cabling as Ethernet. Some other Ethernet standards, such as the 100BaseT4 and 1000BaseT standards (discussed later in this chapter), also require all eight wires. The moral of this story: don't give in to the temptation to connect only the wires needed by 10BaseT. When installing UTP cabling, connect all the wires so they can be used for other applications in the future.

Each wire inside a UTP cable must connect to the proper pin on the RJ-45 connector at each end of the cable. Manufacturers color-code each wire within a piece of four-pair UTP to assist in properly matching the ends. Each pair of wires has a solid-colored wire and a striped wire: blue/blue-white, orange/orange-white, brown/brown-white, and green/green-white. Because signals sent down pin 1 on one end of a cable must be received on pin 1 on the other end, the same wire must connect to pin 1 on both ends. Industry organizations have developed a variety of standard *color codes* to facilitate installation. Figure 6-9 shows the EIA/TIA 568A color code standard. Note that the pairs used by Ethernet (1 through 2 and 3 through 6) come from the same color pairs (green/green-white and orange/orange-white). Using the RJ-45 connector to match the twisted pairs from the cable with the pairs used by 10BaseT helps minimize interference between the wires. Following an established color-code scheme such as EIA/TIA 568A ensures that the wires match up correctly at each end of the cable.

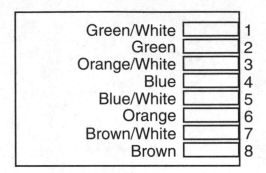

Figure 6-9 The EIA/TIA 568A standard

 NOTE: The EIA/TIA is the Electronics Industry Association/Telecommunications Industry Association.

The EIA/TIA 568A standard is not the only game—or color code—in town. The EIA/TIA 568B standard also sees a fairly high quantity of use, but the 568A standard seems to be the most common in today's networks. Theoretically, as long as each end of each cable uses the same color code, many color codes could be used within the same building and everything would still work. 10BaseT devices do not care what color the wires are, they just need to have the pins on the RJ-45 connector match up at each end. Despite the fact that multiple color codes can work, the wise network tech will use a single color code throughout his or her organization. Consistency makes troubleshooting and repair easier by enabling network techs to assume the proper color code. If an end user trips over a cable and breaks the connector (of course, savvy network techs such as ourselves would never do such a thing), putting a new connector on the cable takes much less time if the tech knows in advance the color code being used. If no standard color code exists, then the poor network tech has to find the other end of the cable and figure out what color code was used on that particular cable. To save wear and tear on your techie tennis shoes, pick a standard color code and stick with it!

 EXAM TIP: For the Network+ exam, do not worry about memorizing the EIA/TIA 568A color code. Just know that it is an industry standard color code for UTP cabling.

10BaseT Limits and Specifications

Like any other Ethernet cabling system, 10BaseT has limitations, both on cable distance and on the number of computers. The key distance limitation for 10BaseT is the distance between the hub and the computer. The twisted pair cable connecting a computer to the hub may not exceed 100 meters in length. A 10BaseT hub can connect no more than 1024 computers, although that limitation rarely comes into play. It makes no sense for vendors to build hubs that large and, more to the point, that expensive, because Ethernet performance typically bogs down from excessive collisions with far fewer than 1024 computers.

Connecting the Segments

Sometimes, one hub is just not enough. Once an organization uses every port on its existing hub, adding additional nodes requires additional hubs. Even fault tolerance can motivate an organization to add more hubs. If every node on the network connects to the same hub, that hub becomes a *single point of failure*—if it fails, everybody drops off the network. The 10BaseT standard provides two methods for connecting multiple hubs: coaxial cable and crossover cables.

Coaxial cabling, either 10Base2 or 10Base5, can link together multiple 10BaseT hubs. By definition, a 10BaseT hub is a repeater. It brings in signals from one port and repeats them on all other ports (see Figure 6-10). With the addition of an AUI or BNC port, it

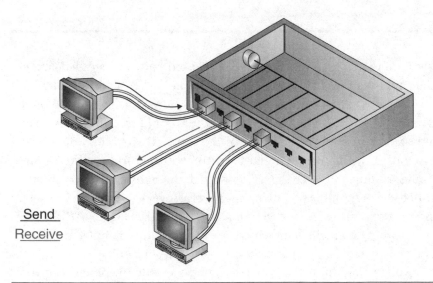

Send
Receive

Figure 6-10 A hub acts as a repeater.

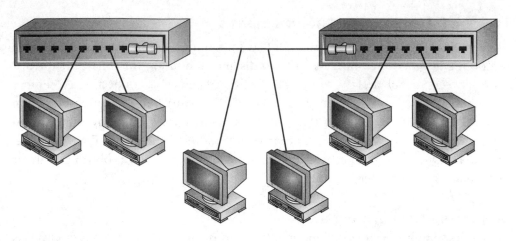

Figure 6-11 The segment connecting two hubs can be populated with machines.

can repeat packets onto a coaxial segment just as easily as it can repeat them on UTP cabling. The coaxial segment can be used to connect two 10BaseT hubs, or it can have nodes directly attached to it, as shown in Figure 6-11.

NOTE: A populated segment has one or more nodes directly attached to it.

Hubs can also connect to each other via special twisted pair cables called *crossover cables*. A standard cable cannot be used to connect two hubs, because both hubs will attempt to send data on the first pair of wires (1 and 2) and will listen for data on the second pair (3 and 6). A crossover cable reverses the sending and receiving pairs on one end of the cable (see Figure 6-12). One end of the cable is wired according to the EIA/TIA 568A standard, while the other end is wired according to the EIA/TIA 568B standard. With the sending and receiving pairs reversed, the hubs can hear each other. To spare network techs the trouble of making special crossover cables, most hubs have a specific crossover port that crosses the wires inside the hub (see Figure 6-13). Unfortunately, when describing and labeling their crossover ports, hub manufacturers use a wide variety of terms, including *crossover, uplink, in port,* and *out port*.

In addition to connecting through a hub, you can use a cable to connect two computers together using 10BaseT NICs with no hub between them at all. This is handy for

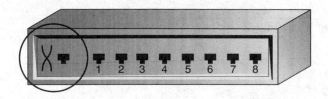

Figure 6-12 A crossover cable reverses the sending and receiving pair.

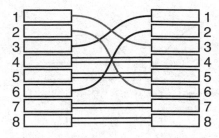

Figure 6-13 Special crossover ports cross the pairs internally.

the quickie connection needed for a nice little home network or when you absolutely, positively *must* chase down a friend in a computer game!

Be careful when using crossover ports. Connecting two crossover ports with a regular piece of twisted pair cabling is among the most common Ethernet misconfigurations. The first crossover port crosses the pairs, while the second uncrosses them, resulting in a standard, straight-through cable connection that will not work.

Multiple segments in a network provide greater fault tolerance than a single segment. Each segment functions or fails on its own. Figure 6-14 shows three segments: A, B, and C. Segments A and B are 10BaseT hubs; segment C is a 10Base2 segment. A failure of one segment does not cause other segments to fail. The failure affects only transmissions that rely on the failed segment. For example, if Cindy's pet rat Gidget escapes and chews through segment C, computers on segment A cannot communicate with computers on segment B, but computers on segment A can continue to communicate with each other, and computers on segment B can also continue to communicate with each other (see Figure 6-15). Of course, the poor computers on segment C must sit idle and twiddle their thumbs until some kind network tech repairs the damage wrought by the evil Gidget.

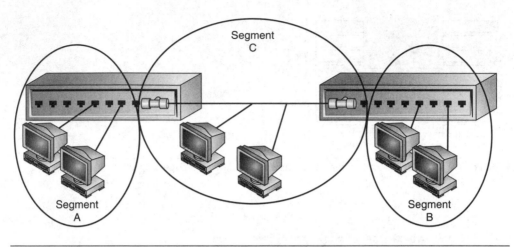

Figure 6-14 Two hubs connected by a 10Base2 segment

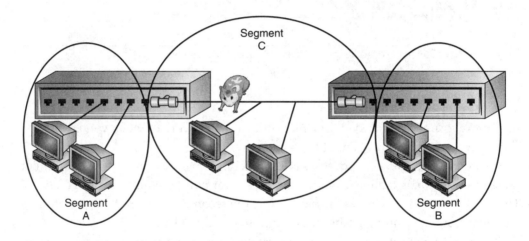

Figure 6-15 Segment C's failure prevents communication between segments A and B, but does not affect communication within segments A and B.

10BaseT Summary

- Speed: 10 Mbps

- Signal type: Baseband

- Distance: 100 meters between the hub and the node

- No more than 1024 nodes per collision domain

- Star bus topology: physical star, logical bus
- Uses CAT3 or better UTP cabling with RJ-45 connectors (see Figure 6-7)

10BaseFL

Just a few years after the introduction of 10BaseT, a fiber optic version appeared, called *10BaseFL*. Fiber optic cabling transmits data packets using pulses of light instead of electrical current. Using light instead of electricity addresses the three key weaknesses of copper cabling. First, optical signals can travel much farther. The maximum length for a 10BaseFL cable is up to two kilometers, depending how it is configured. Second, fiber optic cable is immune to electrical interference, making it an ideal choice for high interference environments. Third, the cable is much more difficult to tap into, making it a good choice for environments with security concerns. 10BaseFL uses a special type of fiber optic cable called *multimode*, and employs one of two types of fiber optic connectors called *SC* or *ST* connectors. Figure 6-16 shows examples of both of these types of connectors.

The presence of two connector standards has led to a bit of confusion in 10BaseFL, as well as later versions of networking that use fiber optic cabling. As a result, most manufacturers of fiber products are moving toward the SC connector over the

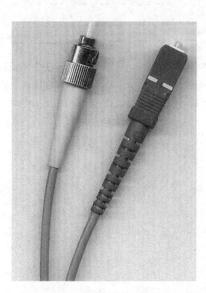

Figure 6-16   ST (left) and SC (right) connectors for fiber optic cable

Figure 6-17   Typical 10BaseFL card

ST connector, although both types are still in common use. Figure 6-17 shows a typical 10BaseFL card. Note that it uses two fiber connectors—one to send, and one to receive. While 10BaseFL enjoyed some popularity for a number of years, most networks today are using the same fiber optic cabling to run far faster network technologies.

10BaseFL Summary

- Speed: 10 Mbps
- Signal type: Baseband
- Distance: 2000 meters between the hub and the node
- No more than 1024 nodes per hub
- Star bus topology: physical star, logical bus
- Uses multimode fiber optic cabling with ST or SC connectors

How Big Can an Ethernet Network Be? The 5-4-3 Rule

When multiple Ethernet segments connect to each other with hubs and repeaters, they remain part of the same collision domain (see Figure 6-18). As discussed in Chapter 5, a collision domain is a set of Ethernet segments that receive all traffic generated by any node within those segments. A set of restrictions known as the 5-4-3 rule limits the size of an Ethernet collision domain.

The 5-4-3 Rule Is Only an Approximation

For Ethernet networks to function properly, each node must detect when its own transmissions collide with those of another node. When a node detects a collision, it waits a random period of time and then re-sends the packet. (See Chapter 5 for a more detailed discussion of CSMA/CD.) If the sending node fails to detect a collision, it won't know to re-send the packet and the packet will be lost. Ethernet nodes cease checking for collisions once they send the last byte of each data packet. If the network is large enough that the last byte leaves the sending node before the first byte reaches every other node on the network, an undetected collision can occur. In the event of a collision between

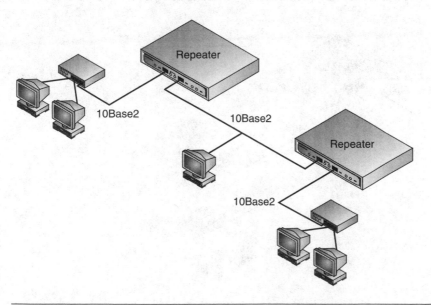

Figure 6-18   An Ethernet collision domain

two machines on the extreme edges of the network, neither node retransmits its data packet, causing the data packets to be lost.

To arrive at a precise answer to the question, "How big is too big?" requires a series of arcane calculations that determine variables with thrilling names like *round trip signal propagation delay* and *inter-packet gap*. Fortunately, the average network tech does not need to do these difficult calculations. The networking industry has developed a rule of thumb that enables technicians to build networks within safe size limits without requiring the poor techs to earn advanced math degrees. It's called the *5-4-3 rule*.

The 5-4-3 Rule

The 5-4-3 rule approximates the more precise and complex calculations that determine the maximize size of an Ethernet collision domain. The rule says that in a collision domain, no two nodes may be separated by more than

- 5 segments
- 4 repeaters
- 3 populated segments

To calculate a network's compliance with the 5-4-3 rule, trace the *worst case* path between two machines—in other words, the path between two machines that will yield the highest number of segments, repeaters, and populated segments. Figure 6-19 shows

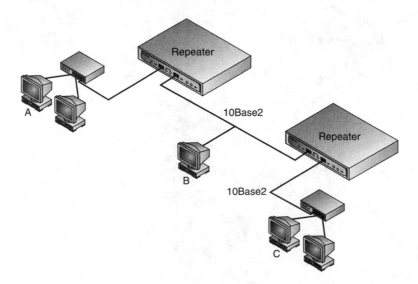

Figure 6-19 A network with 5 segments, 4 repeaters, and 3 populated segments

a network with 5 segments, 4 repeaters, and 3 populated segments. The path between machines A and C represents the worst-case path because the packets must pass through all of the segments and repeaters on the network. The paths between A and B, or B and C, are irrelevant for calculating compliance with the 5-4-3 rule because a longer path exists between two other machines. The path between machine A and machine C uses all five segments, all four repeaters, and all three populated segments.

NOTE: When calculating the 5-4-3 rule, a hub counts as both a repeater and a segment.

The 5-4-3 rule's limitations do not apply to the entire network, but rather to the paths within the network. Figure 6-20 shows a network that complies with the 5-4-3 rule but has 6 segments, 6 repeaters, and 5 populated segments within the entire

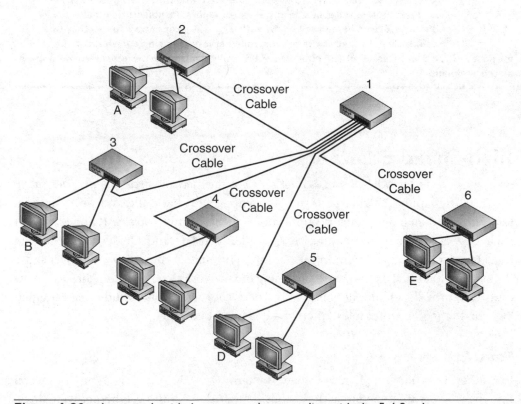

Figure 6-20 A network with 6 segments that complies with the 5-4-3 rule

network. Hub 1 counts as both a segment and a repeater, but not as a populated segment because no computers attach directly to it. Segments that link other segments together but have no computers directly attached to them are called *link segments*. This network follows the 5-4-3 rule because no path between two machines ever traverses more than 5 segments, 4 repeaters, or 3 populated segments. For example, the path between computers A and C runs through 3 segments (hubs 2, 1, and 4), 3 repeaters (hubs 2, 1, and 4) and 2 populated segments (hubs 2 and 4).

The 5-4-3 rule imposes limits on the size of an individual Ethernet collision domain, but the limits are generous. The network shown in Figure 6-20 can contain thousands of individual machines. Remember that each hub can support up to 1024 PCs; because of the demands of modern operating systems and applications, however, 10 Mbps Ethernet networks with far fewer than 1024 machines can become too busy and congested to function well. Two tools exist to relieve this congestion and achieve larger networks: traffic management and high-speed Ethernet.

 NOTE: Rather than make 1024-port hubs that would have a limited market and be expensive to replace in the event of failure, manufacturers make stackable hubs. Stackable hubs are hubs with a special proprietary connection that enables them to function in groups, called stacks, as a single device. For the purposes of the 5-4-3 rule, all of the hubs in a stack are a single segment, repeater, and populated segment.

High-Speed Ethernet

As any fighter pilot will tell you, sometimes you just *feel the need, the need for speed*. While plain vanilla Ethernet performs well enough for basic file and print sharing, today's more demanding network applications, such as Lotus Notes, SAP, and Microsoft Exchange, as well as other key office apps like Half-Life and Quake III Arena, can quickly saturate a network running at 10 Mbps. Fortunately, those crazy kids over at the IEEE keep expanding the standard, providing the network tech in the trenches with new tools that provide additional bandwidth. These cool new tools include Fast Ethernet, Switched Ethernet, Full-duplex Ethernet, and Gigabit Ethernet.

Fast Ethernet

Fast Ethernet is not a single technology. The term *Fast Ethernet* refers to any of several Ethernet flavors that operate at 100 Mbps. Rather than limiting Ethernet to a single high-speed solution, the IEEE endorsed multiple standards for Fast Ethernet and allowed the marketplace to choose from among them. The major variations include 100BaseT and 100BaseFX.

100BaseT

The IEEE supports two variations of 100BaseT: 100BaseTX and 100BaseT4. Both flavors physically resemble 10BaseT, using a star bus topology and connecting to hubs with UTP cabling. The *100* in their names reflects the fact that the cable connecting a device to a hub can send data up to 100 Mbps. The difference between 100BaseTX and 100BaseT4 lies in the quality of the cable used. 100BaseTX requires CAT 5 cabling to achieve a speed of 100 Mbps using only two pairs of wires. Like 10BaseT, 100BaseTX ignores the remaining two pairs. 100BaseT4 uses all four pairs to achieve 100 Mbps performance using lower quality CAT 3 cabling. Think of the cable as a highway: 100BaseTX increases capacity by raising the speed limit, while 100BaseT4 increases capacity by adding additional lanes.

 NOTE: 100BaseVG, also known as 100BaseVGAnyLAN, is not a flavor of Ethernet. Designed to run over Category 3 (Voice Grade) cabling, it does not use CSMA/CD to determine access to the cable. The IEEE 802.12 committee controls the standards for 100BaseVG. As the popularity of 100BaseTX has grown, the importance of competitors like 100BaseVG has diminished dramatically.

Both 100BaseTX and 100BaseT4 allow organizations to take advantage of their existing UTP cabling. If the existing UTP wiring was properly installed, you can upgrade the network from 10BaseT simply by replacing hubs and network cards, with no re-cabling.

UTP cabling cannot meet the needs of every organization, however, for three key reasons. First, the 100-meter distance limitation of UTP-based networks is inadequate for networks covering large buildings or campuses. Second, UTP's lack of electrical shielding makes it a poor choice for networks functioning in locations with high levels of electrical interference. Finally, the Maxwell Smarts and James Bonds of the world find UTP cabling (and copper cabling in general) easy to tap, making it an inappropriate choice for high-security environments. To address these issues, the IEEE 802.3 standard provides for a flavor of 100-megabit Ethernet using fiber optic cable, called 100BaseFX.

100BaseFX

The 100BaseFX standard saw quite a bit of interest for years, as it combined the high speed of 100Base Ethernet with the reliability of fiber optic. Outwardly, 100BaseFX looks exactly like 10BaseFL—both use the same multimode mode fiber optic cabling, and both use SC or ST connectors. 100BaseFX is an improvement over 10BaseFL, however, supporting a maximum cable length of 400 meters.

Migrating to Fast Ethernet

Upgrading an entire network to 100BaseTX can be a daunting task. 100BaseTX requires new hubs, new NICs, and often upgrades to the existing wiring. For organizations with more than a few machines, upgrading every node can take months or even years. Fortunately, the conversion can be done slowly. In fact, organizations that wish to do so can purchase 10/100BaseT devices. A 10/100BaseT device automatically functions as a 100BaseTX device when plugged in to another 10/100BaseT or 100BaseTX device, but will function as a 10BaseT device when plugged in to another 10BaseT device. The existence of these hybrid devices enables organizations to roll out 100BaseT in batches, providing high-speed access to the machines that need it.

Switched Ethernet

Don't feel like upgrading all your NICs and hubs to get more speed? How would you like to dramatically improve performance just by replacing your hub? Switched Ethernet may be the solution for you! An *Ethernet switch* is a special hub that can place some devices into their own collision domains. In essence, an Ethernet switch is a hub with a bridge built in. Switches, like bridges, work at the OSI Data Link layer, or layer two, and are often referred to as *layer two switches*. Physically, an Ethernet switch looks much like any other Ethernet hub, except for the addition of one or more switched ports (see Figure 6-21). Logically, an Ethernet switch puts devices plugged into one of its switched ports into their own collision domain. As one system begins to send data to another system, a switch looks at the incoming MAC addresses and creates a single collision domain (see Figure 6-22).

Using an Ethernet switch provides two benefits. First, if both the sender and the receiver are on their own switched ports, the full bandwidth of that connection (10 or 100 megabits) is available to them—no other machine can cause a collision. Second, the switch can act as a buffer, enabling 10- and 100-megabit devices to communicate.

Ethernet switches can also connect segments to a backbone. A *backbone* is a segment, usually a high speed one, that connects other segments. Figure 6-23 shows a network that supplies 10BaseT to networked desktops, and connects the hubs to a 100BaseT backbone segment. In some cases, heavily accessed machines such as file servers plug directly into the backbone, as shown in Figure 6-24.

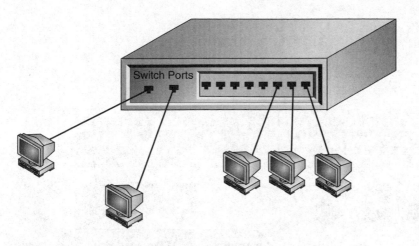

Figure 6-21   An eight-port switch with two switched ports

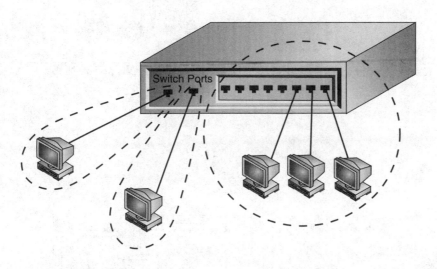

Figure 6-22   Devices plugged into switched ports are isolated on their own collision domains.

Full-Duplex Ethernet

Ethernet switching opens up another avenue for improving the performance of the network: Full-duplex Ethernet. *Full-duplex* means that a device can send and receive data simultaneously. Normally, Ethernet transmissions are half-duplex—in other words, at

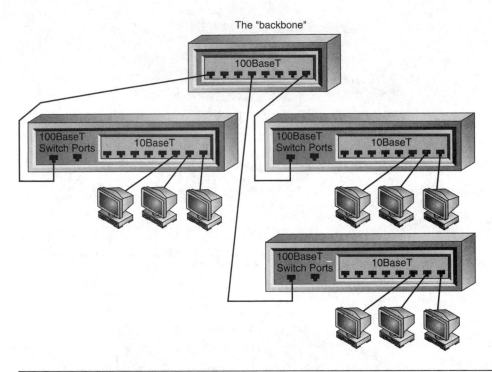

Figure 6-23   Desktop machines run at 10 Mbps, but the backbone runs at 100 Mbps.

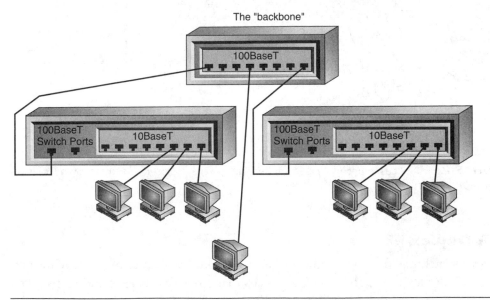

Figure 6-24   Heavily accessed machines can be plugged directly into the backbone.

any given moment, a machine can either send or receive data, but not both. If a machine sends and receives simultaneously, a collision occurs. In the event of a collision, the CSMA/CD rules kick in, causing the machine to stop sending and wait a random period of time before trying again. CSMA/CD allows many machines to share the same segment, but requires all communication to be half-duplex.

A Switched Ethernet connection running over UTP, however, not only creates a two-machine-only segment, it uses separate pairs of wires for sending and receiving. Each pair of wires acts as a separate channel, enabling the devices at each end to communicate with one another in full-duplex mode. If the Ethernet NICs on each end of a switched connection support full-duplex mode, turn it on and enjoy the benefits! Note that not all Ethernet NICs support full-duplex operation; however, those that do will have a full-duplex option you can turn on using their setup programs (see Figure 6-25).

Full-duplex Ethernet offers impressive performance gains. A 10BaseT full-duplex connection has a theoretical bandwidth of 20 Mbps (2 × 10 Mbps), while a 100BaseT

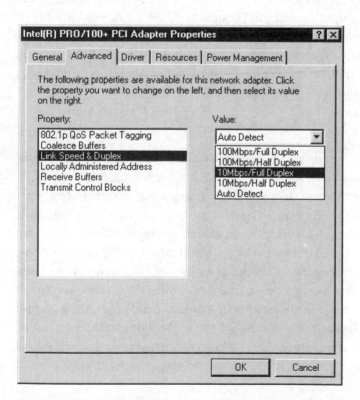

Figure 6-25   If a card supports full-duplex, its setup program will have an option to switch between half- and full-duplex.

full-duplex connection has a theoretical bandwidth of 200 Mbps (2 × 100 Mbps). Because there should never be collisions on a full-duplex connection, the real-world speeds of full-duplex Ethernet actually approach these theoretical maximums. Unfortunately, many older 10BaseT devices do not support full-duplex operation; however, most 100Base and 1000Base Ethernet standards require full-duplex operation, making it an assumed function on those devices.

 EXAM TIP: For the exam, know that in half-duplex communication a device cannot send when it is receiving and vice versa. In full-duplex communication, however, a device can send and receive at the same time.

Here's a thought: if a switched network creates separate collision domains for all the nodes, does the 5-4-3 rule still apply? Good question, if I say so myself, and I do. If you answered *No*, you win a new car! (*Juuuust* kidding!) Once you start using switches, the entire concept of 5-4-3 goes out the window, because there are no limitations due to collisions, except for within individual collision domains.

The wonderful benefits of switches make them extremely common today. By replacing a hub with a switch, your network can take advantage of collision-free, full-duplex communication to achieve much higher speeds.

Gigabit Ethernet

For the true speed junkie, an even more powerful version of Ethernet exists: Gigabit Ethernet. The IEEE approved the official standard for Gigabit Ethernet, a.k.a. 1000BaseX, in 1998. Since then, Gigabit Ethernet has been divided into a series of standards that enjoy growing acceptance in the real world. Gigabit Ethernet is an important backbone technology, but only a few very high-end systems generate enough traffic on their own to justify implementing it between individual PCs. Gigabit Ethernet does not use hubs; instead it relies completely on switches. Because, as we just learned, in a switched network there are never more than two systems in the same collision domain, no gigabit standard has a maximum number of segments rule. A typical network utilizing Gigabit Ethernet would have three layers of speed: 10BaseT to the desktop, 100BaseT between the first level of routers, and some form of Gigabit Ethernet between the second level of routers (see Figure 6-26). Let's look at the most common Gigabit Ethernet standards.

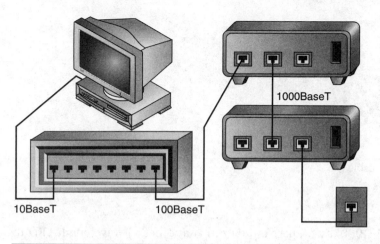

Figure 6-26   Network using Gigabit Ethernet

1000BaseT

1000BaseT is really 1000BaseX. 1000BaseT uses four-pair CAT 5 cabling in full-duplex mode to achieve gigabit performance. Like 10BaseT, 1000BaseT has a maximum cable length of 100 meters. 1000BaseT connections and ports look exactly like the ones on a 10BaseT network. 1000BaseT comes under the IEEE 802.3ab standard. In many cases, when you see a card or switch labeled simply as Gigabit Ethernet, they really mean 1000BaseT, which is easily the most common type of gigabit Ethernet available today.

1000BaseCX

1000BaseCX uses a unique shielded cable known as twinaxial cable (see Figure 6-27). Twinaxial cables are special shielded 150-Ohm cables with a length limit of only 25 meters. As of this writing, 1000BaseCX has yet to make much of an impact in the Gigabit Ethernet market. 1000BaseCX is under the IEEE 802.3z standard.

1000BaseSX

Many networks upgrading to Gigabit Ethernet use the 1000BaseSX standard. 1000BaseSX uses multimode fiber optic cabling to connect between systems, with a generous maximum cable length of over 500 meters (the exact length is really up to the

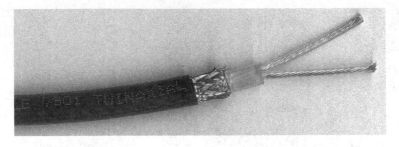

Figure 6-27   Twinaxial cable

various manufacturers). 1000BaseSX uses an 850nm (nanometer) wavelength LED to transmit the light on the fiber optic cable. Like 1000BaseCX, 1000BaseSX comes under the 802.3z standard. 1000BaseSX devices look exactly like the 100BaseFX products seen earlier in this chapter, and rely exclusively on the SC type of connector.

1000BaseLX

1000BaseLX is the long distance carrier for Gigabit Ethernet, and uses single-mode (laser) cables to shoot data at distances of up to five kilometers! Some manufacturers use special repeaters to increase that to distances as great as 70 kilometers! The Ethernet folks are trying to position this as the Ethernet backbone of the future, and already some large carriers are beginning to adopt 1000BaseLX. You may live your whole life and never see a 1000BaseLX device, but odds are good that you will encounter connections that use such devices in the near future. 1000BaseLX looks like 1000BaseSX and is also part of the 802.3z standard.

Conclusion

While 10Base2 and 10Base5 continue to fill valuable niches, the use of the star bus hybrid topology for UTP- and fiber optic-based Ethernet networks enables techs to build more robust and flexible networks. The ability to use high-speed segments, full-duplex operation, bridging, routing, and switching gives the network architect a full tool kit with which to build fast, stable networks.

Chapter Review

Questions

1. Star bus networks use a _____ star and a _____ bus.
   a. physical, logical
   b. logical, physical
   c. hub, Ethernet
   d. Ethernet, hub

2. The T in 10BaseT refers to:
   a. Topology
   b. Ten Mbps
   c. Twisted pair cable
   d. Transport technology

3. Fault tolerance is the key advantage of what topology?
   a. Bus
   b. Ring
   c. Star Bus
   d. Bus Ring

4. The maximum distance that can separate a 10BaseT node from its hub is:
   a. 50 meters
   b. 100 meters
   c. 185 meters
   d. 200 meters

5. When used for Ethernet, unshielded twisted pair uses what type of connector?
   a. RG-58
   b. RJ-45
   c. RJ-11
   d. RS-232

6. What is the maximum number of nodes that can be connected to a 10BaseT hub?
   a. 1024
   b. 500
   c. 100
   d. 185

7. Which of the following is *not* true of crossover cables?
   a. They are a type of twisted pair cabling.
   b. They reverse the sending and receiving wire pairs.
   c. They are used to connect hubs.
   d. The ends of a crossover cable are wired according to the EIA/TIA 568B standard.

8. Which two of the following connectors are used by 10BaseFL cable?
   a. SC
   b. RJ-45
   c. RJ-11
   d. ST

9. Which of the following cable types does *not* use CAT 3 cabling?
   a. 100BaseTX
   b. 10BaseT
   c. 100BaseT4
   d. 100BaseVG

10. Within an Ethernet collision domain, the 5-4-3 rule limits 10-megabit Ethernet networks to _____ between any two machines.
    a. 5 populated segments, 4 repeaters, and 3 hubs
    b. 5 segments, 4 repeaters, and 3 populated segments
    c. 5 tokens, 4 packets, and 3 broadcasts
    d. 5 segments, 4 repeaters, and 3 hubs

Answers

1. **A.** Star bus networks use a physical star that provides improved stability and a logical bus that maintains compatibility with existing Ethernet standards.

2. **C.** The T in 10BaseT refers to its use of twisted pair cabling. This differs from 10Base2 and 10Base5, where the 2 and 5 refer to the maximum segment lengths. The 10 in 10BaseT is what refers to its 10-Mbps speed.

3. **C.** Fault tolerance is the key advantage of the star bus topology. Fault tolerance refers to a system's ability to continue operating when part of it is not working. In this case, a break in a network cable affects only the machine connected to that cable; the others can continue to communicate.

4. **B.** The maximum distance between a 10BaseT node and its hub is 100 meters.

5. **B.** UTP cable uses an RJ-45 connector when used for Ethernet. RG-58 is the type of coaxial cable used with 10Base2. RJ-11 is the standard four-wire connector for regular phone lines. RS-232 is a standard for serial connectors.

6. **A.** 10BaseT hub can connect no more than 1024 nodes (computers).

7. **D.** One end of a crossover cable is wired according to the EIA/TIA 568B standard; the other is wired according to the EIA/TIA 586A standard. This is what *crosses* the wire pairs and enables two hubs to communicate without colliding.

8. **A, D.** 10BaseFL uses one of two types of fiber optic connectors called *SC* and *ST* connectors.

9. **A.** 100BaseTX requires CAT 5 cabling. 10BaseT, 100BaseT4, and 100BaseVG can all use CAT 3 cabling.

10. **B.** Within a collision domain, the 5-4-3 limits 10-megabit Ethernet networks to 5 segments, 4 repeaters, and 3 populated segments between any two machines.

## CHAPTER 7

Non-Ethernet Networks

In this chapter, you will

- Understand the concept of Token Ring
- Learn how Token Ring works
- Understand Token Ring cabling
- Understand the difference between Token Ring and Ethernet
- Learn about ARCNET
- Understand FDDI and ATM technologies
- Learn about wireless networking

No one denies Ethernet's virtual monopoly as the network technology of choice in today's world. Depending on your choice of source, something like 80 to 90 percent of all the network cables in the world run some derivation of Ethernet. But just as Yoda said in *The Empire Strikes Back*, "There is another." Actually we should say, "There are many others," and Network+ expects you to know them as well as you know Ethernet. Some of these network technologies, in particular IBM's famous Token Ring, still enjoy strong followings, especially in organizations that have invested heavily in installing these technologies. But despite their substantial installed bases, the chances of the average networking tech seeing any of these technologies during the course of his career is pretty slim. So, look at this chapter as fulfilling two goals: introducing you to the final days of rapidly fading technologies, and getting you past the Network+ questions that address them. Read this chapter carefully—after the test you may never hear of these technologies again!

Historical/Conceptual

Token Ring

Token Ring, also known as IEEE 802.5, competed directly, and in the long run unsuccessfully, with Ethernet as an option for connecting desktop computers to a LAN. Although Token Ring possesses a much smaller share of the market than Ethernet, Token Ring's installed base has remained extremely loyal. Token Ring offers greater speed (16 Mbps) and efficiency than 10BaseT Ethernet, and the Token Ring folks have even established 100 and 1000 Mbps Token Ring standards. The Network+ test, however, has no interest in any Token Ring standards above 16 Mbps.

Token Ring networks can look much like 10BaseT Ethernet networks, even using identical UTP cabling in some cases. But although they share the same physical star topology, Token Ring uses a logical *ring* topology rather than a logical bus topology.

 NOTE: Although it began as a proprietary IBM technology, today the IEEE 802.5 committee defines the standards for Token Ring. Just as there are minor differences between the original Xerox Ethernet standard and IEEE 802.3, there are minor differences between the original IBM standard for Token Ring and the IEEE 802.5 standard. These differences have little impact on the average network tech, and for all intents and purposes Token Ring and IEEE 802.5 should be considered synonyms.

Test Specific

Logical Ring Topology

Token Ring networks use a logical ring topology (see Figure 7-1). Unlike Ethernet nodes, which broadcast their packets across a shared cable, Token Ring nodes only communicate directly with two other machines: their upstream and downstream neighbors (see Figure 7-2). Token Ring employs a token passing system to control access to the ring; its nodes only transmit data when they receive a special packet called the *token*. Token passing operates more efficiently than Ethernet's CSMA/CD system, preventing collisions entirely so that Token Ring nodes can make full use of the network's bandwidth.

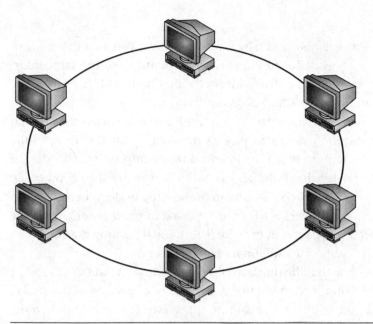

Figure 7-1   Token Ring networks use a logical ring topology.

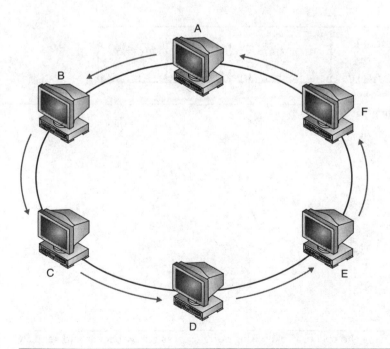

Figure 7-2   Node A's downstream neighbor is Node B and its upstream neighbor is Node F.

Token Passing

Token passing preserves network bandwidth by never allowing more than one node to transmit data at a given time. Most Token Ring packets contain much the same information as Ethernet packets: the source MAC address, the destination MAC address, the data to be transmitted, and a *Frame Check Sequence* (FCS) used to check the data for errors (see Figure 7-3). When receiving a packet, a Token Ring node checks the destination MAC address to determine whether to process the data it contains or send the packet to its downstream neighbor. When the intended recipient processes the data, it adds a special code to the packet that indicates the packet was received in good order. The receiving node then sends the packet around to the sending node. When the sending node receives its original data packet with the "received in good order" mark, the sending machine removes the packet from the wire. The original sending machine then generates a new packet with a special additional field, the token.

The *token* tells the next node that the ring is available. A node with data to send waits until it receives the token. After receiving a free token, the node creates a data packet and sends the new packet on to its downstream neighbor (see Figure 7-4). When the

Recipient's MAC address	Sender's MAC address	Data	CRC	Token
11011000111010011	0001010111101101010	101010101011110111	01111011110001	11110111110

Figure 7-3 A Token Ring packet

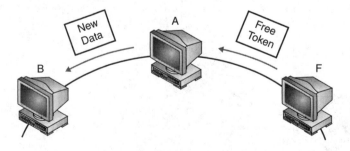

Figure 7-4 After receiving the token, a Token Ring node creates a new packet and sends it to its downstream neighbor

sending node receives confirmation that the intended recipient received the packet, it generates a new token, giving the next machine in line access to the ring.

A token passing network sends data packets more efficiently than one using CSMA/CD because no collisions occur. A station may have to wait for the token before it can send, but if it has the token, it knows no other station will try to send at the same time. In contrast, a CSMA/CD-based network, such as Ethernet, can waste significant bandwidth resolving collisions. Token passing is a deterministic method to resolve which machine should have access to the wire at a given moment. *Deterministic* means that access to the wire is granted in a predictable way, rather than through a random process like CSMA/CD. No virtual dice rolling here!

Token Ring Speed

Token Ring networks can run at either 4 or 16 Mbps, speeds that sound slow compared to the 10- and 100-Mbps Ethernet standards (again, newer versions of Token Ring improve on these speeds but the Network+ exam has little interest, so for the moment at least, neither do we). The raw numbers, however, do not tell the full story. Token Ring networks use every bit of their bandwidth to send data. Ethernet networks, in contrast, waste significant amounts of bandwidth resolving collisions. Because of the wasted bandwidth inherent in Ethernet networks, many well-informed techs argue that 4-Mbps Token Ring performs almost as fast as 10-Mbps Ethernet, and that 16-Mbps Token Ring performs significantly faster. The speed at which the ring operates, however, depends on the slowest device on the ring. A Token Ring network consisting of five 4/16-Mbps Token Ring nodes and one 4-Mbps Token Ring node will run at 4 Mbps (see Figure 7-5).

Token Ring networks can be configured to give some systems higher priority access to the token. Conceivably, a network architect could set a high priority for a particular PC, ensuring that it would get access to the token more often than others. Real-life Token Ring networks rarely take advantage of the ability to prioritize traffic, making the feature less useful than it might seem.

Physical Star

Physical ring topology shares the same vulnerability to cable breaks as physical bus topology. When the cable used by a physical bus topology such as 10Base2 breaks, the entire network shuts down due to electrical reflections. A physical ring topology would also fail completely from a cable break, but for a different reason. In a ring topology, all

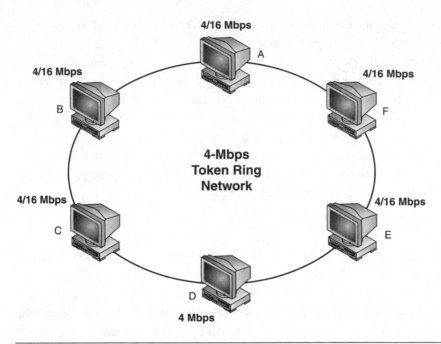

Figure 7-5   The slowest device on the ring determines the speed of the ring.

traffic travels in one direction. If the ring breaks, traffic can never complete the round trip around the network, so no node will generate a free token (see Figure 7-6). To avoid the problems inherent in a physical ring topology, Token Ring uses a physical star topology.

Token Ring hides the logical ring inside a hub, technically referred to as a *Multistation Access Unit (MAU)* (see Figure 7-7). You will also see the abbreviation *MSAU*—use them interchangeably. Individual nodes connect to the hub via either *Unshielded Twisted Pair* (UTP) or *Shielded Twisted Pair* (STP) cabling (Figure 7-8).

 NOTE: Terminology Alert! To make our lives difficult, Token Ring documentation can refer to Multistation Access Units by two different acronyms: MAU and MSAU. The terms Token Ring hub, MAU, and MSAU are synonymous.

Token Ring over STP

Originally, Token Ring networks used a heavily shielded version of twisted-pair cabling referred to as Shielded Twisted Pair (STP). STP consists of two pairs of copper wires sur-

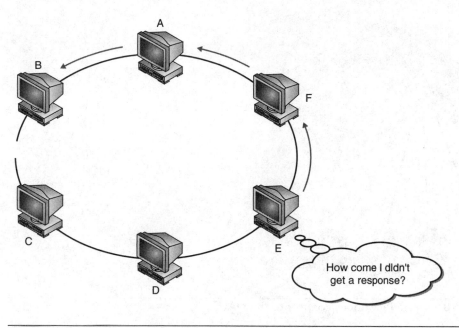

Figure 7-6   A physical ring topology cannot function if the ring breaks.

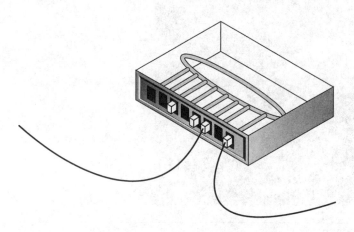

Figure 7-7   The MAU contains the logical ring.

rounded by a metal shield (see Chapter 4, Figure 13). Token Ring uses a special Type 1 connector for STP (see Figure 7-9). STP's metal shield serves the same function as the shield used in coaxial cables: preventing electrical interference from affecting the wires used to send signals. When using STP, a single Token Ring MAU can support up to

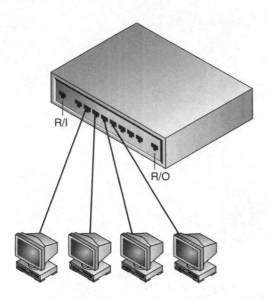

Figure 7-8   Token Ring nodes connect to the MAU.

Figure 7-9   An IBM Type I connector

260 computers. The STP cable connecting the computer to the hub may not be longer than 100 meters. While the heavy shielding of STP cabling makes it an ideal choice for environments with high levels of electrical interference, the high cost of that shielding makes it too expensive for most installations.

Token Ring over UTP

Unshielded Twisted Pair (UTP) offers a cost-effective alternative to STP for normal business environments. Because it lacks the heavy shielding of STP and is manufactured for use in a variety of applications, UTP cabling costs relatively little.

Token Ring can run over UTP using the same cable and RJ-45 connectors as Ethernet. Like 10BaseT, Token Ring uses only two of the four pairs in the typical UTP cable: the 3-6 pair and the 4-5 pair, as shown in Figure 7-10. Provided the cable installer uses a proper wiring color code (such as the EIA/TIA 568A standard discussed in Chapter 6), the UTP cable and connectors used for Token Ring are identical to those used for Ethernet. Token Ring MAUs using UTP can support up to 72 nodes, each of which must be within 45 meters of the MAU.

Connecting MAUs

To connect multiple Token Ring hubs to form a larger network requires the extension of the ring. Token Ring MAUs, whether using UTP or STP, have two special ports on the MAU, labeled *Ring In* and *Ring Out*. These special connections link multiple MAUs together to form a single ring. Both UTP and STP Token Ring MAUs use Ring In and Ring Out ports. The Ring In port on the first MAU must connect to the Ring Out port on the second MAU, and vice versa, in order to form a single logical ring. Figure 7-11 shows two MAUs connected using the Ring In and Ring Out ports. *Logically*, the two MAUs look like a single ring to the devices attached to them (see Figure 7-12). Up to 33 MAUs can combine to form a single logical ring. Building a network with more than 33 MAUs requires the use of bridges or routers. Routers can also connect Token Ring LANs to other types of LANs, such as Ethernet.

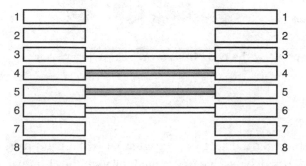

Figure 7-10   Token Ring uses two of the four pairs of available wires.

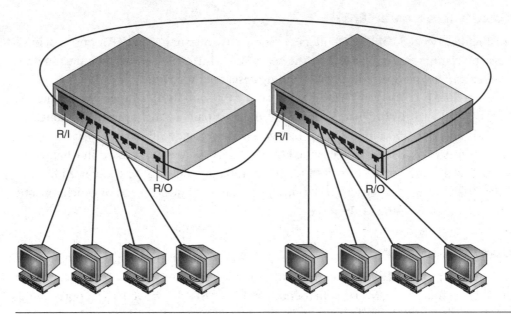

Figure 7-11 Two MAUs connected via Ring In and Ring Out ports

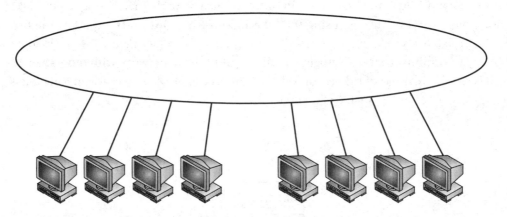

Figure 7-12 When linked together properly, the two MAUs form a single logical ring.

Token Ring vs. Ethernet

The Token Ring vs. Ethernet debate has been a fixture in computer networking journals for many years. As with many technology debates that have raged through the IT industry (PC vs. Macintosh, Microsoft vs. Novell, paper vs. plastic), proponents can invest an amazing amount of emotion into what seems from the outside to be a purely technical debate. Token Ring advocates argue that Token Ring's token passing system utilizes available bandwidth more efficiently than Ethernet's random CSMA/CD process. In addition, the token passing system guarantees that every node will get some amount of bandwidth. In an Ethernet network, the network can get so busy that some machines never get to send their data because of excessive collisions. Advocates also argue that Token Ring is more *scaleable*, meaning that it handles growth better.

Ethernet advocates argue that it does not matter if Token Ring has technical advantages, because it costs too much to implement. Ethernet technology has always been cheaper than Token Ring for two reasons. First, Ethernet devices are simpler than Token Ring devices. CSMA/CD is a very simple algorithm to program into a device, whereas Token Ring devices must deal with more complex issues, such as differing priority levels among the nodes on the ring. Second, economies of scale make Ethernet even less expensive. Because the market for Ethernet devices dwarfs the market for Token Ring devices, Ethernet manufacturers can make a smaller profit on each piece sold and still make money.

In addition, Ethernet overcomes the efficiency advantages of Token Ring by throwing bandwidth at the problem. While 16 Mbps Token Ring may be faster than 10BaseT, it runs significantly more slowly than 100BaseT. Plus, although high-speed Token Ring standards exist, Fast Ethernet and Gigabit Ethernet have achieved a far greater penetration of the market. Most industry pundits agree that Token Ring is a dying technology. While it will continue to exist in niche markets and in organizations with a large installed base of Token Ring equipment, Ethernet will retain its dominance in the marketplace for the foreseeable future.

ARCNET

During the late '70s and early '80s, a company called Datapoint Corporation invented a networking technology it named *Attached Resource Computer Network (ARCNET)*. For many years, ARCNET enjoyed some degree of popularity in smaller networks and still has enough of an installed base to make it interesting for the Network+ exam. Let's take a look at the venerable ARCNET.

The original ARCNET standard defines a true star topology—both the physical and logical topologies work as stars. ARCNET uses token passing to get frames from one system to another. Originally, ARCNET used RG62 coaxial cable. Later versions, however, used good old UTP cable, although it only needed two wire pairs to transmit data. ARCNET runs at a whopping 2.5 Mbps—acceptable in the early '80s, but far too slow to be

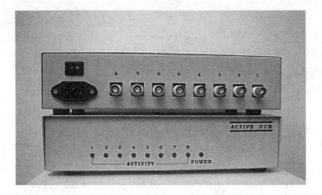

Figure 7-13 An ARCNET hub

of any interest for a modern network application. Faster ARCNET standards, called ARCNET Plus, that ran at speeds up to 20 Mbps were not successful in making ARCNET a serious competitor to either Ethernet or Token Ring.

ARCNET uses hubs to propagate the data between nodes (see Figure 7-13). These hubs provide either 8 or 16 ports, and like 10BaseT hubs, they can daisy-chain to handle more nodes. ARCNET networks can use more basic hubs called *passive hubs*. These do not repeat the signal like regular (*active*) hubs, they just pass the signal along without re-creating the data. Because of this, passive hubs are much less common. Using RG62 and regular hubs, ARCNET supports segment lengths up to 600 meters. Many folks found this substantial segment distance highly attractive—the majority of the remaining ARCNET implementations involve networking scenarios that need to span longer distances.

Like most other network technologies, ARCNET now supports UTP and fiber optic cabling, and has increased its speed and cable length dramatically. As with Token Ring, certain niches continue to support ARCNET, although it too will eventually succumb to the overwhelming popularity of Ethernet.

LocalTalk

When the folks at Apple decided to add networking to their computers, they created a unique networking technology called *LocalTalk* (see Figure 7-14). LocalTalk used a bus topology with each device daisy-chained to the next on the segment, and proprietary

PART II

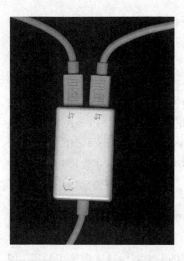

Figure 7-14 LocalTalk connectors

cabling with small round DIN-style connectors. A later version called PhoneTalk, produced by a company called Farallon, used RJ-11 cables and saw widespread popularity. The rise of Ethernet, along with LocalTalk's very slow speed, led to the demise of LocalTalk.

NOTE: Many people confuse the terms AppleTalk and LocalTalk. LocalTalk is a networking technology, whereas AppleTalk is a network protocol.

FDDI and ATM

The increase in demand for bandwidth in the '80s motivated the creation of more powerful network technologies. Two different types of technologies appeared in the early '90s, called FDDI and ATM, that were the de facto high-speed networking standards (at least for a few years) until the emergence of high-speed Ethernet. Like so many other network technologies, FDDI and ATM continue to lose market share to Ethernet, but still have enough of an installed base to make them of interest. Let's look at both of these technologies.

FDDI

Fiber Distributed Data Interface (FDDI) stands as one of the few network technologies that did not spring directly from private industry (although private industry had a lot of impact on its development). Instead, FDDI came directly from American National Standards Institute (ANSI) as a high-speed, highly redundant technology, specifically designed to work as a high-speed backbone to support larger networks. FDDI uses a unique dual token passing ring unlike any other network technology. Originally designed to run on fiber optic cable, later versions of FDDI used—you guessed it— CAT5 UTP. FDDI was the first networking technology to run at 100 Mbps. Using fiber optic cable, FDDI segments can reach up to two kilometers; using CAT 5, the maximum length is 100 meters.

ATM

Asynchronous Transfer Mode (ATM) came into development at roughly the same time as FDDI. ATM runs at 155 Mbps using fiber optic cabling or CAT5 UTP. Just make sure you don't respond, "Ain't that a bank machine?" when asked about ATM and you'll be happy on the test!

Wireless

For years, the networking world dreamed of getting rid of cables altogether. But the technology for reliable, inexpensive wireless networking proved elusive for many years. Many attempts were made using radio and infrared signals, but it wasn't until the adoption of the IEEE 802.11 standard that practical wireless networking finally became a reality.

The 802.11 standard covers a number of sub standards, one of which, the 802.11b sub standard, blossomed into a network technology that now has real products on the shelves.

The best way to appreciate how 802.11b works is by understanding the two different modes it uses. The *infrastructure* or *client/server* mode requires a device called a Wireless Access Port (WAP) that connects to a wired network. Figure 7-15 shows a typical WAP.

Figure 7-15   Linksys WAP

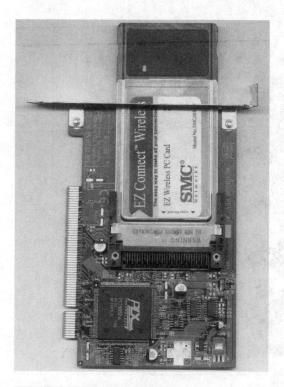

Figure 7-16   A wireless NIC

Figure 7-17   A wireless NIC installed in a PC

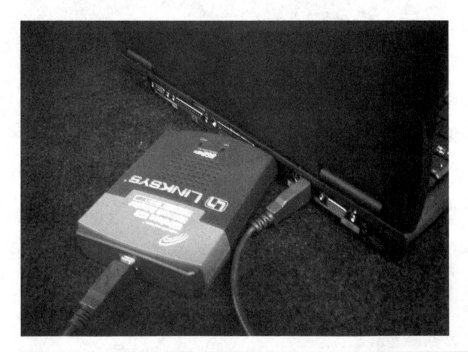

Figure 7-18   An external USB wireless NIC

Each PC on the wireless network gets network access through a wireless NIC that speaks to the WAP. Figure 7-16 shows one of many types of wireless NICs. Figure 7-17 shows a wireless NIC installed in a PC. Figure 7-18 shows an external USB wireless NIC.

In *Ad-hoc* mode, the individual NICs communicate directly with each other instead of working through the WAP. Ad-hoc mode works great for small networks but does not allow the wireless network to connect to larger wired networks.

Setting up a wireless network involves only a few simple steps. Each device on a single wireless network must use the same channel and network name. While the process of setting these values varies from brand to brand, almost all wireless makers provide software or web access to perform this setup task (see Figure 7-19). The primary way to lose a connection is by roaming too far from the other devices on your ad-hoc wireless network.

802.11b enjoys tremendous popularity. Many sources consider it the fastest growing network technology today. Networking without wires is every technogeek's dream!

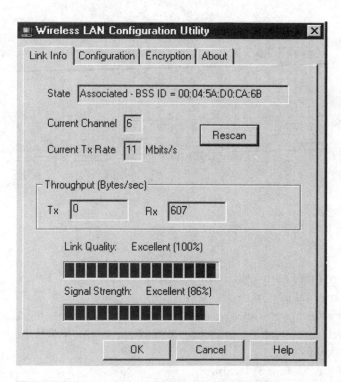

Figure 7-19 Configuring a wireless network

Don't Be an Ethernet Snob!

For all of Ethernet's popularity, failing to recognize that other network technologies exist can turn you into an Ethernet snob. Although Ethernet definitely rules the vast majority of the installed networks today, by keeping an open mind towards other network technologies, you'll be more likely to notice when the next great thing in networking technology presents itself. Don't follow the unfortunate path worn bare by so many other network administrators, who blindly follow only the networking technologies they know. One day Ethernet will no longer enjoy its current predominance, and when that happens, you, the alert network tech, will be prepared to use the technology that most suits you and your network.

Chapter Review

Questions

1. Which of the following standards defines Token Ring networks?
   a. IEEE 802.3
   b. IEEE 802.5
   c. EIA/TIA 568A
   d. IEEE 1284

2. Token Ring networks use a _____ physical topology and a _____ logical topology.
   a. Mesh, ring
   b. Ring, star
   c. Star, ring
   d. Ring, bus

3. Which of the following are true about Token Ring networks?
   a. Collisions occur as a normal part of their operation.
   b. Only a machine with a free token can transmit a new data packet.
   c. In the event of a break in the cable connecting a machine to the MAU, the entire network shuts down.
   d. Token Ring can use either UTP or STP cabling.

4. Token Ring nodes only transmit data when they receive a special packet called a:
    a. Ring
    b. Packet
    c. MAU
    d. Token

5. Philip calls Bob, a tech support technician, for help with a networking problem. Bob asks Philip to tell him what kind of network he uses. Philip responds that he uses UTP. This tells Bob that Philip:
    a. Uses a Token Ring network.
    b. Uses a 10BaseT network.
    c. Uses a 10Base5 network.
    d. Has not provided enough information for Bob to know what kind of network Philip uses.

6. Token Ring MAUs using STP can support up to _____ nodes.
    a. 1024
    b. 260
    c. 100
    d. 72

7. Token Ring MAUs using UTP can support up to _____ nodes.
    a. 1024
    b. 260
    c. 100
    d. 72

8. Token Ring MAUs use special ports called _____ to connect to other MAUs.
    a. Crossovers
    b. Uplinks
    c. Ring In and Ring Out
    d. Repeaters

9. A node connected to its MAU using UTP can be _____ from the MAU.
    a. 100 meters
    b. 100 feet
    c. 45 meters
    d. 45 feet

10. Which of the following standards defines Wireless networks?
    a. IEEE 802.3
    b. IEEE 802.5
    c. IEEE 802.11
    d. IEEE 802.13

Answers

1. **B.** IEEE 802.5 is the IEEE standard for Token Ring. IEEE 802.3 is the standard for Ethernet. EIA/TIA 568A is a cabling standard for UTP cabling. IEEE 1284 is the IEEE standard for parallel communication.

2. **C.** Token Ring networks use a star physical topology and a ring logical topology.

3. **B and D.** Token Ring nodes only transmit new data packets if they have a free token. Token Ring can use either UPT or STP cabling. Although collisions are a normal part of the operation of an Ethernet network, Token Ring's token passing system prevents collisions from occurring. Because Token Ring uses a physical star topology, a break in the cable between the MAU and a device affects only that device, not the rest of the network.

4. **D.** Token ring nodes only transmit data when they receive a special packet called a token.

5. **D.** Both Token Ring and Ethernet networks can use unshielded twisted-pair cabling.

6. **B.** Token Ring MAUs using STP can support up to 260 nodes.

7. **D.** Token Ring MAUs using UTP can support up to 72 nodes.

8. **C.** Token Ring MAUs use special ports called Ring In and Ring Out to connect to other MAUs.

9. **C.** A Token Ring node using UTP can be up to 45 meters from the MAU.

10. **C.** IEEE 802.11 is the IEEE standard for wireless networks. IEEE 802.5 is the IEEE standard for Token Ring. IEEE 802.3 is the standard for Ethernet. IEEE 802.13 is presently not used.

Network Interface Cards

In this chapter, you will

- Learn the different types of NICs
- Understand about Token Ring converters
- Learn the cable types and speeds of most Ethernet cards
- Understand NIC installations
- Learn about assigning resources to the NIC and getting the correct drivers
- Understand the different types of connectors

The network interface card (NIC) provides the PC with a method of sending data to, and receiving data from, other systems, by connecting the PC to the network's cabling structure. A good NIC acts much like a good refrigerator—you set it up once and happily ignore it for the next few years. But like a refrigerator, when a NIC stops working, it causes a tremendous amount of trouble. In this chapter, you'll take an in-depth look at the most common NICs used in a network and appreciate what it takes to install, configure, and troubleshoot them.

Historical/Conceptual

Knowing Your NICs

Every combination of networking technology and cabling has its own type of NIC. For the most part, these cards cannot be interchanged. Every PC in a 10BaseT network, for example, uses a 10BaseT network card. Every PC in a 100BaseTX network uses a 100BaseTX card. A 4-megabit Token Ring network uses nothing but 4-megabit Token Ring NICs. Each combination of topology, cable, and connections for a particular network technology requires a different NIC, and they are in no way compatible.

But what fun would a rule be without the inevitable exceptions? We rarely find out in the PC world! So it is with this technology, where you'll find that some NICs work with more than just one network technology/cable/connection. Figure 8-1 shows a common example. Note the BNC and the RJ-45 connector. This card works with either a 10BaseT or a 10Base2 Ethernet network. Such multiple-connector cards are referred to generically as *combo cards*.

There are a number of different types of combo cards. Figure 8-2 shows a card that can run 10BaseT, 10Base2, and 10Base5.

Combo cards are for the most part limited to Ethernet NICs. This stems from the simple fact that while Ethernet uses a variety of cabling options, all flavors use the same Ethernet frames, so it's relatively easy to make one card that supports many different Ethernet technologies. Non-Ethernet network technologies rarely employ combo cards. Instead, they either use one type of connector exclusively or, as in the case of Token Ring, tend to use converters at the MSAU to enable differently connected cards to work together (see Figure 8-3).

The ability to support more than one type of network technology isn't confined to combo cards. Many NICs operate at more than one speed using the same network tech-

Figure 8-1   A typical Ethernet combo card

Figure 8-2   An Ethernet three-way combo card

Figure 8-3   A Token Ring converter

nology. Any NIC that can run at more than one speed is called—are you sitting down for this?—a *multi-speed* NIC. Breathtakingly imaginative, these networking folks! Names aside, these cards are very popular today, especially NICs that run in 10BaseT and 100BaseT networks. Most multi-speed NICs will automatically detect and adjust themselves to the speed of the network, without requiring any special configuration. These cards are often referred to as *auto-sensing* NICs. Many network administrators prefer to use these cards in 10BaseT networks as a hedge against the possibility that they might one day upgrade their networks to 100BaseT. You can upgrade a network of PCs using auto-sensing 10/100BaseT NICs from a 10BaseT to a 100BaseT simply by changing out the hubs. The card shown in Figure 8-4 is a multi-speed, auto-sensing NIC that works on either a 10BaseT or a 100BaseTX network.

Figure 8-4   A multi-speed NIC

Multi-speed NICs are in no way limited to Ethernet networks! Many Token Ring NICs can switch between 4-megabit and 16-megabit speeds. These Token Ring NICs also employ auto-sensing.

Many networks employ combo and/or multi-speed NICs—the only limitation is that they must all use the same networking technology! No NIC yet invented can operate with more than one network technology. For example, no one has yet made a NIC that can handle both Ethernet *and* Token Ring. If you have a Token Ring network, you must buy Token Ring NICs; if you have an Ethernet network, you must purchase Ethernet NICs.

As you might imagine, there are hundreds of different types of NICs. While most NICs are unique to a particular network technology, cabling type, or speed, some NICs handle more than one type of cable, more than one speed, or both. As a person who wants to pass the Network+ exam and hopefully also work on networks, you must be able to identify these different network cards quickly. In some cases, different network cards look absolutely identical at first glance and you must inspect them closely to make a correct identification. In this chapter, I will match up the different types of NICs to the different network technologies, cables, and speeds. I'll set out some rules and show you some identification tricks, so that you won't, to take a random example, buy 2200 100BaseT4 cards when you should have purchased 2200 100BaseTX cards. (Not that anyone *I* know has actually *done* this . . .)

Test Specific

Ethernet NICs

Ethernet NICs are by far the most common NIC used today. It's tough to get an absolutely dependable statistic, but it's probably safe to say that most of all new installations use Ethernet in one way or another. Ethernet installations are also the most complicated, because of the vast variety of cable types and speeds.

In this chapter, I'll consolidate all of the different connectors and take a detailed look at their different nuances. I'll also throw in a few new types of Ethernet not on the test (yet), but which you may see in the future. Here's a rundown of the different types of Ethernet and their connections.

10Base5 (Thicknet)

10Base5 (Thicknet) NICs use a female, 15-pin DB connector, as shown in Figure 8-5. Officially, this connector is called a *Digital-Intel-Xerox (DIX)* connector. The Ethernet drop cable runs from the DIX connector on the NIC to the *Attachment Unit Interface (AUI)*, which also happens to have a DIX connector. The AUI is also known as a *transceiver*. Many techs erroneously refer to the DIX connector as the AUI, as in, "Hey, plug in the AUI before the coffee gets cold!"

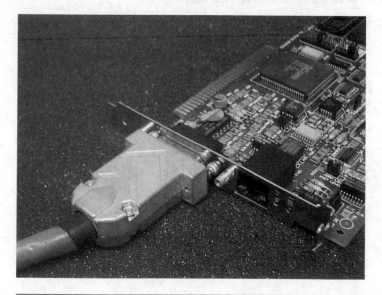

Figure 8-5 A DIX connector

10Base2

10Base2 (Thinnet) NICs have a BNC connector (as shown in Figure 8-6) that attaches to the network cable via a T-connector.

10BaseT

10BaseT NICs all use the RJ-45 connector. The cable runs from the NIC to a hub or a switch (see Figure 8-7).

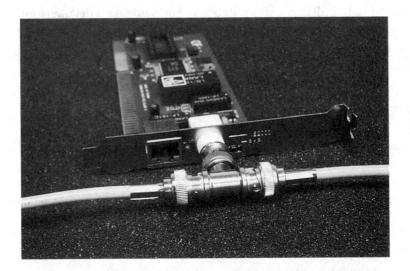

Figure 8-6   A BNC connector

Figure 8-7   An RJ-45 connector

100BaseTX, 100BaseT4, and 100BaseVGAnyLAN

100BaseTX, 100BaseT4, and 100BaseVGAnyLAN are three competing networking technologies designed to run Ethernet at 100 Mbps. All of them use RJ-45 connectors. The difference between these technologies is in the quality and the number of wires used in the network cabling. (See Chapter 7 for more details.) 100BaseVGAnyLAN, by the way, is not an Ethernet technology but can handle the packets.

10BaseFL and 100BaseFX

The 10BaseFL and 100BaseFX standards are the most common (over 99 percent) of the implementations for running Ethernet over fiber optic cable. As their names suggest, 10BaseFL runs at 10 Mbps while 100BaseFX clips along at 100 Mbps. As with most fiber networking standards, you may encounter either SC or ST connections on these NICs, so be alert to variations even among cards from the same manufacturer (see Figure 8-8).

Token Ring NICs

In this Ethernet-centric world, many network folks tend to look at IBM's Token Ring as yesterday's news. This is a mistake. Granted, finding a new Token Ring installation is about as easy as getting 50-yard line seats at the Super Bowl, but Token Ring continues to enjoy a huge installed base. If you need proof that Token Ring is alive and well, simply browse any of the leading NIC manufacturers' web sites. Notice that they all

Figure 8-8   100BaseFX cards

continue to sell Token Ring cards, because the demand still exists, suggesting that Token Ring is doing just fine.

Token Ring NIC connectors come in only two types. The older and still quite common connector is a female DB-9. This cable runs from the back of the PC to an MSAU (Multi-Station Access Unit). Figure 8-9 shows a typical Token Ring DB-9 connector.

The newer, and increasingly more common connector is—can you guess?—an RJ-45. The Token Ring powers that be realized that if they wanted to keep market share, they needed to make Token Ring more compatible with the existing UTP cables in the walls of so many offices today. Thus, Token Ring has incorporated the RJ-45 connector (see Figure 8-10).

Gee, this Token Ring card suddenly looks a lot like a 10BaseT card, doesn't it? The problem of figuring out what type of connector goes with what NIC is complicated by the fact that lots of networking technologies use the same connector—in particular the RJ-45. How can you tell whether the NIC in your hand with an RJ-45 connection is for 10BaseT, 100BaseTX, or Token Ring? The bad news is that you can't always tell; the good news is that there are some clues. If you see an RJ-45/BNC combo card, for example, you can be pretty sure that the RJ-45 is for 10BaseT. In addition, most cards will have some information printed on them that can provide clues. Everybody who makes Token Ring cards gives them a Token Ring-sounding name. So, if you see a word like *TokenLink* printed on a card, you should at least start with the theory that it's a Token

Figure 8-9   A Token Ring DB-9 connector

Figure 8-10   A Token Ring RJ-45 connector

Ring card. Finally, there's the small factoid that the NICs you're examining are probably part of a Token Ring or an Ethernet network—a big clue indeed, wouldn't you say?

Distinguishing between Token Ring and Ethernet is usually fairly easy. But now that you know you have an Ethernet RJ-45 NIC, how do you know if it is 10BaseT, 100BaseTX, or something else altogether? This is tougher. First of all, know your network and the cards you buy. If you don't buy 100BaseTX cards, then it's not going to be 100BaseTX. Second, know your model numbers. Every NIC has a manufacturer's model number you can use to determine its exact capabilities. The model number is nearly always printed on the card. Finally, pray that the NIC is Plug and Play (PnP) and stick it in a Windows 98/ME or Windows 2000/XP system. If you're lucky, the PnP application will recognize the card and give you some text clue as to what type of card it is (see Figure 8-11).

The *model number* is the real key to knowing your NICs. As you will soon see, if you have the model number of a NIC, you also know the right driver for that NIC. You need to deal with this issue before you drop the NIC into a system, however, because once the NIC is installed in a PC, it's difficult to determine the model number from a Windows screen. Many network techs use one of two methods for remembering the types of cards used in their systems. The best way is simply to ensure that the model number of the NIC is printed on the card. If the manufacturer chose not to put the model num-

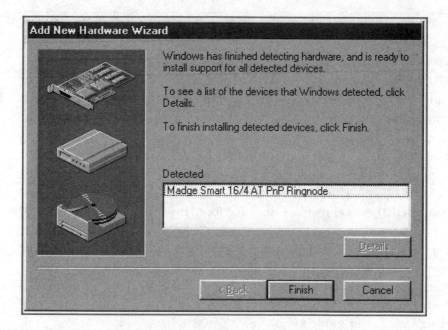

Figure 8-11   Windows 98 Plug and Play

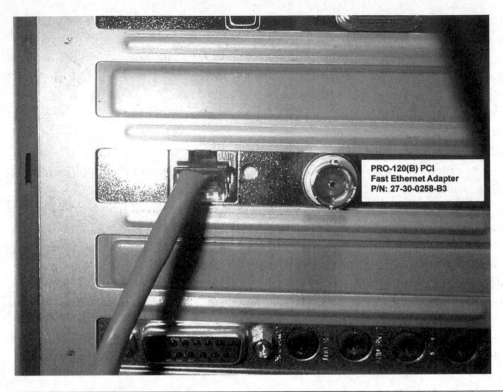

PRO-120(B) PCI
Fast Ethernet Adapter
P/N: 27-30-0258-B3

Figure 8-12   A NIC with model number label added to outside

ber on the NIC, a good network admin takes the time to attach the model number or some other number physically to the NIC, as shown in Figure 8-12.

Granted, some folks will complain, "What good is having the model number on the card once you close the PC?" Well, in the real world, NICs tend not to stay in PCs, and you will be glad you put the model number on the NIC when you have to swap it out later and no longer have any clue what it is. Sometimes PnP doesn't work, and the model number will tell you which driver you need—so slap it on there and save yourself some hassle later! The other method, one used for many years but increasingly difficult to do, is to buy only certain models of NICs. Only buying one model of NIC makes knowing what you have trivially easy. For years, the predominance of 10BaseT gave certain models of NICs a multi-year lifespan, making it easy for NIC purchasers to pursue this method, and making dealing with NICs much easier. The recent influx of new technologies such as 100BaseT and even Gigabit, however, has caused most purchasers to move into newer models, especially 10/100 Ethernet cards—making this strategy less convenient.

Installing NICs

Now that you have a basic understanding of the different types of NICs, let's march through the process of installing a NIC in a PC. Installing a NIC in a PC involves three distinct steps. First, you must physically install the NIC. Second, the NIC is assigned unused system resources—either by Plug and Play or manually. Third, you (or PnP) must install the proper drivers for the card.

Physical Connections

One thing to be clear on: if you don't plug the NIC into the computer, it just isn't going to work! Many users happily assume some sort of quantum magic when it comes to computer communications, but as a tech, you know better. Fortunately, physically inserting the NIC into the PC is the easiest part of the job. Most PCs today have two types of expansion slots. The first, and most common, of the two expansion slots is the Peripheral Component Interconnect (PCI) type (see Figure 8-13). PCI slots are fast, 32-bit, self-configuring expansion slots; virtually all new NICs sold today are of the PCI type, and with good reason. A PCI's speed enables the system to take full advantage of the NIC.

Still around—but fading quickly—are the old Industry Standard Architecture (ISA) slots (see Figure 8-14). These slots date back to the old IBM AT computer, and haven't changed one bit since then. They are 16-bit and very slow. Most modern PCs still have a few of these old expansion slots, primarily to ensure compatibility with the few remaining ISA cards out there. ISA is definitely on its way out, but it's not yet gone.

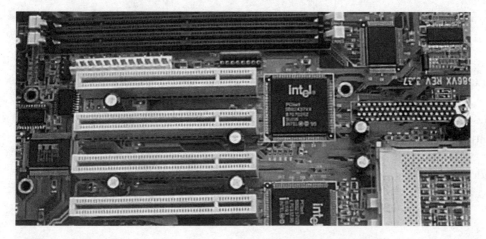

Figure 8-13 PCI slots

Figure 8-14 ISA slots

Although a few of the old ISA-type NICs exist, all new NICs made today use PCI connections. Since PCI fully utilizes PnP, and since all operating systems also use PnP,
installing a NIC usually involves little more than snapping the new NIC into an unused
PCI slot and letting the PnP software do the rest. Remember to treat a NIC as you would
any expansion card: use good anti-ESD procedures, and never touch anything but the
edges of the card!

Once you've installed the card, go right ahead and plug the NIC into the network. In
most cases, this will enable you to test the NIC as soon as it is fully installed, and in any
event, it won't hurt a thing. You'll understand this more as you progress through this
chapter.

Assigning Resources

NICs, like any other device in your PC, require the use of system resources, like I/O
addresses, IRQs, DMA, and memory addresses. Before PnP, assigning system resources
was a laborious process of using jumpers, switches, or software programs to configure
the NIC. Blessedly, these days are behind us—at least in the eyes of the Network+
exam. If a major exam like Network+ no longer requires us to understand the nuances
of manually assigning all those pain in the [insert your favorite bit of anatomy here]
resources, then I think we too should say goodbye and good riddance to the world of
I/O address overlaps and IRQ conflicts, and instead move on to more complex network
support issues. Say it with me: "Goodbye IRQ conflicts! And good riddance!" Now,
didn't that feel good?!

EXAM TIP: The Network+ exam no longer requires a detailed understanding of assigning system resources for NICs—huzzah!

Drivers

Well, given that the magic of PnP negates the need for dealing with resource assignment, how happy would you be if I told you that PnP covers drivers, too? Very happy? Well, my little chocolate drops, I live for your happiness, so let me inform you that PnP in Windows 9*x* and Windows 2000/XP does a fine job of automatic driver installation —most of the time. It really depends on how old the NIC is compared to the version of Windows whose PnP is trying to figure out its type. A great example is the 3COM 3C509 10BaseT NIC in my Windows 2000 system. It's been around for many years, and the drivers that come with Windows 2000 work perfectly. If I installed a much newer card into an older operating system, however, I might not enjoy the same luck.

No worries, though. Every NIC comes with a set of drivers on a floppy disk or CD-ROM, which will work just fine with your operating system *du jour*. Just be sure to install the proper driver! Without the correct driver, the device is not going to work. A popular trick is to copy the drivers from the disk to the PC's hard drive and do the install from there. That way, if you ever need the drivers again, you will not need to rummage around for the driver disk. Unless, of course, you're like me and keep your work space pristinely organized at all times! *[Hi, this is Mike's editor, seizing control of your transmission to offer the following picture (see Figure 8-15) of the* **true** *state of his work space. Let's just say* **pristine** *isn't the first word that leaps to mind.]* Watch for updated drivers. Drivers are constantly being updated. Check the manufacturer's web site or at least always use the driver disk that comes with the NIC.

Card Diagnostics

Every NIC's driver disk has a handy and powerful utility you can use to verify that the electronics on the NIC can properly send and receive data. Poke around on the driver disk and find it. Like the configuration utility, the testing utilities are still usually command prompt programs, although some are now Windows-based. Here is an example of a diagnostic program in action (see Figure 8-16).

Figure 8-15 Mike's "pristine" work space, a.k.a. *The Black Hole*

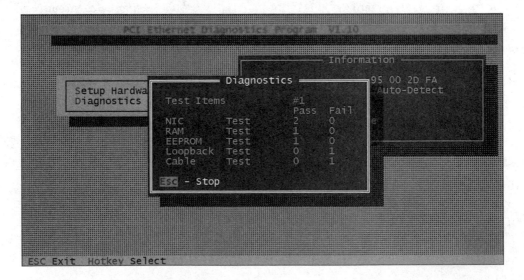

Figure 8-16 A diagnostic program

Do You See the Light?

Most NICs made today have some type of lights—really Light Emitting Diodes (LEDs) —glowing like mini-HALs on the backs of the cards (see Figure 8-17). Now that you know they are really LEDs, call them *lights* just like all of the other network techs. NICs with lights are mostly those for Ethernet network technologies that use RJ-45 (10BaseT, 100BaseT, and so on), and Token Ring cards. Don't be surprised if an old 10Base2 card has no lights. There is no guarantee that a NIC will have lights. In most cases, NICs with lights will have two of them. Sometimes there's only one, and they can be any color. These lights give you clues about what's happening, making troubleshooting a NIC much easier.

One light is a connection light. It tells you that the NIC is connected to a hub (or MSAU in Token Ring). Hubs also have a connect light, enabling you to check the connectivity at both ends of the cable. If a PC can't access a network, look in the back and be sure the cleaning person didn't accidentally unplug the card during the night.

Think I was kidding? Don't laugh—it happens all the time! When a network problem arises, especially a problem with a networked PC that ran well previously, the first item to check (depending on the symptom) is whether or not it's plugged in. There have been too many situations where some fancy pants network muckity-muck doesn't have the common sense to check something basic like whether the connection light is lit! It may sound funny now, but it loses its humor after hours of troubleshooting the

Figure 8-17   Typical lights on a 10BaseT NIC

most complex solutions, only to discover the problem was something trivial that would have taken a few seconds to fix.

The second light is the activity light. This little guy will flicker when the card detects network traffic. The activity light is a lifesaver for detecting problems because, in the real world, the connection light will sometimes lie to you. If the connection light says the connection is good, the next step is to try to copy a file or do something else to create network traffic. If the activity light does not flicker, there's a problem.

Lights are extremely handy troubleshooting tools; you will learn more on how to use lights to detect network trouble in Chapter 21.

Buying NICs

Some folks may disagree with this, but I always purchase name-brand NICs. For NICs, stick with big names such as 3COM or Intel. The NICs are better made, have extra features, and are easy to return if they turn out to be defective. Plus, it's easy to replace a missing driver on a name-brand NIC, and to be sure that the drivers work well. The type of NIC you purchase really depends on the network. Try to think about the future and go for multi-speed cards if your wallet will accept the extra cost. Also, where possible, try to stick with the same model of NIC. Every different model you buy means another set of driver disks you need to haul around. Using the same model of NIC makes driver updates easier, too.

Direct Cable Connections

No doubt, NICs and modems are overwhelmingly the most common method of connecting PCs. But there is one other method—called *Direct Cable Connection*—that should be addressed for completeness. All recent versions of Windows come with software to enable direct serial-to-serial, parallel-to-parallel, or infrared-to-infrared port connections between two PCs. DirectParallel connections require a special bi-directional parallel cable, called rather conspicuously a DirectParallel cable. To connect two PCs using their serial ports, you need to string a special cable called a *null modem cable* between the two PCs. They can then share hard drives, but nothing else. Serial Direct Cable Connections are very slow—a maximum of 115,600 bps—but are a cheap and dirty network option when you don't have a pair of NICs handy.

PART II

Connectors

Have you ever heard the phrase, *don't reinvent the wheel*? Well, the creators of network cards must have this cliché printed on their bedroom ceilings! There are very, very few NIC connections designed from scratch just for PC networks. In fact, specially designed connections are so rare that the Network+ exam doesn't cover them, and you almost certainly will never see one in your entire career. Let's just say therefore that *no* NIC connector is designed from scratch. So, if all NIC connections take the form of previous connector designs—and they do—what are the chances you might have two or three identical connectors on the back of a PC? The probability is very high. Techs must therefore know *all* of the connectors that might connect PCs to networks, even if they aren't currently used in network connections. Later, we will explore which types of connections are commonly used to enable one PC to network to another.

All network connectors fit into one of four different families: BNC, RJ, DB, and fiber. Before you start memorizing which connector goes with what NIC, you need to understand these connectors; it will make the memorization process trivially easy.

BNC Connectors

BNC connectors are one of the oldest connector types used for NICs. (BNC, as I mentioned earlier, stands for all sorts of odd things, depending on whom you ask.) BNC connectors are designed to be used with coaxial cable. They have a very distinct tubular appearance (see Figure 8-18).

Figure 8-18   A BNC connector

If you see a BNC connector on a NIC, you can almost always assume a 10Base2 (thin Ethernet) card. Two other types of cards also use the BNC connector: ARCNET and IBM 3270. *ARCNET*, you'll recall from Chapter 7, is an old, rarely-used network technology not covered on the Network+ exams, although you may see it on the exam as a wrong answer. The other card is in an old IBM terminal emulation adapter known as a *3270*. A 3270 terminal emulation card enabled a PC to switch between being a PC and being a dumb terminal. 3270 emulation is even older than ARCNET and has been rendered completely obsolete in the PC world by network cards. Bottom line: if you see a BNC connector sticking out of the back of a card, assume it is 10Base2 and you'll be right 98 percent of the time—and 100 percent right on any Network+ questions!

RJ Connectors

Registered Jack (RJ) connectors are definitely the most common type seen on NICs. If they look familiar, it's because RJ connectors are also the most common connector used in telephones. RJ connectors are used with unshielded twisted-pair wiring. While RJ connectors come in many different sizes, only two sizes ever appear on the back of a PC. The first of these is the famous RJ-11 connector (see Figure 8-19).

In the wonderful world of networking, RJ-11 is the exclusive domain of modems. Many years ago, RJ-11 appeared on a few proprietary network technologies, but they have all since disappeared. RJ-11 connectors use four-wire cables, the two inner con-

Figure 8-19 An RJ-11 connector

Figure 8-20 An RJ-45 connector

nectors for one phone line, and the outer ones for a second line. Most home phone systems have only one line per jack, so the outer lines do nothing. The six-wire version is known as the RJ-12. RJ-12 connectors certainly do exist, usually for more complex telephone systems, but they are virtually unheard of in the PC world.

Far more common is the RJ-45 connector. As you've been finding out, RJ-45 is the standard network connection for many different types of networks—Ethernet, Token Ring, and even ARCNET networks all have at least one version that uses RJ-45 connectors (see Figure 8-20). RJ-45 connectors have eight wires; however, many network technologies only use four wires, so it is not at all uncommon to see an RJ-45 with only four wires being used.

DB Connectors

DB connectors are the D-shaped connectors used for hundreds of different connections in the PC and network world. DB connectors come in many different forms. They can be *male* (pins) or *female* (sockets); they can have different numbers of pins or sockets (9, 15, and 25 are the most common numbers); and they usually have two rows of pins, although there are a few exceptions. Figure 8-21 shows a 25-pin, female DB connector. We call this, appropriately, a *female DB-25*. Figure 8-22 shows a male DB-25 connector.

The most common DB connectors used in the networking world are the female DB-15 connector used on 10Base5 Ethernet networks, and the female DB-9 connector used on older Token Ring cards. The Network+ exam assumes you know these connectors, in

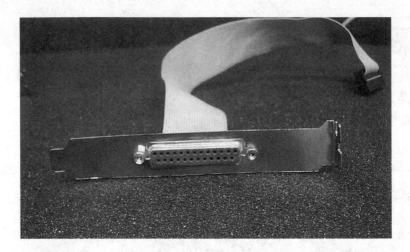

Figure 8-21   A female DB-25 connector

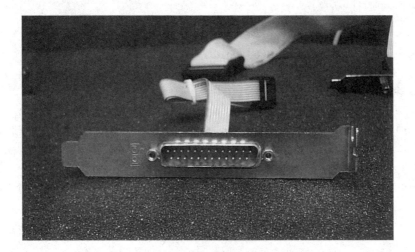

Figure 8-22   A male DB-25 connector

addition to the standard connectors used in the backs of PCs, such as the female DB-25 (parallel port) and the male DB-9 or DB-25 (serial port) connectors (see Figure 8-23).

Be alert for confusion arising from the fact that totally different devices use the same DB connectors. To take just one example, 10Base5 NICs, joysticks, and MIDI (Musical Industry Digital Interface) cards all use female DB-15 connectors. Likewise, if you see a female DB-25 connector, it could be a parallel port or a SCSI connector. How can you

Figure 8-23   Serial and parallel ports on the back of a PC

tell what you're looking at? The first trick is to remember that female DB-25 and female DB-15 connectors are notorious for multiple uses. *Don't assume.* Second, be familiar with the standard functions of these connectors. Almost every PC has a sound card, and that sound card will have a female DB-15 connector. The sound card will also have microphone and speaker connections, the presence of which solves the mystery of what that particular DB-15 connector does. Figure 8-24 shows a typical sound card with microphone and speaker connections.

Figure 8-24   A typical sound card with multiple connections

Figure 8-25   A 10Base5 card

Figure 8-25 shows a 10Base5 card. See any speaker connections? Of course not! If you know the functions of the different connections, it only takes a little common sense to know which connector is which.

Another connector to watch for is the *Centronics* connector. Although these are technically *not* DB connectors, they tend to get lumped in with DBs when techs discuss connectors. Centronics connectors are the D-shaped connectors on the backs of printers. They are distinctive in that they do not have true pins. Instead, they use a single blade containing flat tabs that make the connection. Be aware that the term *pins* is used when discussing what are actually Centronics tabs. Centronics connectors come in both female and male versions, and two common sizes: the famous 36-pin Centronics on the backs of printers, and the increasingly rare 50-pin version used with SCSI devices. Figure 8-26 shows the female 36-pin Centronics printer connector.

Make sure you know all of the DB connectors, even if they are not used for network connections. DB (and Centronics) connectors are very common on every PC, and their multi-function aspects make for some excellent (or tricky, depending on your perspective) Network+ questions that you will get wrong if you are not comfortable with them. Network+ loves to ask questions that include bizarre connector combos like "male DB-35" in an effort to trip up techs who don't know their connectors, so don't be one of them!

Figure 8-26   A 36-pin Centronics printer connector

Fiber Optic

Fiber optic cabling has its own unique connectors. "Whoa there, bucko!" I hear you exclaim. Or maybe that was my cowboy buddy, Finch. Anyway, I know what you're asking. Didn't this whole "Connectors" section start with the premise that no network connections are unique, and that the same connectors used for NICs can be found in other devices? Didn't we just prove this with some great examples of multiple use involving BNC, RJ, and DB connectors? Why yes, yes we did. But what would the computer business be without the obligatory exception?

The combination of fiber optics and PC networks is a pretty recent phenomenon. Fiber optics existed before PC networks, but the existing connectors were a little on the strange and hard to use. The PC industry played a major part in the process of figuring out how fiber would be used to connect PCs. To encourage quick adoption of fiber optic PC cables, it created special connectors that are tough, easy to stick on the end of a piece of fiber optic cable, and easy to insert and remove. In short, this exception to the rule is a good one! Let's look at fiber optic connectors.

The fact that the PC industry participated in the development of fiber optic cabling spared fiber optics from the too-many-different-connectors headache common among earlier types of network connections. There are only two common types of fiber optic connections: *SC* connectors and *ST* connectors (see Figure 8-27). SC and ST connectors

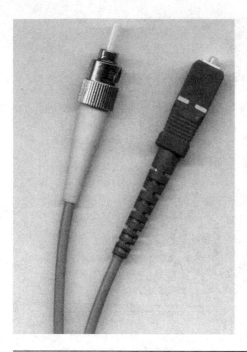

Figure 8-27   ST and SC connectors (from left to right)

are snap-on or push style connectors. Both are quite common, and no fiber optic networking technology is locked into one or the other. 10BaseFL and 100BaseFX networks, for example, can use either or both types of connectors.

In networks, fiber optics are mostly used to connect hubs, switches, and routers, rather than linking directly to PCs. Fiber optic NICs are very expensive! Although it is rare, you will see fiber used for desktop installations in specific situations where speed and security are more important than cost. Figure 8-28 shows a typical fiber optic NIC with SC ports.

Although the overwhelming majority of all fiber installations in the world of PC networking use ST and SC connectors, they are not the only types that exist. Some fiber networks use a very special networking topology called *Fiber Distributed Data Interface (FDDI)*. FDDI networks use a connector unique to FDDI networks (see Figure 8-29). And although FDDI connectors are very rare, they may appear on the Network+ exam as a possible type of fiber optic connection.

PART II

Figure 8-28   A fiber optic NIC with SC ports

Figure 8-29   FDDI connectors

Know Your Connectors!

Adding network connections to a stand-alone PC requires you to know your connectors! Many connectors on a stand-alone PC are very unique. The one-of-a-kind female, three-row DB-15 video connector cannot be confused with any other connector. The classic AT-style keyboard connector looks like no other connector on a PC. But when you add network functions to a PC, the variety of connectors can sometimes get a little confusing. Adding network connections to a stand-alone PC requires you to know your connectors! Mentally separating all of these connectors into four groups—BNC, DB, RJ, and fiber—will make the process of memorizing them for the exam, and for your work, much easier. Armed with an understanding of these many connectors, or at least the ability to tell one from the other, you can look at the ways PCs connect to networks and successfully match up the networking technology to the connector.

Chapter Review

Questions

1. A NIC with both an RJ-45 and a BNC connector is probably a(n) _____ NIC.
   a. Ethernet
   b. Token Ring
   c. ARCNET
   d. Modem

2. John's PC, networked with a 10BaseT NIC, ran perfectly yesterday. Today he can't access the network. Everyone else on the network can see each other, but not John. You look at the NIC and notice both lights are off. You should first:
   a. Try copying a file from another machine over the network.
   b. Verify that the hub is turned on.
   c. Replace the card.
   d. Make sure the NIC is connected to the hub.

3. You have a floppy disk that came with your new NIC. The floppy probably contains all of the following *except*:
   a. Drivers
   b. Configuration Utility
   c. Diagnostic Utility
   d. Driver Update Utility

4. The CEO's office is in the far corner of the building, and his PC cannot connect to the network. There are 107 meters of CAT5 UTP cable between the CEO's system and the network hub. Evaluate the following:

   Required result: Establish connectivity between the computer and the network.

Optional result: Improve network performance and decrease network downtime.

Proposed solution: Replace the CEO's current NIC with a 100BaseFX network card.

  a. The proposed solution produces the required result only.
  b. The proposed solution produces the optional result only.
  c. The proposed solution produces both results.
  d. The proposed solution produces neither of the results.

5. Which of the following network technologies does *not* utilize RJ-45 connectors?
  a. 10BaseT
  b. 10Base2
  c. 100BaseTX
  d. 100BaseT4

6. Wheebo, Inc. has 50 users connected using 10BaseT with CAT3 cabling. The accounting department, the research department, and the sales department share the same hub.

Required result: Increase the network speed from 10 to 100 Mbps.

Optional results: Improve network response time while still allowing all departments to have access to each other. Increase storage capacity of the servers.

Proposed solution: Put auto-sensing 10/100BaseTX NICs in all the systems and in each server. Add a 75GB second hard drive to each server. Separate the accounting department, research department, and sales department by giving each department its own hub.

  a. The solution produces the required result and both optional results.
  b. The solution produces the required result and one optional result.
  c. The solution produces the required result but neither of the optional results.
  d. The solution does not produce the required result. Replace all existing hubs with 100BaseTX hubs.

7. An SC connector is a _____ connector on fiber optic cable.
  a. snap-on
  b. twist-on
  c. BNC type
  d. AUI type

8. When you are setting up a 10Base2 network, you must use a _____ connector with a _____ connector for it to work correctly.
   a. T, RG-58
   b. BNC, RG-58
   c. RJ-45, T
   d. BNC, T

9. You are designing a 10BaseT network. You must use _____ cabling and an _____connector.
   a. STP, RJ-45
   b. UTP, RJ-45
   c. STP, RJ-11
   d. UTP, RJ-11

10. Which of the following is *not* a connector for networking?
   a. Centronics
   b. RJ-45
   c. BNC
   d. DB-15

Answers

1. **A.** The BNC gave it away. Only an Ethernet combo card would have an RJ-45 and BNC connector.

2. **D.** The connect light is off, so the NIC is not connected to a working hub. Everyone else is working, so the hub is fine.

3. **D.** Driver Update Utilities are not commonly found on the floppy disks that come with NICs.

4. **D.** Replacing the NIC with a 100BaseFX NIC would not produce any of the desired results. Changing NICs would require changing the cable and hub, which would then not be compatible with the rest of the network.

5. **B.** All of these choices use RJ-45 connectors except 10Base2, which uses a BNC connector.

6. **D.** To obtain a 100-Mbps speed, the cabling would have to be changed from CAT3 to CAT5 throughout the network.

7. **A.** An SC connector is a snap-on or push style connector that uses fiber.

8. **D.** 10Base2 uses a BNC connector. You must also use a T-connector for the 10Base2 to work properly.

9. **B.** For a 10BaseT network, use UTP cabling and an RJ-45 connector.

10. **A.** You'll find Centronics connectors on older printers and some SCSI devices. They were not commonly used in networking.

Structured Cabling

In this chapter, you will

- Learn what real network hardware looks like
- Learn how to implement network hardware into a real network
- Learn cable basics
- Understand EIA/TIA standards
- Learn about structured cabling
- Understand horizontal cabling
- Learn cabling fire ratings
- Learn about cabling equipment
- Learn how to install a patch panel
- Understand the new basic star

There is a huge difference between what you have learned about network hardware so far and the way hardware is actually implemented in the real world. In previous chapters, you toured the most common network technologies used in today's (and yesterday's) networks. At this point, you should be able to visualize a basic network setup. For bus topologies like 10Base2, visualize a cable running in a ceiling or along the floor with each PC connected somewhere along the bus. For star bus or star ring topologies like 10BaseT or Token Ring, visualize some type of box (hub, MSAU, switch, whatever) with a number of cables snaking out to all of the PCs on the network (see Figure 9-1).

On the surface, such a network setup is absolutely correct, but it does not have enough detail. Certainly, real-world networks (see Figure 9-2) do not look that orderly!

This chapter is designed to turn the conceptual networks I've been discussing into real equipment. You will observe what real network hardware—things like hubs,

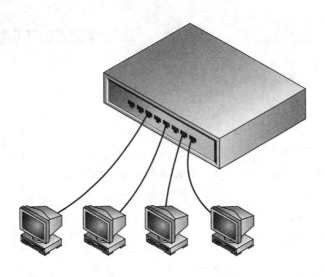

Figure 9-1 What an orderly-looking network!

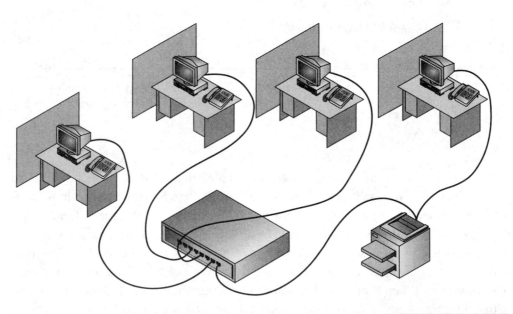

Figure 9-2 A real-world network

switches, and other similarly cool network stuff—looks like, and learn how to implement these components in a physical network. You'll learn how to turn those little lines representing cables into functional wiring systems. Finally, this chapter offers how-to information on cabling and networking devices.

The Network+ exam requires you to understand the basic concepts involved in designing a network and installing network cabling, and to recognize the components used in a real network. Network+ does not, however, expect you to be as knowledgeable as a professional network designer or cable installer. If you analogize networks to automobiles, the goal of Network+ is not to test your abilities as an auto mechanic, but rather to test your ability to talk intelligently to an auto mechanic, based on your solid understanding of how an automobile works.

Historical/Conceptual

Cable Basics—It All Starts with a Star

With that goal in mind, let's explore the world of connectivity hardware, starting with the most basic of all networks: a hub, some UTP cable, and a few PCs; in other words, a typical star network (see Figure 9-3).

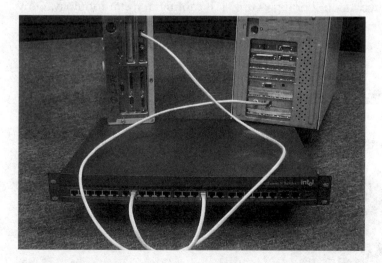

Figure 9-3   A hub connected by UTP cable to two PCs

Okay, pop quiz: is the network in Figure 9-3 a star bus or a star ring? Is it Token Ring, 10BaseT, or 100BaseTX? Gotcha! It's a trick question—you can't tell from this picture. In fact, it could be any of these network technologies. If you have a 10BaseT network and you want to turn it into a Token Ring network, you simply replace the 10BaseT NICs in the PCs with Token Ring NICs, and the 10BaseT hub with a Token Ring MSAU. The cable would stay the same, right? As far as the cabling is concerned, there is *no difference* between these topologies.

Many people find the idea of totally different network technologies like 10BaseT and Token Ring using the same cables just *not right* somehow. They think that because the network technology is different, the cabling should also be different. To them I say, "Open your mind, Grasshoppah, to the idea of cabling options." If you went back in time ten years, you'd find that pretty much every networking technology had its own type of cabling. Over the years, UTP has edged out other cabling options to become the leading type of cabling today. If an organization already has UTP cabling installed, they're not going to be interested in deploying a network technology that doesn't use UTP. If a network technology wants to exist, it must work with UTP. Token Ring originally only used STP cable, but to survive, it changed to UTP. All new network technologies employ UTP—even the new Gigabit Ethernet standards (see Figure 9-4)!

Test Specific

Virtually all of today's network technologies use UTP cabling in a star topology. Only 10Base2 and 10Base5 networks break the pattern of UTP in a star, and they are both dying technologies. The number of PCs using either of these technologies is tiny com-

Figure 9-4   UTP: The king of the world!

pared to those using UTP star technologies. 10Base5 has become so rare it's probably safe to say it is obsolete. (Apologies to the two of you who still use it!) 10Base2 still has a good following, but you will never see it used in a true permanent installation—*in the walls* as network cabling folks say. 10Base2 is still quite popular for temporary networks, or for quick and dirty small networks like a small two-PC office. Nevertheless, when you want a pretty network with the cable in the walls and the nice outlets, star topology UTP is the only way to go. Bus technologies are simply not an option for serious, permanent network installations (see Figure 9-5).

Although the bus is dead, that doesn't mean your older NICs are useless. Almost all older NICs can connect to UTP cables. For example, you can add a *transceiver* to a 10Base5 NIC to convert the 15-pin DIX (AUI) connector to RJ-45. 10Base2 doesn't have a transceiver, but some hubs have an extra 10Base2 port, making that connection a simple matter (see Figure 9-6). For older STP Token Ring cards, there are simple converters that plug into the back of the Token Ring NIC, converting it to RJ-45.

Figure 9-5   The bus is dead.

Figure 9-6   A 10Base2 connection on a hub.

Fiber optic cabling provides a partial exception to the UTP/star dominance in network cabling. Fiber optic uses a star topology, but does *not* use UTP cabling. Fiber optic cabling has properties that UTP just can't match, so it is safe in its own special niche. Later in this chapter you'll see how fiber optics are used within a network.

Okay, so the pure bus topology is dead, leaving us with UTP cable in either a star bus or a star ring topology. The most basic configuration for either of these topologies consists of a hub (or MSAU) with cables running out of it that connect directly to the PCs. Let's call this topology the *basic star*.

NOTE: The rest of the chapter uses the term hub generically to mean either an Ethernet hub or a Token Ring MSAU. Be aware that network techs also often use MAU in place of MSAU.

The Basic Star

The basic star topology looks great in a diagram, but falls apart spectacularly when applied to a real world environment. Four basic problems present themselves to the real-world network tech. First, the exposed cables running along the floor are just waiting for someone to trip over them, causing damage to the network and giving that person a wonderful lawsuit opportunity. Possible accidents aside, simply moving and stepping on the cable will over time cause it to fail. Second, the presence of other electrical devices close to the cable can create interference that confuses the signals going through the wire. Third, this type of setup limits your ability to make any changes to the network. Before you can change anything, you have to figure out which cables in the huge rat's nest of cables connected to the hub go to which machines. Imagine the troubleshooting nightmare, if you dare! Fourth, the only way to *upgrade* this network is to yank out all of the cables and replace them. In a word, *yuck*.

Keep in mind that there are subtle variances in the ways different network technologies use UTP, which, if not addressed through some type of standardized cabling, will prevent you from successfully upgrading your network. The simplest example is the number of wires used. Let's say you've strung a 10BaseT network. 10BaseT uses only two pairs of wires, so you installed two-pair UTP cable in your network. Now you want to upgrade to 100BaseT4. Well, you can forget it! 100BaseT4 requires *four* pairs of wires, not two. Your only option is to throw the old cable out and buy some new four-pair UTP cable.

"Gosh," you're thinking (okay, *I'm* thinking it, but you should be), "there must be a better way to install a physical basic star network." This better installation would provide safety, protecting the star from vacuum cleaners, clumsy coworkers, and electrical interference. This better basic star installation would have extra hardware to create a tight network organization, so that changing the network becomes trivial. Finally, this new and improved star network installation would feature a cabling standard with the flexibility to enable the network to grow according to its needs, and then to upgrade when the next great network technology comes along.

As you have no doubt guessed, I'm not just theorizing here, and in the real world, the people who most wanted improved installation standards were the ones who installed cable for a living. Who were these people? Think about it—what was the first type of cabling (other than electrical cabling) strung in walls? That's right—telephone cabling! The first network cabling installers were all telephone people.

Telephone systems have outlets at each place where you want a telephone. All of the phone cables are run in the walls to a central location. In other words, telephone systems also use a basic star. One day, a very smart telephone installer who was forced to install network UTP cable had this phenomenal idea: since telephone systems use UTP in a basic star, and networks use UTP in a basic star, somebody should come up with some groovy standard for UTP, so the same cables could be used for telephones and networks! That way you could install only one set of cables, significantly reducing the cost of adding cabling to a building. This standard would need to address the requirements and limitations concerning cable quality, distances, and distribution for *both* networks and telephones—no point in doing the same thing twice!

Beyond Network+

Structured Cabling to the Rescue!

The demand for a safe, dependable, and organized network motivated the Electronics Industry Association and the Telephone Industry Association (EIA/TIA) to develop a series of standards that everyone in the network installation business now uses to install cabling. Even though EIA/TIA has developed many standards, the *EIA/TIA 568* standard is considered the centerpiece of all the EIA/TIA cabling standards. This standard defines pretty much every aspect of installing cables in buildings. It standardizes acceptable cable types, the organization of the cabling system, guidelines for installation of the cable, and proper testing methods. The implementation of these standards is called *structured cabling*.

Most importantly, EIA/TIA 568 defines a series of terms, a standardized language for designers of structured cabling systems that is not specific to either telephones or networks. For example, a network designer won't refer to "the network cable that runs to the PC" very often. They have no interest in what you do with the cable—it might be for a telephone! Instead, network designers use phrases like *horizontal cabling* to imply that a cable runs from a closet somewhere out to an outlet in an office. While extremely helpful to the cabling folks, these terms can sometimes confuse a pure network person.

You don't have to learn these standards to pass the Network+ exam, but you do need a passing understanding of structured cabling to answer some of the exam questions. This chapter takes you on an abbreviated tour of network cabling from the structured cable viewpoint—just enough to give you an idea of network cabling, but *not* enough for you to go out and *pull* (install) your own network cables! This abbreviated tour happily ignores critical aspects of EIA/TIA and NEC standards that are important to a real structured cabling system, but of no interest to the Network+ exam. If you are interested in becoming a structured cable designer, an organization called BICSI (www.bicsi.org) provides a series of certifications that are *the* recognized certifications for that industry.

While I'm talking about pulling cable, here's an important piece of advice: *don't*! Installing structured cabling properly takes a startlingly high degree of skill. Thousands of pitfalls await inexperienced network people who think they can install their own network cabling. Pulling cable requires expensive equipment, a lot of hands, and the ability to react to problems quickly. Network techs can lose millions of dollars—not to mention their good jobs!—by imagining they can do it themselves. Unless the network is tiny and the downside is low, let the pros install a solid, tested structured cabling system for you, while you set up the PCs and establish the network. Trust me—your organization will save money, and you'll save your job!

Structured Cable Network Components

The hardest thing to understand about structured cabling is the most basic aspect of the job. Structured cabling works for telephones as well as networks, so take off your Network Tech hat for a moment and just think about getting two cables from every place where a phone or networked PC resides to a central point (see Figure 9-7). Once you begin to think in these terms, structured cabling will make more sense.

Successful implementation of a basic star network requires three essential ingredients: an equipment room, horizontal cabling, and a work area. All the cabling must run to a central location, the *equipment room* (see Figure 9-8). What equipment goes in there —a hub, MSAU, or a telephone system—is not the important thing. What matters is that all the cables concentrate in this one area.

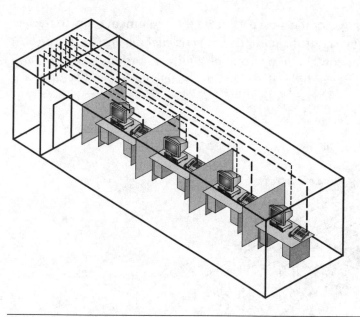

Figure 9-7   Structured cabling

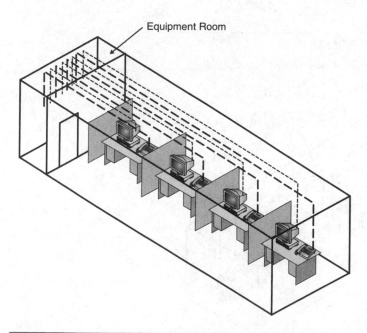

Figure 9-8   The equipment room

All cables run horizontally (for the most part) from the equipment room to the telephones or PCs. This cabling is called, appropriately, *horizontal cabling* (see Figure 9-9). At the other end of the horizontal cabling from the equipment room is the *work area*. The work area is often simply an office that contains the telephones and PCs (see Figure 9-10).

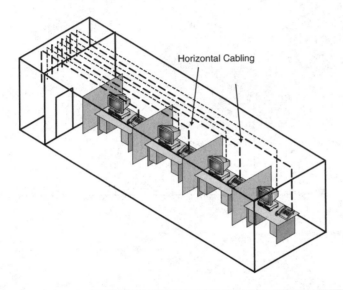

Figure 9-9 Horizontal cabling

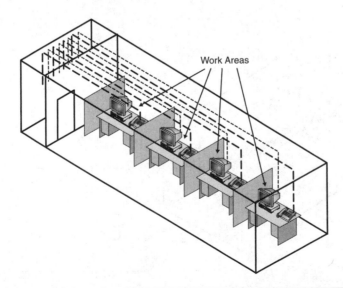

Figure 9-10 The work area

Each of the three parts of a basic star network—the horizontal cabling, the equipment room, and the work area(s)—must follow a series of strict standards designed to ensure that the cabling system is reliable and easy to manage. Let's look at each of the parts individually, starting with the horizontal cabling.

Horizontal Cabling

EIA/TIA 568 recognizes three different types of cable used for horizontal cabling:

- Four-pair, 100 Ohm, 24 AWG, solid-core UTP
- Two-pair, 150 Ohm, 22 AWG, solid-core STP
- Two-fiber, 62.5/125 μm fiber optic

Whew! How much of that did you understand? Not much? Okay, I'll talk about each of these three approved types, but first, did you notice what common type of cable is *not* on the list? That's right, coax. Coax should not be used in structured cabling!

UTP

Because UTP makes up over 95 percent of all the new horizontal cabling installed today, its specs are very interesting to the Network+ folks. Don't bother memorizing all the pretty numbers and unknown acronyms, just familiarize yourself with a few basic terms. *Ohms* is an electronic measurement of the cable's impedance. *Impedance* is (roughly) the amount of resistance to an electrical signal on a wire, and is determined by the physical dimensions and the materials used in the cable. If you use cables with different impedance levels, it will create reflections of data on the line which will confuse the network. Impedance is used as a relative measure of the amount of data a cable can handle. 24 AWG refers to the *gauge*, or thickness of the cable. Do you remember the UTP CAT levels we discussed earlier in the book? Well, when you specify a CAT level of UTP, in reality you are also specifying the Ohms and gauge, as well as a number of other critical criteria. What you need to know are the CAT levels, not gritty details like impedance or wire gauge.

The CAT level alone does not completely describe UTP, because it does not cover critical issues like the number of pairs, and whether the individual wires are stranded (made from lots of tiny wires) or solid (made from one solid piece of copper). EIA/TIA has added these points to the specification. When specifying which cable to use, a network technician should care about the CAT level, the number of pairs, whether it's stranded or solid core, and one other critical feature *not* directly covered by EIA/TIA 568: the *fire rating* of the cable.

Fire Ratings

Did you ever see the movie *Towering Inferno*? Steve McQueen stars as the fireman who saves the day when a skyscraper goes up in flames because of poor quality electrical cabling. The fire reaches every part of the building due to burning insulation on the wires. Although no cables made today contain truly flammable insulation, insulation is made from plastic, and if you get any plastic hot enough, it will create smoke and noxious fumes.

To reduce the fire risk, all cables—UTP, STP, and fiber—have fire ratings. The two most common fire ratings are *PVC* and *plenum*. PVC (Poly-Vinyl Chloride) has no significant fire protection. If you burn a PVC cable, it creates lots of smoke and noxious fumes. Burning plenum cable creates much less smoke and fumes, but plenum costs about three to five times as much as PVC. Most city ordinances require the use of plenum-rated cable for network installations. Bottom line? Get plenum!

Back to UTP

There are different CAT levels for UTP, as discussed extensively in earlier chapters. Here is the chart for review:

Category 1	Regular analog phone lines; not used for data communications
Category 2	Supports speeds up to 4 Mbps
Category 3	Supports speeds up to 16 Mbps
Category 4	Supports speeds up to 20 Mbps
Category 5	Supports speeds up to 100 Mbps
Category 5e	Improved support for 100 Mbps

In the real world, network people only install CAT 5e UTP, even if they can get away with a lower CAT level. Installing CAT 5e is done primarily as a hedge against the day when the network upgrades to technology that requires CAT 5. Networking *caveat emptor* warning: many network installers take advantage of the fact that a lower CAT level will work and bid a network installation using CAT3, so be sure to specify CAT 5 or even CAT 5e!

While CAT levels never seem to pose a problem for folks just getting into network cabling, there always seems to be confusion about the number of pairs. Many people mistakenly assume that CAT 5 means four pairs of cable. There is no correlation between CAT 5 and the number of pairs; in fact, you can purchase CAT 5 in many different pair combinations, so be careful not to confuse them!

The EIA/TIA 568 standard, however, *requires four pairs*, for two reasons. First, most up-and-coming network technologies, particularly the very high-speed ones, require four pairs of wires. Second, many advanced telephone systems require multiple pairs. The smart plan: always get four-pair UTP. In fact, the EIA/TIA standard defines the type of UTP to be used so precisely that the demand for anything *but* four-pair CAT 5 UTP has pretty much collapsed. Almost every place UTP is pulled, you will find four-pair CAT 5. The only choice left to make when buying horizontal UTP cabling is whether to use plenum or PVC. Next time you add a phone line to your house, check the cable— and don't be surprised if what you see is good old CAT 5.

Installing UTP is serious work, but the cabling industry provides thousands of products that make the job fairly easy—for the professional. The most serious consideration when installing UTP is the potential for electronic and radio interference. Cable installers go to great lengths to make sure that UTP stays away from electric motors, fluorescent lights, power cables, and so on. Most UTP installations take advantage of cabling trays or hooks suspended above drop ceilings to keep cables away from potential interference sources.

The EIA/TIA standard sets the maximum distance from the equipment room to any one work area at 90 meters. Those of you who memorized your cable distances from earlier chapters will recall that almost all UTP-based networking technologies allow 100 meters. So where did the other ten meters go? Read on, young Padawan! All will be revealed shortly, but first let's finish our discussion of cable types by looking at the other two types of horizontal cabling: STP and fiber optic.

STP and Fiber Optic

The Network+ exam barely touches shielded twisted-pair (STP) or fiber cabling, but I'll do a quick review for completeness. STP cabling doesn't blend well with the telephone side of structured cabling, thus it's pretty much confined to Token Ring networks plus a few very high-speed networking technologies. Not that there's anything wrong with STP! In fact, STP prices have dropped so much that if you look, you can find STP priced competitively with UTP. But UTP has become so dominant in the market that STP continues to disappear, and it is extremely rare to see it used as horizontal cabling today.

Having to install STP cable makes even the most experienced network tech shudder. Like UTP, STP is usually installed above drop ceilings on racks or hooks. It is less susceptible to electronic interference, diminishing the need to avoid potential sources of interference. One special feature of STP cable installation: you must ground its shielding or the shielding will become, in effect, a 90-meter antenna. Needless to say, this usually causes significant problems for the network!

Fiber optic is rarely used as horizontal cabling due to its high price and the fact that UTP is normally more than enough for most installations. Fiber does have some clear advantages over UTP, however: fiber optics don't use electricity, so electrical interference is a non-issue, and fiber optic cabling can easily reach 1,000 meters. As I mentioned earlier, though, fiber optic cabling is quite fragile and a huge pain in the posterior to install, which is why you should ruthlessly suppress any urge you may develop to do it yourself. Call a professional cable installer instead.

Now that you are more comfortable with horizontal cabling and the types of cabling used, let's concentrate on the ends of the basic star, starting with the equipment room.

The Equipment Room

The equipment room is the heart of the basic star. It contains the hubs and the telephone equipment, and all of the cables from all of the attached PCs and telephones come together in this one area. The concentration of all this gear in one place makes the equipment room potentially one of the messiest parts of the basic star! Even if you do a nice, neat job of organizing the cables when they are first installed, networks change over time. People move computers, new work areas are added, network topologies are added or improved, and so on. Unless you impose some type of organization, this conglomeration of equipment and cables always decays into a nightmarish Gordian knot (see Figure 9-11).

Fortunately, the networking industry has developed a number of specialized components under EIA/TIA guidelines that make organizing the equipment room a snap. It might be fair to say that there are too many options! To keep it simple, we are going to stay with the most common equipment room setup and then take a short peek at some other fairly common options.

Every equipment room should have standard racks for storing the equipment. Equipment racks provide a safe, stable platform for all of the different components inside a telecommunications closet. All equipment racks are 19 inches wide, but vary in height from two- to three-foot high models that bolt onto a wall to the more popular floor-to-ceiling models (see Figure 9-12).

You can mount almost anything into a rack. All hub manufacturers make rack-mounted hubs, switches, and routers that mount into a rack with a few screws. They come with a wide assortment of ports and capabilities. There are even rack-mounted servers, complete with slide-out keyboards, and rack-mounted *uninterruptible power supplies* (UPSs) to power the PCs and NICs (see Figure 9-13).

Figure 9-11   A messy network rack

> **NOTE:**   Most of the devices we call UPSs are not truly uninterruptible power
> supplies. They are standby power supplies (SPSs). An SPS differs from a UPS in
> that it does not provide continuous power. An SPS does nothing until it detects
> a power outage. If the power goes out for more than a few milliseconds, the SPS
> kicks in automatically. There is absolutely nothing wrong with SPSs—just make sure you
> know which type of power supply you are getting, and verify with the manufacturer that it
> will work with your devices.

The first item on the proper equipment room list is the *patch panel*. Ideally, once you install horizontal cabling, it should never be moved. Sure, cables can handle some rearranging, but if you insert a wad of cables directly into your hubs, every time you move a cable to a different port on the hub, or move the hub itself, you will jostle the cable. UTP horizontal cabling has a solid core, making it pretty stiff. You don't have to move it very many times before some of those thin strands of solid copper start breaking, and there goes your network! But lucky for you, you can easily avoid this problem by using a *patch panel*. A patch panel is simply a box with a row of female connectors (ports) on the back, to which you connect the cables.

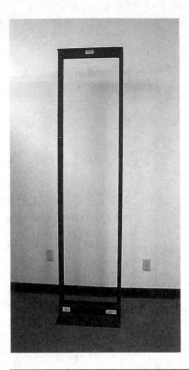

Figure 9-12   A bare equipment rack

Figure 9-13   A rack-mounted UPS

Not only do patch panels prevent the horizontal cabling from being moved, they are also your first line of defense in organizing the cables. All patch panels have space in the front for labels, and these labels are the network person's best friend! Simply place a tiny label on the patch panel identifying each cable, and never will you have to experience that sinking feeling of standing in the equipment room of your non-functioning network wondering, "Where does this cable go?" If you want to be a purist, there is an official, and rather confusing, labeling methodology you can use; but most real-world network techs simply use their own internal codes (see Figure 9-14).

Patch panels are available in a wide variety of configurations that include different types of ports and numbers of ports. Not only can you get UTP, STP, or fiber ports, but some manufacturers combine several different types on the same patch panel. Panels are available with 8, 12, 24, 48, or even more ports. UTP patch cables, meanwhile, come with CAT ratings, which you should be sure to check! Don't blow a good CAT 5 cable installation by buying a cheap patch panel—get a CAT 5 patch panel! Most manufacturers proudly display the CAT level right on the patch panel.

Once you have installed the patch panel, you need to connect the ports to the hub through *patch cables*. Patch cables are short (two- to five- foot) UTP cables, very similar to horizontal cabling (see Figure 9-15). But unlike horizontal cabling, they use stranded rather than solid cable, so they can tolerate much more handling. Patch cables also differ from horizontal cables in that they ignore the EIA/TIA wiring schemes and instead wire straight through: Pin 1 on one connector goes to Pin 1 on the other; Pin 2

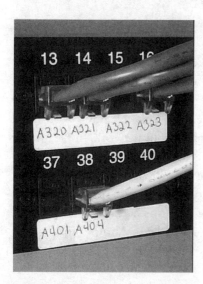

Figure 9-14   A labeled patch panel

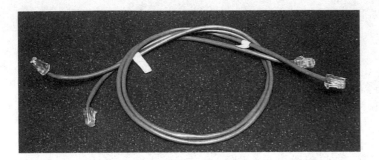

Figure 9-15   Typical patch cables

to Pin 2, and so on. Even though you can make your own patch cables, most people buy pre-made ones. Buying patch cables enables you to use different-colored cables to facilitate organization (yellow for accounting, blue for sales, or whatever).

An equipment room doesn't have to be a special room dedicated to computer equipment. You can use specially-made cabinets with their own little built-in equipment racks that sit on the floor or attach to a wall, or use a storage room, as long as the equipment can be protected from the other items stored there. Fortunately, the demand for equipment rooms has been around for so long, most office space comes equipped with them.

Okay, our basic star installation is really taking shape! We've installed the EIA/TIA horizontal cabling and configured the equipment room. Now it's time to address the last part of the structured cabling system, the work area.

The Work Area

What is a work area? From a cabling standpoint, a *work area* is nothing more than a wall outlet that serves as the termination point for network and telephone cables, and a convenient insertion point for PCs and telephones. A *wall outlet*, itself, is basically a female jack to accept the cable, a mounting plate, and a faceplate. You can buy CAT 5-rated jacks for wall outlets to go along with the CAT 5 cabling in your network. In fact, many network connector manufacturers use the same connectors in the wall jacks that they use on the patch panels. These modular jacks significantly increase ease of installation. Most work area outlets, meanwhile, have two connectors, one for the network and one for the telephone. Some outlets use RJ-45 for both connections because RJ-11 plugs fit into RJ-45 jacks, and these days, many phones use RJ-45 natively. Another tip: be sure you label the outlet to show the job of each connector (see Figure 9-16). A good outlet will also have some form of label that identifies its position on the patch panel. Proper documentation will always save you an incredible amount of work later.

Figure 9-16 A typical phone/data outlet

Figure 9-17 A patch cord connecting a PC to an outlet

The last step is connecting the PC to the outlet box. Here again, most folks use a patch cable. Its stranded cabling stands up to the abuse caused by moving PCs, not to mention the occasional kick (see Figure 9-17).

Now, my young apprentice, let us return to the question of why the EIA/TIA 568 specification only allows UTP cable lengths of 90 meters, even though most UTP networking technologies allow cables to be 100 meters long. Have you figured it out? Hint: the answer lies in the discussion we've just been having. Ding! Time's up! The answer is . . . the patch cables! They add extra distance between the hub and the PC, which we compensate for by reducing the horizontal cabling length.

The work area may be the simplest part of the structured cable system, but it is also the source of most networked failures. When a user can't see the network and you suspect a broken cable, the first place to look is the work area!

The New Basic Star

As you can see, EIA/TIA structured cabling methods can transform the basic star from the cabling nightmare shown at the beginning of this discussion into an orderly and robust network. Sure, you don't have to do any of this to make a network function; you only have to do it if you want the network to run reliably and change easily with the demands of your organization. The extra cost and effort of installing a proper structured cabling system pays huge dividends by preventing the nightmare scenario where you must find one bad cable in a haystack of unlabeled CAT 5, and by protecting the network from clumsy and/or clueless users.

Beyond the Basic Star

The basic single hub with star configuration only works acceptably in the simplest networks. In the real world, networks tend to have many hubs, and often span floors, buildings, states, and even countries. Starting with the basic star, and using structured cabling where applicable, you can progress beyond that rudimentary configuration using certain equipment and strategies designed for larger, more advanced, and more efficient networks. However, in this book we will only touch lightly on networking beyond the basic star. Each of these more advanced network topics deserves its own chapter, if not its own book, which is totally beyond our present scope. Network+ wants you to understand the concepts, but it does not require you to become an expert.

Cascading Hubs

What do you do when your hub runs out of ports? One of the beauties of a network that uses a hub is the ability to *cascade* hubs. Cascading means daisy-chaining two or more hubs together to make, in essence, one big hub. I hate the word *cascade* and would like to apologize for the network industry for using that term, because it confusingly implies that the electrons are flowing in a one-way stream from one hub to the next—*not true!*

Cascading is a *two-way* operation. *Linking* hubs would be a better way to put it, but it's too late to change the terminology, so I'll stick with *cascading* hubs for this book.

Cascading hubs together is a simple process. Remember in Chapter 6 when I discussed crossover cables? All you have to do is connect two hubs with a crossover cable and you've cascaded those hubs! Cascading is so common today that virtually every hub made comes with a built-in crossover port that can be connected to any regular port on another hub, eliminating the need for a special crossover cable (see Figure 9-18). Although in actuality the communication is two-way, a cascaded connection is generally diagrammed as if the cable goes *from* the crossover port *to* the regular port on the attached hub (see Figure 9-19).

Figure 9-18 Hub with crossover port (here labeled "Out to Hub")

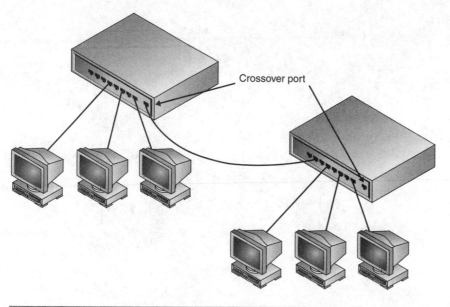

Figure 9-19 Cascaded hubs

Cascading isn't limited to two hubs. Once you've connected Hub A's crossover port to one of Hub B's regular ports, you can grab a third hub—let's creatively name that one Hub C—and connect Hub B's crossover port to one of Hub C's regular ports, making a chain of three hubs that basically operate like one big hub. Be aware that there are limits on the number of hubs you can cascade (refer to the discussion of the 5-4-3 rule in Chapter 6), but the basic concept is essentially this simple.

Let's look at an example. The Bayland Widget Corporation's network has three 10BaseT hubs. Each hub serves a different department: Hub A is for accounting, Hub B is for sales, and Hub C is for manufacturing. Bayland's clever network tech has cascaded the three hubs, allowing any system on any of the three hubs to communicate with any other system on any of the three hubs (see Figure 9-20).

The Switch

As you add PCs to a 10BaseT network, your network traffic will increase. As network traffic increases, your users will begin to notice a perceptible slowdown in network performance. Then they will begin to whine, and you will have to smack them. Okay, not

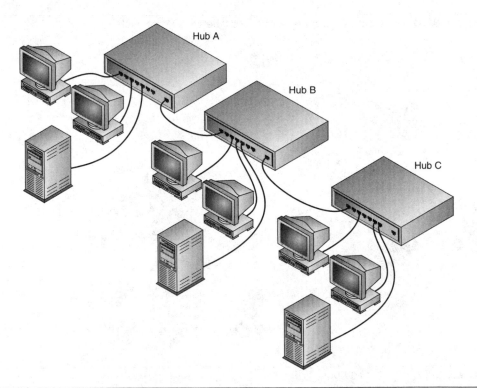

Figure 9-20   Bayland Widget Corporation's three cascaded 10BaseT hubs

Figure 9-21   Switches and hubs look very similar.

really. In fact, let me be clear on this point (as I check over my shoulder for any nearby lawyers): *do not harm your users*! One of the fastest and cheapest hardware solutions for too much traffic on a 10BaseT network is the addition of a switch. To switch (sorry, the pun was just hanging there!) to a switched 10BaseT network, simply remove the hub and replace it with a switch. You don't have to do anything to the cards or the cabling.

Like hubs, switches come in a dizzying variety of shapes and sizes. As you might have guessed, companies that make hubs tend to make switches, too, most of which use the same casing for equivalent hubs and switches. In fact, from 20 feet away, a hub and the equivalent switch look identical. Figure 9-21 shows an Intel small office hub next to a small office switch; note that they are virtually identical.

In the past, switches were tremendously more expensive than hubs, but in the last few years, the price of switches has dropped immensely, from thousands of dollars to hundreds. Switches are still three to four times more expensive than hubs, but this drop in price has transformed the switch from a luxury technology to a viable part of standard office networks.

So now you can buy a switch without selling your house to pay for it, but what do you *do* with it once you have it? There are many possibilities, depending upon the type of network you have, but odds are you'll want to choose between two common implementation strategies. The first option is to switch everything—no more plain hubs; everything is connected to a switch. The second option is to use the switch as a bridge between hubs. Let's look at both of these options, using Bayland Widget as the example.

Bayland's network has three hubs, each of which you can replace with a switch. What this does is eliminate the collision domain problem. With three cascaded hubs, the packets sent from any PC go to all the other PCs on all three hubs. Because switches

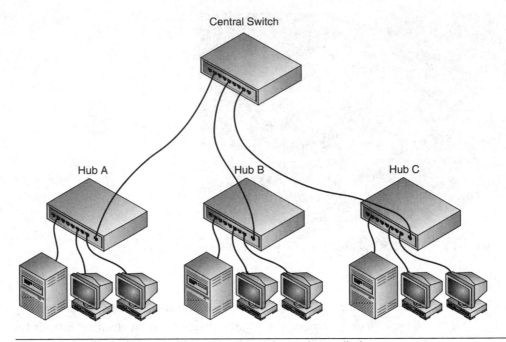

Figure 9-22 Bayland's network with a central switch installed

direct each packet only to the specified recipient PC, there are no collisions. This is wonderful because it means that every connection runs at the full potential speed of the network—in this case, (10BaseT) 10 Mbps. Remember, the moment you start using switches, you can throw the 5-4-3 rule out the window!

Replacing all the hubs with switches will increase network performance, but many networks won't actually see enough of a performance increase to rationalize the relative cost of this option. A more cost-effective option for multihub networks is to keep the hubs but add a central switch to which they all connect. Figure 9-22 shows the Bayland network reconfigured with a shiny new central switch linking the three hubs.

This setup provides two benefits. First, remember that a switch is essentially a multi-port bridge that filters traffic so packets sent between two computers on the same hub don't also get sent to other hubs where they don't belong. By the same token, of course, if a packet *does* need to go to a system on a different hub, the switch will forward that packet to that other hub. Second, you can connect servers *directly* to the switch, so they will receive only the traffic intended for them (see Figure 9-23). This is especially important because servers, by nature, are flooded with traffic; any reduction in the number of packets a server must handle will speed up your network.

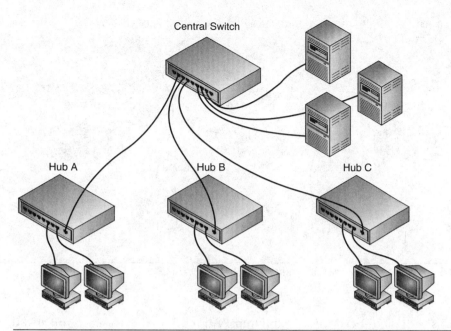

Figure 9-23   Servers connected directly to a central switch

Multispeed Networks

Another great way to combat a slow network is by using higher-speed networking technologies. Replacing all of a network's 10BaseT hubs and 10BaseT NICs with 100BaseT devices will speed up your network, but giving every PC in the network a faster NIC, like making every machine switched, is not necessarily a cost-effective networking solution. A more efficient way to improve network performance is to purchase a *multispeed hub*. Multispeed hubs come in two flavors. Flavor one has a bunch of 10-Mbit ports and one or two special 100-Mbit ports. These special ports are sometimes dedicated 100-Mbit ports, but more commonly they are *auto-sensing* ports that can transmit at either 10 or 100 Mbps. Flavor two hubs have nothing but two-speed auto-sensing ports, meaning you can connect any combination of slower and faster devices to a flavor two hub. The greater convenience of hubs with all auto-sensing ports has made them the overwhelming market choice, causing hubs with only one or two fast ports to fade quickly away.

Let's look again at the Bayland Widget Corp.'s three-department network and apply the concept of multispeed networking. To simplify things, let's forget about the switch we added and go back to the network pictured in Figure 9-20, with three cascaded 10BaseT hubs. The idea is to increase your overall network throughput by using faster networks in conjunction with slower ones. The solution is to replace each of the

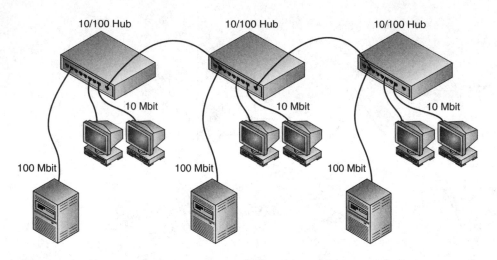

Figure 9-24   Bayland's network with multispeed hubs

10BaseT hubs with multispeed 10/100-Mbit hubs. This enables the servers to run at 100 Mbps, while the PCs continue to communicate at 10 Mbps (see Figure 9-24).

Combining Speed and Switches

There is no law of physics preventing you from combining both switches and multi-speed hubs to make your network *smoke*! Let's use the Bayland example again to see one of many ways to combine high speed and switching. Starting with the basic configuration of three cascaded hubs, Bayland could replace its three 10BaseT hubs with three 10/100 hubs, *and* add a 100BaseT switch, as shown in Figure 9-25. This setup, although more expensive than just adding a switch or multispeed hubs, gives you a very fast network without costing you a dime to install NICs in any of the client systems. If the IT department over at Bayland Widgets decides to make this upgrade to the network, their users will probably buy them all lunch for the next few weeks!

If you look at one of these more complex, multihub networks, you will find a special set of cables operating faster than 10 Mbps. These special cables don't run to individual PCs, only to hubs, switches, and servers. In a sense, there are two totally separate networks here: many individual networks connecting the PCs, and one high-speed network tying together all of those individual networks. This high-speed network is known as a *backbone*. A network backbone is not one cable; it is a group of cables running from a central point (usually a high-speed switch) to a set of other switches and/or hubs. EIA/TIA doesn't give a hoot about hubs vs. switches or high-speed vs. low-speed, but they have a lot to say about backbones—in particular, how those backbones are cabled!

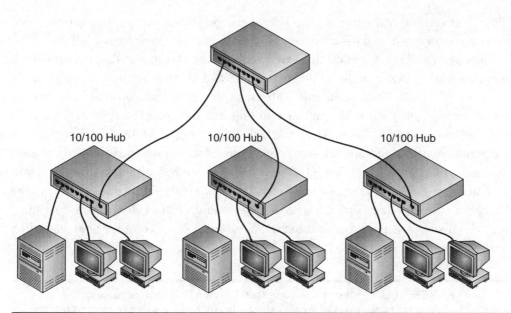

Figure 9-25   Combining switching and high speed

Multiple Floors, Multiple Buildings

Once you begin to expand a network beyond the basic star configuration by adding more hubs and switches, new demands arise. These can be summarized in a single statement: as networks grow, they take up more space! Adding significantly more PCs to a network usually implies adding more offices, cubicles, and other work areas. Adding work areas means adding more switches and hubs in more equipment rooms. Most networks use one equipment room per floor. If the room is centrally located in the building, cabling within the 90-meter limit will completely cover the floor space in most buildings. This, in effect, creates multiple networks on multiple floors, which must be tied together with a backbone cable robust enough to support the demands of combined networks. Adding PCs usually also means adding more (and more powerful) servers to handle the increased demand. It can also mean moving servers to different buildings, which can create relatively long distances between the servers and the PCs that must access them.

As more servers are added to the network, the administrators who tend to them will find it more efficient to group mission-critical servers together in a single—yes, it's back to the future—computer room! The computer room is really nothing more than the main equipment room. A computer room not only provides enhanced safety and security for expensive hardware, it enables administrators to handle daily support chores like backups more efficiently. Bottom line: the larger the network, the larger the space needed to support it, and the more complex your network infrastructure will be.

The concept of structured cabling extends beyond the basic star. EIA/TIA provides a number of standards, centralized on EIA/TIA 568 and another important EIA/TIA standard, EIA/TIA 569. These standards address cabling configuration and performance specifications (568) and cable pathways and installation areas (569) involving multiple equipment rooms, floors, and buildings. Remember, EIA/TIA does not think in terms of networks alone, and it uses its own terminology for structured cabling beyond the basic star. Slightly simplified, EIA/TIA's view of structured cabling breaks down into six main components: the equipment room, the horizontal cabling, the work areas, the backbone, the building entrance, and the telecommunication closets. The first three were discussed earlier and perform the same roles in a more complex network as in a basic star, so I'll concentrate on the last three.

 NOTE: Don't bother memorizing these! Network+ is not going to quiz you on naming the six parts of structured cabling. Do make a point to understand the equipment required for each of these parts, and how the different parts interrelate. This is real-world stuff you will need in the marketplace.

Backbones and Building Entrances

EIA/TIA specifies using UTP, STP, or fiber optics for backbones. UTP and fiber optic are very popular for backbones, whereas STP is rarely used. While any cable that meets the criteria for a backbone can certainly serve as a backbone cable, EIA/TIA conceives of backbones more as cables that *vertically* connect equipment rooms (often called *risers*) or *horizontally* connect buildings (*interbuilding* cables).

EIA/TIA provides some guidelines for backbone cable distances, but the ultimate criterion for determining cable length is the networking technology used. Most riser backbones use either copper or fiber optic cables. Because of its imperviousness to electricity, fiber optic cabling is the only kind you should use for interbuilding cables (see Figure 9-26). Copper cabling *can* be used between buildings, but it requires significant grounding to protect against damage from electrical interference.

The *building entrance* is where all the cables from the outside world (telephone lines, cables from other buildings, and so on) come into a building (see Figure 9-27). EIA/TIA specifies exactly how the building entrance should be configured, but we're not interested in the building entrance beyond knowing that fiber optic cable should be used between buildings.

Figure 9-26 Fiber optic backbone cables connecting into hubs

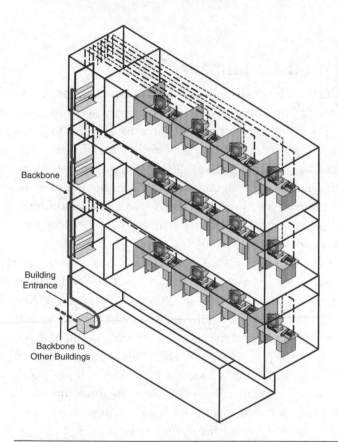

Figure 9-27 Backbone and building entrance

Telecommunications Closets

Telecommunications closets are really more for telephone systems than for networks, but are included here for completeness. Closets are where you connect individual phone cables from work areas to the actual telephone lines of the internal phone system. The cabling for telephones usually looks very different from the cabling for networked computers, so it's not hard to distinguish between them when looking at wire drops around a work area.

Before the advent of advanced telephone systems that handle this electronically, a phone tech had to go into the telecom closet and physically move lines to change phone numbers in an office. Telecommunications closets aren't supposed to have networking equipment in them, so they are not normally used for networks. Instead, larger networks will have a number of equipment rooms. From a networking standpoint, telecommunications closets aren't strictly relevant—especially for our very short dip into structured cabling.

Installer? No. Informed Consumer? Yes!

Network+ does not directly address structured cabling, but understanding structured cabling sure makes a lot of Network+ questions easier. For example, you're not going to be quizzed on the different types of fiber optic cable, but you must be ready to determine, as the Network+ objectives put it, *when they are appropriate*. Similarly, you shouldn't get hung up on how exactly UTP horizontal cable is strung over drop ceilings, but do be aware of its susceptibilities to radio frequency and electronic interference. The goal here is not to turn you into a cable installer, but to give you a solid understanding of the concept of structured cabling—not only so you can pass the Network+ exam, but so you'll be a good network support person!

Cable types, connectors, fire ratings, racks, tools . . . how much of this do you really need to know? I mean, you're just going to get your Network+ certificate and then sit all day in front of a keyboard somewhere, right? Wrong. CompTIA designed the Network+ exam to test for knowledge that anyone working on a network should have. If you work on a network, you *will* need to expand that network at some point, and you will be the first line of defense any time a problem arises. This chapter covers what you need to know to pass the Network+ exam. It barely touches the vast amount of knowledge and training required to become a cable installer. Understanding the components of structured cabling, plus a few basic tools and techniques, won't qualify you as a professional cable installer, but it will enable you to make some basic fixes and to communicate with the pros. In the next chapter, you'll dive into the issues involved in cable installation, not so you can be an installer, but because an understanding of what goes into a cable installation will help you diagnose physical problems with your network.

Chapter Review

Questions

1. Which of the following cables should *never* be used in a structured cabling installation?
   a. UTP
   b. STP
   c. Fiber optic
   d. Coax

2. Which type of fire rating should horizontal cabling have?
   a. Mil Spec
   b. Plenum
   c. PVC
   d. UTP

3. The CAT 5 level defines how many pairs of wires in the cable?
   a. 2
   b. 4
   c. 8
   d. It doesn't specify.

4. The best type of cabling to use for interbuilding connections is:
   a. UTP
   b. Coax
   c. Fiber optic
   d. STP

5. A _____ organizes and protects the horizontal cabling in the equipment room.
   a. Rack
   b. Patch panel
   c. Outlet
   d. 110 jack

6. Which of the following would never be seen in an equipment rack?
   a. Patch Panel
   b. UPS or SPS
   c. PC
   d. All of the above can be seen in an equipment rack.

7. What are patch cables used for? (Choose all that apply.)
   a. To connect different equipment rooms.
   b. To connect the patch panel to the hub.
   c. They are used as crossover cables.
   d. To connect PCs to outlet boxes.

8. Which of the following network technologies use UTP cabling in a star topology?
   a. 10Base2
   b. Fiber optic
   c. 10BaseT
   d. 100BaseT

9. Jane needs to increase network throughput on a 10BaseT network that consists of 1 hub and 30 users. Which of the following hardware solutions would achieve this most inexpensively?
   a. Add a fiber backbone.
   b. Upgrade the network to 100BaseT.
   c. Replace the hub with a switch.
   d. Add a router.

10. What standard addresses cable pathways and installation areas involving multiple rooms, floors, and buildings?
    a. EIA/TIA 586
    b. EIA/TIA 587
    c. EIA/TIA 568
    d. EIA/TIA 569

Answers

1. **D.** Coax cable should not be used in structured cabling networks.

2. **B.** Plenum-rated cabling should be used in horizontal cabling.

3. **D.** CAT levels do not define the number of pairs, only the speed that the cables can handle.

4. **C.**   EIA/TIA specifies fiber optic cabling as the preferred interbuilding cabling.

5. **B.**   The patch panel organizes and protects the horizontal cabling in the equipment room.

6. **D.**   All of these devices can be found in equipment racks.

7. **B and D.**   Patch cables are used to connect the hub to the patch panel and the PCs to the outlet boxes.

8. **C and D.**   10BaseT and 100BaseT use UTP cabling in a star topology. 10Base2 is an older, dying technology that doesn't use UTP in a star. Fiber optic uses star topology, but not UTP (think about it).

9. **C.**   Upgrading to 100BaseT will work, but replacing the hub with a switch is much cheaper.

10. **D.**   EIA/TIA 569 addresses cable pathways and installation areas involving multiple rooms, floors, and buildings. The EIA/TIA 568 standard defines acceptable cable types, the organization of the cabling system, guidelines for installation of the cable, and proper testing methods. The other two choices were made up to confuse you!

Dealing with the Physical

In this chapter, you will

- Learn how to install physical networks
- Understand how to plan an installation
- Understand how to set up an equipment room
- Learn how to install cables
- Learn how to make physical connections
- Understand how to organize cables
- Learn how to test cables
- Learn physical cabling diagnostics and repair, and what tools to use

Physical network problems are some of the most common sources of network failures. On first sight, this sounds like a good thing—in theory we should be able to see a physical network problem, right? A broken cable ought to stand out like a sore thumb, correct? Well, yes and no. Many physical network problems are painfully obvious. An unplugged cable lying next to a NIC makes for an obvious and easy diagnosis and fix. But real structured cabling networks, full of patch panels, hubs, switches, and lots of wire neatly hidden and inaccessible behind the walls, can be much more difficult to troubleshoot. This chapter covers the tools and techniques used to install network cabling and diagnose network problems in an existing network. For the most part, the same tools we use to install a physical network are also used to diagnose it when it fails.

Keep in mind that the physical network is not the only source of network problems —all sorts of software issues can also come into play. Because of the complexity and unique nature of the physical part of a network, diagnosis and repair requires an entire set of tools and techniques. Later in the book, after spending some quality time with the many complex (but also really interesting and fun) software aspects of network troubleshooting, we'll revisit these physical network issues, at which point you will have a complete methodology you can use to fix most network problems. So, raise your right hand and say out loud, "I understand that the physical part of the network is only one source of problems, and I understand that to diagnose and repair networks I must combine the knowledge from this chapter with information I will learn later."

Let's dive into troubleshooting the physical part of a network. Personally, I like working with cables, hubs, patch panels, and all the other physical parts of a network. I like throwing on my old jeans, sneakers, and battered shirt and crawling around in ceiling spaces, behind PCs, and into closets to diagnose and fix networks. If at all possible, this chapter makes more sense if you have an installed network to inspect as you read. Part of the fun of working with networks is to appreciate the sometimes subtle, sometimes dramatic differences between various network installations. So, if you can, go throw on some old clothes (unless you don't mind a little dirt on your good pants) and join me as we deal with the physical network!

Historical/Conceptual

Installing Physical Networks

As you saw in the previous chapter, installation of serious structured cabling is a job best left to the professionals; however, as I also mentioned, you need to be an informed consumer. Personally, I think all good network admins should be comfortable with the actual process of network installation—not to start a new career in the magical world of cable installation, but because it gives you skills that will help you diagnose and repair network problems. With networks (as with any technology), knowing how to put one together is half the battle in understanding how to fix one when it breaks!

In this chapter, we'll be looking at a basic structured cabling system on a single floor in a single building. Installing multifloor or multibuilding (campus) structured cabling systems requires an intimate and detailed understanding of a myriad of standards and codes, as well as a solid knowledge of general construction techniques. Installing a simple structured cabling system provides more than enough knowledge for the average network tech or admin to handle most physical network problems, so we'll keep it simple.

Test Specific

Installing a structured cabling system involves three discrete steps: planning, pulling cable, and connecting. The planning step should be self-evident: not knowing how and where to place and connect the components of the network you wish to install can result in disaster in even the simplest network installations. Pulling cable requires cutting holes in walls, climbing up ladders and pulling out ceilings tiles, working with long strands of ungainly cable, and generally trying to stay organized in a messy, unpleasant, and even dangerous construction site. Connecting cables is the process of connecting the ends of all the cables in the proper locations. This job not only requires skill and special tools, but a good deal of patience as well!

Planning the Installation

In the previous chapter, we learned you can make a basic network using only a NIC, a hub, and a chunk of cabling to connect them. However, we also now know that a real structured network cabling system requires at the very least a series of fixed work areas and an equipment room where all the cables terminate. You need to know if the cables from the work areas can reach the equipment room—is the distance less than the 90-meter limit dictated by the EIA/TIA standard? How will you route the cable? What path (techs use the term *run*) should it take? Don't forget that just because it looks like a cable will reach, that doesn't mean it will! Ceilings and walls always include nasty hidden surprises like firewalls, and I don't mean Internet firewalls! I'm talking about big, thick, concrete walls designed into buildings that require a masonry drill or jackhammer to punch through. Yes, lots of problems await you in the design stage, so let's break this down.

Get a Floor Plan

First, you need a blueprint of the area. If you ever contract an installer and they don't start by asking for a floor plan, fire them immediately and get one who does! The floor plan is the key to proper planning; a good floor plan shows you the location of closets that could serve as equipment rooms, alerts you to any firewalls in your way, and gives you a good overall feel for the scope of the job ahead.

If you don't have a floor plan, which is often the case with homes or older buildings, you need to create your own. Go get a ladder and a flashlight—you'll need them to poke around in ceilings, closets, and crawlspaces as you map out the location of rooms, walls, and anything else of interest to the installation. Figure 10-1 shows a typical do-it-yourself floor plan, created with the popular Visio program.

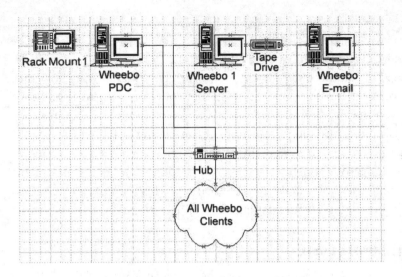

Figure 10-1 The do-it-yourself Wheebo floor plan

Map the Runs

Okay, now that you have your floor plan, it's time to map the cable runs. Here's where you run around the work areas spotting locations of existing systems in order to determine where to place each *cable drop*. A cable drop is the location where the cable comes out of the wall. You should also talk to users, management, and other interested parties to try and understand their plans for the future. It's much easier to install a few extra drops now than to do it a year from now when those two unused offices suddenly find themselves containing users who need networked computers *now*!

This is also the point where the evil word *cost* first raises its ugly head. Face it: Cables, drops, and the people who install them cost moulah. The typical price for a network installation is around $150 U.S. (per drop). Find out how much you want to spend and make some calls. Most network installers price their network jobs by quoting a per drop cost.

Inside or Outside the Walls?   While you're mapping your runs, you have to make another big decision: Do you want to run the cables in the walls or outside them? Many companies sell wonderful external raceway products that adhere to your walls, making for a much simpler, though less neat, installation than running cables in the walls (see Figure 10-2). Raceways make good sense in older buildings, or when you don't have the guts or the rights to go into the walls.

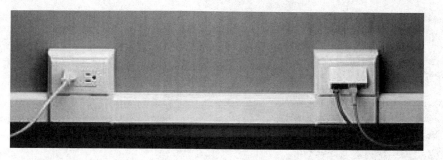

Figure 10-2 A typical raceway

Okay, I know I said you could run cables through a raceway, but let's face it, most of us prefer the nice pretty little outlets with the wires running in the walls. Once we finish mapping the runs, we'll see just what that takes.

The Equipment Room   While mapping the runs, you should decide on the location of your equipment room. When deciding on this location, keep five issues in mind: distance, power, dryness, coolness, and access.

- **Distance**   The equipment room must be located in a spot that won't prompt cable runs in excess of 90 meters. In most locations, keeping runs under 90 meters requires little effort as long as the equipment room is placed in a central location.

- **Power**   Many of the components in your equipment room need power. Make sure you provide enough. If possible, put the equipment room on its own dedicated circuit; that way when someone blows a circuit in the kitchen, it doesn't take out the entire network!

- **Dryness**   I imagine this one is obvious. Electrical components and water don't mix very well. Remind me to tell you about the time I installed a rack in an abandoned bathroom, and the toilet that later exploded. Remember that dryness also means low humidity. Avoid areas with the potential for high humidity, such as a closet near a pool or the room where the cleaning people leave mop buckets full of water. Of course, any well air-conditioned room should be fine—which leads to the next big issue . . .

- **Coolness**   Equipment rooms tend to get warm, especially if you add a couple of server systems and a UPS. Make sure your equipment room has an air-conditioning outlet or some other method of keeping the room cool. Figure 10-3 shows how I installed an air-conditioning duct in my small equipment closet. Of course, I only did this *after* I discovered the server was repeatedly rebooting due to overheating!

Figure 10-3   An A/C duct cooling an equipment closet

- **Access**   Access involves two different issues. First, it means preventing unauthorized access. Think about who you do and don't want messing around with your network, and act accordingly. In my small office, the equipment closet literally sits eight feet from me, so I don't concern myself too much with unauthorized access. You, on the other hand, may wish to consider placing a lock on the door of your equipment room if you're concerned that unscrupulous or thoughtless people might try to access it. Figure 10-4 shows what happened to my equipment room when I allowed access to it!

The second access consideration is making sure the people who need to get at your equipment to maintain and troubleshoot it can do so. Take a look at my equipment room in Figure 10-5. Here's a classic case of not providing good access. Note how difficult it would be for me to get to the back of the server—I literally need to pull the server out to check cables and NICs!

One other issue to keep in mind when choosing your equipment room is expandability. Will this equipment room be able to grow with your network? Is it close enough to be able to service any additional office space your company may acquire nearby? If your company decides to take over the next floor above, can you easily access another equipment room on that floor from this room? While the specific issues will be unique to each installation, keep thinking expansion as you design—your network *will* grow, whether or not you think so now!

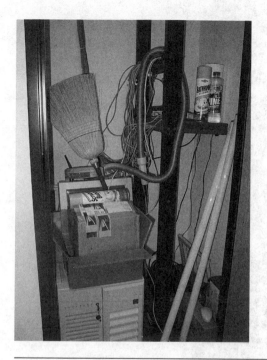

Figure 10-4 Equipment room with mops, brooms, and trash

Most equipment rooms require a true, 19-inch-wide equipment rack, but you do have other options. One option is a shorter rack like the wall-mounted one shown in Figure 10-6.

Serious equipment racks such as these must be mounted to the floor or the wall, usually with big concrete fasteners or other heavy-duty hardware. Installing a rack properly is a big job, and one I never do myself. A really small network can dispense with a rack altogether and use a simple wall-mounted patch panel like the one shown in Figure 10-7. Just be sure that there won't be any serious growth in your network before you try a cheap route like this!

So, you have mapped your cable runs and established your equipment room—now you're ready to start pulling cable!

Figure 10-5   A server wedged in back of a closet

Installing the Cable

Pulling cable is easily one of the most thankless and unpleasant jobs in the entire networking world. It may not look that hard from a distance, but the devil is in the details.
First of all, pulling cable requires two people if you want to get the job done quickly—
three is even better. Most pullers like to start from the equipment room and pull
towards the drops. The pullers draw cable from a reel—many using a handy reel spin-
dle to help the reel turn easily. In an office area with a drop ceiling, pullers will often
feed the cabling along the run by opening ceiling tiles and stringing the cable along the
top of the ceiling. Professional cable pullers have an arsenal of interesting tools to help
them move the cable horizontally, including telescoping poles, special nylon pull

Figure 10-6   A wall-mounted short rack

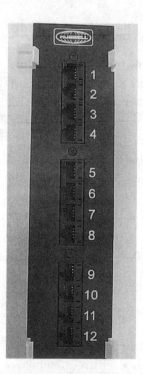

Figure 10-7   A wall-mounted patch panel

Figure 10-8　A tech pulling cable

strings, and even neato little crossbows and pistols that can fire the pull rope long distances! Figure 10-8 shows a tech pulling cable.

Professional installers no longer simply dump cabling onto the top of a drop ceiling. A previous lack of codes or standards for handling cables led to a nightmare of unorganized cables in drop ceilings all over the world. Any cable puller will tell you that the hardest part of installing cables is the need to work around all of the old cable installations in the ceiling! (See Figure 10-9.)

NEC stands for the National Electrical Code, specifications for electrical wiring and such put out by the National Fire Protection Association in the USA. Local codes, the EIA/TIA, and the NEC all have strict rules about how you pull cable in a ceiling. A good installer will use either hooks or trays, which provide better cable management, safety, and protection from ESD (see Figure 10-10). The faster the network, the more critical good cable management becomes. You probably won't have a problem dumping UTP on a drop ceiling if you just want a 10BaseT network, and you *might* even get away with this with 100BaseT—but forget about Gigabit; cable companies are going to make a mint over the next five to six years from all the bad Gigabit network cabling installations that need to be redone!

Running cable horizontally requires relatively little effort compared to running the cable down from the ceiling to a pretty faceplate at the work area, which often takes a lot of skill. In a typical office area with sheetrock walls, the installer first decides on the

Figure 10-9 A tech working in a messy ceiling

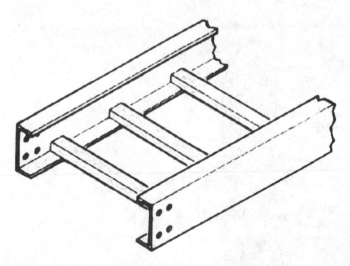

Figure 10-10 A cable tray

position for the outlet, usually using a stud finder to avoid cutting on top of a stud. Once the worker cuts the hole (see Figure 10-11), most installers drop a line to the hole using a weight tied to the end of a nylon pull rope (see Figure 10-12). They then can attach the network cable to the pull rope and pull it down to the hole. Once installers

Figure 10-11   Cutting a hole

Figure 10-12   Dropping a weight

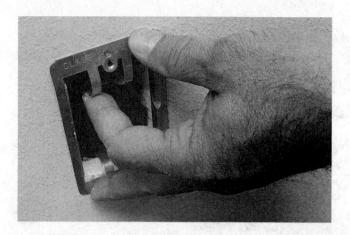

Figure 10-13   Installing a low-voltage mounting bracket

pull the cable through the new hole, they install an outlet box or low-voltage mounting bracket (see Figure 10-13). This bracket acts as a holder for the faceplate.

 NOTE: Keep in mind that the total cable length must not exceed 90 meters! Many do-it-yourself cable installers forget to factor in the vertical distance the cable covers as it runs down from the ceiling to the patch panel in the equipment room, and then down to the outlet in the work area.

Back in the equipment room, the many cables leading to each work area are consolidated and organized in preparation for the next stage: making connections. A truly professional installer takes great care in organizing the equipment closet. Figure 10-14 shows a typical installation using special cable guides to bring the cables down to the equipment rack.

Making Connections

As the name implies, making connections consists of connecting both ends of each cable to the proper jacks. However, this step also includes the most important action in the entire process: *testing* each cable run to ensure that every connection meets the requirements of the network that will use it. We also use this step to document and label each cable run—a critical step too often forgotten by inexperienced installers.

Figure 10-14 Cable guides help organize the equipment closet.

Connecting the Work Areas

Let's begin by watching an installer connect the cable runs. In the work area, that means the cable installer will now crimp a jack onto the end of the wire and mount the faceplate to complete the installation (see Figures 10-15 and 10-16).

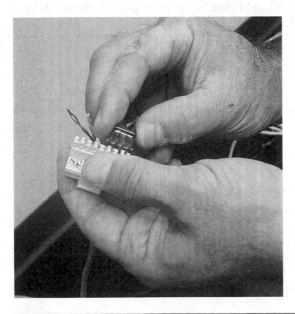

Figure 10-15 Attaching a jack to the wire

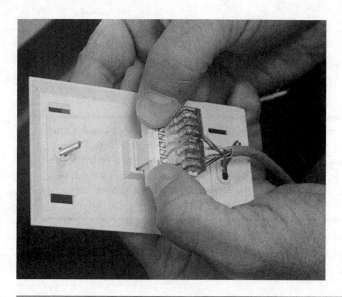

Figure 10-16   Fitting the jack into a faceplate

Note the back of the jack shown in Figure 10-15. This jack uses the very popular *110-punchdown* connection. Other jack makers may use different types, but the 110 is the most common. Most 110 connections have a color code that tells you which wire to punch into which connection on the back of the jack. We use a special 110-punchdown tool to make these connections (see Figure 10-17).

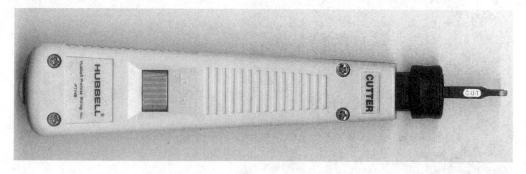

Figure 10-17   The 110-punchdown tool

Connecting the Patch Panels

In most small networks, like the single-floor network we're creating in this example, the other end of each cable run connects directly to the back of a patch panel. Most patch panels use 110 jacks, but some manufacturers use proprietary connectors.

NOTE: Those who know me also know that in almost all cases I despise the word proprietary, and run away from any such device or component. However, I have enjoyed a lot of success using proprietary connectors when stringing up networks. A big reason for this is that an installed structured network cabling system tends not to change much, other than to grow larger. So, if you go proprietary, make adding drops to your network easier by buying lots of extra jacks.

Connecting the cables to patch panels requires you to deal with two issues. The first is patch cable management. Figure 10-18 shows the front of a small network's equip-

Figure 10-18 Bad cable management

ment rack—note the complete lack of cable management! This one is so messy, I challenge you to find the patch panels and the hubs. (Hint: The hubs are in the center of the picture.) Managing patch cables means using the proper cable management hardware. Plastic D-rings guide the patch cables neatly along the sides and front of the patch panel. Finger boxes are rectangular cylinders with slots in the front—the patch cables run into the open ends of the box and individual cables are threaded through the *fingers* on their way to the patch panel, keeping them neatly organized. Creativity and variety abound in the world of cable management hardware—there are as many different solutions to cable management as there are ways to screw up organizing them. Figure 10-19 shows a rack using good cable management—these patch cables are well-secured using cable management hardware, making them much less susceptible to damage from mishandling. Plus, it looks much nicer!

Figure 10-19   Good cable management

The second issue to consider when connecting cables is the overall organization of the patch panel as it relates to the organization of your network. Simply punching cables into a patch panel without rhyme or reason is a recipe for disaster. No exaggeration. Organize your patch panel so that it mirrors the layout of your network. You can organize according to the physical layout, so the different parts of the patch panel correspond to different parts of your office space, for example the north and south sides of the hallway. Another popular way to organize patch panels is to make sure they match the logical layout of the network, so the different user groups or company organizations have their own sections of the patch panel.

Labeling the Cable

After you organize, you must label and document your cable installation if you want to prevent a thousand different network repair nightmares. Professional cabling companies will label and document your network in amazing detail. In fact, some installations document every connector. We don't need to have a master class in network documentation here, however—we'll just go over some of the more critical aspects of organization and labeling.

NOTE: The EIA/TIA 606 standard defines a very detailed methodology for labeling structured networks. It is quite complex, however, and many network installers avoid it unless the customer requests it or codes demand it.

After you have decided on the organizational scheme that best reflects your network, your next task is to design a labeling scheme—for example, you could have all of the connections on the north side of the building start with the letter N followed by a three-digit number starting with 001. After you have a labeling scheme—this part is critical! —you must *use* it! When you make a network connection, label the outlet at the work area and the jack on the patch panel with the same number. Figure 10-20 shows a typical equipment rack with a number of patch panels—a common setup for a small network. In this case, both the color of the patch cables and their placement on the panels tell you where they belong in the network.

You must label, but you don't have to organize to this degree. In fact, many network installers choose *not* to, because they feel it wastes ports on the patch panel. What happens if one side of the network grows beyond the number of assigned ports while the other side gets smaller? My answer: Get another patch panel. Other techs prefer to fill up the existing patch panels, even if it muddies their organizational scheme. This is a

Figure 10-20 Well-organized patch panels

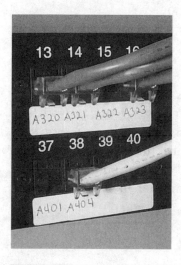

Figure 10-21 Labels on a patch panel

matter of personal choice, of course. Whatever the labeling scheme, only one thing really matters. The most important part of labeling is that *both ends of the same cable say the same thing*. Figure 10-21 shows some labels on a typical patch panel.

Take a look at the wall outlet in Figure 10-22. Note that the label on the outlet corresponds to the label on the patch panel in Figure 10-21. Failure to include this one simple step creates more problems than you can imagine. All good network installers *always* label the runs in this manner, not to mention a lot of other labeling that users do not see, such as labeling on the cable inside the wall. Proper labeling can save you from many potential disasters. Here's a classic example: John wants to install a second

Figure 10-22   Label on an outlet

networked system in the unused office next door. He sees that the unused office has a network outlet, but he wants to make sure the wall outlet connects to the network hub. His problem: he can't determine which port on the patch panel he needs to use. Sure, he could guess, or use a special tool called a toner (we'll get to that next), but think how much faster it would be if all he had to do was read the label on the outlet and find the corresponding label on the patch panel! Make your life simpler than John's—label your patch panels and outlets.

Testing the Cable Runs

Well, in theory, your cabling system is now installed and ready for a hub and some systems. But before you do this, you must test each cable run. Someone new to testing cable might think that all you need to do is verify that each jack has been properly connected. Sure, that's an important and necessary step, but the really interesting problem comes after that: verifying that your cable run can handle the *speed* of your network.

Before we go further, let me be clear: a typical network admin/tech cannot properly test a new cable run. The EIA/TIA provides a series of incredibly complex and important standards for testing cable. Unless you want to get into a 75-page discussion of things like near-end crosstalk and the attenuation-to-crosstalk ratio, this is an area where employing a professional cable installer makes sense. Just the testing equipment alone totally surpasses the cost of most smaller network installations! Advanced network testing tools easily cost over $5000, some well over $10,000! But never fear, there are a number of lower-end tools that work just fine for basic network testing. Let's look at some of them.

The best tool to start with is the cable tester. Can you guess what it does? (I hope so!) Before we talk about cable testers, however, we should answer a key question: what makes a cable *bad*? Clearly, if Gidget the rat chews a piece of UTP in half, that cable should be considered bad. Any time a cable is cut—through *any* of the wires—you have a cable break. But other things can make a cable bad. Suppose someone punched down a cable improperly, so that the individual colored wire pairs weren't in the correct order? Bad cable. What if a perfectly good cable is strung too close to an electric motor, which interferes with its ability to move data correctly? Bad cable. What if the distance between the hub and the PC is too great? Yup, this too will make a cable *bad*.

Now that we've defined the problem, let's talk tools. Cable testers perform a wide variety of functions. Most network admin types staring at a potentially bad cable want to know the following:

- How long is this cable?
- Are any of the wires broken?
- If there is a break, where is it?
- Are any of the wires shorted together?
- Are any of the wires not in proper order (in other words, are there split or crossed pairs)?
- Is there electrical or radio interference?

Various models of cable testers are designed to answer some or all of these questions, depending on the amount of money you are willing to pay. At the low end of the cable tester market are devices that only test for broken wires. A wire that can conduct electricity is said to have *continuity*; thus a broken wire lacks continuity. These cheap (under $100) testers are often called *continuity testers* (see Figure 10-23). Some cheaper cable testers will also test for split or crossed pairs and for shorts. These cheap testers usually require you to insert both ends of the cable into the tester. Of course, this can be a bit of a problem if the cable is already installed in the wall!

Medium price ($\cong$ $400) testers have the additional ability to determine the *length* of a cable, and can tell you *where* a break is located. This type of cable tester (see Figure 10-24) is generically called a *Time Domain Reflectometer* (*TDR*). The medium-priced testers will have a small loopback device that gets inserted into the far end of the cable, enabling them to work with installed cables. These are the types of testers you want to have around.

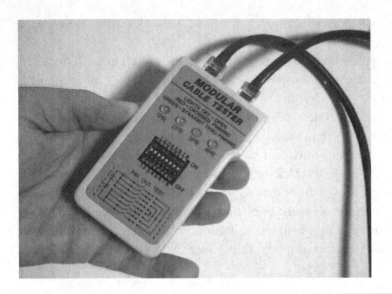

Figure 10-23 A simple cable tester

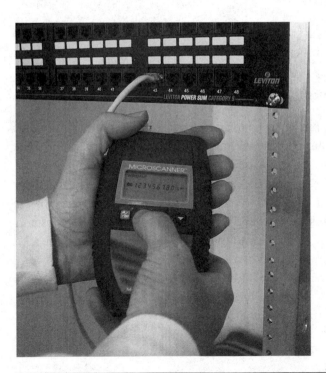

Figure 10-24 A typical medium-priced TDR—a Microtest Microscanner

Figure 10-25   A typical professional tester—a Microtest OMNIScanner

If you want a device that can test the electrical characteristics of a cable, the price shoots up fast. These professional devices test critical EIA/TIA electrical characteristics, and are used by professional installers to verify installations. Some have powerful added features, such as the ability to plug into a network and literally draw a schematic of the entire network for you, including neat information like the MAC addresses of the systems, IP or IPX addresses, and more. These super cable testers might be better described as *protocol analyzers*. (We'll discuss protocol analyzers later in Chapter 11.) Figure 10-25 shows an example of this type, Microtest's *OMNIScanner*. These advanced testers are more than most network techs need. Unless you have some very deep pockets or find yourself doing very serious cable testing, stick to the medium-priced testers.

Diagnostics and Repair of Physical Cabling

When do you need to pull out a cable tester? The first thing to know is that good quality, professionally-installed cable rarely goes bad—unless you have a serious Gidget problem! Always assume software problems first. A key clue that you may indeed have a bad cable is when a user tells you, "I can't see the network!" The user will get an error that tells him, "No server is found," or when he goes into Network Neighborhood he won't see any systems besides his own. Start by double-checking his NIC driver to make sure it hasn't magically decided to die, then run the NIC's internal diagnostic and hardware loopback, if possible. If the NIC checks out, you may have a cable problem.

The next step is to check the *link lights* on the NIC and hub. If they're not lit, you know the cable isn't connected somewhere. Try connecting another patch cable to the outlet. Still no good? Check to make sure other people can access the network, and that other systems can access the shared resource (server) that the problem system can't see. Try the problem user's logon name and password (if possible) on other systems to make sure that account can access the shared resource. Make a quick visual inspection of the cable running from the back of the PC to the outlet. Finally, if you can, plug the system into a different outlet and see if it works. If none of these steps identify the problem, you should begin to suspect the structured cable. Assuming the cable was installed properly and had been working correctly before this event, a simple continuity test will confirm your suspicion in most cases.

Be warned that a bad NIC can also generate this "can't see the network" problem. Worse yet, if the NIC is to blame, there's usually a failure of the port on the NIC, making the NIC's diagnostics useless. Because this is a known issue, most NIC diagnostic programs include a "test the network" diagnostic that makes the NIC send or receive packets. Usually this test requires that you have an identical NIC in another system running the same diagnostic, but sometimes you can insert a hardware loopback plug into the NIC to perform the test.

Ah, if only broken cables were the worst problem! The rarity of this situation, combined with the relative ease of cable diagnostics, makes bad cables both an uncommon and an easily-fixed problem. But another problem, far more common than broken cables, appears in every network installation: tracking cable.

Toners

It would be nice to say that all cable installations are perfect, and that over the years, they won't grow into horrific piles of spaghetti-like, unlabeled cables. But in the real world, you will eventually find yourself having to locate (*trace* is the term installers use) cables. Even in the best-planned networks, labels fall off ports and outlets, mystery cables appear behind walls, new cable runs are added, and mistakes are made counting rows and columns on patch panels. Sooner or later, most network techs will have to be able to pick out one particular cable or port from a stack.

When the time comes to trace cables, all network techs turn to a device called a *toner* for help. Toner is the generic term for two separate devices that are used together: a *tone generator* and a *tone probe*. The tone generator connects to the cable using alligator clips, tiny hooks, or a network jack, and sends an electrical signal along the wire at a certain frequency. The tone probe emits a sound when it is placed near a cable connected to the tone generator (see Figure 10-26). These two devices are often referred to by the brand name *Fox and Hound*, a popular model of toner made by the Triplett Corporation.

To trace a cable, connect the tone generator to the known end of the cable in question, then position the tone probe next to the other end of all of the cables that might be the right one. The tone probe will make a sound when it is next to the right cable. More advanced toners include phone jacks, enabling the person manipulating the tone generator to communicate with the person manipulating the tone probe: "Jim, move the tone generator to the next port!" Some toners have one tone probe that works with multiple tone generators. Each generator emits a separate frequency, and the probe sounds a different tone for each one. Even good toners are relatively inexpensive ($\cong$ \$75), so although cheapo toners can cost less than \$25, they don't tend to work very well. Just keep in mind that if you have to support a network, you'd do best to own a decent toner.

A good, medium-priced cable tester and a good toner are the most important tools used by folks who must support, but not install, networks. A final tip: Be sure to bring along a few extra batteries—there's nothing worse than sitting on the top of a ladder holding a cable tester or toner that has just run out of juice!

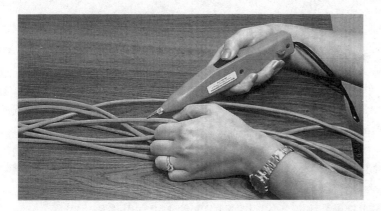

Figure 10-26   A tone probe at work

Chapter Review

Questions

1. Which of the following are factors to consider when deciding on the location of your equipment room? (Choose all that apply.)
   a. Distance
   b. Power
   c. Cool temperature
   d. Comfort

2. In the networking context, a wire that can conduct electricity is said to have:
   a. Impedance
   b. Resistance
   c. Capacitance
   d. Continuity

3. What organizational bodies provide strict standards for pulling cables? (Choose all that apply.)
   a. AMA
   b. EIA/TIA
   c. NEC
   d. ESD

4. What do most installers use to drop a line?
   a. Tape
   b. Paper clip
   c. A stud
   d. A weight tied to the end of a nylon pull rope

5. What is the industry term for the location in the work area where the cable comes out of the wall?
   a. The cable hole
   b. The cable run
   c. The cable drop
   d. The cable port

6. What type of device acts as a holder for the faceplate of an outlet?
   a. A low-voltage mounting bracket
   b. A low-impedance mounting bracket

c. A high-voltage mounting bracket

d. A high-impedance mounting bracket

7. Toner is a generic term for which two separate devices that are used together?

   a. Tone signaler/line probe

   b. Tone generator/tone probe

   c. Signal generator/signal receiver

   d. Line conditioner/tone probe

8. What do 110 connections use as a guide regarding which wire goes into which connection on the back of the jack?

   a. The wires are numbered.

   b. There is no certain order for the wires.

   c. The connections are color-coded.

   d. There is nothing to help you. You must memorize the chart.

9. What EIA/TIA standard defines a very detailed methodology for labeling structured networks?

   a. 606

   b. 706

   c. 506

   d. 306

10. What type of cable tester is used to determine the length of a cable?

    a. A Time Domain Reflectometer (TDR)

    b. A continuity tester

    c. A tone probe

    d. A toner generator

Answers

1. **A, B, and C.**   Distance, power, and a cool temperature are factors that need to be considered when determining the location of the equipment room.

2. **D.**   A wire that can conduct electricity is said to have continuity. An electrician will tell you that all wires that can conduct electricity also have the other three characteristics, but for purposes of the Network+ exam, remember continuity.

3. **B and C.**   EIA/TIA and NEC provide strict standards for pulling cables. ESD stands for electro-static discharge. AMA most commonly stands for the American Medical Association.

4. **D.** Once the worker cuts the hole, most installers use a weight tied to the nylon pull rope to drop a line in the hole.

5. **C.** Cable drop is the industry term for the location in the work area where the cable comes out of the wall.

6. **A.** Once the installer pulls the cable through the new hole, they then place a low-voltage mounting bracket or an outlet box to act as a holder for the faceplate.

7. **B.** Toner is a generic term for two separate devices that are used together—a *tone generator* and a *tone probe*.

8. **C.** 110 connections use a color code as a guide to which wire goes into which connection on the back of the jack.

9. **A.** The EIA/TIA 606 standard defines a very detailed methodology for labeling structured networks.

10. **A.** A TDR is used to determine the length of a cable. Tone probes and tone generators are used to test the continuity of cable.

Protocols

In this chapter, you will

- Understand the concept of protocols
- Learn about the NetBEUI protocol suite
- Learn about the IPX/SPX protocol suite
- Learn about the TCP/IP protocol suite

Every network needs some common method for transferring data. We saw in Chapter 3 that each different network technology uses a different frame type to send data to its systems, but the OSI seven-layer model claims that networks need more than just an Ethernet or Token Ring frame. Networks need packets within those frames to perform other key networking tasks, like controlling the movement of data across routers, and defining non-hardware-dependent naming conventions. Typically, network protocols span the Network and the Transport layers of the OSI seven-layer model, but there is no law of physics or networking standard that requires them to span *only* those two layers. In fact, the term network protocol is a bit deceiving, because it implies that only one protocol exists. In reality, many protocols work together to handle the various jobs associated with the Network, Transport, and possibly other OSI layers, so I'm going to use the term *network protocol suites*.

 NOTE: I'd like to apologize on behalf of the entire networking industry for their horrific use of the term protocol. Webster's defines protocol in the context of computer science as, "A standard procedure for regulating data transmission between computers." You know from the OSI seven-layer model that a network uses many different protocols and procedures to get data from one system to another in the proper format. Try to be patient with the networking uses of the word protocol, because the flexibility of the term can cause a great deal of confusion. When a network tech, book, or FAQ uses the word protocol, take the time to be sure you understand what type of protocol they mean!

Historical/Conceptual

IPX/SPX and TCP/IP are two of the most common network protocol suites used today. Notice that each of these names contains a slash, for a darned good reason. Both of these protocols are actually *groups* of protocols. The TCP/IP label, for example, stands for the Transmission Control Protocol (TCP) and the Internet Protocol (IP). But the TCP/IP suite also includes dozens of other protocols, such as the ubiquitous File Transfer Protocol (FTP), and the Internet Control Message Protocol (ICMP), among others.

Each of the major protocol suites provides a different mix of efficiency, flexibility, and *scalability*, which means the capability to support network growth. NetBEUI works best for small networks without routers; IPX/SPX provides support for integrating with Novell NetWare; and TCP/IP provides a complex, robust, open solution for larger networks. The rest of this chapter dedicates itself to inspecting these and a few other network protocols in order to help you understand which one to use, how to install them in Windows client PCs, how to configure them, and how to deal with network protocol suites when they fail. This is a big job, which we will break down by protocol, but first we need to cover a few critical points about network protocol suites in general.

 NOTE: Some techs make a distinction between the term protocol suite, a set of protocols used together, and a protocol stack, the actual software that implements the suite on a particular operating system. Example: "Windows NT and Windows 98 both use the NetBEUI protocol suite, but they use different NetBEUI stacks." In many contexts, however, writers ignore the distinction and use the terms interchangeably.

Test Specific

You must install a network protocol in each system of your network. Every NOS requires a network protocol. Not too long ago, adding a network protocol involved a sequence of painful steps, but today every operating system installs at least one protocol automatically. Invariably, the system's default choice of protocols is the venerable TCP/IP. This may or may not be an optimal choice for your network, and it may require you to do some configuration, but given the overwhelming presence of TCP/IP in the networking world, it's a sensible choice in most cases.

Every networked system that wants to communicate must use the network's common protocol. Most of the time, every system on the network will use the same proto-

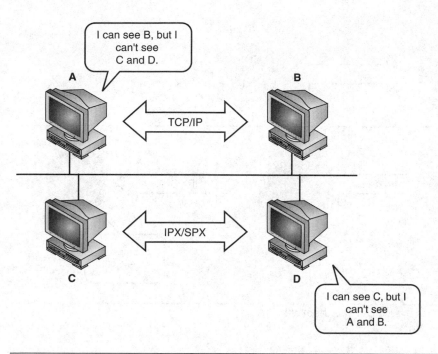

Figure 11-1   Systems A and B use TCP/IP, while systems C and D use IPX/SPX.

col, but situations do exist where some systems are set up on purpose to run a different protocol from others. Figure 11-1 shows networked systems running Windows 98. Systems A and B use TCP/IP, while systems C and D use IPX/SPX. Systems A and B can see each other, but not systems C and D; systems C and D can see each other but not systems A and B. Why would anyone break their network like this on purpose? Simple: security. By using different protocols, a network admin can guarantee that two sets of systems on the same network cannot access each other, unless of course someone adds the other protocol. Which brings us to the next point.

You may have more than one network protocol on the same system. Let's add another system, System E, to the previous diagram. System E has both the IPX/SPX and the TCP/IP network protocols installed. As a result, System E can see every system on the network! (See Figure 11-2.)

Hey! If System E sees both networks, can we fix System E so it acts as a kind of translator between the two sets of systems? Well, yes you can—but hold onto that concept for just a moment as we discuss one more very important concept: *binding*.

Choices are great, but they do complicate matters. In the case of network protocols and adaptor cards, when the rubber hits the proverbial network road, there needs to be

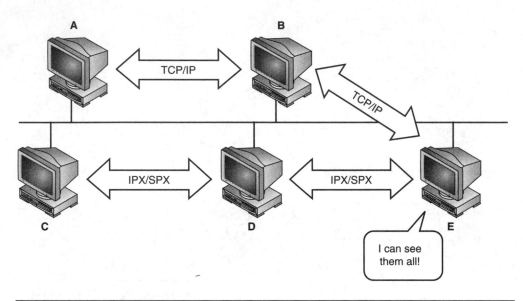

Figure 11-2   System E can see them all!

a way to decide which cards use which protocols for which transactions. The solution to this challenge is called *binding*. Every protocol installed on a system must be *bound* to one or more NICs, and every NIC to one or more specific protocols. Look at Figure 11-2 and think about System E for a moment. You can assume, correctly, that both the IPX/SPX and TCP/IP protocols were bound to System E's NIC. Now look at the situation shown in Figure 11-3. This situation calls for binding IPX/SPX to one NIC, and TCP/IP to the other. Fortunately, Windows makes this binding process extremely easy. We'll save the actual process of binding for later. For now, just remember that at least one protocol must be bound to each NIC in a networked system.

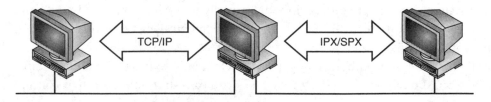

Figure 11-3   IPX/SPX is bound to one NIC, while TCP/IP is bound to the other.

EXAM TIP: At least one network protocol must be bound to each NIC in a networked system.

Before adding a new system to a network, you should check one of the existing systems to determine which network protocol the network uses. Not all network protocols are network-specific. Almost all modern networks use TCP/IP, but it's not 100 percent, and older network operating systems tend to use other protocols. Older versions of Novell NetWare, for example, may use IPX/SPX, while a network containing only Windows 9x systems may use the NetBEUI protocol.

The last general point to make about protocols concerns how they associate with networking hardware. Years ago—many years ago, actually—certain protocols only worked with certain network hardware, but these days, any protocol pretty much works with any network hardware. TCP/IP, for example, runs on Token Ring, Ethernet—even the ancient LocalTalk!

Super! Now that you know some network protocol basics, let's look at each protocol in detail, starting with Microsoft's famous NetBEUI.

NetBEUI

NetBEUI provides a fast, simple set of network protocols appropriate for use in smaller LANs. NetBEUI primarily exists to support Microsoft networking using Windows NT or Windows 9x systems. Although Windows 2000 and XP still support NetBEUI, we rarely see 2000 or XP systems running it. (See Chapter 13 for more on Network Operating Systems.) NetBEUI's speed and ease of use make it a good choice for small networks, but because NetBEUI does not support routing, it is totally unacceptable for any but the smallest networks. Like IPX/SPX and TCP/IP, the NetBEUI protocol suite contains two main protocols—in this case, *NetBIOS* and *NetBEUI*—which operate at the Session layer and the Transport layer, respectively (see Figure 11-4).

NOTE: Be aware that the term NetBEUI can refer either to the NetBEUI protocol suite, or to the NetBEUI Transport layer protocol.

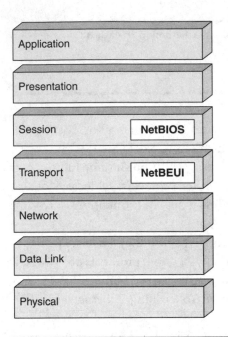

Figure 11-4 NetBIOS operates at the Session layer, while NetBEUI operates at the Transport layer.

One big benefit of NetBEUI, and a big reason this protocol remains popular, is that it requires no real configuration. Once you install the NetBEUI protocol, it pretty much just works. You'll appreciate this more when you see how much configuration TCP/IP takes! Let's look at the two parts of NetBEUI—first NetBIOS, and then NetBEUI—to see how it all works

NetBIOS

NetBIOS handles the Session layer functions for NetBEUI networks. A server often communicates with several machines simultaneously, and must employ some system to track each of the conversations in which it participates. Because of its role in Microsoft networking, NetBIOS often handles the Session layer in other protocol suites as well, as we'll see in the discussion of IPX/SPX and TCP/IP that follows.

NetBIOS manages connections based on the names of the computers involved. Machines using the NetBIOS Session layer protocol adopt a unique *NetBIOS name* for each function that they perform. Each NetBIOS name identifies one specific system performing one specific function. A NetBIOS name is based on a system's *network name*, which you can designate using the Network applet in the Control Panel. Figure 11-5

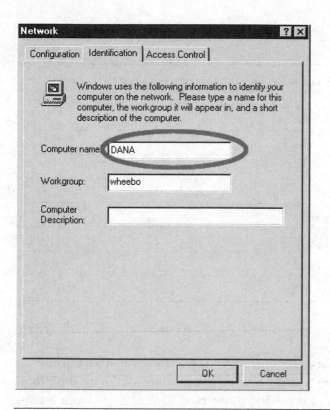

Figure 11-5 The Windows 98 Network Control Panel applet displays the computer's name.

shows an example of the network name of a Windows 98 system, displayed by the Network applet.

NetBIOS names are made up of a system's network name, as specified in the Network applet, followed by a function-specific suffix. The system's network name can contain up to 15 characters. Each character is represented by a single 8-bit (one byte) ASCII code. For example, the 8-bit ASCII code 01100101 (65h in hexadecimal format), represents the capital letter *A*. NetBIOS limits the network name to 15 bytes, or characters, because it reserves the 16th byte for the special suffix code that defines the *role* the machine will play on the network in that particular instance.

The two most common roles played by computers on a network are client and server. A *client* is a machine that can access resources being shared by other computers on a network. A *server* is a machine that can share its resources with other machines on a network. Table 11-1 lists the common 16th byte codes used to define the server and client functions of a machine.

Table 11-1 NetBIOS Names and Functions

16th Byte	Function
<00>	Workstation Service Name. The name registered by *clients* on the network.
<03>	Messenger Service Name. Used by applications such as WINPOPUP and NET SEND to deliver messages.
<1B>	Domain Master Browser
<06>	RAS Server
<1F>	NetDDE Service
<20>	File and Print Server
<21>	RAS Client
<BE>	Network Monitor Agent
<BF>	Network Monitor Utility

Do not worry about memorizing all of the functions and 16th byte codes listed in the table—they will not appear on the Network+ exam. Instead, let's look at the three most commonly used extensions to understand how NetBIOS manages connections between machines.

Hannah, a friendly neighborhood network tech, installs three Windows 98 systems on her network, named WHEEBO, JANELLE, and DANA. Hannah configures the WHEEBO and JANELLE systems to act as both clients and servers, and configures DANA as a client only. According to what we've just learned, WHEEBO has at least two names: WHEEBO<00>, identifying WHEEBO as a client, and WHEEBO<20>, identifying WHEEBO as a file and print server. JANELLE also has two names: JANELLE<00>, identifying JANELLE as a client, and JANELLE <20>, identifying JANELLE as a file and print server. DANA, by contrast, registers only one name, as a client: DANA<00>.

NOTE: Any real machine using NetBIOS on a Microsoft Network will actually register several more names, to support other, less obvious functions. Those additional names have been left out of this discussion for the sake of simplicity.

Hannah does not need to specify these NetBIOS names. She just installs the server or client software, and specifies a network name for each system. A NetBIOS program operating in the background determines the NetBIOS names automatically based on the network names (WHEEBO, JANELLE, and DANA) that Hannah selected for these systems. To specify a network name for the computer, select the **Identification** tab and type the name. You can also specify the Workgroup name here; it must be the same for each system on the network (see Figure 11-5 earlier).

To add the NetBEUI protocol to a Windows 98 system, click Add on the Configuration tab of the Network applet (see Figure 11-6). A *Select Network Component Type* screen appears. Select Protocol and click Add (see Figure 11-7). A *Select Network Protocol* screen appears. Select Microsoft as the Manufacturer and NetBEUI as the Network Protocol (see Figure 11-8). Now WHEEBO is ready to rock and roll!

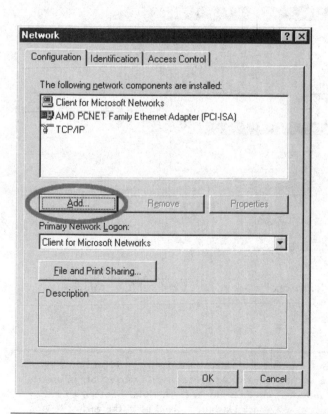

Figure II-6   The Configuration tab of Windows 98's Network applet

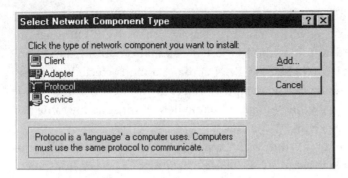

Figure 11-7   The Network Component Type window: select Protocol

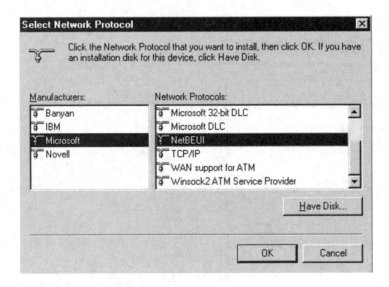

Figure 11-8   The Select Network Protocol window: select Microsoft, NetBEUI

NOTE: The tradition in the industry of referring to entire protocol suites by the name of one or two of their constituent protocols has caused lots of unnecessary confusion, pain, suffering, and gnashing of teeth. Unfortunately, it's not possible to set Mr. Peabody's Way-Back Machine to land us in the early 1980s, so we could force the networking industry to adopt clearer terminology. The moral of the story: Read carefully whenever you see the word protocol—sometimes a writer means a specific protocol, but sometimes he or she means a protocol suite.

To set up WHEEBO and JANELLE as both clients and servers, Hannah installs three protocols: Client for Microsoft Networks, File and Print Sharing for Microsoft Networks, and NetBEUI (see Figure 11-9). Windows 98 calls its server component *File and Print Sharing for Microsoft Networks*. To configure DANA as a client only, Hannah installs NetBIOS and the Client for Microsoft Networks. Hannah has created a three-node network, and she and her coworkers can sit down to do some serious gaming, *errr* . . . work.

When Hannah sits at JANELLE and accesses a file on WHEEBO, both JANELLE and WHEEBO must manage that connection. To open the connection, JANELLE the client, a.k.a. JANELLE<00>, opens up a connection with WHEEBO the server, a.k.a. WHEEBO<20> (see Figure 11-10). As WHEEBO begins to send the requested file to JANELLE, another user, Barbara, sits down at DANA and opens another file on WHEEBO (see Figure 11-11). Each of the computers keeps track of these simultaneous conversations using their NetBIOS names (see Figure 11-12).

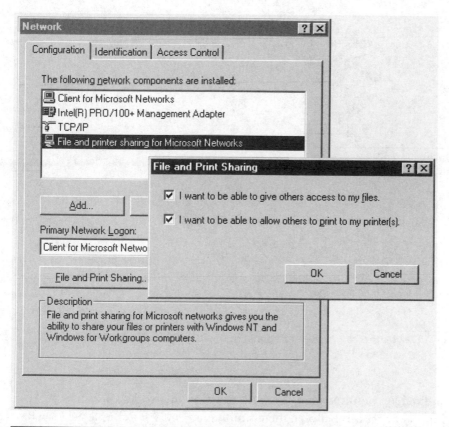

Figure 11-9   Installing File and Print Sharing for Microsoft Networks

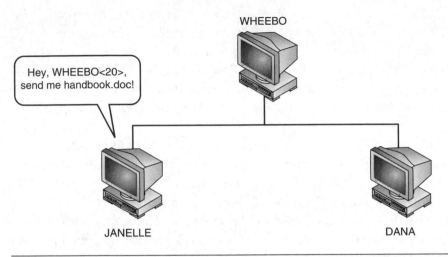

Figure 11-10   JANELLE the client opens a connection with WHEEBO the server.

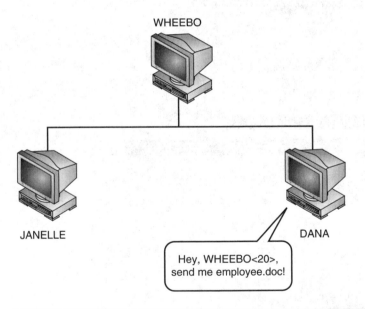

Figure 11-11   DANA the client opens a connection with WHEEBO the server.

By using a different NetBIOS name for each function, networked systems can keep track of multiple connections between them simultaneously. For example, let's say Barbara sits at WHEEBO and opens a file on JANELLE, causing WHEEBO<00> to establish a connection with JANELLE<20>. At the same time, Hannah can sit at JANELLE

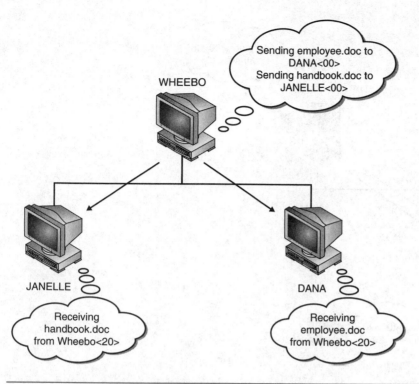

Figure 11-12 WHEEBO, JANELLE, and DANA use NetBIOS names to manage their connections.

and open a file on WHEEBO, causing JANELLE<00> to establish a connection with WHEEBO<20>. The ability to use unique NetBIOS names for each server (<20> suffix) and client (<00> suffix) function enables WHEEBO and JANELLE to hold two (or more) simultaneous conversations (see Figure 11-13).

Without a NetBIOS name for a particular function, a system cannot perform that function when requested by another node on the network. For example, if Hannah sits at JANELLE and attempts to open a file on DANA, JANELLE will not be able to establish the connection. Why? Because DANA is not configured to function as a server. The request from JANELLE for a connection to DANA is addressed to DANA<20>. But the NetBIOS name DANA<20> does not exist; DANA can respond only to the client NetBIOS name DANA<00> (see Figure 11-14). When it sees the message for DANA<20>, DANA just assumes it's for some other system and ignores it; DANA doesn't even send a refusal message back to JANELLE.

While NetBIOS provides an adequate means for managing connections on a small network, it does not scale well for larger networks. NetBIOS uses what is called a *flat name space*, meaning that the names for every machine in a network are drawn from

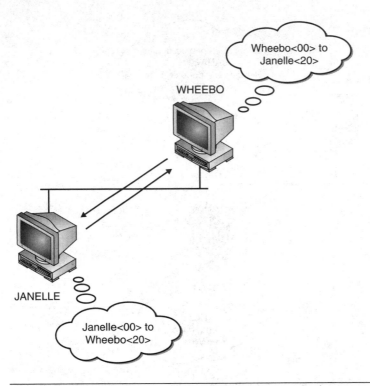

Figure 11-13   JANELLE and WHEEBO can have multiple conversations simultaneously.

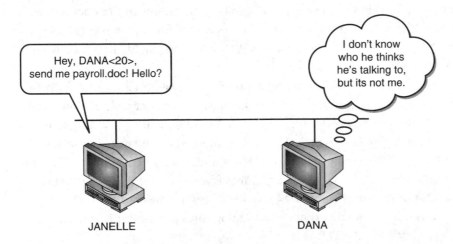

Figure 11-14   DANA ignores JANELLE because DANA<20> is not one of its NetBIOS names.

one pool. Thus the base NetBIOS name for each computer must be unique. Imagine a world without last names. No two people could have the name Mike, or Bob, or Johnny. Instead, people would have to come up with unique names like Johnny5, Fonzie, and Bluto. Finding unique names for a dozen people presents no problem. Placing a few thousand people in the same flat name space creates a big problem. In real life, most people have at least two, and sometimes as many as four or more names, and even then we often need other information, like addresses and identifying numbers, to tell people apart. The designers of NetBIOS created a world where all systems must operate on a first-name basis.

Network administrators working in a first-name-only NetBIOS world are often driven to give their systems bizarre, non-descriptive names, creating many administrative headaches. NetBIOS names are so restricted it's hard to be usefully descriptive. On a network with only one server, simply calling that machine SERVER works fine. But let's take a more realistic example: Simon's network has 20 servers: ten accounting servers, five web servers, four file servers, and an e-mail server. Simon usually refers to one of his servers as "'Accounting Server 7"' in conversation, but he can't use that as the NetBIOS name for the machine. Remember, NetBIOS names must contain 15 or fewer characters (not counting the special 16th character that designates the machine's function). Instead of Accounting Server 7, Simon must name the server ACCOUNTSERV7. Not bad, but not optimal, and Simon's network is a relatively modest one by commercial standards. The problem of ensuring name uniqueness is much more extreme in large WAN environments run by multiple administrators. In a large WAN run by 40 different administrators, guaranteeing that no two administrators ever assign the same name to any two of their 5000+ machines becomes an administrative nightmare requiring extensive planning and ongoing communication. This is why network architects prefer a more scaleable naming scheme, such as the TCP/IP protocol suite's Domain Name Service (DNS), for larger networks.

Within the NetBEUI protocol suite, NetBIOS handles the Session layer function of managing connections. Its reliance on a flat name space makes it difficult to use in large WAN environments, but its simplicity makes it an ideal choice for smaller LANs. As long as the network tech assigns every computer a unique name, NetBIOS does a fine job. Once NetBIOS establishes a connection, it passes the packet down to the NetBEUI protocol, which operates at the Transport layer.

NetBEUI

NetBEUI functions at the Transport layer within the NetBEUI protocol suite, breaking larger chunks of data into smaller pieces on the sending machine, and reassembling them on the receiving end (see Figure 11-15). The NetBEUI protocol requires no setup

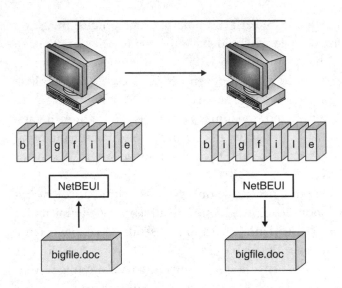

Figure 11-15 NetBEUI breaks the file into smaller pieces for transmission and reassembles the pieces on the receiving end.

beyond installation by the network tech. While its operational simplicity makes NetBEUI attractive for smaller networks, it deprives NetBEUI of a capability vital to larger networks: routing.

The NetBEUI protocol skips the Network layer and communicates directly with the Data Link layer. As discussed in Chapter 3, routing occurs at the Network layer. Network layer protocols add additional addressing information to each data packet. This extra Network layer address tells a router how to find the destination network. By skipping the Network layer, NetBEUI deprives itself of routing capability. When a router receives a NetBEUI packet, it doesn't find the routing information it needs, so it simply discards the packet (Figure 11-16). NetBEUI can work with bridges, however, which operate at the Data Link layer, and can filter and forward NetBEUI packets using the MAC addresses contained in the data packets (see Figure 11-17).

In the early 1980s, network architects frequently used NetBEUI because of its simplicity. As the typical network grew and came to include routers, NetBEUI (both the individual Transport layer protocol and the protocol suite) became an increasingly less common choice, supplanted by more scaleable protocol suites such as IPX/SPX and TCP/IP.

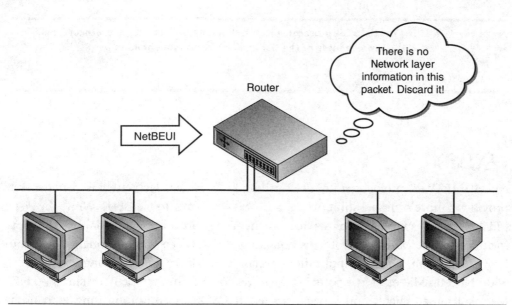

Figure 11-16   Routers discard NetBEUI packets.

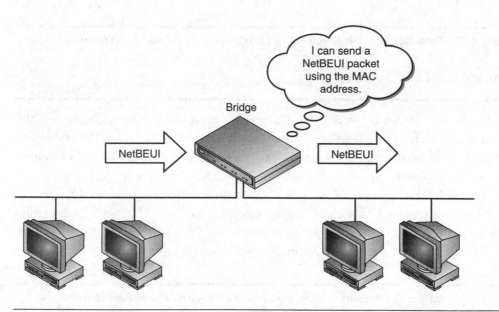

Figure 11-17   Bridges can filter and forward NetBEUI packets using MAC addresses.

NOTE: The NetBEUI protocol suite's lack of any Network layer protocol illustrates the key weakness of the OSI model: not everyone follows it.

IPX/SPX

Novell's IPX/SPX protocol suite, used primarily by Novell NetWare-based networks, provides a more scaleable solution for networks compared to NetBEUI. While the NetBEUI protocol suite provides services at the Transport and Session layers, IPX/SPX includes a wide variety of protocols operating at OSI Layers three through seven (the Network layer through the Application layer). Although IPX/SPX is strongly associated with Novell, Microsoft supports its own version of the protocol called *NWLink*. Microsoft-based clients and servers can use IPX/SPX for communicating with both Microsoft and Novell NetWare servers. Although more scaleable than NetBEUI, IPX/SPX bogs down in very large networks due to excessive traffic. The latest versions of Novell NetWare still support IPX/SPX, but they default to TCP/IP.

EXAM TIP: Make sure you know IPX/SPX is mainly for Novell NetWare!

In a Novell NetWare network, IPX/SPX operates at layers three through seven of the OSI model. Figure 11-18 shows how various IPX/SPX protocols relate to the OSI layers. At the Network layer, the Internetwork Packet eXchange (IPX) protocol handles routing data packets between networks. At the Transport layer, Sequenced Packet eXchange (SPX) handles the process of breaking data into smaller chunks on the sending machine and reassembling the data on the receiving machine. The Service Advertising Protocol (SAP) handles the Session layer, and the NetWare Core Protocol (NCP) handles a variety of Presentation and Application layer issues.

NOTE: The Network+ exam does not require knowledge of the individual protocols that make up the IPX/SPX suite.

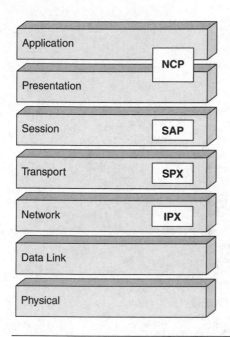

Figure 11-18   IPX/SPX includes protocols operating at OSI layers three through seven.

IPX/SPX has the distinction of being the only protocol other than TCP/IP to be routable. Like TCP/IP (as you will see in a moment), every IPX packet contains special *vector routing* information that routers use when routing packets through large, complex networks. To support routing, every IPX address can be broken into two parts: the network ID and the host name. I'm going to spend an entire chapter on TCP/IP routing issues, so with your kind permission, I'm *not* going to do the same for IPX—they work basically the same way, and while TCP/IP routing issues are of wide interest, few folks care about the gritty details of IPX addresses, packets, and routing (nor does the Network+ exam care).

Microsoft takes advantage of the widespread industry support of IPX/SPX with its own version of the protocol suite, referred to as either *IPX/SPX-compatible Protocol* (Windows 9*x*) or *NWLink IPX/SPX/NetBIOS Compatible Transport Protocol* (Windows 2000/XP) (see Figure 11-19). Adopting a pre-existing, proven routable protocol was a more attractive option for Microsoft than adding routing support to NetBEUI. Microsoft network operating systems, including Windows 9*x*, Windows 2000, and Windows NT, use IPX/SPX for two purposes: to connect to NetWare servers, and to provide the Transport and Network layer functionality for Microsoft Networking. For communication between two Microsoft-based systems, Microsoft does not use the IPX/SPX

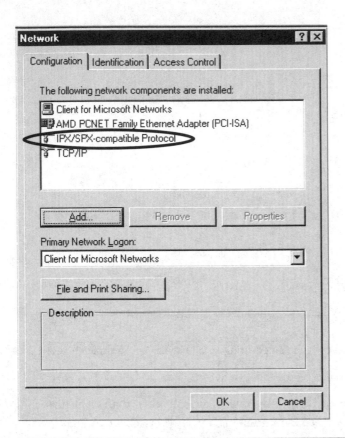

Figure 11-19   Microsoft calls its version of the IPX/SPX protocol suite either IPX/SPX-compatible Protocol or NWLink IPX/SPX/NetBIOS Compatible Transport Protocol.

protocol suite's Application, Presentation, or Session layer protocols, relying instead on traditional Microsoft networking protocols such as NetBIOS (see Figure 11-20).

Unlike NetBEUI, which requires no configuration beyond assigning each computer a name, IPX/SPX requires a network tech to configure the IPX part. IPX packets, created at the Network layer, vary in their format according to the Data Link layer protocol used. IPX running on top of Ethernet, for example, can use one of four data structures, called *frame types*: Ethernet 802.3, Ethernet II, Ethernet 802.2, and Ethernet SNAP. If two IPX/SPX network nodes use different frame types, they will not be able to communicate (see Figure 11-21). In the days of DOS-based network clients, network techs set the frame type manually for each system on the network. Windows 9*x* and Windows NT/2000/XP systems simplify the process by automatically detecting IPX traffic on the

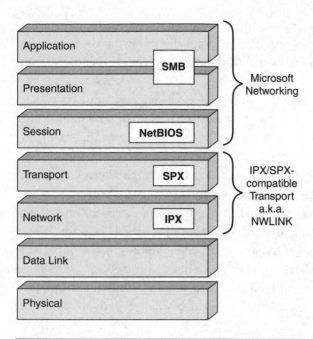

Figure 11-20 Microsoft clients and servers communicate using only part of the IPX/SPX protocol suite.

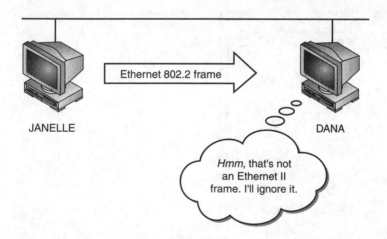

Figure 11-21 Two IPX nodes configured to use different frame types ignore each other's packets.

network and configuring themselves to use the first frame type they detect (see Figure 11-22). Because modern Windows systems automatically use whatever frame type they detect first, however, systems on networks using multiple types can end up trying to communicate using mismatched frame types. To ensure that every system on a network uses the same frame type, a system admin can set each system's frame type manually using the Network (Connections) applet (see Figure 11-23). The structural details of the different frame types do not affect the network tech—simply configure all systems to use the same frame type.

IPX/SPX, although routable, does not scale well for large WANs. Novell designed IPX/SPX to support their NetWare operating system, which treats NetWare servers as the ultimate focus of the network. In a NetWare environment, servers are servers and clients are clients, and never the twain shall meet. Unlike NetBEUI, which assumes that a machine can function as both a client and a server, IPX/SPX assumes that a proper network consists of a few servers and a large number of clients. The servers use the Service Advertising Protocol (SAP) to create and maintain connections. While this configuration works well on small- and medium-sized networks, when a network grows to

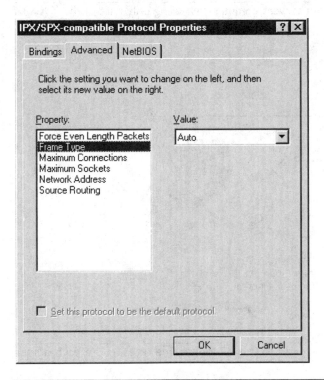

Figure 11-22 Modern Windows systems can auto-detect the frame type being used.

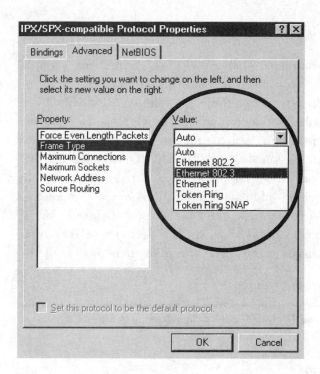

Figure 11-23   Setting the frame type manually

include hundreds of servers and thousands of clients, the increase in SAP traffic will take down the network. Until recently, the danger of excessive SAP broadcasts did not impact the typical network tech, because most networks simply did not have enough servers for SAP broadcasts to cause congestion. But as large networks become more common, IPX/SPX's reliance on SAP broadcasts becomes more of a problem. This has led most WAN designers to adopt a more scaleable alternative: TCP/IP.

TCP/IP

As usual, with greater functionality comes greater complexity. The TCP/IP protocol suite offers a more scaleable solution for the largest networks, but it requires significantly more configuration on the part of the network tech. TCP/IP began as a UNIX networking protocol suite, but its status as the Internet's de facto protocol suite has prompted both Microsoft and Novell to embrace it. Helping this along is the convenient fact that unlike NetBEUI and IPX/SPX, TCP/IP is an open standard, not controlled by any one company.

A series of documents called *Requests for Comment* (RFCs), defines each protocol within the TCP/IP suite. These documents, freely available on the Internet, provide all the information you need to write programs that conform to the TCP/IP standard. The open nature of TCP/IP makes it an attractive environment for developing new protocols. If TCP/IP lacks a protocol to implement some desired function, any skilled programmer can write a new protocol, publish an RFC, and add it to the TCP/IP suite. It was this flexibility that enabled the Internet to evolve rapidly from a simple, geographically dispersed network for transferring e-mail and data files into the immense Internet we have today, with its World Wide Web, real-time audio broadcasts, instant messaging, secure credit card transactions, and who knows what wonders yet to come. This ability to add new protocols to meet new needs gives TCP/IP a flexibility that the other protocols cannot match.

NOTE: Chapters 12, 15, and 16 cover TCP/IP configuration in detail.

TCP/IP now stands as the network protocol suite of choice in most of today's networks, and certainly on any system that wants to use the Internet. This popularity, combined with the fairly high degree of complexity involved in making TCP/IP work properly, and the fact that the Network+ exam really wants you to know TCP/IP in pretty minute detail, motivated me to create several chapters just on the TCP/IP network protocol. Check out the next chapter to find out many of the details about TCP/IP!

AppleTalk

Just as IPX/SPX was invented in-house by Novell for their NetWare NOS, Apple invented the AppleTalk network protocol suite to run on Apple computers. AppleTalk was originally designed to run on top of the old LocalTalk networking technology. Roughly speaking, AppleTalk does for Macs what NetBIOS does for PCs. When two Macs communicate using AppleTalk, their conversation looks quite a bit like a NetBIOS session, in that each name has an associated number function assigned to it. I won't go through this in detail, but you should know that AppleTalk uses a special function called Name Binding Protocol (NBP). NBP binds each system's name to its AppleTalk address so that other systems on the network can see it. Modern Macintosh systems still rely on AppleTalk. All but the very earliest versions of Windows come with the capability to install the AppleTalk protocol, so they can talk to Macintosh systems that still use AppleTalk. For the Network+ exam, at least know that if you want to talk to a Macintosh computer, you'll want to install the AppleTalk protocol on your Windows system.

DLC

The Data Link Control (DLC) network protocol was used for many years to link PCs to mainframe computers. Because Hewlett Packard adopted the DLC protocol for use by network printers, DLC enjoyed a much longer life than it probably should have, given the existence of so many alternatives. All versions of Windows, including Windows XP, still support DLC, but unless you're installing an older network printer that only uses DLC, odds are good you'll never see it. Just know that DLC is a network protocol and that you can install it if needed.

Dealing with Protocols

Dealing with protocols really means three things: installing them, configuring them (as you'll see, configuring and installing are pretty much the same process), and troubleshooting them when they fail. These steps are usually pretty trivial, as long as you don't include TCP/IP. Since the entire next chapter is devoted to TCP/IP, we will skip it for now. NetBEUI, IPX/SPX, and all the other protocols require almost no configuration, so the only topic remaining for this discussion is how you install them on a Windows client. Microsoft makes this very easy, but the Network+ exam expects you to know how to install a protocol—so watch as we go through the steps.

Installing Network Protocols

Windows 95 automatically installs both the IPX/SPX and NetBEUI protocols whenever a network adapter is installed. Windows 98, Windows 2000, and Windows XP automatically install TCP/IP. So which protocol should you use? If the PC is part of a network, the network folks will normally tell you which protocol or protocols to install. Virtually the entire world uses TCP/IP, but Windows comes with lots of other protocols. Should you need to install another protocol, open the Network applet (Windows 9*x*) or select a Local Area Connection in the Network Connection applet (Windows

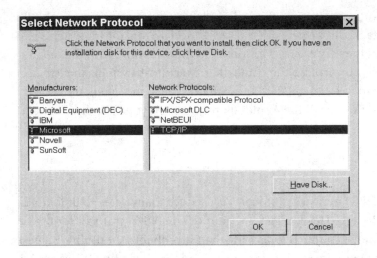

Figure 11-24 Adding a network protocol

2000/XP) in the Control Panel; select Add Protocol, and choose the protocol you wish to install (see Figure 11-24).

In many networks it is common for a system to have several installed protocols in order to support different network operating systems. Figure 11-25 shows a system with three protocols installed: NetBEUI, TCP/IP, and IPX/SPX.

If you're using anything *other than* the TCP/IP protocol, that's all you need to do. If you're using TCP/IP—and everybody is using TCP/IP these days—you need to do a lot more! As I mentioned, I've given TCP/IP its own chapter where we'll learn about all the fun configuration work you need to do.

Well, that's how you install a network protocol on a Windows client. I told you it was trivial! If you thought that was easy, you'll love how simple it is to troubleshoot a non-TCP/IP network in almost all situations.

Troubleshooting Network Protocols

Properly installed network protocols rarely fail. Given that non-TCP/IP protocols need almost no configuration, the chance that some system's IPX/SPX or NetBEUI protocol will fail is perhaps one of the most remote possibilities you may ever encounter on a networked system. Troubleshooting non-TCP/IP protocols usually means just uninstalling and reinstalling the protocol in question. In most cases, I simply delete *everything* in the Network Neighborhood or Local Area Connection properties and start over, thus assuring that any corrupted file is removed. That's it! Beyond that, there's little to

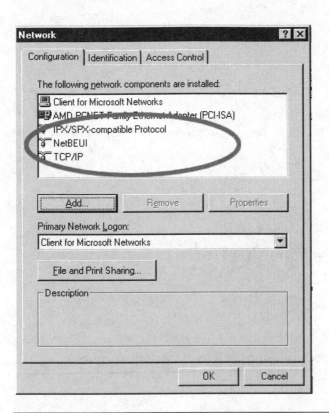

Figure 11-25 A Network Configuration tab showing three installed protocols

do at the network protocol level—unless of course that protocol is TCP/IP. Lucky for you, we'll start on TCP/IP in the next chapter!

Chapter Review

Questions

1. What is the maximum length of a NetBIOS computer's network name?
   a. 8 characters
   b. 23 characters
   c. 15 characters
   d. 256 characters

2. NWLink is Microsoft's version of which protocol suite?
   a. NetBEUI
   b. NetBIOS
   c. IPX/SPX
   d. TCP/IP

3. What are the documents that define the various protocols of the TCP/IP protocol suite called?
   a. The Knowledge Base
   b. TLAs
   c. RFCs
   d. RFAs

4. The NetBIOS protocol operates at which OSI layer?
   a. Data Link
   b. Network
   c. Transport
   d. Session

5. What part of the NetBEUI protocol suite operates at the Transport Layer?
   a. IPX
   b. NetBIOS
   c. NetBEUI
   d. SPX

6. Travis, using a Windows 95 computer named TRACK3, complains that he cannot connect with another Windows 95 computer named SALES3. Jim, the friendly neighborhood network technician, determines that TRACK3 can connect successfully with other machines that reside on the same side of the router, but not with any machines on the far side of the router. Which of the following is the most likely cause of Travis's problem?
   a. TRACK3 is connected to the network with a bad cable.
   b. TRACK3's network card has failed and needs to be replaced.
   c. TRACK3 is running NetBEUI.
   d. TRACK3 is running NetBIOS.

7. Which of the following protocols are routable?
   a. NetBEUI
   b. IPX/SPX
   c. TCP/IP
   d. NetBIOS

8. What do routers do with NetBEUI packets?
   a. Send the packets out over the Internet.
   b. Send the packets back to the sending machines.
   c. Hold the packets until they receive a re-send request.
   d. Discard the packets.

9. The IPX/SPX protocol was originally designed for use with which network operating system?
   a. Novell NetWare
   b. Windows 3.1
   c. UNIX
   d. Linux

10. What are Ethernet 802.3, Ethernet II, Ethernet 802.2, and Ethernet SNAP?
    a. Types of NIC cards
    b. IPX/SPX data structures
    c. TCP/IP protocols
    d. OSI model layers

Answers

1. **C.** The maximum length of a NetBIOS computer's network name is 15 characters. NetBIOS reserves the 16th byte for a special code that defines the function of the machine on the network.

2. **C.** NWLink is Microsoft's version of the IPX/SPX protocol.

3. **C.** RFCs are the documents that define the various protocols of the TCP/IP protocol suite. RFC stands for Request for Comment. Microsoft's Knowledge Base is an online information repository covering all Microsoft products.

4. **D.** The NetBIOS protocol operates at the Session layer.

5. **C.** The NetBEUI protocol operates at the Transport layer. IPX and SPX are parts of a different protocol.

6. **C.** TRACK3 is running NetBEUI. NetBEUI is a non-routable protocol. Because TRACK3 can communicate with some other machines on the network, a bad cable or NIC is unlikely to be the cause of the symptoms described.

7. **B, C.** IPX/SPX and TCP/IP are both routable protocols. NetBEUI is not a routable protocol, and NetBIOS is part of the NetBEUI protocol suite.

8. **D.** Routers discard NetBEUI packets because the packets lack the OSI Network layer routing information the routers use to do their job.

9. **A.** IPX/SPX was originally designed for use with Novell NetWare.

10. **B.** IPX running on top of Ethernet can use one of four data structures, called frame types: Ethernet 802.3, Ethernet II, Ethernet 802.2, or Ethernet SNAP.

## CHAPTER 12

TCP/IP

In this chapter, you will

- Understand the IP protocol and IP addresses
- Learn how to convert binary numbers to decimal numbers
- Understand subnet masking
- Learn to calculate IP addresses and subnet masks
- Know the functions of DNS, DHCP, and WINS and how they work
- Learn about the TCP protocol and TCP ports
- Learn about the UDP protocol
- Learn about NetBIOS
- Understand IPv6

Go up to virtually anyone these days and ask them if they have heard the term TCP/IP and you'll almost certainly get an answer like, "Yeah, I've heard of it. Doesn't it have something to do with computers or the Internet?" Many people in our Internet-saturated society have heard of TCP/IP, but very few of them actually know what it is or what it does. In this chapter, I will lead you out of this land of Internet Ignorance, so you can begin to get your hands dirty in the magical world of TCP/IP!

NOTE: You must be warned that understanding this chapter will hurl you headlong into a life of total geekdom. By the time you finish this chapter you'll be well on your way to trashing TCP/IP networks with wild abandon! Don't worry—trashing TCP/IP configurations is part of the growth process. Just do me a favor: Make sure the systems you trash are your own!

Historical/Conceptual

TCP/IP has the unique distinction of being the only popular network protocol designed from the ground up by the government of the United States. Like many government endeavors, TCP/IP is big, messy, ponderous, hard to configure (relative to other protocols, at least) and tries to be all things to all users. Compared to IPX/SPX, TCP/IP is a pain in the posterior at best. So why does every computer on the Internet use TCP/IP? If what I'm saying is true, why is it overwhelmingly the most popular network protocol on the face of the earth? Well, you need to appreciate the history of TCP/IP to see how we got where we are today.

The History of TCP/IP

Back in the early 1970s, the world was waking up to the possibility of taking computing beyond individual systems to realize the dream of vast *interconnected networks* of systems—what we now call the Internet. The U.S. Defense Advanced Research Projects Agency (DARPA) began to create a series of protocols to support just such an Internet. These became the now-famous TCP/IP protocol suite. The goal of DARPA was not just to make another network protocol; their goal was to make a network protocol that did some very cool things. First, the protocol was designed from the ground up to support groups of separate networks. In fact, the creators of the TCP/IP protocol suite literally invented the concept of routers. The IP part of TCP/IP knows how to work with routers to get data from one system to any other system on the Internet. This is no small feat! IP packets must contain special data to facilitate this routing, and network techs must perform certain configuration tasks. For routing to work, local systems must be told which addresses are for their local network, and what to do when they need to send data to a system that is not a part of their local network, called a *remote system*. We'll go through all these steps shortly.

Second, DARPA intended this new protocol to be able to handle a crisis. If one or more of its component networks suddenly went down, the TCP/IP internetwork should be able to re-route network traffic to avoid the downed areas. The Internet therefore can literally heal itself! We'll get into this latter topic in Chapter 16.

In this chapter, we'll go over some TCP/IP basics, including IP addresses and subnet masking. Then we'll take a look at some other parts of the TCP/IP suite, including the all-important TCP and UDP protocols, to see what role they play in setting up systems to run in TCP/IP networks. Finally, we'll review the functions of various key ports, and take a first quick look at the IPv6 protocol.

Test Specific

What Is TCP/IP?

We know from the previous chapter that TCP/IP is not a single protocol but rather a set of protocols that work mainly at the Network and Transport levels of the OSI model. The IP part of TCP/IP has the job of getting the packets from one system to another. The TCP part handles the individual sessions and makes sure all the data gets where it needs to go on the receiving system. While both parts of TCP/IP are critical, the key installation and configuration issues involve the IP part, so let's start with a nice long look at what IP is, and what we need to do to make it work.

IP Protocol

The Internet Protocol (IP) handles the naming conventions for the entire TCP/IP protocol suite. Every system in an IP network (in TCP/IP parlance, every *host*) must have a unique IP address. IP addresses look complex, but are actually quite simple and obvious once you know how they work.

IP Addresses

Hopefully you've seen an IP address. If you haven't, go to a system that is on the Internet (so you know it's using TCP/IP) and run WINIPCFG (Windows 9*x*) or IPCONFIG (Windows NT/2000) to see what its IP address looks like. Figure 12-1 shows the IP address for a Windows 98 system.

An IP address consists of four numbers, each number being a value between 0 and 255. We use a period to separate the numbers. No IP address may be all 0s or all 255s (I'll explain this in a moment). Here are a few valid IP addresses:

216.30.120.3

224.33.1.66

123.123.123.123

And here are a few invalid IP addresses:

216.30.120   (Must have four numbers)

255.255.255.255   (Can't be all 255s)

6.43.256.67   (Every number must be between 0 and 255)

32:1:66:54   (Must use periods between numbers)

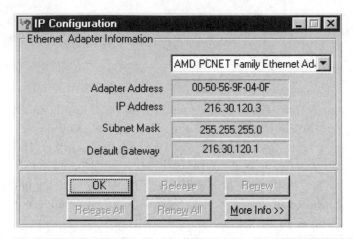

Figure 12-1 WINIPCFG showing a system's IP address

These numbers are entered into every system on the IP network. Figure 12-2 shows where to enter these values in a Windows system: the TCP/IP Properties dialog box.

Looking at Figure 12-2, you will also see a value labeled Subnet Mask, as well as tabs to the left of the one being displayed that say Gateway, DNS Configuration, and WINS Configuration. What are these all about? Hey, I told you IP is by far the messiest of all protocols to configure! That's what this chapter is all about: understanding these IP entries. But in order to understand how to configure these settings, you must understand what an IP address really is. So, let's grab an arbitrary IP address and start tearing it up into its real components: binary numbers.

 EXAM TIP: Windows 98 SE and Windows ME have both WINIPCFG and IPCONFIG utilities, but for the exam assume that all versions of Windows 9x only use WINIPCFG!

Converting IP Addresses

While we commonly write IP addresses as four digits separated by periods, this is just a convenient representation of what is actually a *32-bit binary address*. Let me explain. Here's a typical IP address in its primeval binary form:

11000101101010010101111001010010

While computers have no difficulty handling long strings of ones and zeros, most humans can't handle speaking in these terms. Instead, techs use a special shorthand for IP addresses called *dotted decimal notation*. Dotted decimal notation works as follows. First, divide the IP address into four pieces of eight bits:

11000101 10101001 01011110 01010010

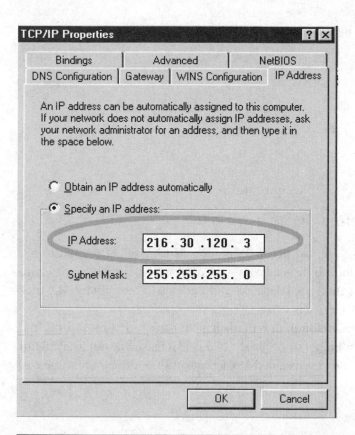

Figure 12-2 TCP/IP Properties dialog box showing IP addresses

A group of eight bits (called an *octet*) has a limited number of permutations of ones and zeros ranging from all zeros (00000000) to all ones (11111111), with a lot of different combinations of ones and zeros in between. The exact number of permutations is 2^8 or 256 different patterns of ones and zeros. Each combination of ones and zeros corresponds to a number between 0 and 255. The list starts like this:

00000000 = 0

00000001 = 1

00000010 = 2

00000011 = 3

00000100 = 4

I'll skip about 246 entries here, bringing us to the end of the list:

11111011 = 251

11111100 = 252

11111101 = 253

11111110 = 254

11111111 = 255

Let's take a look at the first example I just gave you:

11000101   10101001   01011110   01010010

We represent this number in dotted decimal notation as 197.169.94.82. While you may have some idea how I did this, let's take a moment to work through how to convert a true binary IP address into dotted decimal, and back again into binary. The trick is to convert the individual 8-bit octets.

The problem with using decimal notation to display an octet is that most folks find it difficult to convert between binary to decimal notation, at least without a calculator handy. The secret to success is to appreciate that each position in the binary value corresponds to a decimal value. Look at this list:

00000001 = 1

00000010 = 2

00000100 = 4

00001000 = 8

00010000 = 16

00100000 = 32

01000000 = 64

10000000 = 128

If you can memorize these eight binary/decimal equivalents, you can convert any binary octet into its decimal equivalent—not only useful in your networking duties, but an excellent trick you can use to amaze your friends at parties! To make conversion easier, every good IP network person memorizes the form in Figure 12-3.

To convert an octet from binary to decimal, *enter* the binary number into the empty spaces at the bottom of the form, *copy* down the decimal values of the columns where

Position	8th	7th	6th	5th	4th	3rd	2nd	1st
Value	128	64	32	16	8	4	2	1

Figure 12-3   Form to help with binary/decimal conversion

Position	8th	7th	6th	5th	4th	3rd	2nd	1st
Value	128	64	32	16	8	4	2	1
	1	0	0	1	0	0	1	1

$$128 + 0 + 0 + 16 + 0 + 0 + 2 + 1 = 147$$

Figure 12-4   Converting the binary value of 10010011 into a decimal value

there are ones in the binary number, and *add* those decimal values together to get a final answer. Let's convert the binary value 10010011 to a decimal number (see Figure 12-4). In the 8th position enter a 1, and write down 128, which is the decimal value in that column. 128 is the first number in your decimal addition problem. In the 7th and 6th positions enter 0s, and for completeness, write down zeros. Your decimal addition problem now reads $128 + 0 + 0$. Enter a 1 in the 5th position, and write down 16, the decimal value of that column. In the 4th and 3rd positions, enter two more 0s, and write those down. In the 2nd position enter a 1, and add its value, 2, to your equation that follows. Finally, place a 1 in the 1st position, which we know equals 1. Add a 1 to the end of your addition problem, and then do the math! The decimal equivalent of 10010011 is 147. Converting binary numbers to decimal is easy with this handy form!

Now let's return to our binary IP address example, and convert each binary octet to decimal:

11000101=197   10101001=169   01011110=94   01010010=82

Then separate the values with dots, like this:

197.169.94.82

You've now translated an IP address from binary to the more familiar dotted decimal IP address format! Go drink the beverage of your choice in celebration—but only one, because you'll need your wits about you for the next step: converting a decimal value into binary!

You can use the same form to convert numbers from dotted decimal to binary. Let's use a sample decimal value of 49. Whip out a nice blank form and write the number 49 at the top. Start on the far left-hand side of the form and ask yourself, "How many 128s are there in 49?" You should answer yourself, "None, because 128 is larger than 49!" Since zero 128s fit into 49, place a zero in the 128 spot. Repeat this exercise with the next value, 64. Each time you hit a value that produces an answer of one, place a one in the corresponding position. Subtract that value from the decimal value and continue the procedure with the remainder.

Here's how it works with the 49 example:

- How many "128s" in 49? None, so put a zero in the 128s place.
- How many "64s" in 49? None, so put a zero in the 64s place.
- How many "32s" in 49? One! Put a one in the 32s place and subtract 32 from 49, leaving 17.
- How many "16s" in 17? One! Put a one in the 16s place and subtract 16 from 17, leaving 1.
- How many "8s" in 1? None, so put a zero.
- How many "4s" in 1? None, so put a zero.
- How many "2s" in 1? None, so put a zero.
- How many "1s" in 1? One! Put a one in the 1s place and subtract 1 from 1, leaving—ta-da!—zero!

This does—and because you've reached the end of the procedure, it most definitely should—leave you with zero (see Figure 12-5). If you don't get zero at this point, you made a mistake. No big deal—it can take some practice to get the hang of it. Try it again!

Using our handy form, we've deduced that the decimal value 49 is 00110001 in binary. Since every IP address has four values, you must go through this process three more times to convert a typical IP address. You'll find that with practice this becomes a very fast process. Stop here, make up some IP addresses, and practice converting back and forth with values you create until you're comfortable.

Now that you've toiled to learn conversion by hand, I have a confession to make: You can use the calculator applet that comes with every version of Windows (Start | Run, type **Calc**, and press ENTER). The Scientific mode of the calculator has a nice series of radio

Position	8th	7th	6th	5th	4th	3rd	2nd	1st
Value	128	64	32	16	8	4	2	1
	0	0	1	1	0	0	0	1

```
How many   128s  in  49?    0
How many    64s  in  49?    0
How many    32s  in  49?    1    49 − 32 = 17
How many    16s  in  17?    1    17 − 16 = 1
How many     8s  in   1?    0
How many     4s  in   1?    0
How many     2s  in   1?    0
How many     1s  in   1?    1    1 −1 = 0   Did yours come out to zero?
```

Figure 12-5   Did yours come out to zero?

buttons on the top left. Make sure that the Decimal radio button is checked, type in the octet's decimal value, and then click the Binary radio button. Voilà! Instant conversion!

> **NOTE:**   The Network+ exam does not expect you to know how to convert dot-ted decimal IP addresses into binary and back, although any network tech worth his salt can do this in his sleep. Also, it's a skill you need to truly under-stand a number of other aspects of TCP/IP that we are about to learn.

I always laugh when I think about the first time I tried converting IP addresses from decimal to binary and back. When I first had to learn all this, it took me three solid days to get the whole thing straight in my head, while my friend Taylor had it nailed in about five minutes. Even though a calculator will do the conversions for you, don't give up too quickly on doing it yourself—you'll find that being able to do this manually brings some big benefits out in the real world!

Okay, hold on tight to your new knowledge about converting IP addresses, and bear with me a moment as I head off on a brief tangent into the wonderful world of ARP!

ARP

We've been discussing IP addresses, but you know that networks use frames to move data from one system to another, and that frames use *MAC addresses* to do that job, not IP addresses. So how does the sending system know the MAC address of the receiving system? The TCP/IP protocol suite has a very neat little function called *address resolution protocol (ARP)* that performs this task.

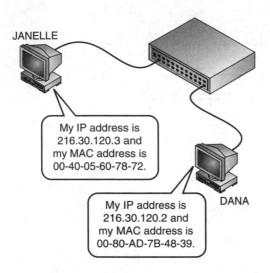

Figure 12-6   Wheebo network showing IP and MAC addresses for each system

To see how ARP works, let's add TCP/IP to Hannah's Wheebo network we saw in the previous chapter. In this case, she configured DANA to use the IP address 216.30.120.2 and JANELLE gets the IP address 216.30.120.3. We also know that each system has a MAC address—let's give each system a MAC address as shown in Figure 12-6.

Let's say DANA wants to send data to JANELLE. It knows the IP address (216.30.120.3) but does not know the MAC address, and without the MAC address, it cannot make a frame. So, DANA sends out a very special frame, addressed to a very special MAC address called the *multicast address*. It's special because *all* systems on the network receive and process frames sent to the multicast address. This frame asks every system on the local network: "What is the MAC address for IP address 216.30.120.3?" We call this frame an *ARP request*. The system with that IP address replies to DANA with an ARP reply (see Figure 12-7).

Once DANA gets the MAC information for JANELLE, it stores this in a cache. You can see the ARP cache in your system by typing the command **ARP -a** (note: the -a is case sensitive) from a command prompt in any version of Windows. Figure 12-8 shows the **ARP** command in action!

TCP/IP works perfectly well as a network protocol for individual networks, but the real power of TCP/IP doesn't come into play until networks start to get really big. TCP/IP is designed to work in really large networks—I'm talking *Internet*-large, here—but TCP/IP handles those big networks a bit differently. This is where a special system called a *gateway* comes in.

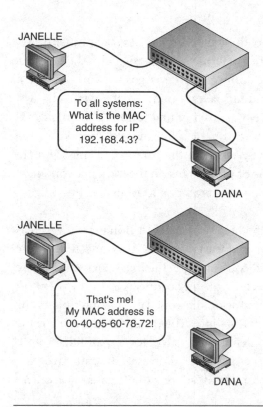

Figure 12-7   DANA sending an ARP request and getting an ARP reply

```
C:\WINNT\System32\cmd.exe

C:\>arp -a

Interface: 192.168.4.15 on Interface 0x1000003
  Internet Address       Physical Address      Type
  192.168.4.17           00-20-18-8b-54-80     dynamic
  192.168.4.18           00-40-95-00-2e-1c     dynamic
  192.168.4.21           00-c0-f0-2c-f7-0c     dynamic
  192.168.4.28           00-a0-c9-98-97-9e     dynamic
  192.168.4.150          00-01-02-c8-95-41     dynamic
  192.168.4.152          00-04-5a-d0-ca-6b     dynamic
  192.168.4.155          00-40-05-60-73-a6     dynamic

C:\>_
```

Figure 12-8   The ARP command in action

Gateways

ARP works great when one IP system needs to know the MAC address of another IP system in the same small network, but remember that one of the cornerstones of IP is its assumption that your local network will be connected to a larger network—in most cases the Internet itself. TCP/IP assumes—and this is important—that a system knows, or at least can find out on the fly (see the DNS discussion that follows), the *IP address* of any system on the Internet. It is not possible, however, for one system to know the MAC addresses of all the millions of other systems on the Internet. If messages are going to move across the Internet, at least one of the systems on the local network must know how to address packets for other systems that are not part of its local network— we call this system the *gateway*.

In most networks, the gateway is a router, but a PC can also function perfectly well as a gateway. The only thing a gateway *must* have is at least two network connections—one connecting to the local network and a second connecting to the bigger network. Figure 12-9 shows the gateway system in my office. This little box connects to (a) my network and (b) the DSL line to my ISP. Note the two thicker network cables—one runs to the hub for my network and the other runs to my DSL line. (The third, thinner cable is the power cable. The other two projections are antennae for its wireless capabilities.)

When setting up a local network, you must enter the IP address of the gateway in the TCP/IP Properties dialogue box of every system. The IP address of the gateway is called,

Figure 12-9   The Totalsem Gateway

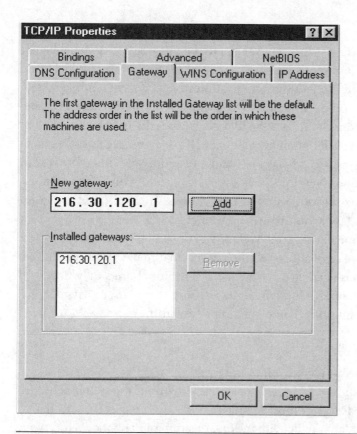

Figure 12-10   The TCP/IP Properties dialogue box showing the default gateway setting

somewhat confusingly, the *default gateway*. Figure 12-10 shows my TCP/IP Properties dialogue box with the default gateway setting added.

If DANA wants to talk to another system that is not part of the local network, it cannot ARP that far away system, because the Internet does not allow any form of broadcast frames. My gosh, imagine if it did! That would mean that DANA would have to ARP *every other computer on the Internet*! Now imagine *every* system on the Internet doing this—there'd be no bandwidth left for data! Don't worry about this happening; every router on the Internet is designed to block ARP requests. Instead, DANA must send its data to its network's gateway, which will work with all of the other routers on the Internet to get the packet to the proper location. The issue this brings up is how DANA can tell whether an address is local or remote.

Local vs. Remote

Any system that wants to send a data packet over a network must be able to tell whether the recipient system is local or remote, because it handles locally and remotely bound IP packets in two completely different ways. If the address is local, the sending system can use ARP. If the address is on a remote network, it must send the packet to its gateway, which will strip off the frame and send the IP packet across the Internet to the right system. TCP/IP networks add a special binary value called a *subnet mask* to each system to enable them to distinguish between local and remote IP addresses. But before we can dive into subnet masks (sounds weird, I know, but tastes great!) you need to understand how TCP/IP can organize networks into distinct chunks. Think about it, we've got all these IP addresses, from 0.0.0.0 all the way up to 255.255.255.255; clearly it's not optimal to treat them all as one big network. We need an organizational scheme we can use to divvy up this huge pool of IP addresses into chunks that make sense and that we can use. And lucky us, this has been done! The official term for chunks of addresses is *network IDs*. (Personally, I'd rather call them chunks—much more fun to use in a sentence—but unfortunately, I'm not in charge of naming this stuff.)

Network IDs

In the earlier discussion, we configured DANA to use the IP address 216.30.120.2 and JANELLE to use the IP address 216.30.120.3. Notice anything about these two IP addresses? Look carefully. They are almost identical—only the final octet is different, and that is *not* a coincidence! It has to do with the organization of networks. Why is your address 305 Main Street, and your next-door neighbor's 306 (or 307, depending on how your street is numbered) Main Street? How about if we make your address 1313 Mulberry Lane, and his address 451 Bradbury Avenue? Imagine the horror on the face of your mail carrier! For the same reason we group street addresses using street names and sets of consecutive numbers, we divide network addresses into parts designating groups of computers, and parts designating individual computers. Okay, here's an IP address: 11010101101010010101111001010010. Which part is which? Ha! Not easy, is it? Actually, it's easier than it looks. The answer to "which is which" lies in the subnet mask!

Look at those two IP addresses again. The first part, 216.30.120, is the same for each system. In fact, it's the same for *every* machine in the Wheebo network! This part of the address, the part that's the same for all the Wheebo systems, is called the *network ID*. It's the number by which the rest of the Internet knows the Wheebo network. The last part of the IP address, the part that is—and must be—different for each host system on the Wheebo network, is called—catch this originality—the *host ID*. So how many hosts can the Wheebo network support, given that each one must have a unique IP address?

Remember the binary conversion stuff we just did (I hope)? Each binary octet translates into a decimal number between 0 and 255, for a total of 256 possible IP addresses using Wheebo's network ID, starting with 216.30.120.0 and running through 216.30.120.255.

Great. Only there's a small complication, courtesy of those quirky folks who designed the Internet: no host ID can be either all zeros or all ones. So 216.30.120.0 and 216.30.120.255 are actually invalid IP addresses. The rest of them are okay, however, so the range of IP addresses available to the Wheebo network starts at 216.30.120.1 and runs to 216.30.120.254, for a whopping total of 254 unique IP addresses.

If some other network admin asks the Wheebo network admin for his network ID, the answer will be: 216.30.120.0. This is just a convention among network folks—any time you see an IP address with a final octet of zero, you are looking at a network ID, not the address of any individual system.

Okay, you're thinking, so the first three octets are the network ID, and the last one is the host ID, right? In Wheebo's case that's true, but not always! Here are two more IP addresses, for systems that share the same network ID: 202.43.169.55 and 202.43.67.123. Uh oh, this time only the first *two* octets are the same! Care to guess what the network ID is for this network? It's the first two octets: 202.43. Why would one network have a three-octet network ID, and the other only two? Because the one with the two-octet network ID needs a lot more IP addresses for its host systems. The two-octet network's IP addresses range from 202.43.0.1 to 202.43.255.254. Now, look carefully—what part of 202.43.0.1 is the host ID? The 1? Nope, it's the final *two* octets: 0.1!

Oh no, a zero! A host ID can't have all zeros or all ones, right? Right, and this one doesn't. The first octet is 00000000 (all zeros), but the second octet is 00000001 (*not* all zeros). The IP address 202.43.0.0 won't fly, but 202.43.0.1 works just fine. By the same token, we can't use 202.43.255.255, because the final two octets would be 11111111 and 11111111 (all ones), but we *can* use 202.43.255.254, because its final two octets are 11111111 and 11111110 (not all ones). I never said that no octet in an IP address can be all zeros or all ones; what I said was that a *host ID* can't be all zeros or all ones. Big difference!

We've established that Wheebo has a network ID of 216.30.120.0. Where did it come from, and why is it a different size from the other one we just looked at? Since no two systems anywhere in the world on the Internet can have the same IP address, we need a single body to dispense IP addresses. The Internet Assigned Numbers Authority (IANA) is the ultimate source of all network IDs. You can't just call them up and ask for one, however; only the big boys play in that arena. Most small networks get their network ID assignments from their ISPs; the ISPs and some large end-users can go directly to one of the IANA-authorized Regional Internet Registries that collectively provide IP registration services to all regions around the globe. Okay, so Wheebo probably got its network ID from its ISP, but who decided what size it would be? Wheebo's network admin did, by deciding how many individual IP addresses Wheebo needed. Wheebo is a small company, so it only asked its ISP for 254 IP addresses, and the ISP gave Wheebo a three-octet network ID.

Subnet Mask

Now that you know where network IDs come from, let's return to an earlier question: how does a host system tell whether an IP address is local or remote? It compares the IP address to its own IP address to see if they have the same network ID. All machines with the same network ID are by definition on the same network, so if the IDs match, it knows the other system is local, not remote. Comparing two network IDs sounds simple, but it's not as easy for computers as it is for people; computers need help, and this is where the subnet mask comes in.

Subnet masks are always some number of ones, followed by enough zeros to make a total of 32 bits. This is—not coincidentally—the same length as an IP address. Every network has a subnet mask, determined by the length of its network ID. Your system uses the subnet mask like a filter. Everywhere there is a 1 in the subnet mask, you are looking at part of the network ID (see Figure 12-11). Everywhere there is a zero, you are looking at part of the host ID. By placing a subnet mask on top of an IP address, a computer can tell which part of the IP address is the network ID and which part is the host ID. A sending system holds up its local network's subnet mask to both its own and the recipient's IP addresses, to see whether the part of the address under the 1s (the network ID) is the same for both systems. If the other system shares the sending system's network ID, it's local; if it does not, it's remote (see Figure 12-12).

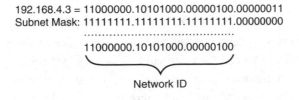

Figure 12-11   The part of the IP address under the 1s is the network ID.

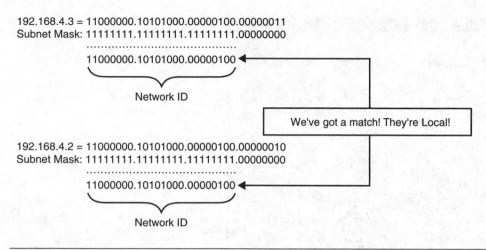

PART II

Figure 12-12   Comparing two network IDs using the subnet mask

Subnet masks are represented in dotted decimal just like IP addresses—just remember that both are really 32-bit binary numbers. All of the following (shown in both binary and dotted decimal formats) can be subnet masks:

11111111111111111111111100000000 = 255.255.255.0

11111111111111110000000000000000 = 255.255.0.0

11111111000000000000000000000000 = 255.0.0.0

Most network folks represent subnet masks using a special shorthand: a "/" character followed by a number equal to the number of *ones* in the subnet mask. Here are a few examples:

11111111111111111111111100000000 = /24 (24 ones)

11111111111111110000000000000000 = /16 (16 ones)

11111111000000000000000000000000 = /8 (8 ones)

An IP address followed by the "/" and number is telling you the IP address and the subnet mask in one statement. For example, 201.23.45.123/24 is an IP address of 201.23.45.123 with a subnet mask of 255.255.255.0. Similarly, 184.222.4.36/16 is an IP address of 184.222.4.36 with a subnet mask of 255.255.0.0.

Fortunately, computers do all of this subnet filtering automatically. Network administrators need only to enter the correct IP address and subnet mask when they first set up their systems, and the rest happens without any human intervention.

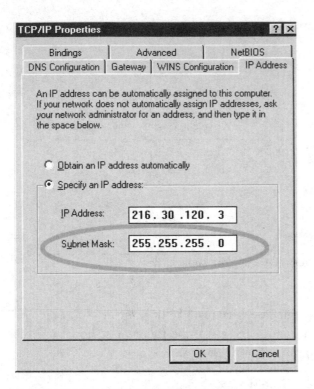

Figure 12-13 The TCP/IP Properties dialog box showing subnet mask

Let's take another peek at the TCP/IP Properties dialog box on my system to see the subnet mask (see Figure 12-13). Are you getting the impression that this dialog box is a really important place for configuring your IP settings? You bet it is!

Subnetting

At first glance you may discount the network ID as relatively unimportant; most of us have never had to enter a network ID into anything. We enter the IP address, the gateway, and the subnet mask on each PC, but there's no place to type in the network ID. Nevertheless, the network ID is critical to making an IP network function. Individual systems don't use network IDs, but routers need them badly! Why do the routers need network IDs? Because routers use router tables, and router tables use network IDs. Let me explain. Figure 12-14 shows a typical router setup at a small office. I even added the IP addresses for each NIC in the router (NICs built into a router are usually referred to as *interfaces*). Below the diagram is the *router table* for that router. The router uses this

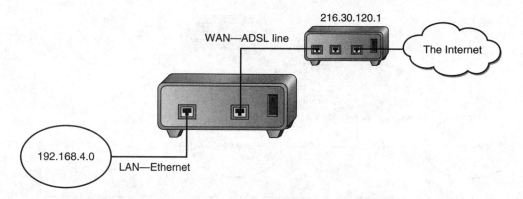

Routing Table Entry List

Destination LAN IP	Subnet Mask	Default Gateway	Hop Count	Interface
0.0.0.0	0.0.0.0	216.30.120.1	1	WAN
192.168.4.0	255.255.255.0	0.0.0.0	1	LAN
216.30.120.0	255.255.255.0	0.0.0.0	1	WAN

Figure 12-14   Router setup and corresponding router table

table to determine the interface (the far right column) through which it should route packets, based on the network ID of the recipient (the left-most column). As you can see, it needs the network ID of the receiving system to know how to route the packet. What if a packet's network ID doesn't match any of the routes in the table? Ah, those clever network designers are way ahead of you! If a router doesn't know what to do with a packet, it sends it along to its *own* default gateway, which will then distribute it to other routers, one of which will eventually know exactly where it should be routed. Very clever, and quite efficient, if you think about it for a minute!

This data in the router table doesn't just appear magically in the router. Someone needs to enter this information into the router when the router is first installed. But once this data is entered, the router will get the packets to the network.

Now that you appreciate the importance of network IDs, let's complicate the networking situation. Let's use a more advanced router with three NICs to create two separate networks (see Figure 12-15). This type of setup is commonly used to reduce network traffic or increase security. We need to make all of this work!

Let's also assume for a moment that you are in charge of setting up this network. You have been given a total of 256 IP addresses: 216.30.120.0/24. This means you are in control of all the IP addresses from 216.30.120.0 to 216.30.120.255. If this were only

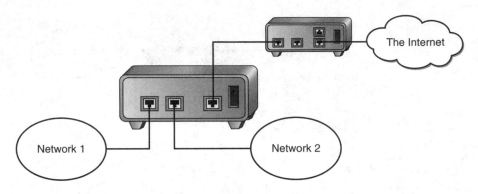

Figure 12-15   Adding another router to make separate networks—how does this work?

one network, you wouldn't have any problems. You could simply set up each system with a unique IP address between 216.30.120.1 and 216.30.120.254.

In this case, however, you can't do that. This router has *two* NICs—if each host system is randomly assigned an IP address from the total, how does the router decide which NIC to route packets through to be sure they get to the correct system? No, you can't just route everything through both NICs! The solution: divide those 256 IP addresses into *two distinct groups* in such a way that your router person can configure the router table to ensure that packets get to the right system. Just as we divide our neighborhoods into streets, we need to take this one Network ID and turn it into two distinct subnetwork IDs. Friend, you need to subnet!

Subnetting breaks a contiguous set of IP addresses into contiguous subgroups of addresses, called *subnets*. Subnets conform to router standards, so the subnetted systems remain accessible to the Internet. Subnetting is simple in concept but complex in practice, largely because it requires us to break away from dividing our network IDs "at the periods." What does "at the periods" mean? I'm referring to the periods in a dotted decimal IP address, which you will recall are nothing more than a handy method for representing a set of binary values. So far, every network ID you've seen stops at either /8, /16, or /24—that is, the first one, two, or three octets are the network ID. I didn't show you any addresses in which, say, the first *two and a half* octets were the network ID, and the remaining one and a half were the host ID. But actually, there is no reason network IDs must end "on the periods." The computers, at least, think it's perfectly fine to have network IDs that end at points between the periods, such as /26, /27, or even /22. The trick here is to stop thinking about IP addresses, network IDs, and subnet masks just in their dotted decimal format, and instead go back to thinking of them as binary octets.

Remember the binary/decimal conversion form? If I were you, I'd put this book on a photocopier right now and make yourself a bunch of copies of that form—you will need them!

We need to divide the 216.30.120.0/24 network ID into two subnets. We always start the subnetting process by writing out the default subnet mask in binary. The subnet mask equal to /24 is

11111111111111111111111100000000

To make subnets, we must *extend* the subnet mask to the right, thereby turning our one network ID into multiple network IDs. The only downside is that we will have fewer host numbers in each of our little subnets. That's the cornerstone of understanding subnetting: you take the network ID you get from your ISP and then chop it up into multiple, smaller network IDs, each of which supports fewer host numbers. The final step in this process is changing the IP addresses and subnet masks on all your systems, and entering the two (in this case) new network IDs into your gateway system. The hard part is knowing *what* to enter into the systems and routers.

Okay, let's stop and work from what you know. You know you need two subnets, right? So let's extend the subnet mask one place to the right (see Figure 12-16). This creates a three-section IP address: (1) the *original* network ID; (2) the now one digit smaller host ID; and (3) nestled in between, what I call the *subnet ID*.

Uh oh. Sorry, you can't do that—by rule of the Internet powers that be, you're not allowed to have a *subnet ID* that is all ones, or all zeros either! We get around this by moving the subnet mask *two* places, as shown in Figure 12-17. How many new network IDs does that create? That would be 2^2, which is four, did I hear you say? Careful—remember the "all ones or zeros" prohibition! Two of the subnets (00 and 11) are useless according to the rules of subnetting, so actually we only get two new network IDs.

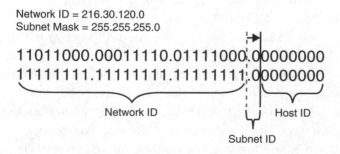

Network ID = 216.30.120.0
Subnet Mask = 255.255.255.0

11011000.00011110.01111000.00000000
11111111.11111111.11111111.00000000

Network ID   Host ID

Subnet ID

Figure 12-16 An IP address in three sections

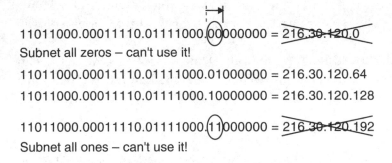

11011000.00011110.01111000.00000000 = 216.30.120.0
Subnet all zeros – can't use it!

11011000.00011110.01111000.01000000 = 216.30.120.64

11011000.00011110.01111000.10000000 = 216.30.120.128

11011000.00011110.01111000.11000000 = 216.30.120.192
Subnet all ones – can't use it!

Figure 12-17   Extending the subnet mask two places

NOTE: Even though the official rules do not allow subnets with all zeros or all ones, most networking systems—certainly all versions of Windows—run just fine if you use them. But for the test, stick to the rules!

Take a good hard look at the two new dotted decimal network IDs. Do you see how they no longer end in a zero? Didn't I say earlier that you can tell a dotted decimal network ID because it ends in a zero? True enough, and yet these network IDs don't . . . or do they? Why sure they do, when you look at their binary form—but not in *eight* zeros. They still *end* in zeros, but not at the periods. Only the last *six* digits of the IP address, which in this example are the host ID, are zeros.

Now think about the subnet masks for each of the new subnets—how would you write a subnet mask of /26? That would be 255.255.255.192! Hey, these new subnet masks don't end in a zero either . . . or do they? Yes indeedy, they do, too! Remember that we count zeros in the *binary* version of the address. The last six values in the fourth binary octet *are* zeros. 11000000 equals 192 (128 + 64) in decimal, so we represent that subnet mask in dotted decimal as 255.255.255.192.

This "dotted decimal ID must end in a zero" issue drives a lot of folks crazy when they're first learning this stuff—they just can't "get past the periods," as I like to put it. But you, you my young apprentices, will conquer your fear, and we will rule the galaxy . . . sorry, wrong story . . . long, long ago and all that. What I mean to say is, I'm sure with some effort you will be able to appreciate that whether or not the subnet masks and network ID end in a zero when you write them as dotted decimal, everything still works the same way. It's useful to memorize the fact that any time you see a dotted decimal ID ending in 128, 192, 224, or 240, you are looking at an ID which, in its binary format, ends in zero.

> **NOTE:**   Confession: This drove me crazy when I first learned subnetting years ago. Roll with it and you too can spend the rest of your life huddled next to a computer at odd hours writing books.

So we now have two subnets: 216.30.120.64/26 and 216.30.120.128/26. If that isn't clear, stop reading now and go back to the previous text and graphics until it *is* clear. How do you use these two subnets in our example network? Well, the new subnet mask for every system is /26, so first we need to update the subnet mask settings in all our systems. We also know that our resident router geek must update the router to reflect the two new network IDs. The only question left is: which IP addresses go to each subnet? Well, every IP address must include the Network ID, leaving only six places for unique host numbers. In network ID 216.30.120.64/26, that gives us 64 different unique IP addresses. Just as no subnet may contain all zeros or all ones, no host ID may be all zeros and all ones, leaving a total of 62 usable IP addresses: 216.30.120.65 to 216.30.120.126 (see Figure 12-18). Contrast those with the IP addresses for the 216.30.120.128/26 network ID (see Figure 12-19).

Clearly there is a relationship between the number of network IDs you create and the number of unique IP addresses available for each subnet. This is the tradeoff of subnetting: the more subnets, the fewer available host numbers per subnet. Also notice

Network ID: 216.30.120.64 =
11011000.00011110.01111000.01000000

11011000.00011110.01111000.01000001 = 216.30.120.65
11011000.00011110.01111000.01000010 = 216.30.120.66
11011000.00011110.01111000.01000011 = 216.30.120.67
11011000.00011110.01111000.01000100 = 216.30.120.68
....
11011000.00011110.01111000.01111011 = 216.30.120.123
11011000.00011110.01111000.01111100 = 216.30.120.124
11011000.00011110.01111000.01111101 = 216.30.120.125
11011000.00011110.01111000.01111110 = 216.30.120.126

Figure 12-18   Showing the IP addresses for 216.30.120.64

Network ID: 216.30.120.128 =

11011000.00011110.01111000.10000000

11011000.00011110.01111000.10000001 = 216.30.120.129
11011000.00011110.01111000.10000010 = 216.30.120.130
11011000.00011110.01111000.10000011 = 216.30.120.131
11011000.00011110.01111000.10000100 = 216.30.120.132
....
11011000.00011110.01111000.10111011 = 216.30.120.187
11011000.00011110.01111000.10111100 = 216.30.120.188
11011000.00011110.01111000.10111101 = 216.30.120.189
11011000.00011110.01111000.10111110 = 216.30.120.190

Figure 12-19   Showing the IP addresses for 216.30.120.128

that subnetting has reduced our original complement of 256 unique IP addresses to only 124. Here's why:

  256 IP addresses to start
−128 (the two subnets that would be all zeros or all ones)
−   4 (two host numbers in each subnet that would be all zeros or all ones)
=124 usable IP addresses

Wow! Subnetting sure costs you a lot of IP addresses! No wonder most systems let you cheat the official subnetting rules and use subnets that contain all zeros or all ones! If your systems allow it (Windows, NetWare, and Linux do, although you may need to tweak them), and if your router allows it (most do but your router person may have to configure some special settings), you don't have to lose all these IP addresses. But remember, for the test, follow all the rules strictly.

Let's now plug some real values into our example network. Note that we had the router person update the router table for each subnet (see Figure 12-20).

Class Licenses

In the early days of the Internet, in fact until fairly recently, if you wanted to put some computers on the Internet, you (or your ISP) asked for a block of unused IP addresses from the IANA. The IANA passes out IP addresses in contiguous chunks called *class licenses* (see Figure 12-21). Classes D and E addresses were not distributed (only Classes A, B, and C were).

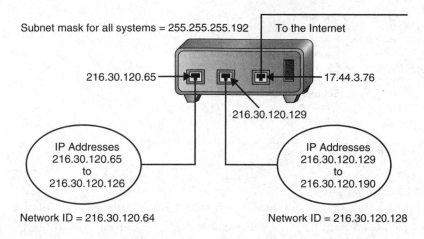

Figure 12-20   Working subnet router settings

	First Decimal Value	Addresses	Hosts per Network
Class A	1—126	1.0.0.0—126.0.0.0	16.7 Million
Class B	128—191	128.0.0.0—191.255.0.0	65,534
Class C	192—223	192.0.0.0—223.255.255.0	254
Class D	224—239	224.0.0.0—239.255.255.255	Multicast addresses
Class E	240—255	240.0.0.0—255.255.255.254	Experimental addresses

Figure 12-21   IP classes

 EXAM TIP: Make sure you memorize the Class A, B, and C IP class licenses! You should be able to look at any IP address and tell its class license. A trick to help: The first binary octet of a Class A address always begins with a 0 (0xxxxxxx); for Class B, it's 10 (10xxxxxx), and for Class C, 110 (110xxxxx).

In most cases, you get an address class that you need to subnet, which means the subnet always hits at one of the dots (/8, /16, or /24). Using this, you can make a chart showing the number of subnets created by moving the subnet mask from zero to eight

```
.00000000 =                          0 Subnets      2⁸ − 2 = 254 Hosts
.10000000 = .128 = 2¹ − 2 =          0 Subnets      2⁷ − 2 = 126 Hosts
.11000000 = .128 = 2² − 2 =          2 Subnets      2⁶ − 2 =  62 Hosts
.11100000 = .128 = 2³ − 2 =          6 Subnets      2⁵ − 2 =  30 Hosts
.11110000 = .128 = 2⁴ − 2 =         14 Subnets      2⁴ − 2 =  14 Hosts
.11111000 = .128 = 2⁵ − 2 =         30 Subnets      2³ − 2 =   6 Hosts
.11111100 = .128 = 2⁶ − 2 =         62 Subnets      2² − 2 =   2 Hosts
.11111110 = .128 = 2⁷ − 2 =        126 Subnets      2¹ − 2 =   0 Hosts
.11111111 =                          0 Subnets
```

Figure 12-22   Subnet possibilities

places (see Figure 12-22). It makes subnetting a lot faster! Note that there are only certain numbers of subnets. If you need 22 subnets, for example, you need to move the subnet mask over 5 places to get 30. You then only use 22 of the 30 subnets.

The previous example used a class C license, but subnetting works the same for class A and class B licenses, just with a larger number of hosts and subnets. Let's say you get a network ID of 129.30.0.0 and need to create 12 subnets. All IP addresses starting with 128.0.xxx.xxx up to 191.255.xxx.xxx are by definition class B, so we can represent our network as 129.30.0.0/16. Just as you did before, first write out the starting subnet mask and start moving it to the right until you have enough subnets. If you move it over 3 places, you get $2^3 = 8 - 2$ (the two you can't use) = 6 subnets. Not enough. If you move the subnet mask four places, you get $2^4 = 16 - 2$ (again, minus the two you can't use) = 14 subnets (see Figure 12-23).

Just out of curiosity, can you figure out how many host numbers you get for each new network ID? That's easy! As you can see from the previous figure, the host ID has a total of 12 places. For each network ID, you get $2^{12} - 2$ or 4094 hosts. Figure 12-24 lists some of the IP addresses for one of the new network IDs.

There are three secrets to subnetting. First, remember to start with the given subnet mask and move it to the right until you have the number of subnets you need. Second, forget the dots. Never try to subnet without first converting to binary. Too many techs are locked into what I call *Class-C-itis*. They are so used to working only with Class C licenses that they forget there's more to subnetting than just the last octet. Finally, practice subnetting. Use the questions at the end of this lesson as a guide. You should be able to create your own scenarios for subnetting. Stick to these three secrets and you'll soon find subnetting a breeze to do.

[*Mike switches to Evil Overlord Mode*] Cackle! Muhawhawhaw! Now that I've had some fun torturing your pathetic little minds with subnets, I'm going to let you in on a little secret. Very few network administrators deal with subnetting anymore, because most systems nowadays don't need their own unique IP addresses. Instead, they use

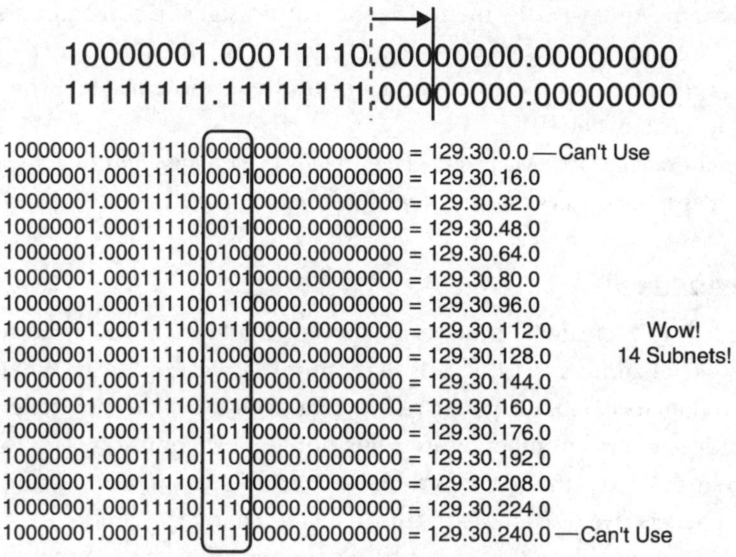

```
      10000001.00011110.00000000.00000000
      11111111.11111111.00000000.00000000
```

```
10000001.00011110|0000|0000.00000000 = 129.30.0.0 —Can't Use
10000001.00011110|0001|0000.00000000 = 129.30.16.0
10000001.00011110|0010|0000.00000000 = 129.30.32.0
10000001.00011110|0011|0000.00000000 = 129.30.48.0
10000001.00011110|0100|0000.00000000 = 129.30.64.0
10000001.00011110|0101|0000.00000000 = 129.30.80.0
10000001.00011110|0110|0000.00000000 = 129.30.96.0
10000001.00011110|0111|0000.00000000 = 129.30.112.0        Wow!
10000001.00011110|1000|0000.00000000 = 129.30.128.0     14 Subnets!
10000001.00011110|1001|0000.00000000 = 129.30.144.0
10000001.00011110|1010|0000.00000000 = 129.30.160.0
10000001.00011110|1011|0000.00000000 = 129.30.176.0
10000001.00011110|1100|0000.00000000 = 129.30.192.0
10000001.00011110|1101|0000.00000000 = 129.30.208.0
10000001.00011110|1110|0000.00000000 = 129.30.224.0
10000001.00011110|1111|0000.00000000 = 129.30.240.0 —Can't Use
```

Figure 12-23   Moving the subnet mask four places

```
10000001.00011110.10010000.00000001 = 129.30.144.1
10000001.00011110.10010000.00000010 = 129.30.144.2
10000001.00011110.10010000.00000011 = 129.30.144.3
10000001.00011110.10010000.00000100 = 129.30.144.4
10000001.00011110.10010000.00000101 = 129.30.144.5
.......
10000001.00011110.10010000.00011110 = 129.30.144.30
10000001.00011110.10010000.00011111 = 129.30.144.31
10000001.00011110.10010000.00100000 = 129.30.144.32
10000001.00011110.10010000.00100001 = 129.30.144.33
10000001.00011110.10010000.00100010 = 129.30.144.34
.......
10000001.00011110.10010000.11111010 = 129.30.144.250
10000001.00011110.10010000.11111011 = 129.30.144.251
10000001.00011110.10010000.11111100 = 129.30.144.252
10000001.00011110.10010000.11111101 = 129.30.144.253
10000001.00011110.10010000.11111110 = 129.30.144.254
```

Figure 12-24   Some of the IP addresses for network ID 129.30.0.0/16

special IP addresses that are invisible outside of their local network, thanks to the machinations of special systems called NATs (I cover NATs in a later chapter). Is that whimpering I hear? How satisfying! All that pain for nothing! Well, nothing except passing the Network+ exam. And actually, the folks who administer the real Internet, and that includes the thousands of techs who work at every ISP, do this stuff every day. So, learn subnetting—and come visit me in my underground volcano complex when you've figured it out! Muhawhawhaw!!!

[*Mike returns to Normal Friendly Geek Mode. Filled with remorse for having tortured innocent newbie techs so mercilessly, he decides to switch to a much simpler topic.*]

Special IP Addresses

The folks who invented TCP/IP created a number of special IP addresses you need to know about. The first special address is 127.0.0.1, the famous *loopback* address. When you tell a device to send data to 127.0.0.1, you're telling that device to send the packets to *itself*. The loopback address has a number of uses; one of the most common is to use it with the **PING** command. We use the command **PING 127.0.0.1** to test a NIC's ability to send and receive packets (we'll see more of this in a later chapter).

Lots of folks use TCP/IP in networks that either aren't connected to the Internet, or that want to hide from the bad guys on the Internet, like hackers and spies. Certain groups of IP addresses, known as *private IP addresses*, are available to help in these situations. All routers are designed to destroy private IP addresses so they can never be used on the Internet, making them a very handy way to hide systems! Anyone can use these private IP addresses, but they're useless for systems that need to access the Internet—*unless* you use one of those mysterious NAT things to which I just referred. (Bet you're dying to learn about NATs now!) For the moment, however, let's just look at the ranges of addresses that are designated *private* IP addresses:

- 10.0.0.0 through 10.255.255.255 (One class A license)
- 172.16.0.0 through 172.31.255.255 (16 class B licenses)
- 192.168.0.0 through 192.168.255.255 (256 class C licenses)

We refer to all other IP addresses as *public* IP addresses.

 EXAM TIP: Make sure you can quickly tell the difference between a private and a public IP address for the Network+ exam!

DNS

Anyone who's ever used a web browser is used to seeing Internet addresses like www.totalsem.com, ftp.microsoft.com, and so on; these invariably end with .com, .org, .net or some other usually three-character name. Now just a minute here—haven't we spent the last several pages explaining how every computer on the Internet has a unique *IP address* that distinguishes it from every other computer on the Internet? What's with this *name* business all of a sudden? Well, the folks who invented the Internet decided early on that it was way too painful for human beings to refer to computer systems using dotted decimal notation. There had to be some sort of Internet naming convention that allowed people to refer to systems by human-friendly names, rather than cryptic but computer-friendly numbers. They couldn't just do away with the numbers, however, unless they were planning to teach the computers to read English, so they developed a procedure called *name resolution*. The idea was to have a list of IP addresses matched up with corresponding human-friendly names, that any computer on the Internet could use to translate a computer name into an IP address.

The original IP specification implemented name resolution using a special text file called HOSTS. A copy of this file was stored on every computer system on the Internet. The HOSTS file contained a list of IP addresses for every computer on the Internet, matched to the corresponding system names. Remember, not only was the Internet a lot smaller then, there weren't yet rules about how to compose Internet names, like they must end in .com or .org, or start with www or ftp. Anyone could name their computer pretty much anything they wanted (there were a few restrictions on length and allowable characters) as long as nobody else had snagged the name first. Part of an old HOSTS file might look something like this:

192.168.2.1   fred

201.32.16.4   school2

123.21.44.16   server

If your system wanted to access the system called fred, it looked up the name fred in its HOSTS file, and then used the corresponding IP address to contact fred. Every HOSTS file on every system on the Internet was updated every night at 2 A.M. This worked fine when the Internet was still the province of a few university geeks and some military guys, but when the Internet grew to about 5,000 systems, it became impractical to make every system use and update a HOSTS file. This motivated the creation of the Domain Name Service (DNS) concept.

Believe it or not, the HOSTS file is still alive and well in every computer. You can find the HOSTS file in the \WINDOWS folder in Windows 9*x* and in the \WINNT\SYSTEM32\DRIVERS\ETC folder in Windows NT/2000. It's just a text file that you can open with any text editor. Here are a few lines from the default HOSTS file that comes with Windows. See the "#" signs? Those are *remark* symbols that designate lines as comments rather than code—take them off and Windows will read the lines and act on them. While all operating systems continue to support the HOSTS file, it is rarely if ever used, and you should leave it alone!

```
# Additionally, comments (such as these) may be inserted on individual
# lines or following the machine name denoted by a '#' symbol.
#
# For example:
#
#      102.54.94.97      rhino.acme.com          # source server
#       38.25.63.10      x.acme.com              # x client host
127.0.0.1            localhost
```

How DNS Works

The Internet guys, faced with the task of replacing HOSTS, first came up with the idea of creating one super computer that did nothing but resolve names for all the other computers on the Internet. Problem: Even now, no computer is big enough or powerful enough to handle the job alone. So they fell back on that time-tested bureaucratic solution: delegation! The top dog DNS system would delegate parts of the job to subsidiary DNS systems, who in turn would delegate part of their work to other systems, and so on, potentially without end. These systems run a special DNS server program, and are called, amazingly enough, *DNS servers*. This is all peachy, but it raises another issue: you need some way to decide how to divvy up the work. Toward this end, they created a naming system designed to facilitate delegation. The top dog DNS server is actually a bunch of really powerful computers dispersed around the world and working as a team, known collectively as the *DNS root*. The Internet name of this computer team is "."—that's right, just "dot." Sure it's weird, but it's quick to type, and they had to start somewhere! DNS root has the complete definitive name resolution table, but most name resolution work is delegated to other DNS servers. Just below the DNS root in the hierarchy is a set of DNS servers that handle what are known as the *top-level domain names*. These are the famous COM, ORG, NET, EDU, GOV, MIL, and INT. (Even these are getting full—you may have seen news stories about new additions to this top level domain list.) These top-level DNS servers delegate to thousands of second-level DNS servers; they handle the millions of names like totalsem.com and whitehouse.gov that have been created within each of the top-level domains.

These domain names must be registered for Internet use with an organization called *Internic* (www.Internic.net). They are arranged in the familiar "Second level.Top level" domain name format, where the top level is COM, ORG, NET, and so on, and the second level is the name of the individual entity registering the domain name. For example, in the domain name microsoft.com, "microsoft" is the second-level part and "com" is the top-level part. As we just learned, the Internet maintains a group of very powerful and very busy DNS servers that resolve the top-level parts of domain names. The second-level parts of domain names are resolved by the owners of those domain names, or by an ISP.

A DNS network may also have subdomains. The subdomain names are added to the *left* of the domain name. Let's use our standard example: the Wheebo network, which has the domain name "wheebo.com," may have subdomains with names like north .wheebo.com and south.wheebo.com. The owner of the second level domain, Wheebo in our example, maintains any subdomains on its own DNS servers or its ISP's DNS servers. Subdomains may also contain a further layer of subdomains (for example, bravo.north.wheebo.com), but this is rare, and usually handled by in-house DNS servers where it does exist.

Every system on the Internet also has a *host name* added on to the left of its domain name. A *fully qualified domain name* (FQDN) contains the complete DNS name of a system, from its host name to the top-level domain name. I have a system in my office with an FQDN of vpn.totalsem.com that handles my virtual private network. I also have a system with the FQDN of www.totalsem.com that runs my web site. How about that—seems you've been using FQDNs for years and didn't even know it!

When a system needs to resolve a domain name to an IP address, it queries the DNS server listed in its DNS server settings. If the DNS server cannot resolve the name, the DNS server asks the root server. The root server then redirects your DNS server to a top-level DNS server. The top-level DNS server in turn points you to a second-level DNS server that will actually resolve the domain name. We'll look at how DNS works in much more detail in Chapter 15; right now, let's see how you configure a Windows client system to use DNS.

You configure DNS in Windows using the TCP/IP Properties dialog box. Figure 12-25 shows the DNS settings for my system. Note that I have more than one DNS server setting; the second one is a backup in case the first one isn't working. Two DNS settings is not a rule, however, so don't worry if your system shows only one DNS server setting, or perhaps more than two. Also notice the Host and Domain settings in Figure 12-25.

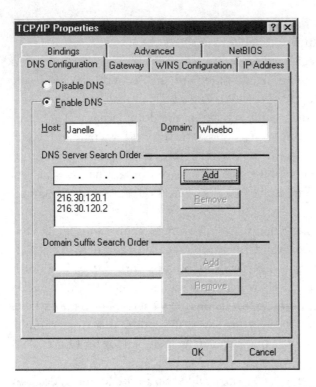

Figure 12-25 DNS settings in Windows 98

These are used to identify your system on the Internet. Your system gives the DNS server whatever names you enter in these boxes. You can check your current DNS server settings in Windows using either the **WINIPCFG** or the **IPCONFIG** command.

That's pretty much all we need to talk about right now. What you need to know about DNS for the Network+ exam is how to set up the DNS server for your system if given the configuration information.

DHCP

Before you read this, you must promise not to hit me, okay? So far we've discussed four items that must be configured for every system in an IP network: the IP address, the default gateway, the subnet mask, and the DNS server. Does this sound like a bit of a hassle? Imagine being informed by some network muckety-muck that your organization is changing its DNS servers, requiring you to reset the DNS server settings on every system in the network. Doesn't sound like too much fun, eh?

Fortunately for you, there's something called the Dynamic Host Configuration Protocol (DHCP). DHCP enables individual client machines on an IP network to configure all of their IP settings automatically. DHCP requires a special system running a special program called a *DHCP server*. Auto-configuration has been a boon to networks that change a lot (like mine), systems that travel around (like laptops), and dial-up systems. DHCP is extremely popular and heavily used in almost all IP networks.

 EXAM TIP: DHCP is used mainly by Windows networks. There's another auto-configuration protocol called BOOTP that is popular in UNIX/Linux networks. They both work basically the same way.

How Does DHCP Work?

All of this DHCP automatic self-configuration doesn't let administrators completely off the hook, of course. Somebody has to set up the DHCP server before it can make the magic happen throughout the network. The DHCP server stores all of the necessary IP information for the network, and provides that information to clients as they boot into the network.

You also have to configure your network *clients* to use DHCP. Configuring a Windows system for DHCP is really easy. Yes, once again go to the TCP/IP Properties dialog box. This time, set the IP Address to *Obtain an IP address automatically*, and you're ready to go (see Figure 12-26)! Just be sure you have a DHCP server on your network!

Any IP setting that relies on a DHCP server is called a *dynamic* setting. Any setting that you manually configure in a client is called a *static* setting. You can use a combination of dynamic and static settings on a single client. You can tell the client to get its IP address dynamically from a DHCP server, for example, but manually input static DNS server address information.

WINS

Years ago, Microsoft and TCP/IP didn't mix too well. Microsoft networks leaned heavily on the NetBIOS/NetBEUI protocols, and NetBIOS used a completely different naming convention than TCP/IP. To implement an IP network protocol in Windows NT, the programmers realized that NT needed some way to resolve NT's NetBIOS names into IP addresses. At the time, Microsoft didn't foresee the impact of the Internet; it seemed to make more sense to ignore DNS, thereby avoiding a major redesign of Windows NT, and instead come up with an equivalent that used the already existing NetBIOS functions. This decision resulted in the creation of the *Windows Internet Naming Service* (*WINS*).

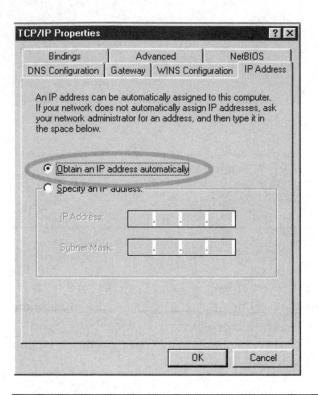

Figure 12-26 Configuring a Windows 98 system for DHCP

 NOTE: Windows 2000 systems no longer need NetBIOS; they now use DNS, although they can support WINS if needed. Windows 9x and NT systems, however, still need WINS!

As we saw in the previous chapter, name resolution in Windows has always depended on individual hosts broadcasting to the network their desire to use a particular NetBIOS name. Clearly, broadcasting is a really poor way to interface in an IP environment that does not like broadcasting. Microsoft solved this dilemma by creating WINS.

WINS is a hierarchical naming system, similar to DNS in many ways. Just as DNS depends on DNS servers, WINS revolves around special WINS server software. A WINS server tracks all of the requests for NetBIOS names on a Windows TCP/IP network. When computers first log on to a WINS network, they register with the WINS server, and the server puts the client's NetBIOS name and IP address into its WINS database. Any system on the network can query the WINS server for NetBIOS name resolution.

Happily for network techs, Microsoft automated many aspects of WINS, making the actual setup and configuration of WINS almost trivially easy. Setting up WINS on a Windows client requires little more than a quick trip to the WINS Configuration tab in —can you guess?—the TCP/IP Properties dialogue box, where you can select *Use DHCP for WINS resolution* (see Figure 12-27). There are other setup options as well which we will discuss in Chapter 15.

Don't Panic!

Holy Acronyms, Batman! How are you supposed to remember all of these different IP functions? Don't panic, my young friend—let's review what each one does.

- **IP Address** The unique address required for every system on the Internet or other TCP/IP network; a 32-bit binary number, it is commonly expressed in dotted decimal notation.

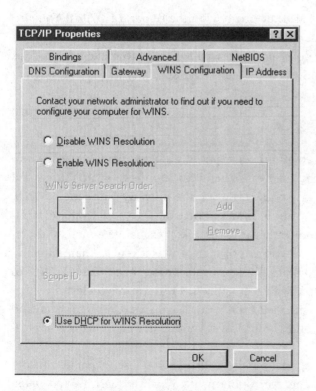

Figure 12-27 WINS settings in Windows 98

- **Gateway** A system that acts as the router for a local network. Its IP address is called the Default Gateway.

- **Subnet Mask** A special binary value used by a networked system to determine if the recipient's address on an IP packet is local or remote.

- **DNS** A feature of IP that resolves domain names (for example, www.totalsem .com) into actual IP addresses.

- **WINS** A Windows-only protocol used to resolve NetBIOS names into IP addresses.

- **DHCP** A protocol that automatically configures all of this crap for you!

You may have noticed that DNS, WINS, and DHCP all require a *server*. Be careful with this terminology. In this context, server does not mean a physical computer—it means a *program* that handles DNS, DHCP, or WINS requests from client computers. It's fairly common, especially on smaller networks, for one server system to run all three of these server programs simultaneously.

Everything we've covered so far has dealt strictly with the IP part of TCP/IP. You also need to know some information about TCP for the Network+ exam, however, so let's now move to TCP and see what it does, and what we have to do to make it work. Plus we'll take a brief glance at UDP, a protocol that functions similarly to TCP, although at a much lower level.

TCP

Most folks who work in a network environment, especially a network with systems running Microsoft Windows, think that a network's main function is to share folders and printers. Back when the Internet was young, however, the folks who designed TCP/IP didn't think exactly in those terms. They looked at a network as a way to share terminals (remember this discussion from earlier in the book?), exchange e-mail, and perform other functions unrelated to our concept of networks as a way to share files and printers. But lucky for us, they also realized they would probably be using TCP/IP to share things they hadn't yet invented, so they designed it with a degree of flexibility that enables you and me today to share files, surf the WEB, listen to streaming media, and play Everquest online with a thousand of our closest buddies at once. This is TCP's reason for being.

The inventors of TCP/IP assign a special number called a *port* to each separate network function, such as e-mail, web browsing, even online games like Everquest. This *port number* is placed inside every IP packet and is used by the sending and receiving systems to figure out which application to give the packet to. Possibly the most famous TCP port of all is good old port 80. If a packet comes into a computer with the port number 80 embedded in it, the system knows that the packet needs to go to your web browser. Packets sent to port 80 use a special protocol called HyperText Transfer Protocol (HTTP).

UDP

If you get a chance, take a look at the link light on your NIC when you first start your system. You'll notice that the light is flickering away, showing that some kind of communication is taking place. Granted, not all of that communication is for your system, but trust me, a lot of it is—and you haven't even started your e-mail or opened a web browser! Clearly your PC is talking on the network even though you haven't asked it to do anything! Don't worry—this is a good thing. TCP/IP does lots of boring maintenance-type stuff in the background that you neither need nor want to care about. Most of these maintenance communications are simple things like an ARP request, or any one of about 500 other little maintenance jobs that TCP/IP handles for you automatically.

While these things are important, they do not require all the TCP information in an IP packet. Knowing this, the folks who designed TCP/IP created a much simpler protocol called User Datagram Protocol (UDP). UDP transmits much less information than TCP. UDP packets are both simpler and smaller than TCP packets, and do most of the behind-the-scenes work in a TCP/IP network. UDP packets are what is called *connectionless*—that is, they don't worry about confirming that a packet actually reached its destination. TCP packets, in contrast, are *connection-oriented*—in other words, they must create a connection between the sending and receiving systems to ensure that the packet actually reaches its destination successfully. Important functions like e-mail will never use UDP. Some older applications, most prominently TFTP (Trivial FTP), use UDP to transfer files. But even TFTP is quite rare today; these days UDP is almost completely relegated to behind-the-scenes jobs.

Table 12-1 shows a list of the most famous of all the TCP and UDP ports and their uses. Keep in mind that Table 12-1 shows only the most common ones—there are literally hundreds more than these! For the Network+ exam, at least be sure you memorize this table.

Here are brief explanations of these ports, most of which I'll revisit in detail in later chapters.

HTTP (Port 80)   Web servers use HyperText Transfer Protocol (HTTP) to send Web pages to clients running web browsers such as Internet Explorer or Netscape Navigator.

FTP (Ports 20 and 21)   File Transfer Protocol (FTP) transfers data files between servers and clients. All implementations of TCP/IP support FTP file transfers, making

Table 12-1 TCP Ports

Port Number	Service	Description
20	FTP DATA	File Transfer Protocol – Data. Used for transferring files.
21	FTP	File Transfer Protocol – Control. Used for transferring files.
23	TELNET	Telnet. Used to gain "remote control" over another machine on the network.
25	SMTP	Simple Mail Transfer Protocol. Used for transferring e-mail between e-mail servers or from client to server.
69	TFTP	Trivial File Transfer Protocol. Used for transferring files without a secure login.
80	HTTP	HyperText Transfer Protocol, used for transferring HyperText Markup Language (HTML) files (in other words, Web pages).
110	POP3	Post Office Protocol, ver. 3. Used for transferring e-mail from an e-mail server to an e-mail client.
119	NNTP	Network News Transfer Protocol. Used to transfer Usenet news group messages from a news server to a news reader program.
123	NTP	Network Time Protocol. Used to synchronize the time of a server or workstation to another server.
137	NETBIOS-NS	NetBIOS Name Service. Used by Microsoft Networking.
138	NETBIOS-DG	NetBIOS Datagram Service. Used for transporting data by Microsoft Networking.
139	NETBIOS-SS	NetBIOS Session Service. Used by Microsoft Networking.
161	SNMP	Simple Network Management Protocol. Used to monitor network devices remotely.
443	HTTPS	HyperText Transfer Protocol, Secure.

FTP an excellent choice for transferring files between machines running different operating systems (Windows to UNIX, UNIX to Macintosh, and so on). FTP uses port 21 for control messages and sends the data using port 20. FTP servers can require users to log in before downloading or uploading files. Most operating systems include a command line FTP utility.

TFTP (Port 69)   Trivial File Transfer Protocol (TFTP) transfers files between servers and clients. Unlike FTP, TFTP requires no user login. Devices that need an operating system but have no local hard disk (for example, diskless workstations and routers) often use TFTP to download their operating systems.

SMTP (Port 25)   Simple Mail Transfer Protocol (SMTP) sends e-mail messages between clients and servers or between servers. From the end user's perspective, SMTP handles outgoing mail only.

POP3 (Port 110)   Post Office Protocol version 3 (POP3) enables e-mail client software (for example, Outlook Express, Eudora, Netscape Mail) to retrieve e-mail from a mail server. POP3 does not send e-mail; SMTP handles that function.

SNMP (Port 161)   Simple Network Management Protocol (SNMP) enables network management applications to remotely monitor other devices on the network.

Telnet (Port 23)   Telnet allows a user to log in remotely and execute text-based commands on a remote host. Although any operating system can run a Telnet server, techs typically use Telnet to log in to UNIX-based systems.

NetBIOS (Ports 137, 138, 139)   Networks using NetBIOS in an IP network use ports 137, 138, and 139 for name resolution and other NetBIOS-specific tasks.

In most cases, you will never have to deal with ports. When you install an e-mail program, for example, your system will automatically assume that all packets coming on ports 110 and 25 are e-mail and will send them to the e-mail application. You don't have to do anything special to configure the port values—they just work. In later chapters, we will discuss configuring TCP/IP applications, and we'll see that in some cases you may have to change port numbers, but for now just be sure to memorize the port numbers in Table 12-1.

Managing Connections at the Session Layer

TCP/IP networks currently support two distinct Session layer protocols: NetBIOS and Sockets. Microsoft operating systems using TCP/IP employ NetBIOS names to track connections, while basic Internet functions such as web browsing use Sockets, the traditional TCP/IP Session layer protocol. Network techs and architects must understand the distinction between NetBIOS and Sockets applications to secure their networks properly and to configure WINS and DNS correctly.

EXAM TIP: Although CompTIA claims to be vendor-neutral, TCP/IP questions on the Network+ exam generally assume that the client system uses a Microsoft operating system such as Windows 9x, NT, or 2000.

NetBIOS

NetBIOS, discussed in more detail in Chapter 11, manages connections between machines using NetBIOS names. NetBIOS names combine the computer's name with special codes specifying each role the machine is performing on the network, such as server or client. A machine named WHEEBO, for example, that functions as both a client and a server, would have at least two names: WHEEBO<20> as a server and WHEEBO<00> as a client.

Microsoft operating systems prior to Windows 2000 use NetBIOS for file and print sharing functions regardless of the protocol suite they employ. By maintaining Net-BIOS as the Session layer protocol, Microsoft avoided having to rewrite programs operating at higher layers that rely on NetBIOS; however, the overwhelming predominance of DNS finally forced Microsoft to abandon NetBIOS starting with Windows 2000.

Sockets

Sockets functions much like NetBIOS names, defining both the host on the other end of a connection and its role in the connection. Where NetBIOS would define a connection with a NetBIOS name and an extension designating a function, a Sockets application defines a connection in terms of a *socket*, made up of an IP address and a port number. When Clara uses her web browser to connect to www.microsoft.com, her computer sends a request to Microsoft's web server requesting a connection at port 80, the default port number for HyperText Transfer Protocol (HTTP). The server sends the requested page, using the socket to keep track of the connection (see Figure 12-28).

IPv6

One of the big problems with TCP/IP stems from the fact that we seem to be running out of IP addresses. In theory, the 32-bit IP address under the current IP specification (we officially call it IPv4) allows for 2^{32} or over 4 billion addresses. However, due to many restrictions, only about 1.7 billion are available, and many of those are wasted by

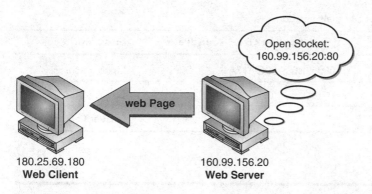

Figure 12-28   Sockets track connections using an IP address and port number.

organizations that take more IP addresses than they need. As a result, the Internet Engineering Task Force (IETF) developed a new IP addressing scheme, called *IP version 6*, abbreviated *IPv6* (first known as *IP Next Generation* [*IPng*]), that is expected to gradually replace IPv4 in coming years. IPv6 extends the 32-bit IP address to 128 bits, allowing up to 3.4×10^{38} addresses! Probably enough to last us for awhile, eh?

Remember that the IPv4 addresses are written as 197.169.94.82 using four octets. Well, IPv6 has now changed all that. IPv6 addresses are written like this:

```
FEDC:BA98:7654:3210:0800:200C:00CF:1234
```

IPv6 uses a *colon* as a separator, instead of the period used in IPv4's dotted decimal format. Each group is a *hexadecimal* number between 0000 and FFFF. As a refresher for those who don't play with hex regularly, one hexadecimal character (for example, F) represents four bits, so four hexadecimal characters make a 16-bit group. When writing IPv6 addresses, leading zeros can be dropped from a group, so 00CF becomes simply CF, and 0000 becomes just 0. To write IPv6 addresses containing strings of zeros, you can use a pair of colons (::) to represent a string of consecutive 16-bit groups with a value of zero. For example, using the :: rule you can write the IPv6 address FEDC:0000:0000:0000:00CF:0000:BA98:1234 as FEDC::CF:0:BA98:1234. Notice that I could not use a second :: to represent the third-to-last group of four zeros—only one :: per address! There's a very good reason for this rule. Can you see what it is? Hint: Think about expanding an abbreviated IPv6 address.

Table 12-2 shows some of the reserved IPv6 addresses.

Table 12-2   IPv6 addresses and their function

IPv6	:: rule applied to IPv6 address	Function
1080:0:0:0:8:800:200C:417A	1080::8:800:200C:417A	Unicast address
0:0:0:0:0:0:0:1	::1	Loopback address
0:0:0:0:0:0:0:0	::	Unspecified address

NOTE: **The unspecified address (all zeros) can never be used, nor can an address that contains all ones.**

Chapter Review

Questions

1. A host is:
   a. Any server on a TCP/IP network
   b. Any device on a TCP/IP network that can send or receive data packets
   c. A device on a TCP/IP network that forwards data packets to other networks
   d. A device on a TCP/IP network that resolves names to IP addresses

2. Before it can communicate with another host on a different network, a TCP/IP host must have which of the following settings configured correctly? (Select all that apply.)
   a. IP address
   b. Subnet mask
   c. DNS server
   d. Default gateway

3. What port number does HTTP use?
   a. 443
   b. 110
   c. 80
   d. 43

4. The binary number 11000101 has the decimal equivalent of:

    a. 197

    b. 169

    c. 94

    d. 82

5. What is the loopback address for IPv4?

    a. 127.0.0.1

    b. 0:0:0:0:0:0:0:0

    c. ::1

    d. 0:0:0:0:0:0:0:1

6. The protocol that enables network management applications to remotely monitor devices is known as:

    a. SNMP

    b. SMTP

    c. POP3

    d. TFTP

7. John is running Windows 98. He wants to find out his MAC address and IP address. What utility can he use that provides him with this information?

    a. ARP

    b. WINIPCFG

    c. IPCONFIG

    d. MACIP

8. Mike is running Windows 2000. He wants to find out his MAC address and IP address. What utility can he use that provides him with this information?

    a. ARP

    b. WINIPCFG

    c. IPCONFIG

    d. MACIP

9. Scott's system wants to send data to Roger's system. Scott's system knows Roger's IP address, but it doesn't know the MAC address, which it needs. What does the system use to make to request a MAC address for a known IP address?

    a. ARP

    b. WINIPCFG

    c. IPCONFIG

    d. MACIP

10. The IP address 192.23.45.123 has a default subnet mask of:
    a. 255.0.0.0
    b. 255.255.0.0
    c. 255.255.255.0
    d. 255.255.255.255

Answers

1. **B.** Any device on a TCP/IP network that can send or receive data packets is called a host.

2. **A, B, and D.** A host on a TCP/IP network must have its IP address, subnet mask, and default gateway correctly configured before it can communicate with hosts on other networks.

3. **C.** HyperText Transfer Protocol (HTTP) uses port 80.

4. **A.** The binary number 11000101 has the decimal equivalent of 197.

5. **A.** The loopback address for IPv4 is 127.0.0.1.

6. **A.** Simple Network Management Protocol (SNMP) enables network management applications to remotely monitor devices.

7. **B.** On a Windows 98 system, the WINIPCFG utility gives the MAC address and IP address currently used by that system.

8. **C.** On a Windows 2000 system, the IPCONFIG utility gives the MAC address and IP address currently used by that system.

9. **A.** The sending system sends out an address resolution protocol (ARP) request to get the MAC address for a known IP address.

10. **C.** The IP address 192.23.45.123 is in Class C and has the default subnet mask of 255.255.255.0.

## CHAPTER 13

Network Operating Systems

In this chapter, you will

- Learn about the major network operating systems
- Understand network operating system features
- Understand client/server and peer-to-peer networks and the differences between them
- Learn about network security issues relating to network operating systems and passwords
- Understand the concepts of resource-, server-, and organization-based networks

Once upon a time, in a land far, far away, building a network was a simple task. The intrepid network tech went to a single large company like IBM and said, "Give me a network!" The vendor would then provide everything the tech needed: servers, clients, NICs, hubs, the lot. Everything worked together, at least in theory, because everything came from a single company that controlled the design of all the components. Today, network techs don't get to live in that fairy-tale world; these days a typical large-scale network includes products from many different vendors. On the hardware level, a network designer can select Ethernet or Token Ring hardware from a wide variety of vendors, trusting that the products comply with standards such as IEEE 802.3 and IEEE 802.5 (see Chapters 3 and 4). A computer with a 10BaseT NIC from 3Com needs no special tweaking to communicate with a computer using a 10BaseT NIC from Intel, and the NICs will have no problem communicating with a 10BaseT switch made by Cisco. As long as you stick to standards, getting hardware from different vendors to work together is a breeze.

The choice of a network operating system for your network is more complex. Odds are good you've heard of some or all of the variations of Microsoft Windows, but you do have other choices, like Novell NetWare and Linux. The lofty goal of this chapter is to give you a basic overview of these various network operating systems so that you can appreciate their strengths and weaknesses. The Network+ exam has very low expectations of what you need to know about the different network operating systems—a basic understanding of each is more than sufficient to pass the exam. Given these low expectations, I'm going to concentrate mostly on a few basic issues, such as the types of network protocols each NOS uses and how each provides security for shared resources.

One aspect of network operating systems I hope you don't find too surprising is that all of these products do the same basic job: sharing resources. Each of the major operating system choices offers its own unique approach to accomplishing common network tasks. While each of the major network operating systems offers similar features, the implementations vary greatly in the nitty-gritty details. Before I go into all the details, let's make sure you understand what a network operating system is supposed to do, so you can more easily appreciate the differences among the major competitors for your networking allegiance.

Historical/Conceptual

All network operating systems share the same fundamental goal: to enable *users*, the human beings who sit at the computers, to get work done by sharing resources. The routes to that goal vary, of course, depending on the nature of the work. Some networks simply enable users to share files and printers, while others supply users with access to literally hundreds of sophisticated applications such as web servers.

Network Operating System Features

Before choosing the right network operating system for your network, you must evaluate the networking functions you want to use, the level of security you require, and the types of any other networks that your network will be communicating with.

To help facilitate these decisions, the networking industry uses the concept of *roles* to determine the functions of a single system. I've used the terms client and server already, but now you'll see how to apply those terms when a network gets down to business.

Roles

The idea of a client system is pretty easy to grasp. The majority of systems on most networks are *clients*, the machines at which users sit and work (or play Half-Life, as the case may be). Client systems run applications such as word processors, spreadsheets, and web browsers, and generally accessing resources on the network. Most networks today use a Microsoft operating system such as Windows 9*x* or Windows 2000 as their client operating system, although UNIX workstations dominate in some settings.

Servers, on the other hand, are not nearly as easy to grasp conceptually—unless, of course, you just happen to be one of the smart, beautiful, cleverer-than-average people who bought the best Network+ book this side of Bespin! Since you must be one of those people, let me explain that the term server has two separate meanings, both of which we use quite heavily in the networking world. The definition of *server* that comes quickest to most folks' minds is a great, big, heavy-duty computer that uses a really big CPU, lots of RAM, and gazillions of hard drives to share resources. I've devoted an entire chapter to the hardware aspects of servers, and all the neato details involved in making those beasts work, so be patient and you will get to see lots of cool stuff!

But there's another definition for *server*, one that you need to understand to appreciate the power of networking roles. Ready? Here we go! Servers are systems that use special serving programs to provide clients access to certain resources. Different serving programs provide access to different resources. Ever heard of a web server? Well, when you fire up your web browser and type in www.totalsem.com, you're actually contacting another computer that's running some type of web-serving software. Many companies make web-serving software, but two of the most common are Microsoft Internet Information Server (IIS) and the very popular and free Apache web server. Apache has fairly boring configuration files, but you can use a third-party web-based utility to spruce it up. Figure 13-1 shows a web-based utility for Apache called Comanche.

If lots of people try to access the www.totalsem.com web site, that server system is going to get pretty busy, isn't it? That's why server systems tend to have lots of RAM, powerful CPUs, and big hard drives. Serving systems need that extra hardware to handle their high workloads, not because the server software itself needs it. In fact, many serving programs will run just fine on regular computers. For instance, consider the Microsoft Personal Web Server (PWS) program. Figure 13-2 shows the PWS Personal Web Manager screen running on a Windows 98 SE system. Granted, PWS doesn't do all the cool things the more powerful web servers do, but it is most certainly a functional web server and it runs on my Windows 98 system with no problems.

This second definition for a server begs an obvious question: If a server is any computer running serving software, can more than one serving program run on the same

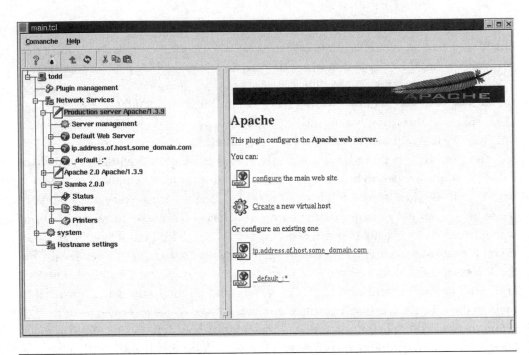

Figure 13-1 Comanche in action

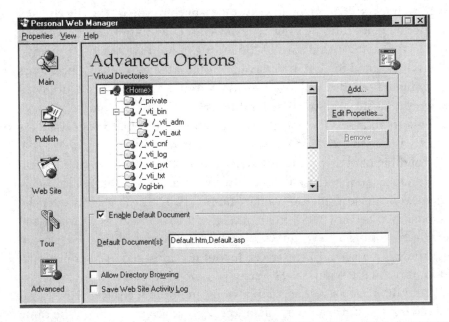

Figure 13-2 PWS running on a Windows 98 system

computer? Absolutely! In fact, that's the more common way to use serving programs. My Windows 2000 server, for example, runs about 13 different serving programs all at once. A single system running multiple server programs is very common in today's networks, especially smaller ones.

Can a system running a server program also act as a client? In most cases, yes—although you'll see one major exception when I show you Novell NetWare in a moment. Using my Windows 98 system as an example, it's acting as a web server but I can use it to access other servers at the same time. I can browse the Web (another system's web server), and I can access other servers' files or printers. In most cases, one system can be both a client and a server, but there are situations where you may not want to do that for security reasons.

Test Specific

Why is it so important to understand this concept of server and client roles? Different network operating systems have very different ways of handling which systems can act as servers and which as clients. If you don't understand the differences in how Novell NetWare handles servers and clients as compared to Microsoft Windows 2000, you could find yourself making a major mess by asking your NOS to do something it isn't designed to do! Networking folks use the terms client/server and peer-to-peer to categorize network operating systems. Let's look at how these two terms define the functionality of different network operating systems.

Client/Server

The earliest network operating systems used a client/server model. In that model, certain systems act as *dedicated servers*. Dedicated servers run powerful server network operating systems that offer up files, folders, web pages, and so on to the network's client systems. Dedicated servers are called *dedicated* because that's all they do. You cannot go up to a dedicated server and run Word or Solitaire. Client systems on a client/server network never function as servers. One client system can't access shared resources on another client system. Servers serve and clients receive, and never the twain shall meet in client/server land! The classic example of this type of network operating system is the popular and powerful Novell NetWare. Figure 13-3 shows a typical client/server network. As far as the clients are concerned, the only system on the network is the server system. The clients cannot see each other nor can they share data with each other directly. They must save the data on the server so other systems can access it.

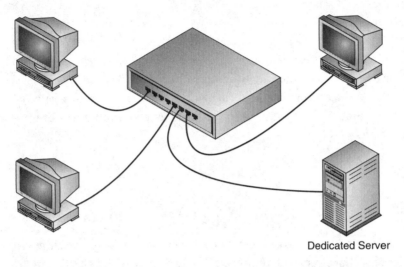

We can only access the
server. We can't access
each other.

Dedicated Server

Figure 13-3   In a pure client/server network, the clients cannot access each other directly.

Novell NetWare servers are true dedicated servers. You cannot go up to a Novell Net-Ware server and type a letter; there is no Windows, there are no user applications. The only thing Novell NetWare servers know how to do is share their own resources, but they share those resources extremely well! Novell NetWare's operating system is totally different from Windows. It requires you to learn an entirely different set of installation, configuration, and administration commands. Figure 13-4 shows a screen from Novell NetWare. Don't let the passing resemblance to Windows fool you—it is a completely different operating system!

 EXAM TIP: Fortunately, the Network+ exam does not expect you to know how to install, configure, or administer a NetWare server, or any other high-end NOS for that matter. Good thing, too, because if they did, this book would be about 5,000 pages!

Peer-to-Peer

In a *peer-to-peer* network operating system, any system can act as a server or a client or both, depending on how you decide to configure it (see Figure 13-5). PCs on peer-to-peer

```
Loading module ZIP.NLM
  Java Zip (based on 1.1.7B) Build 00032109
  Version 1.01q March 21,2000
  (C) Copyright 1998-2000 Novell,Inc.   All Rights Reserved.
Loading module  NWBG.NLM
  NW Background
  Version 1.00  March 7, 2000
  Copyright (c) 1999 Novell,Inc.
Loading module JPEG.NLM
  Java JPEG (based on 1.7.7B)
  Version 1.01q March 21, 2000
  (C) Copyright 1998 Novell, Inc. All Rights Reserved.
java: Class SetBG exited successfully


01-01-2002    2:17:25 pm:   SLP -1.7-0
SLP UA WARNING: Unable to contact directory agent Verify DA availability,
IP connectivity, DA, discovery options and configuration.


NETWARE51:
```

Figure 13-4   Novell NetWare—this ain't Windows!

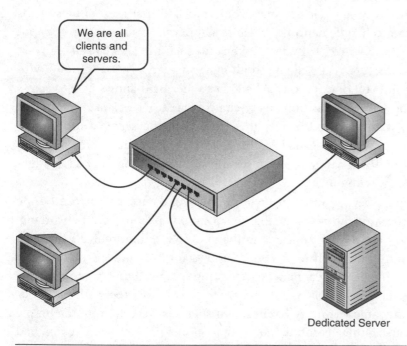

Figure 13-5 In a pure peer-to-peer network, the clients may all act as servers.

networks frequently act as both clients and servers. One of the most common examples of a peer-to-peer network is the venerable Windows 9*x* series of operating systems.

Client/Server vs. Peer-to-Peer

At first glance, it would seem that peer-to-peer is the way to go—why create a network that doesn't allow the clients to see each other? And besides, in today's Windows-dominated world, we're all running Windows already, so why bother with this Novell NetWare thing? Good questions! Let's answer them by going back in time to around 1983.

Back in the early 1980s, networking didn't really exist in the PC world. These were the days of the first processors, CPUs like the Intel 8088 and 80286. Just the demands of running a PC worked those poor CPUs to death. Then folks started to get the bright idea of adding networking to these systems. This was great in concept, but adding networking also meant adding lots of extra software, and networking software had to run continuously in the background while other activities were taking place. Those early systems had a *very* limited amount of processing power with which to tackle such networking challenges. Oh, and did I mention this was back in the days of DOS, the simplistic, single-tasking operating system of your forefathers? All the same, folks were determined to make 8088 systems running DOS handle networking. Clearly, this was going to take some doing!

The answer came in the form of client/server networking. Novell NetWare was invented back in the DOS days. Novell knew good and well that these little systems didn't have the power to handle networking *and* run application software, so they put all the functionality in the server software. There is no such thing as Novell NetWare client operating systems. A NetWare client is nothing more than a DOS, or (now) Windows system with a little bit of extra software added so the client knows how to access the server. By keeping the server functionality separate from the client systems, the Novell folks could add whatever functionality they wished to the server without overwhelming the clients. Novell servers had (and still have) tremendous power and great security because the only thing they do is run serving software. In the early days of networking, client/server was king!

CPU power advanced beyond those first wimpy chips, of course, so Microsoft came up with a new answer to the resource sharing question: peer-to-peer networking. Although peer-to-peer networking appeared in the mid 1980s, it didn't really become popular until the introduction of Microsoft Windows for Workgroups in the early 1990s. Early versions of peer-to-peer network operating systems didn't have nearly the strength of Novell's client/server NOS, but they worked fairly well for small networks. They *couldn't* have the same security, reliability, and speed as NetWare running on the same hardware, for the simple reason that every system in a peer-to-peer network had to provide both server and client networking support, *and* still let users do things like run word processors.

For years, we divided network operating systems into the client/server and peer-to-peer camps. Client/server networks used dedicated servers and allowed only the servers to share resources. Peer-to-peer networks allowed any system to act as a server and/or a client, but at the price of impaired reliability, security, and speed. The ability to pigeon-hole all network operating systems into these two network types made us happy and content. All was well with the networking world until Microsoft (who else?) came out with Windows NT. Windows NT totally messed up our lovely division of networks into client/server and peer-to-peer, because an NT (and Windows 2000 and Windows XP) system can be part of *both* a client/server network and a peer-to-peer network at the same time! A system running Windows NT gives you all the power of a dedicated server, while enabling that system to act as a client as well. Okay, it's actually not quite that simple, and I'll go into more detail in the next section, but the main point stands: NT messed up the entire client/server vs. peer-to-peer concept.

In my opinion, client/server and peer-to-peer are no longer useful ways to organize different types of networks. Unfortunately, the terms peer-to-peer and client/server are still tossed around by network folks like dice at a craps table. So how do we manifest the concepts of client/server and peer-to-peer networking in a world that has outgrown these categories? I use a totally different concept to organize network operating systems, based on how they handle security. Let's take a moment and make sure you understand what I mean by network security, so you can understand how my concept works.

Security

Network security involves protecting a network's users from their two greatest enemies: "bad guys" and themselves. When most people think about security issues, they immediately visualize some evil hacker attempting to break into a network and steal company secrets. For many organizations, especially those connected to the Internet, such threats are no joke. Network security, however, must also include Pogo's admonition that we've seen the enemy, and he is us. *User-proofing* a network—preventing users from accidentally destroying data or granting access to unauthorized individuals—is a key part of network security.

NOTE: What you are about to learn is not on the Network+ exam, nor is it part of common network vernacular. It is my way of understanding networks, an idea I developed with my good friends Brian and Libby Schwarz a few years ago. Even though this concept is not directly on the Network+ exam, it has withstood a lot of criticism and is starting to supplant the old and obsolete client/server and peer-to-peer terminology. I think it will help you tremendously on the exam.

How do we secure our network shares? Well, that begs the question, "What aspects of the shared resource need to be secured?" Think about this for a second: If you're sharing a folder, what exactly do you want to protect? You could just stop anyone from doing anything to that folder—that's certainly secure—but you can slice the issue a lot more finely than just blocking everyone and everything. For example, you could set up security so users could *read* the files in a particular folder but not *delete* them. Or, slicing things even more finely, you could set it up so users could add information to files but not delete any. It's this fine level of detailed control that really makes a network powerful.

These security issues don't just apply to shared folders. Security comes into play with any type of resource you want to share! Every time you access a web site, you run headlong into security. I can set my web server up so some visitors can only view web pages, others can edit certain pages, and a very few others can do anything they want, including delete the entire site if necessary. This control of what users can do to resources is called *permissions* or *rights*, depending on the brand of NOS you use. In the next chapter, I'll spend plenty of time discussing permissions and rights, types of protected resources, and how to share and secure them, but for now, what I want to discuss is *how* the NOS handles all this security. The different approaches network operating systems take in handling security is an easy and clear way to distinguish them. I call these different approaches *security types*.

Security Types

Odds are good you've heard of terms like user accounts, passwords, groups, domain controllers, and the like. These terms are critical to understanding how a network secures resources. Don't worry if you don't understand any or all of them right now—I'll cover them all in detail in this chapter and the next. Whether you know these terms or not, do know this: each NOS uses these tools in different ways. This is what my *security types* concept is all about—it separates the different network operating systems by the way they secure the network's resources.

My scheme divides networks into three different security types, based on which part of the NOS handles the security: Resource, Server, and Organization. Think about this—some part of the NOS must keep track of who can do what on the network. Some part of the NOS must check particular databases whenever someone opens a folder or tries to print to a printer in order to make sure that person is allowed to do whatever they are trying to do with that resource. My security model identifies three parts of the NOS that do the dirty job of handling security. As I describe my three security types, I'll pause to define things like user accounts and groups. Let's get busy learning about the most basic type: resource-based security.

EXAM TIP: Even though the Network+ exam doesn't discuss my security types, this section of the chapter is crammed with critical definitions you need to understand for the exam! Don't even think about skipping this!

Resource-based Security

The simplest network operating systems use what I call *resource-based* security. In a resource-based NOSs, the individual resources themselves store the information about who can access the resource and what they can do (see Figure 13-6). This information is usually stored within some data structure that is part of the actual shared resource, although it can also be stored in some arbitrary part of the NOS itself. The important thing to understand is that there's no central storage facility for such information—each resource is in charge of its own security storage. The most common example of a resource-based NOS is the Microsoft Windows 9x series of operating systems. Most of what the traditional model calls peer-to-peer network operating systems belongs in my resource-based security type.

Storing security information within individual resources is a simple security solution, but one that can handle only simple security issues. As an example, let's take a look at my Windows 98 system. If I want to share a folder called C:\WheeboPersonnelRecords,

Figure 13-6 In resource-based network operating systems, the resources themselves store the security information.

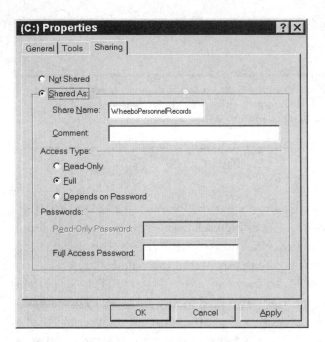

Figure 13-7 The Sharing folder in Windows 98

I alternate-click (right-click) that folder and select Sharing. I click the Shared As radio button to see the folder's sharing properties (see Figure 13-7).

Note that I can choose from a whopping three levels of sharing. I can set up the folder so anyone who uses it gets full access to do anything they want; I can set it up so everyone gets only Read access, or I can set a password on the resource to control full vs. read-only access. Feel the networking Force flowing through you, my young apprentice! These are your first examples of permissions/rights! Microsoft calls these *network rights*.

While this type of sharing works perfectly well as far as it goes, it has some serious limitations. First, unless I use a password, I have to give everyone who accesses this folder the same level of access. What if I want some people to have full access and others just Read access? I can use a password, of course, but consider the problem from an administrator's standpoint: everyone with the same level of access has that password. Suppose I want to change just one person's access—I have to change the password and then give the new password to everyone who needs access to that folder. This is not only wildly annoying, it's just asking for problems, because you're trusting those who know this one common password not to tell anyone else. Uh-huh. Not on the planet I call home. Now imagine there are 30 or 40 more shared folders and printers you need to protect this way—every one of those shared resources will get its own password! At this rate, a single system could use 60 to 70 different passwords! No problem, you say, if you make them all the same. Well, you could, but then how would you give different users different levels of access? But if you must have different passwords for different users of different resources, how can one lonely admin keep track of them all? Write it all down on a piece of paper? Make a spreadsheet? Let's face it, resource-based security may be fine for simple networks, but this is just not going to hack it in a more complex network.

Server-based Security

Server-based security employs a central database on each server to track who gets what level of access to the resources on that server. Most folks give Novell the nod for inventing this security type since it first appeared in the early versions of NetWare. Novell wasn't constrained to using a DOS system for its server, because it was literally its own operating system. Novell could design every part of the dedicated server specifically to optimize its ability to handle sharing, including the file system. Novell's file system is nothing like DOS or Windows. Novell invented it from the ground up to share files. By creating its own file system, Novell could add resource sharing directly to the file system. No other operating system can read a hard drive formatted for NetWare, although NetWare knows how to make the folders and files on the server visible over the network —a big difference.

To access a shared resource on a NetWare server, you must have a *user account*. A user account contains lists of user rights that tell the network what the user can and cannot do on the network, and file system rights that determine which shared resources the user can access. Each user account also has a password. A person who wants to access the shared resources on the server must go through a process called *logging on* to the server. Figure 13-8 shows a classic example of a person logging on to a NetWare server. As soon as the person logs on to a NetWare server, all of the access privileges for every shared resource on the network are set for the duration of that session.

Server-based security makes life a lot easier from an administrative standpoint. Still, in a large organization, assigning specific rights to each user individually makes for an excessive workload for the network administrator. The solution: Organize users with similar needs into *groups*. For example, Alice, the administrator of the network, assigns Greg, Bobby, and Peter's user accounts to the ACCOUNTING group and Jan's user account to the SALES group. Alice then assigns the ACCOUNTING group permission to access the accounting database and any other appropriate resources. By virtue of their membership in ACCOUNTING, Greg, Bobby, and Peter's user accounts have access to the ACCOUNTING group's resources, without Alice having to touch the individual

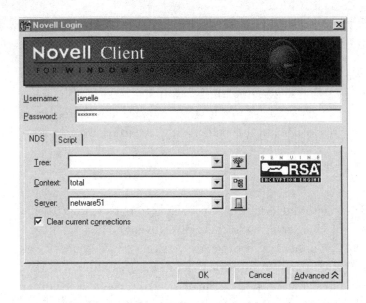

Figure 13-8 The NetWare logon screen

accounts. If the company hires more accountants, Alice simply creates new user accounts and adds them to the ACCOUNTING group. Alice creates groups for whatever different work specialties her company employs, and then assigns user accounts to the appropriate groups. In large organizations with hundreds of employees who have similar needs, the time and effort saved becomes significant.

In most instances, a user account's rights are *cumulative*, that is, a user receives the sum total of the rights granted to his individual user account and the rights granted to any of the groups to which he belongs. Greg, for example, belongs to both the MANAGERS and ACCOUNTANTS groups. Suppose Alice sets up a shared folder on a server and assigns the MANAGERS group the right to add files to the folder, the ACCOUNTANTS group the right to read (but not alter or delete) files in that folder, and Greg (as an individual) the right to modify files that already exist in that folder. To see what Greg can do, add up the rights: Greg can add files (MANAGERS), read files (ACCOUNTANTS), and modify files (Greg) in that directory because of his cumulative individual and group rights.

Server-based networks work great for more advanced networks, unless a network has more than one server. To use a server-based network, you must first have a user account on every server you want to use, and then you must log onto each one before you can use its resources. If your network only has a few servers, this isn't *too* much of a hassle for the user or the admin, but when the network has many servers, you've got an administrative nightmare once again.

Organization-based Security

In an organization-based network, a single database acts as the logon point for all the shared resources of the network. Different brands of network operating systems call this database by different names, but all of them work basically the same way. One system stores this database, and when a user logs on, that one system handles authentication of the user account and determines that user's level of access to every serving system on the network (see Figure 13-9).

Naturally, networks that use organization-based security have many methods to back up this database, in case the system it lives on crashes. For example, Windows NT designates one system as the Primary Domain Controller, but good NT administrators configure a second NT system to be a Backup Domain Controller. All serious (that is, *not* resource-based) network operating systems use some form of organization-based security. In fact, both Microsoft and Novell now use an even more advanced type of database called a *directory*. A directory goes beyond just providing authentication for the user accounts—a directory literally maps out the entire network. A good directory implementation describes every system, every printer, every user, and every group on its network, providing a central repository of all that is the network in one big database.

Mixing Types

As you will soon see, every network operating system fits nicely into one of these three security types. Do understand, however, that these types can and do work happily

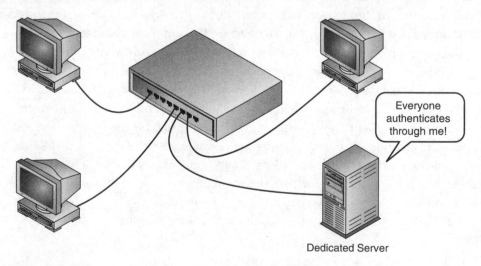

Figure 13-9   Everyone authenticates through me!

together in one physical network. Networked Windows 98 systems that operate in a resource-based mode when communicating amongst themselves can also communicate in a server-based mode with a NetWare server on the same physical network. Microsoft did an amazing job enabling Windows systems to act as clients for multiple server types. Better yet (but confusing to new techs), all this complexity is hidden from the user. Looked at from Network Neighborhood in a Windows 98 system, a NetWare server looks no different than another Windows 98 system. You can't tell them apart just by looking at the icons in Network Neighborhood—unless you know what to look for. To the untrained eye, it looks like one network, but to your trained tech's eye, the NetWare server icon tells you this system is actually connected to two different networks using two different types of security.

Client/Server Part Deux

Okay, Mike, you say client/server and peer-to-peer no longer mean anything, but anyone who's into networking at all hears these terms now more than ever. So what do client/server and peer-to-peer mean in the context of today's networks? Well, these terms have taken on new, or rather updated, definitions. Client/server and peer-to-peer now refer more to *applications* than to network operating systems. Consider e-mail for a moment. Most of us easily accept that for e-mail to work, you need an e-mail *client* like Microsoft Outlook or Netscape Messenger. But you also need an e-mail *server* program like Microsoft Exchange to handle the e-mail requests from your e-mail client. When we talk about client/server today, we mean what happens between the serving application and the client application.

Client/server networking works pretty much the same way regardless of function. The client program starts by formatting a request to perform some task and then sending it to the server program. The client program handles the user interface of the application and validates any data entered by the user. When the serving program responds with the requested data, the client software displays the result to the user.

The server program handles the client software's requests and responds with whatever information the client software needs. The server program receives the request from the client program, executes the necessary database retrieval, management, and update functions, produces the requested data, and sends it back to the client. The vast majority of network applications are considered client/server applications.

Peer-to-peer applications are very much a part of most networking environments as well, but they are relegated mostly to hidden functions handled automatically by the NOS.

Creating Servers and Clients

After choosing the best NOS for your network, you must install the operating system software on your networked systems. You will confront a number of critical issues at various steps during the installation process. While each operating system handles these issues differently, either you or the NOS must take care of each of them.

Network Interface Every system on the network must have some device by which to access the network. In most cases, this will be a NIC or a modem. Fortunately, the world of Plug n Play (PnP) now predominates, and installing a NIC or modem has pretty much been reduced to plugging in the device and then kicking back while the NOS handles everything else for you. The only issue you need concern yourself with is making sure the device installed properly. That means knowing where in the operating system you go to check on this. In almost all versions of Windows, it means a trip to the good old Device Manager. Figure 13-10 shows a perfectly functioning NIC in the Windows 2000 Device Manager.

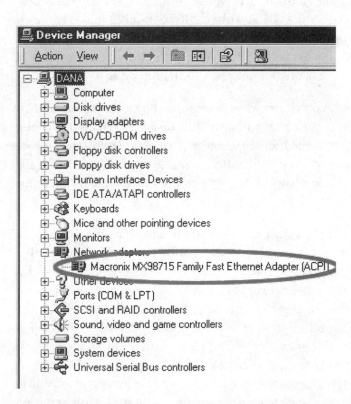

Figure 13-10   A functioning NIC in the Windows 2000 Device Manager

```
[root@localhost /dev]# ifconfig eth0
eth0    Link encap:Ethernet HWaddr 00:40:F4:23:0C:51
        inet addr:192.168.4.19 Bcast:192.168.4.255 Mask:255.255.255.0
        UP BROADCAST RUNNING MTU:1500 Metric:1
        RX packets:14 errors:0 dropped:0 overruns:0 frame:0
        TX packets:14 errors:0 dropped:0 overruns:0 carrier:0
        collisions:0 txqueuelen:0
        Interrupt:10 Base address:0x1000

[root@localhost /dev]#
```

Figure 13-11   Running IFCONFIG eth0 in Linux

Other operating systems like Linux aren't nearly as pretty, but they're just as functional. Figure 13-11 shows someone running the **IFCONFIG** command and looking for eth0—the universal name for an Ethernet adapter in the UNIX/Linux world.

If a NIC isn't working correctly, you'll get some type of error information. Windows adds a pretty **X** or **?** to the graphic of the device, while Linux just gives you some text, but either way you can tell whether the NIC is working. Keep in mind that every operating system invariably provides more than one way to check the NIC. The two examples I just gave aren't the only ways to check a NIC in either Windows or Linux—they're just the ones I use. Refer back to Chapter 8 for more information on installing NICs.

Protocol   Along with the NIC comes the network protocol. Since everyone and their dog uses TCP/IP, you can bet that your NOS will invariably install TCP/IP as the default protocol, unless you're running something a tad older. This is a *big deal* in the Network+ exam's eyes—make sure you know the different protocols that install with the different network operating systems, including some of the older ones! I'll describe them all in this chapter.

Naming   Okay, this is a big one! In most networks you need to give every system, or at least every system that shares resources, a "friendly name," which is to say, one that isn't 192.168.43.2 or something else cryptic and hard to remember. You see this friendly name when you view shared network resources. In Windows, you can view shared resources using the ever-popular Network Neighborhood/My Network Places. (Novell NetWare also calls its application Network Neighborhood.) All network operating systems have some similar application. Figure 13-12 shows my Windows 2000 system's My Network Places displaying my Novell NetWare Server, called NETWARE51.

As I've said, organization-based networks name *groups* of computers for organizational purposes. Luckily, creating these group names is the realm of the folks who set up servers, an area Network+ doesn't expect you to know. However, if a network

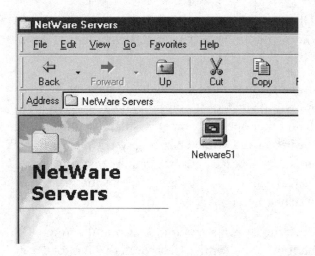

Figure 13-12   The Novell NetWare server displayed in My Network Places

administrator tells you to set up a Windows 2000 client system, Network+ does expect you to understand organizational groups and group names, and it expects you to know how to assign a client to a group. Figure 13-13 shows five groups on my network. These groups are called *domains* because, well, that's what Microsoft decided to call its groups of computers. The actual names of the domains are ones I created.

Different organization-based network operating systems use different names for these groups. Windows calls them *workgroups* or *domains*. NetWare, meanwhile, calls them *trees*. These groupings of computers have very different capabilities, depending on

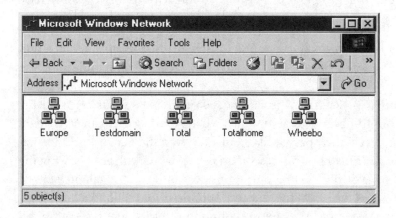

Figure 13-13   Domains on Mike's system

the operating system using them. I'll go into these in a bit more detail later. For now, whatever they are, you need to know how to set up a Windows client so it can access them.

Server or Client   Every NOS can perform either as a server or as a client. In most cases, this is determined by what you buy. If you buy Novell NetWare, it will automatically set up as a server. Pretty much all other operating systems, such as Windows 98, automatically perform as clients. The trick is that some operating systems, particularly Windows 9x clients, when running in resource-based networks, require that you also set them up to act as servers. All this really means is you must turn on File and Print Sharing, so the Windows 9x systems can share.

User Accounts   Most network operating systems require user accounts. Any NOS that requires this will come with a built-in, all-powerful user account that has total control of everything in the network. This account is called *supervisor* or *admin* in NetWare, *Administrator* in Windows NT/2000, and *root* in UNIX/Linux. When a system is first installed, you must set the password for this account. As you might imagine, this account's password is something you want only the most trusted people to know! Most operating systems require you to use this account, or an equivalent (you can usually make more accounts with the same power), to do most of the network administrative tasks. Most of the time the network admin herself will create user accounts; however, most network operating systems enable an administrator to delegate her power to create accounts to other user accounts—a nice way to delegate administrative work!

Groups   Most network operating systems have default groups. For example, Windows NT/2000 has a group called *All Users*. Anyone with a valid user account automatically becomes a part of this group. Your network admin will almost certainly have made such groups for your network.

Passwords   Passwords are now pretty common to all network operating systems, and the folks who give the Network+ exam want you to have a good general understanding of passwords.

Network security only works well when users keep their passwords secure. Passwords, for example, should never be written down where another user can find them, and users should never reveal their passwords to anyone, even the network administrator! In most cases, the administrator can reset a user's password without knowing the old one. Many users, however, remain unaware of this possibility and so fall prey to one of the oldest hacker tricks in the book: the fake tech support phone call. In a large organization, most users will not know every network support technician. A hacker can call up one of these hapless users and say, "This is Howie from tech support. We're upgrading the forward deflector array and we need your password so we can reset it when we're done." A shocking number of users will simply give out their password when asked over the phone. Getting humans to think is never easy, but it's a vital part of network security!

Educating network users about the proper care and feeding of their passwords is a critical part of any network security plan. First, teach users to pick good passwords. A good password cannot be guessed easily. They should never be based on any information about the user that a bad guy can obtain easily. For example, if Herman lives at 1313 Mockingbird Lane, is married to Lily, and has a pet named Spot, he should never use the following passwords:

- mockingbird
- dribgnikcom (mockingbird spelled backwards)
- lily
- ylil (lily spelled backwards)
- spot
- tops (spot spelled backwards)

Ideally, a password should not be a real word at all. Hackers probing a network often run password-guessing utilities that try common dictionary words at random. Network administrators can reduce the effectiveness of such password-guessing programs by requiring that all passwords be longer than six to eight characters. Hackers have a more difficult task guessing longer passwords because there are so many more possible combinations. The most secure passwords contain a combination of letters and numbers. Users hate them because they are also the hardest to remember. The following list contains strong passwords:

- gr78brk
- tnk23wqk
- 100bobotw

A good network administrator should assume that, given enough time, some users' passwords will become public knowledge. To limit the impact of these exposed passwords, a careful network administrator sets passwords to expire periodically, usually every 30 days at the most. Should a password become public knowledge, the gap in network security will automatically close when the user changes his password. One of the most frustrating aspects of implementing passwords is the stream of support calls from users who can't log onto the network. If I only had a dollar for every time a user left on the Caps Lock key, or just didn't type in the password correctly!

 EXAM TIP: A strong password should be longer than six to eight characters, contain both letters and numbers, be changed on a regular schedule, and not be based on easily guessed information.

Most network operating systems also allow you to disable a user's account. A disabled user account is simply an account whose access has been disabled but which hasn't been removed from the system. Many network administrators will disable an account while a user is on extended leave or on temporary assignment. Of course, somebody is sure to hear about it when the user comes back and can't log on because their account is disabled! While the Network+ exam isn't interested in whether you know how to enable and disable user accounts for your particular NOS, you do need to know that they *can* be disabled.

The Major Network Operating Systems

Microsoft, Novell, and UNIX all provide strong network operating system solutions that address the goals of networking, including access to shared resources and security. While Microsoft clients dominate the role of desktop client, Microsoft, Novell, and UNIX compete for the server NOS market. In this section, I'll cover all the different variations of these network operating systems, and discuss a few of the more important aspects of each.

Microsoft Windows

Microsoft competes for NOS market share with two distinct product lines: Windows 9*x* and Windows 2000. Another version of Windows called Windows NT was the predecessor to Windows 2000. Even though Windows NT is gone in Microsoft's eyes, its large installed base makes it of interest to the Network+ exam. Windows 9*x* functions as a flexible desktop NOS, capable of connecting to virtually any type of server. Windows NT and Windows 2000, in contrast, can function both as powerful client systems and as full-featured server network operating systems.

Microsoft has two different lines of both Windows NT and Windows 2000. Windows NT Workstation and Windows 2000 Professional are the client versions of their respective operating systems—they can act as servers but lack some of the more powerful features of the server versions, Windows NT Server and Windows 2000 Server. Since the client versions of NT and 2000 are so different from the server versions, I'll treat each of them as a separate product in this section.

NOTE: While the text may refer to Windows XP from time to time, the Network+ exam does not explicitly refer to Windows XP. Windows XP is the latest client version of the NT/2000 line of operating systems, so you can think of it as analogous to Windows 2000 Professional.

Windows 9x

Microsoft Windows 95, 98, and ME, collectively known as Windows 9x, provide basic file and print sharing functions, but little security by themselves. A network tech can configure a Windows 9x system as a client, or as both a client and a server. When operating as a server, however, Windows 9x uses share-level control, making it significantly less secure than more sophisticated server operating systems like Windows NT, Novell NetWare, and UNIX. Overall, Windows 9x has very weak security. Neither passwords nor user accounts provide much, if any, security in a pure Windows 9x network.

Windows 9x's key feature is its ability to connect to virtually any kind of server, including Windows 9x, Windows NT, Novell NetWare, and UNIX servers. To connect to a server running any Microsoft NOS, a Windows 9x client must have the Client for Microsoft Networks installed, as shown in Figure 13-14. You don't have to worry about installing it, however—Windows installs Client for Microsoft Networks automatically when it detects a modem or a NIC. Because Microsoft maintains a high degree of compatibility with its older network operating systems, Client for Microsoft Networks enables a Windows 9x system to communicate with any of the following types of servers:

- Windows 95
- Windows 98
- Windows ME
- Windows NT 3.x
- Windows NT 4.x
- Windows 2000
- Windows XP

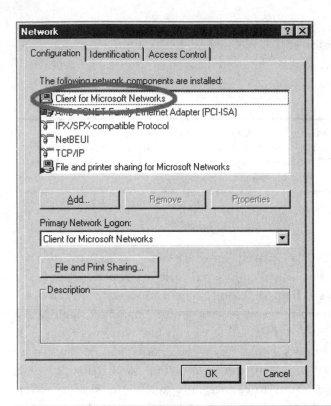

Figure 13-14 Client for Microsoft Networks is installed.

Windows 9x's amazing server compatibility stems in part from its tremendous number of network protocols. Windows 9x supports NetBEUI, IPX/SPX, TCP/IP, AppleTalk, and even a few lesser-known protocols, giving it the ability to converse with almost any other NOS. But keep in mind that these protocols do not all install by default, that the Microsoft protocols may not be as good as others, and that you may have to install extra client software before the Windows system can connect to some networks. For example, Windows 9x ships with the Microsoft Client for NetWare Networks, which provides connectivity with Novell NetWare servers. The Microsoft Client for NetWare Networks requires the IPX/SPX-compatible Protocol. It enables a Windows 9x client to connect to resources on a NetWare server. However, the Microsoft Client for NetWare Networks that comes with Windows 9x has two key weaknesses. First, it cannot connect to Net-Ware servers using TCP/IP. As Novell joins the rest of the networking industry in its headlong stampede toward TCP/IP, Windows 9x clients running the Microsoft Client for NetWare Networks gets left behind. Second, the Microsoft Client for NetWare

Networks does not understand Novell Directory Services (NDS), NetWare's default security, and the directory systems for NetWare 4 and 5.

Novell thoughtfully provides an alternative to Microsoft's Client for NetWare Networks. Novell's Client32 enables Windows 9*x* clients to connect to a NetWare server using either IPX/SPX or TCP/IP, and provides full support for NDS. Novell calls the current version, which replaces the original Client 32, *Client v3.1 for Windows 95/98*. Most techs, who as a general rule prefer shorter names, simply refer to all Novell client software for Windows 9*x* clients as *Client32*.

NOTE: To download Novell client software, go to: http://www.novell.com/download/.

Windows 9*x* systems can be grouped into what are called *workgroups*. These workgroups have little purpose other than providing a way to organize slightly more complex networks. When you set up a Windows system, you give it a workgroup to join. Putting systems in workgroups makes it easier for other systems to find them in Network Neighborhood.

Again, workgroups don't really *do* anything other than organize. There's no security aspect to them that would stop an unauthorized user from accessing a workgroup or control what a user might do in a workgroup. Workgroups are actually a throwback to the early days of Microsoft networking, and have been replaced in more advanced Microsoft network operating systems with the much more powerful domains.

NOTE: Later versions of Windows all still support workgroups, but only for compatibility purposes!

Windows NT Workstation

Windows NT Workstation offers the same user interface as Windows 95 but with greatly enhanced security and stability. In Windows 95, a knowledgeable power user can defeat most security measures. He or she might, for example, directly access the registry (to refresh your memory, that's the database that defines all settings, including security settings, on a Windows 9*x* system). Windows NT Workstation, by contrast, follows a more robust security model, and an able network administrator can prevent even power users from digging into the innards of the system. Windows NT Workstation also provides a more stable platform for running applications. While applications can still lock up, Windows NT Workstation does a better job of protecting programs from each other. Rarely will the failure of one program on an NT Workstation crash other programs.

Windows NT provides native support for NetBEUI and TCP/IP, as well as strong security by using robust user accounts. You cannot log onto a Windows NT system without a valid user account. Every Windows NT (and Windows 2000 and Windows XP) operating system comes with a special account called *administrator*. Anyone who logs in using the administrator account of a Windows NT, 2000, or XP system has complete and total control over the entire system. Clearly, very few people should ever have access to the administrator account!

Windows 2000 Professional

Windows 2000 Professional combines the Windows 98 user interface with the underlying power of Windows NT. Windows 2000 Professional is identical to Windows NT in terms of security and users, and it has the more up-to-date features of Windows 98, like Plug and Play and the more advanced Windows 98 user interface. Windows 2000 installs only TCP/IP by default, although through extra configuration it can support NetBEUI, IPX/SPX, and AppleTalk.

Windows NT Workstation and Windows 2000 Professional also function effectively as NetWare clients. Microsoft provides its own NetWare client software for NT and 2000, called *Client Services for NetWare* (*CSNW*). Unfortunately, as with Windows 9*x*'s Client for NetWare Networks, CSNW cannot connect to NetWare servers via TCP/IP and does not fully support NDS. Once again, Novell provides its own client software for NT and 2000, usually referred to simply as Client32. Novell's Client32 can connect to a NetWare server using TCP/IP, and fully supports NDS.

User Profiles

Windows 9*x*, NT, and 2000 all support the use of user profiles, which enhance both the usability and security of a network. A *user profile* is a collection of settings that corresponds to a specific user account and follows the user to any computer she uses on the network. User profiles enable users to customize their working environments. The server checks the user profiles to determine each user's wallpaper, desktop layout, and other environment preferences. Each time the user logs onto the network, the client system retrieves the profile and displays the OS accordingly. Here's an example.

Roger, Chris, and Cindy work different shifts and share the same Windows 9x computer. When each of them logs onto the computer at the beginning of their respective shifts, Windows 9x loads the appropriate configuration from their profile. If the profiles exist on the local hard drive, they only affect that computer. But a savvy network administrator will store the profiles on a network server (2000, NetWare, or other NOS), enabling the profiles to follow the users regardless of where they sit. When Roger transfers to the day shift, he can use a different computer and still enjoy all of his customized settings. As much as Roger, Chris, and Cindy enjoy the benefits of user profiles, John, the network admin, likes them even more. John can use profiles to place restrictions on how Roger, Chris, and Cindy use their computers. When their boss, Dudley, complains that employees spend too much time playing Solitaire, John edits their profiles so they cannot run the Solitaire program anymore. John can also restrict their use in other ways, to prevent them from

- Running other programs
- Changing their desktop icons and wallpaper
- Loading new programs

User profiles offer a consistent look and feel to the end user, and control to the network administrator.

 EXAM TIP: A profile is a set of configuration settings specific to an individual user. Profiles can be stored locally or on a server. Administrators can use profiles to place restrictions on what users can do with their computers.

Windows NT Server and Domain-based Networking

Windows NT Server offers all of the features of Windows NT Workstation, plus enhancements that strengthen its ability to work as a server. Microsoft optimized Windows NT Server so that, by default, it puts a higher priority on serving requests coming to it over the network than on serving requests from a user sitting at the server itself. Windows NT Server can fill a variety of needs on the network in addition to its file and print sharing functions.

Windows NT enables any Windows system to join a group of computers, called a *domain*, that share a common security database. This sounds like a workgroup, but domains are much more powerful. In the bad old days of computer networking, a user needing to access more than one server would need a separate user account on each server. Maintaining multiple user accounts for each user created a huge burden on both administrators (who had to create and maintain all those accounts) and end users (who had to remember multiple user account names and passwords). Fortunately, some forgotten genius came up with the idea of a *single login*, which enables a user to log in once and access all of their resources, regardless of the server on which the resource resides. Microsoft implements the single login through domains.

EXAM TIP: Windows NT enables users to log in once and access all their resources by logging onto the NT domain.

In an NT domain, a group of special servers known as *domain controllers* store a common security database called the *Security Accounts Manager (SAM)* database. When users log onto the domain, they log onto a domain controller that checks their usernames and passwords. When Kathy logs in successfully to the domain, the domain controller issues her an *access token*, the electronic equivalent of an ID badge. Whenever she attempts to access a resource on any server in the domain, her computer automatically shows the server her access token. Based on the access token, the server then decides whether or not to grant her access (see Figure 13-15).

NOTE: In Windows NT, all computers in the same domain share a common security database. Each user logs in once to access all of his resources within the domain.

Windows 2000 Server and Active Directory

Directory services are centralized storage areas for information about a network's resources, including users, applications, files, and printers. Directory services applications enable network administrators to centrally manage and share information about their networks' users and resources, and to centralize network security authority. Not until Windows 2000 did Microsoft finally create an NOS with directory services. Windows 2000's directory services are called *Active Directory*. All of the domain functions of Windows NT still work—they've just been incorporated into Active Directory. Windows

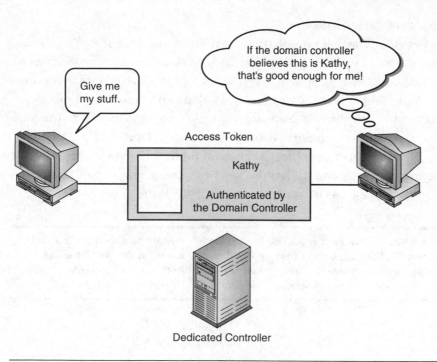

Figure 13-15 An access token at work

2000 Server still only supports TCP/IP natively, but it can, through extra configuration, support NetBEUI, IPX/SPX, and AppleTalk.

Novell NetWare

The continued use of older versions testifies to the power and stability of Novell Net-Ware. Many organizations upgrade their client software, but continue to use their existing NetWare 3.x and 4.x servers, following those ancient words of wisdom: "If it ain't broke, don't fix it!" Network techs should familiarize themselves with three significant versions of NetWare: NetWare 3.x, NetWare 4.x, and NetWare 5.x.

 EXAM TIP: The Network+ exam assumes all Novell Networks use IPX/SPX unless specifically stated otherwise.

NetWare 3.x and the Bindery

NetWare 3.*x* offers solid file and print sharing capabilities using the IPX/SPX protocol suite, but lacks a centralized security database. Each NetWare 3.*x* server maintains its own security database, called the *Bindery*. When a user logs in, the NetWare server compares the username and password to its Bindery database and then determines which resources it will share with the user. NetWare 3.*x* works best in networks that require only a single server, because each server maintains its own independent Bindery database (see Figure 13-16). A user accessing resources on three different servers must have three separate user accounts and passwords. NetWare 3.*x*'s reliance on IPX/SPX also limits its use, as more and more networks move to TCP/IP as the protocol of choice.

 EXAM TIP: Although it is possible to add TCP/IP support to a NetWare 3.*x* server, NetWare 3.*x* servers running TCP/IP rarely occur "in the wild." For the purposes of the Network+ exam, assume that all NetWare 3.*x* servers use IPX/SPX as their sole networking protocol.

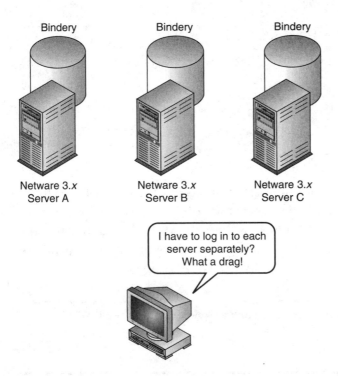

Figure 13-16 NetWare 3.*x* servers maintain separate Bindery databases.

NetWare 4.x and NDS

NetWare 4.x built on the success of NetWare 3.x by adding two key features: Novell Directory Services (NDS) and TCP/IP encapsulation. *Novell Directory Services (NDS)* organizes all user and resource information in a database referred to as the *NDS tree*. The NDS tree acts as a centralized security database, enabling users who "log onto the directory" to access all of their resources anywhere on the network. NetWare 4.x also supports TCP/IP, allowing NetWare servers and clients to place IPX packets inside of TCP/IP packets, a process known as *encapsulation* (see Figure 13-17). Although Net-Ware's basic design assumes the use of IPX/SPX, encapsulation enables NetWare to use TCP/IP without a massive redesign. Unfortunately, encapsulation hurts performance by adding an additional layer of protocol information to each packet.

EXAM TIP: NetWare 4.x (and 5.x) enable users to log in once and access all of their resources by logging onto the NDS tree.

NetWare 5.x

NetWare 5.x runs TCP/IP natively, removing the need for TCP/IP encapsulation. Having *native TCP/IP* means that NetWare 5.x no longer needs to use IPX/SPX at all (although it can for backward compatibility). Because NetWare 5.x can speak TCP/IP natively, it performs far more efficiently than NetWare 4.x when using TCP/IP.

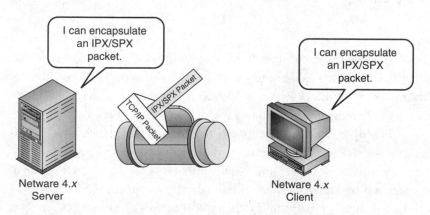

Figure 13-17 NetWare 4.x can encapsulate IPX packets in TCP/IP packets.

Table 13-1   NetWare Security Databases and Protocols

NetWare Version	Security Database	Protocol(s)
NetWare 3.x	Bindery	IPX/SPX
NetWare 4.x	NDS	IPX/SPX or TCP/IP
NetWare 5.x	NDS	IPX/SPX or TCP/IP

For the Network+ exam, familiarize yourself with the protocols and security databases used by each version of NetWare, as shown in Table 13-1.

Novell calls its version of the Windows NT/2000/XP administrator account—an account that provides total and complete access to the system—the *supervisor* or *admin* account, depending on the version of NetWare. Make sure only a few administrators have access to the supervisor/admin account!

UNIX and Linux

As the importance of the Internet continues to grow, the UNIX operating system, long a mainstay of university and scientific computing, is becoming more important for the average network tech in the trenches. Originally, the Internet consisted of a few UNIX-based systems at a handful of universities spread around the world. The basic Internet protocols, like FTP, HTTP, DNS, and ARP, actually originated in the world of UNIX and were only later ported to other operating systems. UNIX comes in many versions, but they all share certain features. The flexibility of UNIX, and the rise of open source variants like Linux and Free BSD, make UNIX a network operating system that network techs ignore at their own peril.

Many Flavors

The wide variety of UNIX versions, commonly referred to in geek-land as *flavors*, arose because Bell Labs made UNIX available to universities, and allowed the universities to modify the operating system to meet their own needs. This freedom to adapt the operating system encouraged innovation, leading to the development of critical technologies such as TCP/IP-based networking, but it also resulted in many flavors of UNIX possessing significant differences. Today, major variations include Sun's Solaris, IBM's AIX UNIX, Hewlett-Packard's HP UNIX, and BSD. While all versions of UNIX share a similar look and feel, a program written for one flavor often requires significant revision before it can run on another. Fortunately, the typical network tech can safely leave the variations among UNIX flavors to the programmers. From the network tech's point of view, all versions of UNIX are more alike than different.

EXAM TIP: The Network+ exam does not cover the differences between versions of UNIX/Linux.

Web Applications

Although it faces increasing competition from Windows NT and NetWare, UNIX remains the server of choice for providing Internet-based services such as web browsing and e-mail. The protocols used for Internet-based services mostly originated in UNIX versions, and many organizations that use NetWare or Windows NT for their file and print sharing needs still rely on UNIX for their Internet services.

Open Source UNIX

If you haven't heard of Linux yet, you need to read the newspaper a little more often. Linus Torvalds, while a student, expressed his frustration over the high cost of most versions of UNIX by building his own. What makes this story special is that Torvalds licensed his UNIX clone, dubbed *Linux*, in a unique way. Linux is an *open source* operating system, meaning that anyone who purchases a copy receives full access to its *source code*, the building blocks of the operating system. Free access to the source code gives software developers the power to modify the operating system to meet their needs. This has led to the rapid development of a wide variety of applications, including some of the most commonly used web and e-mail servers on the Internet. In most cases, both the Linux operating system and Linux applications are available for free download from the Internet, although vendors like Red Hat and Caldera sell boxed versions, and charge for support services. For all intents and purposes, Linux is a full-featured clone of UNIX.

Does UNIX have a super account like Windows and Novell? You bet it does! The all-powerful account in all versions of UNIX/Linux is called *root*. Again, giving someone the password to the root account gives them the ability to log onto a UNIX/Linux system with complete access to anything they want to do on that system. So give out the root password sparingly!

Mac OS

Apple Computer was one of the earliest adopters of network functions for its systems. In keeping with Apple's long-term attitude of "we can do it better," Apple implemented networking very differently from the other network operating systems. Adding to the confusion, over the years Apple has made a number of upgrades to the networking functions of the Macintosh operating system. All of these incremental changes make it difficult to give a brief overview of Macintosh networking without going way, way outside the scope of the Network+ exams. Instead, I'm going to concentrate on current Macintosh NOS functions, with a small nod to a few critical historical points that CompTIA wants you to know.

The key to the uniqueness of Macintosh networking is AppleTalk, Apple's do-it-all family of networking protocols. AppleTalk handles tasks ranging from Transport Layer packet creation to establishing sessions between systems to support for network applications. One can reasonably compare the functionality of AppleTalk with the territory covered by Microsoft's NetBIOS and NetBEUI (although any good Mac networking tech will probably cringe when I say that). Like NetBIOS, AppleTalk was designed primarily for file and printer sharing. Its naming conventions are very similar to what you see in NetBIOS, although AppleTalk supports very long system names. The practical limit for an AppleTalk name, however, is about 20 characters. Like NetBEUI, AppleTalk does not support routing and instead uses a NetBIOS-like broadcast function to enable systems to recognize each other.

AppleTalk still rules on Macintosh systems. Even though Macs have pretty much dumped the ancient and slow LocalTalk for Ethernet and added IP support, if you want to connect Macs, you will use AppleTalk.

Macintosh systems also use a grouping function called *zones*. A zone works for the most part just like a Microsoft Workgroup. Zones do not provide any real network security and simply act as a tool for organization.

Not surprisingly, given its overwhelming popularity, all modern Macintosh systems implement TCP/IP, using a program called AppleShare IP. AppleShare IP's mission is to connect your Macintosh system to IP networks, including the Internet. Apple also makes an add-on product called AppleShare IP Server that adds lots of neato TCP server features and built-in tools to facilitate interconnectivity with Windows and Linux. It also greatly enhances network security, in particular by implementing groups and robust user accounts. So, networking in Macintosh involves two products: the basic networking functions of AppleShare IP, which are built into all Macintosh systems, and AppleShare IP Server, which is installed only on specialized server systems.

Conclusion

As a person supporting networks, you must have basic understanding of the different makes and models of network operating systems available today. Become familiar with the many variations of Novell, Microsoft, and Linux/UNIX products, and be sure you can explain the differences between client/server and peer-to-peer networking.

Chapter Review

Questions

1. Your network consists of a Novell NetWare 4 server and a UNIX system. Sally cannot access the server, so you go to My Network Places and discover that Sally only has the NetBEUI protocol installed. Which of the following protocols should you install so Sally can communicate with the NetWare server and the other systems using UNIX?
   a. Banyan VINES
   b. TCP/IP
   c. IPX/SPX
   d. NetBEUI

2. Of the following NOS server programs, which one can only be a server and never a client?
   a. Novell NetWare
   b. Microsoft Windows 2000
   c. Microsoft Windows 98
   d. UNIX

3. What type of system accesses a resource?
   a. MAC
   b. Server
   c. Client
   d. Terminal

4. Novell NetWare, Windows NT/2000, and UNIX/Linux all have a built-in, all-powerful user account that has total control of anything on the network. Each NOS uses a different name for this all-powerful user. UNIX/Linux calls it a(n) _____; Windows NT/2000 calls it a(n) _____; and NetWare calls it either _____ or _____.
   a. Root, Administrator, Admin, Supervisor
   b. Supervisor, Root, Administrator, Admin
   c. Admin, Supervisor, Root, Administrator
   d. Administrator, Admin, Supervisor, Root

5. Your network is made up of ten Windows 98 systems, and you installed the TCP/IP protocol on all the systems. Melissa wants to share her hard drive. She

goes to My Computer and alternate-clicks on the C: drive, but Sharing is not listed as one of her choices. You know that her cable and NIC are working, and she can see everyone on the network. What could be the problem?

a. IPX/SPX needs to be installed on Melissa's system.

b. File and Print Sharing has not been installed on Melissa's system.

c. Client for Microsoft Networks has not been installed on Melissa's system.

d. Melissa is not running the sharing protocol.

6. May wants to allow Mary Jane and Peter to view and modify a database stored on her server. She wants Betty to be able to view the database but not modify it, and she wants Jonah to have no access to the database whatsoever. Each user should have his or her own password. What kind of security should May implement?

a. High level

b. Share level

c. User level

d. SMTP level

7. NetWare 3.*x* servers store user account and password information in a database called the:

a. Domain

b. NDS tree

c. Bindery

d. Registry

8. You are running a Linux system on your network. In order for you to access *root* on this system you need to know the:

a. Location of the directory

b. Computer's name

c. Password

d. Root code

9. You are running a Windows 2000 server on your network. You need to make sure that the TCP/IP protocol suite, IPX/SPX protocol suite, and NetBEUI protocol suites are installed. Which of these protocols does Windows 2000 install by default? (Select all that apply.)

a. NetBIOS

b. NetBEUI

c. TCP/IP

d. IPX/SPX

10. When using a common security database, Novell NetWare servers must be organized into a(n):
    a. NDS tree
    b. Domain
    c. Ring
    d. Web

Answers

1. **B and C.** You need to make sure you have the IPX/SPX protocol for the NetWare server and the TCP/IP protocol for the UNIX systems installed on Sally's system.

2. **A.** With the exception of Novell NetWare, every operating system capable of networking (Windows, UNIX/Linux, and Macintosh) allows systems to act both as servers and clients at the same time. Novell NetWare cannot act as both a server and a client on the same system.

3. **C.** A client is a system that accesses the shared resource.

4. **A.** UNIX/Linux calls its all-powerful user account Root. Windows NT/2000 calls it Administrator. NetWare calls it either Admin or Supervisor.

5. **B.** Melissa must turn on File and Print Sharing before her Windows 98 system can function as a server and share her hard drive.

6. **C.** May should implement user-level security, which lets her assign different rights and permissions to each user, and give each user a unique password. Share-level security assigns a password to each resource, but would not fulfill May's needs because Mary Jane and Peter would use the same password to access the database. Simple Mail Transfer Protocol (SMTP) is an e-mail protocol that has nothing to do with securing files on a server. High-level security is a bogus term that I hope you didn't fall for!

7. **C.** Each NetWare 3.*x* server has its own security database called the Bindery. NetWare 4.*x* and 5.*x* servers share a common NDS database, and Windows NT servers share a domain database. The Registry is a central hierarchical database used in Windows 95, 98, NT, and 2000 to store information necessary to configure the system for one or more users, applications, and hardware devices.

8. **C.** You need to know the password to the root account to log onto a UNIX/Linux system with complete access to that system.

9. **C.** Windows 2000 installs TCP/IP by default. NetBEUI and IPX/SPX come with Windows 2000, but you must install them manually.

10. **A.** Novell NetWare servers use Novell Directory Services when sharing a common security database. Servers sharing that database exist within an NDS tree.

PART III

Beyond the Basic LAN

Resources

In this chapter, you will

- Understand the naming of shared resources and the Universal Naming Convention (UNC)
- Learn about permissions for Windows 9x, Windows NT, Windows 2000, NetWare 3.x, NetWare 4.x/5.x, and UNIX/Linux
- Understand sharing resources as it applies to the preceding operating systems
- Understand accessing shared resources

An installed network of servers and client computers is useless without resources for the serving systems to share and the client systems to access. In this chapter, we'll look at the different ways the different brands of network operating systems enable servers to share resources. Then we'll see how clients—actually just Windows clients since that's what Network+ stresses—get access to those shared resources. The Network+ test is most interested in the process of sharing folders and printers, so we will focus exclusively on the steps needed to share them. The basic steps of making *any* resource sharable are pretty much the same whether you're sharing a folder on your C: drive to a small network or a huge Web site to the entire Internet. So before we learn the specifics of how NetWare shares a printer or Windows 2000 shares a folder, we need to cover two important sharing issues universal to all networks: naming and permissions.

Naming

Tim decides to share his C:\GAMES folder; how do his pals on the network know this resource is available for use? We're assuming that his system is running the correct protocol, is properly connected to the network, and even has a server name: TIM. It's fairly common for a serving system to have a name that reflects its user, especially if that system is also a client PC. For the same reason each serving system gets a name, each shared resource must also have a name. That way others wishing to use that resource have a method to point at and select that resource. Windows clients use the Network Neighborhood/My Network Places tool to browse a network for available resources. Figure 14-1 shows the My Network Places folder on my PC. I can see all of the systems currently sharing resources, including Tim's PC. Double-clicking TIM displays all the shared folders on his system, as shown in Figure 14-2.

NOTE: Windows 9x and NT call this folder Network Neighborhood; Windows 2000 and XP call it My Network Places. For the remainder of this chapter, I'm going to keep things simple and call it Network Neighborhood regardless of the operating system.

One of the shared folders we can see must be Tim's C:\GAMES folder—but which one? None of the shares is called C:\GAMES! That's because Tim's shared folder has a *network name*. Almost all network operating systems insist that shared resources have network names separate from their real names. A shared resource's network name is not and often cannot be the same as its real name. Tim's shared C:\GAMES folder has the network name GAMES—now can you find it in the figure? To access this folder, just

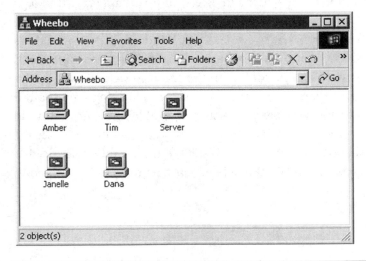

Figure 14-1 Network Neighborhood showing Tim's PC

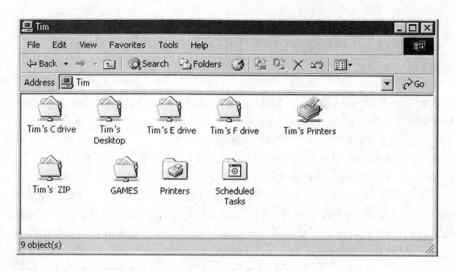

Figure 14-2 Shared Folders on Tim's PC

double-click it; then, assuming no security restrictions prevent it, we can access the files and subfolders on this share.

Historical/Conceptual

UNC

Window's Network Neighborhood makes browsing through a network very easy to do. Simply by clicking a group, serving system, or shared resource, you can access whatever you want—or at least whatever you're allowed to access. But networking hasn't always been about *Windows* client systems. Long ago, before Windows even existed, Microsoft championed the concept of the *Universal Naming Convention* (*UNC*), which describes any shared resource in a network using the convention

```
\\<server name>\<name of shared resource>
```

DOS programs (pre-Windows, remember?) accessed shared resources using commands typed at a command prompt. DOS systems needed UNC names to access shared resources. Let's say someone wanted to access Tim's C:\GAMES folder. The UNC name you'd type to access his system would be \\TIM, and the UNC name for the shared folder would be \\TIM\GAMES. If you were using the old DOS-based NOS called LAN Manager, you'd have to type strange commands at the C: prompt, like

```
NET use g: \\Tim\games
```

This command, in a process known as *mapping*, creates a G: drive on the client system's hard drive that's really the \\TIM\GAMES folder. All versions of Windows still support drive mapping. Fortunately, you no longer need to type strange commands at command prompts. You just alternate-click (right-click) the folder in Network Neighborhood and select *Map Network Drive* to get a wizard (see Figure 14-3). Select a drive letter for the drive, and the mapped share will appear like magic in your My Computer folder! Figure 14-4 shows the shared folder Tim's games mapped as Mike's I: drive. Windows is even nice enough to change the icon slightly so you know the folder is mapped—can you see the difference?

Although Windows systems still support mapping, you no longer need to map a shared folder to a drive letter, because Windows applications can access shares directly by their UNC names. Even though mapping is not nearly as common as it once was, you'll still see it used in some networks, usually for security reasons or to support some

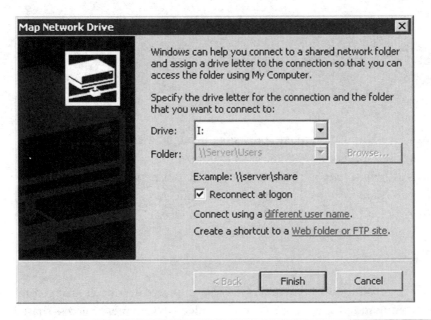

Figure 14-3   The Map Network Drive wizard in Windows 2000

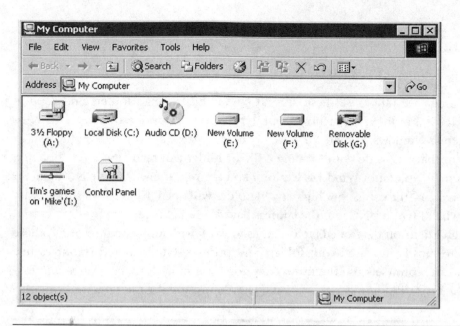

Figure 14-4   The Tim's games folder mapped as Mike's I: drive

older application that needs to access a drive letter and not a UNC name. Mapping, as well as a number of other share functions, simply would not work without UNC.

Make sure you can recognize a valid UNC name. They always begin with a double-slash "\\" followed by the name of the serving system, then a single slash "\" followed by the name of the shared resource.

EXAM TIP: **Make sure you can tell a valid UNC name from an invalid one!**

UNCs are not limited to shared folders and drives. You can also use a printer's UNC to connect to a shared printer. This process, similar to mapping, is called *capturing* a printer. A captured printer uses a local LPT port that connects to the networked printer. Like mapping, this is usually only done to support older programs that are not smart enough to know how to print directly to a UNC-named printer; it's quite rare today.

Back in the old days we could capture a printer just like a shared folder, using the **NET** command:

```
NET use LPT1 \\Tim\Printer
```

Even though we rarely use these ancient commands to map folders and capture printers, UNCs are still very much part of the networking world, especially with Windows systems. Windows support for UNCs goes very deep; almost any application in your system that has to do with locating a file or folder will read UNCs. Try opening either Internet Explorer or Windows Explorer and typing a known valid UNC name in the address area—the corresponding network folder will open. Figure 14-5 shows what happens when I type a UNC into the address bar of Internet Explorer.

Although Microsoft developed UNC names to work with any shared resource, these days they're mostly just used with folders and printers. Other shared resources like e-mail and web browsers use the more common, and more Internet-aware, *Universal Resource Locator* (*URL*) nomenclature. You'll learn more about URLs later in the book.

NOTE: You will find that the "U" in URL can stand for either Uniform or Universal. Universal was the early choice, but Uniform is probably ahead in usage now. Neither one is "wrong" per se.

The rest of this chapter details how different network operating systems share resources and then shows how to access those shared resources. We'll be messing with

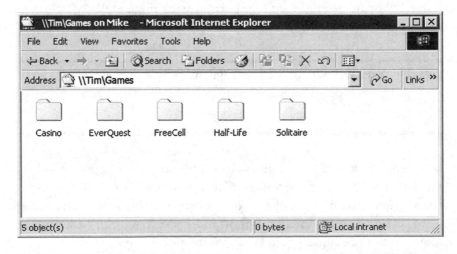

Figure 14-5 A UNC typed into the address bar of Internet Explorer

URLs like crazy, but before we do that you need to understand the major concept of *permissions*.

Test Specific

Permissions

Once you've set up a resource for sharing and given it a network name, how do you control who gets to access it and what they can do to it? You know the answer to this one from Chapter 13, right? Permissions, of course! I touched on permissions—or *rights*, as they're called in Novell NetWare—in Chapter 13, but now it's time to go into them in more detail. I've included a bit of background here that'll sound familiar, but could be a useful refresher if you've slept since reading the last chapter.

As you know, permissions are sets of attributes network administrators assign to resources to define what users and groups can do with them (the resources, not the admin!). A fairly typical permission used in all network operating systems is a permission assigned to folders called *execute*. The execute permission, as its name implies, enables the user or group that has it to execute, or run, any programs in that folder.

Types of permissions vary depending on the resource being shared. If I share a printer, I certainly don't need a permission called execute, although I do admit wishing I could have executed a few troublesome dot-matrix printers in the past! Instead, printers usually have permissions like *manage printer* that let certain users or groups reset the printer or start and stop print jobs.

There are many, many more permission types than the two I described here. I just wanted you to get an idea of what a couple looked like. One of the most fascinating aspects of permissions is the different way certain network operating systems utilize them. Let's look at the more common network operating systems and appreciate how they use permissions.

Dueling Security Models

The first thing to understand here is that Windows 9*x* is a freak of nature when it comes to networking and permissions. It does permissions one way, and all the other operating systems we'll be discussing do them another (better) way. It all boils down to the difference between the resource-based security model, and the server- and organization-based models. The server- and organization-based models have two layers of security in between a user and the resource he wants to access, while the resource-based model has only one.

As you'll recall from Chapter 13, in the server and organization models, every user must log on before they can access shared resources. In the server-based model, users log in to each server for access to the resources it controls; in the organization-based model, users log in once for access to the entire network. Either way, after a user has logged on successfully, that user account receives an electronic key it can show to serving systems on the network when it wants access to specific resources. Hillary works for a super-secret spy agency. When she walks in the front door, she shows the badge to a guard to prove that it's okay to let her in. The guard then gives her a special electronic card with a secret code on it. The code specifies where she can go and what she can do during that particular visit. Every time Hillary wants to access a particular area, a security device checks her card to see what permissions she has. The type and extent of her access to the resources in that area will be determined by the specific permissions encoded on her card. What I've just described is a two-layer security model: First you must get in the door of the building (log in to the network), and second, you must have the necessary permissions to access the various resources inside (see Figure 14-6).

In resource-based security models, there's only one layer of security. Returning to my hypothetical situation, it would be as if there was no guard at the door—absolutely anyone could walk in to the building without anyone knowing who they were or when they came and went. The only security barrier between them and any particular area in the building would be the door to that area, which would either be locked, unlocked, or protected by a password code.

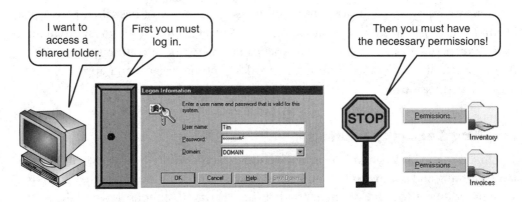

Figure 14-6   Two-layer security: Log on to the network and have permissions.

Windows 9x Permissions

All Windows 9x systems use the resource-based security model. The only security options are Full (the door is open—do what you want), Read-Only (you can look but not touch), and Depends On Password (Full access requires a password). Interestingly, Windows 9x doesn't have a No Access option. Think about it—there's really no point in having a resource *nobody* can access ever, but because 9x doesn't have real user accounts, it doesn't know who's knocking at the door, so it's only choices are (a) let everyone in to do whatever they want, (b) let everyone in but only let them look (Read-Only access), or (c) let everyone in to look, but only those who know the password can do whatever they want.

Additionally, these permissions, called *share permissions*, only control the access of *other* users on the network with whom you share your resource; they have no impact on you (or anyone else) sitting at the computer whose resource is being shared. These Windows 9x permissions are prehistoric in networking terms; they date from the days of LANMan 1.0 (the very first NOS for PCs), before anybody could imagine a need for more than this basic amount of security.

Clearly, they were wrong about that. Gone are the days when computer security meant locking the computer room door! Today's networks have to be secured against all enemies, foreign and domestic. Network admins need to be able to keep track of who can use their networks, and in what specific ways, regardless of whether the person is sitting at the serving system itself, or dialing in from a country half-way around the world. Truly useful security also requires a more powerful and flexible set of permissions. Modern network operating systems like Windows NT/2000 and Novell NetWare implement robustly featured user accounts. User accounts enable a network admin not only to control initial access to the network, but to fine-tune any user's access to each and every resource being shared.

 NOTE: Yes, Windows 9x has user accounts, but their only reason for being is so a user on a 9x box on a network can log into a Windows NT/2000 server. The user account login provides absolutely no protection for the local machine itself —if you didn't know this, let me tell you a secret: Just hit ESC at the logon screen and Windows 9x will shrug its shoulders and let you have full access to its local resources.

Windows NT Permissions

If Windows 9x is a freak of nature, Windows NT has multiple personalities. Windows NT can handle security in two completely different ways.

Windows NT file and folder permissions are based on the powerful *NT File System* (NTFS) file format. When you format a partition in Windows NT, you can choose from two file formats: the old FAT partition used by Windows 9x systems, or NTFS (Windows 2000 and XP also give you the choice of FAT32). Figure 14-7 shows the Windows NT Disk Administrator tool—note the two NTFS partitions and one FAT partition. You don't have to use NTFS to format an NT volume, but if you choose not to format a partition on a Windows NT system with NTFS, you will lose all of the security that NTFS provides. You will be reduced to the Windows 9x share permissions just described. Needless to say, pretty much everyone uses NTFS on their Windows NT/2000/XP systems nowadays!

NOTE: Windows 2000 and Windows XP also use NTFS. Everything discussed in this section about NT's use of NTFS also holds true for Windows 2000 and XP.

NTFS embeds the powerful NTFS permissions into each shared resource. However, the resource itself is not in charge of security. That job goes either to the individual NT serving system or to the NT domain, depending on how the NT network is configured. This is a critical point and one that is often lost on folks new to more advanced network operating systems. If the network isn't running any copies of Windows NT server or Windows

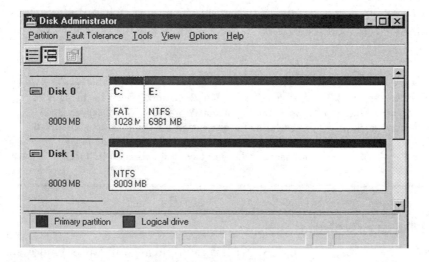

Figure 14-7 The Windows NT Disk Administrator tool

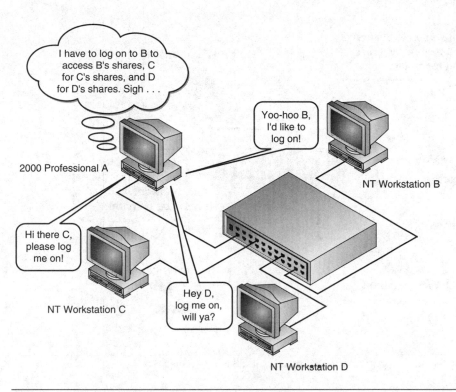

Figure 14-8 Logging on to each sharing system separately

2000 Server, each system on the network must act as its own server; this means users must have an account on each system they want to access (see Figure 14-8). Once you install a copy of Windows NT Server or Windows 2000 Server, each user gets a domain user account that gives them access to the network in one quick logon (see Figure 14-9). In a domain-based network, no one has a local user account—all users get domain user accounts that must be set up by a special program on the Windows NT or 2000 server system. Local accounts still exist in a Windows NT or 2000 domain-based network but are rarely used except for perhaps an occasional maintenance function. In order to logon locally to a system that uses a domain, you must perform a special local logon. In fact, the Windows NT logon gives you the ability to log in to the domain or just to the local system (see Figure 14-10). We often log in to a local system only to perform maintenance.

Table 14-1 lists Microsoft's standard NTFS permissions for files and folders under Windows NT. These standard permissions are actually groupings of what Microsoft calls *special permissions* that have names like Execute, Read, and Write. These special permissions are rarely accessed directly in most NT environments, but you can find these

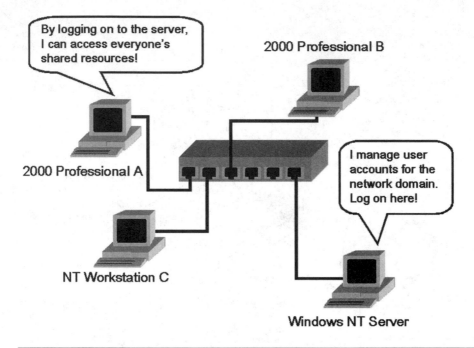

Figure 14-9   One logon to the server does it all!

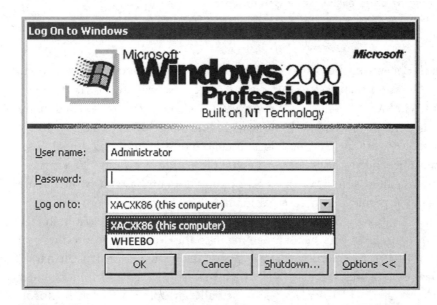

Figure 14-10   The Windows NT logon screen showing both local and domain logon options

Table 14-1 NTFS Permissions for Files and Folders under Windows NT

Permission	Folders?	Files?	What Does It Allow?
No Access	Yes	Yes	Denies all access to the file or folder. Users can see the file or folder but cannot access it in any way.
List	Yes	No	Users can only see the contents of the folder and go to subfolders.
Read	Yes	Yes	Users can read files and folders, open files and subfolders, but cannot change any files.
Add	Yes	No	Users can add files or subfolders to the folder but cannot open or change any files.
Add & Read	Yes	No	Users can read and add files or subfolders to the folder. Users can also open files in the folder.
Change	Yes	Yes	Users can do anything but delete the file or folder. They cannot change permissions on any files or subfolders.
Full Control	Yes	Yes	Users can do anything they want.

permissions in a resource's Properties. Figure 14-11 shows the special permissions for a folder.

The beauty of NTFS is that it really doesn't matter to the serving system if you log in locally, log in to the server over the network, or log in to a domain. NTFS permissions work the same way whether the NT/2000 system is on a network or running as a stand-alone system. If only one Windows NT or Windows 2000 system existed in the universe, you would still need a user account and NTFS permissions to access anything on the system. To differentiate these permissions from the share permissions, we call them *NTFS permissions* or *local permissions*.

So how can NTFS be used in a network? Simple! NTFS resources can store information on *any* user account. The account can be local just to that system or, if the system is part of a Windows NT/2000 domain, it can be a *domain* user account. The only difference is whether the local system handles the user account logons, or the domain does—either way, it doesn't matter to NTFS!

Whoa! Wait a minute, Mike! Are you telling me that Windows NT/2000 systems have *two* different types of user accounts? Yup, that's right! You get two types: local users and domain users. (Actually there are more than two, but we don't need to cover that here.) However, to use domains, you have to buy a special server version of Windows, either Windows NT Server or Windows 2000 Server.

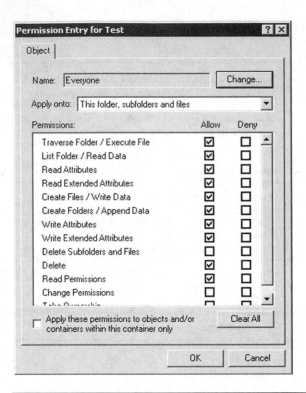

Figure 14-11 NTFS special permissions for a folder

All of this security is invisible to the network user as long as he has a good user account and the necessary NTFS permissions. This process is not unique to Windows networks—NetWare and Linux networks use the same two-step security method.

Windows 2000 Permissions

From the permissions standpoint, Windows 2000 works pretty much exactly the same way as Windows NT; however, if you look at Table 14-2, you will find there are a few subtle distinctions between the standard permission types. Take a good hard look at the Windows 2000 permissions. Look at the Write permission—why would anyone want that? You can add or edit a file, but you can't open it? That sounds crazy! Actually, it makes a lot of sense to folks who administer more complex networks. Imagine a network full of users who need to add files to a folder but by the same token we don't want them to see files others are adding. Trust me, it happens. NTFS permissions give administrators incredible control over exactly what a user can or cannot do to a file or folder,

Table 14-2 Windows 2000 Standard Permission Types

Permission	Folders?	Files?	What Does It Allow?
Deny Access	Yes	Yes	Denies all access to the file or folder. Users can see the file or folder but cannot access it in any way.
List Folder Contents	Yes	No	Users can only see the contents of the folder and go to subfolders.
Read	Yes	Yes	Users can read files and folders, open files and sub-folders, but cannot change any files.
Write	Yes	Yes	Users can add files or subfolders to the folder but cannot open or change any files or subfolders.
Read & Execute	Yes	Yes	Users can read and add files or subfolders to the folder. Users can also open files in the folder.
Modify	Yes	Yes	Users can do anything but delete the file or folder. They cannot change permissions on any files or sub-folders.
Full Control	Yes	Yes	Users can do anything they want.

even though it may not be obvious *how* these permissions work. If you really want to get into NTFS permissions, go for your MCSE or MCSA certification!

NetWare 3.x Rights

Novell NetWare 3.x was the first NOS to adopt more advanced permissions. Novell calls its permissions *rights*. Unlike Windows's NTFS, each Novell NetWare 3.x server stores this information in its Bindery (see Chapter 13).

Table 14-3 shows the NetWare 3.12 rights. Compare these to the Windows NT and 2000 permissions. At first they may seem quite different, but if you take your time and compare them, you'll see they're almost exactly the same.

NetWare 4.x/5.x

NetWare 4.x and 5.x dispense with the Bindery, replacing it with NetWare Directory Services (NDS). NDS controls access to network resources using network-wide permissions, rather than the file server-specific permissions used by NetWare 3.x's Bindery. NetWare 5.x introduces a new file format called Novell Storage Services (NSS). From the standpoint of sharing files and folders, NetWare has never changed from its

Table 14-3 NetWare 3.12 Rights

Right	Folders?	Files?	What Does It Allow?
Read	Yes	Yes	Users can read files and folders, open files and subfolders, but cannot change any files.
Write	Yes	Yes	Users can open and write to files.
Create	Yes	Yes	Users can add files or subfolders and can open or change any files.
Erase	Yes	Yes	Users can delete any file or subfolder.
Modify	Yes	Yes	Users can change the attributes of or rename files or subfolders.
File Scan	Yes	Yes	Users can see the file or the contents of the folder.
Access Control	Yes	Yes	Users can modify other users' and groups' rights to this file or folder.
Supervisory	Yes	Yes	Users can do anything they want.

original permissions. Isn't it nice when you can count on something to stay the same? Microsoft, are you listening? Hello? Oh well, let's move on.

UNIX/Linux

Permissions is one of those areas that can really get confusing when switching between Linux and Windows. UNIX/Linux systems do have local file and folder permissions like NetWare and NT/2000, but they look quite different than the ones we've just seen. They do share one common feature with Windows, however: permissions are the same for both networked and local users. File-serving programs like FTP use the local permissions to handle network access permissions.

Unlike NetWare and Windows, UNIX/Linux provides only three permissions (see Table 14-4). Because they lack the more detailed permissions available in NetWare and Windows, most network admins don't like to use UNIX/Linux systems for pure file sharing. I realize in saying this I'm risking an avalanche of indignant e-mail from the million or so UNIX/Linux users out there, but what can I do? When I'm right, I'm right! (I just won't have any friends.)

Table 14-4   UNIX/Linux Permissions

Permission	Folders?	Files?	What Does It Allow?
Read	Yes	Yes	Users can read files and folders, open files and sub-folders, but cannot change any files.
Write	Yes	Yes	Users can open and write to files.
Execute	Yes	Yes	Users can execute the file

Sharing Is Sharing

For all the differences in names and functions among the different types of permissions, the bottom line is they all perform roughly the same functions: enabling those who administer networks to control the level of access to shared files and folders. Keep in mind that permissions are not at all limited to just files and folders—pretty much any shared resource on any network will have some type of permissions to assign to users and groups. However, files and folders are still the thing we love to share the most, and once you appreciate the variations in the ways different network operating systems share files and folders, sharing other resources like printers will seem pretty anti-climactic!

Now that we've got a grip on permissions, let's put this knowledge to work and actually start sharing some files and folders. Oh, and by the way, let's go ahead and start sharing some printers too while we are at it!

Sharing Resources

Sharing a resource involves three distinct steps. First, we must make sure our system is capable of sharing. Second, we need to share the resource and name it. Third, we need to set permissions on that shared resource.

Let's get one thing settled right now: No network NOS allows you to share individual files. Sure, you can share entire volumes or you can share folders in those volumes, but you absolutely cannot share a file! Don't confuse the ability to place permissions on a file with sharing a file. Just because you can't share a file doesn't mean you can't place permissions on it. Sharing is a network function; permissions are unique to a resource. When we share a folder, we apply permissions to the shared folder which are then attributed to the files and subfolders in that shared folder. This subtle difference can cause confusion in the unwary.

Sharing Folders

Since sharing folders is the area of biggest interest to most techs, let's start with them. We'll look at the network operating systems we just discussed and see what we need to do to set up a resource for sharing. This is going to look a bit redundant—but who cares? The process never really changes. Once you know what you have to do, all that remains are the specific details of how to create a share on a particular NOS.

Windows 9x

Remember when I said the first step in sharing a resource is to ensure that your system is capable of sharing? Well, every NOS we discuss in this book is preset to share resources automatically, except Windows 9x. All Windows 9x systems require you to install and activate a special service called File and Print Sharing. To install this service on a Windows 9x system, access the Network Neighborhood Properties dialog box (see Figure 14-12). You can also access these settings by running the Network applet in the

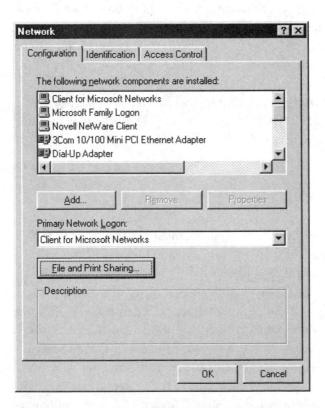

Figure 14-12 The Network Neighborhood Properties dialog box showing the system's network settings

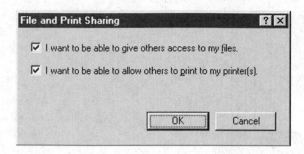

Figure 14-13 The File and Print Sharing options

Control Panel. Make sure you know how to get to the Network settings in a Windows 9*x* client—we're going to be doing this a lot over the rest of the book! Do you see the File and Print Sharing button? Click it to see the sharing options (see Figure 14-13).

This is pretty simple stuff here. If you want to share your files and folders, click the *I want to be able to give others access to my files* check box. Let's see if you get the idea. What should you check to allow others to access your printers? Hey! You are a genius! Once you've checked the boxes you desire, click OK and be ready with your installation CD —Windows will want it. And you can pretty well count on a reboot, too (hey, it's Windows). But that's it! You've completed the first step in sharing a resource: making sure the system is configured to share by installing the File and Print Sharing service. A *service* is any program that runs on Windows that you don't normally see. Your Windows 9*x* system may look the same as before, but trust me, a new set of programs is now running, even if you can't see them. We're all done setting up systems to share. You won't see this step again since all the other network operating systems do this automatically. Hooray!

Let's assume you've installed the File and Print Sharing service on your system (see Figure 14-14). You can go back to Network properties to see if it's there. Once this is installed, you're ready to start sharing some files and folders! *Wheeee!*

Windows 9*x* lets you share folders and entire hard drives—whatever you're sharing, you configure it in the exact same way. Just use My Computer or Windows Explorer to select the resource you want to share, alternate-click the resource and select Sharing (see Figure 14-15).

If you don't see the Sharing menu option, you've either forgotten to add the File and Print Sharing service, or you didn't select the *I want to be able to give others access to my files* check box. Go ahead and select Sharing to see the dialog box in Figure 14-16.

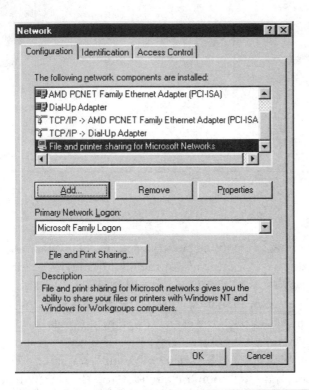

Figure 14-14 File and Print sharing installed

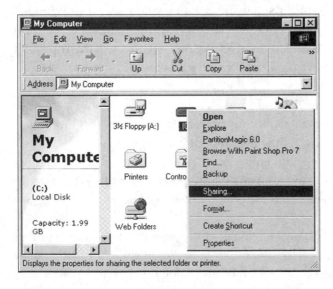

Figure 14-15 Selecting Sharing in My Computer

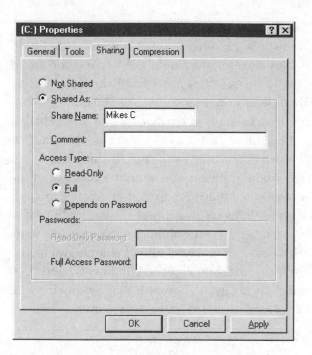

Figure 14-16   The Sharing dialog box

Remember seeing this dialog box earlier when we looked at how networks share? Well, this time click the box labeled Shared As and enter a name. Since this is Windows 9*x* and you are using NetBIOS names, you would think the name could be up to 15 characters long, as we learned in Chapter 11. Yeah, well, you'd think that, but try it—you only get 12 characters, because Windows 9*x* systems are limited to the old DOS 8.3 filename size.

After you've given the share a name, you need to set the share permissions for this share. In most cases, you wouldn't be that interested in security (or you'd be using something besides Windows 9*x* for networking!) so just leave the permissions set to Full. Click OK and you will see the little hand icon appear that indicates a resource is shared (see Figure 14-17).

Figure 14-17   A shared folder showing the hand icon

Windows NT and Windows 2000

Remember what you just learned about sharing a folder or drive in Windows 9x? Well, it works pretty much the same way in Windows NT and Windows 2000. You don't need to configure any version of NT or 2000 to share—they are preconfigured to share by default—so you just need to worry about setting up the share. Just as you did with Windows 9x, select the drive or folder you wish to share, alternate-click and select Sharing to see the sharing dialog box. Figure 14-18 shows this box in Windows NT, while Figure 14-19 shows the same box in Windows 2000. They look basically the same.

If you don't see the Sharing menu option, it means you are not a member of the Administrators (NT/2000) or the Power Users (2000) group. A user account that is a member of the Power Users group has the ability to do many of the basic administrator functions; this is a handy way to give other users the ability to do things like share folders, without making them members of the all-powerful Administrators group.

Just like with Windows 9x, you must name the shared folder. Windows NT and 2000 allow share names of up to 80 characters. Be aware, however, that any shares with names longer than 12 characters will *not be visible* to Windows 9x systems.

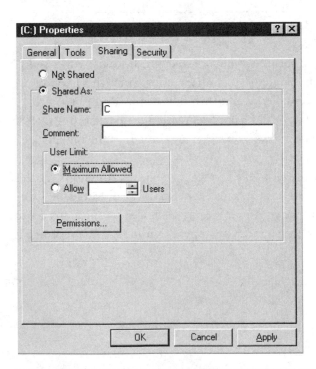

Figure 14-18   The Windows NT Sharing dialog box

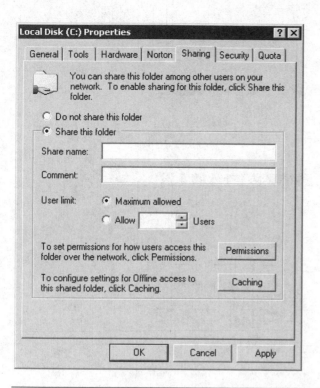

Figure 14-19   The Windows 2000 Sharing dialog box

Even in Windows NT and 2000, you still need to set share permissions before you can actually share a resource. Click the Sharing tab on the Properties dialog box of the shared resource. Since we're going to use NTFS permissions to do the actual security work, we really don't need to do anything here at all. Just leave this at the default full-control settings; that's the normal process on NTFS systems.

Now let's have some fun and start playing with NTFS permissions! In Windows NT, click the Security tab, then click the Permissions button (see Figure 14-20). In Windows 2000, just click the Security tab to see the NTFS settings (see Figure 14-21).

By default, everyone has complete access to a new share in Windows 2000, and Read access in Windows NT. All network operating systems start a new share with some default permissions applied to everyone, so your first job is to start limiting who gets access. Let's concentrate on Windows 2000 for a moment since Windows NT does all this in roughly the same fashion. Let's say we only want the Accounting group to be able to read documents, and we want Mike Meyers to have full control. Microsoft does a nice job of making this easy to set up. Start by clicking Add to see a list of users and

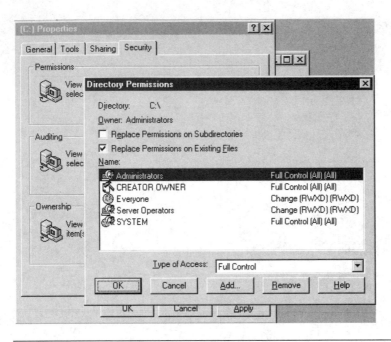

Figure 14-20   Windows NT permissions

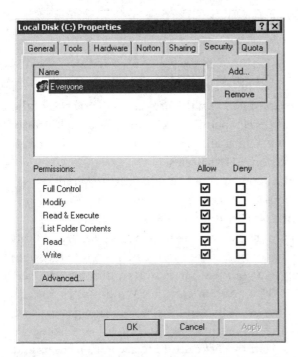

Figure 14-21   Windows 2000 NTFS settings

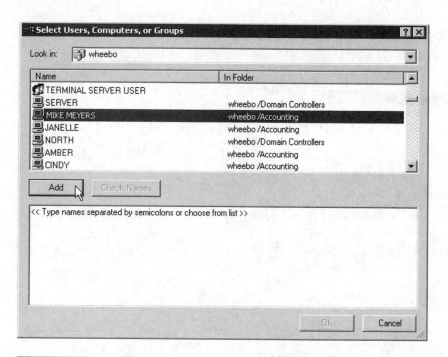

Figure 14-22   Finding Mike Meyers and Accounting in the list

groups. Find the Mike Meyers user account in the Accounting group in the list (see Figure 14-22). Pretty much all network operating systems let you add multiple users and/or groups in one shot.

Click OK to return to the Security tab. You'll see Mike Meyers is now listed. Take a look at the default permissions. Like most other network operating systems, Windows 2000 provides only limited permissions by default. We'll need to click Full Control to let Mike Meyers do whatever he wants. The Accounting group's default settings are just fine for what we want, so we'll leave them alone.

Oops! You can't leave yet! Remember the Everyone group? It has full control! As long as that's the case, everyone has full access—better deny access to the Everyone group before you exit (see Figure 14-23).

Hey, this brings up an interesting issue: What if a user account is a member of two different groups, and these two groups have different permissions for the same folder? Or what if a user account has certain permissions for a folder—what permissions do they have for any subfolders and any files in those subfolders? All network operating systems have different ways of handling these more complex permissions issues—you could easily make a career out of being little more than a permissions expert. Luckily, the Network+ exam isn't too interested in more than a basic understanding of the

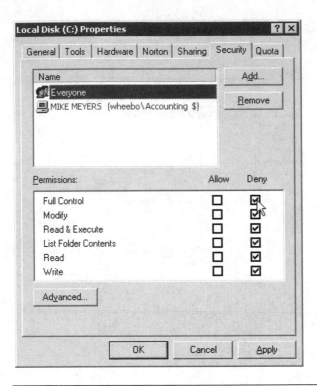

Figure 14-23   The Everyone group is denied access

existence of permissions, so you can blissfully ignore these fascinating questions until you decide to go for your more advanced certifications.

NetWare 3.x

The first thing to appreciate about Novell networks is the fact Novell servers do not use the classic drive letters we see on Windows systems. If you were to look at a Novell Server, you would see drive volumes with names like SYS: and VOL:. The SYS: volume is roughly equivalent to the Windows C: drive—by default, the SYS: volume stores all of the critical programs that make up the NetWare NOS itself.

There are a number of interesting aspects to network administration using Novell NetWare. One of the most interesting, and one shared by all versions of NetWare, is that almost no administrative work is actually done from the server itself. NetWare comes with a series of utilities that you run from the server to perform almost every network task, including creating users/groups, and setting rights to shared folders. These utilities are located by default in a special folder called \public on the SYS: drive; however, most NetWare administrators will move this folder to a less sensitive area.

How can users access these programs if they can't see volumes with weird names like SYS:? The answer lies in special mapping that is automatically done for any system that needs to access a NetWare server. Every NetWare client has a special drive premapped to a drive letter—in the case of Windows systems this drive is usually called the F: drive, but that can easily be changed. When a Windows PC loaded with the correct NetWare client software boots up, this F: drive is automatically mapped, whether or not the client is logged into the server. Figure 14-24 shows an example of this mapped drive on a Windows system. Using this mapped drive, the client system can run utilities without even logging into the network. The mapped drive also acts as a public folder where certain files and utilities are made available to all regardless of the level of rights that client has to other areas of the server.

There is no specific step you must perform to start sharing folders in NetWare. All folders on all drives are ready for sharing—you only need to set up the *trustee rights*. A trustee right is NetWare lingo for user and group permissions to a shared folder. Any user or group with rights to a certain shared folder are said to have trustee rights to that folder. Don't let these terms throw you—it's the same as setting permissions on a Windows NT or 2000 system!

We set up trustee rights in NetWare 3.*x* by running the ancient but completely functional SYSCON program. There are other methods, but SYSCON is the most famous and most common way to set up trustee rights in NetWare 3.*x*. SYSCON does far more than just make shares available—this same program handles a number of administrative

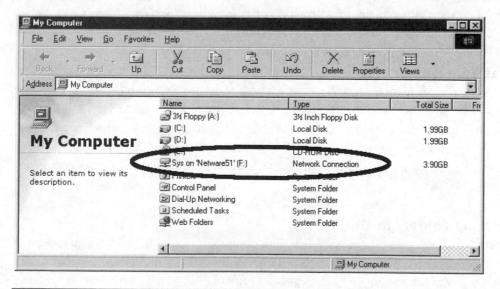

Figure 14-24 A mapped NetWare drive on a Windows system

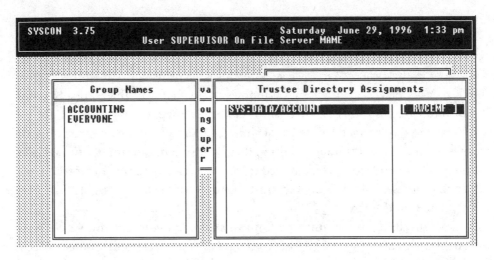

Figure 14-25   SYSCON in action

tasks, such as creating users and groups. SYSCON is a text mode utility that runs at a command prompt—a testament to the DOS era of networking. While SYSCON is powerful, it is also an absolute pain to use, and more than a little practice is required to get it to work properly. Figure 14-25 shows SYSCON being used to set up trustee rights to a folder. Note the names of the two groups and the rights assigned to them. Can't tell which is the trustee right? That's okay—it's RWCEMF, on the right side. Go back to the permissions section of this chapter and check the NetWare rights table to see which rights are assigned to the users in this example.

NetWare 4.x/5.x

NetWare 4.x/5.x work basically the same way as NetWare 3.x, but happily the tools you have for assigning trustee rights have improved dramatically. The current tool we use to assign trustee rights is NWADMIN. Unlike the old SYSCON, NWADMIN is a Windows-based application that lets you click the folder you wish to share and easily assign trustee rights. Figure 14-26 shows NWADMIN in action, configuring trustee rights for a shared folder.

Sharing Folders in UNIX/Linux

UNIX/Linux systems do not have a sharing option that easily fits into the paradigm of Windows and NetWare systems. UNIX/Linux systems share files across a network in a variety of ways. These include File Transfer Protocol (FTP), Network File System (NFS), and SAMBA. FTP, as discussed in Chapter 12, enables two TCP/IP hosts to transfer files

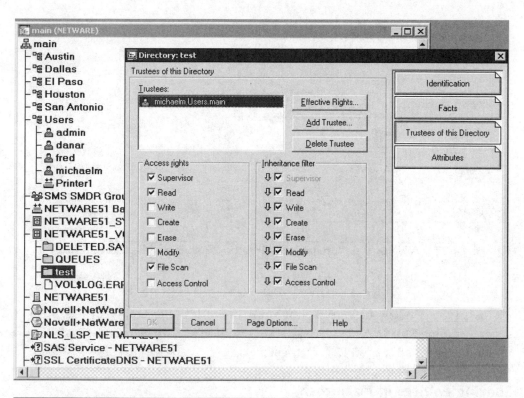

Figure 14-26 NWADMIN in action

across a network. All implementations of TCP/IP support FTP, making it an excellent choice for moving files from a UNIX host to a machine running another operating system such as Windows 9x, Windows NT, a different flavor of UNIX, or even a Macintosh.

Network File System (*NFS*) enables a UNIX system to treat files and directories on another UNIX host as though they were local files. Let's say Fred needs to access the /mark/projects/current directory on Mark's UNIX system, named MARK1. Fred *mounts* the /mark/projects/current/ directory to his own file system as /markstuff/, adding it to his local directory structure. As far as any program on Fred's UNIX machine can tell, the files in the /markstuff/ directory are local files. NFS enables his UNIX machine to share files transparently by adding network directories to its local directory structure. Unfortunately, Windows-based machines don't get to play, because they don't come with an NFS client. Although there are some fine third-party NFS tools available for Windows, most of us just use FTP or SAMBA for Windows-to-UNIX/Linux file transfers.

UNIX systems, however, can pretend to be Microsoft clients and servers using *SAMBA*, which enables UNIX systems to communicate using Server Message Blocks

Figure 14-27 A UNIX system running SAMBA looks just like a Microsoft server.

(SMBs). To a Windows-based system running Client for Microsoft Networks, a UNIX system running SAMBA looks just like a Microsoft server (see Figure 14-27). We'll see more of SAMBA, NFS, and FTP in later chapters.

Sharing Folders in Macintosh

Macintosh networks have very rudimentary networking functions, similar to Windows 9x networking. Unlike a Windows 9x system, a Macintosh is ready to share folders immediately. To share a folder on a Macintosh, you select the folder, click File/Get Info, and click the *Share this item and its contents* check box. Like Windows 9x, you only have three share permissions, which Apple calls Read & Write, Read only and interestingly enough, Write only (see Figure 14-28). A shared folder manifests itself with a different icon, as shown in Figure 14-29. Unfortunately, these shares are only good for Mac-to-Mac communication—we'll see how to get Mac to talk to Windows clients in Chapter 19.

Follow the Steps

Regardless of the NOS, the steps you take to share a folder are basically the same. First, you make sure the system is capable of sharing—this is done for you in all but Windows 9x systems. Second, you decide what you want to share, and make that folder available for sharing. Finally, you set whatever share/permissions/rights you want the share to have. Remember these three steps and sharing a folder is always easy!

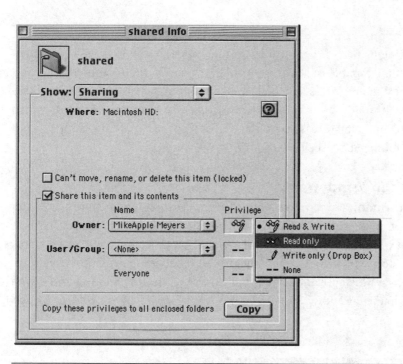

Figure 14-28 Sharing a folder on a Macintosh

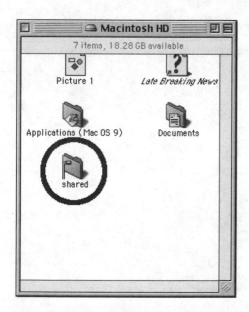

Figure 14-29 A shared folder on a Macintosh

Sharing Printers

The process of sharing printers is very similar to the folder sharing process—you must make sure the system is capable of sharing a printer, give the printer a share name, and set permissions. The actual process by which network operating systems share printers varies dramatically, although the sharing process doesn't vary nearly as much between versions of Windows and NetWare, so we won't have to go into quite the same level of detail we saw with folders. Let's see how they do it!

Sharing Printers in Windows 9x

Sharing a printer in Windows 9x requires almost the exact same steps as sharing a folder in Windows 9x. First, make sure the sharing system has added the File and Print Sharing service, and that you have clicked the *I want to share my printers with others* check box. Having done those steps, you actually share the printer by opening My Computer, finding the printer you want to share and—yup, that's right!—selecting Sharing and giving the printer a share name, as shown in Figure 14-30. Windows 9x has no form of per-

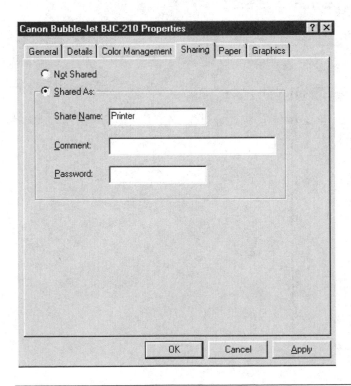

Figure 14-30   Sharing a printer in Windows 9x

missions for shared printers, but does at least allow you to set a password for the network share. Like all network shares, this password only affects network users.

Sharing Printers in Windows NT/2000

Windows NT and 2000 share a printer exactly like Windows 9*x*, but they do provide more substantial permissions. A Windows NT/2000 system provides three levels of print permissions: Print, Manage Printer, and Manage Documents. The Print permission allows users and groups to print to the printer. Manage Printer lets users control the printer properties, and Manage Documents gives users the right to delete, pause, and restart print jobs. Like folder permissions, these settings are found on the Security tab of the printer's Properties dialog box. Figure 14-31 shows the Printer sharing Security tab in Windows 2000.

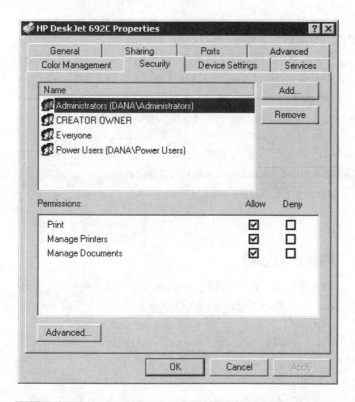

Figure 14-31   The Windows 2000 Printer Properties Security tab

Sharing Printers in NetWare

Novell NetWare has a bit of a problem with printers. While Windows NT/2000 can allow any system to act as a printer server, Novell NetWare can only control printers installed on a NetWare Server. Unfortunately, printers don't tend to hang around servers—they're installed around the network at user systems or as stand-alone network printers. Novell realized this long ago and developed complex but powerful methods for print serving that break away from the only-servers-serve attitude, and instead allow any system on any NetWare Network to act as a print server. All versions of Novell Net-Ware share basically the same two methods. The first is to allow a NetWare server to act as a print server. The second is to configure a client system to act as a print server. Novell allows virtually any type of OS client to act as a NetWare print server. This includes all versions of Windows, UNIX/Linux, and Macintosh computers, although you will need to install special NetWare printer server software on them to enable this to happen.

Sharing Printers in UNIX/Linux

Once again, UNIX/Linux does not have the same concept of actively sharing a printer that we saw in both Windows and NetWare. Instead, Linux uses two TCP/IP functions, Line Printer Daemon (LPD) and Line Printer Remote (LPR). The LPD program works as the server and runs on the system sharing the printer. Meanwhile, LPR runs on any system wanting to access a printer under the control of LPD. As a matter of fact, almost every operating system capable of supporting TCP/IP also includes the LPD and LPR programs, or at least something similar enough to support them. Go to a command prompt in Windows and type LPR—it's almost certainly there!

Accessing Shared Resources

Once a folder or printer has been shared by a serving system the next step is for the client systems to access that device and start to use it. The steps involved in accessing a shared resource usually include browsing to locate the shared resource, then connecting to it to make it seem as though it were a local resource; neither of these steps is completely necessary in all situations, however.

In this section, we will concentrate exclusively on Windows client systems. That's about as much as the Network+ test wants to you to know. We'll save most of the UNIX/Linux connection issues for other chapters.

Accessing Files in Windows

There are literally about six different ways to access a shared resource in Windows, but the most common method is to browse through My Network Places to locate the shared resource you desire. Tim wants to store some files in a folder on the server. He talks to the person who shared the folder on the server and they tell him to use the *tim-stuff* share on the server. Tim uses My Network Places to locate the share, as shown in Figure 14-32. Once he has found the share, he has some choices. He can just leave the share open in My Network Places and use it like any other folder, but this has a downside. He'll have to do this every time he uses it. Being a clever fellow, he instead decides to map the shared folder and give it a drive letter, checking the box that orders the share to reconnect at logon. We call this a *persistent connection* (see Figure 14-33). Any time you map a drive only to have it disappear after a reboot, you can be pretty sure you did not make a persistent connection.

Keep in mind that Windows doesn't care what type of server is providing this share. As long as you have the right user account with the right permissions, you'll be able to treat a share the same way, whether it comes from a Windows NT Server system, a Linux box, or a NetWare server. All shared folders manifest the same way (see Figure 14-34).

Beginning with Windows 95, you could create a desktop shortcut to a network share as an alternative to mapping the share to a drive letter. Just right-click and drag the

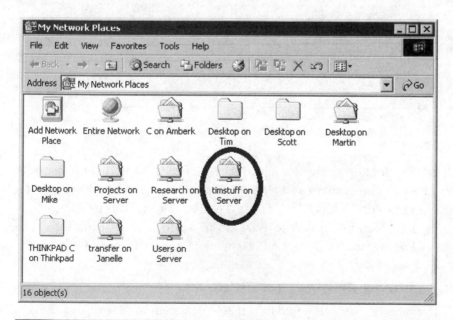

Figure 14-32 Finding the share in My Network Places

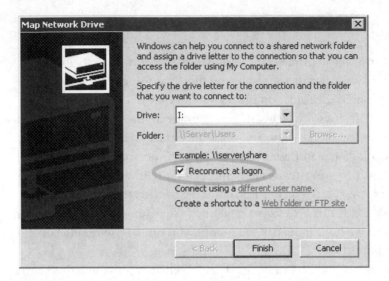

Figure 14-33 Setting a persistent connection

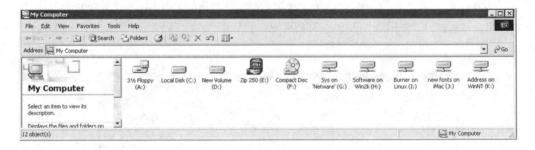

Figure 14-34 All shared folders look alike.

shared folder to the desktop to create a shortcut. Windows 2000 added the Network Place concept. Basically just a shortcut, a Network Place points to a shared folder, but it is not limited just to shared folders—you can make a Web site, an ftp site, almost anything you can share, a Network Place. The usual way to create these shortcuts is to open the My Network Places folder and select Add Network Place (see Figure 14-35).

Accessing Shared Printers in Windows

One aspect of printers not shared by folders is that your system needs printer drivers to send print jobs. Back in the old days, we would capture the printer to an LPT port and

Figure 14-35   The Add Network Place Wizard in My Network Places

then install the printer drivers onto our local systems. We would then tell the printer to install to the captured port. Today, Windows makes all of this much easier—when we access a network printer, the printer drivers install automatically on the local system, a big benefit of Windows networking! NetWare has a similar feature.

Troubleshooting Shared Resources

Almost all problems with sharing or accessing shared resources stem from some mistake in the process of creating the share, as opposed to a problem with the shared resource itself. In fact, most of what appear to be sharing errors have nothing to do with the sharing process—they are actually lower level errors like severed cables, incorrectly installed protocols, or attempts to access the wrong system. For the moment, let's assume none of these is the culprit, and look at some of the classic sharing errors that do take place on a network. We'll divide the most classic errors into two groups: sharing errors and access errors.

Sharing Errors

Sharing errors are problems that take place as you try to share a resource. Whenever I have a sharing error, I make a point to mentally review the steps required to create a share. Usually I realize that I skipped a step or failed to do a step properly.

The most frequent mistake people make is not sharing the right resource. This isn't exactly a sharing error but it happens so often that I simply must mention it. One folder that folks really like to share on a Windows system is the Desktop. That makes sense— I love to dump junk on my Desktop and then tell others to "Get it off my Desktop!" The problem with Windows Desktops is that many people don't know where they are actually located. Do you remember? On a Windows 9*x* system, you'll find the Desktop in \Windows\Desktop. Windows NT and Windows 2000 make life more difficult, because they create a separate Desktop for each user. In Windows NT, each user's Desktop is hidden under the \WINNT\PROFILES folder. To find the Desktop of my Windows 2000 system, you have to dig down to \Documents and Settings\michaelm\Desktop. Desktops are not the only folders people have a problem finding to share. There are zillions of ways to mess up sharing a folder, so the wise user will double-check each folder before they start sharing it!

The other sharing issue that will bust you on more advanced network operating systems like Windows NT, 2000, and NetWare, stems from permissions. The complexities of permissions make it way too easy to give someone insufficient permissions, preventing them from doing what they need to do on that share. Getting this right requires a bit of patience on your part as you experiment with different permission combinations to find the one that will let the user do what they need to do without unnecessarily sacrificing security.

Finally, watch out for share name incompatibilities. You can make a share in Windows 2000 called "This is the share Mike made on 12-1-02. Please use freely but send me an e-mail when you do!" but many other systems, especially Windows 9*x* systems, won't be able to see it. Always think about the other systems on your network before you create share names!

Access Errors

As with sharing errors, almost all access errors are due to configuration problems, not some corrupt piece of software. The single biggest error flows directly from permissions: if you can't access a shared resource in the way you think you should be able to, ask the person who controls the share to give you the permissions you need. It's not uncommon to hear a conversation like this:

"Hey Alison, I can't make any changes to the Accounting database!"

"Yeah, well, you're not supposed to be able to! You don't have the right permissions!"

"Okay, well, either I make these changes or the boss is gonna yell at me—can you change my permissions?"

"Okay, gimme a sec."

"Thanks!"

I know some folks in more formal offices will laugh at this, because they have very rigid procedures for changing permissions, but the basic process is still the same. Check to be sure you have the permissions you need. Just because you had the right permissions yesterday is no guarantee that some network guru isn't going to change them today! Always assume permission problems first!

Chapter Review

Questions

1. Which of the following operating systems can use the file and folder permissions based on NTFS?
   a. NetWare
   b. Windows 2000
   c. Linux
   d. Windows 98

2. Your network consists of a NetWare server and a mixture of Windows 98 systems and Windows NT workstations. You add a Windows NT server to the network. All systems have the TCP/IP protocol suite installed. Samantha is unable to access a shared file on the NT server, but she is able to print from the shared printer. What could be the problem?
   a. Samantha's system and the Windows NT server are not connected to the same hub.
   b. Client for NetWare Networks has not been installed on Samantha's system.
   c. Client for Microsoft Networks has not been installed on Samantha's system.
   d. You have not given Samantha permission to access the shared file on the NT server.

3. Chris needs to work on a folder on the Desktop of your Windows 98 system. He is unable to access the folder and you realize that you haven't shared the folder. You alternate-click the folder, but you don't get the Sharing option. What has happened?

   a. Chris hasn't been given the correct permissions to access the folder on your Desktop.

   b. At the logon screen, you clicked Cancel instead of entering a password.

   c. You did not install File and Print Sharing services on your system.

   d. The server is down.

4. The office's expensive laser printer is connected to Karen's Windows 98 system. Previously, other users have been able to print from that printer with no problem, but today they can't access it. What could be the problem?

   a. At the logon screen, Karen clicked Cancel instead of entering a password to log on to the network.

   b. File and Print Sharing services have not been installed on Karen's system.

   c. The server is down.

   d. Karen's system doesn't have the proper permissions set so other users can use the printer.

5. James is running a Windows 2000 system. He has shared his C: drive, but no one is able to access it. What could be causing this problem?

   a. He needs to be the Administrator before he can share the drive.

   b. He is set up as Power User and Power Users can't set permissions.

   c. After he shares a device, he still needs to go into Security and set the permissions.

   d. Everyone else's system has a problem. Only James' system is set up correctly.

6. Which of the following client systems can act as a printer server on a Novell NetWare network? (Choose all that apply.)

   a. UNIX/Linux

   b. Macintosh

   c. Windows 9x and 2000

   d. NetWare Server

7. In order for client systems to act as a printer server on a Novell NetWare network, each of the client systems must have the NetWare printer server software installed.

   a. True

   b. False

8. To share printers on a UNIX/Linux network, you must have which two printing services installed?
   a. EPP
   b. PPT
   c. LPD
   d. LPR

9. When one Windows 98 PC (*System A*) accesses a printer shared by another Windows 98 system, *System A* doesn't need printer drivers installed.
   a. True
   b. False

10. Joe does a lot of work in a network folder, so he mapped the network drive. The next morning when he boots up his system, the mapped network drive isn't there. What has happened?
    a. You must map a network drive each day.
    b. He didn't have the correct permissions to map a network drive.
    c. The server is turned off so the mapped network drive doesn't appear.
    d. He forgot to check the box to have the share reconnect at each logon.

Answers

1. **B.** Windows NT and 2000 can both recognize NT File System (NTFS). (Windows NT wasn't a choice, of course.)

2. **D.** Samantha does not have permission to access the shared file on the NT server.

3. **C.** You did not install File and Print Sharing services on your system.

4. **A.** Karen bypassed signing on to the network by clicking Cancel instead of entering a password at the logon screen. Windows 98 doesn't have permissions. Previously, the users have been able to use the printer so the File and Print Sharing service is installed.

5. **C.** After a resource is shared in 2000, you still need to go to the Security tab and set permissions before others can access the resource. James must already be signed on as an Administrator or Power User because he was able to share the resource. A Power User can share resources.

6. **A, B, C, and D.** All four answers are correct. With NetWare, each of these choices can act as a print server.

7. **A.** True. In order for client systems to act as a printer server on a Novell NetWare network, each of the client systems must have NetWare printer server software installed.

8. **C and D.** The LPD program works on the server and runs on the systems sharing the printer. LPR runs on any system wishing to access a printer under the control of LPD.

9. **B.** False. When you access a printer, you still need printer drivers, but Windows takes care of this automatically so you don't have to worry about it.

10. **D.** He needs to make sure the box is checked to have the mapped network drive reconnect at logon. If the server is down, then the mapped drive will have a big red X across it.

Going Large with TCP/IP

In this chapter, you will

- Understand DNS in detail
- Learn about troubleshooting DNS
- Understand DHCP in detail
- Learn about troubleshooting DHCP
- Understand WINS in detail
- Learn about troubleshooting WINS
- Understand diagnosing TCP/IP networks

Well, no sooner do you think you're done with TCP/IP then I grab you by the collar and we're right back into it harder than ever! You didn't *really* think we were finished with TCP/IP yet, did you? I promise no more subnetting, but we do need to look more at some critical tools we use to make TCP/IP networks function, particularly large ones. In fact, we're going to work with the largest of all networks, the Internet itself!

In this chapter we'll take an in-depth tour of DNS, WINS, and DHCP. Sure, I know you know how to set up your Windows clients for these fellas—if someone tells you what to enter in those TCP/IP Network Properties boxes—but now we're going to look at these in far more detail. In fact, we'll go a good bit beyond Network+ by looking at some real DNS, WINS, and DHCP servers! At the end of this chapter, we'll take a long hard look at the many software utilities (including some you've already seen, but in far more depth) and use them to diagnose and fix a number of the most common problems that occur in TCP/IP networks. That part you'll definitely want to know for the Network+ exam!

Odds are good you've got a system that is connected—or at least can connect—to the Internet. If I were you, I'd be firing that system up, because the vast majority of the programs you're going to learn about here come free with every operating system made. Finding them may be a challenge on some systems, but don't worry—I'll show you where they all hang out!

Historical/Conceptual

DNS

Chapter 12 gave you a brief overview of DNS. Let's now go a bit deeper into DNS and take some time to appreciate how it works, see a DNS server in action, and then explore some of the neat tools you can use to diagnose DNS problems. We're going to revisit a few things, like HOSTS files and domain names, but we'll be looking at them in a more practical way, really getting into them and hopefully having some fun, too!

DNS in Detail

In Chapter 12, you saw that DNS uses a hierarchal naming system and that it needs a magic box called a DNS server to provide FQDN to IP name resolution. But how does this really work? More importantly, if you're having a problem, how can you determine if DNS is the culprit? And if it is, what can you do about it without having to become an expert on DNS servers? Conveniently, it turns out that if you're having a DNS problem, in most cases it's not due to the DNS server crashing or some other problem over which you have no control. Instead, it's usually due to problems with the client systems, or another problem that you most certainly can control—*if* you understand DNS and know your DNS diagnostic tools!

DNS Organization

What does *hierarchal* mean in terms of DNS? Well, the DNS *hierarchical name space* is an imaginary tree structure of all possible names that could be used within a single system. By contrast, NetBIOS names use a *flat name space*—basically just one big undivided list containing all names, with no grouping whatsoever. The HOSTS file that resided on all networked systems in the old days is another example of a flat name space. In a flat name space all names must be absolutely unique. No two machines can ever share the same name under any circumstances. A flat name space works fine on a smaller network, but not so well for a large organization with computers and networks spread among several cities. To avoid naming conflicts, all of its administrators would need to keep track of all the names used throughout the entire corporate network. Even if there was a way to manage a flat name space using very powerful computers, a flat name space still wouldn't provide any way to structure the names of the networked systems to reflect the organization of the business.

A hierarchical name space offers a better solution, permitting a great deal more flexibility by enabling administrators to give networked systems longer, more fully descriptive names. The personal names people use every day are an example of a hierarchical name space. Most people address our town postman, Ron Samuels, as simply Ron. When his name comes up in conversation, people usually refer to him as Ron. The town troublemaker, Ron Falwell, and Mayor Jones's son, Ron, who went off to Toledo, obviously share first names with the postman. In some conversations, people need to distinguish between the good Ron, the bad Ron, and the Ron in Toledo (who may or may not be the ugly Ron). They could use a medieval style of address, and refer to the Rons as Ron the Postman, Ron the Blackguard, and Ron of Toledo, or they could use the modern Western style of address and add their surnames: "That Ron Samuels—he is such a card!" "That Ron Falwell is one bad apple." "That Ron Jones was the homeliest child I ever saw." You might visualize this as the People Name Space illustrated in Figure 15-1. Adding the surname creates what you might call a Fully Qualified Person Name—enough information to prevent confusion among the various people named Ron.

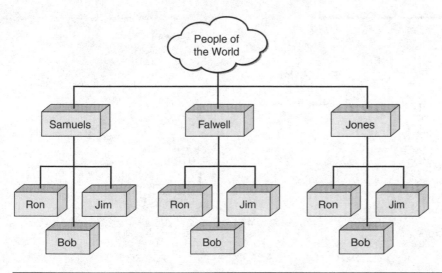

Figure 15-1   People Name Space

A name space most of you are already familiar with is the hierarchical file name space used by hard drive volumes. Hard drives formatted using one of the popular file formats, like FAT, NTFS, or Linux, use a hierarchical name space; you can create as many files named DATA.TXT as you want, as long as you store them in different parts of the file tree. In the example shown in Figure 15-2, two different files named DATA.TXT can exist simultaneously on the same system, but only if they are placed in different directories, such as C:\PROGRAM1\CURRENT\DATA.TXT and C:\PROGRAM1\BACKUP\ DATA.TXT. Although both files have the same basic filename—DATA.TXT—their fully qualified names are different: C:\PROGRAM1\CURRENT\DATA.TXT and C:\ PROGRAM1\BACKUP\DATA.TXT. Additionally, multiple subfolders can use the same name. There's no problem with having two folders using the name DATA, as long as they reside in different folders. Any Windows file system will happily let you create both C:\PROGRAM1\DATA and C:\PROGRAM2\DATA folders. We like this since we often want to give the same name to multiple folders doing the same job for different applications.

In contrast, imagine what would happen if your computer's file system didn't support folders/directories. It would be as if Windows had to store all the files on your hard drive in the root directory! This is a classic example of a flat name space. Because all

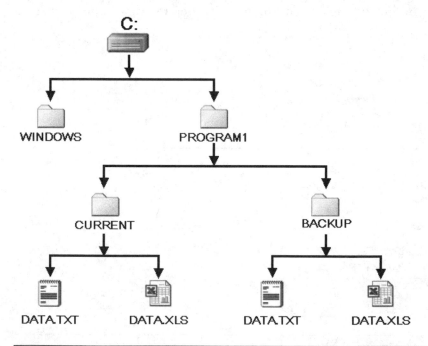

Figure 15-2   Two DATA.TXT files in different directories on the same system

your files would be living together in one directory, each one would have to have a unique name. Needless to say, naming files would be a nightmare. Software vendors would have to avoid sensible descriptive names like README.TXT, because they would almost certainly have been used already. You'd probably have to do what the Internet does for IP addresses: An organization of some sort would assign names out of the limited pool of possible file names. With a hierarchical name space, on the other hand, which is what all file systems really use (thank goodness!), naming is much simpler. Lots of programs can have files called README.TXT, because each program can have its own folder and subfolders.

The DNS name space works the same way. The vast majority of web servers are called WWW. If DNS used a flat name space, only the first organization that created a server with the name WWW could use it. Because DNS naming appends domain names to the server names, however, the servers www.totalsem.com and www.microsoft.com can both exist simultaneously. DNS names like www.microsoft.com must fit within a worldwide hierarchical name space, meaning that no two machines should ever have the same *fully qualified* name.

The DNS name space must be managed manually by network administrators. In order to allow decentralized administration, the DNS name space is broken up into domains. A *DNS domain* is a specific branch of the DNS name space, which starts at the root, and is often represented by a dot (.). Figure 15-3 shows the host named ACCOUNTING with a fully qualified domain name of ACCOUNTING.TEXAS .MICROSOFT.COM.

NOTE: Technically, the TEXAS.MICROSOFT.COM domain shown in Figure 15-3 is a subdomain. Don't be surprised to see the terms domain and subdomain used interchangeably, as it's a common practice.

This root named dot drove me crazy when I first saw it. Not only was I raised on a C:\ command prompt from my beginnings as a DOS user in a galaxy far far away, but all Windows file systems *still* use the *<drive letter>*:\ nomenclature when talking about disk volumes. *<Old Fogey Rant Mode on>* To me, a directory begins with a C:\ prompt, which is to say the good old root directory I learned so long ago. Shouldn't the root directory have a name, or at least a *letter*? *<OFRM off>* Well, it doesn't, and DNS isn't the only offender, either—man oh man did I get a shock when I first saw how the UNIX (and Linux) file systems work! Instead of a C: prompt, there was nothing but a /! Yikes! How can a directory structure be based on nothing but a /? Now I can admit it— I was stuck in my DOS/Windows frame of reference as to what a directory structure

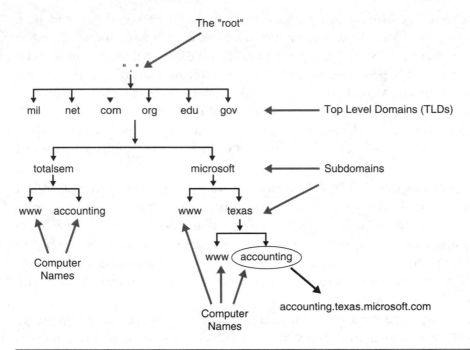

Figure 15-3 DNS domain TEXAS.MICROSOFT.COM containing the host AC-COUNTING

should look like. When you get right down to it, why not just have a / for a directory structure? It took a little mental practice but I was quickly able to appreciate that instead of thinking my hard drive started at C:\, I just thought in terms of a simple / and now I love Linux. Having a root of simply / doesn't change the way Linux stores folders. For example, essential program libraries are stored in the /lib directory, temporary files and directories created by users and/or applications are stored in the /tmp directory, and configuration and administration files that are specific to the system live in the /etc directory.

You're probably saying, "That's just fine for folders on one volume but wait, without drive letters, UNIX/Linux can't support floppy or CD-ROM drives!" Not true, mis amigos—UNIX/Linux only has one root, but it places other devices such as floppy drives and CD-ROM drives under that one root. So what is the equivalent of the A: and D: drives that most Windows systems use for floppy and CD-ROM drives? UNIX/Linux has a directory called /mnt, which stands for *mount*, available for mounts of file systems. What's a mount, you say? Well, back in the days of mainframes, you mounted a tape on one of those big fridge-sized tape drives and then typed some commands at a terminal to tell the mainframe to go read that tape. That's where the term mount comes from—remember, UNIX goes *way* back! The concept of mounting a floppy or CD-ROM drive in UNIX/Linux systems works roughly the same way today. If you want to access a floppy drive, for example, you must first mount it. To mount a floppy means simply to make the floppy drive appear as a folder. You then access the floppy by opening its mount folder. Believe me, it makes more sense if you see it happen. Figure 15-4 shows the process of mounting a folder to the /mnt folder. I decided to call the folder that is actually my floppy drive /mnt/floppy—most UNIX/Linux systems use this convention. Figure 15-4 shows the results of typing the **LS** command to see the contents of a floppy disk.

NOTE: In this example, I mounted the floppy drive to the /MNT/FLOPPY folder but I can mount it to any folder I wish. It's just that most folks like to use the /MNT/FLOPPY as the folder for the mounted floppy – if for no other reason than that others will know where to find the floppy quickly!

Okay, well that explains things like floppy drives and CD-ROMs, but what about a system with more than one partition? A Windows system handles this by giving each partition a drive letter like C:, D:, and so on, but if UNIX/Linux systems only have a /, how does this work? Actually, we can do this the same way we handle floppy drives and CD-ROMs. A UNIX/Linux system simply places these drives in a subdirectory.

This brings up an interesting point. Every IP network that uses DNS must be part of the same DNS naming system, or *DNS tree*. Any network that is part of the Internet becomes part of the great big Internet DNS tree. But not all networks using DNS are part of the Internet, and that's fine—nowhere is it written that all of the systems in the universe have to be part of the big Internet tree system! There's nothing wrong with creating your own little DNS tree that has nothing to do with the Internet. In the same way,

```
[Linux1@localhost /]$ mount /mnt/floppy
[Linux1@localhost /]$ cd / mnt/floppy
[Linux1@localhost floppy]$ ls
aspi2dos.sys    btcdrom.sys    ebd.sys        flashpt.sys    ramdrive.sys
aspi4dos.sys    btdosm.sys     ebdundo.exe    hibinv.exe     readme.txt
aspi8dos.sys    checksr.bat    extract.exe    himem.sys      setramd.bat
aspi8u2.sys     command.com    fdisk.exe      io.sys
[Linux1@localhost floppy]$
```

Figure 15-4   Contents of a floppy drive on Mike's Linux system

a Windows system can have multiple directory trees. This will become very important in a moment! Keep it in mind as we look at how DNS works in detail.

Name Resolution

You don't have to use DNS to access the Internet, but it sure makes life a lot easier! Programs like Internet Explorer accept names such as www.microsoft.com as a convenience to the end user, but utilize the IP address that corresponds to that name to create a connection. If you know the IP address of the system you wish to talk to, you don't need DNS at all. Figure 15-5 shows Internet Explorer displaying the same web page when given the straight IP address as it does when given the DNS name www.microsoft .com. In theory, if you knew the IP addresses of all the systems you wanted to access, you could turn off DNS completely. I guess you could also start a fire using a bow and

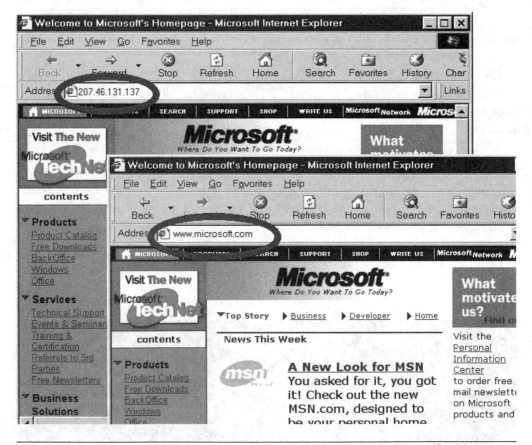

Figure 15-5   Sockets-based applications like Internet Explorer can accept IP addresses or DNS names.

drill too, but most people wouldn't make a habit of it if there were a more efficient alternative, which in this case, DNS definitely is! I have no trouble keeping hundreds of DNS names in my head, but IP addresses? Forget it! Without DNS, I might as well not even try to use the Internet, and I'd wager that's true of most people.

When you type in www.microsoft.com, Internet Explorer must resolve that name to the IP address 207.46.131.137 to make a connection to Microsoft's web server. It can resolve the name in three ways: by broadcasting, by consulting a locally stored text file we discussed earlier, called HOSTS, or by contacting a DNS server.

To *broadcast* for name resolution, the host sends a message to all the machines on the network, saying something like, "Hey! If your name is JOESCOMPUTER, please respond with your IP address." All the networked hosts receive that packet, but only JOESCOMPUTER responds with an IP address. Broadcasting works fine for small networks, but it is very limited because it cannot provide name resolution across routers. Routers do not forward broadcast messages to other networks, as illustrated in Figure 15-6.

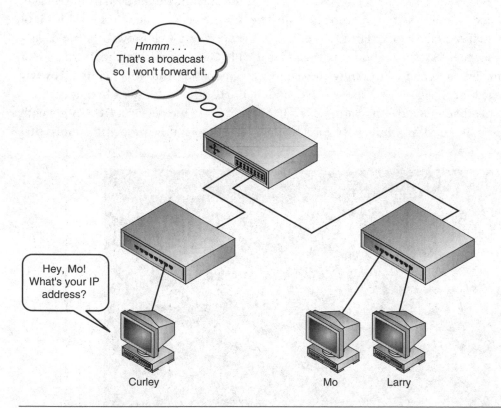

Figure 15-6   Name resolution by broadcast does not work across routers because routers do not forward broadcasts.

As we discussed earlier, a HOSTS file functions like a little black book, listing the names and addresses of machines on a network, just like a little black book lists the names and phone numbers of people. A typical HOSTS file would look like this:

```
109.54.94.197      stephen.totalsem.com
138.125.163.17     roger.totalsem.com
127.0.0.1          localhost
```

NOTE: Notice that the name "localhost" appears in the HOSTS file as an alias for the loopback address, 127.0.0.1.

When a program needs to resolve a name, its first stop is the local machine's HOSTS file to see if it contains an entry for the name specified. The secret knowledge here is: the HOSTS file takes precedence over DNS! This little factoid can be used by the sneaky-minded among you to have some fun—just be *sure* the person you select for this bit of mischief can take a joke! First, find out what they use for a web browser home page—let's say they use www.yahoo.com. Next, use the PING program to get the IP address for some amusing and/or irritating web site (my personal favorite for this trick is www.barney.com). Figure 15-7 shows PING finding the IP address for www.barney.com.

Now that you know the Barney site's IP address, open the person's HOSTS file with a text editor and substitute www.barney.com's IP address for the proper IP address that

```
C:\WINDOWS>cd..

C:\>ping www.barney.com

Pinging barney.com [216.46.231.162] with 32 bytes of data:

Reply from 216.46.231.162: bytes=32 time=40ms TTL=118
Reply from 216.46.231.162: bytes=32 time=25ms TTL=118
Reply from 216.46.231.162: bytes=32 time=28ms TTL=118
Reply from 216.46.231.162: bytes=32 time=35ms TTL=118

Ping statistics for 216.46.231.162:
    Packets: Sent = 4, Received = 4, Lost = 0 (0% loss),
Approximate round trip times in milli-seconds:
    Minimum = 25ms, Maximum =  40ms, Average =  32ms

C:\>_
```

Figure 15-7   Pinging www.barney.com

would normally be used to resolve www.yahoo.com. It doesn't matter where you add it in the file. Here's what the entry would look like in a typical Windows HOSTS file, assuming they don't change the IP address for www.barney.com by the time you read this:

```
127.0.0.1          localhost
216.46.231.162     www.yahoo.com
```

Now all you have to do is save the HOSTS file, sit back, and enjoy! Every time the person tries to access www.yahoo.com, the HOSTS file will send them instead to www .barney.com. Final piece of advice: a joke like this doesn't *stay* funny for long, so have a laugh, but then be sure to change the HOSTS file back to its proper state without delay.

The final way to resolve a name to an IP address is to use DNS. We've seen what a wonderful thing DNS is for the user; now let's look at how it actually does the job. To resolve the name www.microsoft.com, the host contacts its DNS server and requests the IP address, as shown in Figure 15-8. The local DNS server may not know the address for www.microsoft.com, but it does know the address of a DNS root server. The root servers, maintained by the Internic, know all of the addresses of the top-level domain DNS servers. The root servers don't know the address of www.microsoft.com, but they do know the address of the DNS server in charge of all .com addresses. The .com DNS server also doesn't know the address of www.microsoft.com, but it knows the IP address of the microsoft.com DNS server. The microsoft.com server does know the IP address of www.microsoft.com, and can send that information back to the local DNS

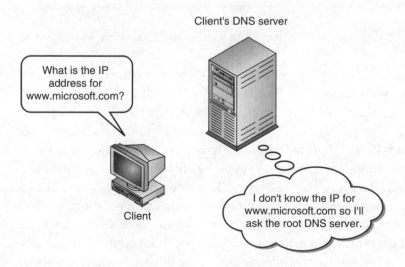

Figure 15-8   A host contacts its DNS server.

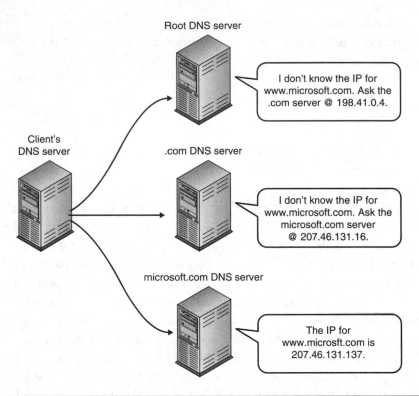

Figure 15-9 A DNS server contacts other DNS servers to resolve a FQDN into an IP address.

server. Figure 15-9 shows the process of resolving a fully qualified domain name into an IP address.

No single machine needs to know every DNS name, as long as every machine knows who to ask for more information. The distributed, decentralized nature of the DNS database provides a great deal of flexibility and freedom to network administrators using DNS. DNS still requires an administrator to type in each name and address, just as they do with a HOSTS file. There are two key advantages, however, to maintaining this information in a DNS database, compared to maintaining the same information in the form of HOSTS files. First, because the database is centralized on the DNS server, an administrator can add new entries just once, rather than walking around the network to add new entries to each machine. Second, the database is distributed, meaning that no single administrator must maintain a database that knows about every other machine in the world. A DNS server simply has to know about the other DNS servers where it can go for more information.

PART III

The DNS Cache

Most web browsers and Windows 2000/XP systems keep track of DNS via a cache, logically called the *DNS resolver cache*. After a web browser or a Windows 2000/XP system has made a DNS request, it keeps that IP address in its own personal DNS cache. If you want to see the DNS cache on a Windows 2000 or XP system, just run the command **IPCONFIG /displaydns** at a command prompt. Internet Explorer and Netscape Navigator also have DNS caches but you need a third-party utility to see their contents. **IPCONFIG /displaydns** creates a rather messy, long output, so be ready to do some scrolling. Figure 15-10 shows just a small bit of the typical output from **IPCONFIG /displaydns**. You can then erase this cache using the **IPCONFIG/flushdns** command.

```
ns.jump.net.

    Record Name . . . . . : ns.jump.net
    Record Type . . . . . : 1
    Time To Live  . . . . : 74548
    Data Length . . . . . : 4
    Section . . . . . . . : Answer
    A (Host) Record . . . :
                    204.238.120.5


1.0.0.127.in-addr.arpa.

    Record Name . . . . . : 1.0.0.127.in-addr.arpa
    Record Type . . . . . : 12
    Time To Live  . . . . : 31279767
    Data Length . . . . . : 4
    Section . . . . . . . : Answer
    PTR Record  . . . . . :
                    localhost


sca03.sec.dns.exodus.net.

    Record Name . . . . . : sca03.sec.dns.exodus.net
    Record Type . . . . . : 1
    Time To Live  . . . . : 70340
    Data Length . . . . . : 4
    Section . . . . . . . : Answer
    A (Host) Record . . . :
                    216.32.126.150


ns2.got.net.

    Record Name . . . . . : ns2.got.net
    Record Type . . . . . : 1
    Time To Live  . . . . : 67469
    Data Length . . . . . : 4
    Section . . . . . . . : Answer
    A (Host) Record . . . :
                    207.111.232.23
```

Figure 15-10   Some output from the IPCONFIG/displaydns command

Remember this command—you'll be needing it in just a moment! For now, let's take a look at a real DNS server running on a Windows 2000 system.

DNS Servers

We've been talking about DNS servers for so long I feel I'd be untrue to my vision of an All-In-One book unless we took at least a quick peek at a DNS server in action. Lots of network operating systems come with built-in DNS server software, including Windows NT and 2000 Server, NetWare 5.*x*, and just about every version of UNIX/Linux. There are also a number of third-party DNS server programs for virtually any operating system. I'm going to use the DNS server program that comes with Microsoft Windows 2000 Server primarily because (1) it takes the prettiest screen snapshots and (2) it's the one I use here at the office. You start the DNS server by selecting Administrative Tools | DNS from the Start menu. When you first open the DNS server, there's not much to see other than the name of the server itself; in this case, it has the really boring name *Server* (see Figure 15-11).

The first folder is called *Cached Lookup*. Every DNS server keeps a list of all the IP addresses it has already resolved so it won't have to re-resolve a FQDN name it has

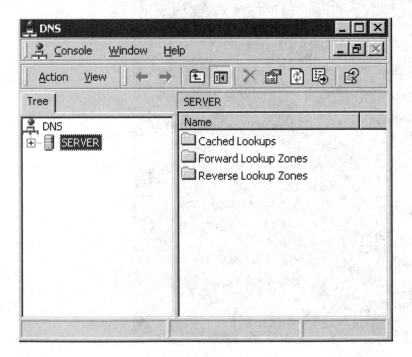

Figure 15-11   Mike's Windows 2000 DNS server when first opened

already checked, within the limit of the size of the cache and the limit you can set on how long the DNS server holds cache entries. Windows does a nice job of separating these cached addresses by placing all cached lookups in little folders that share the first name of the top level domain with subfolders that use the second level domain—sure makes it easy to see where folks have been web browsing! (See Figure 15-12.)

This brings up an interesting point. Basically, there are two types of DNS servers. *Authoritative DNS servers* actually hold the IP addresses and names of systems for a particular domain or domains in special storage areas called *Forward Lookup Zones*. In Figure 15-13, the record called SOA in the folder wheebo.com indicates that my server is the authoritative server for a domain called wheebo.com. You can even see a few of the systems in that domain (note to hackers: these are fake, so don't bother). A tech looking at this would know that server.wheebo.com is the authoritative server for the wheebo.com domain. The "A" records in the folder are the names of the systems on the network.

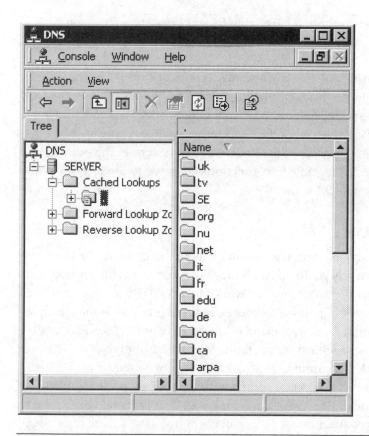

Figure 15-12 The Cached Lookups table

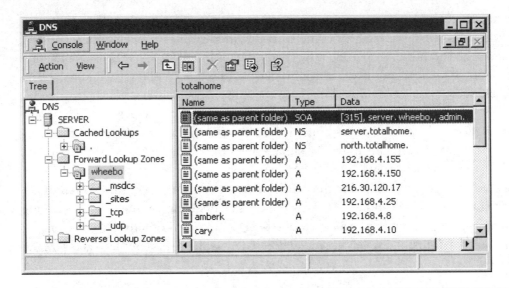

Figure 15-13 The SOA record in the wheebo.com folder of the authoritative server

Many DNS servers are *cache-only*. They will resolve names of systems on the Internet for the network but are not responsible for telling other DNS servers the names of any clients. This is fairly common for DNS servers in smaller networks. The other folder you can see in Figure 15-13 is *Reverse Lookup Zones*. This rather strange setting enables a system to determine a FQDN by knowing the IP address; that is, it does the exact reverse of what DNS normally does! A few low-level functions continue to use reverse lookup zones, so DNS servers all still provide them.

Troubleshooting DNS

As I mentioned earlier, most DNS problems result from a problem with the client systems, because DNS servers rarely go down and if they do, most clients have a secondary DNS server setting that lets them continue to work properly. DNS servers have been known to fail, however, so it's important to know when the problem is the client system, and when you can complain to the person in charge of your DNS server. All of the tools you're about to see come with every operating system that supports TCP/IP, with the exception of the **IPCONFIG** commands, which I'll mention when we get to them.

So how do you know when to suspect DNS as a problem on your network? Well, just about everything you do on an IP network depends on DNS to find the right system to talk to for whatever job the application does. E-mail clients use DNS to find their e-mail servers; FTP clients use DNS for their servers; web browsers use DNS to find web servers, and so on. The first clue is usually a user calling you and saying they're getting a "server not found" error. Server not found errors look different on different applications but you can count on something in there that says "server not found." Figure 15-14 shows how this error appears in a web browser and in an e-mail client.

Before you start testing, you need to eliminate any DNS caches on the local system. If you're running Windows 2000 or Windows XP, run the **IPCONFIG /flushdns** command now. In addition, most web browsers also have caches, so you can't use a web browser for any testing. In such cases, it's time to turn to the **PING** command!

PING is your best friend when you're testing DNS. Run **PING** from a command prompt, first typing in the name of a well-known web site such as www.microsoft.com. Watch the output carefully to see if you get an IP address. You may get a "request timed out" message, but that's fine; you just want to see if DNS is resolving FQDN names into IP addresses (see Figure 15-15).

PART III

![Microsoft Networking dialog box with warning: "No domain server was available to validate your password. You may not be able to gain access to some network resources." with OK and Cancel buttons]

Figure 15-14 "Server not found" errors in web browsers and e-mail clients

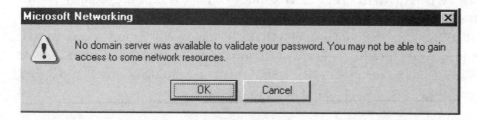

```
C:\WINNT\System32\cmd.exe

Microsoft Windows 2000 [Version 5.00.2195]
(C) Copyright 1985-2000 Microsoft Corp.

C:\>ipconfig/flushdns

Windows 2000 IP Configuration

Successfully flushed the DNS Resolver Cache.

C:\>ping www.totalsem.com

Pinging www.totalsem.com [64.226.214.168] with 32 bytes of data:

Reply from 64.226.214.168: bytes=32 time=50ms TTL=114
Reply from 64.226.214.168: bytes=32 time=60ms TTL=114
Reply from 64.226.214.168: bytes=32 time=41ms TTL=114
Reply from 64.226.214.168: bytes=32 time=40ms TTL=114

Ping statistics for 64.226.214.168:
    Packets: Sent = 4, Received = 4, Lost = 0 (0% loss),
Approximate round trip times in milli-seconds:
    Minimum = 40ms, Maximum = 60ms, Average = 47ms

C:\>_
```

Figure 15-15 Pinging www.totalsem.com

If you get a "server not found" error you need to ping again using just an IP address. Most network techs keep the IP address of a known server in their heads. If you don't have one memorized, try 216.30.120.1. If **PING** works with the IP address but not with the web site name, you know you've got a DNS problem.

Once you've determined there's a DNS problem, check to make sure your system has the correct DNS server entry. Again, this information is something you should keep around. I can tell you the DNS server IP address for every Internet link I own—two in the office, one at the house, plus two dialups I use on the road. You don't have to memorize the IP addresses, but you should have all the critical IP information written down. If that isn't the problem, run **IPCONFIG** or **WINIPCONFIG** to see if those DNS settings are the same as the ones in the server; if they aren't, you may need to refresh your DHCP settings. I'll show you how to do that next.

If you have the correct DNS settings for your DNS server and the DNS settings in **IPCONFIG/WINIPCONFIG** match those settings, you can assume the problem is with the DNS server itself. There's a popular command for working with DNS servers called **NSLOOKUP** (name server lookup). **NSLOOKUP** comes with Windows (except 9*x*), Linux, and NetWare. It's a handy tool that advanced techs use to query the functions of DNS servers. Don't worry about using **NSLOOKUP** now, though—save that for your next big certification!

DHCP

Earlier, you saw that Dynamic Host Configuration Protocol (DHCP) could somehow magically take all your TCP/IP setup blues away by enabling any system to get all its necessary TCP/IP settings automatically from a DHCP server. In this section, we'll take a look at a DHCP server, consider some of the configuration issues, and then review some basic DHCP troubleshooting techniques.

DHCP in Detail

DHCP is Microsoft's answer to TCP/IP client auto-configuration. The DHCP server stores IP information and disperses it to the client systems on the network. At first glance, you might think that DHCP only gives out IP *addresses*, but in fact it can give out all types of IP information: IP addresses, default gateways, DNS servers, and so on. While very useful, it's important to add that it's not mandatory for the network's client systems to use DHCP. It's no problem at all if some systems on the network get their IP information from the DHCP server, while others use static IP information. Finally, a system can use DHCP to obtain some IP information, and use static IP information for other purposes—there's no rule that a single system has to use only DHCP or static IP information.

The beauty of DHCP is that it enables a network to share a relatively small number of IP addresses among a relatively large number of host systems. Let's say your network has only ten available IP addresses. You have about 20 sales people with laptops who plug into the network when they come into the office. Instead of giving each laptop a static IP address, you can *pool* the ten IP addresses on the DHCP server; the salespeople are then assigned IP addresses from this pool only when they actually need them. Of course, you must be sure that no more than ten laptop users will want to connect at any given time.

DHCP Servers

Since only Windows systems normally use DHCP (UNIX/Linux systems use the similar BOOTP function) I'll show you the DHCP server that comes with Windows 2000 Server. At first glance, you might think you're looking at the DNS server program, because you only see the name of the server running the DHCP server program (see Figure 15-16).

If you click the name of the DNS server, you'll see the cornerstone of DHCP: the DHCP scope. A *DHCP scope* is the pool of IP addresses that a DHCP server may allocate to clients requesting IP addresses, or other IP information like DNS server addresses. This DHCP server has a pool of IP addresses running from 192.168.4.1 up to 192.168.4.100 (see Figure 15-17). It passes out these IP addresses in order as they are

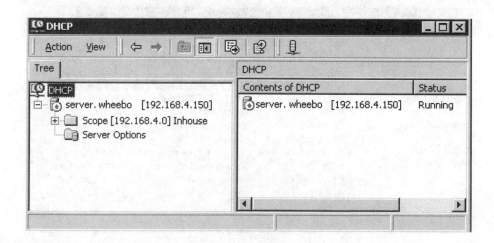

Figure 15-16 The Windows 2000 DHCP server program

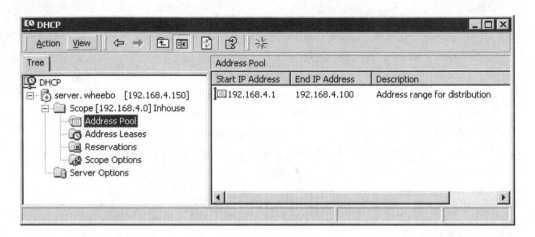

Figure 15-17 DHCP scope—a pool of IP addresses

requested; so the first system that asks for an IP address gets 192.168.4.1, the second one gets 192.168.4.2, and so on.

When a system requests DHCP IP information, the DHCP server creates a *lease* for the requested IP information; this means the client may use these setting for a certain amount of time. Windows sets this to eight days by default. To see the systems currently leasing DHCP IP addresses, look under Address Leases in DHCP (see Figure 15-18).

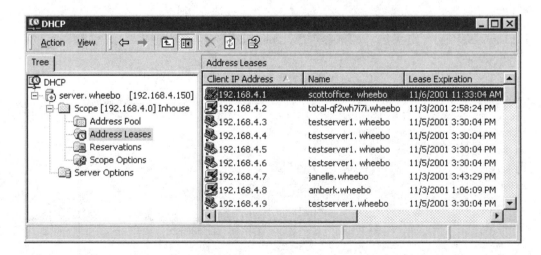

Figure 15-18 Address Leases showing currently leased DHCP IP addresses

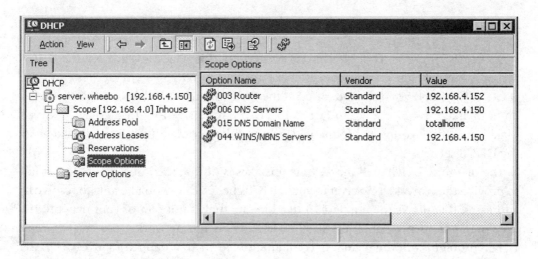

Figure 15-19 DHCP scope options

Remember that DHCP does more than just provide dynamic IP addresses. DHCP is great at dispensing all sorts of IP information your system might need. Figure 15-19 shows these DHCP scope options, and that I have the options for Default Gateway (Router), DNS server, and domain information activated, as well as my WINS server. All of this information is passed to DHCP clients when they get their dynamic IP addresses.

Troubleshooting DHCP

DHCP is a highly automated process that requires little configuration from the client side. This makes DHCP problems rare indeed. Once a system connects to a DHCP server and gets its dynamic IP information, it will run on those settings until the end of its lease period or until it reboots. These are the only times you'll get an error pointing to a DHCP problem. On reboot, you'll see something like the error shown in Figure 15-20.

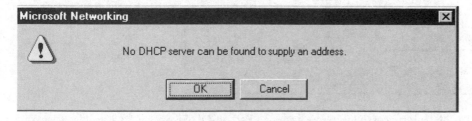

Figure 15-20 Error: No DHCP server present

Any Windows 98 and later Windows client that is configured for DHCP but unable to access a DHCP server will always default to a special IP address starting with 169.254. Use **IPCONFIG** or **WINIPCFG** to check for this IP address if you think DHCP access is the problem. If you do this check and get a 169.254.x.x IP address, run the **IPCONFIG /RENEW** command, or press the RENEW button in **WINIPCFG**. If you get an error like the one shown in Figure 15-21, you're not getting to the DHCP server. Make sure you're connected to the network, and then contact the person in charge of the DHCP server.

The one time DHCP will make some mistakes is during the initial setup. If you fail to provide the correct DNS server to your DHCP clients, they won't be able to resolve IP addresses. If you give them a pool of IP addresses that is not part of your network ID, they may not even be able to see other systems on the network. These really aren't DHCP problems; they're regular IP configuration errors that happen to involve DHCP, which happily disperses them to all your networked systems.

Release or Renew?

WINIPCFG and **IPCONFIG** both come with the handy *Release* and *Renew* options. When do you use Release and when do you use Renew? This one's simple: if you know you're changing to a *new* DHCP server, first Release, then Renew. If you know you're sticking with the same DHCP server, just Renew. Linux users don't have these handy Release and Renew options, so they have to turn the NIC off and back on again to get

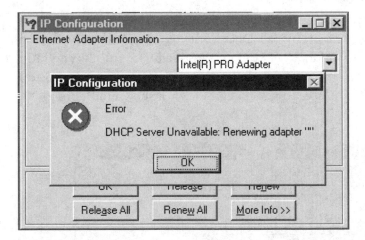

Figure 15-21 Unsuccessful RENEW command error: DHCP Server Unavailable: Renewing Adapter

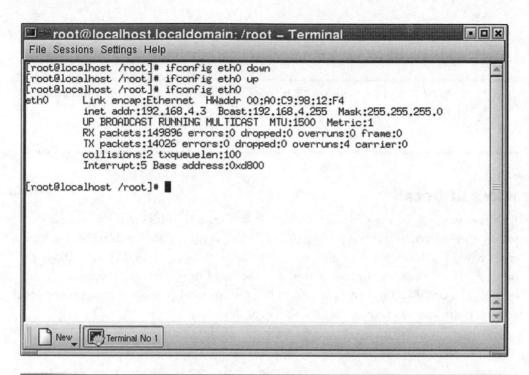

Figure 15-22 Renewing a DHCP lease in Linux using the IFCONFIG up command

the same result. To do this, run the **IFCONFIG eth0 down** command (*eth0* is what Linux names your NIC; if you have multiple NICs, the second would be eth1, and so on) and then the **IFCONFIG eth0 up** command. When the NIC comes back on, it will automatically try to renew the DHCP lease (see Figure 15-22).

WINS

Remember WINS? It resolves NetBIOS names to IP addresses. WINS drives many network types absolutely crazy, because it's one of those services that most networks simply don't need. Since only Windows networks run NetBIOS, WINS only operates in pure or nearly pure Windows networks. A Windows network must be running both IP and NetBIOS in order to need WINS, and even in those cases, you may not need WINS, because NetBIOS clients broadcast over a single segment. The latest versions of Windows—2000 and XP—have dumped native support for WINS, instead relying completely on DNS, except when running in networks with Windows 9*x* or NT systems. Bottom line? If you've never seen a WINS server before, this may be your only chance.

 EXAM TIP: Even though WINS is fading away, the Network+ exam still expects you to know it!

WINS in Detail

Let's review what we know about NetBIOS. In a simple NetBIOS network—no matter what protocol you're running—a NetBIOS system claims a NetBIOS name for itself simply by broadcasting out to the rest of the network (Figure 15-23). As long as no other system is already using that name, it works just fine. Of course, broadcasting can be a bit of a problem for routers and such, but remember that this example presumes a single network on the same wire, so it's okay in this context.

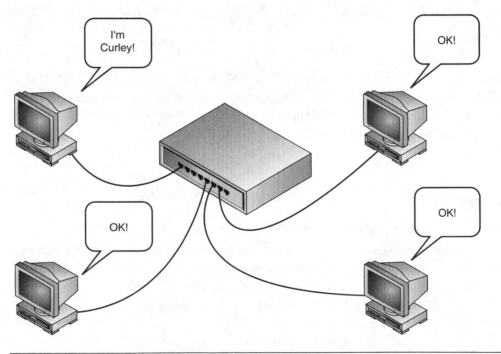

Figure 15-23   A NetBIOS system broadcasting its name

Remember that NetBIOS was invented way back in the early 1980s. Microsoft had a big investment in NetBIOS, and had to support a large installed base of systems, so even after NetBEUI (the network protocol NetBIOS was designed for) began to lose market share to TCP/IP, Microsoft had to continue to support NetBIOS or incur the wrath of millions of customers. What happened next seems in retrospect more a comedy than the machinations of the most powerful software company in the world. Microsoft did something that should not have been possible: they redesigned NetBIOS to work with TCP/IP. Let's look at some of the strategies and techniques they used to make NetBIOS and TCP/IP coexist on the same network.

One very early strategy Microsoft came up with to reduce the overhead from NetBIOS broadcasts was to use a special text file called LMHOSTS. LMHOSTS contains a list of the NetBIOS names and corresponding IP addresses of the host systems on the network. Sound familiar? Well, it should—the LMHOSTS file works exactly the same way as the DNS HOSTS file. Although Microsoft still supports LMHOSTS file usage, I'm happy to say that LMHOSTS files have gone the way of DNS HOSTS files, which is to say they are no more.

Microsoft quickly replaced the LMHOSTS files with WINS servers. WINS servers let NetBIOS hosts register their names with just the one server, eliminating the need for broadcasting and thereby reducing NetBIOS overhead substantially. Figure 15-24 shows the copy of the WINS server that comes with Windows 2000 Server. Note that the PCs on this network have registered their names with the WINS server.

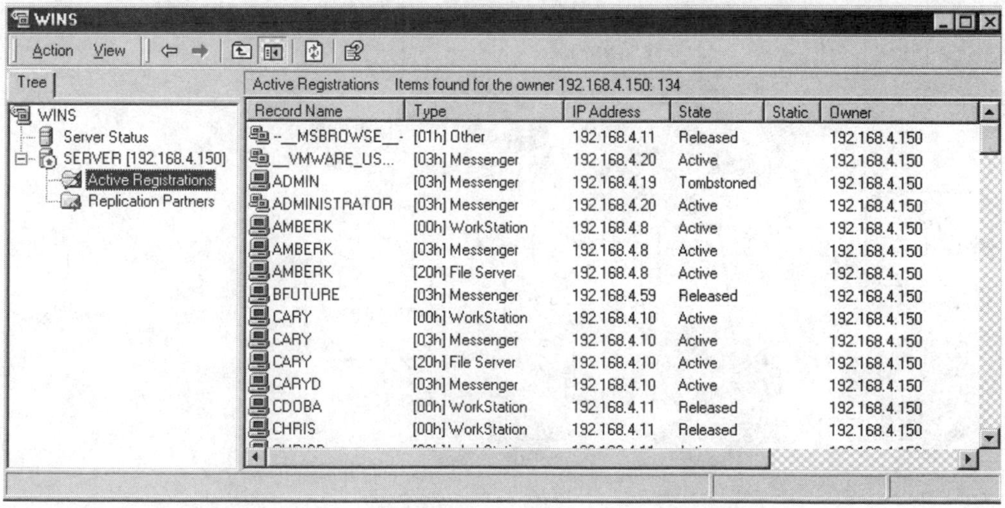

Figure 15-24 The WINS server that comes with Windows 2000 Server

There are only two good reasons to use a WINS server: (1) to reduce overhead from broadcasts; and (2) to enable NetBIOS name resolution across routers. What does a WINS server have to do with routers, you ask? Just this: The WINS server enables Net-BIOS to function in a routed network. IP routers are programmed to *kill* all broadcasts, remember? To get around this problem, you can configure a system to act as a *WINS relay agent*, forwarding WINS broadcasts to a WINS server on the other side of the router (see Figure 15-25).

The bottom line with WINS is this: Larger or routed networks that run NetBIOS still need them. As long as we have Windows NT and Windows 9*x* systems out there in those types of networks, don't be surprised to find that some system somewhere is running a WINS server.

Configuring WINS Clients

You don't need to do much to get a Windows client to use WINS. In fact, every Windows system is designed to look for the IP address of a WINS server in its WINS settings

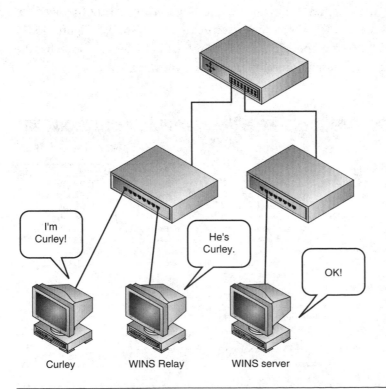

Figure 15-25 A WINS relay agent forwarding broadcasts across a router

under Network Properties. If it finds one, it will send out a registration to the WINS server; if it doesn't, it will automatically start broadcasting. You can add WINS information to DHCP if necessary, so unless you're running static IPs, you may never have to enter anything into your Windows clients to get WINS to work.

Troubleshooting WINS

Most WINS problems are not WINS problems at all. They are NetBIOS problems. By far, the most common problem is having two systems share the same name. In that case, you get a pretty clear error. It looks different in different versions of Windows, but it usually says about the same thing: another system has this name. How do you fix it? Change the name of the system!

The program we turn to for help with NetBIOS problems is called *NBTSTAT*. NBTSTAT will do a number of jobs, depending on the switches you add to the end of the command. The -c switch, for example, tells NBTSTAT to check the current NetBIOS name cache (yup, NetBIOS caches names just like some systems cache DNS names). The NetBIOS name cache contains the NetBIOS names and corresponding IP addresses that have been resolved by a particular host. You can use NBTSTAT to see if the WINS server has supplied inaccurate addresses to a WINS client. Here's an example of the **NBTSTAT –c** command and its results:

```
C:\ >NBTSTAT -c

Node IpAddress: [192.168.43.5] Scope Id: []
              NetBIOS Remote Cache Name Table

    Name             Type      Host Address     Life [sec]
    ---------------------------------------------------------
    WRITERS       <1B>  UNIQUE    192.168.43.13      420
    SCOTT         <20>  UNIQUE    192.168.43.3       420
    VENUSPDC      <00>  UNIQUE    192.168.43.13      120
    MIKE          <20>  UNIQUE    192.168.43.2       420
    NOTES01       <20>  UNIQUE    192.168.43.4       420
```

Diagnosing TCP/IP Networks

I've dedicated an entire chapter to network diagnostic procedures, but TCP/IP has a few little extras that I want to talk about here. TCP/IP is a pretty tough little protocol, and in good networks, it runs like a top for years without problems. Most of the TCP/IP problems you'll see come from improper configuration, so I'm going to assume you've run into problems with a new TCP/IP install, and we'll look at some classic screw-ups common in this situation. I want to concentrate on making sure you can ping anyone you want to ping. If you can ping a system by its DNS name, any application should work just fine. So let's start pinging!

I've done thousands of IP installations over the years, and I'm proud to say that in most cases they worked right the first time. My users jumped on the newly configured systems, fired up their Network Neighborhoods, e-mail software, and web browsers, and were last seen typing away, smiling from ear to ear. But I'd be a liar if I didn't also admit that plenty of setups didn't work so well. Let's start with the hypothetical case of a user who can't see something on the network. You get a call: "Help!" they cry. First troubleshooting point to remember here: it doesn't matter *what* they can't see. It doesn't matter if they can't see other systems in Network Neighborhood, or they can't see the home page on their browser, because you go through the same steps in any event.

Remember to use common sense and more than one brain cell at a time wherever possible. If the problem system can't ping by DNS name, but all the other systems can, is the DNS server down? Of course not! If something—*anything*—doesn't work on one system, *always* try it on another one to determine if the problem is specific to one system or affects the entire network.

One thing I always do is check the network connections and protocols. We're going to cover those topics in greater detail later in the book, so for now we'll assume our problem systems are properly connected and have good protocols installed. Here are some steps to take:

1. *Diagnose the NIC.* First, use PING with the loopback address to determine if the system can send and receive packets. Specifically, you run **PING 127.0.0.1** or **PING localhost** (remember the HOSTS file?). If you're not getting a good response, your NIC has a problem!

2. *Diagnose locally.* If the card's okay, diagnose locally by pinging a few neighboring systems, both by IP address and DNS name. If you're using NetBIOS, use the **NET VIEW** command to see if the other local systems are visible (see Figure 15-26). If you can't ping by DNS, check your DNS settings. If you can't see the network using **NET VIEW**, you may have a problem with your NetBIOS settings.

   If you're having a problem pinging locally, make sure you have the right IP address and subnet mask. Oh, if I had a nickel for every time I entered those incorrectly! If you're on DHCP, try renewing the lease—sometimes that will do the trick. If DHCP fails, call the person in charge of the server.

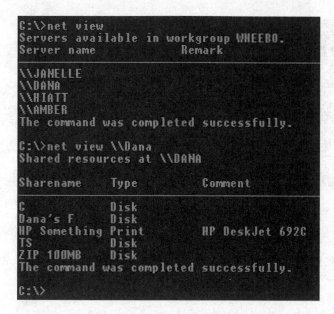

Figure 15-26 NET VIEW shows other local systems.

EXAM TIP: A good testing trick is to use the **NET SEND** command to try sending messages to other systems. Not all versions of Windows support **NET SEND**, however.

At this point, another little handy program comes into play called *NETSTAT*. NETSTAT has a number of options. The two handiest ways to run **NETSTAT** are with no options at all, and with the "-s" option. Running **NETSTAT** with no options will show you all of the current connections to your system. Look for a connection here that isn't working with an application—that's often a clue to an application problem, such as a broken application or a sneaky application running in the background. Figure 15-27 shows a NETSTAT program running.

Running **NETSTAT** with the "-s" option displays several statistics that can help you diagnose problems. For example, if the display shows you are sending but not receiving, you almost certainly have a bad cable with a broken receive wire.

3. *Diagnose to the gateway.* If you can't get out to the Internet, check to see if you can ping the router. Remember, the router has two interfaces, so try both: first the

```
Microsoft Windows 2000 [Version 5.00.2195]
(C) Copyright 1985-2000 Microsoft Corp.

C:\>netstat

Active Connections

  Proto  Local Address          Foreign Address               State
  TCP    dana:microsoft-ds      CHRISD:2546                   ESTABLISHED
  TCP    dana:3832              VPN:1376                      ESTABLISHED
  TCP    dana:3837              VPN:1376                      ESTABLISHED
  TCP    dana:4164              AMBERK:microsoft-ds           ESTABLISHED
  TCP    dana:4168              server.totalhome:microsoft-ds ESTABLISHED
  TCP    dana:4235              VPN:netbios-ssn               TIME_WAIT
  TCP    dana:4237              VPN:microsoft-ds              TIME_WAIT

C:\>_
```

Figure 15-27 NETSTAT

local interface (the one on your subnet), and then the one to the Internet. You *do* have both of those IP addresses memorized, don't you? You should! If you can't ping the router, it's either down, or you're not connected to it. If you can only ping the near side, something in the router itself is messed up.

4. *Diagnose to the Internet.* If you can ping the router, it's time to try to ping something on the Internet. If you can't ping one address, try another—it's always possible that the first place you try to ping is down. If you still can't get through, you can try to locate the problem using the **TRACERT** (stands for "trace route") command. **TRACERT** will mark out the entire route the ping packet traveled between you and whatever you were trying to ping, and even better, it will tell you where the problem lies (see Figure 15-28).

```
C:\>tracert 216.115.108.243

Tracing route to img3.yahoo.com [216.115.108.243]
over a maximum of 30 hops:

  1    30 ms    30 ms    30 ms  houston-interface-static-01.redback.jump.net [21
6.30.120.1]
  2    20 ms    20 ms    20 ms  hou-core-01-f1-0-0.jump.net [206.196.64.1]
  3    20 ms    30 ms    30 ms  gigabitethernet5-0-178.hsipaccess2.Houston1.Leve
l3.net [209.247.109.113]
  4    20 ms    20 ms    20 ms  ge-6-0-1.mp1.Houston1.Level3.net [209.247.11.185
]
  5    60 ms    71 ms    60 ms  so-3-0-0.mp2.SanJose1.Level3.net [64.159.1.130]
  6    60 ms    70 ms    60 ms  gigabitethernet10-2.ipcolo4.SanJose1.Level3.net
[64.159.2.170]
  7     *         *         *    Request timed out.
  8    80 ms    90 ms    90 ms  ge-3-3-0.msr1.pao.yahoo.com [216.115.101.42]
  9    80 ms    90 ms   100 ms  v120.bas1.snv.yahoo.com [216.115.100.225]
 10     *        90 ms    90 ms  img3.yahoo.com [216.115.108.243]

Trace complete.

C:\>
```

Figure 15-28 Simple TRACERT

Chapter Review

Questions

1. NetBIOS uses what type of name space?
   a. Hierarchical name space
   b. People name space
   c. DNS name space
   d. Flat name space

2. The DNS root directory is represented by what symbol?
   a. . (dot)
   b. / (forward slash)
   c. \ (back slash)
   d. $ (dollar sign)

3. What command do you use to see the DNS cache on a Windows 2000 or XP system?
   a. WINIPCFG /showdns
   b. IPCONFIG /showdns
   c. IPCONFIG /displaydns
   d. WINIPCFG /displaydns

4. What do you call the set of IP addresses that a DHCP server may allocate to client systems?
   a. DHCP group
   b. DHCP scope
   c. DHCP array
   d. DHCP lease

5. What folder in the DHCP program lists the systems currently leasing DHCP IP addresses?
   a. Reservations
   b. Address Pool
   c. Address Leases
   d. Current Addresses

6. The users on your network haven't been able to connect to the server for 30 minutes. You check and reboot the server, but it's unable to ping either its own loopback address or any of your client systems. What should you do?
   a. Restart the DHCP server.
   b. Restart the DNS server.
   c. Replace the NIC on the server, because it has failed.
   d. Have your users ping the server.

7. What are the two reasons to use a WINS server?
   a. To reduce overhead from broadcasts
   b. To facilitate broadcast of NetBIOS names
   c. To support Windows XP systems on IP networks
   d. To enable NetBIOS name resolution across routers

8. What command do you use to check the current NetBIOS name cache?
   a. NETSTAT –n
   b. NETSTAT –c
   c. NBTSTAT –n
   d. NBTSTAT –c

9. A user calls to say she can't see the other systems on the network when she looks in Network Neighborhood. You are not using NetBIOS. What are your first two troubleshooting steps?
   a. Ping the address of a known web site.
   b. Ping the loopback address to test her NIC.
   c. Ping several neighboring systems using both DNS names and IP addresses.
   d. Ping the IP addresses of the router.

10. When troubleshooting a network using NetBIOS, what command do you use to see if the other local systems are visible?
    a. NBTSTAT
    b. NET VIEW
    c. NBT VIEW
    d. VIEW LOCAL

Answers

1. **D.** NetBIOS uses a flat name space, while DNS servers use a hierarchical name space.

2. **A.** The DNS root directory is represented by dot (.).

3. **C.** To see the DNS cache on a Windows 2000 or XP system, run the command **IPCONFIG /displaydns** at a command prompt. The others are all there just to fake you out!

4. **B.** *DHCP scope* is the pool of IP addresses that a DHCP server may allocate to client systems.

5. **C.** The Address Leases folder in the DHCP program lists the systems currently leasing DHCP IP addresses. The Address Pool folder lists the range of available IP addresses.

6. **C.** You should replace the server's NIC, because it's bad. It doesn't need either DNS or DHCP to ping its loopback address. Having the users ping the server is also pointless, as you already know they can't connect to it.

7. **A and D.** Two reasons to use a WINS server are to reduce overhead from broadcasts, and to enable NetBIOS name resolution across routers. WINS servers eliminate the need for broadcasts. They are needed by Windows 9x and NT systems running on IP networks; WINS is not even native to Windows 2000 and XP.

8. **D.** You use the **NBTSTAT –c** command to check the current NetBIOS name cache. The others are just there to confuse you!

9. **B and C.** Your first two troubleshooting steps are (1) ping the loopback address to check her NIC and (2) ping neighboring systems. If her NIC and the local network check out, then you might try pinging the router and a web site, but those are later steps.

10. **B.** When troubleshooting a network using NetBIOS, use the **NET VIEW** command to see if the other local systems are visible.

PART III

## CHAPTER 16

TCP/IP and the Internet

In this chapter, you will

- Understand routers
- Learn about static and dynamic routers
- Understand Network Address Translation (NAT)
- Understand proxy servers
- Understand HTTP, HTTPS, FTP, and Telnet

I've spent a lot of time in this book discussing the many parts of TCP/IP, and have covered a lot of the underpinnings that make TCP/IP work. This chapter looks at the function of real-world routers and examines some of the issues involved in making them work in environments ranging from a simple home Internet connection to full-blown serious office environments. After giving you a big picture view of routers, this chapter drills down to the LAN level for a look at ways to leverage multiple connections to the Internet through a single IP address. You will also learn how to configure and troubleshoot some of the most common applications used on the Internet, such as web browsers and e-mail.

Test Specific

Routers, routers, routers! The word router invariably seems to send chills down the spines of folks just starting out in the networking world as they contemplate these magic boxes that create all the connections that make up the Internet. Although I've referenced routers in numerous spots—you've even had a peek at a router table—you need to know more. Let's look at how routers work and what you can expect from them.

What on Earth Is a Router, Anyway?

A *router* directs incoming network protocol packets from one LAN to another based on OSI Network layer information stored in the incoming packets. Routers make this determination by reading internal router tables. In order to route these packets, a router by definition must have at least two interfaces, although some routers have three or more, depending on the needs of the network. If you think about it for a moment, a router acts a lot like a switch, except it works on the OSI Network layer (Layer 3), while a typical switch works on the OSI Data Link layer (Layer 2). That's why you hear a lot of network folks call a regular switch a *layer 2 switch* and a router a *layer 3 switch*. Be comfortable using both terms, as techs tend to use them interchangeably, even in the same sentence (see Figure 16-1).

Routers come in a dizzying variety of shapes, sizes, and functions. You find little routers used in homes and small businesses, like the handy-dandy Linksys router I use at my house (see Figure 16-2), and mid-sized routers used to connect a couple of buildings. At the top end are the massive routers that literally make the big connections on the Internet (see Figure 16-3).

You don't necessarily need special hardware to have a router. Pretty much every modern operating system enables you to turn a PC into a router by adding an extra NIC, modem, or some other device to connect to another LAN. Figure 16-4 shows a screen

Figure 16-1   I'm a router! I'm a layer 3 switch! I'm both!

Figure 16-2   Little routers

Figure 16-3 Big routers

```
        Coyote Linux Gateway -- configuration menu


   1 ) Network settings          4) Change system password

   2 ) System settings
   3 ) Package settings

   c) Show running configuration  b) Back-up configuration

                                  h) Help
q) quit
------------------------------------------------------------------
   Selection:
```

Figure 16-4 Coyote Linux configuration screen

shot on my old router, a beat-up old Pentium 166 system with two NICs, no hard drive or CD-ROM drive, running a handy little Linux-based router program—called Coyote Linux (www.coyotelinux.com)—completely from the floppy drive.

Even though a router may use more than just two interfaces, the vast majority of routers seen in the small- to medium-sized networks act as nothing more than a method to link your LAN to the Internet via your local ISP. In almost all cases, these routers, whether a special box or just a PC in the network, will have two interfaces: a NIC that connects to your LAN and some other connection that links to a regular phone line, a more advanced telephone connection like ISDN, ADSL, or T1, or maybe a cable modem. Whatever the connection type, these two-interface-only routers are extremely common.

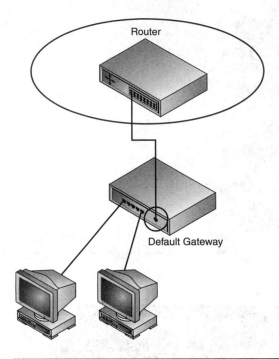

Figure 16-5 A default gateway

A *gateway*, in contrast to a regular router, connects two LANs that use different hardware/protocols. You wouldn't refer to a router that connects two Ethernet LANs, for example, as a gateway. However, a router that connects an Ethernet LAN to a DSL router, for example, or an Ethernet LAN to a Token Ring LAN, *would* be called a gateway. So, don't get too confused when a fellow tech looks at your router and asks, "Is that your gateway?" This is a perfectly legitimate question.

People often become confused when they hear the terms gateway and default gateway. They sound like more or less the same thing, but they aren't at all. A router may be a gateway, but the router itself can never be the default gateway! The term *default gateway* refers not to any piece of hardware, but rather to the *IP address* of the router interface that connects to your LAN, called the *local side* or the *local interface* of your router (see Figure 16-5).

How Routers Work

The Network+ exam doesn't expect you to know how to configure a router, but you should be familiar with some of the ways those who do configure routers do it. To use an analogy, if this were an exam about automobiles, you wouldn't actually have to drive a car, but you would need to be able to explain how drivers steer and brake. Get it?

A key basic feature of the router is the *router table*. All routers have a built-in router table that tells them how to send packets. Where does this router table information come from? Let's look at how router tables get created.

Static Routes

In the bleak old days of the Internet, router tables were composed entirely of static entries. In other words, somebody who really understood routers (and subnetting) had to type this information into the router table. The router person would link into the router using a serial cable or something called Telnet (see "Telnet" section later in this chapter) and type in a command to add or remove static routes from the router table. Would you like to see a router table? If you're sitting at a Windows or UNIX/Linux system, get to a prompt and type in one of these two commands: **NETSTAT –NR** or **ROUTE PRINT**. Both of these commands result in basically the same output as shown in Figure 16-6.

Every IP client has a router table. Does that mean that every IP client is a router? Well, sort of. IP clients are routers in the sense that they need to know how to address their outgoing packets. An IP client refers to its router table when it sends packets. Now, you may be thinking that it seems kind of silly for a client to have a router table when it only

```
Microsoft(R) Windows DOS
(C)Copyright Microsoft Corp 1990-1999.

C:\>route print
===========================================================================
Interface List
0x1 ........................... MS TCP Loopback interface
0x1000003 ...00 80 ad 7b 48 39 ...... PCI Bus Master Adapter
===========================================================================
===========================================================================
Active Routes:
Network Destination        Netmask          Gateway       Interface  Metric
          0.0.0.0          0.0.0.0    192.168.4.152    192.168.4.15       1
        127.0.0.0        255.0.0.0        127.0.0.1        127.0.0.1       1
      192.168.4.0    255.255.255.0     192.168.4.15     192.168.4.15       1
     192.168.4.15  255.255.255.255        127.0.0.1        127.0.0.1       1
    192.168.4.255  255.255.255.255     192.168.4.15     192.168.4.15       1
        224.0.0.0        224.0.0.0     192.168.4.15     192.168.4.15       1
  255.255.255.255  255.255.255.255     192.168.4.15     192.168.4.15       1
Default Gateway:       192.168.4.152
===========================================================================
Persistent Routes:
  None

C:\>_
```

Figure 16-6 ROUTE PRINT output

has one interface—I mean, where else is it going to send these packets? Good question, but there is an answer.

First of all it treats the loop back address as a different interface. Note how 127.0.0.1 shows up as one of the interface options. Also, keep in mind that there's nothing to stop a client from having more than one NIC. I often put a second NIC in my system when I want to test some network thingy without trashing my real network. In that case, my router table is going to look a lot more complex, as you can see in Figure 16-7. Now, don't panic looking at all this gooblety-gook. Just look at the Interface column. You'll see I now have two IP addresses: 192.168.4.1 and 192.168.4.54, one for each NIC. Without the router table, my system wouldn't know which NIC to use to send packets.

By the same token, a regular IP client is not a router in that both NICs are completely separated on the routing table. If you look at the router table, you won't see any rows that say to send anything with a network destination of network ID 192.168.4.1 to Interface 192.168.4.54. If this were a router you would see rows that instructed the system to pass data from one interface to the other and trust me, there are none here. So, even though IP clients do have router tables, they don't route by default (although nothing stops you from turning the client into a router).

The question now becomes: Where did this router table come from? Was it entered statically? Thank goodness no! Static IP addresses are rarely used in client systems unless there's something very unique taking place. Real routers have static routes.

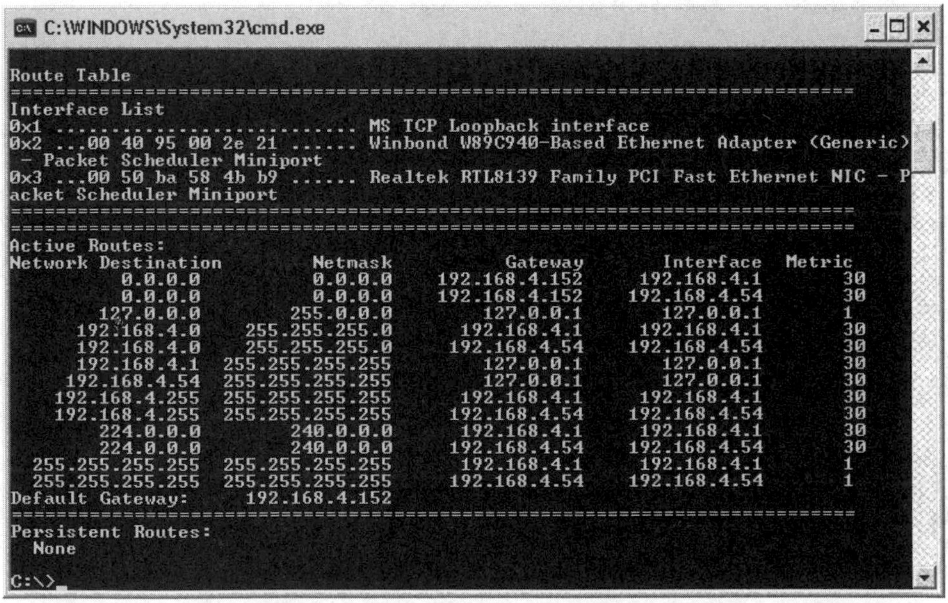

Figure 16-7   Route table for Mike's PC with two NICs

Remember the subnetting scenario discussed in Chapter 12 where you had to configure the router table to split one subnet into two? That would be one place where you need to do this—but leave that to the router gurus!

Dynamic Routing

Early on in the life of the Internet it became painfully clear that routers using only static IPs were incapable of handling the demands of anything but a network where nothing changed. If a new router was introduced to the network, it was useless until humans could get in and update not only the new router but also all of the new router's neighbors. While this might have worked when the number of routers on the Internet was small, it simply did not work as the number began to grow past a few dozen.

Furthermore, neither TCP/IP nor the Internet was ever designed to run on only static routers. When DARPA first created the entire concept of TCP/IP and the Internet, they were tasked by the U.S. military to create a network that could survive having any single part disappear under a mushroom cloud. In reality, the Internet invented routers more than routers invented the Internet. The Internet's designers visualized a mesh of routers, each having at least three connections, to provide a large level of redundancy in the case of multiple connection failures. They never realized just how large this mesh of routers would someday become!

All these routers needed to be able to communicate with each other in such a way that they could detect changes to the network and redirect routes to new interfaces without human intervention. Certainly, a router would initially have a few routes listed on its router table, but once the router started operating, it would need to update the table. The answer: dynamic routing.

Like every other aspect of the Internet and TCP/IP, dynamic routing methods have grown in number and complexity over the years. The variety of these methods—with fun acronyms and initials such as RIP, OSPF, BGP, and IGRP—has reached a point where we categorize them into two types: interior routing methods and exterior routing methods. Interior routing methods are used primarily in routed private networks and smaller Internet ISPs. The main Ethernet backbone and large ISPs use exterior gateway routing methods. Let's check them out.

The oldest of all routing methods is called Routing Information Protocol (RIP). Developed in the late '70s and early '80s, RIP stood alone as the only routing method for many years. RIP uses a *distance vector algorithm*—basically just a nice way to say that neighboring routers share their routing tables. RIP is now only used as an interior routing protocol, having long been kicked off the more critical Internet routers. RIP has a number of shortcomings. In particular, RIP routers do not respond rapidly to changes and tend to flood the network with information as they update. However, you can count on any router knowing how to do RIP. Most interior routers still use RIP, but it is slowly being replaced by OSPF.

The Open Shortest Path First (OSPF) methodology is a much newer and far better way to update routers dynamically. OSPF routers use a *link state* algorithm: routers constantly monitor their neighbors with tiny messages—called *hellos*—and share more detailed information—called *link state advertisements*. If a connection is lost or created, the routers share this information with their neighboring routers.

 EXAM TIP: Don't forget about IPX/SPX in the world of routing! All higher-end routers fully support IPX/SPX routing, too. Anyone with a Cisco certification can work with IPX/SPX packets as easily as they work with IP packets!

Knowing that an exterior gateway protocol is used on the Internet backbone, and that there's only one Internet, you shouldn't be too surprised to learn that the Internet uses only one exterior gateway routing protocol: Border Gateway Protocol (BGP). BGP has been also around for quite some time, but it has gone through a number of iterations. The current one is BGP-4. BGP works using a distance vector methodology like RIP, but once the routers have initially exchanged router tables, they only pass changes in their tables, rather than entire tables, dramatically reducing router traffic.

I couldn't discuss routing methods without at least mentioning Interior Gateway Routing Protocol (IGRP) and its successor, Enhanced Interior Gateway Routing Protocol (EIGRP). Cisco developed these protocols to work in enterprise-wide routing environments. If Cisco had their way, EIGRP would replace BGP-4 as the primary Internet protocol!

Routing protocols are not simply for the big daddy of networks, the Internet. Many LANs use routing to handle connections with the outside world, enabling several machines to connect to the larger Internet using only a single IP address. Two technologies handle the majority of these chores: NATs and proxy servers.

NATs

The Internet has a real problem with IP addresses, or rather a lack of IP addresses. Not only is it difficult to get public IP addresses for every system in your network, but most ISPs charge you for them. Additionally, any system using a public IP address is susceptible to hacking, requiring the use of protection devices called firewalls (see the firewall discussion in Chapter 18). Network Address Translation (NAT) was created in an effort to reduce the demand for public IP addresses, and to provide more security to systems.

Network Address Translation is a process whereby a NAT program running on a system or a router translates a system's IP address into a different IP address before it's sent out to a larger network. A network using NAT will provide its systems with private IP addresses—192.168.1.x addresses are the most popular, but other private IP addresses work equally well. The system running the NAT software will have two interfaces, one connected to the internal network and the other connected to the larger network. The NAT program takes packets from the client systems bound for the larger network and translates their internal private IP addresses to its own public IP address, enabling many systems to share that single IP address (see Figure 16-8).

The NAT adds a small bit of information to the outgoing IP packet so that when the packet returns from the larger network, the NAT remembers which system should receive the incoming packet (see Figure 16-9).

NAT is not the perfect solution for everything. It works well for networks where the clients access the Internet but are not themselves accessed by systems on the Internet. You *don't* place web servers as NAT clients, for example, because systems outside the network cannot access systems on the NAT. If you want a browser to be able to access your web server, you need to place the web server *outside* the NAT-controller area. Figure 16-10 shows a typical placement for a web server in a NAT network.

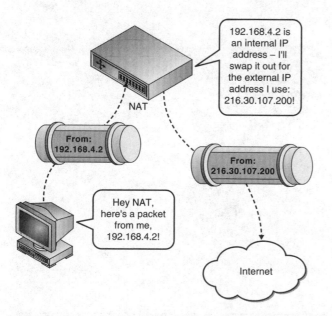

Figure 16-8   NAT swapping private and public IP addresses with wild abandon

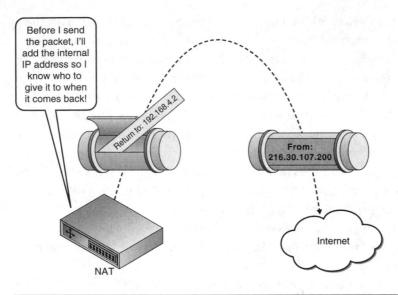

Figure 16-9 NAT adds more information to packet to tell which system should receive it.

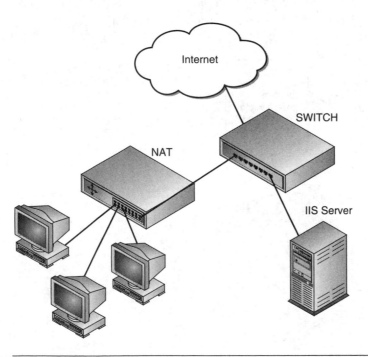

Figure 16-10 Typical placement of a web server in a NAT network

There are an amazing number of ways to implement NAT. You can use the NAT functions built into the OS (nearly every operating system comes with NAT capabilities) or you can buy a third-party NAT program to make any system with two interfaces a NAT server. You can even buy a router with buit-in NAT. Many operating systems come with NAT programs, but in many cases you simply do not see them—they just work! Many of the popular gateway routers come with DHCP and NAT built into the same box. Even my little Linksys router has NAT built in. I just give it an IP address and a subnet mask for its internal interface and it automatically translates any IP address from my network. There simply aren't any NAT settings in many cases! (see Figure 16-11).

NAT also provides a strong defense against hacking since outsiders simply cannot see any of the systems behind the NAT system. To other systems on the Internet, your entire private network looks like just one system—the NAT system. Any system running a NAT gets labeled with the term *firewall*, since it acts as a protector of the private network. You'll learn that a firewall means much more than simply NAT when you get to Chapter 18.

NAT has become extremely popular for networking. In fact, it has become so popular that the long-anticipated day when the world runs out of IP addresses has thus far

Figure 16-11   Where are the NAT settings? There aren't any!

failed to materialize. A NAT's ability to enable multiple systems to share an IP address, combined with strong protection against hacking, have made NATs as common as servers in most networks.

Proxy Server

A *proxy server* also translates addresses, but it does so in a very different way. While a NAT simply translates incoming and outgoing IP packets, a proxy server can translate the TCP port number to another port number. Because proxy servers translate port numbers, applications like web browsers and e-mail clients must be proxy aware (that is, they must be able to change their standard ports to whatever the proxy server uses). For example, HTTP uses TCP port 80 by default, but we can change the proxy server to accept only certain TCP port numbers, like port 88 for HTTP requests from clients. When it receives those requests, the proxy server will change the client system's IP address to its own, change the port back to 80 and then send the request out to the Internet (see Figure 16-12).

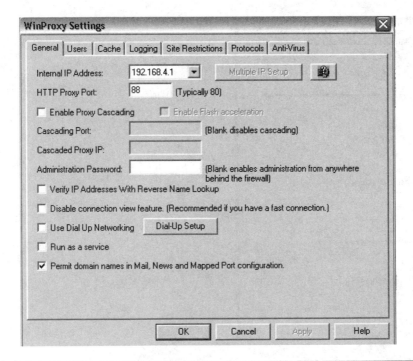

Figure 16-12   A proxy server at work

Port changing by proxy servers adds security to a network, because the sky's the limit when it comes to assigning ports to web pages. Most browsers automatically default to port 80 when looking up HTML pages. When you assign a different port to a web page, you pretty well ensure that it is not going to be found by the general browsing public.

Proxy servers can dramatically improve performance for groups of users. This is because a proxy server can *cache* requests from users, greatly reducing network traffic. Most businesses access a few web sites very frequently. Proxy servers can hold on to the information resulting from user requests for a prespecified amount of time, eliminating the need to reaccess that information from the remote site that contains the HTML document.

Proxy servers can also be used to filter requests. This can further secure a network by limiting the types of web sites and Internet resources its users can access. For instance, you can use a proxy server to eliminate IRC chatting on a network.

So What's the Big Difference between NAT and a Proxy, Anyway?

As you know by now, both proxies and NAT mask IP addresses, enabling a network to have a set of internal private IP addresses that use one public IP address to communicate with the Internet. The difference between using proxies and NAT is where they operate in the network structure. Proxies work at the application level, which means the relevant applications must know how to interact with a proxy, whereas NAT works at the router level, providing transparent Internet access to users.

Think of a proxy server as an old-time telephone operator in a hotel. Just as the hotel operator receives incoming calls for hotel guests and forwards them to the proper room, a proxy server takes incoming requests for Internet services (such as FTP) and forwards them to the actual applications that perform those services. Conversely, just as a guest needing an outside line would go through the hotel operator, a network user needing an Internet service goes through the proxy to the Internet. Because proxies provide replacement connections and act as gateways, they are sometimes known as *application-level gateways*.

Now that we know *how* information travels outside of your network, lets take a look at the information your users have been trying so hard to find.

The Web

Where would we be without the World Wide Web? The Web functions as the graphical face for the Internet. Most of you have used it, firing up your web browser to surf to one cool site after another, learning new things, clicking links, often ending up somewhere completely unexpected . . . It's all very fun! This section of the chapter looks at the Web and the tools that make it function, specifically the protocols that enable communication over the Internet.

You can find an HTML document on the Internet by entering a *URL* in your web browser. A *URL*, short for *Uniform Resource Locator,* is a global address that all documents and other resources on the Web must have. When you type the URL of a web page, such as www.wheebo.com, you are typing the address by which your browser locates the HTML document on a remote computer.

A web address is made up of several different parts, each of which carries an instruction for the computer on how to deal with the web resource whose address it is. The first part of the address indicates what protocol to use—*www*, for instance, indicates that the resource will be an HTML document accessed by using HTTP. The second part of the web address specifies the IP address or the domain name where the resource is located. In www.wheebo.com, *wheebo* is the registered name of the server that contains the HTML document.

To help you understand this a little better, let's take a closer look at the HTTP protocol.

HTTP

HTTP is short for HyperText Transfer Protocol. It is the underlying protocol used by the World Wide Web, and it runs by default on TCP/IP port 80. Notice the HTTP at the beginning of the URL in Figure 16-13. The HTTP at the beginning of the URL defines how messages are formatted and transmitted, and what actions web servers and browsers should

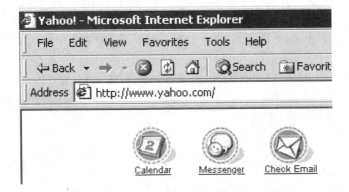

Figure 16-13 A regular run-of-the-mill URL

take in response to various commands. When you enter a URL in your browser, it sends an HTTP command to the web server directing it to find and return the requested web page. Currently, most web browsers and servers support HTTP version 1.1.

HTTP has a general weakness in its handling of web pages: it relays commands executed by users without reference to any commands previously executed. The problem with this is that web designers continue to design more complex and truly interactive web pages. HTTP is pretty dumb when it comes to remembering what people have done on a web site. Luckily for web designers everywhere, other technologies exist to help HTTP relay commands and thus support more interactive, intelligent web sites. These technologies include JavaScript, Active Server Pages, and cookies.

Publishing Web Pages

Once you've designed and created a web document, you can share it with the rest of the world. Sharing a page on the World Wide Web is quite an easy matter. Once the web document is finished, you need to find a server that will host the site. Most ISPs provide web servers of their own, or you can find relatively inexpensive web hosting elsewhere. The price of web hosting usually depends on the services and drive space offered. You can typically find a good web host for around $10 a month.

One option that has been available for a while is free web hosting. Usually the services are not too bad, but you will run across a few limitations. Nearly all free web hosts will insist on the right to place ads on your web page. This is not as much of an issue if you are posting a vanity or fan web page, but if you are doing any sort of business with your web site, this can be most annoying to your customers. The worst sort of free web host services place pop-up ads over your web page. Beyond annoying!

Once you have selected your web host, you need to select your domain name. Domain names have to be registered through InterNIC; this enables your web site name to be resolved to the IP address of the server that has your web site. Fortunately, registering your domain name is a breeze. Most web hosts will offer to register your domain name for you (for a nominal fee). The cost of registering your domain name is usually about $30 a year.

The trickiest aspect of registering your domain name is finding a domain name that has not already been taken. The last time I checked, the Web had about 11 million registered domain names, and that number has undoubtedly climbed steadily since. Many web sites that offer registration for domain names (such as www.register.com) offer a search that will check to see whether a name has already been registered.

Once you have your domain name registered and your web hosting covered, it's time to upload your web page to the web server. What's a web server? I'm glad you asked!

Web Servers and Web Clients

A web server is a computer that delivers (or *serves up*) web pages. Every web server has at least one static IP address and at least one domain name. For example, if you enter the URL **www.wheebo.com/index.html**, your browser sends a request to the server whose domain name is *wheebo.com*. The server then fetches the page named *index.html* and sends it to your browser. A web server *must* have a static IP address, because once you register your domain name, browsers must be able to resolve that domain name to a steady, unchanging IP address.

You can turn any computer into a web server by installing server software and connecting the machine to the Internet, but not just any old operating system can run the programs needed to serve a web page. Windows 95/98/ME systems cannot be web servers, because they limit the number of people who can connect at any one time to no more than ten users. A program called Personal Web Server allows Windows 95/98/ME systems to share one web page out to a limited number of users. The Windows NT Workstation OS has similar limitations. The Windows 2000 Professional OS can run a light version of Microsoft's Internet Information Server (IIS) (see the following), but as with Personal Web Server, it can only host one web page and has a ten-connection limit.

Windows 2000 Server and UNIX/Linux-based operating systems can serve as full-blown web servers. This means they can host multiple web pages with multiple domain names, as well as multiple FTP and newsgroup servers. The two most popular web server software applications are Apache and Microsoft's Internet Information Server (IIS). As of this writing, Apache serves about 60 percent of the web sites on the Internet. Apache is incredibly popular because it's full-featured and powerful, runs on multiple operating systems (including Windows), and best of all, it's *free*! Better yet, you can add on a GUI called Comanche that makes administering Apache a breeze. Figure 16-14 illustrates the wonderful simplicity that is Comanche.

Microsoft's IIS is both easy to use and very powerful. IIS not only serves web pages, it also can create FTP servers and newsgroup servers, and offers a large number of administrative options. You can even administer your IIS server remotely using an administrative web page. The IIS console runs from the Microsoft Management Console, and it's very simple to use, as you can see in Figure 16-15. Alas, IIS is only available on Windows NT-based systems. There are many other web server solutions to choose from besides Apache and IIS, however, including Netscape Enterprise, iPlanet Web Server, and Enterprise for NetWare.

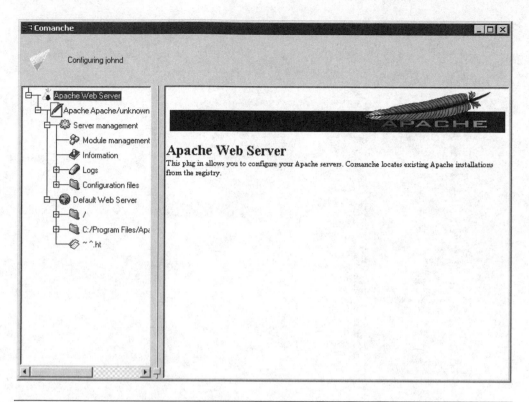

Figure 16-14   The Comanche GUI

Web Clients

Web clients are the users who surf the Internet. A user uses a client program (an Internet *browser*) to read web pages and interact with the Internet. Most browsers can handle multiple functions, from reading HTML documents to offering FTP services and even serving as an e-mail or newsgroup reader. The two biggest Internet browsers out there are Microsoft's *Internet Explorer* and Netscape's *Netscape Communicator*. Both are full-featured browsers that offer nearly identical services. Another fine Internet browser is Opera Software's *Opera*. Opera offers many options for the more experienced Internet surfer, and accesses information from the Internet very quickly. The best thing about all of these browsers is they're free!

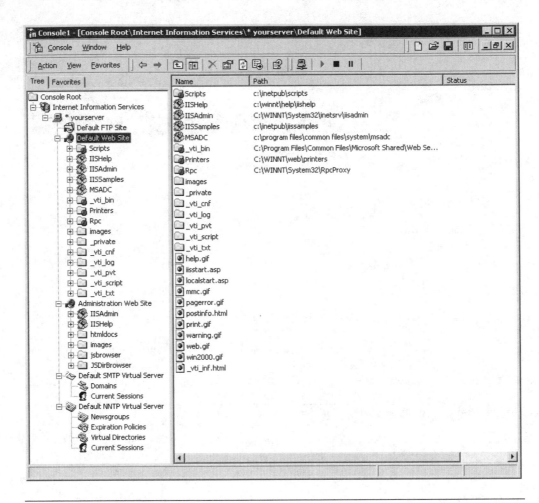

Figure 16-15   The IIS console

Secure Sockets Layer and HTTPS

Since the Web has blossomed into a major economic player, the concern over security has become a near panic. In the early days of e-commerce, people feared that a simple credit card transaction on a less-than-secure web site could transform their dreams of easy online buying into a nightmare of being robbed blind and ending up living in a refrigerator box.

I can safely say that it was *never* as bad as all that. And nowadays, there are a number of safeguards on the Internet that can protect your purchase *and* your anonymity. One such safeguard is called *Secure Sockets Layer* (*SSL*).

SSL is a protocol developed by Netscape for transmitting private documents over the Internet. SSL works by using a public key to encrypt sensitive data. This encrypted data is sent over an SSL connection, then decrypted at the receiving end using a private key. Both Netscape Navigator and Internet Explorer support SSL, and many web sites use the protocol to obtain confidential user information, such as credit card numbers. One way to tell if a site is using SSL is by looking at the URL. By convention, URLs that use an SSL connection start with *https* instead of *http*.

Configuring a Web Browser

Configuring your web browser to run on the Internet is a simple process. In the case of Windows 95/98/ME/NT/2000, an Internet Connection Wizard walks you through all the steps you need to get Internet Explorer to surf the Web with ease. Netscape and Opera are much the same. You need to make sure your TCP/IP settings are correct.

Two things you can control on your browser are the number of cookies the browser uses and the caching of web pages. Each browser has its own particular way of accessing the user configuration areas. In Netscape Communicator, the preferences are set in Edit | Preferences. In Internet Explorer, go to Tools | Internet Options. (see Figure 16-16)

Configuring a Web Server

Configuring a web server is a little more complex. Each web server software application has its own unique way of detailing user and administrator rights, and this information is a little beyond the scope of the Network+ exam. Suffice to say, if you plan to host more than one web page on your web server, you need more than one static IP address. Remember that each web page needs its own static IP address to be visible to other systems on the Internet. How can you get more than one static IP address on one computer? You can assign more than one IP address to one NIC. Ideally, if you expect a high load of traffic, you might want to install more than one NIC in your web server and have those NICs balance the load among the multiple pages. But if you are on a budget (and aren't we all?), assigning more than one static IP address to one NIC will work fine.

Troubleshooting

If you're having problems connecting to the Internet, one of the first things to try is *pinging* a domain using the **PING** command at a command prompt. This command will tell you if there are connectivity problems.

When using your browser to see if there are connectivity issues, either call up a web site you have not accessed for a long time, or reload the page once or twice, because

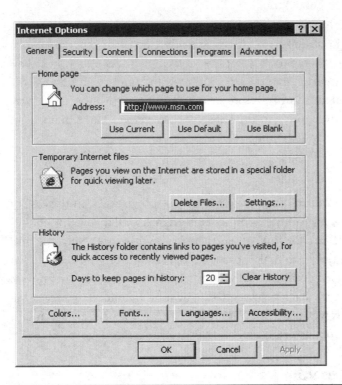

Figure 16-16 Internet Options in Internet Explorer

browsers are usually set to cache frequently accessed web pages, which can therefore appear even when your Internet access isn't working.

Whether you are using a dial-up modem or a cable modem (to a lesser degree), your connection is likely to slow down during peak usage times on the Internet when masses of people are trying to access the same information at once. Lunchtime, suppertime, and evenings are popular times for surfing and checking e-mail. If you must join the crowd, you may have to be patient.

When buying on the Internet from a secured web page using SSL, be careful to follow the instructions exactly about not over-clicking buttons. Occasionally, information travels a little more slowly over an SSL connection than over a regular unsecured connection, due to the time it takes to encrypt and decrypt the information. If you keep clicking the order button over and over again, you may be sending in order after order to the server. However, if you don't mind paying for the same item fifty times, go right ahead!

Now that we've taken a look at the World Wide Web, it's time to learn about the second most popular feature of the Internet: e-mail.

E-mail

E-mail, short for *electronic mail*, has been a major part of the Internet revolution, and not just because it has streamlined the junk mail industry. E-mail provides an extremely quick way for people to communicate with one another, letting you send messages and attachments (like documents and pictures) over the Internet. It's normally offered as a free service by ISPs. Most e-mail client programs provide a rudimentary text editor for composing messages, but many can be configured to let you edit your messages using more sophisticated editors.

When you create an e-mail message, you must specify the recipient's e-mail address, consisting of the user's name and a domain name: for instance, MyName@Wheebo .com. When you send an e-mail message, it travels from router to router until it finds the domain in question. Then your message is directed to the specific user to whom it's addressed. If you want to, you can also send the same message to several users at the same time. This is called *broadcasting*.

When a message is sent to your e-mail address, it is normally stored in an electronic mailbox on your ISP's server until you come and get it. Some ISPs limit the amount of time they keep messages around, so always check this aspect of your user agreement! Most e-mail client programs can be configured to signal you in some way when a new message has arrived. Once you read an e-mail message, you can archive it, forward it, print it, or delete it. Many e-mail programs are configured to automatically delete messages from the ISP's server when you download them to your local machine, but you can usually change this configuration option to suit your circumstances.

E-mail programs use a number of application-level protocols to send and receive information. Specifically, the e-mail you find on the Internet uses either SMTP to send e-mail, and POP3 or IMAP to receive e-mail.

SMTP, IMAP, and POP3, Oh My!

The previous discussion might lead you to think e-mail is directly connected with the World Wide Web, but in fact, the two are quite separate and different. HTML pages use the HTTP protocol, whereas e-mail is sent and received using a number of different protocols. The following is a list of the different protocols that the Internet uses to transfer and receive mail.

SMTP

The *Simple Mail Transfer Protocol* (SMTP) is used to send e-mail between servers. SMTP travels over TCP/IP port 25, and is used to send messages, but not receive them. Thus you need to specify the POP or IMAP server as well as the SMTP server when you configure your e-mail application.

POP3

POP3 is the protocol that receives the e-mail from the server. It stands for *Post Office Protocol Version 3*, and uses TCP/IP port 110. Most e-mail clients use this protocol, although some use IMAP.

IMAP

IMAP is an alternative to POP3. IMAP stands for Internet Message Access Protocol, and like POP3, it retrieves e-mail from an e-mail server. The main difference is that IMAP uses TCP/IP port 143. The latest version, *IMAP4*, supports some features that are not supported in POP3. For example, IMAP4 enables you to search through messages on the mail server to find specific keywords, and select the messages you want to download onto your machine.

Other Internet protocols include Extended Simple Mail Transfer Protocol (ESMTP), Authenticated Post Office Protocol (APOP), Multipurpose Internet Mail Extensions (MIME), and Directory Access Protocol (DAP). Many mail servers are also adding S/MIME, SSL, or RSA support for message encryption; and Lightweight Directory Access Protocol (LDAP) support to access operating system directory information about mail users.

E-mail Servers and E-mail Clients

To give you a clearer idea of how the whole enchilada works, I'm now going to describe an e-mail server and an e-mail client.

E-mail Server

Many people have heard of web servers and know what they do, but for some reason e-mail servers remain a mystery. This is odd, because e-mail servers are nearly as prevalent on the Internet as web servers. E-mail is used daily by millions of people, both within private networks and on the Internet. This means that e-mail servers are a vital part of any large network.

E-mail servers accept incoming mail and sort out the mail for recipients into *mailboxes*. These mailboxes are special separate holding areas for each user's e-mail. An e-mail server works much like a post office, sorting and arranging incoming messages, and kicking back those messages that have no known recipient.

Perhaps one reason e-mail servers are so little understood is that they're more difficult to manage than web servers. E-mail servers store user lists, user rights, and messages, and are constantly involved in Internet traffic and resources. Setting up and administering an e-mail server takes a lot of planning, although it's getting easier. Most e-mail server software runs in a GUI interface, but even the command-line-based interface of e-mail servers is becoming more intuitive.

E-mail Client

An e-mail client is a program that runs on a computer and enables you to send, receive, and organize e-mail. The e-mail client program communicates with the e-mail server and downloads the messages from the e-mail server to the client computer.

Configuring an E-mail Client   Configuring a client is an easy matter. You need the POP3 or IMAP address and the SMTP address for the e-mail server. Usually the SMTP address looks like *mail.wheebo.net*. Besides the e-mail server addresses, you must also enter the username and password of the e-mail account the client will be managing. The username will usually be part of the e-mail address. For example, the username for the e-mail address *ghengizsam@wheebo.com* will usually be *ghengizsam*.

Troubleshooting

If you encounter a problem with an SMTP or POP3 name, it's likely you have a problem with the DNS not recognizing the name of the mail server you have entered. Figure 16-17 shows you the error screen in Microsoft Outlook resulting from a bad SMTP connection. In this case, you can check to see if there is a problem with the mail server. Since an SMTP or POP3 name is a name resolved in DNS, how can you check to see if that server is online? You can **PING** it. **PING** the mail server to see if you can find it online. If it is not responding to the **PING**, you have your answer right there.

Another common problem is a bad password. A mail server is like any other server: You need permission to access its resources. If you can't get access, your password may not be correct. Most e-mail client programs will prompt a dialog box to appear if your e-mail password is set incorrectly, as seen in Figure 16-18.

I would like to take this opportunity to reveal a very common Internet hoax. One of the most prevalent hoaxes on the Internet concerns some legislative body pushing a bill that would charge rates for e-mail on a per–e-mail basis. The supposed reason is to help the Postal Service recoup some of its losses. If any friend, family member, or co-worker tells you about this horrible new bill, you should do what any good network expert would do: make fun of them for being so gullible. Just kidding! E-mail is a free service,

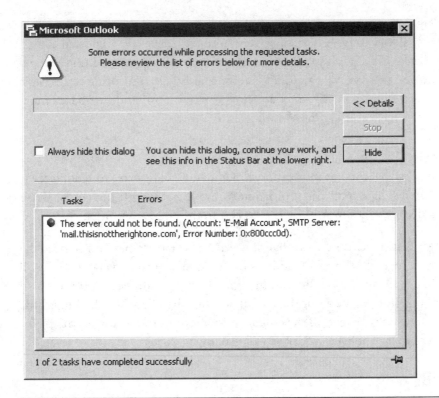

Figure 16-17 Bad SMTP!

Figure 16-18 What was my password again?

which is not owned by any one nation or corporation. It would be nearly impossible for one nation to tax what essentially is a worldwide service. If they need proof, you can send them to one of the Urban Legend web sites, like **www.snopes.com**, where this and many other types of hoaxes are cataloged.

FTP

File Transfer Protocol (FTP) is the protocol used on the Internet for transferring files. Although HTTP can be used to transfer files as well, the transfer is often not as reliable or as fast as with FTP. In addition, FTP can do the transfer with security and data integrity. FTP uses TCP/IP ports 21 and 20 by default, although you can often change the port number for security reasons.

FTP sites are either anonymous sites, meaning that anyone can log on, or secured sites, meaning that you must have a username and password to be able to transfer files. You can use the Archie system (**http://archie.emnet.co.uk/services.html**) to obtain a list of anonymous FTP sites and the files available on each site.

FTP Servers and FTP Clients

Like many Internet applications, FTP uses a client and server arrangement. The FTP server does all the real work of storing the files, keeping everything secure, and transferring the files. The client logs on to the FTP server (either from a web site, a command-line, or a special FTP application) and downloads the requested files onto the local hard drive.

FTP Servers

Most web servers come with their own internal FTP server software, allowing you to set up an FTP server with a minimum of fuss. These bundled versions of FTP server are robust, but do not provide all the options one might want. Luckily for you, many specialized FTP server software applications provide a full array of options for the administrator.

One aspect of FTP servers you should be aware of concerns FTP passwords. Although it may sound like a good idea to set up a secure, user-only FTP server, in the end this is actually *less* secure than an anonymous FTP server. How can this be? The problem is that FTP passwords are unencrypted (that is, they are sent over the Internet as plain text). Suppose you are an administrator setting up an FTP server for a company. You decide to extend user rights and login permissions to your FTP server so your company employees may access and download some important programs. When a remote user enters a username and password to log on to the FTP server—the *same* data they use to log on and off the network—they send this data in *clear text* to the FTP server. Anyone who happens to be eavesdropping on the network can intercept this username and password and use it to log on to the *network* as if they were an authorized user. This, as you can see, is very, *very* bad for security! In the end, it's safer just to set up a general FTP server with anonymous access, and then change the ports it uses. That way only people you authorize to know about the FTP server can find out which port their FTP client software must use to access the data. This is still not foolproof—someone taking the trouble to tap into your dial-up line can retrieve the FTP port information and then log in anonymously—but it certainly deters casual mischief.

Another thing to check when deciding on an FTP server setup is the number of clients you want to support. Most anonymous FTP sites limit the number of users who may download at any one time to around 500. This protects you from a sudden influx of users flooding your server and eating up all your Internet bandwidth.

FTP Clients

FTP clients, as noted before, can access an FTP server though a web site, a command-line, or a special FTP application. Usually special FTP applications offer the most choices for accessing and using an FTP site.

Configuring an FTP client Using an FTP client to upload content is a very simple process. In order to transfer files via FTP, you must have an FTP client installed on your PC. Most FTP sites require a username of *some* sort in order to log in, even if the FTP server allows anonymous logins. In the case of anonymous FTP, it's common for the username to be anonymous and the password to be your e-mail address. You must also know the host name of the FTP server. This name is an IP address, which is resolved to a host name using DNS. Usually a host name looks something like: *ftp.wheebo.com*.

When you first start up an FTP client program, a dialog box will appear in which you can enter this information (as shown in Figure 16-19). After you log in, you will have access to the files on the FTP server's hard drive. One pane will display the contents of your hard drive, and the other will show you the FTP site's hard drive (see Figure 16-20).

Your FTP client should allow you to select which file transfer mode you want to use, either ASCII or BINARY. ASCII mode is used to transfer text files, while BINARY mode is used to transfer binary files, like programs and graphics. Most FTP clients have an Automatic transfer mode option, which automatically detects which transfer mode is correct for each file.

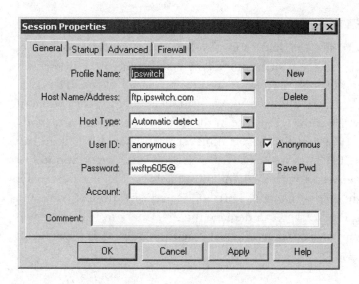

Figure 16-19 FTP login using WS_FTP LE

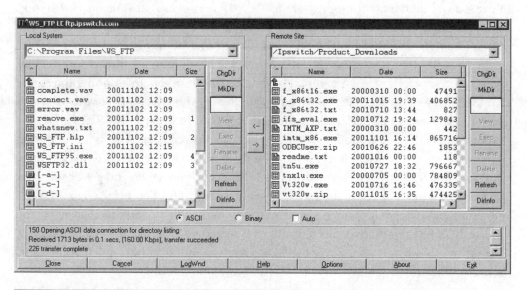

Figure 16-20 Downloading fun with WS_FTP LE!

Troubleshooting FTP

If you can't connect to an FTP site, first make sure you have an *active* dial-up or direct Internet connection. FTP programs are not automatic dialers. If your connection closes after a certain number of minutes of inactivity, you have run afoul of the FTP server. This is actually a feature for system administrators: you can set an FTP server to boot out users who have been inactive for some number of minutes or hours. This is particularly important on anonymous FTP servers that have a limit regarding how many users can be on simultaneously. Most FTP sites will close a connection after a few minutes of inactivity. If the files you transfer are corrupted, the most likely problem is the transfer mode you (often unwittingly, by not changing a previous selection) chose. If you try to transfer a binary file in ASCII mode, you can damage the file. Check to make sure you have selected the proper mode, and do so manually if you think Automatic mode is not working correctly.

Telnet

Telnet is a terminal emulation program for TCP/IP networks that runs on TCP/IP port 23. Telnet allows you to connect to a server and run commands on that server as if you were sitting right in front of it. This way, you can remotely administer a server and communicate with other servers on your network. As you can imagine, this is sort of risky. If you can remotely control a computer, what is to stop others from doing the same? Thankfully, Telnet does not just allow *anyone* to log on and wreak havoc with your network. You must enter a special username and password in order to run Telnet.

Telnet is mostly used nowadays to control web servers remotely. This is rather important since web servers often need extra care and attention. Suppose you're the administrator for your company's web server. You are sitting at home when you get a call. There is a problem with your company's web page: a hacker has broken into your web server and replaced the web page with a picture of someone . . . ah . . . *fabricly challenged*. You can use Telnet to remotely connect to the web server and remove the offending page, then run processes and administer the Web server without ever having left your comfy chair. A wonderful capability for the overworked system admin!

Telnet Servers and Clients

A Telnet server enables users to log on to a host computer and perform tasks as if they're actually working on the remote computer itself. Users can access the host through the Telnet server from anywhere in the world using a Telnet client. When you create a Telnet server, you can also create a web page that handles server management. Most web server software will do this for you. For instance, IIS enables you to manage an IIS Web server via a secured web page.

A Telnet client is the computer from which you log on to the remote server. In order to use Telnet from the client, you must have the proper permissions. If you do not have a web site that will handle the remote connection for you, you can select from a number of terminal emulators that enable you to operate from a GUI.

Configuring a Telnet client

When you configure a Telnet client, you must provide the host name, your user logon name, and the password. As I mentioned previously, you must have permission to access the server in order to use Telnet.

Host Name   A *host name* is the name or IP address of the computer to which you want to connect. For instance, you might connect to a web server with the host name *websrv.wheebo.com*.

Login Name   The user *login name* you give Telnet should be the same login name you'd use if you logged into the server at its location. Some computers, usually university libraries with online catalogs, have open systems that allow you to login with Telnet. These sites will either display a banner before the login prompt that tells you what login name to use, or they'll require no login name at all.

Password   As with the login name, you use the same password for a Telnet login that you'd use to log in to the server directly. It's that simple. Computers with open access will either tell you what password to use when they tell you what login name to use, or they'll require no login name/password at all.

Online Gaming

All work and no play makes the Internet a dull world-wide network. Luckily, there is more to do on the Internet than just look at web pages, spam people with junk e-mail, download programs, and control a server remotely. You can chase people around a darkened castle as well!

An important part of the Internet is Internet gaming. Most of the best-selling computer games allow multiple players to log into a central gaming server and participate in the same game at the same time. These multiplayer computer games may include anywhere from two to thousands of players, all sharing in the gaming experience. It's a beautiful thing, really. Beautiful. (Excuse me while I wipe the tears from my eyes.)

Computer games often push the limits of hardware and network bandwidth in a way that most other applications only dream of. This is why whenever you see *any* kind of benchmark testing of processors, memory, or graphics and sound cards, you will see a computer game (such as Quake III or Unreal Tournament) playing a vital part in the testing. Multiplayer games seriously test the capabilities of any computer and network because the server has to keep constant track of the position of many players at the same time, all of whom are issuing their own commands.

Although multiplayer gaming has come a long way in the last decade, we are still at the very brink of the multiplayer gaming revolution. A recent contender in this field is something called a *Massively Multiplayer Online Role-Playing Game* (MMORPG). MMORPGs use servers that handle thousands of players across a huge virtual world, each with thousands of quests and choices. A few great examples of this new genre are EverQuest and Dark Ages of Camelot, both of which employ a 3-D first-person perspective to immerse the player in the game.

As fresh as this technology is, it still uses the same old tried-and-true client/server architecture. When you first sign into an MMORPG, you establish a user account, from which you can sign into one of the many game servers. Each server presents its own virtual world, which does not affect any of the other servers. This ensures you do not overload one game with too many players. This is a very real issue, given the huge number of people who are getting into the massive multiplayer gaming world. One recent count suggests that the game EverQuest alone has over 400,000 players worldwide!

Each of these games employs good old TCP/IP to send information using special ports either reserved by the game itself, or reserved by DirectX. For instance, the Quake series of games uses port 26000, and DirectX uses ports 47624 and 2300 through 2400.

Online computer gaming pushes the envelope of computer and network capabilities. The system requirements needed to run a new word processing program are nothing compared to the system requirements needed to run a new 3-D combat game. Games help push the industry to produce faster networks and systems.

In fact, computer gaming has become so serious that there are now competitive leagues that hold contests. For instance, the CyberAthlete Professional League holds worldwide contests where the best online gamer can win up to $150,000. So brush up your mousing skills . . . it can *really* pay off!

Chapter Review

Questions

1. What device directs incoming network protocols packets from one LAN to another based on OSI Network layer information stored in the incoming packets?
   a. Hub
   b. Switch
   c. Bridge
   d. Router

2. In order to route packets, a router must have at least _____ interfaces.
   a. One
   b. Two
   c. Three
   d. Four

3. What device connects two LANs that use different hardware?
   a. Gateway
   b. Switch
   c. Bridge
   d. Router

4. The IP address of the router interface that connects to your LAN is called a:
   a. Subnet mask
   b. IP address
   c. DNS
   d. Default gateway

5. What device, acting at the router level, translates a system's IP address into another IP address before sending it out to the larger network?
   a. A firewall
   b. A NAT
   c. A router
   d. A proxy server

6. What device, acting at the Application level, translates port numbers to a different port number to add more security to the system?
   a. A firewall
   b. A NAT
   c. A router
   d. A proxy server

7. The protocol developed by Netscape for transmitting private documents over the Internet is known as:
   a. SSS
   b. SSA
   c. SSL
   d. NSSL

8. SSL was developed by Netscape therefore Internet Explorer does not recognize it.
   a. True
   b. False

9. An SSL URL connection starts with:
   a. HTTP
   b. WWW
   c. FTP
   d. HTTPS

10. Joe likes to surf the Web instead of doing his work. He calls you and tells you he can't connect to the Internet. Which of the following would be one of the first utilities you would use to diagnose his problem?
    a. NBSTAT
    b. TRACEROUTE
    c. ROUTE PRINT
    d. PING

Answers

1. **D.** Routers direct incoming network protocol packets from one LAN to another based on OSI Network layer information stored in the incoming packets.

2. **B.** In order to route these packets, a router by definition must have at least two interfaces, although some routers have three or more, depending on the needs of the network.

3. **A.**   A *gateway*, in contrast to a regular router, connects two LANs that use different hardware. You wouldn't refer to a router that connects two Ethernet LANs, for example, as a gateway. A router that connects an Ethernet LAN to a DSL router or to a Token Ring LAN, in contrast, is a gateway.

4. **D.**   The *default gateway* is the IP address of the router interface that connects to your LAN. That interface is called the local side or the local interface on your router.

5. **B.**   A NAT translates a system's IP addresses into another IP address before sending it out to the larger network. NATs work at the network layer.

6. **D.**   Proxy servers translate port numbers to a different port number to add more security to the system. Proxy servers work at the application layer.

7. **C.**   Secure Sockets Layer (SSL) is a protocol developed by Netscape for transmitting private documents over the Internet. SSL works by using a public key to encrypt sensitive data.

8. **B.**   False. Internet Explorer supports SSL.

9. **D.**   URLs that use an SSL connection start with HTTPS instead of HTTP.

10. **D.**   One of the first things to try is pinging a domain using the **PING** command at a command prompt. This command checks to see if there are connectivity problems.

Remote Connectivity

In this chapter, you will

- Understand the different kinds of LAN connections
- Understand the different kinds of WAN connections
- Learn about the SLIP, PPP, and PPTP protocols
- Understand remote access
- Learn about Internet connection sharing

Local area networks (LANs) provide organizations with abilities essential for today's business needs. LANs offer access to important databases, e-mail, printers, fax machines —all the resources a modern business uses to get the job done. In the vast majority of organizations, if employees want to get work done, they need to have access to a LAN (see Figure 17-1).

A LAN is a static item. You don't move a LAN very often, if at all. Organizations and the people that populate them, on the other hand, are not static. People need to fly to a sales meeting in Topeka, they need to train new employees in Austin, and they need to open a new office in Smyrna. Most organizations start as a single entity—with a single LAN—but inevitably grow in such a way that people end up being far away from the precious LAN (see Figure 17-2).

The people in your organization need to be able to access the LAN regardless of where they are working. In particular, they need access to the company's data. Other network resources, like printing, are less important to a person who is 500 miles away from the office. Although there are many methods to access this information from far away, most people want to be able to access their office network exactly as though they were sitting at a local system on the LAN. To appreciate the many methods of accessing a LAN remotely, you must understand two very basic and very abused terms: *Local* and *Remote*.

Figure 17-1 I love my LAN!

Figure 17-2 I miss my LAN!

Historical/Conceptual

Local vs. Remote

The "L" in LAN stands for "local." In a classic LAN, all of the systems are local to each other, physically connected via some type of *dedicated* connection, usually a cable. Each system is linked permanently to the network, and when a computer boots, it logs on to the network. As long as the machine is running, it stays connected to the network. The user can automatically access the network's shared resources as long as the machine has booted properly. If for some reason the system is logged off the network, a user can reconnect to the network simply by logging back on. It is unusual in this scenario for the system *not* to be connected to the network. Physically disconnecting the system creates an error scenario (see Figure 17-3).

A remote system, in contrast, accesses your LAN via a connection that your organization does not own, often through the public telephone lines. Remote access requires two devices: a server and a client. The remote access server has a dedicated connection to a LAN, some type of modem or modem equivalent, and special software that works with the modem to listen for rings, authenticate the user, and provide network access. The remote access client has a modem or equivalent, plus software to enable it to link into the server (see Figure 17-4).

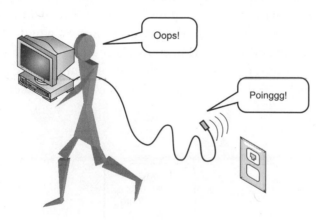

Figure 17-3   Don't unplug while connected!

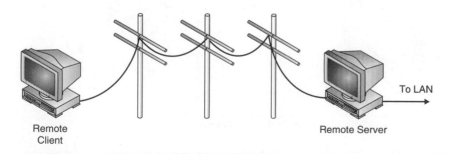

Figure 17-4   Remote client and server

Okay, you have a remote access server and a remote access client—which is the local system and which is the remote one? You will hear people use these terms in two different ways. Many people use the terms remote and local in a relative way. The local system is the system that is physically where you're at. The remote system is the one physically remote from your system. Imagine a salesman with a laptop in North Zulch, TX trying to access a server in Intercourse, PA. From the salesman's standpoint, his laptop is the local system and the server is the remote system. From the servers' point of view, the server is the local system and the laptop is the remote system. The preferred way to define local and remote is not relative at all—the remote access server is always the local system and the remote access client is always the remote system. This more absolute definition makes understanding remote access easier. Just be prepared for Network+ to throw questions at you that use either definition (see Figure 17-5).

Remote access uses telephone lines. If you want to understand remote access, you need to understand another badly abused word: telephony. *Telephony* technically is the science of converting sound into electrical signals, moving those signals from one location to another, and converting those signals back into sounds. This includes modems, telephone lines, the telephone system, and the many products used to create a remote access link between a remote access client and a server. Unfortunately, many people use the word telephony the way they use "thing-a-ma-bob"—when they can't think of the right word. Be aware that some people use the term sloppily, but don't do the same yourself!

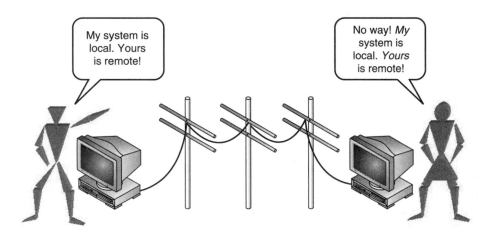

Figure 17-5   "Local" and "remote" can be relative terms.

Test Specific

LAN Connections

Becoming an expert on how one computer can use telephone lines to link to another is a totally separate career path from network tech. Network+ doesn't want to turn you into a telephony expert, just an informed consumer. You need to know the different types of telephone lines, and in particular, the amount of data they can carry. Also, you need to know what hardware goes with what lines, and how they work together to get the PC connected to the telephone line.

Your first and most important decision when creating a remote connection is choosing the type of line that will connect the two systems. The most basic types of telephone lines are cheap and require little effort to install. More advanced types of lines are very expensive to install and have high monthly costs. The telephone line you choose should be no more expensive than necessary, but fast enough to handle your remote connectivity needs.

There are many different types of telephone lines available, but all the choices break down into two groups: dedicated and dial-up access. *Dedicated* telephone lines are always off the hook (that is, they never hang up on each other). A true dedicated connection does not have a phone number. In essence, the telephone company creates a permanent, hard-wired connection between the two locations, rendering a phone number superfluous. Dial-up lines, by contrast, do have phone numbers; they must dial each other up to make a connection. When they're finished communicating, they hang up. Telephone companies hate it, but many locations use dial-up lines in a dedicated manner. If a dial-up connection is made and the two ends never disconnect, you have basically the same function as a dedicated connection. But it is still a dial-up connection, even if the two sides rarely disconnect.

In this section, we look at the most common types of dial-up lines—PSTN and ISDN —and briefly discuss two new high-speed consumer Internet access technologies: ADSL and cable modems. Most of the expensive, dedicated types of phone lines (including ADSL and Cable) are of no interest to Network+, but I include them here for completeness.

Public Switched Telephone Network

The oldest, slowest, and most common phone connection is the Public Switched Telephone Network (PSTN). PSTN is also known as Plain Old Telephone Service (seriously! —you see it all the time, often abbreviated POTS). PSTN is just a regular phone line, the same line that runs into everybody's home telephone jacks. Because PSTN was designed long before computers were common, it was designed to work with only one type of data: sound. PSTN takes the sound—usually your voice—that you are transmitting, which has been translated into an electrical analog waveform by the telephone's microphone, and transmits it to the phone on the other end of the connection. That phone translates the signal into sound on the other end using its speaker. The important word here is *analog*. The telephone microphone converts the sounds into electrical waveforms that cycle 2400 times a second. An individual cycle is known as a *baud*. The number of bauds per second is called the *baud rate*. Pretty much all phone companies' PSTN lines have a baud rate of 2400. PSTN uses a connector called RJ-11. It's the classic connector you see on all telephones (see Figure 17-6).

Computers, as we know, don't speak analog—only digital (ones and zeros) will do. To connect over phone lines, they need a device that can convert (modulate) digital signals from the computer into analog waveforms that can travel across PSTN lines and demodulate the analog signals from the PSTN wall jack into ones and zeros the computer can understand. This device is called a *MOdulator DEModulator* (modem). Modems connect to serial ports to provide the interface to the PC. Refer back to Chapter 8 for a discussion of modems and serial ports (see Figure 17-7).

V Standards

Modems utilize phone lines to transmit data, not just voice, at various speeds. These speeds cause a world of confusion and problems for computer people. This is where a little bit of knowledge becomes dangerous. Standard modems you can buy for your

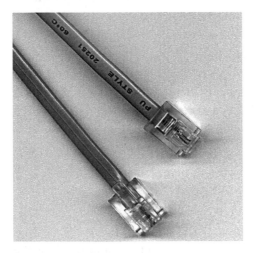

Figure 17-6 An RJ-11 connector

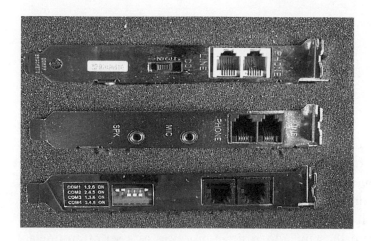

Figure 17-7 Typical modems

home computer normally transmit data at speeds up to 56 Kbps. That's 56 kilobits per second, *not* 56 kilo-baud! Many people confuse the terms *baud* and *bits per second*. This confusion arises because the baud rate and bps are the same for modems until the data transfer rate surpasses 2400 baud.

A PSTN phone line takes analog samples of sound 2400 times a second. This standard was determined a long time ago as an acceptable rate for sending voice traffic over phone lines. Although 2400-baud analog signals are in fact fine for voice communication, they are a big problem for computers trying to send data. As I said, computers hate analog signals; in fact, they work only with digital signals. The job of the modem is to take the digital signals it receives from the computer and send them out over the phone line in an analog form, using the baud cycles from the phone system. The earliest modems—often erroneously called 300-baud modems—used four analog bauds just to send one bit of data. As you should already have realized, they weren't 300-baud modems at all—they were 300 *bps* modems; however, the name baud kind of stuck for describing modem speeds.

As technology progressed, modems became faster and faster. To get past the 2400 baud limit, modems would modulate the 2400 baud signal twice in each cycle, thereby transmitting 4800 bits per second. To get 9600 bps, the modem would modulate the signal four times per cycle. All PSTN modem speeds are always a multiple of 2400. Look at the following classic modem speeds:

- 2400 baud/sec × 1 bit/baud = 2400 bits/sec
- 2400 × 2 = 4800 bps
- 2400 × 4 = 9600 bps

- 2400 × 6 = 14400 bps
- 2400 × 8 = 19200 bps
- 2400 × 12 = 28800 bps
- 2400 × 24 = 57600 bps (56K)

So, if someone comes up to you and asks, "Is that a 56K baud modem?" you can look them straight in the eye and say, "No, it's a 2400-baud modem. But its bits per second rate is 57600!" You'll be technically correct, but soon you will have no friends.

For two modems to communicate with each other at their fastest rate, they must modulate signals in the same fashion. The two modems must also negotiate with, or *query*, each other in order to determine the fastest speed they share. The modem manufacturers themselves originally standardized these processes as a set of proprietary protocols. The downside to these protocols was that unless you had two modems from the same manufacturer, modems often would not work together. In response, a European standards body called the CCITT established standards for modems. These standards, known generically as the V standards, define the speeds at which modems can modulate. The most common of these speed standards are as follows:

V.22	1200 bps
V.22bis	2400 bps
V.32	9600 bps
V.32bis	14400 bps
V.34	28000 bps
V.90	57600 bps

A new modem standard now on the market is the *V.92 standard*. V.92 has the same download speed as the V.90, but upstream rates increase to as much as 48 Kbps. If your modem is having trouble getting 56K rates with V.90 in your area, you will not notice an improvement. V.92 also offers a Quick Connect feature which implements faster handshaking to cut connection delays. Finally, the V.92 standard offers a Modem On Hold feature, which enables the modem to stay connected while you take an incoming call-waiting call or even initiate an outgoing voice call. This feature only works if the V.92 server modem is configured to enable it.

In addition to speed standards, the CCITT, now known simply as ITT, has established standards controlling how modems compress data and perform error checking when they communicate. These standards are as follows:

V.42	Error Checking
V.42bis	Data Compression
MNP5	Both error checking and data compression

The beauty of these standards is that you don't need to do anything special to enjoy their benefits. If you want 56K data transfers, for example, you simply need to ensure that the modems in the local system and the remote system both support the V.90 standard. Assuming you have good line quality, the connections will run at, or at least close to, 56K.

NOTE: Many people get a little confused by the concept of port speed vs. modem speed. All versions of Windows give you the opportunity to set the port speed. Port speed is the speed at which the data travels between the serial port (really the UART) and the modem, not between the local and remote modems. As a rule, always set this speed to the highest setting available (this should be 115200 bps, assuming your UART is a 16500 or better).

ISDN

There are many pieces to a PSTN telephone connection. First, there's the phone line that runs from your phone out to a Network Interface Box (the little box on the side of your house), and into a central switch. (In some cases, there are intermediary steps.) Standard metropolitan areas have a large number of central offices, each with a central switch. Houston, Texas, for example, has nearly 100 offices in the general metro area. These central switches connect to each other through high-capacity *trunk lines*. Before 1970, the entire phone system was analog, but over time, phone companies began to upgrade their trunk lines to digital systems. Nowadays, the entire telephone system, with the exception of the line from your phone to the central office, is digital.

During this upgrade period, customers have continued to demand higher throughput from their phone lines. The old PSTN was not expected to produce more than 28.8 Kbps (56K modems, which were a *big* surprise to the phone companies, didn't appear until 1995). Needless to say, the phone companies were very motivated to come up with a way to generate higher capacities. Their answer was actually fairly straightforward: make the entire phone system digital. By adding special equipment at the central office and the user's location, phone companies can achieve a throughput of up to 64K per line (see the following) over the same copper wires already used by PSTN lines. This process of sending telephone transmission across fully digital lines end-to-end is called *Integrated Services Digital Network* (ISDN) service.

ISDN service consists of two types of channels: "Bearer" or "B" channels and "Delta" or "D" channels. B channels carry data and voice information at 64 Kbps, while D channels carry setup and configuration information, as well as data, at 16 Kbps. Most providers of ISDN allow the user to choose either one or two B channels. The more common setup is two B/one D, usually called a *Basic Rate Interface* (BRI) setup. A BRI setup uses only one physical line, but each B channel sends 64K, doubling the throughput total to 128K. ISDN also connects much faster than PSTN, eliminating that long, annoying, modem mating call you get with PSTN. The monthly cost per B channel is slightly more than a PSTN line, and there is usually a fairly steep initial cost for the installation and equipment. The other limitation is that not everyone can get ISDN. You usually need to be within about 18,000 feet of a central office to use ISDN.

The physical connections for ISDN bear some similarity to PSTN modems. An ISDN wall socket is usually something that looks like a standard RJ-45 network jack. The most common interface for your computer is a device called a *Terminal Adapter* (TA). TAs look very much like regular modems, and like modems, come in external and internal variants. You can even get TAs that are also hubs, enabling your system to support a direct LAN connection (see Figure 17-8).

NOTE: There is another type of ISDN, called Primary Rate Interface (PRI), composed of 23 64-Kbps B channels and one 64-Kbps D channel, giving it a total throughput of 1.5 Mbps. PRI uses a special type of telephone line called a T1 and is very expensive. PRI ISDN lines are rarely used as dial-up connections—they are far more common on dedicated lines.

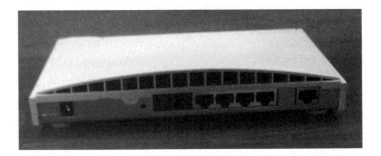

Figure 17-8   A Terminal Adapter that is also a hub

While this chapter concentrates on the two most common remote access telephony options—PSTN (POTS) and ISDN—keep in mind that there are others. In particular, two other technologies—ADSL and cable modems—deserve a few quick words. Keep in mind that as of this writing, Network+ does not include either of these technologies in the objectives list; however, the fast-growing popularity of these powerful new remote connectivity technologies is certain to cause the CompTIA folks to update the Network+ exams sooner or later.

ADSL

Asymmetric Digital Subscriber Line (*ADSL*) represented the next great leap forward for telephone lines. ADSL is a fully digital, dedicated (no phone number) connection to the telephone system that provides download speeds up to 9 Mbps and upload speeds up to 1 Mbps over PSTN lines. Even more attractive to the consumer, the same ADSL line you use for data can simultaneously transmit your voice (telephone) over the same line. The only downside to ADSL is that you can't use it unless your ISP specifically supports ADSL. A lot of ISPs currently do support ADSL, so most customers have a wide array of choices.

ADSL operates using your preexisting telephone lines (assuming they are up to spec). This is wonderful, but also presents a technical challenge. In order for ADSL and your run-of-the-mill POTS line to coexist, you need to filter out the ADSL signal on the POTS line. An ADSL line has three information channels: a high-speed downstream channel, a medium-speed duplex channel, and a POTS channel. Segregating the two ADSL channels from the POTS channel guarantees that your POTS line will continue to operate even if the ADSL fails. This is accomplished by inserting a filter on each POTS line, or a splitter mechanism that allows all three channels to flow to the ADSL modem, but sends only the POTS channel down the POTS line.

ADSL is actually only one type of a group of similar technologies known as xDSL. The *asymmetric* part of ADSL is the fact that the upload and download speeds are different (most home users are primarily concerned with fast *downloads* for things like web pages, and can tolerate slower upload speeds). Other xDSL technologies provide equally fast upload and download speeds. ADSL has become the most common type of xDSL by far, due in part to the support of big ISPs such as the Baby Bells, GTE, and Sprint. ADSL has roughly the same distance restrictions as ISDN—around 18,000 feet.

ADSL service is packaged in a variety of upload/download speed combinations and prices, depending on the telephone company providing the ADSL service. Southwestern Bell, for example, provides two levels of ADSL service. The more basic service provides a maximum download speed of 1.5 Mbps, with a guaranteed minimum of 384 Kbps, and an upload speed of 128 Kbps. The faster—and much more expensive—service provides a maximum download speed of 9 Mbps, with a guaranteed minimum of 1.5 Mbps, and an upload speed of 384 Kbps.

The most common ADSL installation consists of an *ADSL modem* connected to a telephone wall jack, and to a standard NIC in your computer (see Figure 17-9). An ADSL modem is not actually a modem—it's more like an ISDN terminal adapter—but the term stuck, and even the manufacturers of the devices now call them ADSL modems. The installation, equipment, and monthly service for basic ADSL service usually costs about the same as, or possibly a little less than, ISDN service. This competitive price point, combined with the fact that you can use the same line for your phone (ISDN requires a special ISDN telephone or adapter), should make ADSL a very attractive option for the future.

NOTE: The one potentially costly aspect of ADSL service is the ISP link. Many ISPs add a significant surcharge to use ADSL. Before you choose ADSL, make sure that your ISP provides ADSL links at a reasonable price. Most telephone companies bundle ISP services with their ADSL service for a very low cost.

Cable Modems

The big competition for ADSL comes from the cable companies. Almost every house in America has a big chunk of coax cable running into it for cable TV. In a moment of

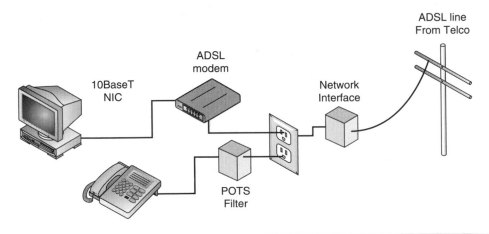

Figure 17-9 An ADSL modem connected to a PC and Telco

genius, the cable industry realized, hey, they could put the Home Shopping Network and the History Channel into every home, so why not provide Internet access? The entire infrastructure of the cabling industry had to undergo some major changes to deal with issues like bidirectional communication, but most large cities now provide cable modem service. By the time you read this, cable modems will be well on their way to becoming as common as cable TV boxes, or at least such is the dream of the cable companies.

The single most impressive aspect of cable modems is their phenomenal top speeds. These speeds vary from cable company to cable company, but most advertise speeds in the (are you sitting down?) *10 to 27 megabits per second* range! Okay, now that you've heard this exciting news, don't get too excited, because there is a catch: You have to *share* that massive throughput with all of your neighbors who also have cable modems. The problem: As more people in the neighborhood connect, the throughput of any individual modem will drop. How significant is this drop? Some early installations showed that the throughput of a heavily used cable line can drop to *under* 100 Kbps! A more realistic projection would be a throughput speed of 1 to 3 Mbps. In the upstream direction (from computer to network), theoretical cable modem speeds can reach 10 Mbps. However, most modem producers have selected a more optimum speed in the range of 500 Kbps to 2.5 Mbps, and some service providers limit upstream access speeds to 256 Kbps or less.

A cable modem installation consists of a cable modem connected to a cable outlet. The cable modem gets its own cable outlet, separate from the one that goes to the television. It's the same cable line, just split from the main line as if you were adding a second cable outlet for another television. As with ADSL, cable modems connect to PCs using a standard NIC (see Figure 17-10).

Take your time when choosing the type of remote connection you need. Be sure to consider upload/download speeds, equipment and installation costs, monthly service

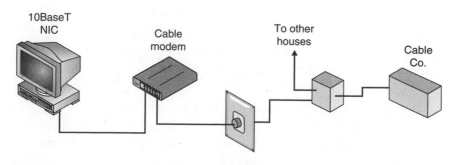

Figure 17-10   A typical cable modem configuration

costs, and availability. When studying for the Network+ exam, be sure to watch for these same criteria. Remember, Network+ wants informed consumers, not telephone/cable experts!

WAN Connections

A wide area network (WAN) is a computer network that spans a relatively large geographical area. Typically, a WAN consists of two or more LANs connected together over a distance. Computers connected to a WAN are often connected through a public network, such as the telephone system. They can also be connected through leased lines or satellites. The largest WAN in existence is—can you guess?—the Internet.

As I hope you realize by now, mystical packet gnomes do not magically whisk information from one LAN to another. Packets travel over a variety of connection media. Because a large quantity of information needs to travel between LANs in a speedy and reliable fashion, WAN connections are faster and *far* more expensive than any LAN connection. You're not going to find a typical home user connecting their computer to an ATM or a T3 connection (we'll discuss these in a moment); those are for businesses and universities that have many computers connecting to other LANs across the globe.

High-speed networks are networks with a link capacity of 100 Mbps and above, and a high end-user capacity, meaning that they can handle a large number of users connecting at the same time. Despite these greater capabilities, their behavior is not fundamentally different from that of lower-speed LAN networks.

T1 and T3 Connections

A *T1 line* is a dedicated phone connection that can run at 1.544 Mbps. A T1 line actually consists of 24 individual channels, each of which supports 64 Kbps and can be configured to carry voice or data traffic. An entire T1 bundle can be expensive, so most telephone companies allow you to buy just some of these individual channels. This is known as *fractional T1 access*. T1 lines (sometimes known as DS1 lines) are a popular leased line option for businesses connecting to the Internet, and for Internet service providers (ISPs) connecting to the Internet backbone. The Internet backbone itself consists of faster T3 connections.

A *T3 line* is a dedicated telephone connection supporting a data rate of about 43 Mbps. A T3 line actually consists of 672 individual channels, each of which supports 64 Kbps. T3 lines (sometimes referred to as DS3 lines) are used mainly by ISPs connecting to the Internet backbone, and by the backbone itself.

Similar to the North American T1 line, *E1* is the European format for digital transmission. An E1 line carries signals at 2 Mbps (32 channels at 64 Kbps), compared to the T1's 1.544 Mbps (24 channels at 64 Kbps). Both E1 and T1 lines may be interconnected for international use. There are also E3 lines, which are similar to T3 lines, with a bandwidth of 45 Mbps.

CSU/DSU

A *Channel Service Unit/Data Service Unit* (CSU/DSU) is a piece of equipment that connects a leased line from the telephone company to a customer's equipment (such as a router). It performs line encoding and conditioning functions, and often has a loopback function for testing. Although CSU/DSUs look a lot like modems, they are not modems, because they don't modulate/demodulate. All they really do is interface between a 56K, T1, or T3 line and a serial interface (typically a V.35 connector) that connects to the router. Many newer routers have CSU/DSUs built into them. CSU/DSUs for 56K, T1, and T3 lines are *not* the same, and are generally not interchangeable.

The CSU part of a CSU/DSU is designed to protect the T1 line and the user equipment from lightning strikes and other types of electrical interference. It also stores statistics and has capabilities for loopback testing. The DSU part supplies timing to each user port, taking the incoming user data signals and converting the input signal into the specified line code, then framing the format for transmission over the provided line.

ATM

Most people think an ATM is an automatic teller machine, and so it is, but not in this case. ATM is short for *Asynchronous Transfer Mode*. ATM integrates voice, video and data on one connection, using short, fixed-length packets called *cells* to transfer information. Every cell sent with the same source and destination travels over the same route, giving ATM the potential to remove the performance bottlenecks that exist in today's LANs and WANs. The key problem ATM addresses is that data and audio/video transmissions have different transfer requirements. Data can tolerate a delay in transfer, but not signal loss. Audio and video transmissions, on the other hand, can tolerate signal loss but not delay. Because ATM transfers information in cells of one set size (53 bytes long), it is scalable and can handle both types of transfers very well. ATM transfer speeds range from 155.52 to 622.08 Mbps and beyond.

SONET

Short for *Synchronous Optical Network*, SONET is a standard for connecting fiber-optic transmission systems. Communication between different networks once required a complicated multiplexing/demultiplexing, coding/decoding process to convert a signal from one format to another format. To solve this problem, SONET was proposed in the middle 1980s, and is now an ANSI standard. SONET defines interface standards at the physical layer of the OSI seven-layer model. The standard defines a hierarchy of interface rates that allow data streams at different rates to be multiplexed. Earlier rate standards used by different countries specified rates that were not compatible for multiplexing. With the implementation of SONET, communication carriers throughout the world can interconnect their existing digital carrier and fiber optic systems.

Optical Carriers

The Optical Carrier (OC) specification is used to denote the optical data carrying capacity (in Mbps) of fiber optic cables in networks conforming to the SONET standard. The OC standard is an escalating series of speeds, designed to meet the needs of medium-to-large corporations. SONET establishes OCs from 51.8 Mbps to 13.2 Gbps (OC-255). Here are some of the more common ones:

- OC-1 = 51.85 Mbps
- OC-3 = 155.52 Mbps
- OC-12 = 622.08 Mbps
- OC-24 = 1.244 Gbps
- OC-48 = 2.488 Gbps
- OC-192 = 9.952 Gbps
- OC-255 = 13.21 Gbps

The *Synchronous Transport Signal* (STS) is the basic building block of SONET optical interfaces. The STS consists of two parts: the STS *payload* (which carries data), and the STS *overhead* (which carries the signaling and protocol information). STS calculates overhead by measuring the *electrical* level of the fiber optic cable. The STS overhead rating and the OC rating are the same. For example, OC-1 and STS-1 have the same megabits per second.

X.25

X.25 Packet Switched networks enable remote devices to communicate with each other across high-speed digital links without the expense of individual leased lines. Packet switching (you should recall) is a technique whereby the network routes individual packets of data between different destinations based on addressing within each packet. X.25 encompasses the first three layers of the OSI seven-layer architecture, and gives you a virtual high-quality digital network at low cost. It is inexpensive because you are sharing the infrastructure with other people who are using the service. In most parts of the world, users pay for X.25 by way of a monthly connect fee plus packet charges. There is usually no holding charge, making X.25 ideal for organizations that need to be online all the time.

Store-and-forwarding is another nice aspect of X.25. In store-and-forwarding, as a message passes from node to node, each node stores the entire message. After examining the message header, the node forwards it on to the appropriate link. If a blockage appears, messages are held until it clears. If a blockage is there for too long, however, messages can accumulate. Another useful feature is speed matching: because of the store-and-forward nature of packet switching, plus excellent flow control, you do not have to implement the same line speed across your entire network. You can save the faster, more expensive lines for the parts of your network that really have a need for speed, and give slower lines to the rest of your remote users.

X.25 is considerably slower than the other WAN communications discussed here, but it's still out there. The big reason, aside from its continued large presence in Europe, is that X.25 is used by Automatic Teller Machines in the United States. So, oddly enough, X.25 *is* used with ATM, just not the ATM previously discussed. X.25 has been around since the mid-1970s, so it's very thoroughly debugged and stable. You literally never encounter data errors on modern X.25 networks.

Frame Relay

Frame relay is an extremely efficient data transmission technique used to send digital information such as voice, data, LAN, and WAN traffic quickly and cost-efficiently to many destinations from one port. It is especially effective for the off-again/on-again traffic typical of most LAN applications. Frame relay switches packets end-to-end much faster than X.25, but without any guarantee of data integrity at all. The network delivers the frames whether the CRC check matches or not. You can't even count on it to deliver all the frames, because it will discard frames whenever there is network congestion. In practice, however, a frame relay network delivers data quite reliably. Unlike the analog communication lines that were originally used for X.25, the modern digital lines that use frame relay have very low error rates.

The Protocols

Telephone lines need a Data Link layer protocol to handle the non-voice data sent between computers. Existing Data Link protocols, like Ethernet and Token Ring, simply won't work on a telephone line. They are designed to run too quickly, and they don't address a multitude of telephone-only issues. For many years, every type of Data Link protocol was proprietary. There was no way to make one system talk to another brand's system. This was okay in the days of mainframe computers, but the world of generic PCs, especially PCs trying to connect to the Internet, needs a generic Data Link protocol that will work over telephone lines. The first Internet-supported Data Link protocol for telephone lines was known as Serial Line Internet Protocol (SLIP).

SLIP

SLIP was the network community's first effort to make a Data Link protocol for telephony, and it shows. About the only thing good you can say about SLIP is that it worked—barely. SLIP had a number of major limitations. First, it only supported TCP/IP. If you had a NetBEUI or IPX network, you were out of luck. Second, SLIP could not use DHCP, so any system that used SLIP required a static IP address. This wasn't too much of an issue in the early days of the Internet, but today's shortage of IP addresses makes SLIP an unacceptable choice. As if this were not enough, SLIP provided no error checking and instead relied on the hardware making the connection to do any error correction. SLIP also did not natively support compression, which meant that there was no way to streamline your network protocol. There were later versions, such as CSLIP (or Compressed SLIP), which supported a little bit of compression, but it did not fit the bill. Perhaps worst of all (at least from a security standpoint), SLIP transmitted all authentication passwords as clear text. That's right; there was no encryption on the password. To make matters even more interesting, you usually had to create a script to log on to a server using SLIP. So aside from no security, no support for other protocols, no compression, no compatibility with DHCP, and a pain-in-the-rear login system, SLIP was not such a bad protocol.

SLIP continues to be supported by most remote access programs, primarily as a backward-compatibility option. But in reality, time and technology have moved away from SLIP and into the brighter, better days of PPP.

PPP

SLIP's many shortcomings motivated the creation of an improved Data Link protocol called *Point-to-Point Protocol* (PPP). PPP addressed all of the shortcomings of SLIP, and has totally replaced SLIP in all but the oldest connections. Although PPP has many powerful features, its two strongest assets are its ability to support IPX and NetBEUI as well as IP, and its ability to support dynamic IP addresses. All remote access software comes with the PPP protocol, so PPP *is* the one to use!

PPTP

An offshoot of PPP is Microsoft's *Point-to-Point Tunneling Protocol* (PPTP). Buying ISDN or T1 lines is an expensive proposition compared to PSTN. If the remote location is fixed, like a satellite office, the extra cost of ISDN or T1 often makes good sense. But what about the person who needs to access the company network in New York from a hotel room in Chicago? Well, there are two choices. First the company can set up its own remote access server and the person can dial in over a long distance line. This works great but can be very expensive. (Have you ever paid for a long distance call from a hotel room? Yikes!) All of the bigger ISPs have accounts that allow a person to dial into the Internet using local access numbers. They have local access numbers all over the United States, even all over the world in some cases. Wouldn't it be neat if the user could dial into the Internet using a local phone number and access the company's network through the Internet? You bet it would, and that's PPTP's job.

NOTE: PPTP is currently supported only by Microsoft products and the popular UNIX clone, Linux.

PPTP does not replace PPP. It works *with* PPP to create an encrypted tunnel—a direct link through the Internet between the remote system and the PPTP server. PPTP is *not* a Data Link protocol. Both the remote access server and the remote access client need special PPTP software to accomplish this connection. Once the PPTP connection is made, the Internet functions as nothing more than the cable linking the client with the server.

The only downside to using the Internet, or even directly dialing into a remote server, is that your login ID, password, and potentially valuable data must travel over public telephone lines, which can be tapped and your information intercepted. With PPTP, the data is also moving through routers, where it can easily be intercepted by the wrong people. To prevent information from falling into the wrong hands, remote access usually includes encryption options to scramble the data. Depending on the type of encryption, you can encrypt the login ID, the password, and even the data *before* they are sent across the network. The server and the client set up the encryption before any important data is sent, even before the client has the opportunity to log in. Encryption is an important part of remote access. One benefit of PPTP is its powerful, automatic encryption. Other remote access software usually requires the user to specify the level of encryption, if any, to be used.

Remote Access

Since most businesses are no longer limited to a simple little shop like you would find in a Dickens novel, there is a great need for people to be able to access files and resources over a great distance. Enter remote access. Remote access uses WAN and LAN connections to enable a computer user to log on to a network from the other side of a city, a state, or even the globe. As people travel, information has to travel with them. Remote access allows users to dial into a server at the business location and log in to the network as if they were in the same building as the company.

A major problem with this little slice of heaven is security. An old truth when it comes to security is if you give your employees a pathway into your system, someone else can find it, too. Luckily, there are many ways you can secure your servers from unwanted attention. A lot of it has to do with how you set up remote access to begin with.

Remote Access Servers

A *remote access server* (RAS) is a server dedicated to handling users who are not directly connected to a LAN but who need to access files and print services on the LAN from a remote location. For example, when a user dials into a network from home using an analog modem or an ISDN connection, she is dialing into a RAS. Once the user is authenticated, she can access shared drives and printers as if she were physically connected to the office LAN.

First, you must enable the chosen system as a RAS (see Figure 17-11). That system becomes your RAS server, accepting incoming calls and handling password authentication. Because TCP/IP is the dominant (and best) remote connection protocol, you must ensure that your remote access server is using the TCP/IP protocol for its network communications. Many remote servers have separate sets of permissions for dial-in users and local users. You must also configure the server to set the dial-in user's rights and permissions (see Figure 17-12). If there are any encryption requirements, you arrange them now as well.

Remote access server is, in a way, a catchall phrase. It refers to both the hardware component (servers built to handle the unique stresses of a large number of clients calling in) and the software component (programs that work with the operating system to allow remote access to the network) of a remote access solution. For instance, Windows 2000 has an optional software component called *Routing and Remote Access Server*

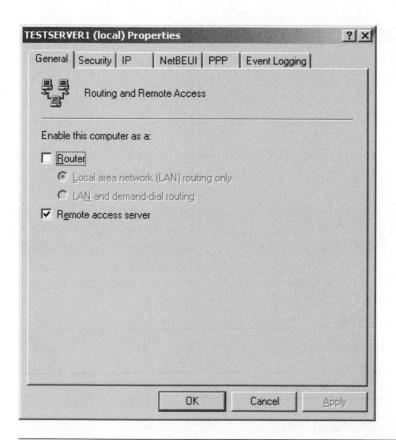

Figure 17-11 Enabling a RAS

(RRAS), which you could install on your specially designed RAS (see Figure 17-13). Remote access server software like RRAS manages remote users and deals with their permissions and rights on the network. It also handles network resources such as DHCP and DNS (see Figure 17-14).

Remote Access Clients

On the client side of remote access networking, the Big Kahuna of all remote access clients is Microsoft's *Dial-Up Networking* (*DUN*). Figure 17-15 shows a Windows 2000 system's remote access client, DUN, with PPP installed. Like all remote access clients,

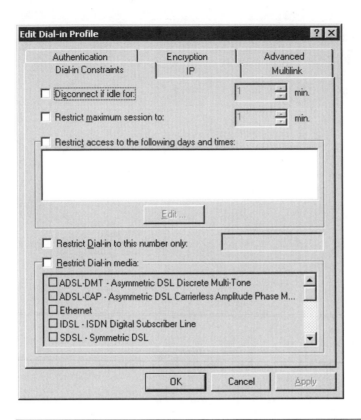

Figure 17-12 Configuring a dial-in profile

DUN needs a device to use, a phone number to dial, and, depending on the network protocol, special settings like an IP address, a gateway, and so on (see Figure 17-16).

The secret to success on the remote access Network+ questions is to *keep it simple*. What do you need to make remote access work? You need a telephone link, hardware, a Data Link protocol, and the correct software. Make sure you know the difference between PSTN and ISDN, and understand that you want to use PPP instead of SLIP. Finally, know that encryption exists, and that the type of remote access software you use will determine the amount of encryption you can have. Remember these basics and you'll do fine!

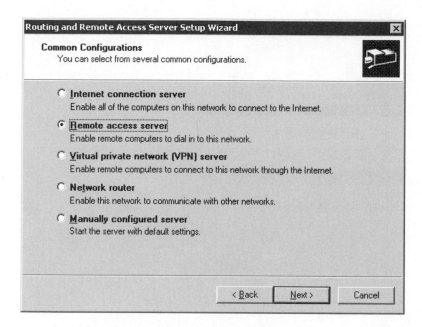

Figure 17-13   Microsoft's RRAS Setup Wizard

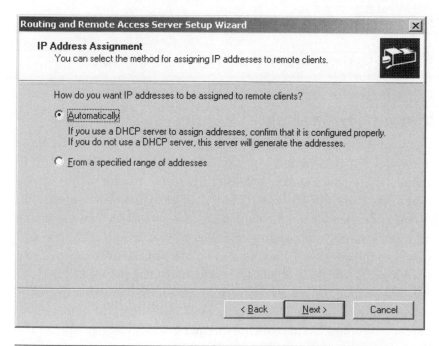

Figure 17-14   Selecting DHCP for IP address assignment in RRAS

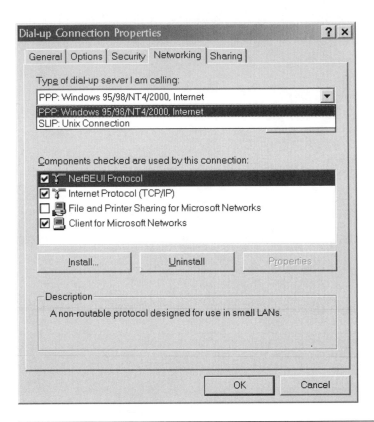

Figure 17-15   The Dial-Up Networking remote access client with PPP installed

Internet Connection Sharing

When a computer is connected to the Internet, it is assigned an IP address, which allows it to communicate with other computers on the Internet. As you know, public IP addresses are unique. This enables routers and other Internet hardware to direct packets of information to the correct destination. Public IP addresses, however, are in limited supply. They are getting scarcer and therefore more expensive, which means getting a unique IP address is becoming more and more difficult. Does this mean that eventually IP addresses will go the way of the dinosaur and no one not already connected will have access to the Internet? Not at all, thanks to *Internet connection sharing* (ICS).

Internet connection sharing, or just *Internet sharing*, is a term used to describe the technique of allowing more than one computer to access the Internet simultaneously using a single Internet connection. When you use Internet sharing, you actually connect an entire LAN to the Internet using a single *public* IP address. All of the computers on

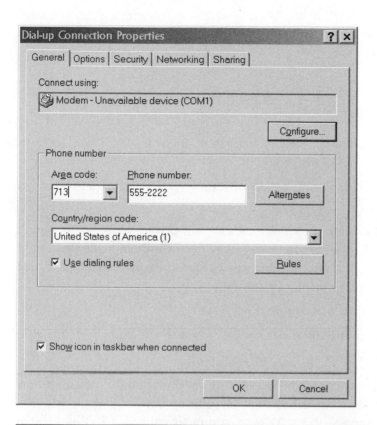

Figure 17-16 The Dial-Up Networking remote access client has many needs.

the LAN except one can use *private* IP addresses, which only reference computers within the private network. The network has only one connection leading out, using one public IP address. This connection to the Internet may be via modem, cable modem, ADSL, ISDN, leased line, or T1. In most cases, Internet sharing software uses *Network Address Translation* (NAT) to achieve this sharing.

There are many benefits to using ICS. For starters, having only one Internet account reduces costs. ICS also protects your data by putting your computers behind a firewall, and by enabling administrators to control user access to Internet services and resources. If you have multiple computers on a LAN, you can use ICS to allow different computers on the LAN to perform different tasks simultaneously. For example, one person can send and receive e-mail messages, while another person downloads a file, and another person browses the Internet. ICS uses DHCP and DNS to automatically configure TCP/IP information for clients in the LAN. Any IP-attached device can connect to the LAN, including older Windows-based clients, non-Windows-based clients, Microsoft

Windows 98-based clients, and Microsoft Windows 2000-based clients, without any additional client software.

Internet Connection Sharing Components

ICS has the following components:

- **DHCP Allocator** A simplified DHCP service that assigns the IP address, gateway, and name server on the local network.

- **DNS Proxy** Resolves names on behalf of local network clients and forwards queries.

- **Network Address Translation (NAT)** Maps a set of private addresses to a set of public addresses. NAT tracks private-source IP addresses and public-destination IP addresses for outbound data flows. It changes the IP address information and edits the required IP header information dynamically.

- **Auto-dial** Automatically dials connections.

- **Application programming interfaces (APIs)** Used by programs for configuration, status, and dial control.

An ICS system usually consists of an Internet connection via an ISP, and a gateway computer connected to the ISP via dial-up modem, cable modem, or DSL modem. The other computers are connected to the gateway computer using NICs. This is often implemented using a hub to connect multiple systems to the gateway computer.

ICS for Linux

Linux can do Internet sharing right out of the box. Most versions of Linux you buy in a computer store (for example, Mandrake or Red Hat) have wizards that enable you to set up Internet connection sharing very easily.

For those of you (I know you're out there) who like to do things the hard way, there's a utility called *ipchains* that knows how to distribute an Internet connection to all the computers within the network. One central computer is connected to the Internet; it runs the ipchains utility, and can then act as the firewall to the Internet. Client systems must be configured to use ipchains. There are two crucial steps involved in setting up clients for Linux:

1. Set the gateway to the IP address of the server.

2. Set the DNS numbers to the DNS numbers of the Internet provider (the same DNS as the server).

ICS for NetWare

Novell has a product called *BorderManager* that handles ICS. BorderManager also has security, bandwidth, and caching features to help your NetWare clients dial into your NetWare server. BorderManager runs on the NetWare 4.11 and NetWare 5-x operating systems, and uses the NetWare server utilities or the NetWare Administrator utility for server configuration. Server configurations are stored in the NDSTM database. NDS enables you to control user and user group access to the Web. BorderManager is so called because it enables you to manage and protect the border where networks meet. Why they had to be cute and leave out the space between the words is beyond my feeble brain's ability to speculate.

Remote Access Security

Companies have disparate workforces, applications, and security and network architectures. All of these factors can make it difficult to implement end-to-end remote access solutions. Let's face it: maintaining a secure LAN already takes a tremendous amount of time and effort, and this is destined to increase when you decide to implement remote access for employees and corporate partners.

A good place to start is to review all the connections into (and out of) your LAN. Identify all of your remote users and determine how they are getting to your network. This can be a fairly simple and straightforward task in a small organization. In larger organizations, however, you will need to plan out and keep track of the way in which your remote access is set up.

If you've planned out your remote access before setting it up, you should have a good idea of who needs to access your network and how they will do so. The most important point is to maintain a centralized access point into the network. The fewer pathways into your network, the easier it is to troubleshoot. Every exception you make to this rule creates a potential back door into your network.

Use the smallest possible number of authentication processes. If you require multiple authentications, there is a great chance your users will choose simple passwords, or write them down and leave them on their PC. Most network operating systems allow authentication over an entire network using one password.

Securing the data that is passed from the remote user to the corporate LAN server is another vital part of a remote access solution. A good way to do this is to implement IPSec and packet authentication for your server. Data encryption secures the packets that are being sent over the remote connection. This way, if packets are intercepted, they will have to be decrypted to be read by an unauthorized user.

Protecting your network from viruses and other malicious code is a vital part of ensuring secure remote access. The remote access server, as well as the remote devices, should have anti-virus software installed and kept up to date with the newest anti-virus definitions. Remote users connected to the Internet must also protect their machines from hacker exploits. Personal or distributed firewalls help protect remote devices that are connected to the Internet. Without this protection, a hacker could possibly take control of a remote device and ultimately get into your corporate LAN.

Creating and enforcing the appropriate policies and procedures concerning remote access can be a difficult task. Ideally, technology will dictate and enforce security policy, but any time humans are involved, nothing is easy. Security procedures should be easy for your users to understand, and security policies should hold end users accountable when appropriate. The best security policies and procedures meet your company's security needs, no more and no less.

Last of all, you need to decide how you will handle security incidents. It is a good idea to create an Incident Response Team as well as Incident Handling Procedures. Designate individuals responsible for documenting all incidents and bringing them to an acceptable level of resolution, as defined by your Incident Handling Procedures.

Configuring a Remote Access Client

When a remote client logs into the network via a modem, that modem acts as the NIC for that machine. Thus it's important to know how to configure a client machine so it can log in with no problems. This configuration task is much the same across multiple platforms: they all need a gateway address to communicate with the remote server, a dial-in number that will let them access the server and the appropriate permissions to do so. You must configure the remote access server to recognize the client asking for access as a legitimate user.

Troubleshooting Remote Access

Here are a few tips for troubleshooting remote access problems. Before we get to specific suggestions, remember that the number of modems installed on your server determines the number of simultaneous dial-up modem connections the server will support —one modem, one connection; two modems, two connections. The number of dial-up VPN connections is more flexible: You can decide how many simultaneous VPN connections you want to allow. Sometimes your system may simply be under-configured for its current usage load!

Okay, on to some specific suggestions:

- If you are dialing the Internet via a remote access account on a computer that is configured for your LAN, you may sometimes find that other machines on your LAN are unreachable. This is because Windows has become confused by having more than one TCP/IP configuration in the Network Control panel.

- The **TRACERT** command can help you troubleshoot connectivity issues. At the DOS prompt, type **tracert w.x.y.z**, where w.x.y.z is the IP address of the local LAN machine. If the trace times out on the first hop, there's probably a TCP/IP configuration problem.

- If there is still a problem, check to be sure the remote host is on line. The best way to do this is to use the command **PING <hostname>**. If the **PING** fails, there's a problem with the network connection from your client machine to the server. You will need to contact your network administrator to resolve this problem before proceeding.

- If you are on the remote machine and notice that there is no dial tone coming from the modem, the modem protocols may not be configured properly. This is the easiest thing to check. If your modem protocols are configured correctly, you may have a bad modem or a bad telephone line.

Chapter Review

Questions

1. Which of the following is *not* a Data Link protocol for telephone lines? (Select all that apply.)
   a. SLIP
   b. IP
   c. PPP
   d. PPTP

2. Which of the following provides the fastest throughput?
   a. PSTN
   b. ISDN BRI
   c. ISDN PRI
   d. POTS

3. The popular Microsoft remote access client is called:
   a. RAS
   b. Dial-Up Networking
   c. Dial-Up Server
   d. Microsoft Client for Networks

4. Thor is concerned that e-mail sent from his laptop to the RAS system in his home office could be read by others. He needs to use:
   a. A password
   b. Encryption
   c. A login name
   d. SMTP

5. BRI ISDN uses:
   a. One B channel and 24 D channels
   b. 24 B channels and one D channel
   c. One B channel and two D channels
   d. Two B channels and one D channel

6. The V.90 standard defines a modem speed of:
   a. 56 Kbps
   b. 33.6K baud
   c. 28.8 Kbps
   d. 2400 baud

7. Which of the following V standards defines error checking?
   a. V.42
   b. V.42bis
   c. V.34
   d. MNP 8

8. The ISDN equivalent of a modem is called a:
   a. terminal point
   b. network interface device
   c. terminal adapter
   d. network adapter

9. Which of the following are benefits of ISDN over PSTN? (Select all that apply.)
   a. ISDN is more widely available
   b. ISDN is faster.

    c. ISDN connects more quickly.

    d. ISDN is cheaper.

10. Generally, how close do you need to be to a central office to use ISDN?

    a. 1,800 feet

    b. 1,800 meters

    c. 18,000 feet

    d. 18,000 meters

Answers

1. **B** and **D.**   SLIP and PPP are Data Link protocols for telephone lines.

2. **C.**   ISDN PRI has a throughput of 1.5 Mbps. The next closest is ISDN BRI at 128 Kbps.

3. **B.**   The popular Microsoft remote access client is called Dial-Up Networking. RAS is remote access server software.

4. **B.**   Thor needs to use some form of encryption.

5. **D.**   BRI ISDN uses two B channels and one D channel.

6. **A.**   The V.90 standard defines a 56 Kbps modem speed.

7. **A.**   The V.42 standard defines modem error checking.

8. **C.**   The ISDN equivalent of a modem is called a terminal adapter.

9. **B** and **C.**   ISDN is faster than PSTN and connects more quickly.

10. **C.**   You generally need to be within 18,000 feet of a central office to take advantage of ISDN.

## CHAPTER 18

Protecting Your Network

In this chapter, you will

- Understand the various types of network threats
- Learn about protecting networks from internal threats
- Learn about protecting networks from external threats
- Understand firewalls, hiding IP addresses, port filtering, packet filtering, encryption, and authentication
- Learn about virtual private networks (VPNs)
- Learn about implementing external network security

The very nature of networking makes networks vulnerable to a dizzying array of threats. By definition, a network must allow for multiple users to access serving systems, and as we all know from painful experience, the more people who get their hands on something (not just networks), the greater the chance it will get messed up in one way or another. I used to enjoy going to my local health club to use the nice aerobic stepping machines, but I got tired of finding half of them broken. I bet it didn't even occur to most of you that I might be saying vandals got into the gym after hours and trashed the steppers. And you're right—the legitimate patrons of the gym are more than capable of turning these expensive pieces of equipment into giant hunks of pop art. I finally purchased my own stepper, and after two years of use it still works perfectly. Why? [*Because he was very careful both times*—Ed.] Ha, ha—jolly joker. No, because 50 different people haven't been using it every day, that's why—only one person uses it, a person who has a sense of ownership that motivates better maintenance and generally lower levels of abuse. Your personal home PC is like my stepper. Networks are like the gym's steppers.

The news may be full of tales about hackers and other evil people with nothing better to do than lurk around the Internet and trash the peace-loving systems of good folks like us, but in reality hackers are only one of many serious network threats. You will learn about protecting your networks from hackers, but first I want you to appreciate that the average network faces plenty of threats from the folks who are *authorized* to use it! Users are far more likely to cause you trouble than any hacker. So, the first order of business is to stop and think about the types of threats that face the average network. After we define the threats, we can discuss the many tools and methods we use to protect our precious networks from all this evilness.

Historical/Conceptual

Defining Network Threats

What really is a threat? What makes something bad for our network? In my opinion, anything that prevents users from accessing the resources they need to get work done is a threat. Clearly that includes the evil hacker who reformats the server's hard drive, but it also includes things like bad configurations, screwed up permissions, viruses, and unintentional corruption of data by users. To make the security task more manageable, I like to sort these possibilities into two groups: internal threats and external threats.

Internal Threats

Internal threats are all the things our own users do to networks to keep them from sharing resources properly. Internal threats may not be as sexy as external threats, but they are far more likely to bring a network to its knees; they are the ones we need to be most vigilant to prevent. The most common internal threats are described as follows:

Unauthorized Access

The most common of all network threats, unauthorized access, occurs when a user looks at data they should not see. The unauthorized access itself does no actual damage to data; the person is usually just looking at data that's supposed to be secret—employee personnel files, say, or maybe confidential notes from the last board of directors meeting. Usually this problem arises when users who are randomly poking around in the network discover that they can see data the administrators don't want them to see.

Accidental Data Destruction

Destruction means more than just intentionally or accidentally erasing or corrupting data. Consider the case where users are authorized to access certain data, but what they do to that data goes beyond what they are authorized to do. A good example is the person who legitimately accesses a Microsoft Access product database to modify the product descriptions, only to discover he can change the prices of the products, too. This type of threat is particularly dangerous where users are not clearly informed about the extent to which they are authorized to make changes. Users will often assume they're authorized to make any changes they believe are necessary when working on a piece of data they know they're authorized to access.

Access to Administration

Throughout this book you've seen that every NOS is packed with administrative tools and functionality. We need these tools to get all kinds of work done, but by the same token we really need to work hard to keep these capabilities out of the reach of those who don't need them. Clearly giving regular users Administrator/Supervisor/root access is a *really* bad idea, but far more subtle problems can arise. I once gave a user Manage Documents permission for a very busy laser printer in a Windows 2000 network. She quickly realized she could pause other users' print jobs and send her print jobs to the beginning of the print queue—nice for her but not so nice for her co-workers. Protecting administrative programs and functions from access and abuse by users is a real challenge, and one that requires an extensive knowledge of the NOS and of users' motivations.

System Crash/Hardware Failure

Like any technology, computers can and will fail—usually when you can least afford for it to happen. Hard drives crash, servers lock up, the power fails—it's all part of the joy of working in the networking business. We need to create redundancy in areas prone to failure (like installing backup power in case of electrical failure) and perform those all-important data backups. Chapter 20 goes into detail about these and other issues involved in creating a stable and reliable server.

Theft

I once had a fellow network geek challenge me to try to bring down his newly installed network. He had just installed a powerful and expensive firewall router and was convinced that I couldn't access his data. After a few attempts to hack in over the Internet, I saw that I wasn't going to get anywhere that way. So I jumped in my car and drove to his office, having first outfitted myself in a techy looking jumpsuit and an ancient ID badge I just happened to have in my sock drawer. I smiled sweetly at the receptionist, walked right by my friend's office (I noticed he was smugly monitoring incoming IP traffic using some neato packet sniffing program) to his new server. I quickly pulled the wires out of the back of his precious server, picked it up, and walked out the door. The receptionist was too busy trying to figure out why her e-mail wasn't working to notice me as I whisked by her carrying the 65-pound server box. I stopped in the hall and called him from my cell phone.

Me (cheerily): "Dude, I got all your data!"

Him (not cheerily): "<Expletive>! You rebooted my server! How did you do it?"

Me (smiling): "I didn't reboot it—go over and look at it!"

Him (really mad now): "YOU <EXPLETIVE> THIEF! YOU STOLE MY SERVER!"

Me (cordially): "Why yes. Yes, I did. Give me two days to hack your password in the comfort of my home, and I'll see everything! Bye!"

Never forget that the best network software security measures can be rendered useless if you fail to physically protect your systems!

Virus

Networks are without a doubt the fastest and most efficient vehicle for transferring computer viruses between systems. News reports focus attention on the many virus attacks from the Internet, but a huge number of viruses still come from users who bring in programs on floppy disks, writeable CDs, and Zip disks. We could treat viruses as an external threat as well, but instead of repeating myself, I'm going to cover internal and external issues together, both the various methods of virus infection, and what we need to do to prevent virus infection of our networked systems.

External Threats

Ah, here's the part I know you want to talk about—those infamous network threats from outside, the evil hacker working out of his basement in Germany, using satellite uplinks to punch into networks using sophisticated Internet worms and other arcane geek weapons. Hollywood wants us to visualize Hugh Jackman hacking a 128-bit encrypted password in 60 seconds with a gun to his head and a babe in his lap at the same time. (*I* did not make this up—it's in the movie *Swordfish*.) Lots of people assume that hacking is a sexy, exciting business, full of suspense and beautiful people. I hate to break this to those of you inclined to such a view, but the world of hackers is really a pathetic sideshow of punk kids, Internet newbies, and a few otherwise normal folks with some extra networking knowledge who for one reason or another find a motivation to try to get into areas of public and private networks where they have no business.

The secret to preventing hacking is to understand the motivations of hackers. I divide hackers into four groups, each with different motivations.

Inspector

An inspector is a person who wants to poke around on your serving systems like a regular user. They look for vulnerabilities in your permissions, passwords, and other methods to gain access to your network. Their motivation ranges from the casual—a person who notices open doors to your network—to the serious—hackers looking for specific data. This is the type of hacker most of us visualize when we think of hacking.

Interceptor

An interceptor doesn't try to hack into systems. They just monitor your network traffic looking for intercept information. Once they find the traffic they want, they may read or redirect the traffic for a number of nefarious purposes. Inspecting is often done to collect passwords for later invasion of a network.

Controller

A controller wants to take control of one particular aspect of your system. One of the controller's favorite gambits is taking control of SMTP servers and using them for other purposes—usually evil purposes. Other popular targets are FTP and Telnet servers.

Flooder

Flooding attacks, more commonly called denial of service attacks, are the work of hackers whose only interest is in bringing a network to its knees. They do this by flooding it with so many requests that they overwhelm it and force it to cease functioning. These attacks are most commonly performed on Web sites and mail servers, but virtually any part of a network can be attacked via some denial of service method.

Test Specific

Protecting from Internal Threats

The vast majority of protective strategies related to internal threats are based on policies rather than technology. Even the smallest network will have a number of user accounts and groups scattered about with different levels of rights/permissions. Every time you give somebody greater access, you create potential loopholes that can leave your network vulnerable to unauthorized accesses, data destruction, and other administrative nightmares. Let's start with probably the most abused of all areas: passwords.

Passwords

Passwords are the ultimate key to protecting your network. A user account with a valid password will get you into any system. Even if the user account only has limited permissions, you still have a security breach. Remember: For a hacker, just getting into the network is half the battle.

Protect your passwords. Never give out passwords over the phone. If a user loses a password, an administrator should reset the password to a complex combination of letters and numbers, and then allow the user to change the password to something they wish. All of the stronger network operating systems have this ability. Figure 18-1 shows the *User must change password at next logon* setting in User Account Settings on a Windows 2000 Server.

Make your users choose good passwords. I once attended a network security seminar, and the speaker had everyone stand up. She then began to ask questions about our

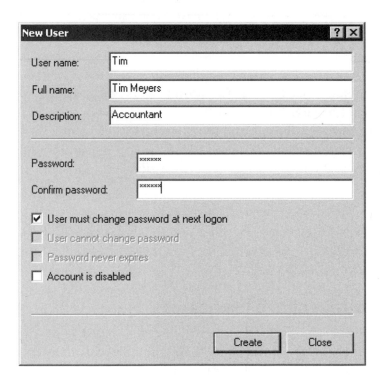

Figure 18-1   The User must change password at next logon setting in User Account Settings on a Windows 2000 Server.

passwords—if we responded positively to the question we were to sit down. She began to ask questions like

"Do you use the name of your spouse as a password?"

"Do you use your pet's name?"

By the time she was done asking about 15 questions, only about 6 people out of some 300 were still standing! The reality is that most of us choose passwords that are amazingly easy to hack. Make sure you use strong passwords: at least six to eight characters in length, including both letters and numbers, and possibly at least one capital letter.

Once you've forced your users to choose strong passwords, you should make them change passwords at regular intervals. While this concept sounds good on paper, and for the Network+ exam you should remember that regular password changing is a good idea, in the real world it is a hard policy to maintain. For starters, users tend to forget passwords when they change a lot. One way to remember passwords if your organization forces you to change them is to use a numbering system. I worked at a company that required me to change my password at the beginning of each month, so I did something very simple. I took a root password—let's say it was "elvis5," and simply added a number to the end representing the current month. So when, let's say, June rolled around, I would change my password to "elvis56." It worked pretty well!

User Account Control

Access to user accounts should be restricted to the assigned individuals, and those accounts should have permission to access only the resources they need, no more. Tight control of user accounts is critical to preventing unauthorized access. Disabling unused accounts is an important part of this strategy, but good user account control goes far deeper than that. One of your best tools for user account control is groups. Instead of giving permissions/rights to individual user accounts, give them to groups; this makes keeping track of the permissions assigned to individual user accounts much easier. Figure 18-2 shows me giving a group permissions for a folder in Windows 2000. Once a group is created and its permissions set, we can then add user accounts to that group as needed. Any user account that becomes a member of a group automatically gets the permissions assigned to that group. Figure 18-3 shows me adding a user to a newly created group in the same Windows 2000 system.

Groups are a great way to get increased complexity without increasing the administrative burden on IT, because all network operating systems combine permissions.

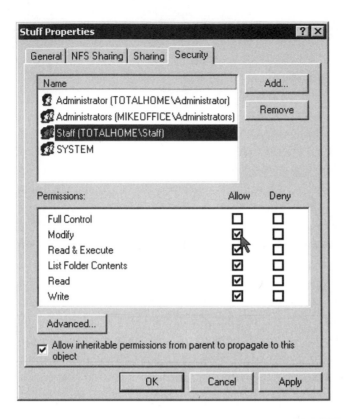

Figure 18-2   Giving a group permissions for a folder in Windows 2000

When a user is a member of more than one group, which permissions does he have with respect to any particular resource? In all network operating systems, the permissions of the groups are *combined*, and the result is what we call the *effective permissions* the user has to access the resource. Let's use an example from Windows 2000. If Timmy is a member of the Sales group, which has List Folder Contents permission to a folder, and he is also a member of the Managers group, which has Read and Execute permissions to the same folder, Timmy will have both List Folder Contents *and* Read and Execute permissions to that folder.

Another great tool for organizing user accounts in network operating systems using organization-based security is the *organizational unit*. Organizational-based network operating systems like NetWare 4.*x*/5.*x* and Windows 2000 store the entire network structure—computers, groups, printers, users, shared resources—as one big directory tree. This is great for administration, but having all your groups in one big directory tree can become unwieldy when networks grow past a certain size. Large organizations tend

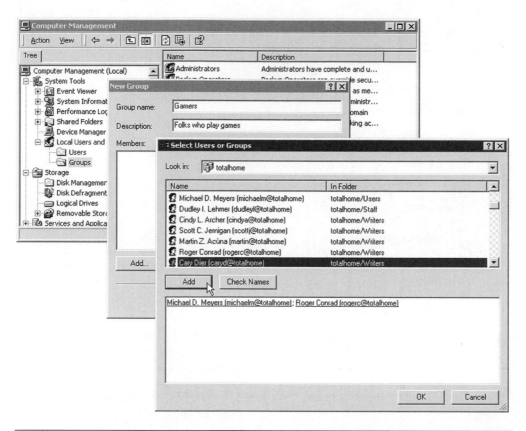

Figure 18-3   Adding a user to a newly created group in Windows 2000

to be geographically dispersed and organizationally complex. For example, most large companies don't just have *an* Accounting organization, they have *many* Accounting organizations serving different locations and different organizations. Organizational units are a tool to help network administrators group the groups. An organizational unit usually does not get rights or permissions; it is only a storage area for users and groups. Figure 18-4 shows the Dallas organizational unit, containing the Sales and Accounting groups, on a Windows 2000 Server system.

Both Windows 2000 and NetWare 5.*x* provide powerful applications that enable you to see and manipulate various parts of the network tree. Figure 18-5 shows me using the NetWare 5.*x* NWADMIN application to add users to the Accounting group in the directory tree. Figure 18-6 shows the same activity in the equivalent Windows 2000 Server tool, called Active Directory Users and Computers. Pretty similar interfaces for such different network operating systems!

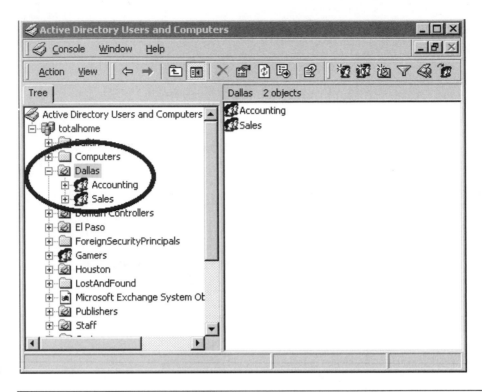

Figure 18-4 Dallas organizational unit containing Sales and Accounting groups

Watch out for *default* user accounts and groups—they can become secret backdoors to your network! All network operating systems have a default Everyone group, and it can easily be used to sneak into shared resources. This Everyone group, as its name implies, literally includes anyone who connects to that resource. All of the default groups—Everyone, Guest, Users—define broad groups of users. Never use them unless you really intend to permit all those folks to access a resource. If you do use one of these groups, remember to configure them with the proper rights/permissions to prevent them from doing things you don't want them to do with that shared resource!

All of these groups and organizational units really only do one thing for you: They let you keep track of your user accounts, so you know they are only available for those who actually need them, and they only access the resources you want them to use. Before we move on, let me add one more tool to your kit: diligence. Managing user accounts is a thankless and difficult task, but one that you really must stay on top of if you want to keep your network secure. Most organizations integrate the creation, disabling/ enabling, and deletion of user accounts with the work of their human resources folks.

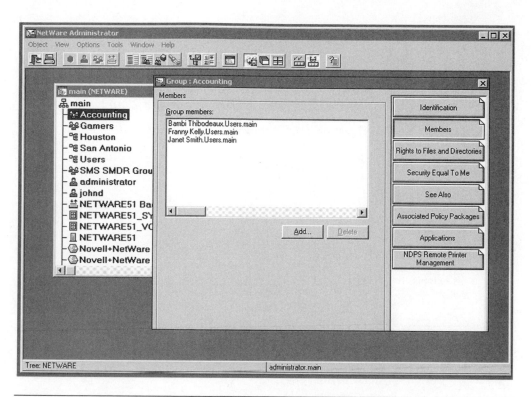

Figure 18-5 Adding users to a group in NetWare 5.x NWADMIN

Whenever a person joins, quits, or moves, the network admin is always one of the first to know!

Careful Use of Permissions

I have to admit that I gave most of this part away in the previous section when I discussed groups. The administration of rights/permissions can become incredibly complex even with judicious use of groups and organizational units. You now know what happens when a user account has multiple sets of rights/permissions to the same resource, but what happens if the user has one set of rights to a folder, and a different set of rights to one of its subfolders? This brings up a phenomenon called *inheritance*. We won't get into the many ways different network operating systems handle inherited permissions. Lucky for you, Network+ doesn't expect you to understand all the nuances of combined or inherited permissions—just be aware that they exist. However, those who go on to get their CNE or MCSE will become extremely familiar with the many complex permutations of permissions.

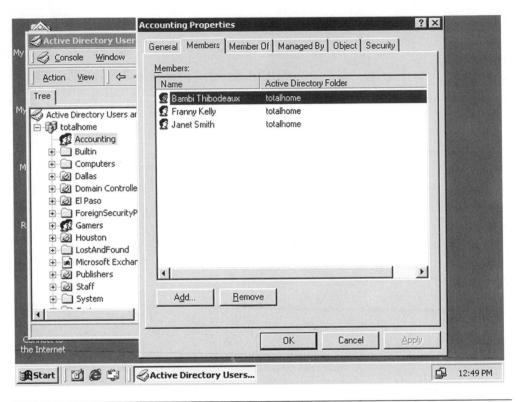

Figure 18-6 Adding users to a group in Windows 2000 Active Directory Users and Computers

Policies

While rights/permissions control how users access shared resources, there are a number of other functions it would be useful to control that are outside the scope of resources. For example, do you want users to be able to access a command prompt at their Windows system? Do you want users to be able to install software? Would you like to control what systems or what time of day a user can log in? All network operating systems provide you with some ability to control these and literally hundreds of other security parameters, under what both Windows and NetWare call *policies*. I like to think of policies as permissions for activities as opposed to true permissions, which control access to resources. The actual process of performing and using policies varies not only from NOS to NOS, but even among different versions of a single NOS. In concept, however, they all work the same way.

A policy is usually applied to a user account, a computer, a group, or an organizational unit—again this depends on the make and model of NOS. Let's use the example of a network composed of Windows 2000 Professional systems with a Windows 2000 Server. Every Windows 2000 system has its own Local Policies program, which enables policies to be placed on that system only. Figure 18-7 shows the tool we use to set Local Policies on an individual system, called *Local Security Settings*, being used to deny the user account Danar the ability to log on locally (I'm tired of her using my system when I'm out of the office!).

Local policies work great for individual systems, and policies get even better when you add a Windows 2000 Server system. Windows 2000 Server-based networks use the concept of *group policies*. This is a bit of a misnomer, because these super policies are actually applied to domains, organizational units, and another special type of unit called a *site*. You apply group policies to your network in a bundle called a *Group Policy Object* (GPO). GPOs perform all kinds of powerful functions under Windows 2000. Not only do GPOs cover everything local policies do, you can use GPOs for tasks like installing programs, providing logon scripts—literally hundreds of small but critical jobs. There are several programs you can use to apply these GPOs, but the most common is the *Active Directory Users and Computers* program. In this case, I want to keep the writers from eating up too much disk space on the Server, so I created a GPO called Enable Disk Quotas and applied it to the Writers organizational unit (see Figure 18-8). That will keep my editor from storing all her MP3s on the server! [*Pot calling the kettle black there, methinks! –Ed.*]

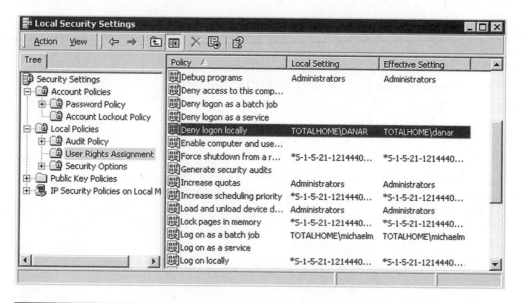

Figure 18-7 Local Security Settings

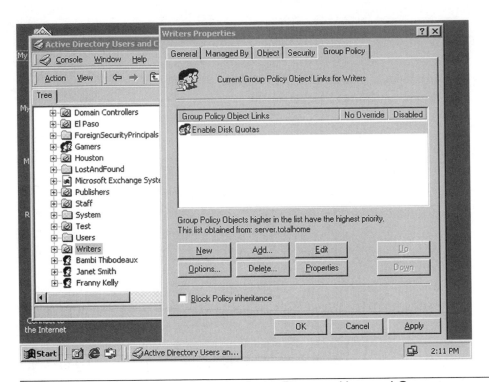

Figure 18-8   GPOs being applied using Active Directory Users and Computers

NetWare doesn't do a lot with policies. NetWare is content to add some of their own policies to the Windows policy list, which is actually a pretty smart way to handle things, given that NetWare is not that interested in the goings-on of client systems.

Linux doesn't provide a single application that you open to set up policies, like Windows does. In fact, Linux doesn't even use the name policies. Instead, Linux relies on individual applications to set up policies for whatever they're doing. This is very much in keeping with the Linux paradigm of having lots of little programs that do one thing well, as opposed to the Windows paradigm of having one program try to be all things for all applications. For the Network+ exam, you can safely say that Linux does not have policies. Certainly not in the Microsoft sense of the word!

Although I could never name every possible policy you can enable on a Windows system, here's a list of some of those more commonly used:

- **Prevent Registry Edits**   If you try to edit the Registry, you get a failure message.
- **Prevent Access to the Command Prompt**   This policy keeps users from getting to the command prompt by turning off the Run command and the MS-DOS Prompt shortcut.

- **Log on Locally**   This policy defines who may log on to the system locally.

- **Shut Down System**   This policy defines who may shut down the system.

- **Minimum Password Length**   This policy forces a minimum password length.

- **Account Lockout Threshold**   This policy sets the maximum number of logon attempts a person can make before they are locked out of the account.

- **Disable Windows Installer**   This policy prevents users from installing software.

- **Printer Browsing**   This policy allows users to browse for printers on the network, as opposed to using only assigned printers.

While the Network+ exam doesn't expect you to know how to implement policies on any type of network, you are expected to understand that policies exist, especially on Windows networks, and that they can do amazing things in terms of controlling what users can do on their systems. If you ever try to get to a command prompt on a Windows system, only to discover the **Run** command is grayed out, blame it on a policy, not the computer!

Protecting a Network from External Threats

So far, I've stressed that internal threats are far more likely to cause network failures than external threats, but in no way am I suggesting you should take external threats lightly. Hacking has reached epidemic proportions as the Internet has expanded beyond the wildest fantasies of network pioneers, and easy access to hacking tools and information has made virtually any 13-year-old with a modem and time on his hands a serious threat to your network.

Securing networks from external threats is an ever-evolving competition between hackers and security people to find vulnerabilities in networking software and hardware. It can be a horse race—hackers finding and exploiting network vulnerabilities, neck and neck with security experts creating fixes. Newly discovered vulnerabilities always make the news, but the vast majority of intrusions are not due to a hacker discovering a new vulnerability and using it. In almost all cases, hackers take advantage of well-known vulnerabilities that network administrators have simply failed to fix. These well-known vulnerabilities are what we'll concentrate on in this section.

Firewalls

I always fear the moment when technical terms move beyond the technical people and start to find use in the non-technical world. The moment any technical term becomes part of the common vernacular, you can bet that its true meaning will become obscured, because without a technical background people are reduced to simplistic descriptions of what is invariably a far more complex idea. I submit the term *firewall* as a perfect example of this phenomenon. Most people with some level of computer knowledge think of a firewall as some sort of thing-a-ma-bob that protects an internal network from unauthorized access to and from the Internet at large. That type of definition might work for your VP as you explain why you need to get a firewall, but as techs, we need a deeper understanding.

We must begin our definition of a firewall by appreciating how it goes about protecting a network. Actually, there is no one way; firewalls use a number of methods to protect networks. Any device that uses any or all of the techniques we are about to define is by definition a firewall. The first order of business here is defining these protection methods. then you will learn how to implement them. I hate to remove the drama here, but you should already know most of these methods!

Hide the IPs

The first and most common technique for protecting a network is to hide the real IP addresses of the internal network systems from the Internet. If a hacker gets a real IP address, they can then begin to probe that system, looking for vulnerabilities. If you can prevent a hacker from getting an IP address to probe, you've stopped most hacking techniques cold. We already know how to hide IP addresses: either via a NAT or a proxy server. Choosing between a NAT and a proxy server requires some analysis, because each has its advantages and disadvantages. NATs only translate IP addresses. This means a NAT has no interest in the TCP port or the information and it can work fairly quickly. A proxy server can change the port numbers; this adds an extra level of security but at the cost of slower throughput because this involves more work by the system. For this reason, many networks only use NATs; however, plenty of networks, especially in corporate environments where security is of a higher concern, make significant use of proxy serving.

We've already seen examples of proxy servers and NATs in previous chapters; now you know another reason why most routers have built-in NATs. Not only do NATs reduce the need for true IANA-supplied public IP addresses, but they also do a great job protecting networks from hackers (see Figure 18-9).

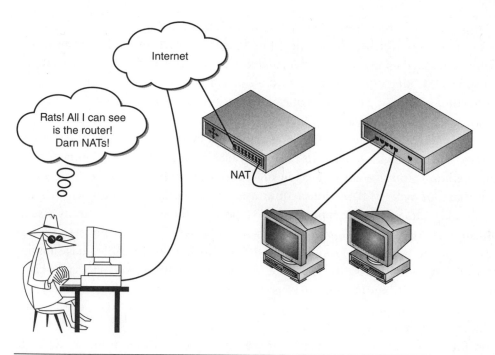

Figure 18-9 Hacker stopped cold by NAT!

Port Filtering

The second most common tool used to protect a network is port filtering. Hackers will often try less commonly used port numbers to get into a network. Port filtering simply means preventing the passage of any IP packets through any ports other than the ones prescribed by the system administrator. Port filtering is very effective, but it requires some serious configuration in order to work properly. The question is always, "Which ports do I allow into the network?" No one has problems with the well-known ports like 80 (HTTP), 20/21 (FTP), 25 (SMTP), and 110 (POP), but there are a large number of lesser-known ports that networks often want opened.

I recently installed port filtering on my personal firewall and everything worked great —until I decided to play the popular game Half-Life on the Internet. I simply could not connect to the Internet servers, until I discovered that Half-Life required TCP ports 27010 and 27015 in order to work over the Internet. After reconfiguring my port filter I was able to play Half-Life, but when I tried to talk to my friends using Microsoft Net-Meeting, I couldn't log on to a NetMeeting server! Want to guess where the problem lay? Yup, I needed to open ports 389, 522, 1503, 1720, and 1731! How did I figure this out? I didn't know which ports to open, but I suspected that my problem was in the port arena so I fired up my web browser (thank goodness that worked!) and went to the Microsoft NetMeeting Web site, which told me which ports I needed to open. This constant opening and closing of ports is one of the prices you pay for the protection of port filtering, but it sure stops hackers if they can't use strange ports to gain access!

Most routers that provide port blocking manifest it in one of two ways. The first way is to have port filtering close *all* ports until you open them explicitly. The other port filtering method is to leave all ports open unless you explicitly close them. The gotcha here is that most types of IP sessions require *dynamic port* usage. For example, when my system makes a query for a web page on HTTP port 80, the web server and my system establish a session using a *different* port to send the web pages to my system. Figure 18-10 shows the results of running the **NETSTAT –n** command while I have a number of web pages open—note the TCP ports used for the incoming web pages (the Local Address column). Dynamic ports can cause some problems for older (much older) port filtering systems, but almost all of today's port filtering systems are aware of this issue and handle it automatically.

Port filters have so many different interfaces that it boggles the mind. On my little gateway router, the port filtering uses the pretty web-based interface shown in Figure 18-11. Contrast that nice interface with the IPCHAINS text file used by many Linux systems. Linux does a great job of port filtering, but ooh that's a real pain to configure! (see Figure 18-12).

```
Microsoft Windows 2000 [Version 5.00.2195]
(C) Copyright 1985-1999 Microsoft Corp.

C:\>netstat -n

Active Connections

  Proto  Local Address          Foreign Address        State
  TCP    192.168.4.10:1707      207.46.144.86:80       ESTABLISHED
  TCP    192.168.4.10:1710      207.46.238.24:80       ESTABLISHED
  TCP    192.168.4.10:1711      207.46.144.86:80       ESTABLISHED
  TCP    192.168.4.10:1712      207.46.144.86:80       ESTABLISHED
  TCP    192.168.4.10:1713      207.46.144.86:80       ESTABLISHED
  TCP    192.168.4.10:1741      216.239.33.100:80      CLOSE_WAIT

C:\>
```

Figure 18-10 NETSTAT –n command showing HTTP connections

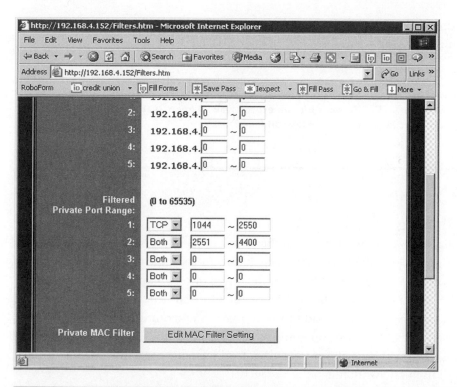

Figure 18-11 Web-based port filtering interface

```
ipchains  -A output -d 197.95.207.0/24 -j REJECT
ipchains  -A output -d 199.95.208.0/24 -j REJECT
ipchains  -N ppp-out
ipchains  -A output -i ppp0  -j ppp-out
ipchains  -A ppp-out  -p TCP -d proxy.virtual.net.au 8080  -t 0x01  0x10
ipchains  -A ppp-out  -p TCP -d 0.0.0.0/0 telnet  -t  0x01  0x10
ipchains  -A ppp-out  -p TCP -d 0.0.0.0/0 ftp-data -t  0x01  0x02
ipchains  -A ppp-out  -p TCP -d 0.0.0.0/0 nntp  -t  0x01  0x02
ipchains  -A ppp-out  -p TCP -d 0.0.0.0/0 pop-3  -t  0x01  0x02
ipchains  -N ppp-in
ipchains  -A input -i ppp0  -j ppp-in
ipchains  -A ppp-in -s 192.168.1.0/24  -l  -j DENY
ipchains  -A ppp-in -p UDP -s 203.29.16.1 -d $LOCALIP dns  -j ACCEPT
ipchains  -A ppp-in -p TCP -s 0.0.0.0/0 ftp-data -d $LOCALIP 1024:5999  -j ACCEPT
ipchains  -A ppp-in -p TCP -s 0.0.0.0/0 ftp-data -d $LOCALIP 6010:  -j ACCEPT
ipchains  -A ppp-in -p TCP -d $LOCALIP ftp -j ACCEPT
ipchains  -A ppp-in -p TCP -y -j ACCEPT
ipchains  -A input -i lo  -j ACCEPT
```

Figure 18-12 The IPCHAINS configuration file

So, can one system have both a NAT and port filtering? You bet it can! Most gateway routers come with both—you just need to take the time to configure them and make them work!

 EXAM TIP: The Network+ exam expects you to know that NAT, proxy servers, and port filters are typical firewall functions!

Packet Filtering

Port filtering deals only with port numbers; it completely disregards IP addresses. Packet filtering works in the same way, except it only looks at the IP addresses. *Packet filters*, also known as *IP filters*, will block any incoming or outgoing packet from a particular IP address or range of IP addresses. Packet filters are far better at blocking outgoing IP addresses, because the network administrator knows and can specify the IP addresses of the internal systems. Blocking outgoing packets is a good way to prevent users on certain systems from accessing the Internet, while allowing those same systems to take advantage of useful network functions like DHCP.

Systems that can block incoming IP addresses are usually high-end dedicated firewall boxes, which automatically detect dangerous behavior from incoming packets and start blocking those packets. These high-end firewalls are designed to stop denial of service attacks or other threats that require a fast response. Systems powerful enough to block IP addresses dynamically usually employ an even more powerful function called *stateful inspection*, by which suspicious packets are inspected at many layers, providing very powerful—and very expensive—firewall protection.

Encryption

Firewalls do a great job controlling traffic coming into or out of a network from the Internet, but they do nothing to stop interceptor hackers who monitor traffic on the public Internet looking for vulnerabilities. Once a packet is on the Internet itself, anyone with the right equipment can intercept and inspect it. Inspected packets are a cornucopia of passwords, account names, and other tidbits that hackers can use to intrude into your network. Since we can't stop hackers from inspecting these packets, we must turn to encryption to make them unreadable.

Network encryption occurs at many different levels and is in no way limited to Internet-based activities. Not only are there many levels of network encryption, but each encryption level provides multiple standards and options, making encryption one of the most complicated of all networking issues. You need to understand where encryption comes into play, what options are available, and what you can actually use to protect your network.

Authentication

Throughout this book, I've used examples where users type in usernames and passwords to gain access to networks. But have you ever considered the process that takes place each time this authentication is requested? If you're thinking that when a user types in a user-name and password, that information is sent to a server of some sort to be authenticated, you're right—but do you know how the username and password get to the serving system? That's where encryption becomes very important in authentication.

In a local network, encryption is usually handled by the NOS. Since NOS makers usually control software development of both the client and the server, they can create their own proprietary encryptions. However, in today's increasingly interconnected and diverse networking environment, there is a motivation to enable different network operating systems to authenticate any client system from any other NOS. Modern network operating systems like Windows 2000 and NetWare 4.*x*/5.*x* use standard authentication encryptions like MIT's Kerberos, enabling multiple brands of servers to authenticate multiple brands of clients. These LAN encryptions are usually very transparent and work quite nicely even in mixed networks.

Unfortunately, this uniformity falls away as you begin to add remote access authentications. There are so many different remote access tools, based on UNIX/Linux, NetWare, and Microsoft serving programs that most remote access systems have to support a variety of different authentication methods.

PAP

Password Authentication Protocol (PAP) is the oldest and most basic form of authentication. It's also the least safe, because it sends all passwords in clear text. No NOS uses PAP for a client system's login, but almost all network operating systems that provide remote access service will support PAP.

CHAP

Challenge Handshake Authentication Protocol (CHAP) is the most common remote access protocol. CHAP has the serving system challenge the remote client, which must provide an encrypted password.

MS-CHAP

MS-CHAP is Microsoft's variation of the CHAP protocol. It uses a slightly more advanced encryption protocol.

Configuring Dial-up Encryption

It's the server not the client that controls the choice of dial-up encryption. Microsoft clients can handle a broad selection of authentication encryption methods, including no authentication at all. On the rare occasion when you actually have to change your client's default encryption settings for a dial-up connection, you'll need to journey deep into the bowels of its Properties. Figure 18-13 shows the Windows 2000 dialog box where you configure encryption, called Advanced Security Settings. The person who controls the server's configuration will tell you which encryption method to select here.

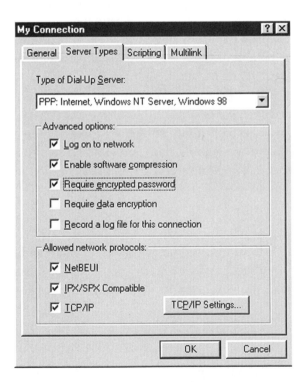

Figure 18-13 Setting dial-up encryption in the Windows 2000 Advanced Security Settings dialog box

Data Encryption

Encryption methods don't stop at the authentication level. There are a number of ways to encrypt network *data* as well. The choice of encryption method is dictated to a large degree by the method used by the communicating systems to connect. Many networks consist of multiple networks linked together by some sort of private connection, usually some kind of telephone line like ISDN or T1. Microsoft's encryption method of choice for this type of network is called *IPSec* (derived from IP security). IPSec provides transparent encryption between the server and the client. IPSec will also work in VPNs (see next), but other encryption methods are more commonly used in those situations.

VPNs

Many networks forego the idea of using private long distance lines and instead use the Internet itself as a way to connect LANs both to individual systems and to each other. The obvious danger (I hope) with this is the complete exposure of all network data to the Internet. This has led to the development of encryption methods designed to protect data moving between systems. A network employing encryption to use the Internet as if it were a private network is referred to as a virtual private network (VPN). Currently two encryption methods are the most popular for this purpose: L2TP and PPTP. L2TP is championed by Cisco; it is most commonly seen on dedicated VPN boxes like the one shown in Figure 18-14. PPTP is the Microsoft solution embedded into most Windows network operating systems.

Application Encryption

When it comes to encryption, even TCP/IP applications can get into the swing of things. The most famous of all application encryptions is Netscape's Secure Sockets Layer (SSL) security protocol, which is used to create secure web sites. Microsoft incorporates SSL into its more far-reaching HTTPS (HTTP Secure—also known as S-HTTP) protocol.

Figure 18-14 A Cisco VPN box

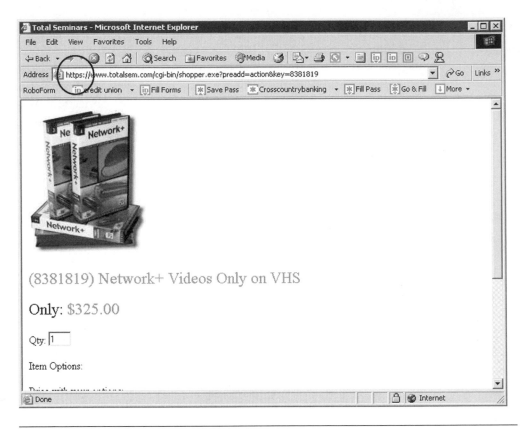

Figure 18-15   A secure Web site

These protocols work together to create those secure web sites we often use when making online purchases over the Internet. HTTPS web sites can be identified by the HTTPS:// included in their URL (see Figure 18-15).

Implementing External Network Security

Now that you understand how to protect your networks from external threats, let's take a look at a few common implementations of network security. I've chosen three typical setups: a single home system connected to the Internet, a small office network, and a large organizational network.

Personal Connections

Back in the days of dial-up connections, the concept of protection from external threats wasn't very interesting. The concept of dial-up alone was more than enough protection for most users. First, systems using dial-up connections were by definition only period-ically on the Internet, making them tough for hackers to detect. Second, all dial-up con-nections use either BOOTP- or DHCP-assigned IP addresses, so even if a hacker could get a bead on a dial-up user during one session, that dial-up user would have a differ-ent IP address the next time they accessed the Internet. As long as they have installed a good anti-virus program, dial-up users really have nothing to fear from hackers.

The onset of high-speed, always-connected Internet links has changed the security picture completely. The user who dumps their dial-up connection for ADSL or a cable modem immediately becomes a prime target for hackers. Even though most ADSL and cable modems use BOOTP/DHCP links, the lease time for these addresses is more than long enough to give even the casual hacker all the time they need to poke around in the systems.

One of the first items on the agenda of Windows users with high-bandwidth con-nections is to turn off File and Print Sharing. Because NetBIOS runs over IP, sharing a folder or printer makes it available to anyone on the Internet. Some hacker groups run port scanner programs looking for systems with File and Print Sharing enabled and post these IP addresses to public sites (no, I will not tell you where to find them!). When I first got my cable modem about two years ago, I absentmindedly clicked Net-work Neighborhood and discovered that four of my fellow cable users had their sys-tems shared, and two of them were sharing printers! Being a good neighbor and not a hacker, I made sure they changed their erroneous ways!

Although you can buy a firewall system to place between your system and the Inter-net, most single users prefer to employ a personal software firewall program like Black-Ice Defender or ZoneAlarm (see Figure 18-16). These personal firewall programs are

Figure 18-16 ZoneAlarm

quite powerful and have the added benefit of being easy to use—and in the case of ZoneAlarm are also free! These days, there's no excuse for individual Internet users not using a personal firewall.

SOHO Connections

The typical small office/home office (SOHO) setup is a few networked systems sharing a single Internet connection. In this situation, you really need a combination firewall/router. You have two choices here: you can drop two NICs in a system and make it a router (expensive, challenging to configure, and yet another system to maintain), or you can buy a SOHO firewall/gateway router like my little Linksys. These routers are cheap, provide all the firewall functions you'll probably ever need, and require little maintenance. There are a number of great brands out there. Figure 18-17 shows the popular Cisco SOHO 70 series router.

These routers all do NAT and or proxy serving with almost no setup; however you'll definitely want to read the instructions carefully to determine their default Network ID. Plus, as your network grows, you can use these same small routers to support separate DNS, DHCP, and WINS servers, although the configuration can become challenging.

Large Network Connections

Once you start to add components to your network like web and e-mail servers, you're going to have to step up to a more serious network protection configuration. Since web and e-mail servers must have exposure to the Internet, you will need to create what we call a *Demilitarized Zone* (*DMZ*). A DMZ is a lightly protected or unprotected network positioned between your firewall and the Internet. There are a number of ways to configure this; Figure 18-18 shows one classic example.

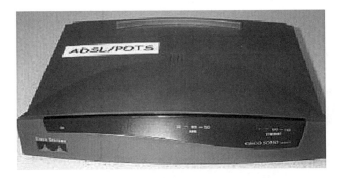

Figure 18-17   Cisco SOHO 70 series router

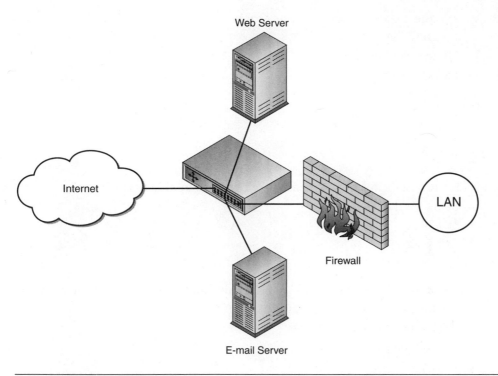

Figure 18-18 A DMZ configuration

Chapter Review

Questions

1. What two encryption applications work together to make secure web sites for online purchases?
   a. HTTP
   b. VPN
   c. HTTPS
   d. SSL

2. Which three basic technologies are used with firewalls?
   a. Proxy servers
   b. Packet filtering
   c. Dynamic routing
   d. Network Address Translation (NAT)

3. What is the most common technique for protecting a network?
   a. Port filtering
   b. Hiding IP addresses
   c. Packet filtering
   d. Encryption

4. Most routers have built-in proxy servers.
   a. True
   b. False

5. Which two of the following methods can you use to hide IP addresses?
   a. Static IP addresses
   b. DHCP
   c. Proxy server
   d. NAT

6. Which of the following blocks IP packets using any port other than the ones pre-scribed by the system administrator?
   a. Hiding IP addresses
   b. Port filtering
   c. Packet filtering
   d. Encryption

7. Which of the following blocks any incoming or outgoing packets from a particu-lar IP address or range of IP addresses?
   a. Hiding IP addresses
   b. Port filtering
   c. Packet filtering
   d. Encryption

8. Firewalls cannot stop which type of hacker?
   a. Inspector
   b. Interceptor
   c. Controller
   d. Flooder

9. Which method prevents hackers from reading packets intercepted on the Inter-net?
   a. Hiding IP addresses
   b. Port filtering

   c. Packet filtering

   d. Encryption

10. Of the following choices, which two are encryption methods?

   a. L2TP

   b. PPTP

   c. VPN

   d. SLIP

Answers

1. **C and D.** HTTP secure (HTTPS) and Secure Sockets Layer (SSL) are used to create secure web sites.

2. **A, B, and D.** Proxy servers, packet filtering, and network address translation are the basic technologies used with firewalls.

3. **B.** Hiding IP addresses is the most common technique for protecting a network.

4. **B.** False. Most routers have built-in NATs, not built-in proxy servers.

5. **C and D.** Both a proxy server and a NAT can hide IP addresses.

6. **B.** Port filtering blocks IP packets using any ports other than the ones prescribed by the system administrator.

7. **C.** Packet filtering blocks any incoming or ongoing packets from a particular IP address or range of IP addresses.

8. **B.** Firewalls can do nothing to stop interceptor hackers who monitor traffic on the public Internet looking for vulnerabilities.

9. **D.** Encryption prevents hackers from reading packets intercepted on the Internet.

10. **A and B.** L2TP is a Cisco encryption method, and PPTP is a Microsoft encryption method.

## CHAPTER 19

Interconnecting Network Operating Systems

In this chapter, you will

- Understand the interconnection issues of Windows 9x, NT, and 2000 with other network operating systems
- Understand the interconnection issues of NetWare relating to other network operating systems
- Understand the interconnection issues of Macintosh with other network operating systems
- Understand the interconnection issues of Linux with other network operating systems

Getting one brand of network operating system (NOS) to share its resources with other NOS brands has been a huge issue in the networking world for many years. During that time, we've seen amazing strides in interconnectivity tools and techniques, so much so that now almost any NOS is able to share with any other NOS. However, there are lots of limitations and gotchas, and you need to understand how interconnection works if you want to make sure your interconnection experience is as smooth as possible.

Historical/Conceptual

Before I even start to discuss the concept of interconnecting network operating systems, you need to understand what it means to interconnect different brands and makes of network operating systems. There's no way you, I, or the Network+ exam can expect you to memorize all the steps necessary to make every type of NOS share every type of possible resource with every type of NOS client that's available. There are just way too many NOS combinations out there! For that matter, I could write an entire book just on the topic "Making NetWare 5 Servers Share Folders with Windows 9*x* Clients." Oh, sure, it would be a great book ('cause I wrote it), but that's going way outside the scope of the Network+ exam, so I'll stick to the basics here.

To make this chapter more manageable, I've selected the network operating systems that we most commonly use to act as servers, and the three most common client systems: Windows (9*x* and 2000), Linux, and Macintosh. In each section, I'll discuss how one type of server connects to each type of client. Since this chapter is about interconnections, I'm not going to include Linux clients when I discuss connecting to Linux servers, nor will I discuss Windows clients in the Windows servers section. Since NetWare is a server-only NOS, I will cover all three client types.

So, what are the serving systems we want to discuss? Clearly we need to cover Windows NT and Windows 2000. These two operating systems have mostly the same interconnection issues, but there's just enough of a difference that I'll handle them in separate sections. I'll also discuss connecting to simple Windows 9*x* systems—don't forget they can share folders and printers, too! Next up: NetWare 3.*x*, followed by NetWare 4.*x*/5.*x* servers. The interconnectivity methods of NetWare 3.*x* are actually quite different from those of NetWare 4.*x*/5.*x*. Macintosh serving systems are next-to-last, followed, finally, by Linux. It's a tall order—but an interesting one, too!

Test Specific

Be prepared for a good bit of review here. I've covered so many different aspects of networking that you should recognize terms from previous sections of the book. The difference is that this chapter looks at these terms exclusively from the perspective of interconnectivity of different network operating systems.

What Are We Interconnecting?

Now that you're clear on which network operating systems we'll be interconnecting, let's get on the same page as to *what* we want to interconnect. The predominance of TCP/IP has made a number of interconnectivity issues moot. For example, a person sitting at a Windows 9*x* system (with properly configured TCP/IP settings) can fire up a copy of Outlook Express and connect to a Linux e-mail server without any special configuration of either the web server or the client. In fact, if you get your e-mail directly from your ISP's e-mail server, you're probably linking to a Linux server every day! By the same token, a Linux system, again with properly configured TCP/IP settings, can access a web server running on a Novell NetWare server. As long as you're using TCP applications and you've got your TCP/IP configuration correct, interconnectivity becomes a non-issue. But this universal TCP/IP interconnectivity only works with TCP applications. The moment you stop using SMTP e-mail, HTTP web programs, or NNTP news programs, and try to make your client system access a non-TCP, totally proprietary folder or print sharing application, you will need special interconnectivity software and configurations. That's what I'll concentrate on here: enabling different clients to access folder sharing and print sharing on NOS servers not using TCP.

Almost all of the interconnection methods you're about to see require that the serving system, the client, or some intermediary system run some form of specialized serving, client, or emulation program. Many network operating systems have this type of software built into them—especially the more robust network operating systems like Windows NT/2000 and Linux. Other network operating systems must rely on third-party programs. These third-party software makers have made a nice market for themselves compensating for shortcomings in the interconnectivity abilities of some network operating systems.

One interconnectivity issue you'll definitely see on the Network+ exam is that of protocol. There's no way that any two systems can communicate unless they are using the same network protocol. Well, I'll take that back—a little bit. There are devices out there called *multi-protocol routers* that can translate, for example, IP packets into IPX packets, but these systems are relatively slow, very expensive, and not too common anymore. Again, the universal adoption of TCP/IP has made interconnectivity much less of an issue than it was in the days when different networks ran IPX/SPX, NetBEUI, LocalTalk, and other mutually incompatible network protocols. Even though TCP/IP is quite common, there are many network operating systems that still run some of these older protocols. If they're not running the same network protocol, they won't interconnect!

Connecting to Windows 9x Systems

Enabling one type of Windows system to access another Windows system's shared folders or printers doesn't fit our definition of interconnectivity. As long as you have a valid user account and password, all versions of Windows have everything they need to access any other type of Windows system. Normally only two types of non-Windows operating system clients may need to connect to a Windows system's shared folders and printers: Macintosh and Linux.

Connecting Macintosh to Windows 9x Shared Resources

The first area where you will get in trouble connecting Macs to any Windows system is in network protocol. Many older Macs use the AppleTalk protocol, while most Windows systems use NetBEUI or TCP/IP. Later Macs all use TCP/IP, but the Network+ seems not to know this—if the test says Macintosh, assume AppleTalk!

Communication between Macintosh and Windows systems is further complicated by the fact that Macs and PCs use different higher-level protocols, too. Macintosh systems use the AppleTalk protocol for roughly the same jobs NetBIOS handles in Windows systems. So, even when your Macintosh and Windows systems are both using TCP/IP, you still have two different protocols handling the sessions, network naming conventions, and other important jobs. Windows 9x systems do not come with the AppleTalk protocol, and Macintoshes don't come with NetBIOS, so you're not going to get a Windows 9x client to talk to a Macintosh without some extra software. No problem! Now that all newer Macintosh systems support TCP/IP, a number of third-party vendors sell excellent programs that enable Macintosh computers to access shared folders and printers on Windows 9x systems. Figure 19-1 shows the popular interconnectivity program PC MACLAN running on a Windows system.

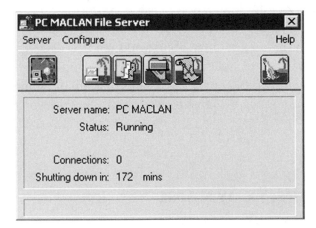

Figure 19-1   PC MACLAN running on a Windows system

Connecting Linux Systems to Windows 9x Systems

Connecting Linux systems to Windows 9x systems for native access to shared folders requires you to run a program called SAMBA on the Linux system. SAMBA makes the Linux box look like just another Windows 9x system to the Windows server. Once you've got SAMBA running on the Linux box, it will have access to the Windows system's shared folders.

For those who just aren't up to the grinding detail of configuring SAMBA on a Linux client, there are a number of third-party tools that install the network file system (NFS) protocol on Windows 9x systems. The NFS protocol is the closest thing the TCP world has to compare to Windows' folder sharing functions. Installing an NFS server program on a Windows 9x system enables that system to share its folders just like a Linux system. Figure 19-2 shows a typical third-party NFS server product running on a Windows system: OMNI NFS server from X-Link Technology.

Connecting to Windows NT/2000 Systems

Unlike Windows 9x, Windows NT and Windows 2000 come with substantial support for Macintosh systems—but only in the server versions. Windows 2000 Professional or Windows NT Workstation systems have exactly the same folder and print sharing options as Windows 9x systems.

Connecting Macintosh to Windows NT/2000 Shared Resources

Windows NT Server and Windows 2000 Server come with both an AppleTalk protocol and the File Sharing for Macintosh service. File Sharing for Macintosh is a bit of a

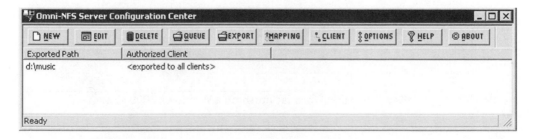

Figure 19-2   OMNI NFS server running on a Windows system

PART III

misnomer—besides enabling Macintosh clients to access *files* on Windows NT/2000 Server systems, it also enables Windows NT/2000 servers to share printers with Macintosh systems. With both AppleTalk protocol support and file Services for Macintosh, Windows NT Server and Windows 2000 Server have all the functionality they need to provide seamless interconnectivity for Macintosh computers (see Figure 19-3). Once you've installed the File Sharing for Macintosh, all of your Macintosh systems will have access to the Windows network's shared folders and printers. When you create a share on the Windows server, you must specify that it is to be shared by Macintosh clients (see Figure 19-4). All of the Macintosh systems will also need to have valid user accounts on the Windows server.

Connecting Linux Systems to Windows NT/2000 Shared Resources

Microsoft also provides a handy service to enable NT and 2000 systems to share their resources with Linux clients, but this product, currently called Services for UNIX (SFU), is only available as an add-on, and at additional cost.

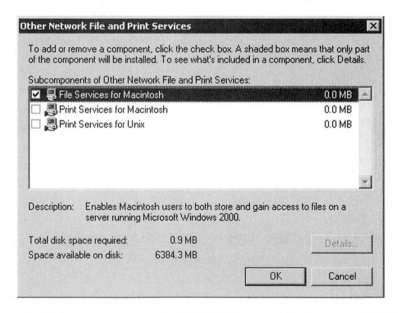

Figure 19-3   Installing File Sharing for Macintosh on a Windows 2000 system

Figure 19-4 Creating a new share for Macintosh systems on a Windows server

Windows Rules!

Windows' interconnectivity functions are a true testament to the overwhelming popularity of Windows as both a client and a server program. If Microsoft itself doesn't provide support for a particular interconnectivity need, you will usually find that some third-party vendor is ready with the product you need to get any client talking to a Windows system, be it 9*x*, NT, or 2000!

Connecting to NetWare

If there's one NOS that makes interconnectivity a snap, it's Novell NetWare—or at least NetWare 4.*x*/5.*x*. Since NetWare is purely a server NOS, it must, by definition, perform interconnectivity every time you use it: there's no such thing as a NetWare *client* operating system. Windows, Macintosh, and UNIX/Linux systems must all use some form of client software to connect to a NetWare server, and Novell has, by necessity, created excellent client software for all of them. You've seen the Windows client for NetWare

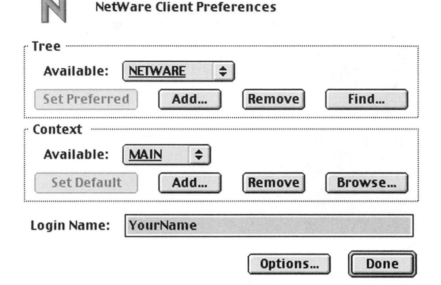

Figure 19-5 Macintosh Client for NetWare

already. Figure 19-5 shows the Macintosh Client for NetWare. The Linux client looks pretty much the same. Once the NetWare client is installed, the OS has full access to the shared resources on the NetWare server, both folders and printers. Figure 19-6 shows a shared folder on a NetWare server being accessed from a Macintosh client. One interesting aspect unique to the Macintosh client is that it's the only one you have to pay to use, because Novell doesn't make a Macintosh client. A third-party vendor called ProSoft does, however (**www.prosoft.com**). Both the Windows (any version) and UNIX/Linux clients are available free from Novell.

There's really no difference between NetWare 3.*x* and NetWare 4.*x*/5.*x* in terms of the client software. Novell constantly updates the client software, and NetWare shops commonly upgrade their client systems every so often to take advantage of some new feature in the latest version of Novell's client software.

NetWare client software can't do the job unless the client system is running the correct protocol. Fortunately, Novell provides IPX drivers for all network client systems to support the occasional NetWare network that still uses IPX as its network protocol. But whether your network runs IPX or IP, the NetWare client will work perfectly for Windows, Macintosh, or UNIX/Linux systems.

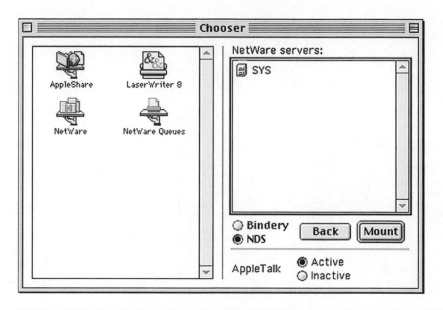

Figure 19-6   Macintosh client accessing shared folder on NetWare server

Microsoft takes NetWare connectivity one step further by providing Gateway Services for NetWare (GSNW). GSNW allows one Windows NT/2000 Server system to act as a gateway to a NetWare server, enabling Windows clients to access the NetWare server as if it were just another Windows server (see Figure 19-7). Individual Windows clients running GSNW do not need to run the NetWare client program; however, GSNW is limited to NetWare systems that run IPX. Since most NetWare 3.*x* systems still run IPX, this is no big deal, but NetWare 4.*x*/5.*x* systems require an IPX-to-IP bridge program to run GSNW.

Connecting to Macintosh

Even though modern Macintosh operating systems all use IP as their network protocol, Apple still relies on the venerable AppleTalk for higher-level network functions, just as Windows 9*x* still relies on NetBIOS even though most Windows 9*x* systems now use IP. This means that any time you have a Macintosh system talking to any other type of system, you must have some form of software on one end or the other that translates the AppleTalk information (like network names) into something the client NOS can understand.

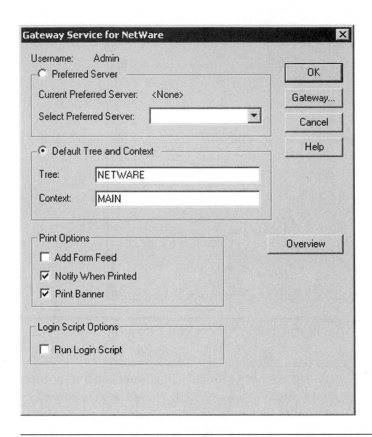

Figure 19-7 Configuring GSNW on a Windows 2000 server

Connecting Windows Systems to Macintosh Serving Systems

The most common way to get a Macintosh system to share its resources with Windows and Linux systems is via the AppleShare IP program. AppleShare IP has built-in SMB support, making it something like a SAMBA for Macintosh. AppleShare also provides printing support, but only to clients running the TCP/IP LPR program. Conveniently, this is no problem as both Windows and Linux clients support LPR.

AppleShare IP is powerful but is an extra cost item and requires fairly serious Macintosh hardware to run. AppleShare IP also includes a web server, an FTP server, and other items that might be more than you need just to connect to a Macintosh or two in a smaller network. For smaller jobs, many networks use the DAVE program from Thursby Software. DAVE runs on a Macintosh, enabling any Windows systems to access shared folders and printers on Macintosh systems. DAVE has the added benefit of not requir-

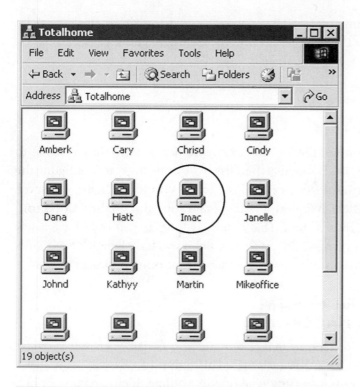

Figure 19-8   A DAVE-shared Macintosh named Imac as seen by Windows

ing the Windows system to run any form of client software—the DAVE software runs only on the Macintosh. Figure 19-8 shows a DAVE-shared Macintosh as seen by a Windows client system.

I should add that DAVE is not just for Windows-to-Mac sharing. It works equally well to enable Mac clients to access shared folders on Windows systems. Actually, a number of companies provide Mac-to-Windows and Windows-to-Mac interconnectivity tools. If you're really interested in getting Mac and Windows systems to work together, check out **www.macwindows.com**.

Connecting UNIX/Linux Systems to Macintosh Sharing Systems

Until the advent of the Mac OS X operating system, Macintosh systems lacked a truly handy way for Linux systems to connect to shared folders on Macintosh systems. Macintosh systems have used various NFS server programs, which worked moderately well. Linux systems can use their built-in NFS-based tools to access NFS shares on Macintosh systems. With the introduction of the UNIX-based OS X, Macintosh systems now share the same UNIX NFS as pure UNIX/Linux systems. As you might guess, UNIX/Linux systems use good old LPR/LPD to share printers.

Connecting to Linux

UNIX/Linux systems rely on SAMBA or NFS to enable non-UNIX/Linux systems to access their resources. SAMBA is popular because you only have to configure the UNIX/Linux system for its resources to be visible to all Windows clients. However, SAMBA only works on NetBIOS (Windows) systems, and you must do the SAMBA configuration on each UNIX/Linux system. This is fine as long as you only have a few UNIX/Linux servers, and are using Windows clients. But if you have lots of UNIX/Linux systems, or if you're using Macintosh clients, you need some other options.

Connecting Windows Systems to UNIX/Linux Sharing Systems

To reduce network congestion and to make configuration easier, Microsoft provides Microsoft Windows Services for UNIX (MWSU). This group of services, really just a toolbox of NFS programs, can access any type of NFS volume, including any from a UNIX/Linux system. MWSU is an add-on product that will run on any Windows NT or Windows 2000 system. To enable a Windows 9x system to access a Linux folder, you need to find a good third-party NFS client program. Figure 19-9 shows the OMNI NFS client program from Xlink Technology running on a Windows 9x system.

One very interesting part of MWSU is the Gateway Services for UNIX. As with Gateway Services for NetWare, MWSU enables a Windows NT/2000 Server system to act as a

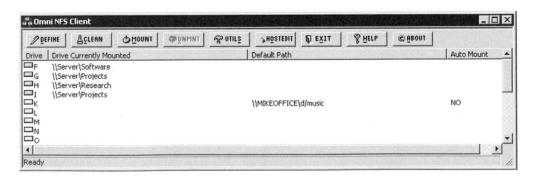

Figure 19-9 The OMNI NFS client running on a Windows 9x system

gateway between a Windows network and UNIX/Linux serving systems. None of the Windows systems need to run an NFS client program, and all of the UNIX/Linux servers appear to the Windows systems as though they're Windows servers.

Connecting Macintosh Systems to UNIX/Linux Sharing Systems

Okay, I've covered almost all of the possible NOS interconnectivity combinations. The last combination I need to cover is getting Macintosh systems to connect to shared resources on UNIX/Linux systems. You should be able to tell me the answer at this point—can you? Remember that Mac OS X has full NFS support for file sharing and LPD/LPR support for accessing shared printers. But I can't end this chapter without at least one more peek at some fun third-party software. Many UNIX/Linux servers that need to provide access to Macintosh systems use a little program called Netatalk. Netatalk creates AppleTalk-compliant folder and printer shares on Linux systems. While Netatalk itself is a text-based program, many folks use it with a graphical front end like the AppleTalk Configurator (see Figure 19-10).

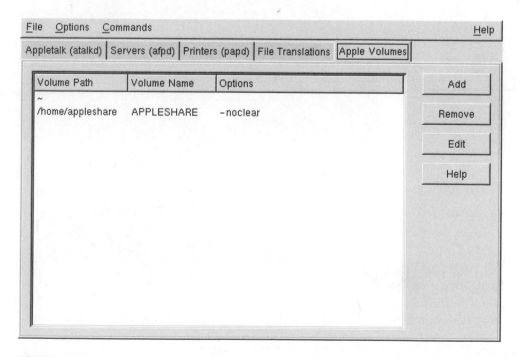

Figure 19-10 The AppleTalk Configurator graphical front end

When All Else Fails, Terminal Emulate!

Terminal emulation has been a part of TCP/IP from its earliest days, in the form of good old Telnet. Even though Telnet is one of the oldest of all the TCP/IP applications, it remains one of the most heavily used. But since it dates from pre-GUI days, Telnet is a text-based utility, and all modern operating systems are graphical. In keeping with the GUI world we live in today, all OSes come equipped with some type of graphical terminal emulator. Some, like Windows and Linux, come with built-in emulators like the very handy Windows 2000 Terminal Services (see Figure 19-11).

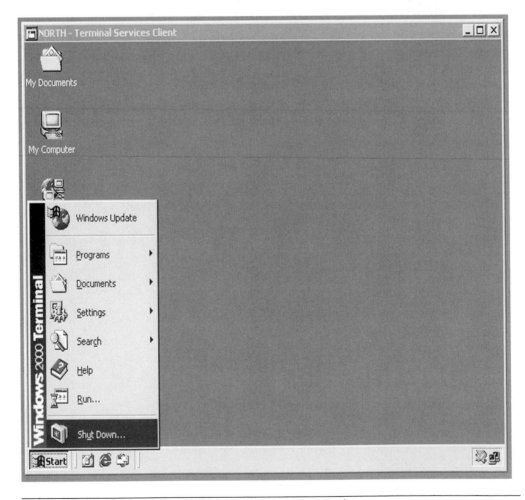

Figure 19-11   Windows 2000 Terminal Services in action!

Unfortunately, Terminal Services only works in the Windows environment; however, a number of third parties make absolutely amazing terminal emulation programs that run on any operating system. One of the best of these is VNC, which stands for virtual network computing. VNC doesn't really let you share folders or printers since it is only a terminal emulator. But it runs on almost every client NOS, is solid as a rock, and even runs from a web browser. Why bother sharing if you can literally be at the screen? (See Figure 19-12.)

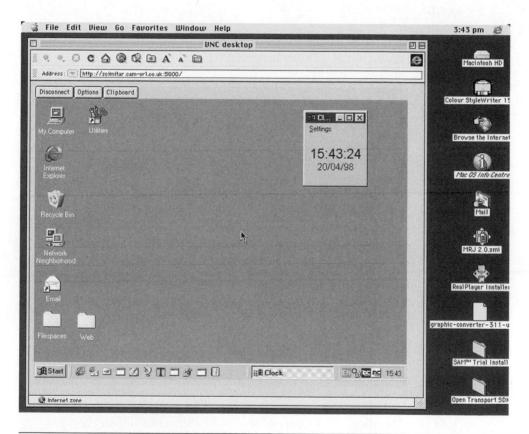

Figure 19-12 The VNC Desktop

Chapter Review

Questions

1. The universal adoption of what protocol suite has made the concept of interconnectivity between network operating systems much easier?
   a. TCP/IP
   b. IPX/SPX
   c. SAMBA
   d. LocalTalk

2. What protocol suite has Macintosh historically used?
   a. TCP/IP
   b. IPX/SPX
   c. SAMBA
   d. LocalTalk

3. What program makes a Linux system look like a Windows 9x system, and enables it to access a Windows system's shared folders?
   a. TCP/IP
   b. IPX/SPX
   c. SAMBA
   d. LocalTalk

4. Which of the following file system protocols must be installed on a Windows 9x system in order for that system to share its folders like a Linux system?
   a. NT file system (NTFS)
   b. FAT32
   c. SAMBA
   d. Network File System (NFS)

5. Which of the following services must be installed on a Windows NT or 2000 server in order for files and printers to be shared with a Macintosh client?
   a. File and Print Sharing
   b. File Sharing for Macintosh
   c. Services for UNIX
   d. Client Services for NetWare

6. Which of the following services must be installed on a Windows NT or 2000 server in order for files and printers to be shared with a Linux client?
   a. File and Print Sharing
   b. File Sharing for Macintosh
   c. Services for UNIX
   d. Client Services for NetWare

7. What client software must be installed on a Macintosh client system to enable it to connect to a NetWare server?
   a. File and Print Sharing
   b. File Sharing for Macintosh
   c. Services for UNIX
   d. Macintosh Client for NetWare

8. When you connect a Windows or Linux system to a Macintosh server, what program is used to share the Mac resources?
   a. Macintosh Client for NetWare
   b. File Sharing for Macintosh
   c. AppleShare IP
   d. Client Services for NetWare

9. What program can you install on a Macintosh serving system in a smaller network, where you don't need all the extras that come with AppleShare IP, to enable a Windows system to access shared resources on that Mac?
   a. TCP/IP
   b. DAVE
   c. WIN2MAC
   d. File Sharing for Macintosh

10. Windows 2000 has a built-in terminal emulator. What is it called?
    a. Windows 2000 Terminal Services
    b. Windows 2000 Terminal Emulator
    c. Windows 2000 Telnet
    d. Windows 2000 Emulation Services

Answers

1. A. The universal adoption of TCP/IP has made interconnectivity much easier than it was in the days when different networks ran IPX/SPX, NetBEUI, LocalTalk, and other network protocols.

2. **D.**   Many older Macs use the LocalTalk protocol and most Windows systems use NetBEUI or TCP/IP. Later Macs all use TCP/IP, but if the Network+ exam says Macintosh, assume LocalTalk.

3. **C.**   SAMBA makes a Linux system look like a Windows 9*x* system, and enables it to access a Windows system's shared folders.

4. **D.**   The NFS protocol is the closest thing the TCP world has to Windows' folder sharing functions. Installing an NFS server program on a Windows 9*x* system will enable it to share its folders just like a Linux system.

5. **B.**   With File Sharing for Macintosh and AppleTalk protocol support, Windows NT Server and Windows 2000 Server have everything they need to provide Macintosh clients with seamless interconnectivity to Windows NT/2000 serving systems.

6. **C.**   Microsoft provides a product called Services for UNIX (SFU) to enable NT and 2000 serving systems to share their resources with Linux clients, but it comes as an add-on, and at additional cost.

7. **D.**   A Macintosh client needs Macintosh Client for NetWare software to connect to a NetWare server.

8. **C.**   The AppleShare IP program enables a Macintosh serving system to share its resources with Windows and Linux clients. AppleShare IP has built-in SMB support, making it something like a SAMBA for Macintosh. AppleShare also provides printing support, but only to clients running the TCP/IP LPR program—which isn't a problem since Windows and Linux clients both support LPR.

9. **B.**   In a smaller network, where you don't need all the extras that come with AppleShare IP, you can install a program called DAVE on a Macintosh serving system, enabling Windows clients to access shared folders and printers on the Mac.

10. **A.**   Windows' built-in terminal emulator is called Windows 2000 Terminal Services.

The Perfect Server

In this chapter, you will

- Learn about connectivity hardware
- Understand methods and hardware used for protecting data
- Master server-specific hardware for boosting speed
- Learn methods and hardware used for server reliability

The job of networking demands fundamental hardware differences between a PC that connects to a network and a PC that does not connect to a network. Arguably, the designers of the Personal Computer never considered the PC as a device to participate in a network. You can't blame them. The original PC simply didn't pack the necessary firepower to function in any but the most primitive of networks. The first PCs used tiny (less than 10 megabyte) hard drives—or only floppy drives—and the 4.77-MHz Intel 8088 simply could not handle the many calculations demanded by even the most basic network operating systems. The mainframe-centric world of IBM created the PC to work primarily as an individual computer, a stand-alone system, or to perform as a *dumb* terminal for mainframe access. While networks were not part of the original PC concept, the ongoing improvements in the power and phenomenal flexibly of PCs enabled them to move easily from a world of individual, stand-alone systems, into the interactive world of connected, networked machines. Even though any stand-alone PC transforms nicely into a networked machine, the very different jobs of a stand-alone vs. a networked machine require significantly different hardware in each. What are these requirements? What hardware does a networked PC need that a stand-alone PC can live without? The network functions themselves supply the answers (see Figure 20-1).

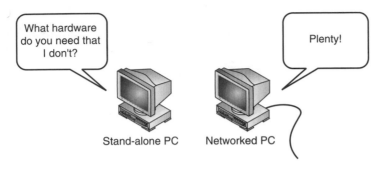

Figure 20-1 Networked PCs need more hardware.

Historical/Conceptual

A networked PC has four significant functions. First, it must connect to the network. This connection usually runs through a cable of some type, but wireless networks are becoming more common.

Second, if the PC shares data, the PC needs to protect that shared data by creating more than one copy of the data. The data is usually copied with multiple storage devices—almost always hard drives—that work together to create multiple copies of data.

Third, and again only if the PC shares data, it needs specialized hardware that enables it to share the data as quickly as possible. A sharing PC often uses a number of different hardware technologies to increase the speed with which it shares its resources. A good example of a speed technology is a specialized network card that enables faster data access.

The fourth and last function unique to a network PC is reliability. The shared resources of the network must be available whenever another system accesses them. The networked PC must use special hardware to prevent a sharing system from failing to provide their shared resources. Were not talking about more hard drives here; we've already covered that! Reliability means methods to make good and sure the PC doesn't stop working due to a failed component. These hardware devices manifest themselves in items such as redundant power supplies or air conditioning units. Together or separately, every network PC has at least one of these four functions (see Figure 20-2).

The process of deciding which functions appear in a network PC is determined by the job of that particular system. The biggest line of demarcation is between systems that share resources (servers) and systems that only access the server's shared resources

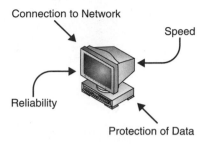

Connection to Network

Speed

Reliability

Protection of Data

Figure 20-2   The four network functions

(workstations). The hardware requirements for a workstation and a server differ fundamentally. The only specialized function of a workstation is connecting to the network via a NIC. Workstations do not share resources, so they have little need for reliability, speed, and data protection beyond that already built into any stand-alone PC. Servers, on the other hand, use all of the functions, creating the need for highly specialized systems full of specialized hardware to provide most, if not all, of these four network functions. The incorporation of the specialized hardware usually makes a server system stand out compared to a workstation, especially if you purchase a pre-ready server system (see Figure 20-3).

Keep in mind that there is no requirement for a serving system to have the extra hardware. Virtually any PC can act as a serving system—as long as you are willing to put up with lack of reliability, slower response times, and the higher potential for data loss. Equally, in peer-to-peer networks, some, most, or all of the systems act as servers. It is usually logistically impractical and financially imprudent to give every user in a peer-to-peer network a powerful server system (although if you did, you'd be extremely popular!). A good network person considers the network functions of a particular system to

Figure 20-3   A typical network server

Figure 20-4 Do I really need this for a workgroup printer?

determine which ones the system actually needs. They then balance the needed network functions against cost, time, and support needs to determine what hardware a particular system needs (see Figure 20-4).

Test Specific

So, all networked PCs need at least one of these four network functions: connections, data safety, speed, and reliability. In this chapter, we explore these four network functions in great detail and tour the wide variety of hardware, software, and organization solutions used in today's networks to fulfill the needs of these four functions. Let's go!

Connecting to a Network

A network PC must communicate with other networked PCs. There can be little argument that the connecting to the network function is the first and certainly the most obvious function of a networked PC. Most PCs connect to a network through a Network Interface Card (NIC) (see Figure 20-5).

Using NICs is the most common, but not the only method, for connecting PCs to networks. Others include using wireless networks (in reality, wireless networks are simply special NICs connected to a radio or infrared transmitter/receiver), modems, and direct serial-to-serial or parallel-to-parallel port connections (Windows calls this a *direct cable connection* [DCC]). In Chapter 8, you learned about NIC cards. In this chapter, we

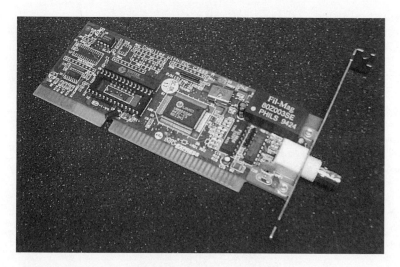

PART III

Figure 20-5 A typical older NIC

will take a look at other connections and learn that they all share many common issues. We can then look at how to use (or not use) these connections in a network, so that when it comes time to plug something in, we do it correctly.

The Modems

Modems stand second only to NICs as the most common way to connect a PC to a network. For some reason, the idea of a modem as a network connection confuses folks new to networking. They want to separate the idea of dialing up from using a NIC. This problem tends to show up more in techs that remember the days when a modem was used to dial up private bulletin boards, before the Internet became so common. Don't do this! All network operating systems look at a modem as nothing more than another type of NIC. Windows 9x even shows the modem as an adapter in the Network Properties window. Go to a networked Windows 9x system with a modem installed and right-click Network Neighborhood, then select Properties. You'll see something like what's shown in Figure 20-6.

Modems take analog serial data (the phone line) and turn it into digital serial data. There are two types of modems, internal and external. Internal modems go inside the PC, while external modems are little boxes that connect to the PC via a serial port (see Figure 20-7).

Once a modem has turned the analog phone signal into a digital signal, the data must then be changed to a digital format that the PC can understand. That's where the

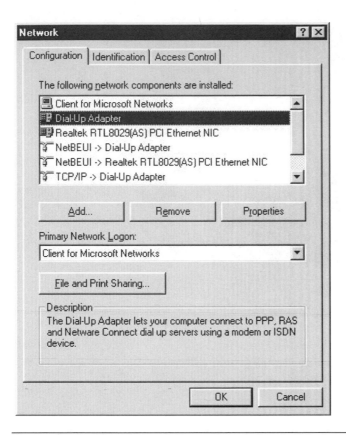

Figure 20-6   The Network Properties window in Windows 98

Figure 20-7   Internal and external modems

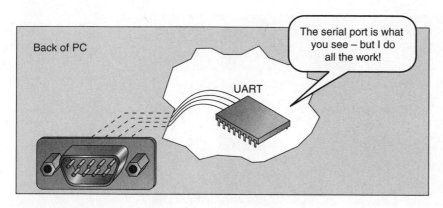

Figure 20-8   A UART and a serial port

serial port comes in. The serial connector leads to a special chip called a Universal Asynchronous Receiver/Transmitter (UART) (see Figure 20-8).

The UART takes digital serial data from the modem and converts it into parallel data that makes sense to the PC. A serial port is really just a connection to a UART. External modems don't have UARTs and must connect to a serial port on the PC. Internal modems, meanwhile, are really a UART and a modem on one card. An internal modem, therefore, brings its own UART to the PC. There are many types of UARTs, but the only one worth purchasing—and by now the only one you can buy—is called a 16550 UART. The 16550 can run the serial ports at 115,600 bits per second—faster than the fastest modems.

Phone lines have a speed based on a unit called a *baud*, which translates as a cycle per second. The fastest baud rate that a phone line can achieve is 2400 baud, And Modems can pack multiple bits of data into each baud. A 33.6 kilobits per second (Kbps) modem, for example, packs 14 bits into every baud (or $2400 \times 14 = 33.6K$). It is technically incorrect to say, "I have a 56K baud modem." You should say, "I have a 56-Kbps modem." But people use the term baud instead of bps so often that the terms have become functionally synonymous.

Looking at a modem as nothing more than another NIC makes sense. Sure, modems have a few extra requirements during installation, but generally they still need the same items a NIC does. The other nice thing about modems is that there is only one type of connection—good 'ol RJ-11 (see Figure 20-9).

One RJ-11 connector goes to the phone jack; the other enables you to install a telephone. Compared to NICs, modems are trivial to identify! Modems come in a number of speeds and other important controls. Refer to Chapter 17 for these details on modems.

Figure 20-9 An internal modem, showing RJ-11

System Resources

This section assumes you know your system resources. If you are not aware of system resources, the short descriptions given here are sufficient to pass the Network+ exam. Any good tech, however, should know them in better detail. For those of you who don't, here's the Reader's Digest version. For a detailed study of system resources, get my *All-in-One A+ Certification Exam Guide*!

Modems and NICs require system resources in order to function properly. Don't worry about *how* to set these resources at this point; just be aware that they exist. We'll get to the process of setting system resources next.

System resources is a Microsoft term, now part of tech vernacular, that describes four totally different PC functions. The first of these functions is the Interrupt Request (IRQ). Every device that wants to tell the CPU that it needs to talk to that particular device must have an assigned IRQ. Virtually every device in the PC uses an IRQ. Certainly, all NICs and modems must have an assigned IRQ. There are a number of IRQs on a PC, but required devices such as hard drives and floppy drives take up many of them. See Table 20-1 for the complete IRQ list and the devices that use them.

Don't let this table deceive you. Only one device can use a particular IRQ. If you have installed a sound card and it is using IRQ 10, for example, you cannot use IRQ 10 for your NIC. Be aware of the fact that if the default device is not using an IRQ, the IRQ is open for use. Looking again at the table, note that IRQ 5 is for a second parallel port. Most PCs do not have a second parallel port. IRQ 5 therefore is pretty much always available on a PC.

The second, and also required, system resource is called the I/O address. *Every* device in the PC has an I/O address. Think of it as the phone number for a particular compo-

Table 20-1 IRQs

IRQ	Default Function	Available?
IRQ 0	System timer	No
IRQ 1	Keyboard	No
IRQ 2/9	Open for use	Yes
IRQ 3	Serial ports	Yes
IRQ 4	Serial ports	Yes
IRQ 5	Second parallel port	Yes
IRQ 6	Floppy drive	No
IRQ 7	Primary parallel port	No
IRQ 8	Real-time clock	No
IRQ 10	Open for use	Yes
IRQ 11	Open for use	Yes
IRQ 12	Open for use	Yes
IRQ 13	Math-coprocessor	No
IRQ 14	Primary hard drive controller	No
IRQ 15	Secondary hard drive controller	No

nent. A four-digit hexadecimal number designates I/O addresses. Following are a few examples of common I/O addresses on a PC:

    0060   Keyboard

    01F0   Primary hard drive controller

    03F0   Floppy drive controller

Both NICs and modems absolutely require I/O addresses and IRQs. If you install either of these, you must give the NIC or modem an unused I/O address and IRQ. There are two other system resources that NICs *might* need: a DMA channel and a memory address. Modems only need an I/O address and an IRQ; they never need these other two system resources.

DMA stands for *Direct Memory Access* and is used by a few devices, notably sound cards and the floppy drive, to talk directly to RAM without any intervention by the CPU.

Many years ago, DMA was a popular method of speeding up a device, but with today's very fast computers, it is rarely used (aside from the two exceptions already noted). A *DMA Channel* is a wire used by the device to perform a DMA. There are seven DMA channels on the PC. Table 20-2 has the complete list.

Modern NICs rarely require DMA, but be aware that DMA is a system resource and that a NIC might need to have a DMA assigned when it is installed. DMA channels should be treated exactly like IRQs: No two devices should ever share a DMA channel.

The fourth and last system resource is the *memory address*. Some NICs must have a tiny amount of RAM set aside for their own use. The memory address is the location of this set aside RAM, and is defined by eight hexadecimal digits. No device uses just one memory address, of course; what you will encounter are *ranges* of memory addresses. As an example, here is a range of memory addresses used by video cards:

000A0000-000AFFFF   Video Graphics

Today, only video cards still use memory addresses in PCs, while most NICs today do not require them at all.

Well, that's it for the Reader's Digest description of system resources. It's not critical to understand exactly *what* a system resource is. Just remember that there are four of them—I/O address, IRQ, DMA, and memory address—and that all NICs and modems will need an I/O address and an IRQ. Only NICs and not modems might need a DMA channel or a memory address.

When IBM first invented the PC, they realized that some people might have trouble setting IRQs and I/O addresses. To make device configuration easier, IBM defined preset combinations of I/O addresses and IRQs for the serial and parallel connectors. IBM

Table 20-2 DMA Channels

DMA Channel	Default Function	Available?
DMA 0/4	System	No
DMA 1	Open for use	Yes
DMA 2	Floppy drive	No
DMA 3	Open for use	Yes
DMA 5	Open for use	Yes
DMA 6	Open for use	Yes
DMA 7	Open for use	Yes

called these preset combinations *ports* to reflect that the serial and parallel ports would function as data *portals*. They called serial ports *COM* ports and the parallel ports *LPT* ports. These ports are still used today. Table 20-3 has the list of ports as defined by IBM so long ago.

Ports enable people to install serial and parallel devices without having to worry too much about resources. If you want to install an external modem, for example, you simply plug it into one of the two built-in serial ports. In the original IBM PC, the first serial port was preset as I/O address 03F8 and IRQ 4 (COM1). The other serial port was preset as I/O address 02F8 and IRQ 3 (COM2)—a common configuration today. Plug the modem into one serial port or the other and then configure the modem software to look on the correct port simply by selecting the appropriate COM port number from a list. Internal modems came (and still do) with their own built-in serial port. Instead of setting an I/O address and an IRQ on an internal modem, you set a COM port on the modem. You do not have to know that selecting a COM port actually sets the I/O address and IRQ, you just set the COM port and it works! COM and LPT ports were a very handy item years ago, and remain useful today.

Ports can also cause confusion. Philip's system has a serial mouse installed on COM1. That means that IRQ 4 is used, correct? No other device can use IRQ 4, so if you accidentally installed, say, a modem and used IRQ 4, his computer would lock up the moment he tried to use either the mouse or the modem. That is, as we say in the business, a bad thing. But it was easy to do since nobody knew that COM1 was, by definition, I/O address 03F8 and IRQ 4! The few techs that understood this back in the bad old days made a mint!

To make matters worse, notice that COM1 and COM3 share IRQ 4 while COM2 and COM4 share IRQ 3. This means you cannot have a device using COM1 and COM3 (or COM2 and COM4) at the same time. If you try, they'll lock up.

Table 20-3 COM and LPT Ports

COM/LPT Port Name	I/O Address	IRQ
COM1	03F8	4
COM2	02F8	3
COM3	03E8	4
COM4	02E8	3
LPT1	0378	7
LPT2	0278	5

PART III

Fortunately, most internal modems can use non-standard IRQs for their COM ports. Mabel's PC, for example, has devices installed on COM1 and COM2. You need to install an internal modem in her system, which must have a COM port. You set it to COM3 (and create a potential IRQ conflict), but then set the IRQ to something like IRQ 10. Assuming no device uses IRQ 10, everything works perfectly.

Before Windows 95, the process of installing devices, including NICs and modems, was only performed by techs with an intimate knowledge of system resources and ports. The introduction of Windows 95 brought a powerful new standard called Plug and Play (PnP), which is a combination of smart PCs, smart devices, and smart operating systems that automatically configure all of the necessary system resources. With PnP operating properly, there is no need to know anything about system resources or ports. The computer handles all of these details automatically. All new—and not so new—NICs and modems are PnP.

If PnP is so great, why even discuss system resources? Three issues require network technicians to have a thorough understanding of resources. First, and perhaps most shocking, PnP does not always work perfectly and occasionally requires a little manual configuration. Second, millions of older devices came out before PnP. These *legacy* devices require you to understand system resources in detail. Third, and possibly most important, the Network+ exam tests you on system resources. Know your resources!

Protection of Data

The single most important part of most networks is the shared data. The main motivation for networks is the ability for many users to access shared data. This shared data might be as trivial as premade forms or as critical as accounts receivable information. The sudden loss of data in their networks would cripple most organizations. Computers can be replaced and new employees hired, but the data is what makes most organizations function. Certainly, any good network must include a solid backup plan, but restoring backups takes time and effort. Unless the data is being continually backed up, the backups will always be a little dated. Backups are a last resort option. Businesses have failed after the loss of data—even with relatively good backups. The shared data of a network therefore should have better protection than the fallback of laboriously having to restore potentially dated backups! A good network must have a method of protecting data such that if a hard drive fails, a network technician can bring the data instantly, or at least very quickly, back online. This requires some sort of instant backup or automatic copy of the data stored on a second drive.

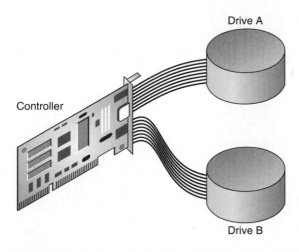

Drive A

Controller

Drive B

Figure 20-10 Mirrored drives

Okay, so you need to come up with a way to make data redundant on the serving system. How do you do this? Well, first of all, you could install some fancy hard drive controller that reads and writes data to two hard drives simultaneously (see Figure 20-10). This would ensure that the data on each drive was always identical. One drive would be the primary drive, while the other drive, called the *mirror* drive, would not be used unless the primary drive failed. This process of reading and writing data at the same time to two drives is called *drive mirroring*.

If you really want to make data safe, you can use two separate controllers for each drive. With two drives, each on a separate controller, the system will continue to operate, even if the primary drive's controller stops working. This super-drive mirroring technique is called *drive duplexing* (see Figure 20-11), and is much faster than drive mirroring since one controller does not write each piece of data twice.

Even though drive duplexing is faster than drive mirroring, they both are slower than the classic one drive, one controller setup. The third and most common way to create redundant data is by a method called disk striping with parity. *Disk striping* (without parity) means to spread the data among multiple (at least two) drives. Disk striping by itself provides no redundancy. If you save a small Microsoft Word file, for example, the file is split into multiple pieces; half of the pieces go on one drive and half on the other (see Figure 20-12).

The one and only advantage of disk striping is speed—it is a very fast way to read and write to hard drives. But if either drive fails, *all* data is lost. Disk striping is not

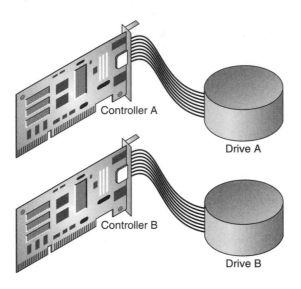

Figure 20-11   Duplexing drives

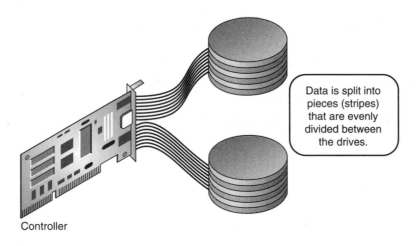

Data is split into pieces (stripes) that are evenly divided between the drives.

Controller

Figure 20-12   Disk striping

something we ever want to do—unless you simply don't care about data. Nobody does disk striping!

Disk striping with parity, in contrast, protects data. Disk striping with parity adds an extra drive, called a parity drive, that stores information that can be used to rebuild data should one of the data drives fail. Let's look at that same Microsoft Word document used earlier. The data is still stored on the two data drives, but this time a calculation is done on the data from each equivalent location on the data drives to create parity information on the parity drive. This parity data is created by a simple, but very accurate calculation. It's similar to dividing two numbers and storing the result of the division. The calculation is not important; the fact that the parity data can be used to rebuild either drive is, however.

Disk striping with parity must have at least three drives, but it's common to see more than three. Unfortunately, the more drives used, the higher the chance one might fail. Disk striping with parity can only recover data if one drive fails. If two drives fail, you're heading for the backup tapes!

Disk striping with parity combines the best of disk mirroring and plain disk striping. It protects data and is quite fast. In fact, the majority of network servers use a type of disk striping with parity.

RAID

The many different techniques of using multiple drives for data protection and increasing speeds were organized by a couple of sharp guys at Berkeley back in the '80s. This organization was presented under the name Random Array of Inexpensive Disks (RAID) or Random Array of Independent Disks. There are seven official levels of RAID, numbered 0 through 6, which are as follows:

- **RAID 0** Disk striping
- **RAID 1** Disk mirroring and disk duplexing
- **RAID 2** Disk striping with multiple parity drives. Unused, ignore it.
- **RAID 3 and RAID 4** Disk striping with parity. The differences between the two are trivial.
- **RAID 5** Disk striping with parity, where parity information is placed on all drives. This is the fastest way to provide data redundancy. RAID 5 is the most common RAID implementation.
- **RAID 6** RAID 5 with the added capability of asynchronous and cached data transmission. Think of it as a Super RAID 5.

No network tech worth her salt says things like "We're implementing disk striping with parity." Use the RAID level. Say, "We're implementing RAID 5." It's more accurate and very impressive to the folks in Accounting!

Drive Technologies

Talking about RAID levels is like singing about Einstein's Theory of Brownian motion. You may sound good, but that doesn't mean you know what you are talking about! Remember that RAID levels are a general framework; they describe methods to provide data redundancy and enhance the speed of data throughput to and from groups of hard drives. They do not say *how* to implement these methods. There are literally thousands of different methods to actually set up RAID. The method used depends largely on the desired level of RAID, the operating system used, and the thickness of your wallet. Before we delve into these solutions, however, let's do a quick run-through of hard drive technologies to make a few terms more clear.

EIDE   If you peek into most desktop PCs, you will find hard drives based on the ultra popular Enhanced Intelligent Device Electronics or Enhanced Integrated Device Electronics (EIDE) standard. EIDE drives are always internal—inside the PC, which is designed to use up to four EIDE drives. EIDE drives can be identified by their unique 40-pin ribbon cable connection (see Figure 20-13).

The price, performance, and ease of installation explain the tremendous popularity of EIDE drives. IDE, the predecessor to EIDE, was exclusively a hard drive technology. EIDE can accept any type of storage device, including CD-ROMs, tape backups, and removable drives. Even with the ability to handle diverse devices, the PC cannot handle more than the maximum of four EIDE devices without special additional hardware. For example, my new high-end motherboard has a total of four EIDE slots, two of which are standard slots, and two of which are RAID-capable.

Figure 20-13   EIDE connections

SCSI   Small computer system interface (SCSI) accomplishes much the same goals as EIDE—making hard drives and other devices available to the PC. SCSI, however, is not a hard drive technology. Think instead of SCSI as a mini network that connects many different types of devices. Any kind of storage device you can imagine comes in a SCSI version—for instance, SCSI manifests itself in PCs via a card called a *Host adapter*. This host adapter then connects to SCSI devices in a daisy-chain (see Figure 20-14). An installed set of SCSI devices is called a *SCSI Chain*.

Each SCSI device on the SCSI chain must have a unique SCSI ID. SCSI devices are numbered 0 through 7, with 7 usually reserved for the host adapter itself. More advanced versions of SCSI can support up to 16 devices (including the host adapter).

SCSI devices can be internal or external. Better host adapters come with an internal and an external connector, enabling both types of devices to exist on the same SCSI chain. Figure 20-15 shows a SCSI chain with both internal and external devices. Note that each device gets a unique SCSI ID.

SCSI Connections   Fortunately, the Network+ exam isn't interested in your ability to configure SCSI. It does, however, demand you know the many connections unique to SCSI devices. No other class of device has as many connections as SCSI. This is because SCSI has been in existence for a long time and has gone through four distinct

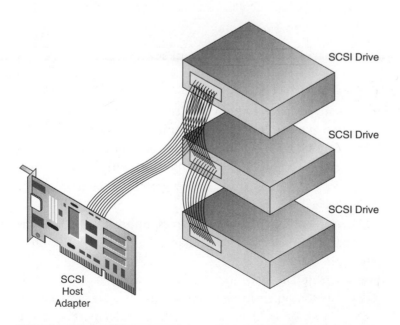

Figure 20-14   A SCSI chain

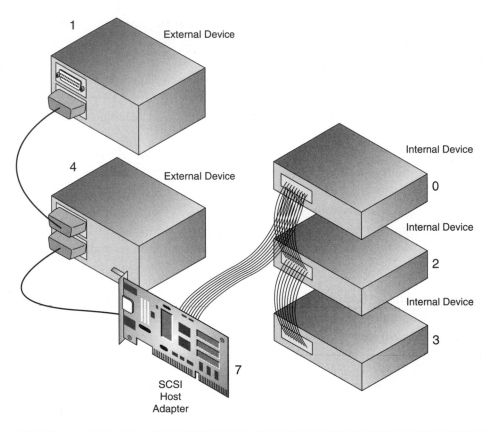

Figure 20-15   A typical SCSI chain with internal and external devices

standard upgrades, fostering many variations within each standard over the years.

SCSI devices can be both external (outside of the PC) or internal (inside the PC), giving SCSI drives an advantage over EIDE. There are two types of internal SCSI connections, both of which are inserted into a ribbon cable, just like EIDE: the 50-pin narrow connection and the 68-pin wide SCSI. Figure 20-16 shows a typical 50-pin narrow connection with a ribbon cable attached.

The oldest external SCSI connection is a 50-pin Centronics. Although dated, a large number of SCSI devices still use this connector. It looks like a slightly longer version of the printer Centronics (see Figure 20-17).

Many host adapters use a female DB-25 connector. Apple has been using female DB-25 connectors for SCSI on its computers for many years, but they are fairly new to PCs. This Apple-style SCSI connector is identical to a PC parallel port (see Figure 20-18), which is unfortunate because they are not electrically compatible. If you

Figure 20-16 The 50-pin narrow SCSI connection

Figure 20-17 The 50-pin SCSI Centronics connection

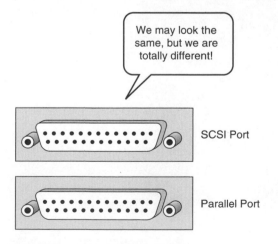

Figure 20-18 Parallel and SCSI connections—both DB-25s

plug your printer into the SCSI port, or a SCSI device into the printer, it definitely will not work—and in some cases may damage devices!

Most modern SCSI devices now come with the special, SCSI-only, high-density DB connectors. High-density DB connectors look like regular DBs at first, but have much thinner and more densely packed pins. High-density DB connectors come in 50- and 68-pin versions, the former being the more common of the two (see Figure 20-19).

They Both Work!   Both EIDE and SCSI drives work beautifully for RAID implementations. People who are new to RAID immediately assume that RAID requires some special, expensive stack of SCSI drives. Such is not the case. You certainly can spend the money on fancy RAID boxes, but you do not have to go that route. You can easily implement RAID using nothing but inexpensive EIDE drives and cheap, sometimes free software. Furthermore, RAID can use combinations of EIDE and SCSI (although trying to keep track of combinations of SCSI and EIDE drives is not recommended!). In fact, EIDE RAID arrays have lately become so stable that they rival the security that only SCSI used to promise. The only real distinction nowadays is a difference in access speed.

Most people prefer SCSI drives for RAID, because they tend to be faster than EIDE drives and you can put more drives into a system (7 to 15, rather than the 4 in EIDE). The only drawback with SCSI is cost—hard drives are more expensive and you often must purchase a host adapter as well. When speed outweighs cost as a factor—and it

Figure 20-19   The high-density DB-50

usually does for servers—SCSI implementations win out. Finally, if you need serious speed and extra bells and whistles, you can install any number of expensive "stack of SCSI drives" solutions.

RAID Implementations

All RAID implementations break down into either hardware or software methods. Software is often used when price takes priority over performance. Hardware is used when you need speed along with data redundancy. The most famous software implementation of RAID is the built-in RAID software that comes with Windows NT/Windows 2000. The NT Disk Administrator can configure drives for RAID 0, 1, or 5, and it works with EIDE and or SCSI (see Figure 20-20).

NT is not the only software RAID game in town. There are a number of third-party software programs available that can be used with other operating systems. There are even third-party software RAID solutions for NT that add a number of extra features above what the Disk Administrator provides.

Most techs and administrators prefer hardware RAID. Software RAID works for very small RAID solutions, but tends to run quite slowly and usually requires shutting down the PC to reconfigure and replace drives. When you *really* need to keep going, when you

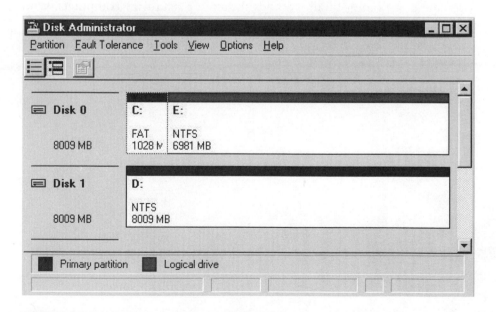

Figure 20-20 The NT Disk Administrator

need RAID that doesn't even let the users know there was ever a problem, hardware RAID is the only answer. Since most organizations fit into this latter category, most RAID in the real world is hardware-based. There are a large number of hardware RAID solutions, and almost all these solutions rely on SCSI. SCSI can do one thing that EIDE still cannot do—assuming that you have the right type of host adapter, you can yank a bad SCSI drive off of a SCSI chain and replace it with another one without even rebooting the server. This *hot-swapping* process is very common in hardware RAID (see Figure 20-21).

RAID provides data redundancy. Implementing RAID requires that you decide the level of RAID you wish to use and whether you want to go the hardware or software route. For the exam, make sure you can quote the different levels of RAID and know your SCSI connections. You'll fly through those questions without any difficulty!

Tape Backup

Various RAID solutions provide data redundancy to a certain degree, but to secure your server data fully, nothing beats a tape backup. If the RAID solution works properly, that tape backup can happily collect dust on an off-site shelf somewhere. In the event of a catastrophic hardware crash, however, such as when two drives in your disk stripe with parity suddenly go to that hardware heaven in the sky, only that tape can save the day.

Magnetic tape is the oldest of all methods for storing data with computers. Who hasn't seen an episode of the old TV shows like Time Tunnel or Voyage to the Bottom of the Sea and watched the old reel-to-reel tapes spinning merrily in the background?

Figure 20-21   Hot swapping a drive

The reel-to-reels are gone, replaced by hard drives; tapes are now relegated to the world of backup. Nothing can beat magnetic tape's ability to store phenomenal amounts of data cheaply and safely.

Every properly designed network uses a tape backup, so every network tech must learn to use them. The type of tape backup implemented varies from network to network, as do the methods for backing up data. This section covers the types of tape backup; refer to the Troubleshooting chapter for the methods.

There are a dizzying number of tape backup options, each with different advantages and disadvantages. They basically break down into three major groups: QIC, DAT, and DLT. All of the groups similarly use cartridge tapes—square tapes like fat audio cassettes —but the physical cartridge size, capacity, recording method, tape length, and speed vary enormously.

QIC

Quarter-Inch Tape (QIC) is an old standard and rarely used in any but the smallest of networks. QIC was one of the first standards used for PC backups, but has gone through many evolutions in an attempt to keep up with the demand for increased capacities over the years. The earliest versions of QIC could store about 40 megabytes—fine for the days when tiny hard drives were the rule, but unacceptable today. There have been a number of increases in QIC capacities, as high as two gigabytes, but QIC has fallen out as a desired tape standard. Imation Corporation created an improved QIC format called Travan that is quite popular, again on smaller networks, with capacities of up to 8 gigabytes. Under the Travan banner, QIC lives on as a tape backup option. Older QIC/Travan drives used a floppy connection, but EIDE or SCSI connections are more common today.

DAT

Digital Audio Tape (DAT) was the first tape system to use a totally digital recording method. DAT was originally designed to record digital audio and video, but has easily moved into the tape backup world. DAT tapes have much higher storage capacities than QIC/Travan tapes—up to 24 gigabytes—and are popular for medium-sized networks. DAT drives use a SCSI connection.

DLT

Digital Linear Tape (DLT) is quickly becoming the tape backup standard of choice. It's a relatively new standard that has massive data capacity (up to 70 gigabytes), is very fast, incredibly reliable, and quite expensive compared to earlier technologies. When the data is critical, however, the price of the tape backup is considered insignificant. DLT drives use a SCSI connection.

Data Redundancy Is the Key

Data redundancy provides networks with one of the most important things they need —security. Improper preparation for the day a server hard drive dies leads to many quickly prepared résumés for the suddenly out of work network technician. When the data is important enough (and when *isn't* it?), providing data redundancy via RAID solutions is required for the properly designed network.

Speed

A system providing a resource to a network has a tough job. It needs to be able to handle thousands, millions, even billions of transactions over the network to provide that shared resource to other systems. All of this work can bring a standard desktop PC to its knees. Anyone who has taken a regular desktop PC and shared a folder or a printer and watched their PC act as though it just shifted into first gear can attest to the fact that sharing resources is a drain on a PC. Systems that share resources, and especially dedicated servers, require more powerful, faster hardware to be able to respond to the needs of the network.

There are a number of methods for making a serving system faster. Making a good server isn't just a matter of buying faster or multiple CPUs. You can't just dump in tons of the fastest RAM. Fast CPUs and RAM are very important, but there are two other critical areas that tend to be ignored—a good server needs fast NICs and fast drives.

Fast NICs

The first place to look when thinking of making a server faster is the NIC. Placing the same NIC in your server that you place in your workstations is like putting a garden hose on a fire hydrant—it just isn't designed to handle the job. There are a number of methods for making the NIC better suited to the task. You can increase the megabits (the data throughput), make the NIC smarter, pickier, and make it do more than one thing at a time. A lot of this was covered in detail in Chapter 6, so let's simply do the high points here.

Increase the Megabits

Mixing 10- and 100-megabit Ethernet on your network can optimize network performance. The trick is to have the server part of the network run at a faster speed than the rest of the network. If you have a 10BaseT network, you can purchase a switch that has a couple of 100 megabit ports. Put a 100BaseT NIC in the server and connect it to one of the 100BaseT connectors on the switch. The server runs at 100 Mbps while the workstations run at 10 Mbps (see Figure 20-22). This optimizes the server speed and, since the server does most of the work in the network, optimizes your network as well.

Smarter NICs

Many NICs still need the CPU to handle most of the network job, but several companies make powerful NICs with onboard processors that take most of the work away from the CPU. Every NIC manufacturer has a different method to provide this support and those methods are way outside the scope of this book. From a network person's standpoint, just buy a special server NIC, plug that sucker in, and enjoy the benefits of faster response times.

Full-duplex NICs

Most network technologies consist of send and receive wires, and most NICs can handle only sending or receiving at a given moment. Full-duplex NICs can both send and receive data at the same time, which practically doubles the speed of the network card.

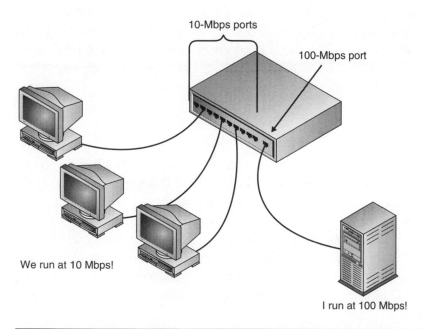

Figure 20-22   The server runs at 100 Mbps; workstations at 10 Mbps.

Make sure your server NICs are full-duplex, but be warned that you may need to upgrade the server's hub to take advantage of full-duplex!

Making the NIC better is one of the easiest upgrades to a server as it usually means simply yanking out an inferior NIC and replacing it with something better. At worst, you may have to replace a hub or switch. Make your NIC better and you'll see the results.

Make the Drives Faster

The other big way to increase a server's speed is to make the process of getting the data to and from the shared drives faster. There are two big options here. First is to get fast drives. Using run of the mill EIDE drives in a busy serving system is not smart. Try using high performance SCSI drives on a fast controller. It makes a big difference. Second, use RAID 5. Since you probably need it for data protection anyway, you'll also enjoy the speed.

It's Not Just Hardware

The demands of networking require servers to have better hardware than your run-of-the-mill stand-alone PC. Improving CPUs, adding RAM, using powerful NICs, and running fast hard drives all work together to make your serving PC more powerful. But hardware is not the only answer. Good maintenance, such as defragging and setting up good disk caches, also plays an important role. Many times, slow resource access is due to poor network design and is not the fault of the serving system. Be careful about throwing hardware at the slow access issues; it can often be a big waste of money!

Reliability

The last network function, primarily for serving systems, is reliability. The shared resource must be there when the user needs it. Reliability is achieved by providing a secure environment for the server and by adding redundant hardware to compensate for failed components. There is a nasty tendency to mistake reliability for data protection. Don't confuse the two. All the pretty RAID systems aren't going to do you any good if somebody steals the server. Tape backups are useless if the power supply dies. Clearly, other technologies are needed to keep the serving system reliable. There is no logical order to explaining these technologies and safeguards, so we will cover them in no particular order.

Good Power

All of the components in the PC run on DC current electrical power. Without clean, steady, DC power, the components stop working. There are a number of steps that electrical power must take between the power company and those components. At any given moment, if one of those steps fails to do its part, the PC no longer works. You can take several actions to safeguard your hardware to make sure this doesn't happen, starting with the power company.

Electrical power in the United States is a wonderful commodity. Electrical service is pretty reliable, and the electricity is generally of high quality. Most folks in the United States can count on a good electrical service 98 percent of the time. It's that other 2 percent that will get you! Electrical power sometimes stops (power outages) and sometimes goes bad (electrical spikes and sags). Additionally, techs (and non-techs alike) can screw up perfectly good electricity on their own by overloading circuits with too much equipment. You can protect the servers from problems of power outages, electrical spikes, and overloaded circuits with several important technologies—dedicated circuits, surge suppressors, UPSs, and backup power.

Dedicated Circuits

A *dedicated circuit* is a circuit that runs from the breaker box to only certain outlets. In most homes and offices, a circuit might have many jobs. The circuit that runs your PC might also run the office water cooler and the big laser printer. Using too many devices on one circuit causes the power to sag, which might cause your computer to do nothing, lock up, or spontaneously reboot. It all depends on how lucky you are at that moment! Dedicated circuits keep this from happening. In most cases, dedicated circuits have outlets with bright orange faceplates to let you know that they are dedicated. This will (theoretically) prevent some uninformed person from plugging a photocopier into the circuit.

Surge Suppressors

It almost sounds silly to talk about suppressors these days, doesn't it? Does anyone really need to be convinced that all PCs, both network and stand-alone, need surge suppressors? An electrical surge—a sudden increase in the voltage on a circuit—can (and will) destroy an unprotected computer. Translation: Every computer should plug into a surge suppressor!

UPS

An uninterruptible power supply (UPS) is standard equipment for servers. Many UPSs also provide protection from spikes and sags. Most only offer a few minutes of power, but it's enough to enable the server to shut down cleanly. All servers will have a UPS.

Backup Power

When you really want to be reliable, get a backup power supply. No, you don't have to put a diesel generator in the basement! There are a number of small battery-based backup systems that will provide a few hours of protection. If you want something that will last for a few days, however, you will need a gasoline/diesel backup system.

The Computer Virus

Ah, would that the only problem you faced was with faulty power. But alas, this is not the case. There are a large number of computer viruses and malicious code just waiting to infect your network. So what do you do when you think your computer has caught a code? In this chapter, you will find out.

The words "I think your machine has a virus" can send shudders down the back of even the most competent technician. The thought of megabytes of critical data being wiped away by the work of some evil programmer is at best annoying—and at worst a serious financial disaster.

So, where do viruses come from? Just like many human viruses, they live in host bodies—in this case, computers. Your computer can only catch one if it interacts with other computers, or with programs or data from an infected computer. Problem is, these days almost everyone's computer (aside from folks like the CIA) is connected to the Internet, and thereby to many, many other computers. Also, many viruses are spread through the sharing of programs or information on floppy disks or CD-ROMs.

How do you know if you've caught a virus? You feel sluggish, start sneezing and coughing, want to sleep—or in this case, the computer equivalents of those symptoms might be as follows: Your computer seems unusually sluggish, generates strange error messages or other odd emissions, or possibly even locks up and refuses to function entirely. All these are classic symptoms, but you cannot assume your computer is virus free just because it seems fine. Some viruses do their work in secret, as we shall discuss shortly.

The secret to avoiding viruses is to understand how they work. A virus is a program that has two functions: 1) *proliferate* (make more copies of itself) and 2) *activate* (at some signal, count, date, and so on, do something—usually something bad like delete the boot sector). A virus does not have to do damage to be a virus. Some of the first viruses written were harmless and downright amusing. Without going into too much of the nitty-gritty, there are basically only four types of viruses—boot sector, executable, macro, and Trojan—plus a fifth type that is really a combination of two others—bimodal/bipartite.

Boot Sector

Boot sector viruses change the code in the master boot record (MBR) of the hard drive. Once the machine is booted, they reside in memory, attempting to infect the MBRs of other drives such as floppy drives, connected network machines, or removable media, and creating whatever havoc they are designed to do by the programmer.

Executable

Executable viruses reside in executable files. They are literally extensions of executables and are unable to exist by themselves. Once the infected executable file is run, the virus loads into memory, adding copies of itself to other EXEs that are subsequently run, and again doing whatever evil that the virus was designed to do.

Macro

Macro viruses are specially written application macros. Although they are not truly programs, they perform the same functions as regular viruses. These viruses will auto-start when the particular application is run and will then attempt to make more copies of themselves—some will even try to find other copies of the same application across a network to propagate.

Trojan

Trojans are true, freestanding programs that do something other than what the person who runs the program thinks they will do. An example of a Trojan would be a program that a person thinks is a game but that is actually a CMOS eraser. Some Trojans are quite sophisticated. It might be a game that works perfectly well, but when the user quits the game, it causes some type of damage.

Bimodal/Bipartite

A *bimodal* or *bipartite* virus uses both boot-sector and executable functions.

Antivirus Programs

The only way to protect your PC permanently from getting a virus is to disconnect from the Internet and never permit any potentially infected software to touch your precious computer. Since neither scenario is likely these days, you need to use a specialized anti-virus program to help stave off the inevitable virus assaults.

An antivirus program protects your PC in two ways. It can be both sword and shield, working in an active seek and destroy mode and in a passive sentry mode. When ordered to seek and destroy, the program will scan the computer's boot sector and files for viruses, and if it finds any, present you with the available options for removing or disabling them. Antivirus programs can also operate as virus shields that passively monitor your computer's activity, checking for viruses only when certain events occur, such as a program executing or a file being downloaded.

Antivirus programs use different techniques to combat different types of viruses. They detect boot-sector viruses simply by comparing the drive's boot sector to a standard boot sector. This works because most boot sectors are basically the same. Some antivirus programs make a backup copy of the boot sector. If they detect a virus, the programs will use that backup copy to replace the infected boot sector. Executable viruses are a little more difficult to find because they can be on any file in the drive. To detect executable viruses, the antivirus program uses a library of *signatures*. A signature is a code pattern of a known virus. The antivirus program compares an executable file to its library of signatures. There have been instances where a perfectly clean program coincidentally held a virus signature. Usually the antivirus program's creator will provide a patch to prevent further alarms. Antivirus programs detect macro viruses through the presence of virus signatures or of certain macro commands that indicate a known macro virus. Now that we understand the types of viruses and how antivirus programs try to protect against them, let's review a few terms that are often used when describing certain traits of viruses.

Polymorphics/Polymorphs

A *polymorph* virus attempts to change its signature to prevent detection by antivirus programs, usually by continually scrambling a bit of useless code. Fortunately, the scrambling code itself can be identified and used as the signature—once the antivirus makers become aware of the virus. One technique sometimes used to combat unknown polymorphs is to have the antivirus program create a checksum on every file in the drive. A *checksum* in this context is a number generated by the software based on the contents of the file rather than the name, date, or size of that file. The algorithms for creating these checksums vary among different antivirus programs (they are also usually kept secret to help prevent virus makers from coming up with ways to beat them). Every time a program is run, the antivirus program calculates a new checksum and compares it with the earlier calculation. If the checksums are different, it is a sure sign of a virus.

Stealth

The term *stealth* is more of a concept than an actual virus function. Most stealth virus programs are boot sector viruses that use various methods to hide from antivirus software. One popular stealth virus will hook on to a little-known but often-used software interrupt, running only when that interrupt runs. Others make copies of innocent-looking files.

Virus Prevention Tips

The secret to preventing damage from a virus attack is to keep from getting one in the first place. As discussed earlier, all good antivirus programs include a virus shield that will automatically scan floppies, downloads, and so on (see Figure 20-23).

Use your anti-virus shield. It is also a good idea to scan a PC daily for possible virus attacks. Again, all antivirus programs include TSRs that will run every time the PC is booted. Last but not least, know where software has come from before you load it. While the chance of commercial, shrink-wrapped software having a virus is virtually nil (there have been a couple of well-publicized exceptions), that illegal copy of Unreal Tournament you borrowed from a local hacker should definitely be inspected with care.

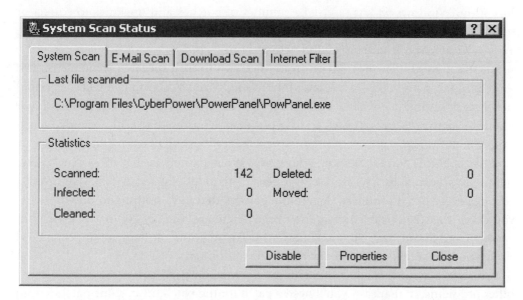

Figure 20-23 A virus shield in action

Get into the habit of keeping around an antivirus floppy disk—a bootable, write-protected floppy with a copy of an antivirus program. If you suspect a virus, use the diskette, even if your antivirus program claims to have eliminated it. Turn off the PC and reboot it from the antivirus diskette. Run your antivirus program's most comprehensive virus scan. Then check all removable media that were exposed to the system, and any other machine that may have received data from it, or that is networked to the cleaned machine. A virus can often go for months before anyone knows of its presence.

Environment

Keep the server room locked at all times. Get a card lock or combination lock doorknob and make sure that only the right people have access. Keep the humidity low, but not too low—around 40 percent is about right for most electronics. Keep the room a little on the cool side—right around 68 degrees is just about perfect, although most PCs can handle about 80 to 85 degrees before overheating becomes a problem. Check with the system's manufacturer for their recommendations.

Service Packs/Patches/ Windows Update

Windows has gone through a number of evolutionary changes over the years. Since its inception, Windows 9x has received a number of patches and upgrades to correct or improve a broad cross-section of problems. There are three different ways to update Windows: patches, service packs, and new versions.

Patches are EXE files that you get from Microsoft to fix a specific problem. You run these programs, and they do whatever they're supposed to do—update DLLs, reconfigure registry settings, or whatever else they need to do to fix a particular problem. For example, Figure 20-24 is a patch to fix a problem Windows had with extended partitions on LBA drives.

What is a TSD Virtual Device? Who cares? What matters is that these patches are required to keep Windows running properly. This does not mean that Windows 9x requires every patch produced. Ignore the patches that have nothing to do with what you do or that fix a problem you don't have. There are roughly 200 patches for Windows 95 and about 10 to 20 for Windows 98. The majority of them are important. I'll show you how to determine what you need in a moment.

Sometimes a patch might not totally fix a particular problem or might even cause other problems. In that case, you'll need a patch for the patch. Also, some patches need to be installed before another patch can be used. This creates a unique situation where the patch order is quite important.

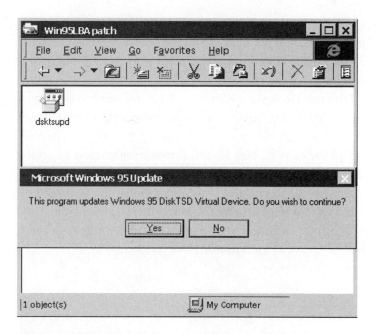

Figure 20-24 A patch to fix a partition problem

NOTE: The order in which you install patches in Windows 95 can be crucial!

The first Windows 95 release was followed by a long series of patches over the next few months, fixing everything from password problems to memory leaks. Microsoft packaged these together into a single EXE file that would perform the patches simultaneously. This grouping of patches is called a *service pack*. There are currently two Windows 95 service packs, predictably called Service Pack 1 and Service Pack 2 (assuming you have an original version of Windows 95).

Microsoft eventually sold Windows 95 with Service Pack 1 already installed. This version was called OEM service release 1 (OSR 1). After OSR 1, more patches were created, and so roughly a year later, another set of patches was combined into OSR 2. There have been a number of patches since then.

As time goes by, Microsoft continues to redefine the names for patches. For example, a patch that fixes a security problem is now called a *security update*. Don't let terminology prevent you from getting what you need!

Windows 98 only had one major update, which they call the Customer Service Pack. Windows 98 SE included the Customer Service Pack, plus a number of other enhancements like new versions of Internet Explorer, Outlook Express, and other applications. A number of minor patches have also been released.

Okay, you're convinced of the need to update Windows. You now need to be able to answer the questions "What service packs/patches are on my system now," and "What should I install?"

This is one area where the power of Windows 98/ME shines through. Just go to the Windows Update and let Microsoft tell you (see Figure 20-25)!

The Windows Update queries your system and provides a list of the updates you require. Simply read about them and select the ones you want. Just know ahead of time that most of these updates are huge—a little tough to download on a 56K modem. Microsoft will gladly provide them on CD for a nominal fee.

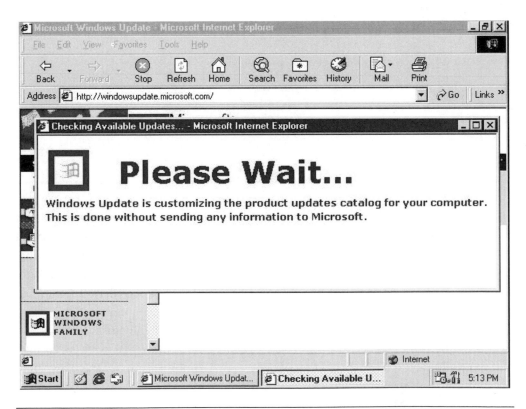

Figure 20-25   The Windows Update tells all . . .

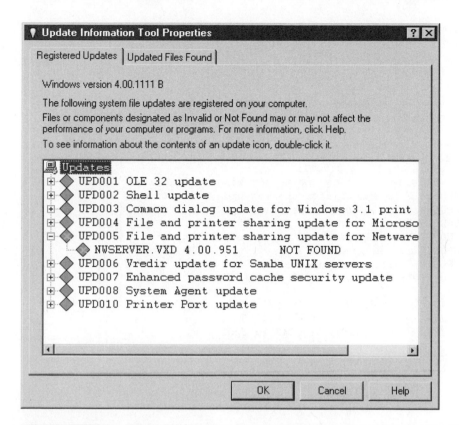

Figure 20-26 QFECHECK

Identifying patches in Windows 95 is tougher. The best way to determine the patches currently loaded on your Windows 95 system is to use Microsoft's QFECHECK (see Figure 20-26).

QFECHECK can be downloaded from the Microsoft Web site, it generates a detailed list of all patches performed on your machine. Note that the listed patches can be expanded to show the details of the files that were updated.

Remember that service packs and OSRs are compilations of patches. When you install a service pack or purchase a machine with an OSR, QFECHECK will show *all* the patches performed by the service pack or OSR. In Figure 20-27, only Service Pack 1 and two patches have been installed, but QFECHECK breaks down Service Pack 1 to show all its separate patches.

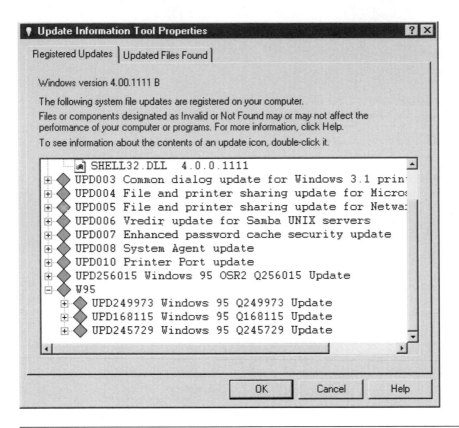

Figure 20-27   Service Pack 1 contains many patches.

Needless to say, Windows 9*x* has not cornered the Service Pack market. Windows NT 4.0 has had six service packs since its release in 1996, and as of this writing, Microsoft has released Service Pack 2 for Windows 2000 and lots of patches for Windows XP.

I Want It All . . . ?

Remember, you don't need every update that Microsoft offers. Make sure you understand the needs of the system before you download that latest security update or service pack. When a new one comes out, let other folks test it for a few weeks, and then do a search on the Internet to see if there are any problems with that update. There's no worse feeling than installing a patch to improve a system, only to find you've made it worse!

Redundant Components

Many components inside the system can be made redundant. It is very common to find servers with redundant power supplies where a power supply can be removed without even shutting down the PC. You can buy NICs that work together in the same PC, covering for one or the other if one dies—there are even NICs that can be replaced without rebooting the PC! Placing hard drives on separate controllers—like the drive duplexing discussed earlier in this chapter—provides excellent redundancy.

Last, there are methods for making the entire server redundant. For instance, there are a number of methods where two or more servers can be mirrored, providing the ultimate in reliability (assuming the cost is bearable)!

How Much Reliability Do You Need?

Reliability is like any security system—expensive, boring, a pain to administer, and you never have enough when you need it. Measure the cost of being down vs. the cost of reliability to make your decision. You might be surprised to find that it's a lot cheaper to be safe than sorry.

Network Attached Storage

If there's one thing no network ever seems to get enough of, it's space for file storage. For many years, the way we increased file storage space was to add larger and bigger hard drives to our servers. This works well and is still the way we increase file storage space on many networks. But as networks grow, the burden of increased file handling begins to take its toll on the servers. This problem is exacerbated by the fact that most servers are already doing a lot of other jobs, such as name resolution, authentication, and e-mail serving—all of them critical jobs that we need servers to do to make our networks run. Over the years, I've seen a trend to spread these many jobs out to different servers. In my network, for example, I have one system that handles DNS, another that takes care of DHCP and WINS, and a third that handles authentication. However, all of these systems are also tasked with providing file sharing. What if we had a server that did absolutely nothing but file sharing?

That, in essence, is the idea behind Network Attached Storage (NAS). If you have a server that only shares files, you can customize that system with powerful RAID and backup hardware to make that server a super file server. Sure, you can add such features to any server, but with an NAS device, you get a file-sharing server that has no responsibilities beyond sharing files. In other words, you get a real powerhouse system that can share files quickly and safely.

So what operating system do you run on these NAS boxes? What type of file systems do they use? Actually, it really doesn't matter, as long as all of the other systems in the network can access the shared folders on the NAS box. Today's NAS servers usually run Windows NT/2000, NetWare, or some version of UNIX/Linux. They invariably use the TCP/IP network protocol, although a few NAS servers running NetWare will also provide IPX/SPX as an option.

NAS provides a number of very nice benefits for networks with high-demand file storage needs. Properly configured, NAS provides total cross-platform support using the techniques we saw in the Network Interconnectivity chapter. NAS servers lift the file sharing workload from your other servers, increasing the resources available to handle the many other serving functions every network needs. NAS also provides transparent backup for your network, because all of the necessary backup hardware is contained in the NAS box itself.

Putting Them All Together

There is no such thing as the Perfect Server. Certainly every network PC needs to connect to the network, but data protection, speed, and reliability are functions that vary tremendously depending on network size, types of data and applications, the existing network cabling system, demands of growth, and of course, your pocketbook. The Network+ exam does not assume you can build the perfect network PC, but it does expect you to have a feel for the options you have. When it comes time to build or buy that system, you can act as an advocate for your network, to ensure that you get as close to that perfect network PC as possible.

Chapter Review

Questions

1. You have installed a new NIC card to a Windows 2000 professional system, but can't get a connection on the network. Which of the following could be the problem? (Choose all that apply.)

   a. A conflict with the IRQs.

   b. The wrong drivers were installed for the NIC card.

   c. NIC speed, cable speed, and network speed may be incompatible.

   d. Link light is not on.

2. A computer virus can be categorized as which of the following? (Select all that apply.)
   a. Always destructive
   b. Self-replicating
   c. Self-activating
   d. Self-destructive

3. If Jack's modem is on COM2, which IRQ is being used?
   a. IRQ 1
   b. IRQ 2
   c. IRQ 3
   d. IRQ 4

4. Which is the most common RAID implementation on servers?
   a. RAID 0
   b. RAID 1
   c. RAID 3
   d. RAID 5

5. John's PC, networked with a 10BaseT NIC, ran perfectly yesterday. Today, however, he can't access the network. Everyone else on the network can see each other, but not John. You look at the NIC and notice both lights are off. You should first:
   a. Try copying a file from another machine over the network.
   b. Verify the hub is turned on.
   c. Replace the card.
   d. Make sure the NIC is connected to the hub.

6. The part of the serial port that converts digital serial data to a format the PC can understand is called the:
   a. COM port
   b. Chipset
   c. UART
   d. Modem

7. Which of the following IRQs would most probably be available for a NIC?
   a. IRQ 4
   b. IRQ 5
   c. IRQ 6
   d. IRQ 7

8. You have a floppy disk that came with your new NIC. The floppy probably contains all of the following *except* the:
   a. Drivers
   b. Configuration utility
   c. Diagnostic utility
   d. Driver Update utility

9. Disk mirroring is under which level of RAID?
   a. RAID 0
   b. RAID 1
   c. RAID 2
   d. RAID 3

10. Which of the following connectors are used with SCSI? (Choose all that apply.)
    a. 50-pin Centronics
    b. 36-pin Centronics
    c. Female DB-15
    d. Female DB-25

Answers

1. **A, B,** and **C.**   Each of the first three choices could cause this problem. The link light not being on may *indicate* a problem, but it would not cause one.

2. **B** and **C.**   In order for a program to be considered a virus, it must be self-replicating and self-activating.

3. **C.**   COM2 uses IRQ 3.

4. **D.**   RAID 5 is the most common RAID implementation on servers.

5. **D.**   The connect light is off, so the NIC is not connected to a working hub. Everyone else is working, so the hub is fine.

6. **C.**   The UART converts digital serial data to a format the PC can understand.

7. **B.**   All of these IRQs have a predefined use, but IRQ 5 is for a second parallel port. As most PCs don't have a second parallel port, IRQ 5 is the most likely to be open for use.

8. **D.**   There is no such thing as a driver update utility.

9. **B.**   Disk mirroring is under RAID 1.

10. **A** and **D.**   Both 50-pin Centronics and Female DB-25 connectors are used with SCSI.

Zen and the Art of Network Support

In this chapter, you will

- Learn about troubleshooting tools
- Understand the troubleshooting process
- Understand backups
- Learn about baselines
- Understand troubleshooting models
- Learn about troubleshooting as an art
- Understand Mike's Four-Layer Model
- Look at troubleshooting scenarios

Have you ever seen a tech who walks up to a network and seems to know all the answers, effortlessly typing in a few commands and magically making the system or network work? It's always intrigued me as to how they do this. I did notice they tended to follow the same steps for similar problems—they looked in the same places, typed the same commands, and so on. When someone does a task the same way every time, I figure they're probably following a plan. They understand what tools they have to work with, and they know where to start and what to do second and third and fourth, until they find the problem. This chapter's lofty goal is to consolidate my observations on how these "übertechs" fix networks. We'll look at the primary troubleshooting tools, formulate a troubleshooting plan, and learn where to look for different sorts of problems. At the end of the chapter, we'll apply this knowledge to some common troubleshooting scenarios.

Troubleshooting Tools

While working through the process of finding the cause of a problem, you will need to use many tools. Some of these tools are difficult to quantify—including things like asking questions, referring to your network baselines and documentation, and synthesizing your network knowledge. Other tools are easier to describe. These are the software and hardware tools that provide information about your network. Many of the tools that fall into this category have been described already, such as hardware or software loopback testing devices, utilities like PING and TRACERT, and hardware tools like tone locators. The trick is knowing when and how to use these tools to solve your network problems.

"Touchy Tools"

The tools that are the most difficult to quantify, because they are mostly within you, are what I call "touchy tools." An example of a touchy tool is asking questions of the person who has the problem. This is touchy because there's no predetermined set of questions to ask—your background knowledge and intuition must tell you which questions are the right ones. The *types* of questions you should ask can be grouped into a few categories:

- *Questions designed to find out exactly what steps the user took that may have caused the symptom.* This information can help you re-create the problem. In addition, these types of questions can provide insight into whether the problem was caused by user error or improper procedures. Note from the Geek Central Human Relations Department: be careful how you phrase these sorts of questions. An annoyed, "What did you do this time, you pinhead?!" tends to cause people to clam up. Your goal, remember, is to extract information.

- *Questions designed to find out exactly what any error messages said.* This information can be critical when you need to search manufacturers' knowledge bases and support lines.

- *Questions designed to find out what the user has tried to do to fix the problem.* This information can help you determine whether you are dealing with multiple layers of problems. Many users will try to fix things, but won't think to write down what they're doing. When at some point in the process they reach a standstill and can't get back to where they started, they will come crying to you for help. Be gentle! Your goal is to get the user to remember most, if not all, of the steps they tried, so you can backtrack to the original problem rather than troubleshooting a multilayered one.

Another touchy tool you can use is to compare the current situation to the baselines and documentation you created for your network. When users complain of slow connections or downloads, for example, you should compare the bandwidth and connection speeds from your baseline to what you are able to test while the problem exists. You may find that the difficulty lies more with the user's expectations than any real network problem. You can then decide whether to upgrade your systems and connectivity, or explain to your users the limitations of the network.

The most complicated touchy tool to describe and quantify is the network knowledge you have that you can apply to your network's problems. The Network+ exam contains many network troubleshooting questions that you should be able to answer not from reading this chapter, but from reading the rest of the book. Troubleshooting often comes down to applying prior knowledge in a new way. You know, for example, that an IP address, a subnet mask, and a default gateway are all necessary if your network is to communicate with the Internet using the TCP/IP protocol. Edgar complains that he cannot connect his Windows 2000 client to the Internet. His hardware seems to be functioning correctly (link lights are on and he connects to the server) and the proxy server is up. At that point, you might check his TCP/IP configuration by using the IPCONFIG utility. If you notice that he has no default gateway, you have solved the problem. The knowledge to solve this problem came partially from understanding how to troubleshoot by eliminating possibilities, but it also came from your knowledge of the elements required to connect a machine to the Internet. As you prepare for the exam, and for administering your company's network, ask yourself how each thing you learn about networking could be applied toward troubleshooting the network. This prepares you for the time when you have to make that leap.

Hardware Tools

In Chapter 10, you read about a few hardware tools you use when configuring your network. These hardware tools include cable testers, protocol analyzers, hardware loopback devices, and toners. These tools can also be used in troubleshooting scenarios to help you eliminate or narrow down the possible causes of certain problems. In addition, there are other pieces of hardware which, although they can't actively be used for troubleshooting, can provide clues to the problems you face.

A cable tester enables you to determine if a particular cable is bad. *Bad* can be defined in a variety of ways, but it essentially means that the cable is not delivering the data for whatever reason—perhaps the cable is broken, crimped badly, or sits too close to a heat or electrical source. In most troubleshooting situations, you will use other clues to determine if you have a hardware or software problem. Then, if you have narrowed down the problem to a hardware connectivity issue, a cable tester can help you determine if the cable is good or bad. Another option, if you are without one of these tools, is to replace the cables (one at a time) and test the connectivity. In the "I can't log on" scenario, for example, if you have determined that everyone else in the area can log on, and that this user can log on from another location, you have narrowed the problem to either a configuration or hardware issue. If all network activity is broken (in other words, nothing is available in Network Neighborhood or you cannot ping the default gateway), you may choose to test cables connecting the PC to the server. This is not the only option, but it is one variable that can be tested and eliminated.

Protocol analyzers come in both hardware and software flavors. Most of the hardware analyzers have an additional software component. These tools enable administrators to determine what types of traffic are flowing through their networks. Most analyzers translate the packets flowing over the network to provide destination, source, protocol, and some information about content. In a situation where you have a network slowdown, you might use a protocol analyzer to determine what types of packets are passing over your network, and where they are originating. In some cases, a dying network card can produce large numbers of packets, often called a *broadcast storm*, which can be detected by using a protocol analyzer and noticing that all of the packets are coming from one location. Once you have narrowed your problem down to a particular machine, you can concentrate on that rather than blaming your servers, bandwidth, or other elements.

Software Tools

Throughout the book, you have read about software tools for configuring your network that can also be applied to troubleshooting. Since most of these have been described in previous chapters, I'll just review the basic purposes of these tools here. Key software troubleshooting tools include the following:

- **Software-based Protocol or Network Analyzers** These include applications such as the Network Monitor (NETMON) provided with most versions of Windows. Also called packet sniffers, these tools collect and analyze individual packets on a network to determine bottlenecks or security breaches. Use these tools when you have unexplained slowdowns on your network, to help determine which machines are sending packets. This enables you to determine if there is a broadcast storm (or just too much broadcasting in general), or if you are the victim of some more sinister event like a hacker attack.

- **System Logs** Applications like Windows NT/2000's Event Viewer display any errors or problems that have occurred in your system. If a user repeatedly failed at their logon, for example, this might be recorded in the appropriate view in the Event Viewer tool. That information could be the clue you need to determine that a user is locked out, either because he forgot his password or because someone has been trying to hack into that account. Logs also provide information on services or components of the Operating System that won't start or are receiving errors. This is a good way to troubleshoot system crashes on a particular machine.

- **Performance Monitors** Tools like the Performance Monitor mentioned earlier in this chapter can provide clues to the utilization pattern of a particular machine. When users complain of slowdowns or logon problems that can be traced to a specific system or server, this tool can often give you clues as to what's happening on that system that could be causing problems. For example, if a system is going to 100-percent memory utilization when a particular application is started, it may mean that you need more RAM, or perhaps that you need to put that application on a dedicated server. Use this tool for troubleshooting when you have tracked the problem to a particular machine, and now must determine where in that machine the bottleneck exists.

- **Systems Management Software Suites** Software suites like Microsoft's SMS server and the Tivoli management tools combine all of the earlier applications with other functions such as user registration, security auditing, software installation, and more. These suites provide a centralized tool for managing and monitoring networks in large corporate environments. These suites usually also include pager or e-mail notification of certain events, such as system outages or network slowdowns.

Your Toolbox

It always amazes me when a person calls me up and asks me what tools they need to become a network tech. My answer is always the same: just your brain—everything else will pretty much appear when you need it. There is no such thing as the correct network tech's toolbox, full of hardware and software tools you haul around to get networks fixed. I certainly don't haul around cable testers, toners, or TDRs. I may bring them along if I suspect a cabling problem, but I normally won't dump them in my backpack until *after* I suspect a problem.

Software tools all come with the network operating systems themselves. I don't need a floppy disk with ping, for example, because it's on every PC in the house! The software tools you need to fix a network are sitting there, ready for you to use. Your task is to know *how* to use them. It's the *know-how* you need to bring, and in most cases, little or nothing else!

My lack of dependence on a toolkit makes some customers unhappy—they just can't reconcile in their minds that I can get their networks up and running without some big toolbox. At times this has become so much of an issue that I have brought along a toolkit just to look good! Seriously! I call that box full of stuff my prop because it's of no more real use than a rubber stage sword.

Now that we're no longer obsessing on carrying the right tools, let's instead concentrate on the real toolbox—your brain. In an amazingly brazen act of self-confidence, I have taken the liberty of quantifying the many mental processes you should use when fixing networks into the following section.

The Troubleshooting Process

Troubleshooting is a very dynamic, fluid process that requires you to make snap judgments and act on them to try and make the network go. Any attempt to cover every possible scenario would be futile at best, and probably also not in your best interests, because any reference that tried to list every troubleshooting problem would be obsolete the moment it was created. If an exhaustive listing of all network problems is impossible, then how do you decide what to do and in what order?

Before you touch a single console or cable, you should remember two basic rules: first, as the Roman physician Galen wisely admonished, "Do no harm." If at all possible, don't make a network problem bigger than it was originally. This is a rule I've broken thousands of times, and you will too. But if we change the good doctor's phrase a bit, it's possible to formulate a rule you can live with: "First, do not trash the data!" My gosh, if I had a dollar for every megabyte of irreplaceable data I've destroyed, I'd be rich! I've learned my lesson, and you should learn from my mistakes: Always make good backups! The second rule is to create *baselines* (that is, data on how the network runs when nothing is broken). Backups enable you to rebuild a trashed system. Baselines enable you to compare your network's current performance to how it behaves when all is well. Both of these steps should precede *any* actual troubleshooting activity on your part.

Once you've done your backups and baselines, and it's time to start typing commands or yanking cable, you need a plan. You need to know what steps to take and in what order. These steps are pretty much universal to all network problems, and you should learn them well. You also need a guide to where you should look in the network for problems. For that job, I will gift you with what I modestly call Mike's Four-Layer Model. As in troubleshooting, so in this chapter—first, backups and baselines, then you can start taking troubleshooting steps, with my model to guide you.

Backups

Think about how much work you have done to create nice, stable servers, responsive workstations, and overall network wonderfulness. Imagine how many hours your users have spent creating data and storing it on those servers. Now imagine a virus deleting critical data or configuration files—not a good situation, for either your blood pressure or your job security. Simple common sense dictates that you create backups of your data. Repeatedly. Backups are useless unless they are current. Your users won't thank you for restoring a three-week-old copy of a file that gets updated daily. You should therefore create a backup schedule for your data that ensures it's backed up often enough that a useful copy can be restored easily. Your backup plan should include the following details:

- When the backups will occur and what the tape rotation schedule will be
- What types of backups will be done at each time
- Where the backups will be stored

Perhaps the most important details are the types of backups and the schedule, or strategy, for the backups.

What Are the Types of Backups?

The goal of backing up data is to ensure that when a system dies, there will be an available, recent copy you can use to restore the system. You could simply back up the complete system at the end of each day—or whatever interval you feel is prudent to keep the backups fresh—but complete backups can be a tremendous waste of time and materials. Instead of backing up the entire system, take advantage of the fact that all the files won't be changed in any given period; much of the time you only need to back up what's changed since your last backup. Recognizing this, most backup software solutions have a series of options available beyond the old Complete (usually called Full or Normal) backup.

The key to understanding backups other than the full backup is a little fellow called the Archive attribute. All files have little 1-bit storage areas called *attributes*. The most common attributes are Hidden (don't show the file when **DIR** is typed), System (it's a critical file for the system), Read-Only (can't erase it), and the Archive bit. These attributes were first used in FAT-formatted drives in the DOS era, but they are still completely supported today by all file formats. The Archive bit works basically like this: Whenever a file is saved, the Archive bit is turned on. Simply opening a file will affect the current state of the Archive bit. Backup programs will usually turn off a file's Archive bit when it's backed up. In theory, if a file's Archive bit is turned off, it means there's a good backup of that file on some tape. If the Archive bit is turned on, it means that the file has been changed since it was last backed up (see Figure 21-1).

Archive bits are used to perform backups that are not full backups. The following backup types are most often supported:

- *Normal* is a full backup. Every file selected will be backed up, and the Archive bit will be turned off for every file backed up. This is the standard "back it all up" option.

- *Copy* is identical to Normal with one big exception: The Archive bits are not changed. This is used (although not often) for making extra copies of a previously completed backup.

- *Incremental* backups only back up the files that have their Archive bit turned on. An incremental backup copies only the files that have been changed since the last backup. It then turns off the Archive bits.

- *Differential* backups are identical to incremental backups, but they don't turn off the Archive bits.

- *Daily*, better known as *Daily Copy*, makes a backup of all of the files that have been changed that day. It does not change the Archive bits.

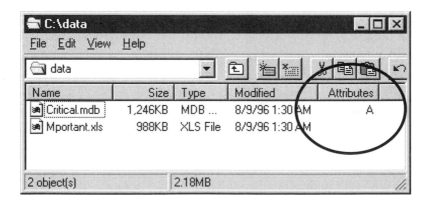

Figure 21-1 The Archive bit

EXAM TIP: Be sure you know the different types of backups, including which ones change the Archive bits and which ones do not.

The motivation for having both the incremental and differential backups may not be clear at first glance—they seem so similar as to be basically the same. Incremental seems the better option at first. If a file is backed up, you would want to turn off the Archive bit, right? Well, maybe. But there is one scenario where that might not be too attractive. Most backups do a big weekly normal backup, followed by daily incremental or differential backups at the end of every business day. Figure 21-2 shows the difference between incremental and differential backups.

Notice that a differential backup is a cumulative backup. Since the Archive bits are not set, it keeps backing up all changes since the last normal backup. This means the backup files will get progressively larger throughout the week (assuming a standard weekly normal backup). The incremental backup, by contrast, only backs up files changed since the last backup. Each incremental backup file will be relatively small and also totally different from the previous backup file. Let's assume that the system is wiped out on a Thursday morning. How can you restore the system to a useful state? If you're using an incremental backup, you will first have to restore the last weekly backup

Incremental

MON	TUE	WED	THU	FRI
Full Backup	All Tuesday Changes	All Wednesday Changes	All Thursday Changes	All Friday Changes

Differential

MON	TUE	WED	THU	FRI
Full Backup	All Changes Through Tuesday	All Changes Through Wednesday	All Changes Through Thursday	All Changes Through Friday

Figure 21-2 Incremental vs. differential

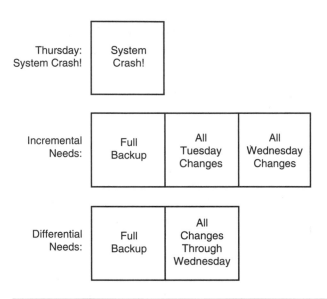

Figure 21-3 Restoring from backups

you ran on Monday, then the Tuesday backup, and then the Wednesday backup before the system is restored to its Thursday morning state. The longer the time between normal backups, the more incremental backups you must restore. Using the same scenario, but assuming you're doing differential instead of incremental backups, you'll only need the weekly backup and then the Wednesday backup to restore your system. A differential backup will always require only two backups to restore a system (see Figure 21-3). Suddenly, the differential backup looks better than the incremental! On the other hand, one big benefit of incremental over differential is backup file size. Differential backup files will be massive compared to incremental ones.

There are a number of possible backup strategies to choose from, some of which make incremental backups more attractive, and some which call for differential backups. The type of backup you perform will determine the type of backups you do.

Backup Strategies

One of the issues you must address to successfully answer questions on backups and recoverability is how to choose strategies that meet your needs for doing backups and restores in your actual network environment. Your goal is to be able to back up and then easily restore all the necessary information from all the necessary machines. This can include both servers and workstations. Decisions about backing up multiple machines can revolve about both hardware and time factors. Another issue to consider when planning your backup strategy is what to do with the all-important tapes. Recognize that you are protecting your network not only against viruses and other computer-related disasters, but also against fire, flood, and man-made catastrophes.

Baselines

The best way to know when a problem is brewing is to know how things perform when all's well with the system. You need to establish a *baseline*: a static picture of your network and servers when they are working correctly. A common tool used to create a baseline on Windows systems is the Performance Monitor utility that comes with Windows NT and 2000. Conveniently, all network operating systems come with similar tools, and you can also create baselines using most network management utilities.

Windows NT/2000—PerfMon

Administrators use Performance Monitor (PerfMon) to view the behavior of hardware and other resources on NT/2000 machines, either locally or remotely. PerfMon can monitor both real time and historical data about the performance of your systems. To access the Performance Monitor applet, choose Start | Programs | Administrative Tools | Performance Monitor from any Windows NT machine. On a Windows 2000 system, choose Start | Settings | Control Panel, then double-click Administrative Tools, and double-click Performance.

Once you access Performance Monitor, you need to configure it to display data. To configure the Performance Monitor, you must understand the concepts of objects, counters, and views. An *object* in the Performance Monitor is the component of your system you want to monitor, such as the processor or the memory. Each object has different measurable features, called *counters*. Counters, in other words, are the aspects of an object you want to track. As you decide which object(s) to monitor, you must also select one or more counters for each object. The Performance Monitor can organize and display selected counter information using a variety of *views*, each of which provides different types of information. The Log view, for example, enables you to store data about your system for later review. This is the view you use to create a baseline. Although it's the only one I'm going to discuss here, the other views—Chart, Alert, and Report—are useful for troubleshooting problems as they arise.

To access the Log view in Windows NT, either click the Log View button or choose View | Log. To add objects to the Log view, either click Add To (the plus sign) or choose Edit | Add To Log. In the Add To Log dialog box, first select the computer you want to monitor. You can choose either the local machine (the default), or a remote machine. To monitor a remote machine, type in the computer name using its Universal Naming

Convention (UNC) name. To monitor a machine named HOUBDC1, for example, you would type **HOUBDC1** in the *Computer* field. You can also use the Select Computer button (at the right end of the Computer field) to view the available machines and select the one you want to monitor, as shown in Figure 21-4.

Although it is usually easier to monitor a machine locally, it is often more accurate to monitor a machine remotely. The Performance Monitor itself as it runs on a machine uses a certain amount of that system's resources to take the measurements and display the data graphically. Especially when you need to troubleshoot problems with disk performance, memory and paging, or processor use, you can corrupt your results by monitoring locally. There are some cases where monitoring locally is preferred or required, however. If you are monitoring network access or networking protocol objects, for example, monitoring locally will affect the readings to a lesser degree than monitoring remotely. Similarly, you must monitor a system locally if you can't access that system over the network. Finally, when you monitor objects created by a specific application, such as Exchange, you should monitor locally, as the objects related to this application are only created locally and will not be available from another system.

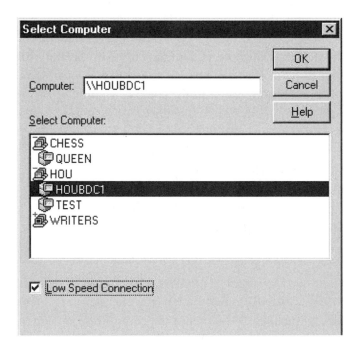

Figure 21-4 Select Computer in Performance Monitor

Once you have selected a system to monitor, either locally or remotely, you must select the object to monitor. Select one or more objects to monitor from the list in the Object field. Note that the Log view is somewhat different from the other views, in that you only add *objects* to the view, not the specific counters for the objects, as shown in the Add To Log dialog box in Figure 21-5.

After you select the objects for the Performance Monitor to track and log, select Options | Log Options to save the data to a log file, then start the logging by clicking the Start Log button, as shown in Figure 21-6. This dialog box also gives you the opportunity to select the update method and time.

After you have configured the Log to save to a particular file, you can see the log file name, status of the logging process, log interval, and file size of the log in the Performance Monitor dialog box. To stop collecting data in a log, open the Log Options dialog box again and click Stop Log. You can then choose to create a new Log file and begin logging again, if necessary. You can also view data from one of these saved log files by selecting Options | Data From. In the Data From . . . dialog box, shown in Figure 21-7, you can choose to continue obtaining data from the current activity, or obtain data from a particular log file.

When you choose to obtain data from a saved log, you go back to that frozen moment in time and add counters to the other views for the objects you chose to save in the log. In our Log options, for example, we chose to store data for the Logical Disk object. After we've loaded that particular log file, we can change to the Chart view, add counters there for the Logical Disk object, and view a static chart for that moment in

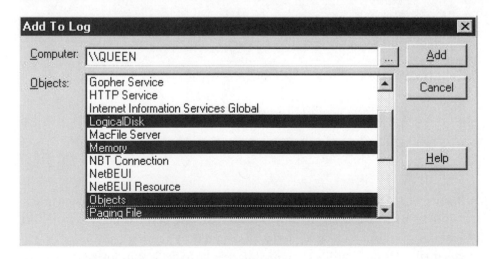

Figure 21-5   Add To Log in Performance Monitor

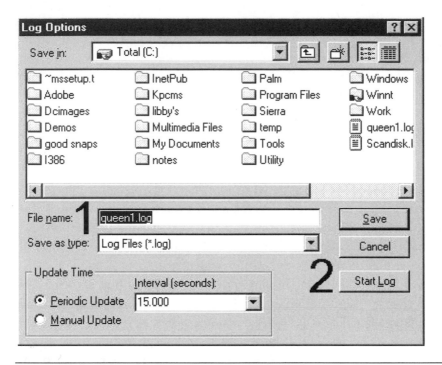

Figure 21-6 Select log file and start logging in Performance Monitor.

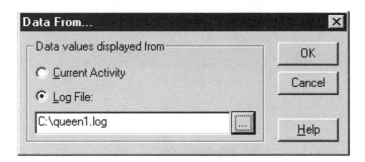

Figure 21-7 The Data From . . . dialog box in Performance Monitor

time (see Figure 21-8). You may want to select a wide variety of objects to save while in Log view, so that when you open the log to display in any of the other views (Chart, Alert, and Report), you can add a wide range of counters.

The Performance Monitor utility described here is specific to Windows NT systems, but you should create baselines for whatever types of systems you have, and they

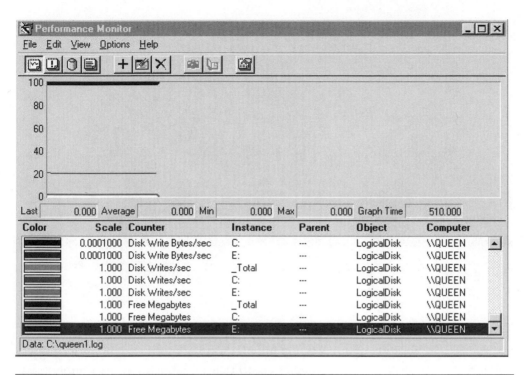

Figure 21-8   Viewing a static chart in Performance Monitor

should cover all aspects of your network. Be certain to create multiple baselines, to show the systems both at rest and in use, using the Performance Monitor as well as other systems management or network sniffer tools.

NetWare—Console Monitor

On a NetWare server, most of the critical information you might need to see and document to establish your baseline can be obtained by loading the Console Monitor application (see Figure 21-9) on the server itself. You can view the program remotely on a client PC, but it only runs on the server. Novell calls a program that runs on the server in this way a *NetWare Loadable Module* (NLM). You issue the command **LOAD MONITOR** at the server's console prompt to start the program.

The Console Monitor NLM can display a wide range of information, from memory use to individual statistics about the NICs installed in the server. Many system managers leave Console Monitor running all the time so they can keep an eye on things. It can also be used to kick users off the server and see which files they're accessing!

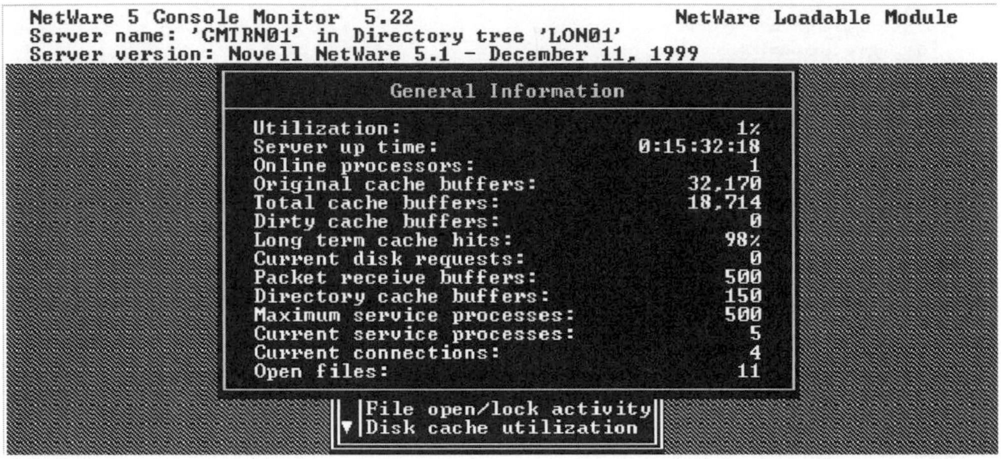

```
NetWare 5 Console Monitor  5.22              NetWare Loadable Module
Server name: 'CMTRN01' in Directory tree 'LON01'
Server version: Novell NetWare 5.1 - December 11, 1999
```
```
                        General Information
        Utilization:                              1%
        Server up time:                    0:15:32:18
        Online processors:                         1
        Original cache buffers:               32,170
        Total cache buffers:                  18,714
        Dirty cache buffers:                       0
        Long term cache hits:                    98%
        Current disk requests:                     0
        Packet receive buffers:                  500
        Directory cache buffers:                 150
        Maximum service processes:               500
        Current service processes:                 5
        Current connections:                       4
        Open files:                               11

              File open/lock activity
            ▼ Disk cache utilization
```

Figure 21-9   The NetWare 5 Console Monitor general information screen

Troubleshooting Model

No matter how complex and fancy, any troubleshooting model can be broken down into simple steps. Having a sequence of steps to follow makes the entire troubleshooting process simpler and easier, because you have a clear set of goals to achieve in a specific sequence. The most important steps are the first three—they help you narrow down the cause of the problem to a specific item. The reason this matters so much is that figuring out what's wrong will also probably tell you how to fix the problem, and how to prevent it from happening in the future.

The basics of any troubleshooting model should include the following steps:

1. Establish the symptoms.

2. Isolate the cause of the problem (identify the scope of the problem).

3. Establish what has changed that might have caused the problem.

4. Identify the most probable cause.

5. Implement a solution.

6. Test the solution.

7. Recognize the potential effects of the solution.

8. Document the solution.

Establish the Symptoms

If you are working directly on the affected system and not relying on somebody on the other end of a telephone to guide you, you will establish the symptoms through your observation of what is (or isn't) happening. If you're troubleshooting over the telephone (always a joy, in my experience), you will need to ask questions based on what the user is telling you. These questions can be *close ended*, which is to say there can only be a yes or no type answer, such as, "Can you see a light on the front of the monitor?" You can also ask *open ended* questions, such as, "Tell me what you see on the screen." The type of question you use at any given moment will depend on what information you need, and on the knowledge level of the user. If, for example, the user seems to be technically oriented, you will probably be able to ask more close-ended questions, because they will know what you are talking about. If, on the other hand, the user seems to be confused about what's happening, open-ended questions will allow him to explain what is going on in his own words.

Isolate the Cause of the Problem

One of the first steps in trying to determine the cause of a problem is to understand the extent of the problem—is it specific to one user or is it network-wide? Sometimes this entails trying the task yourself, both from the user's machine and from your own or another machine.

For example, if a user is experiencing problems logging in to the network, you might need to go to that user's machine and try to use their username to log in. This will tell you whether the problem is a user error of some kind, as well as enable you to see the symptoms of the problem yourself. Next, you probably want to try logging in with your own username from that machine, or have the user try to log in from another machine. In some cases, you can ask other users in the area if they are experiencing the same problem, to see if the problem is affecting more than one user. Depending on the size of your network, you should find out if the problem is occurring in only one part of your company, or across the entire network.

What does all of this tell you? Essentially, it tells you how big the problem is. If nobody in an entire remote office can log in, you may be able to assume that the problem is the network link or router connecting that office to the server. If nobody in any office can log in, you may be able to assume that the server is down or not accepting logins. If only that one user in that one location can't log in, it may be a problem with that user, that machine, or that user's account.

EXAM TIP: Eliminating variables is one of the first tools in your arsenal of diagnostic techniques.

Establish What Has Changed That Might Have Caused the Problem

After determining the extent of a problem, the next step is to eliminate all the extra variables, that is, all the incorrect possible causes of the problem. If you have determined that the problem is specific to that user on that machine, you have already learned a great deal. First, you have learned that this isn't a user account problem, because that user was able to log in from another machine. You have also determined that it isn't user error, because you've tried it yourself. By having other users at other machines successfully try the task, you eliminated the possibility that the server is down.

Ask Isolating Questions

The goal of this step is to isolate the problem to a specific item (hardware, software, user error, and so on), or to identify what has changed that might have caused the problem. You may not have to ask many questions before the problem is isolated, but it can sometimes take quite a bit of time and involve further work behind the scenes. Isolating questions are designed to home in on the likely cause of the problem. Here are some examples:

- "Tell me exactly what you were doing when the problem occurred."
- "Has anything been changed on the system recently?"
- "Has the system been moved recently?"

Notice the way I've tactfully avoided the word *you*, as in "Have *you* changed anything on the system recently?" This is a deliberate tactic to avoid any implied blame on the part of the user. Being nice never hurts, and it makes the whole troubleshooting process more friendly.

You should be asking some isolating questions *internally* of yourself, such as, "Was that machine involved in the software push last night?" or, "Didn't a tech visit that machine this morning?" Note that you will only be able to answer these questions if *your* documentation is up to scratch. Sometimes, isolating a problem may require you to check system and hardware logs (such as those stored by some routers and other network devices), so make sure you know how to do this.

Identify the Most Probable Cause

This step comes down to experience—or good use of the support tools at your disposal, such as your knowledge base. You need to select the most *probable* cause from all the *possible* causes, so the solution you choose fixes the problem the first time. This may not always happen, but whenever possible, you want to avoid spending a whole day stabbing in the dark while the problem snores softly to itself in some cozy, neglected corner of your network.

Implement a Solution

Once you think you have isolated the cause of the problem, you should decide what you think is the best way to fix it, and then try your solution, whether that's giving advice over the phone to a user, installing a replacement part, or adding a software patch. All the way through this step, try only one likely solution at a time. There's no point in installing several patches at once, because then you can't tell which one fixed the problem. Similarly, there's no point in replacing several items of hardware (such as a hard disk and its controller cable) at the same time because then you can't tell which part (or parts) was actually faulty. As you try each possibility, always *document* what you do and what results you get. This isn't just for a future problem, either—during a lengthy troubleshooting process, it's very easy to forget exactly what you tried two hours before, or which thing you tried produced a particular result. Although it may take longer to be methodical, it will save time the next time—and it may enable you to pinpoint what needs to be done to stop the problem from recurring at all, thereby reducing future call volume to your support team—and as any support person will tell you, that's definitely worth the effort!

Test the Solution

This is the part everybody hates. Once you think you've fixed a problem, you should try to make it happen again. If you can't, great! But sometimes you will be able to re-create the problem, and then you know you haven't finished the job at hand. Many techs want to slide away quietly as soon as everything seems to be fine, but trust me on this, it won't impress your customer when their problem flares up again 30 seconds after you've left the building—not to mention that you get the joy of another two-hour car trip the next day to fix the same problem, for an even more unhappy client! In the scenario where you are providing support to someone else rather than working directly on the problem, you should make *them* try to re-create the problem. This will confirm whether they understand what you have been telling them, and will educate them at the same time, lessening the chance they'll call you back later and ask, "Can we just go through that one more time?"

Recognize the Potential Effects of the Solution

Okay, now that *you* have changed something on the system in the process of solving one problem, you must think about the wider repercussions of what you have done. If you've replaced a faulty NIC in a server, for instance, will the fact that the MAC address has changed (remember, it's built in to the NIC) affect anything else, such as the logon security controls, or your network management and inventory software? If you've installed a patch on a client PC, will this change the default protocol or any other default settings that may affect other functionality? If you've changed a user's security settings, will this affect their ability to access other network resources? This is really part of testing your solution to make sure it works properly, but it also makes you think about the impact of your work on the system as a whole.

Document the Solution

It is *vital* that you document the problem, symptoms, and solutions of all support calls, for two reasons. First, you're creating a support database that will be a knowledge base for future reference, enabling everyone on the support team to identify new problems as they arise, and know how to deal with them quickly, without having to duplicate someone else's research efforts. Second, documentation enables you to track problem trends and anticipate future workloads, or even to identify a particular brand or model of an item, such as a printer or a NIC, that seems to be less reliable or that creates more work for you than others. Don't skip this step—it *really* is essential!

 EXAM TIP: Remember these problem analysis steps!

Troubleshooting as Art— Mike's Four-Layer Model

Troubleshooting is not something that can be definitively described in a nice neat list of ten easy steps. It is more of an art—an ability to become "one with the network" and intuit where the problems are hiding. The best troubleshooters are those who have a huge amount of knowledge about every element of the network—hardware, software, connections, and so on. These people can then synthesize all that knowledge into really good guesses about where to start looking for problems. All of the previous steps give you a theoretical concept of where to look and how to proceed when troubleshooting your own network. The theory, however, is easier to implement in real life if you know where (and where not) to look within the network to find the problem.

The troubleshooting model does a great job of describing the steps necessary to get a network problem fixed, but it doesn't really tell you where to look in the first place. So how do you figure out where to look for problems? Some might think to use the OSI seven-layer model, but while the OSI seven-layer model provides a superb tool for those who actually create network hardware and software, it doesn't do a lot for the folks who need to work on a network every day. Instead, I use a model that I modestly call Mike's Four-Layer Model. The Four-Layer Model concentrates on the main components of the hardware and software you need to deal with to make a networking system work, while ignoring the parts of the hardware and software over which you have no control. The core idea behind the four layers of my model is that you can access, change, remove, install, troubleshoot, and fix every layer—unlike most of the layers of the OSI seven-layer model.

The Four-Layer Model breaks all networks into—surprise!—four major areas: Hardware, Protocols, Network, and Shared Resources. No matter what specific networking hardware or software you use, every one of these four layers exists—although some network operating systems like to hide them! If you understand Mike's Four-Layer Model, you should have no problem fixing just about any network, any time. By using the Four-Layer Model when you have a problem with a network, you'll never find yourself saying, "I have no idea why this is happening to my network! What do I do?" Instead, you'll find yourself saying, "I know why this problem exists. I just need to figure out how to fix it!" Trust me, figuring out how to fix a known problem is a lot easier than trying to troubleshoot a mystery problem on your network.

Mike's Four-Layer Model also *ignores the function of the layers* and concentrates instead on *what you need to do to make the layers function* (that is, what you do to verify that a particular layer works correctly or needs diagnosing). For example, if you've installed the hardware correctly, then the hardware layer works. To determine this, you run a certain type of test (like pinging another system), and if you're successful, you in essence check off the hardware layer as good and move on to the next one. Some of my critics suggest that if diagnostic success is the goal, what I've proposed is by definition not a true model—that my Four-Layer Model is nothing more than a diagnostic procedure. Actually, they have a point. If you get technical about it, my Four-Layer Model is nothing more than a diagnostic procedure. To which I must respond, "Oh yeah, well it's the best darn, totally universal, easiest to understand, 100-percent accurate, and most practical diagnostic procedure you'll ever meet! Six weeks after the Network+ exam, you'll probably have forgotten most of the seven OSI layers, but you'll never forget my model!" Why? Because you will use it every day!

> **NOTE** Mike's Four-Layer Model is nothing more than this one tech's opinion of how best to fix a network. It is not an industry standard, nor is it even that well known—yet. It is not part of the Network+ test in any way, but it will help you on the test by providing a framework you can use to analyze the many scenario questions on the exam and quickly generate correct answers.

I once had a reader e-mail me about the Four-Layer Model. She said I should change its name to Mike's Four-Doors Model. Her suggestion for the name change came from the fact that the four layers of my model seemed to her like doorways to the innards of the network, rather than a true definition of all network functions. In a way, she was right—my model does not define all the functions of a network, like the OSI seven-layer model does. I ignore or blend most of the OSI layers into my model because I want to deal with things I can touch in the network. So, I guess the doorway analogy is a decent way to think about my model, but I'm too lazy to change all my work so I'm sticking to the name Four-Layer Model. Let's look at each of its layers.

Hardware

Hardware is probably the most self-explanatory of the four categories. This layer covers the many different ways data can be moved from one PC to another, from copper to fiber to wireless signals. It includes the Physical and Data Link components of the OSI model, but concentrates on the parts that make this all work, like hubs, cables, and connectors. It also includes items that the OSI model does not directly address, like NICs, device drivers for NICs, and how you install and test them.

Protocols

I should really call this section Network Protocols, but I don't want you confusing it with the next one. Protocols are the languages of networks. As you've learned, these languages have interesting names such as NetBEUI, IPX/SPX, and the ever-popular TCP/IP. A protocol is a highly standardized language that handles most of the "invisible" functions on a network, like determining which computer is SERVER1, or disassembling and reassembling data passed over the network. Here we concern ourselves with installing and configuring the protocol so that a system can communicate with other systems on the network. We're not too interested in how this all works in great detail—the point here is that if you install the right protocol and configure it properly, it will work.

Network

Once you install the hardware and the protocol, you need to make two critical determinations. First, you need to decide which systems will share resources. In other words, you must determine which systems will act as servers and which will act as clients, and then configure them accordingly. Second, you need to name the systems, so they can see each other, usually something like *Server1* or *Mike's PC*. In this layer, the concepts of client/server, peer-to-peer, and domain-based networks come into play. Different network operating systems use different methods to name their systems and to determine which systems share and which do not. This layer requires that you appreciate the differences between programs like Windows, NetWare, and Linux.

Shared Resources

The entire reason we network is to share resources, so this final layer encompasses all the steps required to enable a system to share a resource, and to let other systems access that shared resource. This layer includes a number of steps, and unlike the earlier layers, these steps often need to be done fairly frequently, because by their very nature, shared resources and the users who access them change pretty much continuously. This layer includes most of the day-to-day administration of networks and tends to be the place we spend the majority of our time.

Using the Four-Layer Model

The secret to using the Four-Layer Model to diagnose network problems is to use it to structure your analysis when problems occur, and to proceed through the layers as you diagnose the problem. Let me show you how I use it by giving you a scenario.

I recently replaced an ancient router that had an ISDN Internet connection, with a new SOHO gateway DSL router, in a Windows 2000 network. The Windows network had DNS, WINS, and DHCP servers for all the clients on the network. I configured the new router to use the same IP addresses as the old router. When I went to a system to test the setup, I popped right up on the Internet, no problem. I then fired up IPCONFIG and released and renewed the IP address to make sure the new router worked. I got a new IP address and everything looked okay. Then I decided to browse the network—and I couldn't see any other system! Not good. Time to use the Four-Layer Model.

First, the Physical layer—was I disconnected from the network, or was a piece of hardware broken? Not likely, given the fact that I could still get on the Internet. But I used PING to test the router—no problem. Then I pinged the server and didn't get an answer. Hmm, was there a cable problem between me and the server? I checked and saw good link lights all around. Plus, everyone else was still hitting the server just fine. Time to assume the physical layer was okay.

On to the second layer, Protocol. I'm running TCP/IP, and it's unlikely I could get to the Internet if I had a problem there. But I still checked the system with IPCONFIG. Wait a minute! A quick look reveals that my IP address is 192.45.15.10, but the network ID I want is 192.168.4.0! This is weird—where did this strange IP address come from? Well, I set up the router for DHCP—maybe there's a problem with the DHCP server. The network admin checks and tells me it's up and running. I want to verify this so I go to another system and do a release/renew there. Lo and behold, suddenly IT has an IP address of 192.45.15.11! What's going on here? I ask myself the million-dollar question: "What has changed on this network that might have caused this?" The answer was easy: The only recent change to the network was the new router. A quick examination reveals the problem: The router was set up to do DHCP. I quickly shut off the router's DHCP, then do another release/renew on the two systems with the bad IP addresses, and voilà, problem solved, and I'm on to the next job!

By using the Four-Layer Model, I could quickly remove physical issues from the possible problems and move on to examine protocol issues, where I found the problem. Try my Four-Layer Model for yourself—it works!

Troubleshooting Scenarios

I want to end this chapter and the book with some good troubleshooting scenarios. Take some time and really think about these situations and how you would handle them. What questions would you ask? What tests would you do first? The Network+ exam absolutely *loves* to ask scenario questions. The knowledge from the previous chapters combined with the methods you've learned in this chapter should enable you to fix any network!

"I Can't Log In!"

One of the most complex troubleshooting issues is that one set of symptoms, in this case a user's inability to log in, can have many causes. Suppose Woody has called complaining that he cannot log in to the company's intranet. Tina Tech first tries accessing the intranet site from her workstation, and finds she has no problem. Tina might also want to have other users try to log in, or confirm that other users are not having the same problem. Next, Tina should have Woody try to log in from another machine. This will help Tina determine whether the problem lies with Woody's user account's ability to log in, or with Woody's Windows 98 workstation or connectivity.

If Woody is unable to log in from another machine, Tina should probably check to be sure Woody is using the correct login ID, password, and procedure when he logs in. On the other hand, if Woody is able to log in from another user's workstation, Tina should probably focus on determining whether Woody's workstation is working properly and connecting to the network. One step she could try here is pinging Woody's workstation. If Tina is able to ping Woody's machine successfully, she knows that the machine is up, the TCP/IP protocol is configured correctly, and the system is connected to the network. Tina might then check the configuration of the network client on Woody's workstation. If Tina is not able to ping the workstation, however, she might need to test the cables and NIC using cable testers or loopback devices, and verify that TCP/IP was correctly configured using WINIPCFG.

"I Can't Get to This Web Site!"

Reaching external web sites requires that a variety of components be configured correctly. Some of these components are within your company's internal control; many of them are not. When Fatima calls and tells Tina Tech that she cannot reach **www.comptia.org**, Tina's first step is to try to reach that site herself. In this case, Tina was also unable to get a response from the comptia.org site. One of her next steps is to ping the site, first by name, and then by IP address. In this case, she gets no response by name, but she does get a normal response when she pings the site by IP address. This immediately indicates to her that the problem is name resolution, in this case: DNS.

On the other hand, had Tina been unable to ping successfully using either the IP address or host name, she should consider two possibilities. First, if her company uses a firewall or proxy server to reach the Internet, she should ping that machine. This machine usually has the same IP address as the default gateway TCP/IP setting. If Tina can successfully ping her default gateway, she can be almost certain that the problem is not something she or her company has any control over. To verify this, Tina should attempt to reach some other external sites, both by pinging and using a web browser. If she can reach other sites successfully, the problem is most likely with the comptia.org site or the gateway.

"Our Web Server Is Sluggish!"

Slow response from a server can be related to a variety of things. Usually, however, the problem can be traced to a connection to the server, or to the server itself. When Wanda calls in from working at home and tells Tina Tech that she is getting a very slow response from the company's web site, Tina Tech leaps into action. Tina tries to reach the offending server and is immediately connected; this indicates a connectivity problem for that user. She asks Wanda to execute a **TRACERT** command from her workstation to the slow server. This reveals to Tina that the slowdown stems from one of the intermediate steps through which Wanda's system connects to the server. Because of this, the problem is out of Tina's hands, unless she can offer a direct dial-up option for Wanda.

If Tina finds she cannot reach the offending server quickly when she tries from her workstation, then the problem may lie with the server itself. Tina checks the Change Log for the web server, to see if anyone has changed anything recently. She discovers a new anti-virus component was recently added, so she checks the vendor's web site to make sure there are no known problems or patches for that piece of software. She also uses the Performance Monitor to compare the server's current responses to the baseline that she previously recorded. This shows her that the bottleneck is related to excessive paging, indicating that the server may need more physical memory, or RAM.

"I Can't See Anything in Network Neighborhood!"

When a user is completely cut off from the network, the problem is usually limited to that user's workstation or network connection. When Tina gets a call from Johnny saying his Windows 98 machine is on, but that he can't log in and can't see any other machines on the company's TCP/IP network, Tina goes to Johnny's office to run some tests. The first test Tina runs is to ping an external machine. She doesn't expect it to work, but tests just to be certain. Next, she tries to ping Johnny's machine using either **PING Localhost** or **PING 127.0.0.1** (remember the loopback address?). When this ping doesn't work, Tina guesses that the problem is in the TCP/IP configuration. To view the machine's TCP/IP configuration, Tina uses WINIPCFG, and notices the IP address is blank. After checking her network documentation to verify what IP address Johnny's machine should have, she adds the IP address and he is able to connect to the network.

If Tina's **PING 127.0.0.1** had worked, she would have had to assume the TCP/IP and networking configuration of Johnny's machine was correct. She should then check the hardware, using a network card utility to verify that the NIC itself is working correctly, and a cable tester to verify that the cable from Johnny's workstation is operating properly. In this case, the cable tester shows that the cable is bad, so she replaces the cable between Johnny's workstation and the patch panel, and he is able to connect.

Troubleshooting Is Fun!

The art of network troubleshooting can be a fun, frolicsome, and frequently frustrating feature of your network career. By applying a good troubleshooting methodology and constantly increasing your knowledge of networks, you too can develop into a great troubleshooting artist. This takes time, naturally, but stick with it. Begin the training. Use the Force. Learn new stuff, document problems and fixes, talk to other network techs about similar problems. Every bit of knowledge and experience you gain will make things that much easier for you when crunch time comes and a network disaster occurs—and as any experienced network tech can tell you, it will, even in the most robust network.

Chapter Review

Questions

1. You can't connect to your network server. Your system is configured to obtain an IP address automatically. You ran the **IPCONFIG** command to find your default gateway address, which is 192.168.4.152, and you successfully pinged your default gateway. **IPCONFIG** showed your IP address to be 192.168.4.15. You also were able to ping your IP address, but you still cannot connect to your server. What could be causing this problem?
   a. Your hub is malfunctioning.
   b. The cable connecting the hub to the DSL router is bad.
   c. The cable connecting the hub to your system is bad.
   d. The network's SDSL router is also running DHCP, causing a DHCP conflict.

2. This morning you have gotten many complaints about the network being sluggish You are monitoring the network's performance and you notice it is having a high number of collisions. Which of the following could be contributing to this problem?
   a. Your network is connected with old CAT 3 cabling.
   b. There is a loose 50-ohm terminator on the network cabling.
   c. Your network hub has died.
   d. A BNC connector is connected incorrectly without the T-connector.

3. Your boss has decided he wants you to remove WINS from the network and use DNS instead. You have one network segment that has four addresses that are resolved by the WINS server. What is the best way to make this change and make sure your users can reach those addresses by host name?

   a. Add a WINS proxy to your network segment.

   b. Request the addresses be added into DNS.

   c. Enter the four host names and addresses in the HOSTS file.

   d. Enter the four host names and addresses in the LMHOSTS file.

4. You removed an old NT workstation from your network that had been configured with static IP, and placed the old workstation in a closet. You have your network clients obtaining IP addresses automatically, then you notice someone has hooked the old system back up to the network. Meanwhile, the old system and another workstation are experiencing problems getting online. What could be the cause of this?

   a. There is an IP address conflict.

   b. Your LMHOSTS file has become corrupt and is causing network problems.

   c. Your DNS server is down.

   d. The network printer is offline.

5. You have a NetWare network with some Windows 98 systems as workstations. You have installed TCP/IP on your workstation, and add a Windows NT server to the network. The NT server has several resources shared with the network, but not all the Windows 98 workstations can access the NT server's shares. Which of the following are possible reasons for this problem? (Choose all that apply.)

   a. The cable connecting the server to the hub is broken.

   b. The Windows 98 workstations have not been given the needed permissions to access the NT server shares.

   c. The Windows 98 workstations do not have Client for NetWare Networks installed.

   d. The Windows 98 workstations do not have Client for Microsoft Networks installed.

6. Some, but not all of the NICs on your network need to be replaced, so you replace NICs in several of your old workstation systems. Afterward, the workstations with the new NICs can't log on to the server. Which of the following would be a logical step to take to diagnose the problem?

   a. Reboot all the systems on the network.

   b. Check to make sure the appropriate protocols have been installed properly for the new NICs.

    c. Check to see if the server NIC is connected properly.

    d. Test all the cables on the network.

7. The users on your network have been unable to connect to the server for the last ten minutes. You ping the server from several workstations but it times out. You then run the **IPCONFIG** command revealing your IP address to be 169.254.1.16. You reboot the workstations, but they still can't connect to the server. Which of the following would be one of your first steps in diagnosing the problem?

    a. Reboot the DHCP server.

    b. Reboot the workstations again.

    c. Test all the network cables.

    d. Run a diagnostic test on all the server NICs.

8. You are running a Token Ring network, and to increase capacity you've added a new MAU. Afterward, you discover your users can't connect to the LAN. Using a network analyzer, you test connectivity from the NICs to the RJ-45 plugs in the MAU. They appear correct, so what could be causing this problem?

    a. The MAU is set for full-duplex.

    b. CSU/DSU is disconnected.

    c. The Ring In and Ring Out ports are not configured correctly between the MAUs.

    d. You have the workstation cable connected to the wrong port on the hub.

9. Roger is in a hotel room in Virginia trying to access the network in the Houston office, but is having difficulties dialing in to the network. He unplugs the cable from the phone and plugs it into the modem, but gets no dial tone. What is the problem?

    a. The modem on his laptop does not support ISDN.

    b. The dial-up server is not responding.

    c. The wrong protocols are installed.

    d. The dial-up connections are not configured properly.

10. Two of the following devices work together to trace cable by sending an electrical signal along a wire at a particular frequency. One of them emits a sound when it distinguishes that frequency. The devices go by the nickname "Fox and Hound." What are the two devices that compose it? (Choose two of the following.)

    a. Frequency locator

    b. Tone generator

    c. Frequency generator

    d. Tone locator

Answers

1. **D.** The network's SDSL router is also running DHCP, causing a DHCP conflict. The other choices cannot be correct because the pings were successful.

2. **B.** The terminator is loose enough to cause reflection, making it appear that there are many collisions.

3. **B.** The best way to make this change and make sure your users can reach those addresses by host name is to request the addresses be added into DNS.

4. **A.** The most likely answer is an IP address conflict. The old NT workstation is using one of the DHCP-assigned IP addresses, causing a conflict with the other problem workstation.

5. **B and D.** The two possible reasons for this problem are that the Windows 98 workstations have not been given the needed permissions to access the NT server shares, and that they don't have Client for Microsoft Networks installed. The server they can't access is not the NetWare server, so Client for NetWare Networks is irrelevant, and if the cable were broken, the Windows 98 workstations wouldn't be the only ones exhibiting the problem.

6. **B.** The logical step to take in diagnosing why the new NICs can't log on to the server is to make sure all the appropriate protocols have been installed. Since only the new NICs are affected, the problem isn't likely to be the server's NIC, and rebooting all the systems or checking all the cabling are both serious overkill.

7. **A.** The first thing to try is rebooting the DHCP server. You've already rebooted the workstations, and it's unlikely that all the server NICs or cables suddenly failed.

8. **C.** The problem could be that the Ring In and Ring Out ports are connected incorrectly.

9. **D.** Roger's dial-up connections are not configured properly. Neither the server nor any protocols have come into play yet.

10. **B and D.** The tone generator and tone locator work together to trace cables by sending an electrical signal along a wire at a particular frequency.

GLOSSARY

5-4-3 Rule   A general rule for approximating the correct size of a collision domain. In a collision domain, no two nodes may be separated by more than 5 repeaters, 4 segments, and 3 populated segments.

10Base2   An Ethernet LAN designed to run on common coax RG-58 cabling, almost exactly like the coax for cable television. It runs at 10 Mbps and has a maximum segment length of 185 meters. Also known as Thinnet or Thin Ethernet. It uses baseband signaling and BNC connectors.

10Base5   The original Ethernet LAN, designed to run on specialized coax cabling. It runs at 10 Mbps and has a maximum segment length of 500 meters. Also known as Thicknet or Thick Ethernet, 10Base5 uses baseband signaling running on RG-8 coaxial cable. It uses DIX connectors and external transceivers, known as AUIs.

10BaseFL   Fiber-optic implementation of Ethernet that runs at 10 Mbps using baseband signaling. Maximum segment length is 2 km.

10BaseT   An Ethernet LAN designed to run on UTP cabling, 10BaseT runs at 10 Mbps. The maximum length for the cabling between the NIC and the hub (or switch, repeater, and so forth) is 100 meters. It uses baseband signaling.

100BaseFX   An Ethernet LAN designed to run on fiber optic cabling. It runs at 100 Mbps and uses baseband signaling.

100BaseT   A generic term for any Ethernet cabling system that is designed to run at 100 Mbps on UTP cabling. It uses baseband signaling.

100BaseT4   This is an Ethernet LAN designed to run on UTP cabling. It runs at 100 Mbps and uses four pairs of wires on CAT3 or better cabling.

100BaseTX   This is an Ethernet LAN designed to run on UTP cabling. It runs at 100 Mbps and uses two pairs of wires on CAT5 cabling. It uses baseband signaling.

100BaseVG   Also called 100BaseVGAnyLAN. Uses CAT3 cabling and an access method called demand priority.

1000BaseX (Gigabit Ethernet)   Generic term for various Ethernet standards that can transfer data at speeds up to 1000 Mbps. Current standards include 1000BaseT, 1000BaseCX, 1000Base5X, and 1000BaseLX.

16450, 16550, 16550A, 16550AF, 16550AFN   These are incremental improvements in UARTs. The 16550AFN is considered the most sophisticated UART available today. Note: the 16450 should not be used with any modem faster than a 14.4-Kbps modem.

16-bit   Able to process 16 bits of data at a time.

24-bit color   Also referred to as true color, using 3 bytes per pixel to represent a color image in a PC. The 24 bits enable up to 16,777,216 colors to be stored and displayed.

286   Also called 80286. Intel's second-generation processor. The 286 had a 16-bit external data bus and a 24-bit address bus. It was the first Intel processor to achieve protected mode.

386   Also called 80386DX. Intel's third-generation processor. The 386 DX had a 32-bit external data bus and 32-bit address bus.

386SX   Also called 80386SX. This was a hybrid chip that combined the 32-bit functions and modes of the 80386DX with the 16-bit external data bus and 24-bit address bus of the 80286.

486DX   Intel's fourth-generation CPU. Essentially an 80386DX with a built-in cache and math coprocessor.

486DX/2, 486DX/3, 486DX/4   486 CPUs that operate externally at one speed and internally at a speed that is two, three, or four times faster. Although the internal speed can be more than two times as fast as the external speed, these CPUs are known collectively as "clock doublers."

486SX   A 486DX without the functional math coprocessor.

586   This is an unofficial, generic term that describes the Intel Pentium family of CPUs as well as comparable CPUs made by other manufacturers.

8086/8088   These were the first generation of Intel processors to be used in IBM PCs. The 8086 and 8088 were identical with the exception of the external data bus: the 8086 had a 16-bit bus while the 8088 had an 8-bit bus.

8086 mode   *See* real mode.

8237   This is the part number for the original DMA controller. Although long obsolete, the name is still often used in reference to DMA usage.

8259   This is the part number for the original IRQ controller. Although long obsolete, the name is still often used in reference to IRQ usage.

A

access   The reading or writing of data. Also a verb meaning to gain entry to data. Most commonly used in connection with information access, via a user ID, and qualified by an indication of the kinds of access permitted. For example, *read-only access* means that the contents of the file may be read but not altered or erased.

access time   The time interval measured from the moment that data is requested to the moment it is received. Most commonly used in measuring the speed of storage devices.

account   A registered set of rights and/or permissions to an individual computer or to a network of computers.

address bus   The wires leading from the CPU to the memory controller chip that enable the CPU to address RAM. Also used by the CPU for I/O addressing. An internal electronic channel from the microprocessor to random access memory, along which the addresses of memory storage locations are transmitted. Like a post office box, each memory location has a distinct number or address; the address bus provides the means by which the microprocessor can access every location in memory.

address space   The total amount of memory addresses that an address bus can contain.

ADSL (asymmetric digital subscriber line)   A fully digital, dedicated connection to the telephone system that provides download speeds up to 9 Mbps and upload speeds of up to 1 Mbps.

AGP (accelerated graphics port)   A 32-bit expansion slot designed by Intel specifically for video, which runs at 66 MHz and yields a throughput of 254 MBps, at least. Later versions (2X, 3X, 4X) give substantially higher throughput.

AIX (Advanced Interactive Executive)   IBM's version of UNIX, which runs on 386 or better PCs.

algorithm   A set of rules for solving a problem in a given number of steps.

ALU (arithmetic logic unit)   The circuit that performs CPU math calculations and logic operations.

AMD (Advanced Micro Devices)   The manufacturer of chipsets and microprocessors. AMD produces CPUs for computers worldwide.

amplifier   A device that strengthens electrical signals, enabling them to travel farther.

analog   A type of device that uses a physical quantity, such as length or voltage, to represent the value of a number. By contrast, digital storage relies on a coding system of numeric units.

analog video   Picture signals represented by a number of smooth transitions between video levels. Television signals are analog, whereas digital video signals assign a finite set of levels. Because computer signals are digital, video must be converted into analog form before it can be shown on a computer screen. All modern CRTs use analog video standards based on the VGA standard. *See also* VGA.

ANSI (American National Standards Institute)   The body responsible for standards such as ASCII.

ANSI character set   The ANSI-standard character set that defines 256 characters. The first 128 are ASCII, and the second group of 128 contain math and language symbols.

anti-aliasing   In computer imaging, a blending effect that smoothes sharp contrasts between two regions-that is, jagged lines or different colors. This reduces the jagged edges of text or objects. In voice signal processing, it refers to the process of removing or smoothing out spurious frequencies from waveforms produced by converting digital signals back to analog.

API (application programming interface)   A software definition that describes operating system calls for application software; conventions defining how a service is invoked.

APM (automated power management)   The BIOS routines that enable the CPU to selectively turn on and off selected peripherals.

AppleTalk A network protocol suite invented to run on Apple computers. Modern Macintosh systems still support AppleTalk, but most Macintosh systems use TCP/IP in favor or AppleTalk.

application A program designed to perform a job for the user of a PC. A word processor and a spreadsheet program are typical applications.

application servers Servers that provide clients access to software or other applications that run on the server only. Examples include web servers, e-mail servers, and database servers.

archive To copy programs and data onto a relatively inexpensive storage medium (disk, tape, and so forth) for long-term retention.

archive bit An attribute of a file that shows whether the file has been backed up since the last change. Each time a file is opened, changed, or saved, the archive bit is turned on. Some types of backups will turn off this archive bit to indicate that a good backup of the file exists on tape.

ARCNET (Attached Resource Computer NETwork) The original ARCNET standard defined a true star topology, in which both the physical and logical topology work as a star. ARCNET uses token passing to get frames from one system to another. ARCNET runs at 2.5 Mbps.

argument A value supplied to a procedure, macro, subroutine, or command that is required in order to evaluate that procedure, macro, subroutine, or command. Synonymous with parameter.

ARP (Address Resolution Protocol) A protocol in the TCP/IP suite used with the command-line utility of the same name to determine the MAC address that corresponds to a particular IP address.

ARPANET The first practical network ever created. It was conceived by an organization called the Advanced Research Projects Agency (ARPA).

ASCII (American Standard Code for Information Interchange) The industry standard 8-bit characters used to define text characters, consisting of 96 upper and lowercase letters, plus 32 nonprinting control characters, each of which is numbered. These numbers were designed to achieve uniformity among different computer devices for printing and the exchange of simple text documents.

aspect ratio The ratio of width to height of an object. In television, this is usually a 4:3 ratio, except in the new HDTV standard, which is 16:9.

assembler A program that converts symbolically coded programs into object-level machine code. In an assembler program, unlike a compiler, there is a one-to-one correspondence between human-readable instructions and the machine-language code.

asynchronous communication A type of communication in which the receiving devices must send an acknowledgement (ACK) to the sending unit to verify a piece of data has been sent.

ASPI (advanced SCSI programmable interface) A series of very tight standards that enable SCSI devices to share a common set of highly compatible drivers.

AT (advanced technology) The model name of the second-generation, 80286-based IBM computer. Many aspects of the AT, such as the BIOS, CMOS, and expansion bus, have become de facto standards in the PC industry.

AT bus The 16-bit expansion bus used in the IBM Personal Computer and the 32-bit bus of computers using the Intel 386 and 486 microprocessors.

ATA (AT attachment)   A type of hard drive and controller. ATA was designed to replace the earlier ST506 and ESDI drives without requiring replacing the AT BIOS. These drives are more popularly known as IDE drives. *See also* ST506, ESDI, and IDE.

ATAPI (ATA programmable interface)   A series of standards that enables mass storage devices other than hard drives to use the IDE/ATA controllers. Extremely popular with CD-ROMs and removable media drives like the Iomega Zip drive. *See also* EIDE.

ATM (Asynchronous Transfer Mode)   A network technology that runs at speeds between 25 and 622 Mbps using fiber-optic cabling or CAT5 UTP.

authoritative DNS servers   DNS servers that contain forward lookup zones.

AUI (attachment unit interface)   The standard connector used with 10Base5 Ethernet. This is a 15-pin female DB connector, also known as DIX.

AUTOEXEC.BAT   A batch file that DOS executes when you start or restart the system. AUTOEXEC.BAT is not necessary, but when you're running a computer to which you've attached several devices and several different software applications, the file is essential for efficient operation. AUTOEXEC.BAT files commonly include PATH statements that tell DOS where to find application programs, and commands to install a mouse or operate your printer.

B

backbone   A generalized term defining a primary cable or system that connects networks together.

background processing   Users may use a terminal for one project and concurrently submit a job that is placed in a background queue that the computer will run, as resources become available. Also refers to any processing in which a job runs without being connected to a terminal.

backside bus   The set of wires that connect the CPU to level 2 cache. The backside bus first appeared in the Pentium Pro, and most modern CPUs have a special backside bus. Some busses, such as that in the later Celeron processors (300A and beyond), run at the full speed of the CPU, whereas others run at a fraction of this speed. Earlier Pentium IIs, for example, had backside busses running at half the speed of the processor. *See also* frontside bus and external data bus.

back up   To save important data in a secondary location as a safety against loss of the primary data.

backward compatible   Compatible with earlier versions of a program or earlier models of a computer.

bandwidth   A piece of the spectrum occupied by some form of signal, whether it is television, voice, fax data, and so forth. Signals require a certain size and location of bandwidth in order to be transmitted. The higher the bandwidth, the faster the signal transmission, thus allowing for a more complex signal such as audio or video. Because bandwidth is a limited space, when one user is occupying it, others must wait their turn. Bandwidth is also the capacity of a network to transmit a given amount of data during a given period.

bank   The total number of SIMMs that can be simultaneously accessed by the MCC. The width of the external data bus divided by the width of the SIMM sticks.

baseband   Digital signaling that has only one signal (a single signal) on the cable at a time. The signals must be in one of three states: one, zero, or idle.

baseline   Static image of a system's (or network's) performance when all elements are known to be working properly.

BASIC (Beginners All-purpose Symbolic Instruction Code)   A commonly used personal-computer language first developed at Dartmouth during the 1960s and popularized by Microsoft.

baud   One analog cycle on a telephone line. In the early days of telephone data transmission, the baud rate was often analogous to bits per second. Due to advanced modulation of baud cycles as well as data compression, this is no longer true.

BBS (bulletin board system)   A term for dial-up online systems from which users can download software and graphics, send and receive e-mail, and exchange information. Usually run by individuals from their homes. Although once very popular, BBS sites are rapidly diminishing due to the popularity of the Internet.

binary numbers   A number system with a base of 2—unlike the number systems most of us use, which have bases of 10 (decimal numbers), 12 (measurement in feet and inches), and 60 (time). Binary numbers are preferred for computers for precision and economy. Building an electronic circuit that can detect the difference between two states (on-off, 0-1) is easier and more inexpensive than one that could detect the differences among 10 states (0–9).

bindery   Security and account database used by default on Novell NetWare 3.x servers and available to NetWare 4.x and 5.x servers.

BIOS (basic input/output system)   Classically, the software routines burned onto the system ROM of a PC. More commonly seen as any software that directly controls a particular piece of hardware. A set of programs encoded in read-only memory (ROM) on computers. These programs handle startup operations and the low-level control for hardware such as disk drives, the keyboard, and monitor.

bit—binary digit   A bit is a single binary digit, typically represented by 1's and 0's. Any device that can be in an on or off state.

BNC connector   A connector used for 10Base2 coaxial cable. All BNC connectors have to be locked into place by turning the locking ring 90 degrees.

boot   To initiate an automatic routine that clears the memory, loads the operating system, and prepares the computer for use. The term boot is derived from the phrase "pull yourself up by your bootstraps." PCs must do that because RAM doesn't retain program instructions when power is turned off. A cold boot occurs when the PC is physically switched on, while a warm boot enables the system to reset itself without putting a strain on the electronic circuitry. To perform a warm boot, you press the CTRL, ALT, and DELETE keys at the same time, a ritual commonly known as the three-fingered salute.

BOOTP (Bootstrap Protocol)   This is a component of TCP/IP that allows computers to discover and receive an IP address from a DHCP server prior to booting the OS. Other items that may be discovered during the BOOTP process are the IP address of the default gateway for the subnet and the IP addresses of any name servers.

boot sector   The first sector on an IBM-PC hard drive or floppy disk, track 0. The bootup software in ROM tells the computer to load whatever program is found there. If a system disk is read, the program in the boot record directs the computer to the root directory to load MS-DOS.

bps (bits per second)   A measurement of how fast data is moved from one place to another. A 28.8 modem can move 28,800 bits per second.

bridge   A device that connects two networks and passes traffic between them based only on the node address, so that traffic between nodes on one network does not appear on the other network. For example, an Ethernet bridge only looks at the Ethernet address. Bridges filter and forward packets based on MAC addresses and operate at level 2 (Data Link) of the OSI seven-layer model.

broadband   Analog signaling that sends multiple signals over the cable at the same time. The best example of broadband signaling is cable television. The zero, one, and idle states (*see* baseband) exist on multiple channels on the same cable.

broadcast   A broadcast is a packet addressed to all machines. In TCP/IP, the general broadcast address is 255.255.255.255.

BTW (by the way)   Common abbreviation used by BBS, Usenet, and IRC users.

buffer   Electronic storage, usually DRAM, that holds data moving between two devices. Buffers are used anywhere there is a situation where one device may send or receive data faster or slower than the other device with which it is communicating. For example, the BUFFERS statement in DOS is used to set aside RAM for communication with hard drives.

bug   A programming error that causes a program or a computer system to perform erratically, produce incorrect results, or crash. This term was coined when a real bug was found in a circuit of one of the first ENIAC computers.

bus   A series of wires connecting two or more separate electronic devices, enabling those devices to communicate.

bus topology   A network topology in which all computers connect to the network via a central bus cable.

byte   Eight contiguous bits, the fundamental data unit of personal computers. Storing the equivalent of one character, the byte is also the basic unit of measurement for computer storage. Bytes are counted in powers of two.

C

cable modem   High-speed home Internet access that runs through a coax cable laid by a cable company.

cable tester   A device that tests the continuity of cables. Some testers also test for electrical shorts, crossed wires, or other electrical characteristics.

cache   A special area of RAM that stores the data most frequently accessed from the hard drive. Cache memory can optimize the use of your systems.

cache memory   A special section of fast memory chips set aside to store the information most frequently accessed from RAM.

card   Generic term for anything that you can snap into an expansion slot.

CAT3   Category 3 wire, an EIA/TIA standard for UTP wiring that can operate at up to 16 Mbps.

CAT4   Category 4 wire, an EIA/TIA standard for UTP wiring that can operate at up to 20 Mbps. Not widely used, except in older Token Ring networks.

CAT5   Category 5 wire, an EIA/TIA standard for UTP wiring that can operate at up to 100 Mbps.

CAT5e   Category 5e wire, an EIA/TIA standard for UTP wiring with improved support for 100 Mbps.

CD-R (compact disk–recordable)   An improvement on CR-ROM technology that allows for a single write onto the media.

CD-ROM (compact disk–read-only memory)   A read-only compact storage disk for audio or video data. Recordable devices, such as CD-Rs and CD-RWs, are updated versions of the older CD-ROM players.

CD-RW (compact disk–read/write)   CD-RW technology that allows for multiple reads (burns), as compared to CD-R, which allows for only one read.

CHAP (Challenge Handshake Authentication Protocol)   CHAP is the most common remote access protocol. CHAP has the serving system challenge the remote client, which must provide an encrypted password.

chat   A multi-party, real-time text conversation. The Internet's most popular version is known as Internet Relay Chat, which many groups use to converse in real time with each other, moving toward true point-to-point voice communications.

chipset   Electronic chips that handle all of the low-level functions of a PC, which in the original PC were handled by close to 30 different chips. Chipsets usually consist of one, two, or three separate chips to handle all of these functions. The most common chipsets in use today are the Intel family of chipsets (BX, 815e, and so forth).

CHS (cylinder/heads/sectors)   The acronym for the combination of the three critical geometries used to determine the size of a hard drive: cylinders, heads, and sectors per track.

CISC (complex instruction set computing)   A CPU design that enables the processor to handle more complex instructions from the software at the expense of speed. The Intel x86 series (386, 486, Pentium) for PCs are CISC processors.

client   A computer program that uses the services of another computer program; software that extracts information from a server. Your auto-dial phone is a client, and the phone company is its server. Also, a machine that accesses shared resources on a server.

client/server   A relationship in which client software obtains services from a server on behalf of a person.

client/server application   An application that performs some or all of its processing on an application server rather than on the client. The client usually only receives the result of the processing.

client/server network   A network that has dedicated server machines and client machines.

clipboard   A temporary storage space from which captured data can be copied or pasted into other documents.

clock   An electronic circuit using a quartz crystal to generate evenly spaced pulses at speeds of millions of cycles per second. The pulses are used to synchronize the flow of information through the computer's internal communication channels. Most of the chips on a PC synchronize to this clock. The speed of the clock's signal is called the clock rate.

cluster   Groups of sectors organized by the operating system to store files. The number of sectors in a cluster is dependent on the size of the partition and the file system used. When an operating system stores a file on disk, it writes those files into dozens or even hundreds of clusters.

CMOS (complimentary metal-oxide semiconductor)   Originally, the type of nonvolatile RAM that held information about the most basic parts of your PC such as hard drives, floppies, and amount of DRAM. Today, actual CMOS chips have been replaced by Flash type nonvolatile RAM. The information is the same, however, and is still called CMOS-even though it is now almost always stored on Flash RAM.

coax   Short for coaxial. Cabling in which an internal conductor is surrounded by another, outer, conductor, thus sharing the same axis.

code   A language for expressing operations to be performed by a computer.

collision   The result of two nodes transmitting at the same time on a multiple access network such as Ethernet. Both packets may be lost or partial packets may result.

collision domain   A set of Ethernet segments that receive all traffic generated by any node within those segments. Repeaters, amplifiers, and hubs do not create separate collision domains, but bridges, routers, and switches do.

COM   In Microsoft operating systems, a device name that refers to the serial communications ports available on your computer. When used as a program extension, .COM indicates an executable program file limited to 64K.

command   A request, typed from a terminal or embedded in a file, to perform an operation or to execute a particular program.

COMMAND.COM   In DOS and Windows 9x, a file that contains the command processor. This file must be present on the startup disk for DOS to run. COMMAND.COM is usually located in the root directory of your hard drive. Windows NT, 2000, and XP use CMD.EXE instead of COMMAND.COM.

command processor   The part of the operating system that accepts input from the user and displays any messages, such as confirmation and error messages.

communications program   A program that makes a computer act as a terminal to another computer. Communications programs usually provide for file transfer between microcomputers and mainframes.

compression   The process of squeezing data to eliminate redundancies, allowing files to be stored or transmitted using less space.

computer   A device or system that is capable of carrying out a sequence of operations in a distinctly and explicitly defined manner. These operations are frequently numeric computations or data manipulations, but also include data input and output. The ability to branch within sequences is its key feature.

concentrator   A device that brings together at a common center connections to a particular kind of network (such as Ethernet) and implements that network internally.

CONFIG.SYS   An ASCII text file in the root directory that contains configuration commands. CONFIG.SYS enables the system to be set up to configure high, expanded, and extended memories by the loading of HIMEM.SYS and EMM386.EXE drivers, as well as drivers for nonstandard peripheral components.

connectionless protocol   A protocol that does not establish and verify a connection between the hosts before sending data; it just sends the data and hopes for the best. This is faster than connection-oriented protocols. UDP is an example of a connectionless protocol.

connection-oriented protocol   A protocol that establishes a connection between two hosts before transmitting data, and verifies receipt before closing the connection between the hosts. TCP is an example of a connection-oriented protocol.

contiguous   Adjacent; placed one next to the other.

controller card   A card adapter that connects devices, like a disk drive, to the main computer bus/motherboard.

conventional memory   In any IBM PC-compatible computer, the first 640K of the computer's RAM. 640K has proven to be insufficient because of the programs that demand more memory and users who want to run more than one program at a time. Many users equip their systems with extended or expanded memory and the memory management programs needed to access this memory.

copy backup   A type of backup similar to Normal or Full, in that all selected files on a system are backed up. This type of backup *does not* change the archive bit of the files being backed up.

cross-linked files   In DOS, a file-storage error that occurs when the FAT indicates that two files claim the same disk cluster. These occur when the system is abnormally halted. To repair, run Scan Disk or Norton's Disk Doctor.

crossover cable   Special UTP cable used to connect hubs or to connect network cards without a hub. Crossover cables reverse the sending and receiving wire pairs from one end to the other.

crossover port   Special port in a hub that crosses the sending and receiving wires, thus removing the need for a crossover cable to connect the hubs.

crosstalk   Electrical signal interference between two cables that are in close proximity to each other.

CSMA/CA (Carrier Sense Multiple Access / Collision Avoidance)   This access method is used mainly on Apple networks, and is also implemented on wireless networks. With CSMA/CA, before hosts send out data, they send out a signal that checks to make sure that the network is free of other signals. If data is detected on the wire, the hosts wait a random time period before trying again. If the wire is free, the data is sent out.

CSMA/CD (Carrier Sense Multiple Access / Collision Detection)   The access method Ethernet systems use in local area networking technologies, enabling packets of data information to flow through the network and ultimately reach address locations. Known as a *contention* protocol, hosts on CSMA/CD networks send out data without checking to see if the wire is free first. If a collision occurs, both hosts wait a random time period before retransmitting the data.

CPU (central processing unit) The "brain" of the computer. The microprocessor that handles the primary calculations for the computer. Commonly known by names like 486 and Pentium.

CRC (cyclical redundancy check) A mathematical method that is used to check for errors in long streams of transmitted data with very high accuracy. Before data is sent, the main computer uses the data to calculate a CRC value from the data's contents. If the receiver calculates a different CRC value from the received data, the data was corrupted during transmission and is resent. Ethernet packets have a CRC code.

CRT (cathode ray tube) The tube of a monitor in which rays of electrons are beamed onto a phosphorescent screen to produce images. Monitors are sometimes called CRT displays.

CSU/DSU (channel service unit/data service unit) A piece of equipment that connects a leased line from the telephone company to a customer's equipment (such as a router). It performs line encoding and conditioning functions, and often has a loopback function for testing.

cursor A symbol on a display screen that indicates the position at which the next character entered will be displayed. The symbol often blinks so that it can be easily noticed.

Cyrix Company that makes CPUs, in direct competition with Intel.

D

daily backup Also called a daily copy backup, this backup type makes a copy of all files that have been changed on that day without changing the archive bits of those files.

daisy chain A method of connecting together several devices along a bus and managing the signals for each device.

DAT (digital audio tape) Higher storage capacity tape recording system that uses digital recording methods. Used for digital audio and video as well as data backups.

database A collection of interrelated data values that may be integrated permanently into a single connected structure or integrated temporarily for each interrogation, known as a query. In its most technical sense, the term database implies that any of the data may be used as a key for specific queries. In more common usage, it means any accessible collection of information, in which only a limited set of data values may be used to specify queries.

datagram Another term for network packets or frames. *See* packets, frames.

DB connectors D-shaped connectors used for a variety of different connections in the PC and networking world. Can be either male or female, with a varying number of pins or sockets.

DB-15 DB connector (female) used in 10Base5 networks. *See also* DIX and AUI.

DBMS (database management system) A systematic approach to storing, updating, securing, and retrieving information stored as data items, usually in the form of records in one or more files.

debug To detect, trace, and eliminate errors in computer programs.

dedicated circuit A circuit that runs from a breaker box to specific outlets.

dedicated server A machine that does not use any client functions, only server functions.

dedicated telephone line   A telephone line that is an always open, or connected, circuit. Dedicated telephone lines usually do not have numbers.

default   A software function or operation that occurs automatically unless the user specifies something else.

DEFRAG   Defragmentation. A procedure in which all the files on a hard disk are rewritten on disk so that all parts of each file are written in contiguous clusters. The result is an improvement of up to 75 percent of the disk's speed during retrieval operations.

default gateway   In a TCP/IP network, the nearest router to a particular host. This router's IP address is part of the necessary TCP/IP configuration for communicating with multiple networks using IP.

device driver   A subprogram to control communications between the computer and some peripheral hardware.

DHCP (Dynamic Host Configuration Protocol)   A protocol that allows a DHCP server to set TCP/IP settings automatically for a DHCP client.

differential backup   Similar to an incremental backup in that it backs up the files that have been changed since the last backup. This type of backup does not change the state of the archive bit.

DIMM (dual inline memory module)   DIMMs are a type of DRAM packaging, similar to SIMMs, with the distinction that each side of each tab inserted into the system performs a separate function. Comes in 72- and 144-pin SO DIMMs as well as 144- and 168-pin versions.

directory   A logical container of files and other directories; synonymous with folder. Typically implemented as a file that contains pointers (directions) to files or other directories.

disk drive controller   The circuitry that controls the physical operations of the floppy disks and/or hard disks connected to the computer.

disk striping   Process by which data is spread among multiple (at least two) drives. It increases speed for both reads and writes of data. Considered RAID level 0, because it does *not* provide fault tolerance.

disk striping with parity   Provides fault tolerance by writing data across multiple drives and then including an additional drive, called a parity drive, that stores information to rebuild the data contained on the other drives. Disk striping with parity requires at least three physical disks: two for the data and a third for the parity drive. It provides data redundancy at RAID levels 3–5 with different options.

display   A device that enables information, either textual or pictorial, to be seen but not permanently recorded. Sometimes called the monitor, the most widely used kind is the cathode ray tube, or CRT; liquid crystal diode, or LCD, displays are also popular.

dithering   A technique for smoothing out digitized images; using alternating colors in a pattern to produce perceived color detail.

DIX (Digital, Intel, Xerox) connector   The DIX standard was the original implementation of Ethernet. The DIX connector is the standard connector used with 10Base5 Ethernet, also known as the AUI.

DLC (Data Link Control)   A network protocol that was used for many years to link PCs to mainframe computers. Because Hewlett-Packard adopted the DLC protocol for use by network printers, DLC enjoyed a much longer life than it probably should have, given the existence of so many alternatives. All versions of Windows, including Windows XP, still support DLC.

DLL (dynamic link library)   A file of executable functions or data that can be used by a Windows application. Typically, a DLL provides one or more particular functions, and a program accesses the functions by creating links to the DLL.

DLT (digital linear tape)   Huge data capacity tapes used for tape backups.

DMA (direct memory access)   A technique that some PC hardware devices use to transfer data to and from the memory without requiring the use of the CPU.

DMZ (demilitarized zone)   A lightly protected or unprotected network positioned between your firewall and the Internet.

DNS (Domain Name Service [or System])   A TCP/IP name resolution system that resolves host names to IP addresses.

DNS domain   A specific branch of the DNS namespace. First-level DNS domains include .COM, .GOV, and .EDU.

DVI (digital video interface)   While traditional CRT monitors are analog, LCD monitors are digital. DVI is the digital video interface that is most often seen on LCD flat panel monitors.

document   A medium and the data recorded on it for human use; for example, a report sheet or book. By extension, any record that has permanence and that can be read by human or machine.

documentation   A collection of organized documents or the information recorded in documents. Also, instructional material specifying the inputs, operations, and outputs of a computer program or system.

domain   Term used to describe groupings of users, computers, or networks. In Microsoft networking, a domain is a group of computers and users that share a common account database and a common security policy. For the Internet, a domain is a group of computers that share a common element in their hierarchical name. Other types of domains also exist, such as collision domains.

domain controller   A Microsoft Windows NT or 2000 machine that stores the user and server account information for its domain in a central database. On a Windows NT domain controller, the database is called the Security Accounts Manager, or SAM database, and is stored as part of the registry. Windows 2000 domain controllers store all account and security information in the Active Directory directory service.

DOS (disk operating system)   The set of programming that allows a program to interact with the computer. Examples of disk operating systems include Microsoft's MS-DOS, IBM's PC-DOS and OS/2, and Apple's MacOS System 7. Microsoft's Windows 3.1 is not technically an operating system, since it still requires MS-DOS to work, but it is often referred to as one. Windows 9x and Windows NT/2000 are true disk operating systems.

DOSKEY   A DOS utility that enables you to type more than one command on a line, store and retrieve previously used DOS commands, create stored macros, and customize all DOS commands.

DOS prompt   A letter representing the disk drive, followed by the greater-than sign (>), which together inform you that the operating system is ready to receive a command.

Dot-matrix printer   A printer that creates each character from an array of dots. Pins striking a ribbon against the paper, one pin for each dot position, form the dots. The printer may be a serial printer (printing one character at a time) or a line printer.

double word   A group of 32 binary digits. Four bytes.

download   The transfer of information from a remote computer system to the user's system. Opposite of upload.

DPI (dots per inch)   A measure of printer resolution that counts the dots the device can produce per linear inch.

DRAM (dynamic random access memory)   The memory used to store data in most personal computers. DRAM stores each bit in a "cell" composed of a transistor and a capacitor. Because the capacitor in a DRAM cell can only hold a charge for a few milliseconds, DRAM must be continually refreshed, or rewritten, to retain its data.

DSP (digital signal processor)   A specialized microprocessor-like device that processes digital signals at the expense of other abilities, much as the FPU is optimized for math functions. DSPs are used in such specialized hardware as high-speed modems, multimedia sound cards, MIDI equipment, and real-time video capture and compression.

duplexing   Also called disk duplexing or drive duplexing, duplexing is similar to mirroring in that data is written to and read from two physical drives for fault tolerance. In addition, separate controllers are used for each drive, for both additional fault tolerance and additional speed. Considered RAID level 1.

dynamic link   A method of linking data so that it is shared by two or more programs. When data is changed in one program, the data is likewise changed in the other.

dynamic routing   Process by which routers in an internetwork automatically exchange information with all other routers, enabling them to build their own list of routes to various networks, called a routing table. Dynamic routing requires a dynamic routing protocol, such as OSPF or RIP.

dynamic routing protocol   A protocol that supports the building of automatic routing tables, such as Open Shortest Path First (OSPF) or Routing Information Protocol (RIP).

E

EDB (external data bus)   The primary data highway of all computers. Everything in your computer is tied either directly or indirectly to the external data bus. *See also* frontside bus and backside bus.

EDO (enhanced data out)   An improvement on FPM DRAM in that more data can be read before the RAM must be refreshed.

EEPROM (electrically erasable programmable read-only memory)   A type of ROM chip that can be erased and reprogrammed electrically. EEPROMs were the most common BIOS storage device until the advent of Flash ROM.

EIA/TIA (Electronics Industry Association/Telecommunications Industry Association) The standards body that defines most of the standards for computer network cabling. Most of these standards are defined under the EIA/TIA 568 standard.

EIDE (Enhanced IDE) A marketing concept by Western Digital that consolidated four improvements for IDE drives. These improvements included > 528 MB drives, four devices, increase in drive throughput, and non-hard drive devices. *See also* ATAPI, PIO.

EISA (Enhanced ISA) An improved expansion bus, based on the ISA bus, with a top speed of 8.33 MHz, a 32-bit data path, and a high degree of self-configuration. Backward compatible with legacy ISA cards.

e-mail or email (electronic mail) Messages, usually text, sent from one person to another via computer. E-mail can also be sent automatically to a large number of addresses, known as a mailing list.

e-mail server (or mail server) Server that accepts incoming mail and sorts out the mail for recipients into mailboxes. Also sends mail to other servers using SMTP.

EMI (electromagnetic interference) EMI is an electrical interference from one device to another, resulting in poor performance in the device capabilities. This is similar to having static on your TV while running a blow dryer, or placing two monitors too close together and getting a "shaky" screen.

EMM386.EXE An expanded memory emulator that enables DOS applications to use the extended memory as if it were expanded memory. EMM386.EXE also allows the user to load device drivers and programs into the upper memory area.

encapsulation The process of putting the packets from one protocol inside the packets of another protocol. An example of this is TCP/IP encapsulation in NetWare servers, which places IPX/SPX packets inside TCP/IP packets, enabling Novell NetWare to use TCP/IP for transport while still allowing the network operating system to gain the data it needs from IPX/SPX.

encryption A method of securing messages by scrambling and encoding each packet as it is sent across an unsecured medium, such as the Internet. Each encryption level provides multiple standards and options.

EPROM (erasable programmable read-only memory) A special form of ROM that can be erased by high-intensity ultraviolet light and then rewritten, or reprogrammed.

equipment room A central location for computer or telephone equipment and, most importantly, centralized cabling. All cables will usually run to the equipment room from the rest of the installation.

ESD (electrostatic discharge) The movement of electrons from one body to another. ESD is a real menace to PCs as it can cause permanent damage to semiconductors.

ESDI (Enhanced Small Device Interface) Second-generation hard drives, distinct from their predecessors, ST506, by greater data density and lack of dependence on CMOS settings. Completely obsolete.

Ethernet Name coined by Xerox for the first standard of network cabling and protocols. Ethernet is based on a bus topology.

expansion bus   Set of wires going to the CPU, governed by the expansion bus crystal, directly connected to expansion slots of varying types (ISA, PCI, AGP, and so forth). Depending on the type of slots, the expansion bus runs at a percentage of the main system speed (8.33 to 66 MHz).

expansion slot   A receptacle connected to the computer's expansion bus, designed to accept adapters.

external data bus (EDB)   The primary data highway of all computers. Everything in your computer is tied either directly or indirectly to the external data bus. *See also* frontside bus and backside bus.

F

FAQ (frequently asked questions)   Common abbreviation coined by BBS users and spread to Usenet. This is a list of questions and answers that pertain to a particular topic and are maintained so that users new to the group don't all bombard the group with similar questions. Examples are "What is the name of the actor who plays X on this show, and was he in anything else?" or "Can anyone list all of the books by this author in the order that they were published so that I can read them in that order?" The common answer to this type of question is "Read the FAQ!"

Fast Ethernet   Any of several flavors of Ethernet that operate at 100 Mbps.

FAT (file allocation table)   A FAT is a hidden table of every cluster on a hard disk. The FAT records how files are stored in distinct clusters. The address of the first cluster of the file is stored in the directory file. In the FAT entry for the first cluster is the address of the second cluster used to store that file. In the entry for the second cluster for that file is the address for the third cluster, and so on. This table is the only way for DOS to know where to access files. There are two FATs created, mirror images of each other, in case one is destroyed or damaged.

fault tolerance   The ability of any system to continue functioning after some part of the system has failed. RAID is an example of a hardware device that provides fault tolerance.

FDDI (Fiber Distributed Data Interface)   A standard for transmitting data on optical fiber cables at a rate of around 100 Mbps.

fiber optics   A high-speed physical medium for transmitting data, made of high-purity glass fibers sealed within a flexible opaque tube. Much faster than conventional copper wire such as coaxial cable.

file   A collection of any form of data that is stored beyond the time of execution of a single job. A file may contain program instructions or data, which may be numerical, textual, or graphical information.

file format   The type of file, such as picture or text; represented as a suffix at the end of the filename (text = TXT or .txt, and so forth).

file fragmentation   The allocation of a file in a noncontiguous sector on a disk. Fragmentation occurs because of multiple deletions and write operations.

filename   A name assigned to a file when the file is first written on a disk. Every file on a disk within the same folder must have a unique name. Prior to Windows 95, filenames were restricted to 11 characters—8 characters for the filename and 3 characters for the extension—hence the so-called 8.3 naming convention. Starting with Windows 95, you may use up to 255 characters for filenames on a Windows machine. Macintosh filenames are limited to 31 characters. Filenames can contain nearly any character (including spaces). The list of forbidden characters varies according to operating system, but often include the following: \ / : * ? " < > |.

file server   A computer designated to store software, courseware, administrative tools, and other data on a local or wide area network. It "serves" this information to other computers via the network when users enter their personal access codes.

firewall   A device that restricts traffic between a local network and the Internet.

FireWire   An IEEE 1394 standard to send wideband signals over a thin connector system that plugs into TVs, VCRs, TV cameras, PCs, and so forth. This serial bus developed by Apple and Texas Instruments enables connection of 60 devices at speeds ranging from 100 to 400 Mbps.

Flash ROM   A type of ROM technology that can be electrically reprogrammed while still in the PC. Flash is overwhelmingly the most common storage medium of BIOS in PCs today, as it can be upgraded without even having to open the computer on most systems.

flat namespace   A naming convention that gives each device only one name that must be unique. NetBIOS uses a flat namespace. TCP/IP's DNS uses a hierarchical namespace.

floppy disk   A removable and widely used data storage medium that uses a magnetically coated flexible disk of Mylar enclosed in a plastic envelope or case.

font   A set of consistent size, shape, or style of printer characters, including alphabetic and numeric characters and other signs and symbols.

forward lookup zones   Special storage areas that hold the IP addresses and names of systems for a particular domain or domains. Forward lookup zones are contained within authoritative DNS servers.

FPU (floating-point unit)   A formal term for the math coprocessor (also called a numeric processor). This is a specialized processor that handles certain calculations faster than the CPU. A math coprocessor calculates using floating-point math (which allows for decimals), whereas the CPU can only deal with integers. Intel's 486 and Pentium chips and Motorola's PowerPC have an FPU built into the CPU chip, whereas earlier designs, such as Intel's 80387, needed a separate chip to be installed.

FQDN (fully qualified domain name)   The complete DNS name of a system, from its host name to the top-level domain name.

frames   A defined series of binary data that is the basic container for a discrete amount of data moving across a network. Also commonly called a packet.

frame relay   An extremely efficient data transmission technique used to send digital information such as voice, data, LAN, and WAN traffic quickly and cost-efficiently to many destinations from one port. Frame relay switches packets end to end much faster than X.25, but without any guarantee of data integrity at all.

freeware   Software that is distributed for free, with no license fee.

frontside bus   Name for the wires that connect the CPU to the main system RAM. Generally running at speeds of 66 to 133 MHz. Distinct from the expansion bus and the backside bus, even though sharing wires with the former.

FRU (field replaceable unit)   Any part of a PC that is considered to be replaceable in the field —that is, a customer location. There is no official list of FRUs; it is usually a matter of policy by the repair center.

FTP (File Transfer Protocol)   A set of rules that allows two computers to talk to one another as a file transfer is carried out. This is the protocol used when you transfer a file from one computer to another across the Internet.

FUBAR (fouled up beyond all recognition)   Used to describe a system or network that needs to be rebuilt.

full duplex   Describes any device that can send and receive data simultaneously.

function key   A keyboard key that gives an instruction to a computer, as opposed to keys that produce letters, numbers, marks of punctuation, and so forth.

G

gateway   A hardware or software setup that translates between two dissimilar protocols. For example, Prodigy has a gateway that translates between its internal, proprietary e-mail format and Internet e-mail format. Another, sloppier meaning of gateway is to describe any mechanism for providing access to another system—for example, AOL might be called a gateway to the Internet. *See also* default gateway.

GIF (Graphics Interchange Format)   A method of storing graphics developed for CompuServe in the early 1980s. Because GIF is a compressed format, it takes up much less disk space than conventional file formats, and can therefore be transmitted faster over phone lines. GIF is a nonlossy format, meaning that no data is lost when an image is converted to GIF, but the format is limited to 8-bit graphics, or 256 colors.

giga-   The prefix for the quantity 1,073,741,824. One gigabyte would be 1,073,741,824 bytes. Also sometimes means one billion—one gigahertz, for example, is one billion hertz.

gigabyte   1,024 megabytes.

Gopher   A widely successful method of making menus of material available over the Internet. Gopher is a client/server-style program, which requires that the user have a Gopher client program. Although Gopher spread rapidly across the globe in only a couple of years, it has been largely supplanted by HTTP, also known as the World Wide Web. There are still thousands of Gopher servers on the Internet and they will probably be with us for a while.

graphic   A computer-generated picture produced on a computer screen or paper, ranging from simple line or bar graphs to colorful and detailed images.

green PC   A computer system designed to operate in an energy-efficient manner.

groupware   Software that serves the group and makes the group as a whole more productive and efficient in group tasks—for example, group scheduling.

GUI (graphical user interface)   An interface is the method by which a computer and a user interact. Early interfaces were text-based; that is, the user "talked" to the computer by typing and the computer responded with text on a CRT. A GUI, on the other hand, enables the user to interact with the computer graphically, by manipulating icons that represent programs or documents with a mouse or other pointing device.

H

half-duplex   Any device that can only send or receive data at any given moment. Most Ethernet transmissions are half-duplex.

handshaking   A procedure performed by modems, terminals, and computers to verify that communication has been correctly established.

hang   When a computer freezes, so that it does not respond to keyboard commands, it is said to hang or to have hung.

hang time   The number of seconds a too-often-hung computer is airborne after you have thrown it out a second-story window.

hard drive   A data-recording system using solid disks of magnetic material turning at high speeds.

hardware   Physical computer equipment such as electrical, electronic, magnetic, and mechanical devices. Anything in the computer world that you can hold in your hand. A floppy drive is hardware; Microsoft Word is not.

Hayes command set   A standardized set of instructions used to control modems. Examples are

- **AT**   Attention (used to start commands)
- **ATDT**   Attention Dial Tone
- **ATDP**   Attention Dial Pulse
- **ATH** Attention Hang Up

hex (hexadecimal)   Hex symbols based on a numbering system of 16 (computer shorthand for binary numbers), using ten digits and six letters to condense 0's and 1's to binary numbers. Hex is represented by digits 0 through 9 and alpha A through F, so that 09h has a value of 9, and 0Ah has a value of 10.

hierarchical namespace   A naming scheme where the full name of each object includes its position within the hierarchy. An example of a hierarchical name is www.totalseminars.com, which includes not only the host name, but also the domain name. DNS uses a hierarchical namespace scheme for fully qualified domain names (FQDNs).

high resolution   Using a sufficient number of pixels in display monitors or dots per inch when printing, to produce well-defined text characters and smoothly defined curves in graphic images.

HIMEM.SYS   A DOS device driver that configures extended memory and high memory so that programs conforming to XMS can access it.

HMA (high memory area)   The first 64K of memory above 1 megabyte is known as the HMA. Programs that conform to XMS can use HMA as a direct extension of conventional memory. Most of the portions of DOS that must be loaded into conventional memory can be loaded into the HMA.

home page   The web page that your browser is set to use when it starts up or the main web page for a business, organization, or person. Also, the main page in any collection of web pages.

horizontal cabling   Cabling that connects the equipment room to the work area.

host   A single device (usually a computer) on a TCP/IP network that has an IP address; any device that can be the source or destination of a data packet. Also, in the mainframe world, a computer that is made available for use by multiple people simultaneously.

host ID   The portion of an IP address that defines a specific machine.

HOSTS file   A static text file that resides on a computer and is used to resolve DNS host names to IP addresses. The HOSTS file is checked before the machine sends a name resolution request to a DNS name server. The HOSTS file has no extension.

HTML (Hypertext Markup Language)   An ASCII-based script-like language for creating hypertext documents like those on the World Wide Web.

HTTP (Hypertext Transfer Protocol)   Extremely fast protocol used for network file transfers in the WWW environment.

hub   An electronic device that sits at the center of a star topology network, providing a common point for the connection of network devices. In a 10BaseT Ethernet network, the hub contains the electronic equivalent of a properly terminated bus cable; in a Token Ring network, the hub contains the electronic equivalent of a ring.

hypertext   A document that has been marked up to allow a user to select words or pictures within the document—click on them, and connect to further information. The basis of the World Wide Web.

I

IANA (Internet Assigned Numbers Authority)   The organization responsible for assigning public IP addresses.

ICS (Internet connection sharing)   Also known simply as Internet sharing, a term used to describe the technique of allowing more than one computer to access the Internet simultaneously using a single Internet connection. When you use Internet sharing, you actually connect an entire LAN to the Internet using a single public IP address.

IDE (Intelligent [or Integrated] Drive Electronics)   A PC specification for small- to medium-sized hard drives in which the controlling electronics for the drive are part of the drive itself, speeding up transfer rates and leaving only a simple adapter (or paddle). IDE only supported two drives per system of no more than 504 megabytes each, and has been completely supplanted by Enhanced IDE. EIDE supports four drives of over 8 gigabytes each and more than doubles the transfer rate. The more common name for ATA drives. *See also* ATA.

IEEE (Institute of Electronic and Electrical Engineers)   IEEE is the leading standards-setting group in the United States.

IEEE 802.1   IEEE subcommittee that defined the standards for higher-layerlayer LAN protocols.

IEEE 802.2   IEEE subcommittee that defined the standards for Logical Link Control.

IEEE 802.3   IEEE subcommittee that defined the standards for CSMA/CD (a.k.a. Ethernet).

IEEE 802.4   IEEE subcommittee that defined the standards for Token Bus.

IEEE 802.5   IEEE subcommittee that defined the standards for Token Ring.

IEEE 802.6   IEEE subcommittee that defined the standards for MAN (metropolitan area network).

IEEE 802.7   IEEE subcommittee that defined the standards for broadband.

IEEE 802.8   IEEE subcommittee that defined the standards for fiber optic.

IEEE 802.9   IEEE subcommittee that defined the standards for isochronous LAN.

IEEE 802.10   IEEE subcommittee that defined the standards for security.

IEEE 802.11   IEEE subcommittee that defined the standards for wireless.

IEEE 802.12   IEEE subcommittee that defined the standards for demand priority/100BaseVG.

IEEE 802.14   IEEE subcommittee that defined the standards for cable modems.

IETF (Internet Engineering Task Force)   The primary standards organization for the Internet.

IFCONFIG   A command-line utility for Linux servers and workstations that displays the current TCP/IP configuration of the machine, similar to IPCONFIG and WINIPCFG for Windows systems.

IMAP (Internet Message Access Protocol)   An alternative to POP3. IMAP retrieves e-mail from an e-mail server, like POP3; the main difference is that IMAP uses TCP/IP port 143.

IMO, IMHO (in my opinion, in my humble opinion)   Common abbreviation coined by BBS users and spread to Usenet. Used in e-mail messages and real-time chat sessions. IMHO is often used when the speaker wants to convey that this is not their area of expertise, but it also can be used sarcastically when the speaker sees him- or herself as correct.

impedance   The amount of resistance to an electrical signal on a wire. It is used as a relative measure of the amount of data a cable can handle.

incremental backup   A type of backup that backs up all files that have their archive bits turned on, meaning that they have been changed since the last backup. This type of backup turns the archive bits off after the files have been backed up.

interrupt   A suspension of a process, such as the execution of a computer program, caused by an event initiated by a device on the computer and performed in such a way that the process can be resumed. Events of this kind include sensors monitoring laboratory equipment or a user pressing an interrupt key.

interlaced   TV/video systems in which the electron beam writes every other line, then retraces itself to a second pass to complete the final framed image. Originally, this reduced magnetic line paring, but took twice as long to paint, which added some flicker in graphic images.

InterNIC   The organization that maintains the DNS services, registrations, and so forth run by Network Solutions, General Atomics, and AT&T.

intranet   A private network inside a company or organization that uses the same kinds of software that you find on the public Internet, but that is only for internal use.

IPCONFIG   A command-line utility for Windows NT, Windows 2000, and Windows XP machines, which displays the current TCP/IP configuration of the machine; similar to Windows 9x's WINIPCFG and UNIX/Linux's IFCONFIG.

I/O (input/output)   A general term for reading and writing data to a computer. The term input includes data from a keyboard, pointing device (such as a mouse), or loading a file from a disk. Output includes writing information to a disk, viewing it on a CRT, or printing it to a printer.

IP (Internet Protocol)   The Internet standard protocol that provides a common layer over dissimilar networks used to move packets among host computers and through gateways if necessary. Part of the TCP/IP protocol suite.

IP address   The numeric address of a computer connected to a TCP/IP network, such as the Internet. The IP address is made up of four octets of 8-bit binary numbers that are translated by the computer into their shorthand numeric values; for example, 11000000.10101000.00000100.00011010 = 192.168.4.26. IP addresses must be matched with a valid subnet mask, which identifies the part of the IP address that is the network ID and the part that is the host ID.

IPSec (IP Security)   A group of protocols used to encrypt IP packets. IPSec is most commonly seen on virtual private networks. *See also* VPN.

IPX/SPX (Internetwork Packet Exchange/Sequence Packet Exchange)   Protocol suite developed by Novell, primarily for supporting Novell NetWare-based networks.

IRC (Internet Relay Chat)   The Internet Relay Chat, or just Chat, is an online group discussion.

IRQ (interrupt request)   A signal from a hardware device, such as a modem or a mouse, indicating that it needs the CPU's attention. In PCs, IRQs are sent along specific IRQ channels associated with a particular device. It is therefore important to ensure that two devices do not share a common IRQ channel.

ISA (Industry Standard Architecture)   The Industry Standard Architecture design is found in the original IBM PC for the sockets on the motherboard that allowed additional hardware to be connected to the computer's motherboard. An 8-bit, 8.33-MHz expansion bus that was designed by IBM for its AT computer and released to the public domain. An improved 16-bit bus was also released to the public domain. Various other designs such as IBM's MicroChannel and EISA bus tried to improve on the design without much popularity. ISA only supports 8- and 16-bit data paths, so 32-bit alternatives such as PCI and AGP have become popular. Although ISA slots linger on a few motherboards, they are almost never seen in new systems.

ISDN (Integrated Services Digital Network)   The Comité Consutatif Internationale Téléphonique et Télégraphique (CCITT) standard that defines a digital method for communications to replace the current analog telephone system. ISDN is superior to telephone lines because it supports up to a 128-Kbps transfer rate for sending information from computer to computer. It also allows data and voice to share a common phone line.

ISP (Internet service provider)   An institution that provides access to the Internet in some form, usually for a fee.

ISV (independent software vendor)   Firms that develop and market software.

IT (information technology)   The business of computers, electronic communications, and electronic commerce.

J

Java   A network-oriented programming language invented by Sun Microsystems that is specifically designed for writing programs that can be safely downloaded to your computer through the Internet and immediately run without fear of viruses or other harm to your computer or files. Using small Java programs (called applets), web pages can include functions such as animations, calculators, and other fancy tricks.

JPEG (Joint Photographic Experts Group)   A method of formatting images for efficient storage and transfer across phone lines; JPEG files are often a factor of 10 or more times smaller than noncompressed files. JPEG is a lossy format, meaning that some data is lost when an image is converted. Most JPEG conversion software allows the user to decide between more or less compression at the cost of image quality. JPEG supports 24-bit images (up to 16.8 million colors). Because computers running MS-DOS are limited in their filenames, this format is also referred to as JPG.

jumper   A series of pairs of small pins that can be shorted with a shunt to configure many different aspects of PCs. Usually used in configurations that are rarely changed, such as master/slave settings on IDE drives.

K

K-   Most commonly used as the suffix for the binary quantity 1024. 640K means $640 \times 1,024$ or 655,360. Just to add some extra confusion to the IT industry, K is often misspoken as "kilo," the metric value for 1,000. For example, 10KB spoken as "10 kilobytes," actually means 10,240 bytes rather than 10,000 bytes.

Kbps (kilobits per second)   Data transfer rate.

Kerberos   An authentication standard designed to allow different operating systems and applications to authenticate each other.

Kermit   A communications protocol that enables you to transfer files between your computer and online network systems. Kermit has built-in error correction and can handle binary (non-text) files.

kern   The amount of distance between characters in a particular font.

kernel   The core portion of a program that resides in memory and performs the most essential operating system tasks.

L

LAN (local area network)   A group of PCs connected together via cabling, radio, or infrared, and use this connectivity to share resources such as printers and mass storage.

laser printer   An electrophotographic printer in which a laser is used as the light source.

layer   A grouping of related tasks involving the transfer of information. Also, a particular level of the OSI reference model—for example, Physical layer, Data Link layer, and so forth.

layer 2 switch   Also known as a bridge. Filters and forwards data packets based on the MAC addresses of the sending and receiving machines.

layer 3 switch   Also known as a router. Filters and forwards data packets based on the network addresses of the sending and receiving machines.

LBA (logical block addressing)   A translation (algorithm) of IDE drives promoted by Western Digital as a standardized method for breaking the 504-megabyte limit in IDE drives. Subsequently universally adopted by the PC industry, it is now standard on all EIDE drives. Allows drives up to 8.4 gigabytes.

LCD (liquid crystal display)   A display technology that relies on polarized light passing through a liquid medium rather than on electron beams striking a phosphorescent surface.

LED (light emitting diodes)   Solid-state devices that vibrate at luminous frequencies when current is applied.

link segments   Segments that link other segments together but are unpopulated, or have no computers directly attached to them.

Linux   Open source UNIX-clone operating system.

LMHOSTS file   A static text file that resides on a computer and is used to resolve NetBIOS names to IP addresses. The LMHOSTS file is checked before the machine sends a name resolution request to a WINS name server. The LMHOSTS file has no extension.

local bus   A high-speed data path that directly links the computer's CPU with one or more slots on the expansion bus. This direct link means signals from an adapter do not have to travel through the computer expansion bus, which is significantly slower.

localhost   An alias for the loopback address of 127.0.0.1, referring to the current machine.

LocalTalk   A network protocol created by Apple Computers to add networking to their computers. LocalTalk used a bus topology, with each device daisy-chained to the next device on the segment, and a proprietary cabling with small round DIN-style connectors.

logical address   An address that describes both a specific network and a specific machine on that network.

logical drives   Sections of a hard drive that are formatted and assigned a drive letter, each of which is presented to the user as if it is a separate drive.

loopback address   Sometimes called the *localhost*, the loopback address is a reserved IP address used for internal testing: 127.0.0.1.

low-level format   Defining the physical location of magnetic tracks and sectors on a disk.

luminescence   The part of the video signal that controls the luminance/brightness of the picture. Also known as the "Y" portion of the component signal.

M

MAC (Media Access Control)   Unique 48-bit address assigned to each network card. IEEE assigns blocks of possible addresses to various NIC manufacturers to help ensure that each address is unique. The Data Link layer of the OSI model uses MAC addresses for locating machines.

machine language   A programming language or instruction code that is immediately interpretable by the hardware of the machine concerned.

mailbox   Special holding areas on an e-mail server that separates out e-mail for each user.

mail server   *See* e-mail server.

mainframe   The cabinet that houses the central processing unit and main memory of a computer system, separate from peripheral devices such as card readers, printers, disk drives, device controllers, and so forth. The term has come to be applied to the computer itself in the case of large systems.

MAN (metropolitan area network)   Defined as an IEEE 802.6 network, a MAN is a group of computers connected together via cabling, radio, leased phone lines, or infrared, and using this connectivity to share resources such as printers and mass storage. Usually the distance is between that of a LAN and a WAN—different buildings, but within the same city. A typical example of a MAN is a college campus. There are no firm dividing lines dictating what is considered a WAN, a MAN, or a LAN.

mass storage   Hard drives, CD-ROMs, removable media drives, and so forth.

math coprocessor   Also called math unit, floating-point unit, or FPU. A secondary microprocessor whose function is the handling of floating-point arithmetic. Although originally a physically separate chip, math coprocessors are now built into today's CPUs.

MAU (multistation access unit)   A hub used in Token Ring networks. Also abbreviated as MSAU.

MB (megabyte)   1,048,576 bytes. Often abbreviated as a meg.

MCA (MicroChannel Architecture)   Expansion bus architecture developed by IBM as the (unsuccessful) successor to ISA. MCA had a full 32-bit design and was self-configuring.

MCC (memory controller chip)   The chip that handles memory requests from the CPU. Although once a special chip, it has been integrated into the chipset on all PCs today.

mega-   A prefix that usually stands for the binary quantity 1,048,576. One megabyte is 1,048,576 bytes. One megahertz, however, is 1 million hertz. Sometimes shortened to meg, as in a 286 has an address space of 16 megs.

memory   A device or medium that serves for temporary storage of programs and data during program execution. The term is synonymous with storage, although it is most frequently used for referring to the internal storage of a computer that can be directly addressed by operating instructions. A computer's temporary storage capacity is measured in kilobytes (KB) or megabytes (MB) of random access memory (RAM). Long-term data storage on disks is also measured in kilobytes, megabytes, gigabytes, and terabytes.

mesh topology   Each computer has a dedicated connection to every other computer in a network.

MHz (megahertz)   A unit of measure that equals a frequency of 1 million cycles per second.

microcomputer   A computer system in which the central processing unit is built as a single tiny semiconductor chip or as a small number of chips.

microprocessor   Main computer chip that provides speed and capabilities of the computer. Also called a CPU.

MIDI (Musical Instrument Digital Interface)   MIDI is a standard that describes the interface between a computer and a device for simulating musical instruments. Rather than sending large sound samples, a computer can simply send instructions to the instrument describing pitch, tone, and duration of a sound. MIDI files are therefore much more efficient. Because a MIDI file is made up of a set of instructions rather than a copy of the sound, it is easy to modify each component of the file. Additionally, it is possible to program many channels or voices of music to be played simultaneously, creating symphonic sound.

MIME (Multipurpose Internet Mail Extensions)   A standard for attaching binary files (such as executables and images) to the Internet's text-based mail (24-Kbps packet size).

MIPS (millions of instructions per second)   Used for processor benchmarks.

mirroring   Also called drive mirroring. Reading and writing data at the same time to two drives for fault-tolerance purposes. Considered RAID level 1.

MLA (multilettered acronym)   The abbreviation for any object or thought that can be condensed to an abbreviation.

MMU (memory management unit)   A chip or circuit that translates virtual memory addresses to physical addresses and may implement memory protection.

modem (modulator/demodulator)   A device that converts a digital bit stream into an analog signal (modulation) and converts incoming analog signals back into digital signals (demodulation). The analog communications channel is typically a telephone line and the analog signals are typically sounds.

monitor   A television-like screen that shows text, graphics, and other functions performed by the computer.

MPEG (Motion Picture Experts Group)   A sophisticated video standard that enables digital video to be compressed using a form of JPEG image compression and a technique called differencing, in which only the differences between frames are recorded, rather than the frame itself.

MP3 (MPEG-1 audio layer 3)   An audio compression scheme used extensively on the Internet.

MS-CHAP   Microsoft's variation of the CHAP protocol. It uses a slightly more advanced encryption protocol.

MSAU (multistation access unit)   A hub used in Token Ring networks. Also abbreviated as MAU.

motherboard   The primary circuit board that holds all of the core components of the computer.

multimedia   A single work assembled using elements from more than one medium, such as high-resolution color images, sounds, video, and text that contains characters in multiple fonts and styles.

multiplexer   A device that merges information from multiple input channels to a single output channel.

multi-speed hub   Any hub that supports more than one network speed for otherwise similar cabling systems. Multi-speed hubs come in two "flavors." One has mostly dedicated slower ports, with a few dedicated faster ports, while the other has only special auto-sensing ports that automatically run at either the faster or the slower speed.

multitasking   The process of running multiple programs or tasks on the same computer at the same time.

N

NAT (network address translation)   A means of translating a system's IP address into another IP address before sending it out to a larger network. NAT manifests itself by a NAT program that runs on a system or a router. A network using NAT will provide the systems on the network with private IP addresses. The system running the NAT software will have two interfaces, one connected to the network and the other connected to the larger network. The NAT program takes packets from the client systems bound for the larger network and translates their internal private IP addresses to its own public IP address, enabling many systems to share a single IP address.

NBTSTAT   A command-line utility used to check the current NetBIOS name cache on a particular machine. The utility compares NetBIOS names to their corresponding IP addresses.

NDS (Novell Directory Services)   The default security and directory system for Novell NetWare 4.*x* and 5.*x*. Organizes users, servers, and groups into a hierarchical tree.

NetBEUI (NetBIOS Extended User Interface)   A protocol supplied with all Microsoft networking products that operates at the Transport layer. Also a protocol suite that includes NetBIOS. NetBEUI does not support routing.

NetBIOS name   A computer name that identifies both the specific machine and the functions that machine performs. A NetBIOS name consists of 16 characters: the first 15 are an alphanumeric name, and the 16th is a special suffix that identifies the role the machine plays.

NetBIOS (Network Basic Input/Output System)   A protocol that operates at the Session layer of the OSI seven-layer model. This protocol creates and manages connections based on the names of the computers involved.

NETSTAT   A command-line utility used to examine the sockets-based connections open on a given host.

network   A collection of two or more computers interconnected by telephone lines, coaxial cables, satellite links, radio, and/or some other communication technique. A computer network is a group of computers that are connected together and communicate with one another for a common purpose. Computer networks support people and organization networks, users who also share a common purpose for communicating.

network ID   A number that identifies the network on which a device or machine exists. This number exists in both IP and IPX protocol suites.

newsgroup   The name for a discussion group on Usenet.

NFS (Network File System)   A file system that enables UNIX systems to treat files on a remote UNIX machine as though they were local files.

NIC (network interface card)   An expansion card that enables a PC to physically link to a network.

nickname   A name that can be used in place of an e-mail address.

node   A member of a network or a point where one or more functional units interconnect transmission lines.

noise   Undesirable signals bearing no desired information and frequently capable of introducing errors into the communication process.

normal backup   A full backup of every selected file on a system. This type of backup turns off the archive bit after the backup.

NOS (network operating system)   An operating system that provides basic file and supervisory services over a network. While each computer attached to the network does have its own OS, the NOS describes which actions are allowed by each user and coordinates distribution of networked files to the users who request them.

ns (nanosecond)   A billionth of a second. Light travels a little over 11 inches in 1 nanosecond.

NWLink   Also known as IPX/SPX-compatible Protocol, this is Microsoft's implementation of IPX/SPX. *See also* IPX/SPX.

O

OCR (optical character recognition)   The process of converting characters represented in a graphical format into ASCII. This is usually done in conjunction with a scanner to allow for editing of printed material.

OEM (original equipment manufacturer)   Contrary to the name, an OEM does not create original hardware, but rather purchases components from manufacturers and puts them together in systems under its own brand name. Dell Computers and Gateway 2000, for example, are for the most part OEMs. Apple Computers, which manufactures most of the components for its own Macintosh-branded machines, is not an OEM. Also known as value-added resellers (VARs).

ohm   Electronic measurement of a cable's or electronic component's impedance.

OLE (object linking and embedding)   The Microsoft Windows specification that enables objects created within one application to be placed, or embedded, in another application. The two applications are linked, meaning that when the original object is modified, the copy is updated automatically.

open source   Applications and operating systems that offer access to their source code; this enables developers to modify applications and operating systems easily to meet their specific needs.

OS (operating system)   The set of programming that enables a program to interact with the computer. Examples of PC operating systems include Microsoft's MS-DOS, IBM's PC-DOS and OS/2, and Apple's MacOS System 8. Most computers on the Internet use a variant of the UNIX operating system. Microsoft's Windows 3.1 is not technically an operating system, since it still requires MS-DOS to work, but it is often referred to as one. Windows 95/98 and Windows NT are true operating systems.

OSI (Open Systems Interconnect)   An international standard suite of protocols defined by the International Organization for Standardization (ISO) that implements the OSI reference model for network communications between computers.

OSI seven-layer model An architecture model based on the OSI protocol suite, which defines and standardizes the flow of data between computers. The seven layers are listed below:

- **layer 1—The Physical layer** defines hardware connections and turns binary into physical pulses (electrical or light). Repeaters and hubs operate at the Physical layer.
- **layer 2—The Data Link layer** identifies devices on the Physical layer. MAC addresses are part of the Data Link layer. Bridges operate at the Data Link layer.
- **layer 3—The Network layer** moves packets between computers on different networks. Routers operate at the Network layer. IP and IPX operate at the Network layer.
- **layer 4—The Transport layer** breaks data down into manageable chunks. TCP, UDP, SPX, and NetBEUI operate at the Transport layer.
- **layer 5—The Session layer** manages connections between machines. NetBIOS and sockets operate at the Session layer.
- **layer 6—The Presentation layer**, which can also manage data encryption, hides the differences between various types of computer systems.
- **layer 7—The Application layer** provides tools for programs to use to access the network (and the lower layers). HTTP, FTP, SMTP, and POP3 are all examples of protocols that operate at the Application layer.

oscilloscope A device that gives a graphical/visual representation of signal levels over a period of time.

overclocking To run a CPU or video processor faster than its rated speed.

overdrive Generic name given to processors designed as aftermarket upgrades to computer systems.

overscanning Displaying less than the complete area of an image to the viewer. Most monitors may slightly overscan. Also of value when using a Twain Scanner to capture 2K × 2K images, and allowing playback in a smaller window, but moving beyond the normal borders to view close-up detail of portions of the image controlled by the mouse pointer.

P

packet Basic component of communication over a network. A group of bits of fixed maximum size and well-defined format that is switched and transmitted as a complete whole through a network. It contains source and destination address, data, and control information. *See also* frame.

packet filtering Packet filters, also known as IP filters, will block any incoming or outgoing packet from a particular IP address or range of IP addresses. Packet filters are far better at blocking outgoing IP addresses, because the network administrator knows and can specify the IP addresses of the internal systems.

PAP (Password Authentication Protocol) The oldest and most basic form of authentication. It's also the least safe, because it sends all passwords in clear text.

parallel port A connection for the synchronous, high-speed flow of data along parallel lines to a device, usually a printer.

parameter   A variable, or quantity, that can assume any of a given set of values, of which there are two kinds: formal and actual.

parity   A method of error detection in which a small group of bits being transferred is compared to a single parity bit that is set to make the total bits odd or even. The receiving device reads the parity bit and determines whether the data is valid based on the oddness or evenness of the parity bit.

partition   A section of the storage area of a hard disk. A partition is created during initial preparation of the hard disk, before the disk is formatted.

patch cables   Short (2 to 5 ft.) UTP cables that connect patch panels to the hubs.

patch panel   A panel containing a row of female connectors (ports) that terminate the horizontal cabling in the equipment room. Patch panels facilitate cabling organization and provide protection to horizontal cabling.

path   The route the operating system must follow to find an executable program stored in a subdirectory.

PBX (Private Branch Exchange)   A private phone system used within an organization.

PC (personal computer)   A more popular phrase than the more correct term microcomputer, PC means a small computer with its own processor and hard drive, as opposed to a dumb terminal connected to a central mainframe computer. Used in this fashion, the term PC indicates computers of many different manufacturers, using a variety of processors and operating systems. Although the term PC was around long before the original IBM PC was released, it has come to be almost synonymous with IBM-compatible computers, hence the technically incorrect but common question, "Are you a Mac or a PC person?"

PCI (Peripheral Component Interconnect)   A design architecture for the sockets on the computer motherboard that enable system components to be added to the computer. PCI is a local bus standard, meaning that devices added to a computer through this port will use the processor at the motherboard's full speed (up to 33 MHz), rather than at the slower 8-MHz speed of the regular bus. In addition to moving data at a faster rate, PCI moves data 32 or 64 bits at a time, rather than the 8 or 16 bits that the older ISA busses supported.

PCMCIA (Personal Computer Memory Card International Association)   A consortium of computer manufacturers who devised the standard for credit card-sized adapter cards that add functionality in many notebook computers, PDAs, and other computer devices. The simpler term PC Card has become more common in referring to these cards.

PDA (personal digital assistant)   A PDA is a handheld computer that blurs the line between the calculator and computer. Earlier PDAs were calculators that enabled the user to program in such information as addresses and appointments. Newer machines, such as the Palm Pilot, are fully programmable computers. Most PDAs use a pen/stylus for input rather than a keyboard. A few of the larger PDAs have a tiny keyboard in addition to the stylus.

peer-to-peer networks   A network in which each machine can act as either a client or a server.

Pentium   Name given to the fifth generation of Intel microprocessors, distinct with 32-bit address bus, 64-bit external data bus, and dual pipelining. Also used for subsequent generations of Intel processors: Pentium Pro, Pentium II, Pentium II Xeon, Pentium III, Pentium III Xeon, and Pentium 4.

peripheral   Any device other than the motherboard components of the computer. The floppy drive is a peripheral; the CPU is not a peripheral.

permissions   Sets of attributes that network administrators assign to resources to define what users and groups can do with them.

phosphor   An electrofluorescent material used to coat the inside face of a cathode ray tube (CRT). After being hit with an electron, phosphors glow for a fraction of a second.

physical address   A way of defining a specific machine without referencing its location or network. A MAC address is an example of a physical address.

PIM (personal information manager)   A software application designed to hold and manage personal information such as phone numbers, contact notes, schedules, and to-do lists.

PING (Packet Internet Groper)   Slang term for a small network message (ICMP ECHO) sent by a computer to check for the presence and aliveness of another. Also the command used to verify the presence of another system on the network.

PIO Mode   A series of speed standards created by the Small Form Factor committee for the use of PIO by hard drives. The PIO modes range from PIO mode 0 to PIO mode 4.

PIO (programmable input/output)   Using the address bus to send communication to a peripheral. The most common way for the CPU to communicate with peripherals.

Pixel (picture element)   In computer graphics, the smallest element of a display space that can be independently assigned color or intensity.

platen   The cylinder that guides paper through an impact printer and provides a backing surface for the paper when images are impressed onto the page.

platform   Hardware environment that supports the running of a computer system.

plenum   Usually a space between a building's false ceiling and the floor above it. Most of the wiring for networks is located in this space. Plenum is also the fire rating of the grade of cable allowed to be installed in this location.

Plug and Play   Also known as PnP. A combination of smart PCs, smart devices, and smart operating systems that automatically configure all the necessary system resources and ports.

POP (Post Office Protocol)   Also known as point of presence. Refers to the way e-mail software such as Eudora gets mail from a mail server. When you obtain a SLIP, PPP, or shell account, you almost always get a POP account with it; and it is this POP account that you tell your e-mail software to use to get your mail. The current standard is called POP3.

populated segment   A segment that has one or more nodes directly attached to it.

port   That portion of a computer through which a peripheral device may communicate. Often identified with the various plug-in jacks on the back of your computer. On a network hub, it is the connector that receives the wire link from a node.

port filtering   Preventing the passage of any IP packets through any ports other than the ones prescribed by the system administrator.

port number   Number used to identify the requested service (such as SMTP or FTP) when connecting to a TCP/IP host. Some example port numbers include 80 (HTTP), 20 (FTP), 69 (TFTP), 25 (SMTP), and 110 (POP3).

PostScript   A language defined by Adobe Systems, Inc. for describing how to create an image on a page. The description is independent of the resolution of the device that will actually create the image. It includes a technology for defining the shape of a font and creating a raster image at many different resolutions and sizes.

PPP (Point-to-Point Protocol)   A protocol that enables a computer to connect to the Internet through a dial-in connection and enjoy most of the benefits of a direct connection. PPP is considered to be superior to SLIP because of its error detection and data compression features-which SLIP lacks-and the ability to use dynamic IP addresses.

PPPoE (PPP over Ethernet)   A specialized implementation of PPP, specifically designed to allow Ethernet connections to enjoy some of the benefits of PPP, such as encryption. Used exclusively by ADSL.

PPTP (Point-to-Point Tunneling Protocol)   A protocol that works with PPP to provide a secure data link between computers using encryption.

program   A set of actions or instructions that a machine is capable of interpreting and executing. Used as a verb, it means to design, write, and test such instructions.

promiscuous mode   A mode of operation for a network interface card in which the NIC processes all packets that it sees on the cable.

prompt   A character or message provided by an operating system or program to indicate that it is ready to accept input.

protected mode   The operating mode of a CPU to allow more than one program to be run while ensuring that no program can corrupt another program currently running.

protocol   An agreement that governs the procedures used to exchange information between cooperating entities; usually includes how much information is to be sent, how often it is sent, how to recover from transmission errors, and who is to receive the information.

protocol stack   The actual software that implements the protocol suite on a particular operating system.

protocol suite   A set of protocols that are commonly used together and operate at different levels of the OSI seven-layer model.

proprietary   Term used to describe technology that is unique to, and owned by, a particular vendor.

proxy server   A device that fetches Internet resources for a client without exposing that client directly to the Internet. Most proxy servers accept requests for HTTP, FTP, POP3, and SMTP resources. The proxy server will often cache, or store, a copy of the requested resource for later use.

PSTN (public switched telephone network)   Also known as plain old telephone service (POTS). Most common type of phone connection that takes your sounds, translated into an analog waveform by the microphone, and transmits them to another phone.

PVC (polyvinyl chloride)   A material used for the outside insulation and jacketing of most cables. Also a fire rating for a type of cable that has no significant fire protection.

Q

QIC (quarter-inch tape [or cartridge])   Tape backup cartridges that use quarter-inch tape.

queue   The waiting area for things to happen. An example is the print queue, where print jobs wait until it is their turn to be printed.

R

RAID (redundant array of inexpensive devices [or disks])   A way of creating a fault-tolerant storage system. There are six levels. Level 0 uses byte-level striping and provides no fault tolerance. Level 1 uses mirroring or duplexing. Level 2 uses bit-level striping. Level 3 stores error-correcting information (such as parity) on a separate disk, and uses data striping on the remaining drives. Level 4 is level 3 with block-level striping. Level 5 uses block-level and parity data striping.

RAM (random access memory)   Memory in which any address can be written to or read from as easily as any other address.

raster   The horizontal pattern of lines that forms an image on the monitor screen.

real mode   The original 64K segmented memory, single-tasking operating mode of the Intel 8086 and 8088 CPUs.

real time   The processing of transactions as they occur, rather than batching them. Pertaining to an application in which response to input is fast enough to affect subsequent inputs and guide the process and in which records are updated immediately. The lag from input time to output time must be sufficiently small for acceptable timeliness. Timeliness is a function of the total system: missile guidance requires output within a few milliseconds of input, whereas scheduling of steamships requires a response time in days. Real-time systems are those with a response time of milliseconds; interactive systems respond in seconds, and batch systems may respond in hours or days.

refresh   The process of repainting the CRT screen, causing the phosphors to remain lit (or change).

remote access   The ability to access a computer from outside a building in which it is housed. Remote access requires communications hardware, software, and actual physical links.

remote access server   Refers to both the hardware component (servers built to handle the unique stresses of a large number of clients calling in) and the software component (programs that work with the operating system to allow remote access to the network) of a remote access solution.

repeater   A device that takes all of the data packets it receives on one Ethernet segment and re-creates them on another Ethernet segment. This allows for longer cables or more computers on a segment. Repeaters operate at Level 1 (physical) of the OSI seven-layer model.

resistance   The tendency for physical media to impede electron flow. It is classically measured in a unit called *ohms*.

resolution   A measurement expressed in horizontal and vertical dots or pixels for CRTs and/or printers. Higher resolutions provide sharper details, thus displaying better-looking images.

resource   Anything that exists on another computer that a person wants to use without going to that computer. Also an online information set or an online interactive option. An online library catalog or the local school lunch menu are examples of information sets. Online menus or graphical user interfaces, Internet e-mail, online conferences, telnet, FTP, and Gopher are examples of interactive options.

reverse lookup zones   A DNS setting that resolves IP addresses to FQDNs. In other words, it does the exact reverse of what DNS normally accomplishes using forward lookup zones.

RG-58   A type of cable that works with the still quite popular Thin Ethernet network technology. It is rated at 50 ohms.

RG-6   A type of cable that is virtually never installed in networks these days, but still has enough of an installed base that you should at least know about it. The cable used for cable TV is RG-6.

RG-8   Often referred to as Thick Ethernet, RG-8 is the oldest and least-used cabling type still in use. It gets the name Thick Ethernet from the fact that it is used exclusively for 802.5 Thick Ethernet networks. RG-8 is rated at 50 ohms and has a distinct yellow or orange/brown color.

ring topology   A network topology in which all the computers on the network attach to a central ring of cable.

RJ (registered jack)   Connectors used for UTP cable for both telephone and network connections.

RJ-11   Type of connector with four-wire UTP connections; usually found in telephone connections.

RJ-45   Type of connector with eight-wire UTP connections; usually found in network connections and used for 10BaseT networking.

ROM (read only memory)   The generic term for nonvolatile memory that can be read from but not written to. This means that code and data stored in ROM cannot be corrupted by accidental erasure. Additionally, ROM retains its data when power is removed, which makes it the perfect medium for storing BIOS data or information such as scientific constants.

root directory   The directory that contains all other directories.

router   A device connecting separate networks, which forwards a packet from one network to another based only on the network address for the protocol being used. For example, an IP router looks only at the IP network number. Routers operate at layer 3 (Network) of the OSI seven-layer model.

routing table   A list of paths to various networks required by routers. This can be built either manually or automatically.

RS-232C   A standard port recommended by the Electronics Industry Association for serial devices.

S

SAMBA   An application that enables UNIX systems to communicate using server message blocks (SMBs). This in turn enables them to act as Microsoft clients and servers on the network.

scalability   The ability to support network growth.

scanner   A device that senses alterations of light and dark, and enables you to import photographs and other physical images and text into the computer in digital form.

SCSI (Small Computer System Interface)   A powerful and flexible peripheral interface popularized on the Macintosh and used to connect hard drives, CD-ROM drives, tape drives, scanners, and other devices to PCs of all kinds. Because SCSI is less efficient at handling small drives than IDE, it did not become popular on IBM-compatible computers until price reductions made these large drives affordable. Normal SCSI enables up to seven devices to be connected through a single bus connection, whereas Wide SCSI can handle 15 devices attached to a single controller.

sector   A segment of one of the concentric tracks encoded on the disk during a low-level format. A sector holds 512 bytes of data.

segment   The bus cable to which the computers on an Ethernet network connect.

sequential   A method of storing and retrieving information that requires data to be written and read sequentially. Accessing any portion of the data requires reading all the preceding data.

server   A computer that shares its resources, such as printers and files, with other computers on the network. An example of this is a network file system server that shares its disk space with a workstation that has no disk drive of its own.

server-based network   A network in which one or more systems function as dedicated file, print, or application servers, but do not function as clients.

session   A networking term used to refer to the logical stream of data flowing between two programs and being communicated over a network. There may be many different sessions emanating from any one node on a network.

SDRAM (synchronous DRAM)   DRAM that is tied to the system clock and thus runs much faster than traditional FPM and EDO RAM.

share-level security   Security system in which each resource has a password assigned to it; access to the resource is based on knowing the password.

shareware   Software that is protected by copyright, but the copyright holder allows (encourages!) you to make and distribute copies, under the condition that those who adopt the software after preview pay a fee. Derivative works are not allowed, and you may make an archival copy.

shell   A term that generally refers to the user interface of an operating system. A shell is the command processor that is the actual interface between the kernel and the user.

shunt   A tiny connector of metal enclosed in plastic that creates an electrical connection between two posts of a jumper.

SIMM (single inline memory module)   A type of DRAM packaging distinct by having a number of small tabs that install into a special connector. Each side of each tab is the same signal. SIMMs come in two common sizes: 30- and 72-pin.

SL enhanced   A type of CPU that has the ability to turn off selected peripherals as well as run on low (3.3V or less) power. *See also* SMM.

SLIP (Serial Line Interface Protocol)   A protocol that enables a computer to connect to the Internet through a dial-in connection and enjoy most of the benefits of a direct connection. SLIP has been almost completely replaced by PPP, which is considered superior to SLIP because of its error detection and data compression-features that SLIP lacks-and the ability to use dynamic IP addresses.

SMB (server message blocks)   Protocol used by Microsoft clients and servers to share file and print resources.

SMM (system management mode)   A special CPU mode that enables the CPU to reduce power consumption via the selective shutdown of peripherals.

SMTP (Simple Mail Transfer Protocol)   The main protocol used to send electronic mail on the Internet.

SNAFU (situation normal, all fouled up)   A common expression of frustration.

SNMP (Simple Network Management Protocol)   A set of standards for communication with devices connected to a TCP/IP network. Examples of these devices include routers, hubs, and switches.

socket   A combination of a port number and an IP address that uniquely identifies a connection.

software   Programming instructions or data stored on some type of binary storage device.

SONET (Synchronous Optical Network)   A standard for connecting fiber-optic transmission systems. SONET was proposed in the mid-1980s, and is now an ANSI standard. SONET defines interface standards at the physical layer of the OSI seven-layer model.

source code   The program in a language prepared by the programmer. This code cannot be directly executed by the computer and must first be translated into object code. Also, the building blocks of an operating system or application.

spool   A scheme that enables multiple devices to write output simultaneously to the same device, such as multiple computers printing to the same printer at the same time. The data is actually written to temporary files while a program called a spooler sends the files to the device one at a time.

spreadsheet   A software program that enables users to perform mathematical calculations, such as budgeting, keeping track of investments, or tracking grades.

SPS (stand-by power supply [or system])   A device that supplies continuous clean power to a computer system immediately following a power failure. *See also* UPS.

SQL (Structured Query Language)   A language created by IBM that relies on simple English statements to perform database queries. SQL enables databases from different manufacturers to be queried using a standard syntax.

SRAM (static RAM)   A type of RAM that uses a flip-flop type of circuit, rather than the typical transistor/capacitor of DRAM, to hold a bit of information. SRAM does not need to be refreshed and is faster than regular DRAM. Used primarily for cache.

SSL (Secure Sockets Layer)   A protocol developed by Netscape for transmitting private documents over the Internet. SSL works by using a public key to encrypt sensitive data. This encrypted data is sent over an SSL connection, then decrypted at the receiving end using a private key.

ST506   A model of hard drive developed by Seagate. This drive, as well as the WD1003 controller developed by Western Digital, created the standard for the first generation of hard drives and controllers. As a result, drives that copied the connections and BIOS commands of the ST506 came to be known as ST506 drives.

star bus topology   This is a hybrid of the star and bus topologies. This topology uses a physical star, where all nodes connect to a single wiring point such as a hub, and a logical bus that maintains the Ethernet standards. One benefit of a star bus topology is fault tolerance.

star topology   A network topology in which all computers in the network connect to a central wiring point.

static routing   A process by which routers in an internetwork obtain information about paths to other routers. This information must be supplied manually.

storage   A device or medium that can retain data for subsequent retrieval.

STP (shielded twisted pair)   A popular cabling for networks composed of pairs of wires twisted around each other at specific intervals. The twists serve to reduce interference (also called crosstalk). The more twists, the less interference. The cable has metallic shielding to protect the wires from external interference. Token Ring networks are the only common network technology that uses STP, although Token Ring more often now uses UTP.

subnet   In a TCP/IP internetwork, each independent network is referred to as a subnet.

subnet mask   The value used in TCP/IP settings to divide the IP address of a host into its component parts: network ID and host ID.

SVGA (Super Video Graphics Array)   A set of graphics standards that were designed to give a minimum of 800 × 600 resolution and 256 colors.

switch   A device that filters and forwards traffic based on some criteria. A bridge and a router are both examples of switches.

synchronous   Describes a connection between two electronic devices where neither must acknowledge (ACK) when receiving data.

sysop (system operator)   Anyone responsible for the physical operations of a computer system or network resource. A system administrator decides how often backups and maintenance should be performed, and the system operator performs those tasks.

system BIOS   The primary set of BIOS stored on an EPROM or Flash chip on the motherboard. Defines the BIOS for all the assumed hardware on the motherboard, such as keyboard controller, floppy drive, basic video, RAM, and so forth.

T

T-1   A leased-line connection capable of carrying data at 1,544,000 bits per second.

T-3   A leased-line connection capable of carrying data at 44,736,000 bits per second.

TCP (Transmission Control Protocol)   Part of the TCP/IP protocol suite, TCP operates at layer 4 (Transport) of the OSI seven-layer model. TCP is a connection-oriented protocol.

TCP/IP (Transmission Control Protocol/Internet Protocol)   A set of communication protocols developed by the U.S. Department of Defense that enables dissimilar computers to share information over a network.

TDR (time domain reflectometer)   Advanced cable tester that tests the length of cables and their continuity or discontinuity, and identifies the location of any discontinuity due to a bend, break, unwanted crimp, and so on.

telephony   The science of converting sound into electrical signals, moving those signals from one location to another, and then converting those signals back into sounds. This includes modems, telephone lines, the telephone system, and any products used to create a remote access link between a remote access client and server.

telnet   A program that enables users on the Internet to log onto remote systems from their own host systems.

tera-   A prefix that usually stands for the binary number 1,099,511,627,776, which is 2 to the 40th power. When used for mass storage, often shorthand usage for a trillion bytes.

terabyte   1,099,511,627,776 bytes.

terminal   A "dumb" device connected to a computer network that acts as a point for entry or retrieval of information.

terminal emulation   Software that enables a PC to communicate with another computer or network as if it were a specific type of hardware terminal.

terminating resistors   Any device that absorbs excess electrical signals off a wire. Examples include the device used at each end of a coaxial cable to absorb the excess electrical signals-this helps avoid signal bounce or reflection. The level of resistance in RG-58 coaxial cables requires them to have 50-ohm impedance. Another device with the same name is used to terminate the ends of a SCSI chain.

TIFF (Tagged Image File Format)   A graphical file format in which images are divided into discrete blocks or strips called tags. Each tag contains formatting information, such as width, number of colors, and so forth for the entire image. The TIFF format is useful because it can describe many different types of images, but it is also complex, and writing software for it is difficult.

TLA (three-letter acronym)   Any acronym of three letters, such as File Allocation Table (FAT) or Graphics Interchange Format (GIF).

Token Ring   A LAN and protocol in which nodes are connected together in a ring, and a special packet called a token, passed from node to node around the ring, controls communication. A node can send data only when it receives the token and the token is not in use. This avoids the collision problems endemic to Ethernet networks.

toners   Generic term for two devices used together—a tone generator and a tone locator (probe) —to trace cables by sending an electrical signal along a wire at a particular frequency. The tone locator then emits a sound when it distinguishes that frequency. Also referred to as Fox and Hound.

topology   The pattern of interconnections in a communications system among devices, nodes, and associated input and output stations. Also describes how computers connect to each other without regard to how they actually communicate.

TRACERT (also TRACEROUTE)   A command-line utility used to follow the path a packet takes between two hosts.

TSR (terminate and stay resident)   A DOS program that mostly closes immediately after starting up, but leaves a tiny piece of itself in memory. TSRs are used to handle a broad cross-section of DOS-level system needs, such as running hardware (MOUSE.COM) or applying higher-level functionality to hardware already under the control of device drivers. MSCDEX.EXE, for example, assigns a drive letter to a CD-ROM drive after the CD-ROM driver has loaded in CONFIG.SYS.

TWAIN (technology without an interesting name)   A programming interface that enables a graphics application, such as a desktop publishing program, to activate a scanner, frame grabber, or other image-capturing device.

twisted pair   The most overwhelmingly common type of cabling used in networks consists of twisted pairs of cables. The two types of twisted-pair cabling are unshielded twisted pair (UTP) and shielded twisted pair (STP). The twists serve to reduce interference, called *crosstalk*; the more twists, the less crosstalk.

U

UART (universal asynchronous receiver/transmitter)   A device that turns serial data into parallel data. The cornerstone of serial ports and modems.

UDP (User Datagram Protocol)   Part of the TCP/IP protocol suite, UDP is an alternative to TCP. UDP is a connectionless protocol.

UNC (Universal Naming Convention)   Describes any shared resource in a network using the convention \\<server name>\<name of shared resource>.

UNIX   A popular computer software operating system used on many Internet host systems.

UPS (uninterruptible power supply)   A device that supplies continuous clean power to a computer system the whole time the computer is on. Protects against power outages and sags. The term UPS is often used mistakenly when people mean SPS.

URL (uniform resource locator)   An address that defines the location of a resource on the Internet. URLs are used most often in conjunction with HTML and the World Wide Web.

USB (universal serial bus)   A 12-Mbps serial interconnect for keyboards, printers, joysticks, and many other devices. Enables hot-swapping and daisy chaining of devices.

Usenet   The network of UNIX users, generally perceived as informal and made up of loosely coupled nodes, that exchanges mail and messages. Started by Duke University and UNC-Chapel Hill. An information cooperative linking around 16,000 computer sites and millions of people. Usenet provides a series of news groups analogous to online conferences.

user   Anyone who uses a computer. You.

user account   A container that identifies a user to the application, operating system, or network, including name, password, user name, groups to which the user belongs, and other information based on the user and the OS or NOS being used. Usually defines the rights and roles a user plays on a system.

user-level security   A security system in which each user has an account, and access to resources is based on user identity.

user profiles   A collection of settings that corresponds to a specific user account and may follow the user regardless of the computer at which he or she logs on. These settings enable the user to have customized environment and security settings.

UTP (unshielded twisted pair)   A popular cabling for telephone and networks composed of pairs of wires twisted around each other at specific intervals. The twists serve to reduce interference (also called crosstalk). The more twists, the less interference. The cable has *no* metallic shielding to protect the wires from external interference, unlike its cousin, STP. 10BaseT uses UTP, as do many other networking technologies. UTP is available in a variety of grades, called categories, as defined in the following:

- **Category 1 UTP**—Regular analog phone lines, not used for data communications.
- **Category 2 UTP**—Supports speeds up to 4 Mbps.
- **Category 3 UTP**—Supports speeds up to 16 Mbps.
- **Category 4 UTP**—Supports speeds up to 20 Mbps.
- **Category 5 UTP**—Supports speeds up to 100 Mbps.

V

VESA (Video Electronics Standards Association)   A consortium of computer manufacturers that standardized improvements to common IBM PC components. VESA is responsible for the super VGA video standard and the VLB bus architecture.

VGA (Video Graphics Adapter)   The standard for the video graphics adapter that was built into IBM's PS/2 computer. It supports 16 colors in a 640 × 480 pixel video display, and quickly replaced the older Color Graphics Adapter (CGA) and Extended Graphics Adapter (EGA).

virtual   Pertaining to a device or facility that does not physically exist, yet behaves as if it does. For example, a system with 4 MB of virtual memory may have only 1 MB of physical memory plus additional (slower and cheaper) auxiliary memory, yet programs written as if 4 MB of physical memory were available will run correctly.

virus   A program that can make a copy of itself without you necessarily being aware of it. Some viruses can destroy or damage files, and generally the best protection is always to maintain backups of your files.

virus definition or **data file**   These files are also called signature files, depending on the virus protection software in use. These files enable the virus protection software to recognize the viruses on your system and clean them. These files should be updated often.

VLB (VESA local bus)   A design architecture for the sockets on the computer motherboard that enables system components to be added to the computer. VLB was the first local bus standard, meaning that devices added to a computer through this port would use the processor at its full speed, rather than at the slower 8 MHz speed of the regular bus. In addition to moving data at a faster rate, VLB moves data 32 bits at a time, rather than the 8 or 16 bits that the older ISA busses supported. Although VLB was common on machines using Intel's 486 CPU, modern computers now use PCI busses instead.

volatile   Memory that must have constant electricity in order to retain data. Alternatively, any programmer six hours before deadline after a nonstop 48-hour coding session, running on nothing but caffeine and sugar.

volume A physical unit of a storage medium, such as tape reel or disk pack, that is capable of having data recorded on it and subsequently read. Also refers to a contiguous collection of cylinders or blocks on a disk that are treated as a separate unit.

VPN (virtual private network) A network configuration that enables a remote user to access a private network via the Internet. VPNs employ an encryption methodology called tunneling, which protects the data from interception.

VRAM (video RAM) A type of memory in a video display adapter that's used to create the image appearing on the CRT screen. VRAM uses dual-ported memory, which enables simultaneous reads and writes, making it much quicker than DRAM.

W

WAN (wide area network) A geographically dispersed network created by linking various computers and local area networks over long distances, generally using leased phone lines. There is no firm dividing line between a WAN and a LAN.

warm boot A system restart performed after the system has been powered and operating. This clears and resets the memory, but does not stop and start the hard drive.

WAV (Windows Audio Format) The default sound format for Windows.

WB (write back) Defines a certain type of SRAM cache where instructions from the CPU to write changes are held in the cache until there is time available to write the changes to main memory.

web server A server that allows access to HTML documents by remote users.

WIN32 A programming interface or API for an early PC 32-bit mode fully supported by Windows NT. Many functions are supported in Windows 3.x, and written to the Win32 subset to gain improved performance on a 386. Windows 3.x translates the 32-bit calls in an application into its native 16-bit calls.

Windows A set of graphical operating systems produced by Microsoft, including Windows 95, Windows 98, Windows NT, Windows 2000, Windows ME, and Windows XP. Also, in the case of Windows 3.x, a graphical shell for DOS.

WINIPCFG A graphical program used on Windows 95, Windows 98, and Windows ME machines to display the current TCP/IP configuration of the machine; similar to Windows NT/2000/XP's IPCONFIG and UNIX/Linux's IFCONFIG.

WINS (Windows Internet Name Service) A name resolution service that resolves NetBIOS names to IP addresses.

Winsock (Windows Sockets) Microsoft Windows implementation of the TCP/IP sockets interface.

word A group of 16 binary digits, or 2 bytes.

word processor A program used to enter or edit text information in personal computers, often used to create a file before it is uploaded to a network. May also be used to process text after it has been downloaded.

workstation A general purpose computer that is small enough and inexpensive enough to reside at a person's work area for his or her exclusive use.

WWW (World Wide Web) The (graphical) Internet that can be accessed using Gopher, FTP, HTTP, telnet, USENET, WAIS, and some other tools.

X

X.25 A type of packet-switched network that enables remote devices to communicate with each other across high-speed digital links without the expense of individual leased lines.

XGA (Extended Graphics Array) IBM video display to bring 1,024 × 768 resolution to monitors. Can display 65,536 colors at low resolution, and 256 at high resolution.

Xmodem A file transfer protocol (FTP) that provides error-free asynchronous communications through telephone lines.

XMS (extended memory services) The RAM above 1 MB that is installed directly on the motherboard, and is directly accessible to the microprocessor is known as XMS. Usually shortened to simply "extended" memory.

Y

Ymodem A file transfer protocol (FTP) that is more robust than Xmodem; it features a time and date stamp transfer, as well as batch file transfers.

Z

ZIF (zero insertion force) socket A type of socket for CPUs that enables insertion of a chip without much pressure. Intel promoted the ZIF socket with its overdrive upgrades. The chip is dropped into the socket's holes and a small lever is turned to lock it in. Somewhat replaced in modern motherboards by Slot 1 and Slot A architecture, but still in style in Super Socket 7 and Socket 370 motherboards.

Zmodem Streaming asynchronous File Transfer Protocol (FTP) used by communication software. Very popular for downloading.

INDEX

Symbols

10/100BaseT devices, 146
1000BaseCX, twinaxial cabling, 151
1000BaseLX, 152
1000BaseSX, 151
1000BaseT, 151
100BaseFX, 145
100BaseFX NICs, 183
100BaseT Fast Ethernet, 145
100BaseT4 Fast Ethernet, 145
100BaseT4 NICs, 183
100BaseTX, 146
    Fast Ethernet, 145
    NICs, 183
100BaseVGAnyLAN NICs, 183
10Base2, 106–107
    NICs, 107, 182
    repeaters, 113
    shorts, 108
    T-connectors, 109
10Base5
    drop cables, 105
    Ethernet cabling, 102
    NICs, 104, 181
    repeaters, 113
    segments, 103

10BaseFL, 139, 183
10BaseT, 127
    coax cabling, 135
    crossover cabling, 136
    crossover ports, 137
    fault tolerance, 130, 137
    hubs, 129
    limitations, 135
    NICs, 182
    star bus topology, 128
    UTP cabling, 131–134
110 punchdown connections, 255
3270 terminal emulation cards, 194
5-4-3 rule, Ethernet, 141–144
802.11 standard, 170
802.3 standard, 88

A

A+ Certification, 3
access errors, 420
accidental data destruction, 527
Acknowledgement Number, TCP packets, 42
Active Directory, Windows 2000, 370
activity lights, NICs, 192
Ad-Hoc mode, wireless, 173

X–Z

INTERNATIONAL CONTACT INFORMATION

AUSTRALIA
McGraw-Hill Book Company
Australia Pty. Ltd.
TEL +61-2-9900-1800
FAX +61-2-9878-8881
http://www.mcgraw-hill.com.au
books-it_sydney@mcgraw-hill.com

CANADA
McGraw-Hill Ryerson Ltd.
TEL +905-430-5000
FAX +905-430-5020
http://www.mcgraw-hill.ca

**GREECE, MIDDLE EAST, & AFRICA
(Excluding South Africa)**
McGraw-Hill Hellas
TEL +30-210-6560-990
TEL +30-210-6560-993
TEL +30-210-6560-994
FAX +30-210-6545-525

MEXICO (Also serving Latin America)
McGraw-Hill Interamericana Editores
S.A. de C.V.
TEL +525-1500-5108
FAX +525-117-1589
http://www.mcgraw-hill.com.mx
carlos_ruiz@mcgraw-hill.com

SINGAPORE (Serving Asia)
McGraw-Hill Book Company
TEL +65-6863-1580
FAX +65-6862-3354
http://www.mcgraw-hill.com.sg
mghasia@mcgraw-hill.com

SOUTH AFRICA
McGraw-Hill South Africa
TEL +27-11-622-7512
FAX +27-11-622-9045
robyn_swanepoel@mcgraw-hill.com

SPAIN
McGraw-Hill/
Interamericana de España, S.A.U.
TEL +34-91-180-3000
FAX +34-91-372-8513
http://www.mcgraw-hill.es
professional@mcgraw-hill.es

**UNITED KINGDOM, NORTHERN,
EASTERN, & CENTRAL EUROPE**
McGraw-Hill Education Europe
TEL +44-1-628-502500
FAX +44-1-628-770224
http://www.mcgraw-hill.co.uk
emea_queries@mcgraw-hill.com

ALL OTHER INQUIRIES Contact:
McGraw-Hill/Osborne
TEL +1-510-420-7700
FAX +1-510-420-7703
http://www.osborne.com
omg_international@mcgraw-hill.com

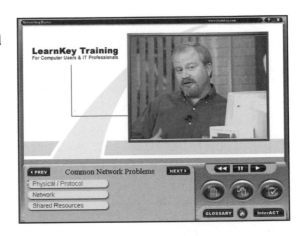

For Reference

Not to be taken from this room